Neil McK. Agnew   Sandra W. Pyke

the
Science
Game

Seventh Edition

AN INTRODUCTION TO RESEARCH
IN THE BEHAVIORAL AND SOCIAL SCIENCES

OXFORD
UNIVERSITY PRESS

OXFORD
UNIVERSITY PRESS

70 Wynford Drive, Don Mills, Ontario M3C 1J9
www.oup.com/ca

Oxford University Press is a department of the University of Oxford.
It furthers the University's objective of excellence in research, scholarship,
and education by publishing worldwide in

Oxford New York
Auckland Cape Town Dar es Salaam Hong Kong Karachi
Kuala Lumpur Madrid Melbourne Mexico City Nairobi
New Delhi Shanghai Taipei Toronto

With offices in
Argentina Austria Brazil Chile Czech Republic France Greece
Guatemala Hungary Italy Japan Poland Portugal Singapore
South Korea Switzerland Thailand Turkey Ukraine Vietnam

Oxford is a trade mark of Oxford University Press
in the UK and in certain other countries

Published in Canada
by Oxford University Press

This book was previously published by Prentice-Hall Inc.

Copyright © Oxford University Press Canada 2007

The moral rights of the author have been asserted

Database right Oxford University Press (maker)

First published 2007

Agnew, Neil McK.
The science game : an introduction to research in the behavioural and social sciences /
Neil McK. Agnew and Sandra W. Pyke.—7th ed.

Includes bibliographical references and index.
ISBN-13: 978-0-19-542321-1
ISBN-10: 0-19-542321-6

1. Social sciences—Research—Methodology—Textbooks.
I. Pyke, Sandra W., 1937– II. Title

BF76.5.A36 2007   300.72   C2006-906000-2

1 2 3 4 - 10 09 08 07
This book is printed on permanent (acid-free) paper ∞.
Printed in Canada

Contents

Preface

Welcome to the seventh edition of The Science Game.

What to Keep, What to Change?

Since the last edition we've seen major theoretical and methodological developments in various fields: cognitive science, neuropsychology, genome mapping, social constructivism, and cross-disciplinary studies, just to name a few! Consequently we've introduced major modifications in the text resulting in a book with more than 50 per cent new material

Those instructors who adopted previous editions list the book's strengths as: (1) being student centered and covering basic material while capturing and holding student interest, (2) not 'dumbing down' the content—in fact some sections have been used as a refresher for graduate students; (3) an emphasis on helping students understand the principals underlying various research designs, and finally, (4) students came away appreciating that science continues to be an exciting *work in progress* pursing the moving horizon of uncertainty. One of our mentors, Don Campbell, called this pursuit a 'healthy addiction', with each new quasi-solution along the way serving as an invigorating 'fix'.

Of course, there's always room for improvement. Previous adopters had suggestions for change as well. One idea that we've pursued while updating the seventh edition is the introduction of a central theme and memory aid throughout the book. We tested several different integrating premises and images and discovered that students found a puzzle-solving theme most helpful, particularly when it progressed from: (1) familiar common-sense problem-solving, (2) to quasi or pre-scientific methods employed by 'experts', the press, and the courts, then (3) to 'normal' science with its emphasis on reliable observations, critical thinking, and rigorous testing, and finally (4) to discussing paradigm shifts in methods and theory.

The student's perspective

Not only have we learned from previous adopters of the book, but students too have been our teachers. From six editions, and thousands of students, we've learned that it's not only what you write and teach—the messages you send—but obviously the messages that students take away with them that determines the value of a book.

We've been both fascinated and frustrated by what students remember, what they forget, and what they transform into weird and wonderful distortions and creations.

Over the years, particularly in our seminars, we've identified those research design concepts that undergo the most imaginative transformations as they travel from the textbook to the student's brain, and then back to us in the form of questions, class discussions, term assignments, and exams. This accumulating flow of feedback has coalesced not only into 'the student's perspective' but has gradually emerged as a virtual student who is now the reincarnation of students past and present. Though unseen, for us she is real; we've even given her a name: Diana Dodds. Yes, she bears a heavy responsibility as she represents the proverbial student perspective, but she has a larger reality; we found that presenting her perspective in both large classes and small seminars resonates with students.

In this edition we include Diana's 'take' in a prologue and as commentaries at the end of each chapter. Their inclusion or exclusion in the pedagogy of the coursework is optional.

The Science Game aims to help students become more sophisticated consumers of the increasing flood of scientific news, to help them discriminate between junk and serious science, and to be able to identify the early—as opposed to mature—stages of scientific explorations. Scientists seek to identify patterns in the flow of human experience, universal patterns in space and time: physical patterns, cultural patterns, and individual psychological patterns. But, as it takes forever to identify universal patterns (to map and connect all the dots in the universe), researches must usually settle for local patterns, patterns unique to certain molecules, certain genes, certain cultures, certain groups, certain individuals.

In a sense scientists are treasure hunters. In order to evaluate the quality of scientific news (reports of found treasure) both consumers of science and budding researchers must learn to identify the quality of the treasure map (clear or fuzzy), the size of the search space (small or large, reasonable, or impossible), and the quality of the tools (precise or crude.)

Additional teaching aids

As well as those mentioned above, the seventh edition includes the following additional teaching and learning aids. Each chapter opens with a clear statement of goals, and contains integrating themes, new graphics, examples of key concepts and methods, a chapter summary, a student's perspective of the chapter, and a self-test quiz. Each section in the book is introduced with a brief overview, which places the material in context for the student. Examination questions and answers are available on an instructor's website (login and password information is available from your sales representative) at http://www.oup.com/ca/he/companion/agnewpyke, along with an instructor's manual that includes additional assignments, readings, and a guide to relevant Internet resources. The website also includes a series of supplemental chapters for student use (no password required), discussing major theoretical and methodological issues across different social science fields (e.g., political science, business, criminology, communication, journalism, social work, and various health sciences such as nursing and emergency services) and additional student resources.

Much has changed since we wrote the first edition of this book, but one thing has not. We still believe that 'sciencing', like the Olympic games, involves pushing our human capacities almost to the breaking point, stretching the boundaries of our rationality, of our imagination, of our ingenuity. Sometimes we win. Sometimes we just get part way there.

Students reading this text may or may not become scientists. But, like it or not, we all bet our lives on science every minute of every hour of every day. So it's smart to know the main rules of the Science Game—the biggest game in town.

Acknowledgements

We had a lot of help.

First and foremost from legions of students, and from course instructors, some of whom have adopted each of the previous six editions—and none of them relatives.

The following friends, family, and colleagues read and provided valuable comments on selected sections of the manuscript: Mary Agnew, Wendy Agnew, Vera and Edward Turner, Lucie Cantrell, Paul Tacon, John Brown, Mike Mahoney, and Frank Farley.

Mary Agnew graciously let Neil use writing this book as an avoidance response for almost everything. Wendy Agnew provided him with references much further out in speculative space than he's ever ventured on his own.

Burke Brown, a wonderful mind, rekindled and greatly expanded Neil's understanding of the neglected (repressed?) role that chance plays in our lives.

Sandra wishes to thank Dr Nicola Brown for permission to use her *informed consent* form, and Dale Pyke for his consistent support and good humour throughout the project.

Once again we gratefully acknowledge Ernest Harberg's permission to use the Island of Research map.

The York University Library and the American Psychological Association made our task not only feasible but also fun in providing 24/7 online access to a massive intellectual candy store.

The folks at Oxford University Press have been wonderful. David Stover, bless his editorial soul, provided the blind faith that got us, and kept us, going. Roberta Osborne reflected his faith, helping to bring the baby to full-term and aiding mightily with the delivery.

We dedicate the seventh edition of *The Science Game* to
Donald Campbell and Elizabeth Bennett, educators who built bridges for their
students into wondrous and constantly unfolding futures.

Note to Instructors for the 7th Edition

If you are teaching students new to university life and social science we recommend that you start them with the Prologue.

Prologue. Our students typically arrive at college or university with two major handicaps: inadequate study habits and an oversimplified view of science. The Prologue tells the story of a student engaging and overcoming both those handicaps while Chapter 1 provides a general introduction to social science.

Structure of the book. The chapters are divided into seven sections, and each section has an introduction designed to prepare the student for the information to follow. Each chapter is organized with a statement of chapter goals, an introduction, discussion of the integrating theme—including graphics, central concepts, and examples—and a chapter summary. Chapters conclude with a detailed student perspective of the chapter, current news reports, and an end of chapter quiz. A student website provides additional teaching aids including suggested Internet explorations of major issues discussed in each chapter.

Target audience. This text has served a mixed audience over the years. It has served as an introduction to research design and methods for undergraduate students in different disciplines, some of whom, while not planning research careers, will hopefully become more discriminating consumers of scientific news—better able to spot 'creative' advertising, better able to identify junk science, and better able to tell the difference between early theoretical explorations, on the one hand, and mature science, on the other.

And of course, over the years the text has also served as a basic introduction to thousands of students heading towards research careers in a variety of fields.

Instructors can emphasize the chapters that best serve their purpose. The instructor's website suggests alternative teaching strategies that we have found useful. The instructor's website also includes supplementary chapters discussing current theoretical and methodological issues, additional assignments, and examples of issues facing different disciplines (e.g. health services, political science, business, social work, journalism, and criminology.)

Prologue

Many students arrive at university burdened by two handicaps: a naïve view of science and grossly inefficient study skills.

In the following prologue, and at the end of each chapter, we show how one student, Diana Dodds, develops a more realistic and animated view of science, and at the same time learns how to study, not necessarily longer but smarter.

THE SOCIAL AND BEHAVIOURAL SCIENCES FROM A STUDENT'S PERSPECTIVE BY DIANA DODDS

I'm a second year university student doing a combined degree in psychology and journalism. As part of my program I serve an apprenticeship at small local paper as a 'go-for' in the newsroom and, when no one else is available, I'm a cub reporter.

I'm supposed to work one day a week but it's always more. I end up cramming for exams. Come to think of it, I always end up cramming no matter what.

My editor called me in. 'I hear you're studying to be a social scientist. Well here's something they won't teach you at University. In spite of all its fancy trappings, Science is just another news service. They dress their reporters up in white coats and call them researchers. And they lock their editors up in ivory towers and call them theorists.'

'But . . .'

'No buts kid, the researchers are just like reporters, they gather bits of local news. And the theorists are just like editors trying to fit the bits into The Big Picture. Enough chatter. It's time to put you to work. It's January, and since you're supposed to be a psychologist put on your white coat and get me a story about New Year's Resolutions. Find out what kinds of things people promise to stop or start doing. Find out if it works. Have the story on my desk by 2 PM, February 5th.'

'Who should I talk to?'

'Anybody you can lay your hands on. Start right here. Interview our staff. Then spread out, get the proverbial cross section of public opinion.'

I nodded and as I was about to leave I asked: 'Mr Wilkens, can I start with you? Did you make a resolution?'

'Sure, every year I give up smoking. It always works.'

'But you're smoking right now.'

'I know. I know. But every year I give it up for one day, January 2nd—just to prove to myself I can do it.'

Over the next few weeks I interviewed sixty-three people: staff at the paper, family, friends, then as my deadline approached I started stopping people on the street.

My results? Fifty-three people admitted they'd made resolutions, mostly about giving up things like too much—junk food, booze, cigarettes, and TV.

Three said that their resolution was 'private'.

Thirty-three people out of fifty-three reported that they kept their resolution for a day or two. Nineteen claimed they hung in for about a week. Only one swore that it was still working in the fourth week of January.

Writing up my story I wondered why people keep doing brainless things even though they 'know better'. Like my own cramming. Obviously knowing it's stupid is not enough.

I highlighted this puzzle in the last paragraph of my story.

I got my copy in by the deadline, but the editor cut my stuff about insight not being enough: 'Just the facts kid. Leave the editorializing to me.'

This project got me wondering, though, how come it's so hard to change a habit, even when you know—really know—that it's a bad habit, even if you know that it's just providing short-term gain for long-term pain?

For answers I went to see Dr Frund, one of my Psychology Professors (I know! What a name!) She's maybe all of five feet tall with red hair and the personality to match; she's really feisty, she hardly ever sits down. She teaches both Social and Clinical Psychology. When she heard about my New Year's Resolution survey and its dismal results she bounced out of her chair, paced around the room, and with rapid-fire talk told me I should do a personal experiment using myself as the guinea pig. She told me to pick a habit I want to change, try changing it, see what happens, and then try to explain the results.

She checked her bookshelves and loaned me a 'how-to' book by Watson and Tharp[1] called *Self-Directed Behavior*. Then she raced on: 'The goal of social science is understanding human behaviour. We test our theories by how

---

[1]Watson and Tharp (2002).

accurately we can predict and modify how people act, think, and feel. So Diana, you'll learn some of the methods and challenges of doing social science research, you'll learn some psychological theory, and you may even break a bad habit.'

Just as Dr Frund paused for breath Professor Creek poked his head in the door. The rest of him followed—toothy, tall, and boney. He nods a lot. He teaches Physiological Psychology. When he found out what we were doing he nodded, laughed, and drawled, 'Lotsa luck, but most human behaviour is bred in the bone. It springs from your genes.'

'Nonsense!' fumed Dr Frund. 'If you want to predict an important piece of behaviour—for example, what language a child will learn to speak—what information would help you the most? Their genetic code or the name of the country in which they were raised? Environment trumps genes almost every time.'

Professor Creek nodded, but followed up by asking, 'And pray tell us my dear Doctor, how come identical twins (same DNA), raised apart (different environments) still end up having almost identical IQ's?'

I left them arguing, bought a cup of coffee, and started planning my project. Wouldn't it be great if I not only got a good grade for a term project, but also wrote it up for the newspaper—a follow-up story. A scientific study with me as the scientist, the subject, and the writer.

I cracked open the book Dr Frund loaned me. The first step, it said, was that you needed to list the bad habits that you want to eliminate. I listed the following: stop cramming for exams and essays, eat less junk food (I'm having trouble buttoning the top button on my jeans), stop letting my boyfriend talk me into things, improve my essay writing skills, and, finally, feel better about myself.

When Dr Frund gave me the book she told me to skim it and then come back at 3 PM Wednesday, when she would help me design a small research study.

As I arrived she was working on her computer. She glanced up and said 'Don't look like someone just shot your dog. Science is an exploration—we should call it "sciencing", acknowledging that it's a verb, a work in progress. No one gets their research right the first time, or even the second. I'm still learning, all scientists are. So, relax, you've just taken out your research "learner's license".'

That was exactly what I needed to hear.

She continued, 'We'll start with something you can manage'. She handed me a list of seven steps to follow. I took her list and went for a double espresso hit.

Avoid Fuzzies, Go for Hard Data

I started with the first step: I needed an 'observable behaviour' to change. I checked my earlier list and chose stop cramming for exams and essays.

I bought myself a small notebook and started to record the time, date, and duration of all my studying. You know what? I found out that my studying is kind of fuzzy—it's sometimes hard to measure. For example, I'm a highlighter, so some of my books look like I used a big yellow paintbrush on the pages. Should I highlight my highlights? Sometimes I sit in front of an open text, but am I studying or daydreaming? How do you measure 'fuzzies'?

I dropped by Dr Frund's office. She gave me five minutes. I told her my problem, and she said 'Diana, the way most students highlight, in fact the way most students study, is pretty much a waste of time. The only way to be certain that you've learned something is to close the book and see if you can recall what you've highlighted or read. Furthermore, since we forget most of what we've heard or read within 24 hours, you should do two recalls, one right after you've studied and again a few hours later. That way you *fix* the new knowledge in your mind.

'So, what you should be recording in your research notebook is how often and how long you spend recalling the main points from your lectures and texts. And Diana, that's *blind recall*—with your *textbook closed* and your lecture notes out of sight.

'In order make your recall activity observable (available to others) you can't just do it in your head, you have to write it down. So write your summaries in your research notebook. Now I have to run. Good luck.'

Well, Dr Frund solved my baseline problem—I never close my textbook or lecture notes and try to recall what I've read, highlighted, or heard, let alone write it out. My baseline for blind recall of stuff I study is a big zero. On the bright side, my target behaviour has no place to go but up.

My record-keeping procedure will include: (1) recording when, where, how often, and how long I spend recalling course material, and (2) at the end of each session I'll record the main points I recalled.

How to Change Your Behaviour

Now I know what I want to change. I want to start recalling and writing down the *main points* of my course material for a few minutes at least twice a day. Hopefully this will help me avoid my usual twenty-four hour meltdown.

When I told my boyfriend Derek about my plan he shook his head. He claims cramming is the only way to go; his theory is that you'll remember just enough to pass the exam and then forget most of it on the way to the pub so you don't clog up your brain with stuff you'll never need again.

Now that I know what I should record, and what behaviour I intend to change, the question is how to I get myself to start and keep doing it? How am I going to make it happen?

Psychologists talk a lot about *reinforcement*. Research and theory both support the idea that the frequency of a given behaviour increases when it's immediately followed by a reward of some kind. So, every time I recall (in writing) some course material I should give myself a reward (e.g., a pat on the back, a gold star in my research notebook, or an M&M).

The Premack principle

Dr Frund had suggested I read about the 'Premack Principle'. I found it on pages 202 and 203 of the Watson and Tharp book. Premack's big discovery is that the reward doesn't have to be a treat at all. Surprise! Instead, it can be another *behaviour*. The principle states: 'any activity that you regularly perform (e.g., standing up and leaving at the end of class) can be used to reinforce (strengthen) any behavior that you are less likely to perform (e.g., recalling course material).'

I know it sounds weird, but apparently it works. What you do is stick a bit of the new behaviour (like recalling course stuff) into the little time gaps between habits (like recalling the main points of one lecture on the way to the next, or for a few minutes before you crack open your novel, or turn on your iPod on the bus). So you sneak the new behaviour into the small gap between two regular events, like between the end of the lecture and standing up to head out.

So I have to record when, where, and for how long I practice blind recall, and what I specifically recalled, so that I will have objective proof that I did it. After some false starts—forgetting to do it and forgetting to record it even when I did it—I started keeping better records.

Now that I think about it, mothers have unwittingly been using Premack reinforcers for centuries: 'You can go play after you clear the table/do your homework/dump the old dinosaur soup bones over the cliff.' But even with the Premack principle, I was discouraged after a few days. I wasn't doing much blind recall. Highlighting? Yes. Blind recall? Not so much.

Shaping: baby steps

Derek came to the rescue by showing me how to do keyword searches in the library—for instance we Googled 'habits' and discovered the idea of *shaping*. The idea is that your starting level, or baseline, indicates your current level of performance (zero in my case for blind recall). And that level is where the shaping process starts. There are two simple rules for shaping: you can never begin too low and the steps upward can never be too small.

Great! Now I won't feel guilty even if I only sneak a minute of blind recall in between the end of one class and leaving for the next one. I've been spending my time on the bus each day catching up on my non-academic reading, but today, before taking my fiction fix, I snuck in a few minutes trying to recall the summaries I scribbled down at the end of each lecture. That means two recalls per lecture before I even got home (one right after the lecture and one on the bus.) And that took maybe ten minutes, at the most. Not bad!

At dinner I made the mistake of telling my dad about my discovery of the Premack principle and shaping—of sneaking bits of new behaviour in between old habits.

'Well, that's just great,' he said, 'Some psychologist has become famous by re-discovering "baby steps"?'

My brother chirped in: 'Yeah, baby steps.'

I got some support from my mother, though. Glaring at my dad and brother she said 'Alright you two, that's enough. There's a big difference between what Diana just explained and your glib remark about baby steps. There's a very big difference between saying "Oh, it's easy, just take baby steps," and telling them specifically what to do, how to do it, and when to do it. It's the difference between telling someone who's hungry to "go bake some bread", as opposed to providing the recipe. That's the difference!' Mum doesn't spout off too often like that—only when the balance of power between the males and females in the family starts getting out of whack.

Up the Crick with Professor Creek

The next day I, almost literally, ran into Professor Creek in the hall. He asked how my project was going and I told him I was focusing my study on summarizing course material and recalling, within 24 hours, what I studied.

He nodded. 'Yes, that'll help prevent memory meltdown, and that'll help strengthen the neurological connections. But what will help even more is to link the new material you're trying to remember to strong, hard-wired, neurological nets in your brain. You try to link the new material to the primitive—biological drives, like sex, food, water, fear, aggression. Get it?'

'Not really.'

'Well, let's say you're trying to remember who broke the genetic code—Watson and Crick. You could tie it to sex by imagining two guys fighting over Julia Robert's DNA, and Julia says: "Sorry, my dear Watson, but you're up the crick." Or link it to a basic aggressive drive. Let's say you're trying to remember the founder of operant conditioning—Skinner—so you think: "For that bad behaviour young man, I'm going to Skinner you alive." Now do you get it?'

'Sort of . . . I guess.'

I met Derek for lunch and updated him on the project, and about how Dr Frund and Professor Creek fight over what's most influential in shaping human behaviour—biology or culture.

B = E + g

Since Derek is majoring in sociology he tends to agree with Dr Frund that environment and culture are the biggest shapers of human behaviour. But he likes to argue too, so he'll take any side just to make things interesting.

For instance, he pointed out, 'The advertisers agree with your guy Creek—go for primitive, animal drives. They try to tie everything to sex in order to grab your attention, so you'll remember the message, whether it's about clothes, or food, or even about what stocks, or socks, to buy. They link sexual imagery to anything and everything.'

But what Derek *really* believes is that culture plays the biggest role in shaping most of what we do: what language you speak, what food you eat, your religion, sexual practices, superstitions. You name it and he's got a cultural explanation.

Recently, though, he admitted that the genome project has given the 'nature' argument a leg up by making intriguing promises about designer babies, curing all kinds of diseases, and changing behaviour merely by injecting snippets of DNA into your body, even into your brain. I could use an injection of 20 or 30 IQ points. Derek's starting to believe that there's probably a larger genetic influence on behaviour than he realized—certainly more than most sociologists will admit.

But, despite all that, he still believes culture, or 'nurture' is the biggie. He even wears a t-shirt with: $B = E + g$ written across the front. It means: Behaviour (B) is the result of big E (environmental) influences and small (g) genetic ones. All the guys who play on the sociology touch football team wear those shirts.

Of course the biology team changes the formula. Their t-shirts read: $B = G + e$, meaning of course that behaviour stems from big genetic factors and little environmental ones. Ever since Einstein's formula: $E = mc^2$ became famous, it seems all sciences are trying to come up with a catchy formula too.

Back to my project. One book recommends that you post keyword cues all around—sticking post-it notes on your coffee cup, on unopened beer bottles in the fridge (Dad will love that!), and on your bathroom mirror—that say things like 'Up the Crick with DNA,' or 'Skinner OD'd on OC' (i.e., Skinner overdosed on operant conditioning.)

I'm nearing the end of the fourth week of my project; two weeks of baseline data collection (zero incidents of blind recall) and two weeks of 'treatment', of trying to summarize and recall lecture notes and text readings. I'm managing to do a few more minutes of blind recall every day.

Another author recommends 'rehearsal'. This is another kind of recall where you tell friends and family what you're learning. My friends may start to avoid me, but my mother will always listen. At the pub I 'rehearsed' my stuff and regaled Derek with the main points from my last lecture. He yawned a lot and said 'Yeah, yeah, the proof of the pudding is in the eating. Let's wait and see how you do on your exams before us lowly peasants start waving and cheering as you drive by in your golden carriage flaunting a grade sheet filled with straight A's.'

Today I slept in. Luckily I couldn't see my face in the mirror, which is covered in post-it notes. Missed a class.

Good News and Bad News

Yippee! I got an A+ on my clinical psychology exam, and even got a B in political science, which is usually my worst subject.

I did my six-week graph—two weeks baseline and four weeks of 'treatment'. Here it is:

■ BEHAVIOUR CHANGE FROM BASELINE USING PREMACK PRINCIPLE

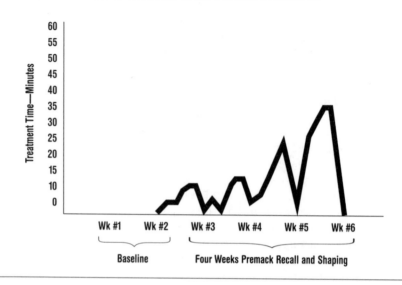

As you can see from the figure, my treatment (including *everything but the kitchen sink*) worked. Except for the third week—when I had a cold—the time spent doing blind, written recalls steadily increased and peaked during the final week. I took time off during weekends; I figured I had earned it.

I wrote up my report, including references. I was like a flea in a fit after handing in my report while I waited for Dr Frund's grade and feedback. I was sure I had aced it.

I met with her at 11:30 Monday morning.

I didn't get an A+. I didn't get an A. I didn't even get a B+

I got a ruddy B!! Why?

Even a psychologist could see I was shocked—Dr Frund picked up on it. She asked me what grade I'd give myself?

I told her I thought that, once I got going, I'd done a good job, that I'd focused on recording objective behaviour (I used my notes and a miniature recorder), and I'd included all my post-it notes in the appendix of my report. Also, I'd searched the literature for critical thinking about studying and included those references. And, finally I'd done conscientious testing of my treatment by comparing it with a baseline. And, most important of all, my grades improved.

She agreed that for a first research project I'd done very well, particularly without any research training. But, she would have liked a bit more critical evaluation of my results, particularly my claim that my new method of study 'caused' my grades to increase.

I said, 'How can you argue with the results? I got an A+ on clinical, and I even got a B in political science—I've never gotten anything higher than a C before. It *had* to be my new method of studying. What other explanation could there be?'

Critical Thinking Gone Missing

Dr Frund shook her head. 'Diana, that's the point. You didn't even consider any other explanations. If you had, even if I hadn't agreed with you, I would have given you an A. Put on your critical thinking hat right now. Can you think of any alternative explanation for you improved grades? Even one?'

I couldn't. It was so obvious that it had to be my new methods of studying that led to my acing the clinical psychology exam and doing unusually well in political science.

'Diana, don't feel too badly', she said. 'You haven't committed a cardinal sin. You've merely made the same mistake that, sooner rather than later, all researchers make. They close their minds to alternative explanations. They work so hard, they become so committed to their theory and their "treatment", that they have difficulty seriously considering that their theory may be wrong or that their "positive results" could have occurred for a variety of reasons in addition to, or rather than, their treatment.'

'LIKE WHAT?' I asked, a little too loudly.

Her eyes narrowed and I thought I was going to be asked to leave immediately. Instead she took a big breath and said: 'Diana, whenever anybody tries to tell you that A causes B a little red sign should light up inside your head that reads: "*Well, maybe?*" Whether it's an advertiser, an expert, or a scientist making the claim, flashing the "Well, maybe?" sign is appropriate. It's also appropriate in your study where you sincerely believe your A (a new method of study) caused B (improved grades). Well, maybe?

'Even experienced scientists fail to see loopholes in their own results, fail to adopt a "Well, maybe?" attitude and so they often end up feeling foolish.

'Since it's difficult to see possible flaws in our own research, let's look for common flaws in a different example and then see if any of them apply to your study.

'Let's say a drug company asks a psychiatrist to test their new wonder treatment for depression. He or she tells the patient that if (A) she takes this pill three times a day for month, then (B) she should feel better. A month later the patient returns, the psychiatrist examines her and decides that the pills have worked, that "If A, then B". But we say: "Well, maybe?" Diana, can you think of why?'

At first I couldn't. Then Dr Frund said: 'Diana, imagine that A and B are elastic measuring sticks; they take different forms and can be different things to different people.'

So I imagined the pill getting bigger and smaller. It got so small it disappeared. Bingo! Sometimes my Gram doesn't take her pills—sometimes she doesn't like the side effects, sometimes she says she can't afford them, and sometimes she just forgets.

'Maybe the patient didn't take all the pills. Maybe A wasn't what it was suppose to be, or maybe it changed during the study?'

Dr Frund almost patted me on the head. 'So one basic question about any "If A, then B" rule is to consider if you really, really know what A consists of throughout the study. Now, what about B?'

I let B go elastic. In the example of the drug study she mentioned B was a kind of yardstick of feeling worse or better. Feelings fluctuate from hour to hour and from day to day. Sometimes I'm not sure how I feel. Bingo!

'Feelings are hard to measure, whether they are your own or those of someone else. How can the psychiatrist be sure he or she just didn't see the patient on one of his good days?'

Dr Frund almost cheered, and added, 'And what did the psychiatrist want to see?'

Bingo! 'He or she wants the treatment to work, maybe he or she is even getting paid by the drug company, and so everyone wants to see positive results.'

'Yes! Yes! He who pays the piper usually calls the tune that could, consciously or unconsciously, influence the psychiatrist in stretching his elastic ruler. One more question: What else besides A (the drug treatment) might be happening during that month the treatment lasted?'

I closed my eyes. Bingo! 'All kinds of things. Maybe better weather, maybe the patient got pay raise, maybe her daughter's soccer team won a tournament, maybe her in-laws moved away.'

'Great! Now, Diana, whenever you encounter an "If A, then B" rule, your automatic response should always be "Well, maybe?" and you should always ask yourself three questions: (1) How elastic is A?, (2) How elastic is B?, and (3) What else is happening besides A? Now go away and apply these three questions to your own study. In particular, consider how elastic B is. Was the class average, by chance, higher on that particular test? That would indicate it was an easier exam. And don't forget to consider fraud.'

It took a minute to sink in: 'You think I cheated!'

'Diana, I didn't say that. But fraud in science is becoming such a major problem that it has to be one of the questions that gets asked when any 'If A, then B' claim is made. If you conscientiously apply the questions to your study I'd be happy to look at your conclusions and reconsider your grade.'

Derek helped me calm down and apply the three questions to my project. We agreed that my A was pretty elastic—a mixed bag of methods. It would be very hard for anyone else to repeat my study. Concerning the elasticity of B, I checked the class average in political science and it was actually lower than the previous test, which would support my original claim. What else happened along with A in the six weeks my study took? Wanting to impress Dr Frund could have been a major motivator. Maybe it was even more important than the blind recall? I wrote up my critical evaluation of my research and dropped into Dr Frund's office.

She said, 'Diana, don't look sad, you did an excellent job on your first research project. On these self-study projects most of my students get a C+ or a B−. Getting a B is rare. And you have what it takes to be a scientist. First, you're curious. Second, you're not afraid of work. Third, and maybe most important, you're committed to your research and excited about your findings.'

I felt a bit better.

Dr Frund added, 'Once you get a research design course under your belt you'll start spotting both phony advertising and loopholes in scientific news.'

Professor Creek stuck his head in the door. 'Sorry, but I couldn't help overhearing that stirring endorsement of my course—I'm teaching research methods next term.' Dr Frund groaned: 'Oh no.'

'Oh yes. And my dear Dr Frund, you can relax, I'll be introducing the students to your brilliant paper on how scientists must walk a fine line. How, on the one hand, they must have enough faith in their theory to invest the blood, sweat, and tears good research demands and, on the other hand, be able to stand back periodically and consider possible flaws and loopholes in their own theory, methods, and conclusions. Although I must confess that, like Diana here, I'm better at the first part—having complete faith in my theory and results. And, although, I'm not great at critiquing my own work, I can find flaws in other people's research. So I can preach even if I can't practice. And I get excited . . . I get completely carried away.'

I left them at that point in the conversation. Next term I'll be taking a course from each of them so maybe I'll end up with a balanced view on nature and nurture, on social science and lab research. Critical thinking here I come!

Meanwhile, Back at the Paper

Back at the paper Mr Wilken's asked how my research project had turned out. I told him I only got a B because I didn't raise alternative explanations for my great results, including, can you believe, cheating?

He snorted: 'I told you, kid; science is like a news service. There's always another angle to the story, including the outside chance of a sloppy or dishonest reporter. The prestigious *New York Times* found that out. For months one of their reporters had been making up stories claiming they were true. When the most respected newspaper in the world can be scammed so outrageously for that long, then you always have to consider fraud, and protect against it. Look what happened to mighty CBS and to "Mr Reliable" Dan Rather! He got scammed, too, in his coverage of the 2004 presidential election. And now we're hearing more and more about scientists fixing their data.'

He shook his head, adding: 'Too bad, because most reporters and researchers are honest—even heroic—but a few bad apples force us go to a lot of extra trouble. But remember, the TRUTH is like the horizon. You know it's there but you can never quite reach it.'

He turned away and coughed, like he was embarrassed to be caught talking philosophy. Then he swung his chair around saying: 'That gives me an idea. With your new-found expertise in research, why don't you pick an important story, say the Prime Minister's last major speech, and identify the different slants three different newspapers take, both in terms of their selection of the facts—the hard news—and in their different interpretations, explanations, and editorializing—the soft news. Of course, I'll have to completely rewrite it, but it'll give you valuable experience."

Here I go again. And, no doubt, without a by-line.

Before the holidays I dropped by to see Dr Frund, to show there were no hard feelings about the lousy B she gave me, to tell her how much I learned on my research project, and to tell her that my editor had given me a couple of new science assignments.

Good news. On the basis of my critical review of my paper Dr Frund raised my grade to a B+! In my original paper I'd given credit for my improved political science grade to my blind recall study method. But maybe that exam was easier than usual. Then, in my critique, I ruled out that alternative explanation by showing the exam had been harder than usual (the class average dropped a grade). She said that was good detective work and produced hard evidence in support of my argument. Yeah!

Dr Frund's been browsing through some newly published textbooks and she handed me one, saying, 'Diana here's some holiday reading for you. You can check it out on slow news days. It's a complimentary copy of a textbook on research methods in the social and behavioural sciences; it's called *The Science Game.*

'While it respects the goals of traditional science—reliable observations, critical thinking, and rigorous testing—it deals with them in a slightly less idealized manner than other texts. It presents science from a human perspective, with peeks behind the unrealistically neat and tidy view that many people have of scientific research. The authors expose some of science's warts, while still displaying its triumphs.

'Actually I'm trying to convince Professor Creek to use this text in his research methods course. I think he's at least considering it. If he does adopt it, you'll have a head start. If not, you'll still benefit by learning the basics of good research. And furthermore, some of the ideas in it should help you provide your readers with a better understanding of how "sciencing" really works.'

Going Beyond Common Sense and Human Limitations

In this section we discuss the strengths and limitations of the common sense methods of puzzle-solving that you and I use every day. It's not just us. Even experts use them. Even scientists use them. We all use them.

Relying on common sense, we jump to conclusions because we have neither the time nor the mental capacity to carefully analyze and evaluate the 101 decisions we make every hour of every day.

In Chapter 1 we introduce you to the Problem-Solving-Triangle (PST). We use it throughout the book as a memory aid in identifying and comparing different pre-scientific and scientific methods. We also provide common sense examples of its application.

In Chapter 2 we make the point that both pre-scientific and scientific methods are problem-solving tools. And, like any tool, they're only as good as the person using them. In order to evaluate the use of a tool we assess it in terms of how well it counterbalances our human limitations in perceiving and connecting the dots. Human problem solvers, including scientists, have certain strengths and limitations. In this chapter we document those limitations.

Even though we provide scientists with extra time, training, and resources, their human nervous system and cultural blinders limit how many dots they can *see*, how many they can remember, and how many they can analyze and connect—just like us.

Understanding these human limits enables us to better evaluate how pre-scientific and scientific methods help us overcome natural restrictions, help us stand on tip toes and *see* more dots, and ultimately make more connections.

1

From Common Sense to Science

Chapter Goal

- To show that the scientific method is an extension of the common-sense problem-solving methods you use every day, the ones enabling you to make sense of the flood of messages flowing from your physical and social environments.

Good problem solvers, whether citizen or scientist, share four qualities: (1) the high anticipation of a child unwrapping gifts, (2) driving curiosity, (3) pig-headed tenacity, and (4) sometimes they're right and sometimes they're wrong.

The difference between what you do and what scientists do is this: society provides scientists with sufficient time, training, and resources so they don't have to jump to as many conclusions.

That's why science is our most trusted news service.

Introduction

What is science?

How would you answer that question? Like many others you might say something like: 'Science consists of white-coated researchers discovering packages of truth.'

How would the two most famous scientists answer the question?

I do not know what I may appear to the world, but to myself I seem to have been only a boy playing on the seashore, and diverting myself in now and then finding a smoother pebble or prettier shell than ordinary, whilst the great ocean of truth lay undiscovered before me. (Sir Isaac Newton)

Whoever undertakes to set himself up as a judge in the field of truth and knowledge is shipwrecked by the laughter of the Gods. (Albert Einstein)

How come these two great scholars see themselves as collecting pretty pebbles and as being ridiculed by the laughter of the Gods?

While exploring their sheltered play-space all scientists: (1) discover small- and medium-sized packages of truth (pretty shells and shell collections); (2) periodically run smack into the hard sides of their playpen, into the boundaries of their own ignorance, into the concrete complexity of nature; and (3) bounce back while cowering at the derisive laughter of the Gods. A fortunate few stumble on big truths, some of them win the Nobel Prize.

> Or is science a wondrous playpen for grown-ups —a protected space spinkled with treasure maps?

But for most scientists their addiction is to the search, not the prize.

But what *is* science? In the following pages we'll explore this question from different perspectives and revisit it at the end of the book.

Science is Like a News Service

Science can be viewed as a news service. Scientific researchers (reporters) collect the news, and scientific theorists (editors) fit it into the big picture—they tell us what it means.

If you view science as a chain of messengers and messages you will appreciate both its astonishing accomplishments and its limitations. Receiving and delivering even a simple message can be tricky. Consider a common experience: somebody gives you a new phone number (message) and you (the messenger) walk across the room to tell it to someone else. First question? Did you deliver the original message? Or, during its passage through you, has that message been transformed, the numbers transposed, or replaced? Conclusion? A simple, clear message passing through one messenger, in a matter of seconds, can be, and often is, embellished or distorted. What would happen to the original message (the phone number) if it had passed through a chain of people?

Second question? How can scientists ever identify original messages flowing through an endless chain of situations, instruments, and human messengers?

Third question? How can we be certain that scientists haven't unwittingly distorted the message?

So, if you view scientists as a chain of messengers who sometimes skillfully enhance and at other times unwittingly distort nature's messages, you'll be suitably astonished by their accomplishments and appropriately patient with their limitations.

You and I face the same challenge scientists do. We perpetually attempt to decode long chains of messages—a mixture of fact and fancy—arriving from family, friends, TV, professors, the Internet, doctors, scientists, etc.

The difference between a typical news service and science is this: we give scientists more time and resources to collect, check, and analyze messages than we give newspapers.

Every day—unlike scientists—reporters and editors have to interrupt their message gathering and analyzing. Every day they have to turn off their learning capacity and send their work to press based on fragments of news. Every day they have to start collecting new messages, weaving them into yet another incomplete story. Day after day traditional news services have to keep jumping to conclusions just to keep up with the flow.

Although we don't have the message gathering and analyzing resources newspapers do, you and I also have to jump to conclusions. We have no choice; life tailgates us. Just to stay in the game we need a fast and mentally affordable way to pick out fragments from the myriad of messages assaulting our senses, flooding our mind.

Fortunately we have one, we call it *common sense*.

Common sense news

The term common sense describes the quick and simple way we collect messages, analyze them, and jump to conclusions as events flow by.

Scientists also have to gather messages, from nature and each other, analyze them, and reach reasoned conclusions. However, because we provide scientists with extra time and resources, they don't have to turn off their learning capacity as soon as we do, they don't have to jump to so many conclusions, and they can afford to practice *uncommon* sense.

Scholars have, over time, added refinements to our common sense method of problem solving. Capitalizing on these refinements, science has become our most trusted method of separating fact from fancy, of reaching valid conclusions.

In order just to keep up with the normal traffic of living you and I have no choice but to jump to most of our conclusions, to practice what we'll call *common-sense-light*. With more time and assets at their disposal, scientists can afford to practice *common-sense-potent*.

For instance, many people believe that stress causes cancer. What's the evidence? Any cancer patient can find evidence of stressful messages and messengers in their past. That's an example of common-sense-light in action. But before you jump to that conclusion, take a minute and think about it. *Everyone*—not just cancer patients—can find stressful messages and messengers in their past. How come everyone doesn't get cancer? That's an instance of critical reasoning generated by *common-sense-medium*.

Now consider the Danish study (Kolato, 2005) of 11,380 parents whose children had cancer (stressful messages galore). These parents had no more cancer than members of the general population. Now that kind of message gathering and analyzing is starting to get into *common-sense-heavy*. Which comes closer to common-sense-potent but, as we'll see later, is not quite there.

Next we'll present a map of common sense problem solving, and then provide examples of common-sense-light, followed by examples of the *uncommon sense* scientists use—common-sense-potent.

The problem-solving triangle (PST)

We solve problems by using our common sense, which involves three linked activities:

1. gathering the messages (observing),
2. analyzing them to reach tentative conclusions (thinking), and
3. evaluating our conclusions (testing).

This chain of activities—of processing messages—can be seen as representing three corners of a triangle around which we cycle while trying to make sense of the flow of experience.[1]

Fig 1.1 ■ THE PROBLEM-SOLVING TRIANGLE

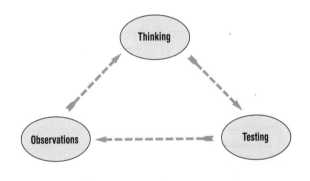

Our triangle, our PST, is a simple map designed to fit easily into your mind and to provide a rough picture of the lay of the land we'll be covering. In the chapters that follow we'll be adding important features to the scientific landscape. That enriched map will still fit inside your head, but it will also help you understand why scientists do what they do, why they sometimes disagree with each other, and why science still remains our most trusted news or message service.

The arrows in Figure 1.1 represent an idealized view of an orderly cycling around the triangle from one corner to another: *from observing to thinking to*

---

[1] Various authors have used triangles to describe different interative information processes (e.g., Casti [1992], Cacioppo, Semin, & Bernston [2004], and Andasht & Michel [2005]). They usually share inductive processes (moving from the particular to the general) and deductive processes (moving from the general to the particular).

testing. Most of the time this happens automatically and requires minimum thinking. If a persistent puzzle is too big for our brains we typically do one of two things. Operating at the lower left corner of our triangle we take a *second look* ('is that a wart or something worse?'). If we can't observe or *see* a solution, we travel up to the top of our PST and explore around inside our heads to determine if we can *think up* or *feel* a solution ('I hope it's not cancer, or AIDS').

What we *see* down at the bottom left corner of the triangle influences what we think up at the top—*seeing-is-believing.* We call this *bottom-up* decision making, with trusted messages flowing from the bottom of the PST up to the top and strongly affecting—or even determining—our conclusion, like the strong messages flowing from skunks or splashed scalding coffee.

But more often than not, we must make decisions on the basis of weak messages, incomplete information, and little, if any, trusted observational evidence. For instance, most decisions concerning our future must be based on guesses; we have no reliable messages to go on, unless you trust teacup readers, TV evangelists, and stockbrokers. We can't *see* the future. No one can.

When we can't see where we're going but have no choice but to travel into the unknown, we must travel on faith, on what we believe. Then we rely on top-down decision making—*believing-is-seeing.* You can't observe it, but you bet your life on the future: your future career, your future health, and your future marriage. You travel on guesses or hope.

When faced with fuzzy, incomplete, or conflicting observations we must rely on messages flowing down from the top that influence, or even determine, what we see (e.g., what's a simple wart for me you see to be skin cancer, what's beautiful to you may appear ugly to me, what's true for you seems false for me, a future that promising to you might look dangerous to me).

Recently a statue of the Virgin Mary appeared to be crying what *looked* like blood. Carrying rosaries and cameras hundreds of believers flocked to the church to witness the miracle.

The Deacon of the mother church is quoted:[2] 'For people individually seeing things through the eyes of faith, something like this can be meaningful. As to whether it is supernatural or a miracle, normally these incidences are not. Miracles are possible, of course.' This is a dramatic example of believing-is-seeing. Repeat polls tell us that a majority of Americans believe in an invisible God.

Top-down decision processes are neither rare nor trivial. Most of our major decisions about the past, present, and future are based on incomplete and conflicting information—seeing provides an incomplete picture. To *get the whole picture* we need to fill in the gaps with beliefs, assumptions, biases, and theories.

---

[2]Associated Press, 29 November 2005.

Fig 1.2 ■ THE COMMON-SENSE PROBLEM-SOLVING TRIANGLE (PST)

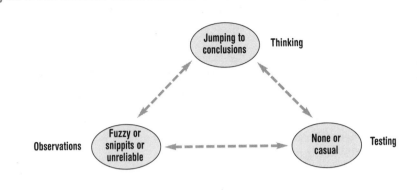

Because what we think or believe can strongly influence what we observe, and visa versa, we must modify Figure 1.1. We do so by using two-way arrows in Figure 1.2. In brief, messages flow in all directions around the PST.

Even when dealing with the present, where you and I can only *see* bits and pieces as they fly by, we rarely have the time to check the accuracy of our observations or messages, or to critically evaluate our decisions. Instead, we toss our quick, casual conclusions out into in the world and hope the worst ones don't catch up with us.

> When navigating large unfamiliar spaces, or the future, biases and beliefs flow down from the top of the PST influencing where we look and what we *see*.

Common-sense-light

You and I, with limited time at our disposal, rely on common-sense-light to *solve*, or a least dispose of, most of our problems.

Occasionally, as we zigzag through life, a surprising observation or idea captures our attention. We pause, take a quick look (observation), devote a bit of time wondering what it means (thinking), and then we may compare our conclusion with past experience or with 'expert' opinion (testing).

For example, consider how two students, Ellie and Carl, unwittingly employ the PST to get common sense answers to nagging personal problems.

Ellie's common sense PST

Ellie suffers from a periodic and itchy skin rash. She starts off at the bottom left corner of her PST with her *observation* of her rash—*itchy* messages, red, *scaly* messages.

These messages flow up to the top of the triangle and trigger stored memories as she travels back in time looking for causes in the long chain of messages. She consciously considers alternative solutions or treatments, trying to decide which message (or messages) are relevant.

She sees a TV ad extolling the magic powers of a new skin lotion. She buys it, and travelling down to the lower right corner of her PST, she starts *testing* it on her rash.

Notice that she has cycled around the three points of the triangle, and lo and behold, a week later she travels across to the lower left hand corner and *observes* that the rash is getting better—the scaly message is getting weaker and weaker.

The treatment *works*. Seeing-is-believing.

Ellie's mother thinks the rash went away because Ellie trusts the magic lotion and so calms down. Her mother thinks the cure is in Ellie's mind, whereas Ellie thinks it's in the jar.

Next consider how another student *solves* a persistent problem.

Carl's common sense PST

Carl—an average basketball player—is 5'11", which is above average height for men but short for a hoopster. Whenever he's on the court he *observes* that he's 'vertically challenged'. He frets, and spends his time dreaming and *thinking* about alternative ways to literally 'grow up'.

Cycling to the peak of his PST, he *thinks* and then he browses the Internet looking for reassuring messages.[3] Sure enough, he finds an exciting advertisement. It promises young people that they can add two to five inches to their height using a combination of stretching exercises and a stringent diet involving a supply of special herbs and vitamins. Carl's not stupid—he *thinks* twice before buying the package but then he notices that a famous National Basketball Association player endorses *the message*. Furthermore the ad *honestly* warns that it can take up to a year for the full benefits to emerge.

Carl signs up, cuts down on beer and movies to cover the costs, and, cycling down to the lower right corner of his PST, he puts the program to the *test*. He conscientiously consumes the foul-tasting herbal tea and suffers through the painful stretching routines.

And just like that, nine months later, he's two and half inches taller. Furthermore, he's made the first string.

He's thrilled. He enrolls for another year of tea and stretching.

Carl has cycled around the PST and, using his common sense, has examined the chain of messages and *knows* he's found 'the answer'.

Are Ellie and Carl kidding themselves?

---

[3]When you do an Internet search on any topic you typically get lots of hits, more than you can handle (it's called information or message overload). Furthermore, there is no 'truth' label provided, no way of differentiating fact from fancy from fraud, of spotting rumours and counterfeit messages.

Common sense can work even when it's wrong

As far as Ellie and Carl are concerned, their common sense problem solving works. Both of them generated mentally affordable and subjectively acceptable *solutions*. While their respective 'solutions' are acceptable to Ellie and Carl, both solutions are naïve, if not dead wrong.

To see why, cycle up to the top of your PST, put on your thinking cap, examine their chains of messages, and come up with one or more likely alternative explanations for their successful results.

Notice that neither Ellie nor Carl is being stupid. They're only doing the best problem solving they can afford with common-sense-light, and with the time, messages, and critical thinking capacity readily at hand.[4]

Jumping to conclusions is the name of the game.

Jumping to conclusions

In jumping to the conclusions that their treatments 'worked', both Ellie and Carl vaulted over some obvious alternative explanations for their 'successful' results. They jumped to naïve conclusions that just a little critical thinking would have exposed.

Here's one such explanation that they both ignored. Have you heard the two old folk wisdoms: 'The doctor keeps the patient busy while nature produces the cure,' and 'Without treatment a cold can last as long as three weeks, but with treatment it only lasts 21 days.'

What happens when you apply these bits of critical thinking to Ellie and Carl's conclusions?

Ellie's solution

Ellie suffers from periodic skin problems. 'Periodic' is the key word. The skin problems come and go. The red rash message (down below) triggers a mental message (up top) to buy the latest magic potion. So when the rash appears Ellie automatically buys, and applies, the latest lotion. When the rash inevitably disappears, two or three weeks later, she gives the salve the credit.

A more accurate conclusion might be: *'Ellie gets skin rashes that last about three weeks, no matter what she does, but she feels in control by buying and applying expensive lotions.'*

Furthermore, we often 'see' what we want to see. So, after the application of her magic potion, when Ellie cycles over to the bottom left corner of her PST she has a vested interest in observing improvements. And, of course, magic lotions are designed to camouflage what they can't cure.

---

[4]As we'll be discussing later, a psychologist recently won the Nobel Prize for research which challenged the traditional view that people usually make rational decisions. He documented the mental and cultural short cuts we take and the biases we use to cut problems and answers down to mind-size.

Therefore Ellie, like the rest of us, speeds around her PST generating mentally affordable and reassuring, but sometimes naïve, answers on the basis of selective message fragments.

Has Carl done any better?

Carl's solution

Generating alternative explanations for Carl's 'successful' solution is a bit more complicated, but the same principles apply. Could time alone have produced his two and half inch growth?

The company peddling the stretching and herbal package pointed out it was designed for *young people*, and that it could take *a year* to work.

Stop and think—what are most teens doing in a year? Along with lots of other things, they're usually growing!

This pattern of normal development has probably not escaped the attention of those selling the package. In fact they probably created a graph similar to the one below and pinned it up on their bulletin board.

Fig 1.3 ■ GROWTH SPURTS IN TEENAGERS

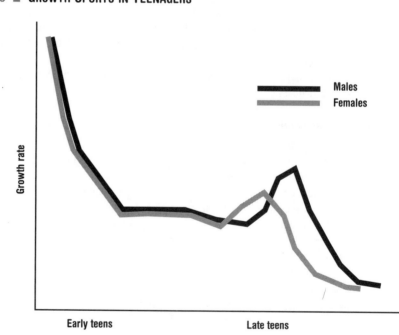

Females, and particularly males, experience a growth spurt in their middle to late teens.

Let's be conservative and say an inch and a half of Carl's growth can reasonably be credited to a normal spurt in his late teens that would have occurred anyway without any special stretching or diet. However, that crucial message is missing from his critical thinking. Scientists have more time than citizens to think critically, to expose hidden messages, and to review the relevant literature.

But what about the other inch Carl added to his height? For some males time alone will produce that too. But what else might explain it? Look down at the left hand corner of the PST and ask the question: how accurate are we in observing/measuring our own height? How accurate are messages about our height?

Even if performed by someone else, measures of height can vary from day to day by at least an inch depending on the measuring instrument used, who's using it, and, of course, height will vary upwards if the person is *standing tall*.

So with a little critical thinking at the top of our PST and a little knowledge about growth patterns, we readily generate alternative and reasonable explanations for the results that Carl had attributed solely to his expensive growth package. But what about his improved performance on the basketball court? Well, if you *think* that you're two and half inches taller, and you are in fact an inch or so taller, and if you're a year older and stronger, and you have invested heavily in a magic treatment while reducing sedentary activities like drinking beer and watching movies, isn't it reasonable to assume that those factors will combine to give you more confidence and energy on the court? And wouldn't this mean that you would be more effective throughout the game?

Again, Carl is not being stupid. He's only trying to generate affordable, reassuring, common sense answers with the time, readily accessible messages, and critical thinking capacity readily at hand.

If he and Ellie had access to more time, more reliable messages, and more training in critical thinking, then they would, no doubt, generate some alternative answers, use the problem-solving triangle more effectively, and avoid jumping to so many naïve answers.

But if they did all that they'd be . . . scientists!

You don't need a PhD to think smarter

You don't need a PhD to significantly improve your critical thinking. In fact, adding just a few basic bits of wisdom to the top of your PST enables you to rapidly spot many major flaws in the 'solutions' proposed by others, including advertisers and experts.

And better still, you may even prevent yourself from jumping to a naïve, or even disastrous, conclusion.

Adding the PST to your supply of critical thinking tools won't win you a Nobel Prize but it will move you from common-sense-light to common-sense-pretty-darn-good (medium). We call this level *pre-scientific*. It involves more conscientious cycling around the PST than we usually do, but still not as effective as scientists do (common-sense-heavy or common-sense-potent).

You and I use this level of pre-scientific problem solving for pet projects. We also provide experts (doctors, lawyers, etc.), news services, and the courts with more time to practice pretty darn good common sense. Nevertheless, even sometimes at work, and certainly as soon as they head home, those same people practice common-sense-light; they jump to a lot of conclusions, just like Ellie and Carl.

Let's take a closer look at pre-scientific problem solving, or common-sense-pretty-darn-good.

The pre-scientific PST: common-sense-pretty-darn-good

Between common-sense-light and common-sense-potent (scientific), lies common-sense-pretty-darn-good. It requires more time and more critical thinking than you and I usually commit to using common-sense-light, but not as much as science requires.

Before discussing the refinements science has made to the PST, we should acknowledge that, on occasion, you and others—including experts such as doctors or lawyers, the news media, and the courts—stretch the boundaries of common-sense problem-solving. People don't jump to conclusions all the time.

For example, you don't have to be a scientist to find the time, on occasion, to make accurate observations, to critically examine a chain of messages, to carefully consider alternatives, and to conscientiously test some of them. Students, amateur cooks, golfers, stamp collectors, and music and sports fans find time to attentively explore bits of their world, that is, to conscientiously cycle around their PSTs.

Although you may not follow all the rules of scientific problem-solving, for special projects you nevertheless stretch your common sense and demonstrate pre-scientific talents. So, if we put our time and our minds to it we can do pretty darn well with small, local puzzles.

So do our experts.

Pretty-darn-good doctors

While we don't provide experts with the time and resources available to scientists, experts can still afford to specialize; they can focus most of their time and critical thinking on a limited set of puzzles, like those arising in the sub-fields of law or medicine for example.

A heart specialist focuses his or her attention on a complex chain of messages concerning your heart. The specialist relies on different messengers: on you to describe your symptoms, medical history, and lifestyle, on various pieces of equipment, on lab tests, on case records, and on the popular medical theories and biases of the day. He or she, under time pressure, analyzes that chain of mixed messages looking for stable patterns, and comparing them with *good-news* and *bad-news* patterns stored in his or her long-term memory. Doctors employ this conscientious but pre-scientific method with the time and tools available.

We call what they do *pre-scientific* for several reasons. First these specialists don't have time to carefully and rigorously check the reliability of your messages concerning symptoms, medical history, and lifestyle. Doctors must rely on fuzzy feedback. Furthermore, once they prescribe a treatment regime, they have no way of knowing how closely you follow it. For instance, patients rarely confess that they stopped taking their pills because of side effects or cost.

Therefore, down at the bottom of their PSTs, these specialists must often rely on an unreliable database in making their diagnosis or judging the value of their treatment. They can't afford to systematically track all their patients, therefore, they don't know how many that they designated as *good news* were false positives[5]—patients who went to another doctor the following week and received bad news, or who dropped dead.

Experts cycle around their PSTs more conscientiously than the rest of us, but, as we'll see, not as conscientiously as scientists.

Reporters and editors

Next, consider the experts who work in traditional news services, like newspapers.[6] They rely on reporters and cameramen to gather reliable messages at the bottom of the PST and send them up to their editors for critical review. But a newspaper has to meet daily deadlines in order to successfully go to press. Unlike scientists, reporters and editors have to turn off their learning capacity, turn off their message-gathering and analyzing, at the same time every day. No matter how conscientious they are they must still rely on relatively quick and dirty message-gathering and editorial bias in order to meet their deadlines.

Even the illustrious *New York Times* is burdened by reporters who make up their stories, by columnists who get seduced by the biases of their sources, and by editors who, while rushing to go to press, miss the false or slanted messages in the flow, or add their own.

---

[5]All measuring instruments, including human yardsticks, send some false messages. For example 'false positives' are patients erroneously labelled by their doctor as healthy. 'False negatives' are patients erroneously labelled by their doctors as sick.

[6]TV news services don't have the same deadline restrictions that newspapers have, and therefore they can afford to keep a part of their learning capacity available for late-breaking news. Internet news even more so. While all these news services frequently make mistakes, they also devote resources to checking the reliability of their news, and at least make gestures toward editorial balance. But the Internet has provided a whole new 'anything-goes-news-service', for example, 'bloggers'. Here you find a raging flood of freewheeling common sense thinking, jumping to conclusions, astonishing examples of top-down problem solving where personal feelings, beliefs, and biases rule the day—an example of freedom of expression in the extreme. Embedded in this massive and perpetual flow of messages you'll find statements from all sorts, ranging from cranks and crazies, to sensible folks like us, and on up to budding geniuses. How can you even begin to sort them? How would you know? Sometimes it takes years to sort fact from fancy.

The courts

Finally, consider the experts working in an institution that sets the gold standard for pre-scientific problem solving—the courts.

Down at the left corner of the PST they commit significant time and resources toward gathering reliable messages, or evidence. At the top of the PST those messages are systematically and critically examined. First, they must pass the court's rules of evidence (hearsay or second hand evidence—the stuff you and I live on—is not accepted). Second, through an adversarial system, the prosecution and the defense challenge each other's interpretations, each side assisted by their own pet experts.[7]

Furthermore, the courts try to test the validity of their conclusions. Down at the right hand corner of the PST they lock up the jury to *test* whether the accused is guilty or innocent. This is a major commitment of social resources in the search for *the truth*.

Individual jury members, however, are not always allowed to cast a secret ballot. Sometimes a show of hands is required. Our courts constrain the testing procedure. They rely upon a combination of politically appointed judges and peer pressure on jury members to force consensus. But, practically speaking, we need constraints to reach closure. Scientists face far fewer constraints and reach far fewer final verdicts. Ideally scientific *solutions* remain open for further modification in the light of new evidence at the bottom and new theory at the top of the PST.

Summarizing, you and I, as well as the experts, the media, and the courts, benefit by periodically stretching our particular common-sense problem-solving methods in order to seek reliable patterns in the noisy flow of mixed messages. Occasionally, in the midst of the rat race, we beg, borrow, or steal enough time to raise our level of problem-solving from quick and dirty common sense to the more conscientious pre-scientific level, where we invest serious attention in a special person, project, or puzzle.

Considering the number and complexity of the problems we regularly face, we do pretty well a lot of the time.

But many of the problems we encounter involve too many dots, or too many possible connections. They lay beyond the reach of common-sense-light and common-sense-pretty-darn-good, and they require a conscientious and sustained commitment of resources at all three corners of the PST. We provide scientists with the resources to extend their senses, enlarge their memory and analytic capacities, and to continue rigorously testing their best bets.

---

[7]The fact that the prosecution and defense can find experts who support almost any interpretation of a piece of evidence suggests that experts work with pretty elastic yardsticks.

Scientists Refine the Triangle

Over the centuries, through trial and error—including some whopping errors—scholars have refined the common-sense PST into a much more powerful tool for separating fact from fancy.

As indicated in Figure 1.4 they've added three very important words, one at each corner of the triangle.

Fig 1.4 ■ THE PROBLEM-SOLVING TRIANGLE (PST)

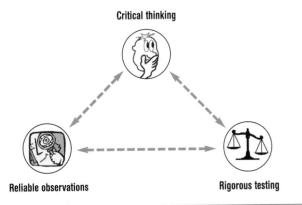

Critical thinking

Reliable observations

Rigorous testing

First, notice that, at the bottom left corner, scientists focus not on just on any observations but rather on *reliable observations*.

How do we define a reliable observation?

If an independent researcher, preferably one who has no loyalty to you or your theory, follows your particular observational or measurement procedure and comes up with same messages you did, then that's a pretty reliable observation (e.g., they find the same growth patterns that you found in a larger sample of North American teens).

Second, it's important to pay attention to how reliable observations simplify the job of theoretical scientists when, at the top of their PSTs, they attempt to do some 'critical thinking'—when they attempt to locate patterns in what's been observed and to make predictions of what might be observed in the future. It's a lot easier to identify patterns (connections between the dots) if you're dealing with clear, stable dots than with fuzzy, shifty ones.

If the observations are reliable then they won't waste time trying to make sense of fuzzy, or imaginary, or distorted observations that might be in the chain of messages. In short, they won't be attempting to make sense out of nonsense; they won't be wasting time playing the GIGO game—*garbage in, garbage out*.

While operating up at the peak of the PST modern scientists have access to an accumulated set of *critical thinking skills*, tools that help them identify alternative explanations of what's been observed, tools that help them separate stable from unstable patterns in the data. For example, they don't have to rely on rough and ready eye-balling of the graphs because they have statistical techniques that enable them to judge the similarities between the growth patterns of two samples of teens drawn from different socio-economic groups. They also have theoretical tools helping them generate alternative interpretations of those patterns, some genetic and some environmental, most a tangled combination of both.

Third, for both *empirical and theoretical science* a most obvious refinement occurs when scientists cycle down to the bottom right corner of the PST. Having selected one or two best bets from the alternative interpretations of message chains and accessible observations, they put their tentative conclusion—their hypothesis—through some rigorous tests, including the toughest tests of all: those conducted by other researchers who don't much like the theory.[8]

For example, empirical researchers check the growth patterns of large samples of teens from different socio-economic groups across the country. If their tests yield similar patterns then they find some support for a genetic influence. That is, regardless of differences in diet, parenting, exercise, climate, etc., similar growth patterns appear across the teenage years. Reliable links have appeared in the chain of messages.

But, those are average growth patterns. And while there may be strong similarities there will invariably also be some group and individual differences that need to be explained. Why are some groups and individuals below or above average? Sciencing is a work in progress. The horizon of complete knowledge keeps moving just out of reach. Scientists walk into that future on theoretical bridges.

Scientific theories and formulae initially appear strange, like E=mc². But if you think of them as promissory notes, or treasure maps, they're not so scary. Einstein's famous formula promised that you could find a huge heap of energy (E) in a small rock (m).

Treasure maps—promissory messages

You can think of scientists as testing treasure maps, or as checking out promissory notes about the future.

On the basis of some *observations* (hopefully reliable) they do some critical *thinking* that results in a mental map of where they believe nature has buried some of her treasure. They start 'digging' and then they start *testing*.

---

[8]Now it must be said that 'theoretical scientists' (those who spend their time at the top of the triangle doing critical thinking), although agreeing that rigorous empirical testing is necessary, won't necessarily agree that it's the most important refinement. Rather, they would claim that first off you had better generate smart hunches and hypotheses worth testing, ones that have already passed some rigorous thought experiments. That's why Einstein claimed that imagination was more important than knowledge. Of course, he was biased; he didn't spend any time sweating it out at the lower right corner of the PST. He stayed up top.

Freud promised we'd find sexy messages buried inside everyone's unconscious, but the digging proved difficult and deep! Freud tried to map the inside of our heads and then dig for repressed sexual messages that would explain why we have weird dreams, anxiety attacks, and depression. When other scholars tested his theory and couldn't *find* messages of repressed sexuality, loyal Freudians claimed that the critical researchers just hadn't dug deep enough. Is it a lousy map, or lazy diggers?

Much of Freud's map of the mind had, and still has, intuitive appeal. Advertisers bet billions on it every year. But most of his theory lacks reliable observations, and independent researchers can't agree about what messages lay buried in the unconscious. The unconscious turned out to be a safe place for Freud to bury his treasure.

As you can see, it's important to understand that an appealing theory issued from the top of the PST may persist for years even if scholars can't agree whether the map leads to real treasure or only fool's gold; that is, whether it leads to true messages or appealing myths.

But it's also important to understand that even the scientifically refined PST runs into trouble, not only when digging for fuzzies but even when digging with hi-tech tools for good solid stuff, like weapons of mass destruction (WMDs).

Here's a lousy map and a bunch of shovels—go dig

Donald Rumsfeld, the hard-nosed former US Secretary of Defense was intensely interested in finding treasure outside the mind, specifically, in finding chemical and nuclear weapons in Iraq. Like Freud's, Rumsfeld's treasure map was vague about just where and how deep to dig. But at least, unlike Freud's, Rumsfeld's diggers would 'know' if their shovel hit something hard.

But, where should the diggers dig?

Answer: well, WMDs could be anywhere in Iraq.

So where should you dig? Everywhere? How deep should you dig? Answer: well, weapons could be buried at various depths, so dig 'deep'. How deep is 'deep?'

So Rumsfeld, like Freud,[9] can't be proved wrong. The treasure is safe. As Rumsfeld told the press, just because WMDs haven't been found doesn't mean they're not there. Maybe we didn't dig in the right place, or deep enough, maybe the enemy keeps moving them around?

Thus, not all treasure maps, not all theories, not all hunches, can be rigorously tested. If the map is too large, and the digging spots and depths aren't specified, don't invest in the map. Yes, it's possible that there might be treasure in 'them thar hills' but let someone else get the blisters.

Understandably then, empirical scientists, working down at the right corner of the PST, are very cautious about maps promising fuzzy treasures, or those

---

[9]With the advent of brain imaging, some researchers will no doubt start looking (digging) for physical locations in the brain of the Id, Ego, and Superego.

promising concrete loot but at unspecified locations in wide open spaces. Those kinds of treasures currently defy rigorous testing.

In contrast, both Einstein and Skinner provided maps promising treasure but also including specific predictions that could be rigorously tested.

Einstein's brief message, $E = mc^2$, produced the atom bomb. Independent observers could agree about that. Einstein's message promised what we'd find in space and time.

Skinner's message was almost as grandiose, promising that we could shape and control all behaviour, from pigeons to people, with precise schedules of reinforcement. And it worked. It worked particularly well with pigeons and with psychiatric patients. It worked as long as experimental participants were locked up in a box or a hospital.

So Skinner's message had to be revised. You could control behaviour as long as the participants were already highly controlled; they were locked up in a Skinner box. Skinner's truth flourished in the laboratory, but unlike Einstein's, it didn't thrive outside the laboratory in the rough and tumble world.

Of course, it's simpler to shape and control the behaviour of a few ounces of purified uranium atoms in a lab than the behaviour of 130 pounds of teenager at a rock festival!

Like Freud looking for the Id, and Rumsfeld looking for WMDs, scientists have to decide what to look for and where to dig.[10] But the universe is a big place. Each scientific discipline stakes out a claim and draws a boundary around a piece of the universe—a tiny piece of the BIG puzzle. Each discipline digs for different *treasure*: for sub-atomic particles, for genes, for brains, for minds, for cultures, or for clues to the future. Of course, scientists disagree about which piece of the puzzle is most important. And, of course, some scholars attempt to fit these different pieces of the puzzle together and explain *everything*. So far, they have been unsuccessful.

Lack of success, however, is not due to lack of effort. Solving complex problems can be like fighting bees—pay attention to one and three others sting you.

Neat and tidy science

Many see science as a neat and tidy method of solving puzzles. They perceive science as the simple process of starting down at the bottom left corner of the PST with reliable observations, cycling up to the top and connecting them together, then sliding down to the bottom right corner to test whether the predicted connection proves to be true.

---

[10] Recall the story about the drunk on his hands and knees, under a lamp post, looking for his car keys. A passerby asked him where he dropped the keys? The drunk replied: 'I dropped them way over there, but it's too dark there so I'm looking here where I can see.' Scientists sometimes have the same problem: they have to look under their disciplinary lamp post, where they can *see*, even though the treasure may lie beyond their boundary, over there in the dark. Maybe the treasure lies in the territory staked out by a different discipline, or even one not yet staked out at all.

For example, a scientist could easily figure out the connection between a stone (a physical object) and the conscious sensation of pain (a psychological experience). You have a stone in your shoe. The stone delivers a clear message to your toe, which delivers a message to a string of nerves and junctions that run up your leg and spinal column to your brain. Then you consciously experience 'pain', your brain sends a message to your vocal cords, and they say 'ouch!' This is a nice simple example of a reliable messenger service. A nice simple example of what *caused*[11] you to say 'ouch!' The cause is the stone.

But wait a minute. How do you explain the observation—the message—that amputees, lacking a stone and a foot, report pain in their toes?

What kind of connection is that? What kind of message service is that?

Just like you and me, scientists are attracted to surprises, to puzzles. How would you explain the above puzzle? What causes pain in missing toes?

Travelling from the known to the unknown

How do we travel from a known message chain, from stones–toes–ouch, to an unknown message change, to no stone–no toes–ouch?

We rely on past experience to provide maps of similar situations. In what familiar situations have we encountered chains of messages? Can they provide clues?

For example, friends create message chains when they talk to each other. Furthermore, very good friends and partners often seem to know ahead of time what the other one is going to say. They only need a look, a gesture, or a few words (message fragments) to *get* the whole message. How can they do that from such an incomplete message chain? And, of course, sometimes they make mistakes.

This example provided a familiar instance from past experience that may help us understand what's happening in the amputee message chain—it may be a bit like old friends getting a clear message from message fragments.

With this hunch in mind, let's revisit the amputee–ouch puzzle and speculate on the chain of events:

1. Before the foot was amputated there were some very familiar, well-established message chains or pathways between his or her toes, at the beginning of the chain, and the 'ouch' issued at the end of the chain.
2. When you have such a familiar chain, where one message bit anywhere in the chain automatically fires another, all that's necessary is to have any messenger above the ankle send a snippet of a message similar to

---

[11]The term 'caused' has become a bad word in science because you can get involved in an infinite regress (what caused the cause). So, instead of the terms 'cause' and 'effect', scientists use the more politically correct terms antecedents and consequences. But, like you and me, scientists still think in terms of cause and effect, so we use those terms.

the stone–toe message, and it triggers others up the line, like a row of dominos.

3. Just as old friends occasionally misread the message fragments you send, so too does our nervous system misread some of the message fragments pouring into our brain.

We've used the analogy of good friends reading—and sometimes misreading—each other's message fragments to help us provide one explanation of how amputees get messages from non-existent toes.

Scientists also rely heavily on analogies and metaphors[12] based on past experience to help them explain puzzles, such as thinking that the human nervous system *is like* a chain of messages, some reliable, some a bit noisy, and some unreliable.

So let's say a scientist follows our hunch, but he or she can afford to give it more time and attention. The steps might go something like this:

1. observation of a number of amputees to make sure it was a common puzzle,
2. use of a qualitative pain scale to measure the intensity, trying to determine under what conditions different degrees of pain did or did not occur,
3. perhaps the use of physical measuring instruments (e.g., electrodes) to trace nerve firing from the ankle up to the brain,
4. use of magnetic resonance images (MRIS) in order to see to which parts of the brain blood flowed when the phantom pain occurred, and
5. testing of different pain-reducing treatment techniques ranging from relaxation and self-hypnosis to drugs and surgery, etc.

The theory being tested is that somewhere, in the chain of messengers above the amputee's ankle, there is a neurological rumour-monger inventing and sending messages along the familiar chain. Remember, all it takes is a snippet of a familiar message in order to fire off a familiar chain above that point.

So, like you and me, scientists help cut complex puzzles down to mind-size by mentally travelling from the known to the unknown using speculative maps, metaphors, and mathematical models *as if* they represented *reality*.

Scientists aren't the only ones drawing speculative maps

Operating at the top of the PST, theoretical scientists draw speculative maps of unknown territories and make specific predictions about what they'll find. Operating down at the bottom of the PST, research scientists test the accuracy of those maps, that is, they test the accuracy of up-top predictions.

---

[12]Metaphors are crude maps that help us travel from the known to the unknown. Like all maps they're *simpler than the territory*, and may or may not be valid; they may or may not accurately describe the lay of the land. Like any map, at best they omit most of the detail—otherwise they wouldn't fit in your glove compartment.

As the research results gradually accumulate, we discover that sometimes those speculative maps are generally right but specifically wrong, or specifically right here and there, but generally wrong. Or just plain wrong, both generally and specifically.

Sometimes we can't tell whether they're right or wrong because researchers can't travel to the problem space to make observations . . . maybe they will never be able to.

Furthermore, most scientific laws apply to groups but not necessarily to individuals. Scientists make predictions about the behaviour of groups; groups of molecules, groups of cells, and groups of patients (e.g., 60 per cent of the patients improved on this treatment).

That's nice, but what I really want to know is: 'Will I improve on this treatment?'

Sorry, science mostly deals with groups and probabilities.[13] In the example above science predicts how many patients will improve, not which patients will improve.

If you're twenty years old, scientific statistics say that you *probably* have 59.3 more years to live. Of course, you may die tomorrow. Or you might live to be 95.

Science can't say.

In the United States, roughly 1 out of every 2 marriages end in divorce. Will you be one of them? In Canada the statistic states that 1 out of 3 marriages fail. Maybe you should you have your wedding in Canada?

Do I really love him? Does he really love me? Science can't say . . . yet. Maybe, in the not too distant future, some scientific entrepreneur will set up a clinic and use an MRI to analyze blood flow in your brain while you look at pictures of your significant other. But is that really a rigorous test of LOVE? Looking at a picture of your prospective mate in a laboratory may indeed get your blood flowing to one particular part of your brain, however, seeing him unwashed and unshaven while shovelling cornflakes into his mouth may make the blood flow to a very different place.

But, every once in a while, science comes up with a finding that covers almost everyone—almost the whole group—like the strong link between smoking and lung cancer. It took a while to discover, but in that case the linkage proved to be so strong that it can now be relied upon to guide your individual decision.

Most scientific discoveries about humans, however, aren't that clear-cut. For most life shaping decisions a high degree of uncertainty remains, which leaves you on your own. Well, almost.

Scientists aren't the only ones working diligently away at the top of the PST, drawing speculative maps about unknown territory. You and I draw them every

---

[13]Later in the book we'll be discussing research on individuals, case studies, and N-of-one studies. Ellie and Carl conducted N-of-one case studies on themselves.

day, particularly about the future. Everyone does, including politicians, poets, and priests.

Because our current collection of speculative and tested scientific maps covers only a tiny portion of our unknown futures, we have no choice but to rely heavily on non-scientific speculative maps.

And in addition to relying on available and relevant science, we have access to a big bundle of speculative maps provided by non-scientific experts and specialists.

Some scientists reject and ridicule these non-scientific maps. But we can't put our lives on hold waiting for the white coats to provide rigorously tested pictures of our particular futures. If we did, we'd never even get out of bed.

Where science has not yet gone, we lack reliable maps. But we can't get off time's conveyer belt and wait. We're carried into the unknown future whether we like it or not. So we must rely on any maps available—those produced by common sense, by experts, and by society's wise and wonderful winnowed wisdom. We must rely on a host of other prognosticators 'seers' leaning over the ramparts, peering into the unknown from the pinnacles of their PSTs.

While we wait for scientists to solve complex problems within their reach, we, and they, must settle for best guesses and promissory notes.

> When travelling from the known to the unknown both citizens and scientists must rely on speculations, hunches, maps, and metaphors.

Where science leaves off, common-sense-light takes over

You should notice that although some puzzles lie beyond the reach of science, perhaps temporarily (like some cancers) or permanently (like what the future holds) no puzzle lies beyond the reach of common-sense-light. That's because that low-level problem-solving method doesn't require reliable observations, critical thinking, or rigorous testing. Common-sense-light can create certainty out of nothing concrete, out of hopes, and out of fears, beliefs, and biases.

In fact, our personal PSTs operate particularly well with fuzzy observations scattered over great spaces, including the past, present, and future (e.g., 'All men are . . .', 'All women are . . .', 'All liberals are . . .'). If your personal hunch or theory doesn't have to pass any rigorous testing then you can afford to believe almost any message in the chain. Visit a random sample of blogs and you will see what we mean. Or, if you're a liberal, listen to a conservative speech.

Millions of Germans believed Hitler's message, millions of Russians (and others) believed Stalin's message, and—closer to home—millions of our ancestors believed the message of slavery. Millions of us still believe get-rich-quick scams and politician's promises. They seemed to make sense at the time, didn't they? That's common sense talking. And if our *conclusions* are wrong—if we choose the wrong friends, the wrong career, the wrong addiction, the wrong mate, the wrong Prime Minister, or the wrong future—it usually takes a while, sometimes years, before the pain (the rigorous test results) comes home to roost.

You and I can provide fuzzy answers to fuzzy questions, and we do. What's more, we get away with it because there are no clear answers to fuzzy questions.

This line of thought is starting to make science look too good to be true. But remember that all maps and models, including the PST, are simplifications. All message chains include weak links. The time has come to pull back the curtains and peek behind the scientific scene.

> Cycling around our PSTs, you and I can 'answer' many more questions than scientists can. We just can't provide as many *valid* answers.

Too good to be true?

If we remove our rose-coloured glasses and take a closer look at science, what do we find? On occasion, we find that as individual scientists navigate around their PSTs they may encounter puzzles too big for their brains. Or, because of a lack of time or technology, scientists must rely on fuzzy observations or unreliable message chains, or jump over plausible explanations, in order to accommodate their pet hunch, the theory promoted by a granting agency, the special interests of a rich drug company, or the popular paradigm of the scientific culture of the day.

So scientists are human? Just like us.

You have to agree that it's hard not to believe, a bit blindly, in a theory you've worked on for months, even years, maybe a lifetime. It's a bit like believing in your child. We're all a bit blind about things we love, our babies, our cherished beliefs, and our pet theories.

Wait a minute! If individual scientists on occasion rely on the same flawed common sense problem solving as the rest of us, what makes scientific news so special? What makes scientific messages so trustworthy?

Scientists challenge each other

How do scientists check the reliability and validity of their pet theories and of the chain of messages they collect and display?

Over centuries, scholars have developed checks and balances to detect errors and correct procedures.

And never fear—the finely tuned capacity for critical analysis of individual scientists remains alive and well. And it is generously applied, lavishly to the work of their opponents—to other scientists with opposing methodological or theoretical views—if not to their own work. And their opponents answer in kind.

Science is a semi-civilized adversarial system. Consequently scientists think very carefully before rushing into print with their findings. They don't want to expose their embarrassing scientific bare spots.

On the other hand, they can't afford to be too cautious or an opponent will beat them into print, maybe to the Nobel Prize.

Scientists face a dilemma. In order to maintain their self-respect—and their jobs—they must publish *or* perish. On the other hand, if they go to press with unreliable science, then they run the risk of publishing and perishing. When is the right time to temporarily turn off their learning capacity, stop cycling conscientiously around their PST, stop gathering and critically analyzing data, and go to press?

There are no simple answers. Science is a work in progress. There is never a final answer to a complex puzzle, each solution raises more questions. Dedicated scientists are reluctant to turn off their learning capacity—to interrupt their explorations—to take time off in order to go to press.

Nevertheless, they must and they do. And that's when the opposition gathers at both the top and bottom of the PST to assault the new research findings and interpretations (theoretical speculations).

We've said that science is an adversarial system. On those occasions when a researcher slips up—when they rely on unreliable observations and messages and jump to rose-coloured conclusions about their *baby*—they can be almost certain that, sooner or later, other scientists will publicly expose those flaws, either at a conference or in the scientific press.

Such ingrained and institutionalized error detection and reporting mechanisms help explain why the products of science remain our most trusted messages.

Maybe we should change the title of this book from *The Science Game* to *The Court of Science*. Certainly science reflects a robust adversarial culture where the prosecution and the defense tenaciously examine each other's observations, thinking, and testing in the ongoing search for *the truth*. Scientists commit their lives to that search, even if in their heart they know that no matter how much ground they cover, they'll never discover *the whole* truth about a big puzzle.

Finally, while rigorously testing theories demands a lot of hard work, it also delivers deep satisfaction. Testing theories is a bit like unwrapping a series of parcels, or taking apart a Chinese puzzle box. And don't forget the 'Ah Ha!' experiences—first, from light-bulb insights that tell you where to dig for treasure, and second, from the wondrous peak experience when you find some.

SUMMARY

Scientists play an exciting, profoundly challenging game with nature in which they try to break nature's codes, locate her hidden truths, and read her endless chain of secret messages.

The rules of the science game are not as mysterious as you may suppose. We've shown how science can be seen as an extension of the common sense problem-solving triangle (PST)—which you use every hour of every day.

With their driving curiosity and tenacity, plus society's support, scientists have refined the PST and, unlike the rest of us, have the time, training, and resources to capitalize on those refinements. They don't have to jump to as many naïve conclusions; they can afford to rigorously test some of their hunches.

In addition, science has institutionalized error-detecting and correcting mechanisms. Scientists critically examine each other's work and, in doing so, help expose unreliable observations, sloppy thinking, less than rigorous testing, and the tricks of chance.

That's why science remains our most trusted news service.

The pre-scientific and scientific methods to be discussed in the rest of the book can be viewed as knowledge-building tools.

Using the PST we've discussed three major tools: reliable observations, critical thinking, and rigorous testing.

As a scientist cycles around his or her PST he or she encounters a chain of messages, all of them filtered through the senses and the brain. And we know from amputees suffering phantom pain that the *defining* message can arise anywhere in the chain—bottom, top, or middle. So, since the scientist operates everywhere in the chain—observing, thinking, and testing—he or she becomes the most likely source of the defining messages, or, of the conclusions.

Therefore, before examining scientific methods or tools, it is imperative that in the next chapter we examine the strengths and limitations of the human tool user—in this case the scientist. We must examine his or her message receiving, transforming, and sending capacity. We must examine to what degree his or her transformations are *truth*-enhancing, *truth*-distorting, or even *truth*-free. Only then can we appreciate their limitations, understand their disagreements, and wonder at their astonishing discoveries.

---

student's notebook[14]

Well, here I am taking the research methods course from Professor Creek. What's more, he decided to use the book Dr Frund lent me, The Science Game. I can understand why Dr Frund liked it—so far it contains a lot of stuff that she believes. She could have written it.

Professor Creek seems to like the book, but he's not too thrilled about the claim in the first chapter that individual scientists, on occasion, rely on unreliable observations, jump to conclusions, and fail to conduct rigorous tests of their hypotheses. Of course, he's admitted to me—in Dr Frund's presence—that he jumps to the odd conclusion and also gets emotionally attached to his hypotheses, to his babies.

---

[14]See the Prologue for Diana's perspective on social and behavioural science, and to see the research study she did of her own behaviour that changed her life, sort of.

Nevertheless, he claims he's the best when operating down at the bottom left corner of the PST, insisting that his observations are super reliable, whether working with rats or people! I guess it's one thing to admit a human frailty in private, and another to see it print.

Our course assignment involves doing a commentary on each chapter of the text. I guess it's not a bad way to force us to learn the course material as we go along. We also have to include two references to current events (e.g., news items) that relate to science. That way we'll gradually become more critical of junk science. He says we'll become 'more sophisticated consumers of scientific news'.

In the commentary we have to pick items of interest from the chapter, do some critical thinking, and read some literature (i.e., related stuff in other texts or journals, in the media, or online). Creek says 'the Internet contains a lot of junk, but increasingly it also contains serious science and critical commentary. So use it!'

A guy sitting next me asked how many pages he expects for these chapter commentaries.

Professor Creek frowned. Apparently he doesn't believe in pages. Students are too foxy. Nodding rapidly he said: 'When I used to give out page lengths, clever students just kept increasing their margins, the type size, and the space between lines so they could get away with saying almost nothing. So let's just say that I want at least 1,500 words—your own words—excluding long quotations and the list of references.'

What can I write 1,500 words about for Chapter 1? One of the ideas in this first chapter that triggered my curiosity was the statement that 'Over the centuries through trial and error—including some whopping errors—scholars have refined the PST, making it a much more powerful tool for separating "fact" from "fancy".'

I'm interested in history, so I wondered what some of those 'whopping errors' were. Also, what did the scientists learn from the errors?

I lucked out. My boyfriend Derek is a sociology major and he took me to a lecture where the visiting professor was talking about the 'Sociology of Science'. I didn't even know there was such a topic. The lecturer discussed the history of scientific thinking. Derek, bless his heart, recorded the lecture so I didn't have to rely on my memory alone, which is like a sieve for new stuff.

So, here's my commentary on whopping 'scientific' errors.

The Evolution of Science: Commentary on Chapter 1,
By Diana Dodds, for Research Methods 201

'To wonder . . . that is the seed of science.'—Emerson

In this chapter the authors write: 'Over the centuries, through trial and error—including some whopping errors—scholars have refined the common-sense PST, making it a much more powerful tool for separating "fact" from "fancy".'

Cave Dweller Science

If Emerson is right, if *to wonder* is the seed, then science was well on its way when Oola the medicine woman stood at the door of her cave, *wondering* about star patterns, about tomorrow's weather, about choosing the location for the next day's hunt, and about curing the ailing tribal chief.

Her methods of finding solutions were simple.

First she checked her memory for previous solutions. The medicine woman was a walking storehouse of accumulated tribal wisdom. If, after making an observation, and if after traveling up to the top of her PST and searching her mental library, she couldn't find an answer, then she looked for new clues by tossing the stones, or by reading animal entrails. These strategies inevitably generated an answer. But how good were her solutions?

Well, if the hunt went well, or if the chief got better, she took the credit. But if the hunt went badly she claimed that some of the hunters must have secretly broken a taboo. If the chief died, she said the Gods were angry.

According to the visiting speaker, we still consult our modern 'shamans', only now we call them experts, physicians, or scientists. He said 'they are schooled in our modern tribal wisdoms and myths, and now search for new patterns by tossing, not stones, but data in their computers, and by reading x-ray or MRI images of our entrails to help them reach (jump?) to conclusions.'

The speaker also claimed that 'successful experts throughout history share two characteristics: (1) They depend on our blind trust that they know what they're talking about most of the time; and (2) they must have publicly and professionally acceptable explanations as a cover when they are blatantly wrong. Now, instead of blaming the Gods, experts usually blame computer error or the government. Scientists blame their research assistants or nature's stingy reluctance to give up her secrets.'

He pointed out that some professions—like medicine—and some scientists are now trying to get us to lower our expectations, to stop expecting 'error-free messages and solutions on demand'. I guess some message chains (e.g., concerning some cancers, or how to break ingrained bad habits) are just too long, too complicated, and too noisy to let even scientists sort out fact from fancy.

The lecturer claims our modern CEOs are masters at damage control. When their firm makes a profit they take the credit and give themselves a big bonus. When their company's stock bombs they claim that they're innocent and blame the market, or their Chief Financial Officer. Of course, the CEO still takes a big bonus for having prevented an even greater loss. Nice job—they can't lose. Oola would be impressed. (And speaking of damage control, there's that old joke about doctor's burying their mistakes.)

The speaker asked us to keep Oola in mind because she represents the ever-present human side of science.

Sciencing, Thousands of Years Later

Let's leap ahead from cave dweller sciencing and consider the mid-1800s. Think about what the medical experts of the day thought about a fever: 'What could it be? Demons? Witches? The weather?'

The learned physicians probably stroked their beards, travelled up to the top of their PSTs and decided to call the fevers 'malaria'. That Latin label reveals what they believed to be the cause of fevers: Mal (bad) and aria (air)—'bad air'. From all the possible causes they jumped to the conclusion that fevers were caused by bad air.

In the bottom left corner of their PST they had one fairly reliable observation—fever—about which different observers, using the touch test, could usually agree on (particularly if it was really high), and one very fuzzy or unreliable 'observation'—bad air. What's it look like? How could they measure it?

Up at the top of the medical PST of that period, they connected the dots. They connected the detectable fever dot to the invisible bad air dot. On the surface, it's not much of a step forward from any other fuzzy dots, like angry Gods, demons, or witches.

But the visiting professor pointed out that a significant shift in critical thinking had occurred; a momentous shift from *supernatural causes* (like demons) to 'natural causes' (like air). That's a battle that still wages today—the creationists versus the evolutionists, with one group looking for supernatural explanations and the other searching for natural explanations.

The guest lecturer stated that some of these ancient experts actually collected evidence. Relating that idea to Chapter 1 of *The Science Game* would mean that they cycled down to the bottom right corner of their PSTs and generated a testable prediction. Not only that, but they found some supporting data along the way.

They figured that if bad air 'caused' fevers, then closing your windows at night should reduce their frequency. And it did! The number of fevers went down.

Of course, from today's enlightened perspective, it's easy to think: 'In their observing, thinking, and testing those old medical experts missed detecting something important. Not only did closing the windows supposedly keep out some "bad air", but it also kept out lots of mosquitoes.'

So, the point to remember is that some problems include a lot more dots, even visible ones, than smart people notice and consider in their observations and thinking—even scientists. Too many dots spoil the science.

Nevertheless, in one sense these would-be scientists were on to an important message: fevers were linked to bad air, specifically the kind of air that harboured mosquitoes. So we learn from history that as long as the answer and the evidence are 'acceptable' to the experts and consumers of that period, those answers count—fuzzy or not. As long as those answers—right or wrong in the long run—help reduce personal, professional, or cultural uncertainty, then they're accepted as true for the time being.

When Bad Theory Gets in the Way of New Knowledge

Not only did the 'bad air' theorists lead us astray concerning the sources of fevers, but they ridiculed a new theory that would eventually lead to medical miracles.

A Ridiculed Theory that Proved to be So Right

In the mid-1800s, Ignaz Semmilweis—a Hungarian physician—courageously challenged the popular theory that illness originated from bad air filled with invisible baddies.

Operating in the left corner of his PST, Ignaz *observed* that many healthy young women were dying of fever following childbirth (dot #1). He also *observed* that the doctors frequently walked from an autopsy in the morgue to the gynecological ward to deliver babies (dot #2).

Out of all the dots floating about, unlike his colleagues, he focused on those two dots. He suspected (theorized) that these two observations were somehow connected.[15]

Cycling to the top of his PST, and ignoring the entrenched fuzzy 'bad air' theory, he speculated that the doctors, after digging into dead bodies, were carrying something bad on their hands and ground under their nails when they went to deliver babies, and that 'something' may be what's causing the lethal fever in otherwise healthy young mothers.

On the basis of his deviant and radical top-of-the-triangle critical thinking, Ignaz cycled down the right corner of his PST, predicting that if the doctors

---

[15]We don't know how to 'produce' creative people—people who think outside the box. We do know how to train researchers to critically analyze and test a new idea or theory once a Semmilweis, or an Einstein, or a Freud generates one. While the Semmilweis and Einstein theories prevailed, much of Freud's theory proved to be untestable. Nevertheless, he helped popularize the concept of the 'unconscious', and he still attracts serious followers.

washed their hands before delivering babies, fewer young mothers would end up dead. He even started carefully washing his own hands, and in doing so was able to provide some supporting personal evidence.

He lectured his colleagues.

They were not amused.

Why on earth should they waste their time washing their hands when everyone *knew for sure* (at the top of the medical triangle of TRUTH) that disease was caused by bad air? Why should the good doctors of the day abandon one familiar and trusted explanation in exchange for a wild, new theory based on other fuzzies—bad things on their hands.

Ridiculous!

But, notice, just as early doctors had shifted attention from supernatural demons and witches to natural air, Ignaz shifted attention from natural but very fuzzy bad air to a natural and specific location, the hands. Hands aren't everywhere, they're at the end of the doctor's arms, and they can be seen. And washed.

The visiting lecturer declared: 'Semmilweis, in his own mind at least, radically reduced the conceptual and empirical space to be searched for the source of childbirth fever.'[16]

Of course, all of this debate took place before the evolution of powerful microscopes, which would ultimately transform the invisible fuzzies on the doctors' hands into visible germs, into detectable dots. But back then the argument boiled down to one fuzzy cause (bad air) versus another ('something' on the doctors hands.)

Finally, not only did Semmilweis's message lie outside the boundary of the acceptable message chains of the period—way outside the box—but the idea was beyond view from the very peak of the PST of the period. The suggestions that the good doctors themselves delivered disease was both personally and professionally insulting.

Ignaz was ridiculed.

He published his theory. It got poor reviews.

Not surprisingly he had a nervous breakdown, and was committed to an insane asylum, thus conveniently 'proving' that he'd been crazy all along.

Modern Times

Common-sense problem solving—layman sciencing—is similar to cave dweller and seventeenth-century science.

---

[16]I'll bet all those people who had to do all that digging in Iraq looking for WMDs wished that Donald Rumsfeld had taken a tip from Semmilweis and been more specific about the empirical space to be searched.

As they did then, we must work at the bottom left corner of the PST and we are limited to readily accessible observations that capture our personal attention.

While it is true that if we had the time and inclination, we would have access to more reliable information, to scientific news. But because that does take time, we tend to move up to the top of our PST and jump to conclusions about what connects to what.

Applying more critical thinking would mean that we would have to ignore deadlines, in essence, pulling out of the traffic of daily living. That would involve changing what we do and when we do it. It would mean messing up other people's schedules so they would try to bring us back in line. It would mean forgetting to take the dog for a walk, offending the dog, and having to clean up a mess.

It's a lot simpler to go with the flow and ignore the bottom right corner of the triangle—to let time and/or others do the rigorous testing.

Yes, we should stop, take a second look, and think for a bit, but then another deadline forces us to jump to yet another conclusion. It's easier to process neat, prepackaged chunks of information, relying on others to string messages together into a simple, comforting story.

Summary

Even this brief peek into history helps us appreciate some of the refinements science has made to common-sense problem solving:

1. The necessity of translating fuzzies into reliable observations that flow up to the top of the PST, and provide a trusted basis for making decisions.

2. The overpowering role that popular theories of the period play in determining what dots are *seen* and linked. These biasing factors highlight the absolute necessity of establishing and protecting an open adversarial arena where alternative perspectives and messages can compete and flourish.

3. A wise society provides its scientists with the time, training, and resources to rigorously *test* the hit parade 'solutions' and treatments of the day.

Well I'm glad that's done. Since it's my first commentary I'm not sure what's expected. I wonder what kind of grade Professor Creek will give me? The student grapevine reports that his grades are usually a bit higher than Dr Frund's.

Professor Creek told us to check the media for interesting scientific news. I noticed one headline screaming 'Science Cures Hemorrhoids', but I don't think that's what he had in mind. Another item reported finding bits of ice-age human teeth and bone fragments.

Using these tiny bits and pieces the archeologists will try to figure out how these people lived, what they ate, their diseases, their medicines, etc.

Here's an interesting item: the President of Harvard University caused an uproar last week when he suggested that one possible reason why women are under-represented in upper-level technology and science jobs may not be solely because of a social bias against promoting women, but could be attributed to a lesser 'intrinsic aptitude'[17] (i.e., gene stuff, as opposed to environment) Wow!

The Harvard 'hypothesis' is sure heating up the nature–nurture debate. I'll bet the opposing sides are busy cherry-picking evidence and waving it about to support their argument. And I'll bet Dr Frund and Professor Creek are having a a battle over this one.

I wonder how researchers untangle the influence of genes and environment? How do they figure out how much of a given behaviour is due to genes and how much due to environmental influences? I remember Creek said something about using identical twins as research subjects, but obviously that doesn't settle the debate. If it did, Dr Frund and Professor Creek wouldn't have anything to keep arguing about.

Treasure Maps

On the student website for *The Science Game* (http://www.oup.com/ca/he/companion/agnewpyke) there are easily accessible Google search results to assist you as you further explore the main themes discussed in each chapter.

For example, when we Googled the word 'truth', we received 18,000,000 results. As we scrolled through the search results, we clicked on the link to a website titled 'Truth—International Encyclopedia of Philosophy'. At the top of the website we noticed the first question: 'Can claims about the future be true *now*?'

You, and I, and scientists are all in the business of daily mapping the future. Can any of these maps be *true*? What do you think? What do your friends think? What did the couple killed in a car accident think two minutes before it happened? What did people think on their commute to the World Trade Center on the morning of 9/11? What did a young mother think the day before she learned she had an inoperable tumour?

What do the experts on this particular website think?

These are not trivial questions because every minute of every hour of every day you bet your life on one of your own maps, or on one of our currently popular scientific maps of the future.

---

[17]S. Dillon, 'Harvard Chief Defends His Talk on Women', *New York Times* 18 January 2005. Available at http://select.nytimes.com/search/restricted/article?res=FA0E1FF8395C0C7B8DDDA80894DD404482.

REVIEW TRUE OR FALSE QUIZ

T	F	1. Stress causes cancer.
T	F	2. The problem-solving triangle involves observing, analyzing, and testing.
T	F	3. 'Seeing-is-believing' is an example of top-down decision-making.
T	F	4. Carl's increase in height was a consequence of improved diet and hormone injections.
T	F	5. The pre-scientific PST is equivalent to common-sense-light.
T	F	6. A false negative is when someone who is sick is erroneously labelled as healthy.
T	F	7. Reliance on Internet 'bloggers' is an example of the application of common-sense-light.
T	F	8. Scientists face far more constraints on their problem-solving process than do news services or the courts.
T	F	9. Scientists' use of the PST is distinctive because they rely on reliable observations, critical thinking, and rigorous tests.
T	F	10. One of the problems with Freudian theory is that it is difficult to test.
T	F	11. Scientists avoid the word 'cause', and instead of talking about cause and effect, they talk about antecedents and consequences.
T	F	12. GIGO is a favourite acronym of computer scientists that means 'garbage in/garbage out'.
T	F	13. All puzzles are potentially solvable using the methods of science.
T	F	14. All puzzles are potentially solvable using common sense.
T	F	15. It is the adversarial process in science that helps to ensure the reliability and validity of scientific claims.
T	F	16. In the battle between the evolutionists and the creationists, the former focus on supernatural explanations while the latter look for natural ones.
T	F	17. The bad air theory gained credibility when the incidence of malaria declined.
T	F	18. Semmilweis theorized that invisible 'fuzzies' on doctors' hands caused childbirth fever.
T	F	19. Diana, reporting on a seminar she attended, states that successful experts are masters at damage control.

2

Big Puzzles, Small Brains

Chapter Goals

- To examine what both you and scientists do when the world sends us chains of messages that are too big to fit into our brains.
- To examine how we automatically cut such puzzles down to mind-size, sometimes brilliantly, sometimes naïvely and sometimes disastrously.

Introduction

In the last chapter Einstein proposed that 'Whoever undertakes to set himself up as a judge in the field of truth and knowledge is shipwrecked by the laughter of the Gods.'

Why would such a successful scientist say such a thing?

One reason may be because, in the second half of his life, he found that the problems he was working on were too big to fit into his brain, no matter how hard he tried. No doubt he knew that we have the same size brain as our cave dwelling ancestors, and yet we must solve problems much more complicated than they ever faced—our cave is much larger, more crowded, and the traffic is awesome.

In this chapter we explore the limitations of the brain and how you and scientists must shrink big problems down to mind-size. Sometimes it works, sometimes the baby goes out with the bathwater.

In subsequent chapters we'll discuss how, through trial and error, scholars have created pre-scientific and scientific methods that extend the reach of our primitive senses and our ancient brains.

In the previous chapter we proposed that science is like a news service with scientists attempting to detect and decode nature's secret messages. But you know that even simple messages—like phone numbers—can become distorted when passing through one person to another.[1] In this chapter we examine how our inherited nervous system and our acquired beliefs automatically transform the messages we receive and deliver.

In subsequent chapters we examine how we, using common sense, and researchers, using both common sense and scientific methods, attempt to correct some of our unwitting distortions and overcome some of our genetic limitations to peek around our acquired cultural blinders.

Both citizens and scientists keep trying to include more facts and less fancy in the messages we receive and transmit while rapidly cycling around our PSTs. You already know that *truth*, like beauty, often resides in the eye of the observer.

Starting with the same array of light and sound waves, down at the bottom of the PST, I often receive radically different messages than you do. For instance, during an election campaign, I might conclude that the politician's speech was short and sweet, providing a clear roadmap into a prosperous future. In contrast, you might conclude that it was a lengthy load of claptrap.

Who's right?

We can probably settle our differences over whether the speech was long or short by consulting the wall clock. But what kind of instrument—physical or human—can we consult to determine who's *right* about the rest of it?

Maybe the politician's message—at 3,642 words—is just too long and fuzzy for anybody's brain to decode it, even the brain of a scientist. Three thousand, six hundred and forty-two words is a long message chain.

But maybe we shouldn't put all the blame on the length of message. Our brains, even scientific brains, can get short messages wrong. For instance, we can unwittingly scramble a ten-digit phone number in four seconds—the time it takes you to walk to a phone or to walk across the science lab. Think of trying to remember a phone number 3,642 numbers long.

In short, it looks like our brains have trouble receiving, and reliably remembering, both long, fuzzy messages and short, clear messages. Not only that, but once we have a message to send—even a short one—we often make mistakes when transmitting it to someone else. Nevertheless, the human brain is a magic loom. It receives light and sound waves at the bottom of the PST and weaves them together into a mental/emotional tapestry of fact and fancy. Yes, it can get things disastrously wrong from time to time, but it can also be wondrously right.

In this chapter we'll examine how our fallible brains can, on the one hand, extract and compile[2] great truths and, on the other, create blinding nonsense

---

[1]For those interested in the debate over whether the brain is a clean slate on which nature writes verid-ical messages, or a messy slate where outside messages get mixed up with and distorted by inside mes-sages, see Khun (1970), Pinker (2003), and Fodor (1998).

[2]See Tversky's classic study *Features of Similarity* (1977), in which he describes how we shrink com-plex visual displays down to mind-size by extracting and compiling simplified images by automatically and radically editing the input.

from the messages it receives. In subsequent chapters we'll examine the common sense and scientific methods we use to increase the odds of getting things right.

The Magic Loom

Although we regularly misperceive *reality*, we still get a lot of messages right. Otherwise, we'd be as extinct as the Dodos! Just think of all the complex things that work, at least most of the time: cars start, planes fly, TVs glow, kids learn, money buys, doctors try, politicians . . . well, they politic. Nothing is perfect.

Why we get things right

From a scientific perspective we get things right for two reasons:

1. through millions of years of evolutionary trial and error we've evolved a nervous system that detects stable patterns in the sound and light waves flowing in from our environment (e.g., a wolf's howl, a baby's cry), and
2. through thousands of years of trial and error, social groups have learned things beyond the capacity of individual nervous systems. Thus, we add cultural wisdom to our inherited neurological smarts.

We also get things right by capitalizing on those special occasions when a driving need to know and creativity magically combine, resulting in personal, cultural, or scientific breakthroughs. In this chapter we focus on our human limitations in order that you can appreciate how the various scientific methods, to be covered in the rest of the book, extend our sensory and cognitive reach. While we concentrate initially on our limitations, remember that's only one side of the coin. The other includes individual epiphanies, cultural wonders, and scientific breakthroughs.

We've acquired technical skills that enable us to establish relatively safe and predictable artificial environments. Since we designed many of those sound and light waves to fit our own nervous systems, it's easier to *get them right* (e.g, enhanced lighting, sound proofing, heating, and cooling all lead to increased predictability by keeping good influences in and bad influences out).

Why we get things wrong

From a scientific perspective, we get things wrong for the same two reasons that we get things right. While we've made life simpler in some respects, we've made it more complicated in others:

1. We now have to deal with patterns of light and sound waves that weren't around during the millions of years our nervous system evolved. Consequently our wired-in neural nets have trouble automatically detecting those novel patterns. As a result, we try to walk through glass doors

and we crash our cars when a rapid change in the pattern of light waves occurs quicker than our inherited nervous system can detect and respond (e.g., another car steaks through a red light).

2. In our artificial and global environments the patterns of many light and sound waves have become longer and increasingly complex (e.g., the politician's speech, computer manuals, health advice, the fine print in insurance contracts, college textbooks, unpredictable terrorism, etc.). And yet we have the same size brains as our hunter/gatherer ancestors had and they lived in a much slower, smaller world consisting of much simpler and shorter messages.

In brief, much of the modern world is too complicated for our primordial brains. Therefore, we must automatically cut intricate messages arriving from the outside down to mind-size. In doing so, we're bound to get some things wrong, to miss some signals, and to transmit some erroneous messages.

To maintain our sanity, we must assume the world is relatively neat and tidy most of the time (Figure 2.1). Whereas, in times of crises, or upon closer study we must acknowledge that it's much more complicated (Figure 2.2). For a tiny demonstration of life's complexity and our simplifications of it let's sit in on an introductory psychology class.

Psychology 101

As we cycle around our PSTs we map and navigate our *physical environment* remarkably well—unless things happen too fast or outside our limited attention span.

However, mapping and navigating our *social environment* is more complicated. When our shared neurological hardware becomes overlaid with different cultural experiences and expectations you and I can construct very different realities.[3] Starting with the same light and sound waves at the bottom of our PSTs, we *see, hear,* and *remember* very different things, as illustrated in the last US election, and in the following demonstration.

To test how accurately we observe and remember social events, psychology professors often stage and videotape a surprising event during a regular classroom lecture. For instance, a screeching woman suddenly bursts through

---

[3]For example, researchers tracked the eye movements of 27 native Chinese and 25 Americans while they were looking at pictures, to determine where they were looking and how long they focused on a given area. They concluded that the two groups were literally seeing different worlds. The Chinese focused on the background and relationships between objects, while the Americans focused on the brightest or most rapidly moving object. The longer a native Chinese person has spent in America the more similar their eye tracking behaviour became to that of Americans. The investigators concluded that the differences were not neurological but were cultural. Chua, Boland, and Nisbett, 'Cultural Variation in Eye Movements during Scene Perception'. Proceedings National Academy of Sciences, 22 August 2005. Available at http://www.pnas.org/cgi/content/.

one door, runs across the front of the class, and out the opposite door. A shouting man waving something in his hand chases her.

Following this brief and unexpected event, students are asked to note their observations on a short questionnaire.

How well do they do? Not very!

Not only do students report 'seeing' and 'hearing' things that never happened, they also miss and distort things that did. The male pursuer is recorded

Fig 2.1 ■ Neat and Tidy View of the World

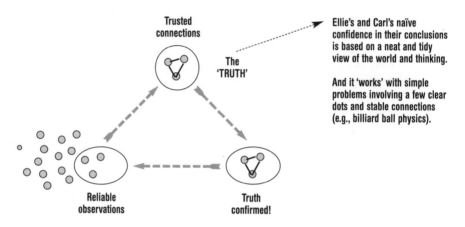

Trusted connections

The 'TRUTH'

Ellie's and Carl's naïve confidence in their conclusions is based on a neat and tidy view of the world and thinking.

And it 'works' with simple problems involving a few clear dots and stable connections (e.g., billiard ball physics).

Reliable observations

Truth confirmed!

Fig 2.2 ■ Too Many Dots, Too Many Possible Connections

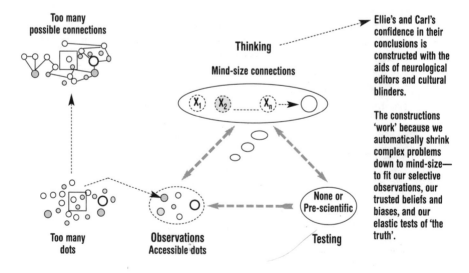

Too many possible connections

Thinking

Mind-size connections

X_1 X_2 ---- X_n ---→ ○

Too many dots

Observations
Accessible dots

None or Pre-scientific

Testing

Ellie's and Carl's confidence in their conclusions is constructed with the aids of neurological editors and cultural blinders.

The constructions 'work' because we automatically shrink complex problems down to mind-size— to fit our selective observations, our trusted beliefs and biases, and our elastic tests of 'the truth'.

as being white, black, or Chinese, and is believed to be carrying a gun, a knife, or a club, and different students hear him shouting different things. Furthermore, each different observer has a high level of confidence in his or her various misperceptions, and will argue vehemently for his or her particular *take on reality*.

Who's right? What *really* happened?

The instructor turns down the lights and replays the dramatic event as seen and heard through the *eyes* and *ears* of the video camera. The camera serves as our *reliable observer*, operating in the bottom left corner of the PST.

What physical or human yardsticks can we trust?

Without the camera's record we have no way of separating the *reliable* dots from the misperceived ones, the distorted messages from the original. Without the film we're left with a mess of conflicting observations and conclusions, whereas with the camera we get an independent (unbiased?) basis for agreement. Such recording devices are tools that help us overcome some of our human limitations by correcting our imperfect senses and extending our limited memory, and therefore serving as extensions to our hunter-gather nervous system.

But notice, when we compare the film to what the students report they witnessed, we discover that different students recorded different bits and pieces of it correctly. Carl, the basketball player, noticed that the male figure was tall, lean, and athletic—maybe even a basketball player—but he missed most of the rest. Ellie, of skin rash fame, noticed that the woman had a poor complexion. But she missed most of the rest. Other students perceived and misperceived other bits.

Thus, what we see at the bottom of our PSTs is constructed from a combination of light and sound waves, our senses, our special interests, and what we expect, or want, to see. Therefore, to provide for this two-way—bottom-up and top-down—traffic we must use two-headed arrows in our pictures of the PST.

Following the class demonstration several students protest, claiming that they know what they saw, that the professor must have edited the film. That is always a possibility to be considered—even when you are relying on physical instruments you can't be certain that the message hasn't been transformed by technical error or human interference. *All evidence eventually rests on our trust in the reliability of the measuring instrument, physical or human.*

Would trained scientists do any better than the students if they were exposed to the same surprising classroom demonstration? We suspect not, however, we know of no such studies. But when caught by surprise, or when operating outside their research contexts—their laboratories, interview rooms, and ivory towers—the scientists we know misperceive information and miss dots right along with the rest of us. Scientists are humans first, and researchers second.

But the point of this story *is not* that humans are lousy observers, and it *is not* that we can't be trusted in the bottom left corner of the PST. Rather, the message to remember is that humans have trouble reliably observing and connecting the dots when they rapidly flow by all at once and without warning. To extend our problem solving capacity we need observational aids (e.g., cameras and other trusted measuring instruments[4]) in the bottom of our PST, and pattern-detecting tools (e.g., logic, mathematics, theories, and computer programs) at the top.

We must appreciate the natural limitations imposed on us by our human neurology and by our acquired cultural blinders in order to be able to judge the power of the various problem-solving tools to be discussed in succeeding chapters.

Not only do humans have trouble with too many dots, we also have trouble with changing or unstable dots—like live things. Live things move and change unpredictably: 'For heaven sakes stand still and make up your mind!'

Our brains may be the same size as our ancient ancestors, but we're not stupid. OK, so we may see things that aren't there, and we might miss seeing things that are there, but our primordial brain also acquired the capacity to protect itself from overload. It acquired the capacity to automatically, and unconsciously, shrink problems down to 'fit' its limited neurological and psychological capacity.

It's not a perfect system. Periodically, the cave dwellers made mistakes and ended up as a saber-toothed tiger's lunch. Our nervous system still makes mistakes (misperceptions and misbeliefs), so from time to time someone ends up injured—or dead—in a car accident, or divorced, or bankrupt. But humans have no choice; the options are limited: shrink problems down to an acceptable size and make a few mistakes along the way, or run around like a chicken with its head cut off, or sit frozen in a state of indecision due to information and decision overload.

Evolution chose the *automatic shrink* option. For the sake of our sanity we oversimplify and jump to conclusions as we cycle around our PSTs.[5] Through their research and theories, behavioural and social scientists help us understand how our small brain deals with big, complex puzzles.

We now briefly examine what four scholars—two Nobel Peace Prize winners—say about how humans reflexively deal with our daily information overload. In subsequent chapters we'll examine how—using common sense and scientific methods—we attempt to overcome some of our neurological limitations and at least loosen our cultural blinders in an effort to incorporate more facts and less fancy in the messages we receive and transmit.

Two Nobel laureates guide our exploration

Research on decision-making by Herb Simon and Daniel Kahneman helps demonstrate the importance of biases, beliefs, and mental short-cuts (top-down

---

[4]Of course, with the arrival of *virtual reality* computer programs we're rapidly losing our trust in a host of devices once used to provide veridical records of reality.

[5]Yes, there's variation in every species—humans included. But notice that we view people who sit in a state of frozen indecision as weak or *sick*, whereas the rest of us, running around jumping to naïve conclusions, are viewed as *normal*.

processes) in human problem solving. When you can't see clearly, believing fills in the gaps. *Believing-is-seeing.*

Simon contributed two major findings:

1. Our capacity to reason is smaller than we thought, so we must simplify; and
2. We simplify by relying heavily on assumptions, beliefs, and biases.

Bounded rationality

Simon (1983) coined the phrase *bounded rationality* to explain our limited attention span and tiny short-term memory. This is a Nobel Prize-winning way of saying that our brains can't process too many dots (words, numbers, messages) at the same time. You've probably noticed this problem when trying to study for exams while watching TV. Carl and Ellie noticed it when trying to report what happened in the psychology classroom demonstration.

Simon, therefore, rejects the popular but naïve presumption that we have enough brainpower, enough rationality, to solve any problem.

Although Simon rejects our naïve optimism about human brainpower, the rest of us retain a soft spot in our hearts for it. We still expect our experts and scientists to solve any problem—simple or complex—and to do it *right now*: 'Come on, hurry up and fix the health care system', 'Come on, hurry up and find a cure for cancer', 'Come on, get the economy rolling', 'Come on, fix the United Nations.'

Simon says that because of our bounded rationality we can't really concentrate on more than one complex message at a time, and usually on only one part of that one message.

However, when dealing with relatively simple problems occurring in familiar and stable physical and social environments, our bounded brain works pretty well, and we usually get things right. When the dots are obviously connected in time and space, like a smoldering cigarette and the burn you get from touching it, we get the message pronto. But when one or more of the dots is fuzzy, or if they're widely separated in time and space—like cigarettes and cancer—it can take a hundred years to make the connection. How many of those complex or delayed-action connections lie just beyond our reach?

When dealing with stable physical environments classic physics has it relatively easy. It works well with objects like billiard balls that travel in nice, predictable straight lines—they obey *the law*.

Billiard balls with brains

However, the rest of us must work with 'billiard balls with brains', better known as people; they don't care what the law won't allow, they're gonna zigzag anyhow! Psychological and social worlds are much more dynamic and unstable, and much harder to predict than the relatively stable world of billiard balls.

When interacting with people, our problems multiply in frequency and complexity. Unlike ordinary billiard balls, humans rarely travel in straight lines.

Trying to predict their behaviour can rapidly overload our mental capacity as we attempt to detect and connect too many moving, fuzzy dots, too many changing connections or relations. Set a billiard ball down, turn your back for a minute, look again, and it's still there. Set a person down, turn your back for a minute, and . . . who knows?

Therefore, to reduce the observational and mental burden, you and I must automatically oversimplify most puzzles. We must make quick and dirty observations at the bottom of our PSTs. Up top, because of time pressures, we jump to conclusions and, in so doing, we understandably sometimes miss important connections or explanations.

In short, we often get it wrong.

Simon's mantra

Not only did Simon introduce the concept of bounded rationality and the need to cut the flow of messages to mind-size, but he also explained how we do it.

Simon shrunk his findings into a simple mantra: 'No conclusions without premises.' This is a Nobel Prize-way of saying that we can't handle too many dots at one time, so we automatically simplify complex problems in order to accommodate our neurology, our bounded rationality, and our cultural expectations. In doing so, most of our thinking becomes neurologically and culturally *affordable*—sort of neurologically and culturally correct, even if scientifically naïve or wrong.

Mind blinks

Emotionally anchored premises, whether they are treasured cultural beliefs or pet scientific theories, are like mental reflexes—a wired-in way of jumping to a response or conclusion. Trying to change an emotionally anchored premise is almost as hard as trying to change an inherited reflex (a genetically wired-in way of jumping to a response). Just as a reflex like the *eye blink* response automatically protects your eye from noxious stimuli, a premise is like a *mind blink* response that protects your mind from *seeing* and *thinking* things that threaten your self-image, your world view, or even your sanity.

It's difficult to identify our own core premises because they fire automatically.[6] It's easier to identify emotionally-anchored blind premises or beliefs that held sway in the past—for example, the belief that the flat earth was the centre of the universe. It's also easier to identify blind beliefs in others, in hard-hearted conservatives or soft-headed liberals, for example.

---

[6]If you can identify and examine one of your basic premises then it has lost its capacity to automatically protect your bounded rationality. Once you become aware that your conclusion depends on a previously blind assumption (premise), uncertainty starts leaking in. Uncertainty takes up rational space. What was once a firm conclusion becomes yet another problem to be reexamined and solved—it takes up some of your bounded rationality, so something else has to go.

Of course, it's the very blindness of a belief that is both its strength and its weakness. Because it fires automatically you don't have to think about it. Such blind premises protect your bounded rationality by radically reducing which dots we observe at the bottom of our PST, and which ones we connect at the top. Unfortunately, and necessarily, there are important dots and connections that we automatically ignore.

But if we buy Simon's proposal that humans are saddled with bounded rationality, and that we protect it with emotionally anchored premises (mental blinders), then it follows that the messages we create as we cycle around our PSTs will often, and unknown to us, include an indeterminate mix of fact and fancy.

Take note that Simon is talking about all humans, including scientists. For example, American scientists were blind—observationally and mentally—to the Australian researchers' theory that most ulcers were caused by germs instead of diet or stress (Forbes, Glaser, Cullen, Warren, Marshall, & Collins, 1994).[7] So, as you progress through this text, you should be looking for ways in which scientists try to extend their rationality and peek around some of the cultural blinders. Using scientific methods (the refined PST) researchers increase the density of fact over fancy in the messages they send both to each other and to the rest of us.

When the strong beliefs of individual scholars determine what they see—a believing-is-seeing bias—we call it a *confirmatory bias*. Some authors go so far as to suggest that 'the history of science can be viewed as the history of confirmatory biases' (Weston & Weimberger, 2004: 609). Others propose that 'science is the history of corrected mistakes' (Wood & Nezworski, 2005: 657) through the adversarial application of scientific methods (Haack, 2003).

Psychology has a healthy array of adversarial premises. For instance, researchers relying on a *biological premise* study how people make risky decisions when the parts of the brain providing emotional anchors are damaged (Shiv, Loewenstein, Bachara, Damasio, & Damasio, 2005), or genetically impaired (Olsen, 2005). Other researchers, relying on an *environmental premise*, explore and argue whether different kinds of training can expand our bounded rationality (McElree, 2001; Cowan, 2005).

We propose that there is something to be said for both sides. However, a scientist can't rigorously test every plausible hypothesis at the same time. He or she has to make a bet, choose one, and give it their best shot.

We next consider our second Nobel Laureate, who built on Simon's concept of bounded rationality and how we cut complex problems down to mind-size.

Accessible dots

Dan Kahneman (2002) has proposed that, with the nervous system we inherited from our cave dwelling ancestors plus our cultural blinders, we simply can not

---

[7] 1998 Mayne Florey Medal award for the discovery of the *Helicobacter Pylori*, the causative agent in gastritis and gastric ulceration. Available at http://www.tallpoppies.net.au/floreymedal/winner1998.htm.

detect and process all available and relevant *facts* or dots. As a result, we typically make do with those that are most readily *accessible* to us—to our eyes, ears, touch, and our bounded rationality from our store of memories.

Kahneman's research helps us understand why 50 million people voted for Bush and a different 50 million people voted for Kerry in the 2004 US presidential election. Conservatives have *easy access* to pro-Bush messages (dots); Conservatives are looking for them, and they're readily available from their conservative media, friends, and mail-outs.

In contrast, Kerry's supporters have easy access to pro-Kerry messages (dots) from liberal friends, media, and mail-outs. Bounded rationality problem-solvers can't mentally afford to study all the messages so they settle for those readily at hand which fit their political premises. As Simon said: no conclusions without premises. No conservative conclusions without conservative premises? No liberal conclusions without liberal premises?

Kahneman's research also helps us understand the results of the classroom demonstration discussed earlier. Carl is forever looking for dots related to basketball, and Ellie for dots related to history—her pet subject—or to her complexion. They cherry-pick them from an endless flood of daily dots. In doing so, they serve their own personal interests while at the same time protecting their bounded rationality from information overload.

At one level you already know the truism that beliefs beat facts almost every time. We've enshrined it in folklore: 'Don't discuss religion or politics at the table,' which reflects the cultural wisdom that you don't change people's emotionally anchored beliefs (premises) by waving facts in their face—all you do is ruin everyone's dinner. Nevertheless, we often ignore such wise advice. In practice we still try to prove *we're right*, and that *they're wrong*, by sweating it out down in the bottom left corner of our PSTs, dipping into readily accessible dots from our biased bags and flinging them at each other.

To summarize, based on the research of our two Nobel Laureates we propose that because of our bounded rationality, humans—including scientists—can't handle too many dots at the same time. Therefore, we must find ways to cut complex problems down to mind-size. We do so by collecting, connecting, and remembering facts that fit our bounded rationality, our beliefs or theories at the top of the PST, and that are readily accessible at the bottom of the PST. You do it. We do it. Scientists do it.

We next consider two more scholars who examined how human problem solvers attempt to navigate to spaces somewhere between pig-headed rigidity, on the one hand, and open-minded idiocy, on the other.

Elegant critical thinking

We repeatedly harp about cutting the size of complex problems down to fit our brains, but, at the same time, we deplore our habit of jumping to conclusions and our lack of critical thinking. But we can't have it both ways. Or can we?

Yoav Shoham's (1998) research paves the way. His elegant model acknowledges our bounded rationality but also allows for some flexible thinking. His model not only accommodates, at the low end of rationality, our on-the-fly common-sense problem solving, but also provides for the increased degrees of critical thinking involved in pre-scientific decision-making and required for scientific problem-solving. While doing so he acknowledges our inability to deal with too many complex messages at the same time by recognizing that we must trade off breadth of thinking for depth of thinking (e.g., the proverbial brilliant but absent-minded professor who forgets to put on his pants before going to give his lecture.)

'If A then B'

For instance, Ellie is in for a surprise. She's about to drive to the drugstore for more lotion on her way to pick up her prize-winning essay in history. She's relying on a nice simple, bounded, rational rule: 'If A then B': 'If A (I turn the key in the ignition) then B (my car will start).'

For those of you whose minds freeze up at the first sign of a formula, you can relax. What we'll be discussing is Mickey Mouse simple. Even Homer Simpson would understand. 'If A then B' is a beautifully simple mind-shrinking rule. Very mentally affordable.

But what happens when the rule doesn't work, when she turns the key and the car does not start?

You're right. She turns the key again . . . and again . . . and again! ✗ — panic

Now we're testing just how emotionally anchored her premise is, that is, how close-minded Ellie is about cars. When her habitual behaviour fails, and she cycles up to the top of her PST, what has she got to work with?

If she knows absolutely nothing about cars she will probably stick with her simple 'If A then B' rule until the car stops 'grrrring'. She'll then get out, kick the door, and call a cab—an instance of primitive critical thinking in action.

But let's assume that Ellie knows a bit about cars. In order to accommodate her bounded rationality she relies on the simple 'If A then B' rule most of the time. But, stored out of awareness, she has a more complex rule in reserve for emergencies, namely: 'If A_1 and (if A_2 and A_3 and A_4) then B'. But notice this more complex, memory-greedy rule only becomes *accessible*—it only intrudes ✗ into her limited conscious space—when the simple rule clearly fails.

So while our conscious, working memory is small (e.g., approximately seven items) our unconscious memory, like the basement of a large house, is spacious. Like a basement, it can store a lot of junk while still being useful for fallback or damage control information, some of which can be automatically triggered, or released, into awareness when our simple rules fail. But it usually takes a toll on your mind to do so. For example, you know some of it's there—it's on the tip of your tongue, but you just can't recall it. And for good reason: if recall were too easy you would be flooding your mind, overloading it with

45

alternatives and exceptions to the rule. Therefore, it requires special keys to unlock stored memories: an emotional arousing rule failure, the 'Ah Ha!' recognition of a familiar situation.

As noted by Rose (2005: 209) 'unlike recall memory, recognition memory seems unbounded.' Recognizing a familiar stimulus is the *key* that unlocks a particular closet: a familiar face, voice, sound, smell, and situation. Then memories—relevant only to that particular stimulus—flow into awareness, therefore not overwhelming our bounded rationality.

Low cost storage of complexity

Shoham keeps this extended rule in 'low cost storage', or out of awareness, until it's needed. He does so by encasing this in-reserve knowledge in brackets. The brackets represent the boundaries of awareness. They protect our conscious bounded rationality from being overloaded by too many alternatives—by the alternative ways our simple rules can fail. The alternatives remain safely out of awareness until the simple 'If A then B' rule actually fails; then the strong negative feedback triggers the brackets to open and the extended rule is released.

So, in addition to her usually reliable 'If A then B' rule, Ellie has a fallback rule in storage, namely: 'If A_1 and (if A_2 and A_3 and A_4) then B.' This more complex, mentally expensive rule translates to mean: 'If A_1 (I turn the key), and if A_2 (there's enough gas), and if A_3 (the battery isn't dead) and if A_4 (the thingamajigs under the hood are dry) then B (the car will start).'

The surprise and emotional frustration of the car not starting (of the trusted rule failing) triggers her bounded, rational mind to open the brackets—a window of awareness—and gain temporary access to her hard earned storage of wisdom about cars. But to do so she has to clear some space in her awareness. In other words, she has to do some forgetting; she has to withdraw some of her limited attention and memory from other things (e.g., she stops thinking about shopping and calling her grandmother).

Ellie is now in the position to utilize her limited supply of critical thinking about her car. She now has temporary access to information enabling her to check two items—the gas and battery—out of her three alternative explanations; she knows nothing about how to test the 'thingamajigs'. At this point she can either solve the problem or rapidly run out of accessible ideas and call a mechanic. The mechanic is an expert with an even more extended rule than Ellie's—a rule with many more alternative 'A's.

Notice how Shoham's model provides for the increased capacity for critical thinking and problem-solving that the expert brings to bear. The expert arrives with a greatly expanded rule for cars that won't start. His or her rule might look like this: 'If A_1 and (if A_2, A_3, A_4, A_5 . . . A_n) then probably B.' Experts learn to list their A_2s, A_3s, A_4s, etc., in order of their probability of relevance to the given problem. The 'A_n' at the end of the extended rule indicates that a list of As can be various lengths, depending on the expert's knowledge and experience.

Experts protect their bounded rationality by trading off breadth of thinking for depth of thinking (complex rules) in a limited area. Obviously, unlike Ellie, the mechanic can mentally afford to acquire and access a larger set of complex rules concerning cars because that's where he concentrates his bounded rationality from 9 AM to 5 PM. Ellie probably has longer and more complex sets of bracketed rules about American History and skin rashes than her mechanic does.

To quickly summarize: according to Simon, we base most of our conclusions on blind premises with low mental costs (e.g., automatic behaviours [habits] and simple rules of thumb supported by ingrained assumptions such as 'If A then B'). According to Kahneman we further protect our bounded rationality by relying mainly on readily accessible observations and ideas. However, in the face of persistent, intrusive surprises, bit-by-bit, we extend our simple 'If A then B' rules to help us deal with a few exceptions.

> Although humans are naturally curious, their limited brain space puts constraints on how many complex rules they can learn and remember. Therefore, we automatically specialize. Both citizens and scientists end up knowing a lot about a few things, and a little, or nothing, about most things.

According to Shoham, we keep this *exceptional knowledge* stored (bracketed) out of awareness. Subsequently, when surprising dots flow up from the bottom of our PSTs they trigger the brackets to open and release stored bits of accumulated knowledge or wisdom. These wise bits start flowing into our awareness carrying with them questions and alternative *solutions*. This oncoming flood threatens our bounded rationality so the thoughts or plans currently occupying our awareness have to be shoved out of the way or forgotten.

Shoham's extended and bracketed rules provide for periodic flexibility even when operating with a bounded rationality brain.

But even experts (mechanics, doctors, scientists) specializing in a particular field can run out of brain space. They can only acquire and access a limited number of complex rules. Therefore, the solution to some complex puzzles remains beyond their rational reach. In subsequent chapters we discuss which of our evolving pre-scientific and scientific methods help specialists decide which puzzles receive priority, which can be postponed, which can be neglected, and which lie beyond their current comprehension.

Simon exposed our bounded rationality and said we protect it by relying on premises or biases to cut complex problems down to mind-size. Kahneman said we further protect it by relying, not on all relevant information, but on readily accessible information. Shoham extended our rationality by providing for the low-cost storage of back-up wisdom that becomes accessible when simple 'If A then B' rules fail.

But what happens when more surprises flow up to the top of the PST than we can manage? What happens when we get a flood of surprises and when neither the simple nor the extended rules work? What happens when we can't locate a stable, trusted belief or bias to guide us?

Defenses against dangerous ways of thinking

In addition to Simon, Kahneman, and Shoham, we rely on a fourth scholar—Marvin Minsky—to help us understand the strengths and limitations of human decision makers.

Minsky (1994), who patented one of the first electron microscopes and who is one of the fathers of artificial intelligence, pondered the kind of cognitive trouble humans can experience when we fail to reduce problems down to mind-size or when life inconsiderately dumps several 'whoppers' onto our relatively small psychological plate at the same time.

Minsky refers to the resulting brain overload as *'dangerous ways of thinking'*. He proposed that one of the most important kinds of knowledge is *knowing 'what not to think'*. Being too open-minded and exploring too far outside our mental boxes is cognitively dangerous. One false step and you could fall out of your mind!

That's why we rely so heavily on the security that comes with Simon's mind-shrinking premises, beliefs, or biases. And that's why we don't wander too far into strange territories looking for new information. It's also why we rely on easily accessible observations and ideas as well as on Shoham's protective brackets to avoid overloading our conscious mind with worry about all the exceptions there are to our repertoire of simple 'If A then B' rules.

Can you think of an obvious *truth* that you keep safely bracketed away, out of awareness? It's an inescapable truth that all of us *irrationally* hide away within brackets, within brackets, within brackets. It's a *truth* that may periodically flit in and out of your awareness. But only under rare circumstances does it break through and push everything else aside as it consumes your complete and continuing attention.

The answer? The immutable truth of facing your own MORTALITY. The older people get the more often they ask: 'How soon will time, on its way into the future, drop me off at the undertakers?'

We use brackets not only to protect ourselves from such scary thoughts, but also to protect against too many thoughts. You overload your curious, but bounded, rationality when you attempt to keep in awareness all the As (A_2s, A_3s, A_4s . . . A_ns) that need to be in working order for your car to start, for your heart to keep beating, for your love life to run smoothly, for you to graduate, for you to lose weight, for you to get a promotion, and for you to make more money.

But Minsky's premise—that the most important kind of knowledge involves *knowing what not to think*—borders on heresy. It goes against everything we've been taught, such as being repeatedly instructed to 'think outside the box', 'look before you leap', and 'consider all your options'.

In contrast, Minsky implies that the walls of the boxes within which we think are there for a good reason—to prevent us from losing our minds. Shoham's brackets are there for good reason—they help us *not to think* about the many assumptions and exceptions linked to our simple rules, at least not until they fail. Brackets and boxes (premises, beliefs, biases) help us avoid overloading our bounded rationality, and therefore help us avoid dangerous ways of thinking. In brief, thinking outside the box should be reserved for special occasions and pet projects. *Otherwise, it can be dangerous!*

As we'll see later, thinking too far outside the box can be dangerous for scientists as well. So we provide them with relatively protected boxes.

But we're getting ahead of ourselves. Let's return for a moment to the classroom demonstration in which we relied on the video to decide what *really* happened. One student challenged this *solution*; he didn't trust it. Thinking outside the box, he suggested that the instructor may have tricked them by altering the film.

Now it's possible that the video was secretly edited. But both Simon's and Minsky question would be: 'What evidence would that student trust?'[8] If someone has an emotionally anchored premise then reasonable evidence seldom works.

Here's another example questioning the validity of onscreen images. After the first televised images of man walking on the moon were broadcast some skeptics proposed that no one went to the moon and that the whole thing was filmed in the Arizona desert. Again, that's possible. But is there any observational evidence, at the bottom of the PST, or logic at the top of it, that those skeptics would accept? Or does their ingrained premise: 'Don't believe any messages coming from official sources' automatically protect the believer from contrary evidence?

Skeptics, in general, also rely on a simple 'If A then B rule': If A (an authority figure makes a statement) then B (it's probably a lie or wrong). And to avoid dangerous ways of thinking they have another rule: Don't question the first rule.

Minsky's point is that almost anything is *possible*, but we can't mentally afford to seriously think that way. Eventually, and sooner rather than later, we have to stop our critical thinking, turn off our questions, turn off our learning capacity, and rely on trusted beliefs and biases in order to make a decision. It's the price of sanity. From this perspective an open mind is an oxymoron.

Additionally, he claims that we learn early warning signs when we're children that we're walking on thin cognitive ice, so to speak, that we're at risk of slipping into risky ways of thinking, or forcing others to do so.

Now, tighten your mental seat belts. You might find some of the twists and turns in Minsky's thinking shake you up a bit.

Three 'whys' in a row

Minsky proposes that we unwittingly, but wisely, restrict children's natural curiosity. We do so by implicitly teaching them not to ask more than three

---

[8]But, as discussed in note 4, since the advent of 'virtual reality', computer programs, pictures, and video recordings—our most trusted forms of evidence—are now open to complete fabrication. It now boils down to the question of whether or not you trust the person who delivers the message. If you can't trust the message, you have to trust the messenger. Or go into hiding. Or go crazy.

'whys' in a row. We do so not to be mean, but because too many 'whys' are dangerous, mentally unaffordable. They force adults to re-examine their premises, beliefs, and biases, and to open too many brackets and flood their brains with exceptions to their mind-sized conclusions. In other words, too many whys threaten to overwhelm our bounded rationality.

A child's persistent probing exposes the underlying ignorance of their parents. We soon run out of brackets, out of backup A_1s, A_2s, and A_3s, and this makes our palms sweat and our heads ache. We then let the child know, one way or another, that asking too many 'whys' in a row is asking for trouble. Each of the child's 'whys' can force us to re-examine a premise, pry open yet another set of protective brackets, and dig even deeper into our mental basements, until we come up empty.

Adults employ a variety of damage control strategies to avoid embarrassment, including invoking authority ('Because I said so!'), delegation ('Go ask your mother'), or the modern and enlightened escape: 'Those are great questions! Go look them up on the Internet.'[9]

If you don't believe Minsky, try throwing a few 'whys' in a row at your mate, or at an 'expert'. For instance, ask your doctor why she's prescribing that particular treatment, the one that the health websites claim produces dangerous side effects. And to every one of her answers ask another why. Of course, before you carry out this little experiment, make sure you have another doctor in reserve.

As noted earlier, in this chapter we've focused on the limitations of the human decision maker—notably, their bounded rationality and their need to shrink problems down to mind-size. We've done so in order for you to appreciate how the evolved scientific methods to be discussed in the remainder of the book help counterbalance our human limitations and extend our perceptual and conceptual reach.

We've also done so to correct what we perceive to be an idealized view of science that leads to false expectations. For instance Charles Sanders Peirce (1955), a famous philosopher, promoted that idealized expectation when he said: 'scientific spirit requires a man to be at all times ready to dump his whole cartload of beliefs, the moment experience is against them' (47). This, obviously, is not our view. Dumping one major premise, let along a cartload, can be dangerous (à la Simon and Minsky). In our view it is not the conceptual flexibility of individual scientists that leads to error correction and innovation, so much as it is the institutionalized adversarial system of SCIENCE—the critical evaluation of each other's theories and research—that makes it our most trusted news service.

---

[9]The Internet is a magnificent invention, however, it has a problem in cutting its answers down to mind-size. Instead it just does keyword screen dumps, too many dots (clear, fuzzy and unreliable), and too many possible and conflicting connections!

The Procrustian bed

In portraying science we would replace Peirce's above caricature with that of a famous Greek myth about Procrustes.[10] He assured his overnight guests that he possessed a special bed, the length of which exactly matched that of whoever lay on it. Procrustes honoured his pledge by stretching the guest on the rack if he was too short, or chopping off his legs if he was too long. Similarly, we believe that both citizens and scientists have a natural tendency (à la Simon, Minsky, etc.) to stretch or shrink their experience to fit their pet premises.

Until? Until along comes the adversarial Theseus who fatally adjusts Procrustes to fit his own bed.

In brief, a Procrustian method is one that tries to force a person, an event, or an idea into a predetermined category or pattern.

Both Peirce's quote and the Procrustian myth represent extreme views (caricatures of science) ranging on a scale from closed to open mindedness. Most problem-solving practices lie somewhere in between. On such a scale we place common-sense problem solving closer to the Procrustian. Between that area and the centre of the scale we place the pre-scientific procedures, with scientific methods straddling the centre, but continuously extending its reach for the truth.

More precisely, while most of us, most of the time, practice Procrustian, common sense, mind-shrinking problem solving, for special projects, we stretch ourselves along the scale intro pre-scientific, and occasional simple scientific practice. In their professional role, experts and specialists rely heavily on pre-scientific methods, with their centre of gravity just below centre, but with individual members ranging from low Procrustian to simpler scientific methods. We place individual scientists straddling the centre point (but ranging from low level Procrustian cheats to high level scientific geniuses). We award the gold star to the adversarial Scientific System, with its centre of gravity above the centre of the scale but still below the high Peircian ideal.

In Figure 2.3 we summarize the main points of this chapter. In subsequent chapters we'll explore how some of our pre-scientific and scientific tools help us locate a middle ground between rigid in-the-box thinking and mentally dangerous ways of thinking too far outside the box.

SUMMARY

Scientific methods have been designed to correct some natural limitations of the human problem solver, and to augment their strengths. In this chapter we discussed those limitations and strengths.

In subsequent chapters we will consider which of those methods or tools, on the one hand, can capitalize on our wondrous natural curiosity, creativity,

---

[10]'Procrustes', from *Encyclopedia of Greek Mythology*. Available at http://www.mythweb.com/encyc/entries/procrustes.html (accessed 6 August 2006).

Fig 2.3 ■ THE HUMAN PROBLEM-SOLVER

Many of our problems have too many dots (clear, fuzzy, moving, and invisible), and too many possible connections to get our heads around.

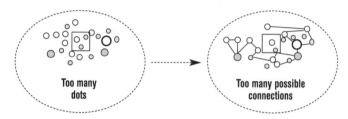

Too many
dots

Too many possible
connections

So, to make sense of our buzzing experience we automatically cut such problems down to mind-size solutions that are linked to trusted beliefs, biases, and rituals.

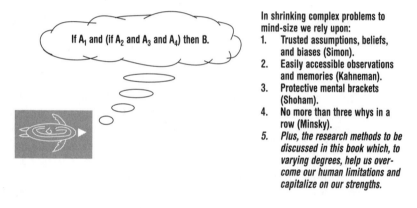

If A$_1$ and (if A$_2$ and A$_3$ and A$_4$) then B.

In shrinking complex problems to mind-size we rely upon:
1. Trusted assumptions, beliefs, and biases (Simon).
2. Easily accessible observations and memories (Kahneman).
3. Protective mental brackets (Shoham).
4. No more than three whys in a row (Minsky).
5. *Plus, the research methods to be discussed in this book which, to varying degrees, help us over-come our human limitations and capitalize on our strengths.*

and driving need to know, and on the other hand, can help us correct or coun-terbalance our human neurological limits and cultural blinders and can extend our rational reach.

Remember that scientists are stuck with the same primordial brain as you or the cave dwellers. They're burdened with the same bounded rationality. They too must rely mainly on simple 'If A then B' rules for most of their decisions. Yes, in a small sub-field of their general area of specialization, they accumulate an impressive set of bracketed complex rules. Nevertheless, most of the pressing and complex questions within the general area of their discipline, and in their small area of their specialization, remain beyond their rational reach. They must rely mainly upon simplifying premises such as the *current beliefs* (theory) and rules of thumb of their discipline, plus their own refinements. But like the hori-zon, complete solutions to complex problems seem to keep moving into the future.

So scientists need all the help they can get. They rely heavily on the same common sense methods we use. In addition society provides them with extra time and resources so they can, in selected space/time domains, check the reliability of their observations in the lower left hand corner of the PST, spend more time critically considering alternative explanations and predictions at the top, and then cycle down to the lower right hand corner to rigorously test their pet hypotheses and best-bet predictions.

Such concentrated and conscientious behaviour works best on small problems, on small slices of behaviour, or on small samples of people. As a result, most scientific research produces small answers. It takes a while before dead ends and many small answers add up to a big solution. Therefore, as consumers of science, we should applaud the dedication of our scientists and their wondrous breakthroughs, while at the same time practicing patience concerning slow progress in solving some of our most pressing problems.

It's not necessarily neat and tidy. Scientists have an endless struggle with their own Procrustian tendencies, and with those of their theoretical and methodological adversaries.

In subsequent chapters we'll consider the problem-solving methods they use in ascending order of power, according to the demands they make upon their bounded rationality at all three corners of their PSTs. We start with those methods requiring relatively little time and resources and work up to an examination of the more powerful but also more mentally demanding, resource-hungry tools.[11]

In the next chapter we introduce the most popular common sense method of problem solving: we call it the *after-the-fact* method. We use it every hour of every day: An event (a fact) is observed and you travel back in time and from the long trail of preceding events you cherry-pick out a cause or causes, while I probably pick out others.

Among all problem-solving tools, this one places the fewest demands on the three corners of the PST: reliable observations, critical thinking, or rigorous testing.

Its strengths? It requires little time or equipment. We can use it on the fly while zipping around our PSTs. Furthermore, since it requires little critical thinking it gives free rein to our natural creativity and imagination. In both the arts and sciences it's a source of exciting new ideas. But since it requires less critical thinking it also lets us jump to naïve conclusions and to generate weird notions. And, unfortunately, it often takes years to decide whether an idea is brilliant or kooky.

---

[11]We concentrate our problem-solving power not only by developing tools that extend our individual capacities, but also by linking and pooling our brains. Families, the courts, and science all represent evolved problem-solving and knowledge-building institutions.

student's notebook

This chapter dropped a lot of dots—a lot of messages—into my bounded rationality. I'm not sure I like what Simon says.

OK, so not everyone is going to agree that my mind is neat and tidy, but at least it felt that way to me, most of the time. After reading the chapter I feel like my head was home to a swarm of bees.

My grandfather used to tell an Abe Lincoln story: On the way out of church Abe complained to Mary that the preacher's sermon had been 'too neat and tidy'. He said 'The world just isn't that way—the Devil makes sure of that; he makes sure that lots of things are unpredictable. Life is like fighting a swarm of bees, protect yourself on one side and they'll sting ya from behind.'

We always saw it as a joke. But according to Minsky, worrying about the future is comparable to fighting a swarm of bees. It's a dangerous way of thinking. And if you stop and really think about it, it is—like thinking about the unthinkable (e.g., dying).

So? So most of the time we keep unpredictable and/or scary knowledge locked away (bracketed) in mental closets (e.g., a loved one cheating on us, the possibility of a bad accident, a fire, house invasion, random violence, etc.). We keep those kinds of real world possibilities in a good safe place—or maybe treat them as a joke. We do a giggle, a quick brain blink, and they're gone—bracketed safely away before they flood into our consciousness, swamp our bounded rationality.

If I didn't have to write a commentary on this chapter, that's where Abe Lincoln's story about the bees would be, bracketed away out of awareness in the basement of my mind. But now it's front and centre in my consciousness, and come to think of it, I've already started to simplify the multiple messages of this chapter, for example by treating Abe's story as a joke. That's what most jokes do—they take some of the sting out of bad things that have happened or scary things that might.

Also, I liked the idea of how we use analogies and metaphors to help make sense of the unknown. Just like the authors helped us travel from the known to the unknown by proposing that 'science is like a news service', I can travel from the known to the unknown by pretending, for a short time, that human thinking is like fighting a swarm of bees. We use premises (biases) as protection against an overwhelming swarm of dots (information) and alternative conclusions.

The analogy is easy to remember, doesn't use up a lot of brain space, and it automatically triggers the main messages of the chapter. It triggers the idea of defending your mind, your bounded rationality, which triggers Simon's mantra—no conclusions without premises—which triggers Kahneman's rule—only pay attention to the most accessible dots (bees). This triggers Shoham's idea of protective brackets against brain attack, which triggers Minsky's idea of dangerous ways of thinking, like letting in swarms of dots.

OK, some of this may seem a bit strange, but that happens when you're exploring unknown territory. That's what analogies and metaphors are for, to provide rough maps of the complex and uncertain,

I think I might be able to use these ideas for a history paper I'm working on. It pro-
vides a nice example of how the past (history) can illuminate the present and future, how
Abe's story is still relevant. His message (analogy) helped me to shrink a lot of buzzing dots
down to mind-size today.

Derek looks down his long nose at History. He says it's like science fiction because
there are only a few facts trying to support pages and pages of speculation.

But as the authors of The Science Game *propose you can't see most of the past, or*
the future. You have no choice but to travel there on premises, beliefs, and theories.
Believing-is-seeing!

Anyway, Derek can't afford a holier-than-thou attitude since sociology isn't all that
high on the scientific totem pole.

On the bus heading home I cracked a book on causality that Dr Frund loaned me, made a
few notes, and—surprise!—could even recall half of them without looking. I'm still rely-
ing on blind recall as my main method of study, except when I panic and flip back into
paintbrush highlighting. By the time I got home, I was ready to start my commentary for
Chapter 2.

Different Beliefs About What 'Causes' Human Behaviour
By Diana Dodds, for Research Methods 201

'The question behind all other questions is the 'why'
of human experience.'—Stephen Kern, 2004: 1

Experts today seek the answer to the question 'what causes what' from different sources. Theologians seek their answers from holy books and prayer, biologists from our genes; physicists from sub-atomic particles; psychiatrists from toilet training and repressed sexual urges; psychologists from our neurology, mother–child relationships, rewards, and peer group pressure; sociologists from institutional rules and concentrations of power; anthropologists from cultural customs and myths.

Not only do our modern experts come up with different answers about the underlying 'causes' of human behaviour, but what they find changes radically through history—today's truths are tomorrow's museum pieces.

As I pointed out in my last assignment, cave-dwelling medicine women looked for causes in friendly and unfriendly gods and demons, and early physicians looked for causes in 'bad air', before reluctantly shifting their search to invisible 'somethings' on doctor's hands.

Stephen Kern, in his book *A Cultural History of Causality*, traces our changing beliefs about causality as reflected in murder novels. He covers various explanations for murder ranging from early experts pointing their fingers at 'bad blood' to modern experts pointing fingers at 'society'—a solution almost as vague as seventeenth century doctors pointing at 'bad air'. 'Society' is one big space–time frame with too many fuzzy dots, too many possible fuzzy connections.

Kern's main point is that throughout history we've gradually moved from focusing on simple causes to investigating complex possibilities; more complex rules, more As, more brackets. The decision about what caused a suspect to murder someone depends on the judge and jury's assumptions; that is to say, it depends on their premises (biases) which control where they're looking for readily accessible clues. Judges and juries used to look specifically at you, at your bad blood, your bad temper, or your bad thoughts: If A (bad blood) then B (bad behaviour).

Increasingly, today's 'experts' are telling juries to look at outside influences: 'It's not their fault!' They're asking you to believe that their client is like an innocent billiard ball, pushed hither and yon by psychological, social, economic, and political forces beyond their control.

These kinds of assumptions may find some scientific support, but such notions put a potentially unsustainable burden on the rational problem-solving capacity of the individuals trying to assign responsibility. What happens when social science comes up with explanations of human behaviour that overwhelm the bounded rationality of judges and juries, explanations that are so complex they can't be understood or remembered at the top of our PSTs, or tested or implemented down at the bottom? Too many fuzzy dots, too many possible connections.

According to Chapter 2, the answer is that judges and juries will still solve complex puzzles the old fashioned way: by doing 'what comes naturally' by finding mentally affordable, even though they may be flawed, ways of shrinking the problem back down to a size that fits the current rules of evidence, prevailing cultural values, readily accessible 'facts', and personal interpretations.

We've gradually moved from simple cause–effect determinism, from 'If A then B' rules, to a string of maybes. We're shifting from 'laws' to probabilities, from nice mentally manageable 'If A then B' chunks, to 'If A_1 and if (A_2, A_3 ... A_n), then maybe (B_1, or B_2 or B_n)'. That kind of complex rule overloads our brains, becomes a dangerous way of thinking for those conscientiously trying to keep it all in mind!

Stephen Kern says that many problems become too big and too complex for our brains—there are too many 'causes', or too many fuzzy, invisible dots.

It's no wonder that Simon says we have to cut problems down to mind-size by shrinking the search space with simplifying assumptions: look at the genes, or look at early experiences. Like Kahneman says, you can't mentally afford to search out all the relevant information so you usually settle for the stuff that's readily accessible to your senses, and that can sneak by your biases. Or, like Shoham says, you keep problems down to mind-size by relying upon simple 'If A then B' rules as much as you can, and keep more complex rules safely out of mind, stored behind brackets, as long as you can Or, like Minsky says, you avoid dangerous thinking by not asking yourself, or others, too many 'whys'.

What we need are problem-solving methods that, on the one hand, are mentally affordable, and, on the other hand, can at least help us survive and at best help us unlock some of nature's biggest secrets.

In spite of the growing complexity, we've done pretty well so far. We're still here. And we've unlocked some very big puzzles (nuclear power) and are knocking on the doors of some others (cures or at least controls for cancer).

I look forward to finding out how we've done it. How *have* we done it with our bounded rationality and with all the challenges we face at each corner of the PST: too many dots to detect (clear, fuzzy and invisible); too many to remember, too many possible connections to critically analyze; too many possible explanations to rigorously test. And yet, with the help of our genetic and cultural smarts, we not only survive but also often thrive?

What do I mean by 'cultural smarts'? I guess those would include the accumulated knowledge and rules of thumb, conscientious guesses, and current functional—if fallible—myths that families, experts, the courts, and science bring to bear on the puzzles that bug them the most.

OK, that's a start. I'll flesh it out a bit with specific examples from Kern's book and from Derek's magazines. It should be done on time for next week's deadline. And I'll Google for news stories about groups with conflicting premises to illustrate Simon's mantra: no conclusions without premises, which I translate into: 'Don't be confused by the cherry-picked "facts", identify the premise or bias that picked the facts. Premises are like sheep, you can trust them to come home dragging their facts behind them.

Creationism versus evolution

Ideational combatants stand emotionally anchored to their premises or beliefs and throw a mixture of clear and fuzzy facts at each other. A current battle rages between the creationists and the evolutionists. The former believe the bible story of our origins—we're God's children—while the latter hold firmly to the premise that, over millions of years, human life evolved from more primitive life forms like aphids and apes.

I came across a recent survey by the Pew Research Centre (New York Times, 31 August 2005), that said 34 per cent of those polled were in favour of replacing evolution with creationism, or its modern version called 'intelligent design.' Intelligent design rests on the premise that life is so complicated and intricate that only a supreme being could have designed it, not random forces rolling genetic dice.

I had always assumed that over the last century or so most Westerners had shifted from trusting religious news to trusting scientific messages, at least about earthly things. I thought the facts were that church attendance was way down, and the churches were having trouble recruiting ministers and priests. But hey, it's the premises not the facts that count.

I guess we need to know how emotionally attached each side is to their respective beliefs. Sixty-three per cent of the creationists are very certain, compared to 32 per cent of the evolutionists. With numbers like that, it feels like it would probably be a waste of time to try to change the minds of true believers on either side.

Derek and I were both brought up to trust scientific news, so we're a bit blind to religious messages. Despite that, at least we can appreciate that if you believe the Bible then angels can defy the laws of gravity by flying and Jesus can ignore both the laws of physics—by walking on water—and of biology, with his virgin birth and his rising from the dead.

It seems that Simon wins. If you accept the biblical story/premise literally then, for you, religion trumps science. At least concerning what's in the bible. One way to see the current dispute between the evolutionists and the creationists is as a battle that is occurring at the top of the pst over premises, regardless of what's happening at the bottom. The creationists buy the premise of supernatural forces and the evolutionists don't.

Since neither side has an iron clad set of rigorously tested facts to support their premise (the evolutionists have more, but even they admit it's incomplete) both sides are standing firm on a believing-is-seeing premise. As I see it, anyway. Derek says that kind of thinking will make you enemies on both sides. But hey, I'm only a little undergrad, burdened with bounded rationality, fragments of accessible information, and crude critical or analytical skills. In spite of all those handicaps, isn't it amazing how often I'm dead certain that I'm right?

According the survey, the majority of Americans are agreeable to teaching creationism in the schools. It's important to remember that those results are based on what people say today, which may be not be what they say tomorrow. But Derek says those stats are fairly stable over time. So the creationism premise seems pretty solid. And if the premise is stable, the resulting conclusions are likely to be stable regardless of what happens down at the bottom of the pst.

But also notice that there are people in both camps who say that they're not certain. In the religious camp, there are people who see the Bible as a moral guide instead of a physics text, and in the scientific camp, there are people who appreciate that there are still big gaps in the fossil record and that science can't answer certain personal and moral questions. These moderates see two worlds: religious premises help them map the one, and science helps them map the other.

Humans launch into ideological crusades when they demand that their particular premises must rule all territories. While adhering to an absolute premise (tolerating no questions) has the advantage of fitting nicely into our bounded rationality, it also creates verbal and physical fights, and at times, body bags.

As with the religion versus science debate there's always debate and news about 'nature versus nurture', about genes versus environment.

Nature versus nurture

Ideological warfare occurs over the nature–nurture premises, over which one should be boss while leaving the other to look after a few of the details. For example, the President of Harvard created a swarm of media attention when he suggested that one reason there were more men than women in top scientific jobs could be, that in addition to social bias favouring them, that men might also have a genetic advantage. I don't consider myself an avid feminist but it made me mad enough to spit!

The President's critics cycled down to the bottom of their PSTs and bombarded him with all the accessible facts they could lay their eyes on, plus all the sacred beliefs from the top, and demanded his resignation. And, eventually, he did resign.

Derek, of course, being a man, defended the President. Derek says rational people—including scientists—are supposed to keep an open mind about complex questions. At least before Simon they were. It looks like many minds are a teensy bit closed on both sides of the nature–nurture debate.

Certainly Dr Frund and Professor Creek had a zinger of a discussion over the Harvard President's speech.

I came across another interesting news item about how the Pentagon is supposedly planting false articles in the Iraq media.[12] If science is like a news service, I wonder how many false messages are planted in the scientific news?

Oh, for the good old days—the pre-Simon days—when brains were bigger, problems were smaller, and facts were facts!

Note

Explore the weird and wonderful mind of Marvin Minsky on your student website at http://www.oup.com/ca/he/companion/agnewpyke.

REVIEW TRUE OR FALSE QUIZ

T F	1.	Individuals experiencing the same stimuli (i.e., light and sound waves) may nevertheless see, hear, and remember very different things.
T F	2.	Exposed to a sudden and unexpected sequence of events, individuals may miss or distort what happened but they don't include things that never happened.
T F	3.	Differences in perception are a function of genetic differences rather than cultural effects.

---

[12]'US is Said to Pay to Plant Articles in Iraq Papers', *New York Times*. Available at http://www.nytimes.com/2005/12/01/politics/01propaganda.html.

T F	4.	As compared with laypersons, scientists are more accurate perceivers.
T F	5.	To cope with vast amounts of information and/or unstable information, humans oversimplify, jump to conclusions, or procrastinate making a decision.
T F	6.	Bounded rationality is a term coined by Daniel Kahneman that refers to our limited attention span and small memory capacity.
T F	7.	It is easier to predict events in the physical world than in psychological and social environments.
T F	8.	The phrase 'no conclusions without premises' refers to reliance on or utilization of reliable observations to inform conclusions.
T. F.	9.	A confirmatory bias is when the beliefs of an individual determine what he or she sees.
T F	10.	Which events are observed, attended to, processed, and remembered is influenced by our belief systems through the mechanism of enhancing their accessibility.
T F	11.	Shoham's model provides for increased complexity in problem solving by trading off depth of thinking for breadth of thinking.
T F	12.	Humans know a lot about a few things and a little or nothing about most things.
T F	13.	Shoham's extended and bracketed rules provide for periodic flexibility even when operating with a bounded rationality brain.
T F	14.	Minsky proposes that one of the most important kinds of knowledge is knowing what not to think.
T F	15.	Failing to respond to a child's persistent probing (i.e., an infinite series of 'whys') is unwise, and even dangerous, since it restricts the child's natural curiosity.
T F	16.	In shrinking complex problems down to mind-size we rely on our innate neurological limitations and our cultural biases.
T F	17.	The information (dots or observations) necessary to solve many problems is often humongous, unclear, inaccessible, and changing.
T F	18.	Collection of and reliance on reliable observations reflects a 'believing-is-seeing' orientation.
T F	19.	Kern postulates that the history of causation reveals a move from complex super natural explanations to more simplistic, concrete explanations.
T F	20.	Intelligent design, which a majority of Americans feel should be taught in the schools, is based on the premise of survival of the fittest.

From Pre-science to Science

In this section we first introduce you to two pre-scientific methods of problem solving: the *after-the-fact* and the *before-and-after* methods. Once you appreciate their strengths and limitations we then discuss the classic scientific method: the *control-group procedure*.

We critically examine the two pre-scientific methods because you and I use them every minute of every day. We bet our lives on them. You and I, the courts, and our doctors all rely on these two methods for generating most of our common sense and pre-scientific *solutions*.

Second, these two flawed tools provide the foundations on which we build our scientific methods. By knowing the foundations of science we can better appreciate its particular strengths and limitations.

Both the 'after-the-fact' and the 'before-and-after' methods share one advantage and one disadvantage. Their advantage is that they help come up with an *answer*, but not necessarily *the answer*, while we zip around our PSTs, trying to keep up with the busy traffic of daily living. Their disadvantage is that, although they are mentally affordable, they frequently lead us to naïve, or even disastrous, conclusions.

You've heard the phrase: 'Putting all the pieces together to get the whole picture?' Well, the problem with these methods is that even though we don't have access to *all the pieces* we erroneously *believe* we've got the whole picture. Without being aware of it, we fill in the gaps with assumptions and biases, while mistaking our construction for *the truth*.

As well as relying on powerful modifications to the after-the-fact and before-and-after tools, scientists still rely on them in their primitive form as well. They rely on them at work, not as a source of *solutions* but rather as a source of interesting questions and hunches. But, like the rest of us, burdened with bounded rationality, they must also rely on these flawed tools when they take off their white coats, leave their laboratories, and come out and join the rest of us zipping around our PSTS.

Once you're familiar with these two flawed but popular methods, we will introduce the Queen-of-all-problem-solving-methods in Chapter 5—the control-group method. A powerful tool that, in one step, helps overcome the major limitations of the after-the-fact and before-and-after methods.

3

The After-the-Fact Method

Chapter Goal

- To introduce you to the *after-the-fact* tool of problem solving.

It is our most user-friendly method. We do it automatically (without thinking). Furthermore, it's so flexible it usually allows us to come up with answers that fit our biases. You use it, doctors use it, the courts use it, and even scientists use it. The results can be wonderful, weird, or disastrous.

Introduction

> *We believe what we want to believe.*
> —Demosthenes

How do we make sense of what we can't see? How do we make sense out of past events, like a broken window or a murder, when we weren't there to witness them?

We rely on reports from those who were there, but can we trust their fallible observations, memory, and honesty? Or, if no one witnessed the event, then we have to rely on whatever bits and pieces of physical evidence we can dig up.

Mapping the past is a tricky challenge involving too many possibilities, too many fuzzy dots, and too many vague connections.

Therefore, following a significant and puzzling observation, we become time travellers. At the top of our PSTs we project ourselves back into the past and, from a myriad of fallible memories, select one or two that connect to our current perplexing observation in a way that fits our personal premises, or our gut, or our culture.

As our dear old Latin teacher used to say: *'post hoc, ergo propter hoc'*, which the smartest kid in the class used to (sanctimoniously!) explain translated into 'after this, therefore because of this'. Which, in ordinary language, means cherry-picking an earlier event and blaming it for a later event.

Minute by minute, you and I rely on the after-the-fact method as we travel around our PSTs jumping to conclusions. The courts and experts use it more conscientiously, committing more time and resources to all three corners.

Scientists use the after-the-fact method too. Not only when they take off their white coats and join the rest of us in the hectic traffic of living, but in their research as well. They must rely on the after-the-fact, cherry-picking, mentally affordable method whenever they select particular observations and ideas from the endless flow of past experience. They use the method not so much as a means of reaching conclusions but rather as a source of hunches, hypotheses, and theories.

The most appealing thing about the after-the-fact method is this: it's usually flexible enough to let us believe whatever we want to believe.

Cutting Puzzles Down to Mind-size

In Chapter 2 we documented, with the help of four scholars, how shrinking complex puzzles down to mind-size produces various results: wondrous, weird, and disastrous.

Wondrously, at the bottom of our PSTs, we miraculously and automatically transform light and sound waves into trusted images: into 'things', into three-dimensional moving, talking, working, singing, and sometimes fighting people.

At the top of our PSTs we infuse those transformed images with feeling and combine them into captivating sagas ranging from Superbowls to symphonies, into hopeful visions of the future, into magical fantasies and delightful stories, into elegant scientific theories which may or may not turn out to be 'true'.

But, in addition to miracles, by *doing what comes naturally* we also manufacture mistakes—small, medium, and lethal. At the bottom of our PSTs we *see* and *hear* things that aren't there, and fail to *see* and *hear* things that are.

At the top of our PSTs we thoughtlessly combine those misperceptions into flawed but trusted conclusions that could result in choosing the wrong mate, in dying from a prescribed but lethal course of treatment, in hanging the wrong man, or in sending our youth to war, yet again, and again, and again.

How can we capitalize on the wondrous products that result from doing what comes naturally but at the same time avoid, or at least minimize, some of our ruinous errors?

Simon's mantra

As noted in Chapter 2, Herb Simon won the Nobel Prize for his research on decision-making. His now famous mantra—'no conclusions without premises'—means that all the decisions we make are based on unproven and perhaps erroneous pre-suppositions, beliefs, or biases.

Can you think of an automatic and fallible premise you rely on every hour of every day?

Here's one. For most problems we implicitly trust the assumption that *seeing-is-believing*. When we *see* little Jimmy throw a rock that breaks the window, we *believe*. When we *see* Harvey slap Sally, we *believe*.

Yes, we believe. And we make mistakes by relying on this fallible *seeing-is-believing* premise or assumption. We make mistakes when we *see* it wrong (e.g., it was Jimmy's brother, who sort of looks like him, who threw the rock, and Harvey didn't really slap Sally, they were merely horsing around). However, it seems, most of the time, that the seeing-is-believing premise works.

But what happens when we can't *see* what happens?

Believing is seeing

When we can't *see* what happens we still make decisions. On the basis of our misperceptions and faulty intelligence we spank the wrong child, marry the wrong mate, hang the wrong guy, and even start the wrong war.

But we shouldn't be too hard on ourselves. What are we supposed to do? We have no choice. Just to keep up with the flow of life as we race around our PSTs, we must depend on incomplete or distorted observations and memories, deadlines, quick and dirty conclusions. How can we make *rational* decisions on the run?

We can't!

Nevertheless, we must make decisions—good or bad—by the minute. Yes, occasionally we take the time to be a bit more critical of faulty perceptions and second hand evidence. But sooner rather than later the time comes when decisions must be made. And, they must be made while we rely on the frequently unreliable after-the-fact method, which involves reconstructing or crudely mapping the past—which almost always involves uncertainty. In the courts we reassure ourselves by calling it 'reasonable doubt'. But in many instances, inside and outside the court, there is nothing reasonable or rational about it.

Like it or not, when using after-the-fact problem solving, *believing* usually has to take the place of *seeing*.

Like it or not, we have no other choice. If we can't trust second-hand evidence (from family, friends, experts and media) then we can't make important decisions, we can't get on with the business of living; we can't decide who to marry, spank, thank, blame, hang, or vote for. Without assumptions, premises, or biases we keep changing our minds, or we procrastinate, or we freeze in place like a hung jury.

Fig 3.1 ■ ELASTIC AFTER-THE-FACT PROBLEM-SOLVING

Shrinking the problem down to mind-size by relying on beliefs and accessible dots to reconstruct the past.

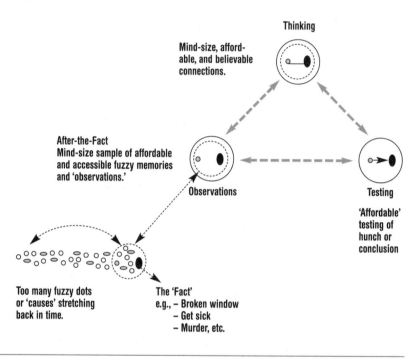

Thinking

Mind-size, afford-
able, and believable
connections.

After-the-Fact
Mind-size sample of affordable
and accessible fuzzy memories
and 'observations.'

Observations

Testing

'Affordable'
testing of
hunch or
conclusion

Too many fuzzy dots
or 'causes' stretching
back in time.

The 'Fact'
e.g., – Broken window
        – Get sick
        – Murder, etc.

As indicated in Figure 3.1, when you pause and think about it, after-the-fact problem-solving presents us with some very interesting challenges:

1. Everyday we must make decisions based on our reconstructions of the past.

2. To do so we must rely on recovered bits and pieces of the past—on faulty memories, and second-, third-, and fourth-hand evidence.

3. For complex questions about what or who 'caused' something (e.g., broken hearts, illness, failure, murder) there are too many dots, too many *possible connections*, scattered over both recent and ancient history.

4. Nevertheless, by assuming—*on the basis of* samples of incomplete and often conflicting evidence, we humans shrink problems down to mind-size, we reconstruct the past, we make important decisions, and we do so with enough confidence to 'bet the farm', punish a child, or hang a man. When we lose confidence in our beliefs and biases, we procrastinate, flip-flop, and experience waves of anxiety, panic, or depression.

We protect our sanity, but not by collecting and critically analyzing *all* relevant information, as the textbooks tell us to. Instead, most of the time we cherry-pick a mind-size sample of affordable and accessible dots, and relying on pet premises of what causes what, we *make* connections; we jump to a conclusion and *test it* using personal, affordable, elastic yardsticks, just as Ellie did in testing her magic lotions.

In brief, when using the flexible after-the-fact method, if you don't have confidence in most of your beliefs—justified or not—your brain hurts.

In this chapter we'll explore how we accomplish this miraculous feat; we'll discuss how to transform incomplete and fuzzy memories into objectively fallible, but subjectively trusted, conclusions. And, we'll explore how we accomplish this feat while zipping around our PST so quickly that we don't have the time to stop and consider how flimsy the evidence on which we base many of our important decisions really is. And it's just as well!

We'll also explore how experts and the courts commit more time and resources, at the bottom left corner of the PST to try to improve the reliability of the elastic, second-hand evidence, and at the top of the PST to critically evaluate alternative interpretations. However, even with such extra effort, the after-the-fact problem-solving tool remains pre-scientific. It doesn't permit the luxury of rigorously testing our conclusions. After all, we don't have the luxury of re-running our lives to see what would have happened if we'd chosen a different career, or a different mate, or if we had different children, or had given up smoking sooner.

To illustrate the after-the-fact method we start with a simple example of doing what comes naturally. And, later in the chapter, we consider more judicious uses of this pre-scientific tool.

On his way to a basketball practice Carl discovers the body of an acquaintance lying beside a car in the college parking lot.

> In brief, after-the-fact puzzles present insurmountable problems at all three corners of our PSTs. They overload our observational abilities, our critical thinking, and our rigorous testing capacities.

How does Carl use the after-the-fact method?

In Figure 3.2 we start in the bottom left hand corner of Carl's PST when he observes Willie lying beside his car. Carl notices a trail of blood on the pavement—it's as though Willie had been trying to crawl away from his own death.

Cautiously Carl reaches down and touches Willie's hand. It's stone cold!

Zipping up to the top of his PST Carl does some quick thinking and connects a few dots. He uses the shorthand mental labels we all use to represent, in our minds, the observations we make down below. Carl's mind automatically connects a few of the many labels floating around in his head and comes to this conclusion:

Fig 3.2 ■ THE FACT: WILLIE IS DEAD

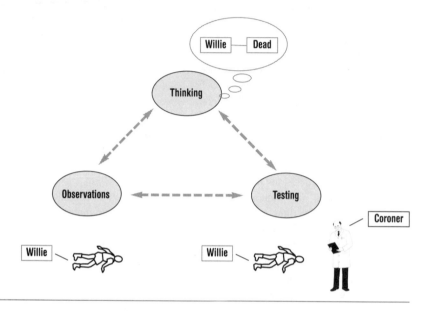

'Willie' + 'blood' + 'stone cold' = 'dead'.

Here we have a triple 'A' mental production, a simple bit of natural logic:

If A_1 (Willie) + A_2 (blood) + A_3 (cold hands) then B (Willie dead).

And then, after connecting the 'Willie' dot to the 'dead' dot, Carl's inner voice spontaneously asks: 'Who did it?' That's something that happens automatically at the top of our PSTs; it's a natural rule: 'if surprised, look for a cause'. So Carl's mind spontaneously starts searching for an image of the *who-done-it* dot.

Detectives realize that in most murder cases there are typically too many suspects, too many dots, and too many possible connections to get their heads and resources around.

But Carl's not a detective. He doesn't worry about complexities. Furthermore he's already late for basketball practice. He can't *afford* the time to get involved so he notifies the parking attendant in the kiosk that 'there's a guy lying by a car over there' and jogs off to the gym.

Carl's satisfied himself that Willie's dead, but that personal conclusion needs official approval, so we travel down to the bottom right corner of the forensic PST, where a coroner is called to the scene. He does 'rigorous testing' on Willie— just in case what Carl saw was actually ketchup instead of blood, and because some people lay down for nap after too much alcohol, furthermore, some people naturally have cold hands. Coroners have to be careful. Dead people sometimes wake up in the morgue and make a fuss. In this case the coroner confirms Carl's casual observation.

Of course, as Carl goes about his business, one part of his mind is still puzzling over who might have done it. That's what our minds do. If there's a B then there has to be an A that caused it.

Too many suspects, too many dots

After poor Willie's funeral, Carl casually keeps one eye on the case. Down at the bottom left corner of his PST, Carl looks for *easily accessible* information (remember Kahneman's Nobel Prize?). The police are digging into Willie's past. Carl scans the papers and peeks at the TV news; he is *seeing* how the investigators are travelling back in time looking for suspects and trying to tie them to Willie.

As is usually the case, lots of people had connections with Willie, and not *everyone* liked him.

In brief there are too many suspects for Carl to actually keep track of, too many to remember, too many with possible connections to Willie, and to each other. So what's a busy, common sense problem-solver in this after-the-fact situation to do?

As indicated in Figure 3.3, Carl cuts the problem down to mind-size in order to fit his bounded rationality—his limited attention span and memory.

He does what we all do: he relies on personal and cultural mind-shrinkers. He automatically protects his bounded rationality by relying on *readily accessible* observations, memories, beliefs, and biases. Commencing in the bottom left corner of his PST, Carl does a quick scan of the suspects paraded on TV and automatically labels these images and cherry-picks pick his favourite (the one who fits his premises, his biases). At the top of his PST he jumps to the conclusion that 'the squinty-eyed guy did it!' He connects the squinty-eyed dot to the dead Willie dot.

He knows in his gut (emotionally anchored premise) that squinty-eye is guilty. Obviously he doesn't have the time or resources to travel down to the right corner of his PST to rigorously test his conclusion. But that doesn't stop him from being certain. That's the appeal of the after-the-fact method—certainty comes cheap.

Carl doesn't even have to wait for the jury's semi-rigorous test. He can 'test' his conclusion effortlessly at the top of his PST. Up there, in his imagination, it's much easier to get away with connecting and disconnecting causes and effects, or 'As' and 'Bs' than it is at the bottom right hand corner. It's much easier to think up a solution than it is to rigorously test it down where the so-called rubber hits the road.

One of Carl's stored dots (one of his long-term memories) floats out of its brackets into his awareness, just as we discussed when explaining Shoham's elegant model in Chapter 2. It's a memory of another squinty-eyed guy, who was a big guard on an opposing basketball team, a mean, dirty player—all elbows

Fig 3.3 ■ CARL'S AFTER-THE-FACT: WILLIE IS DEAD

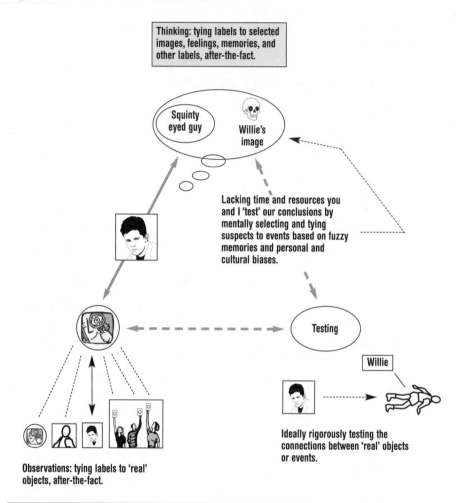

Thinking: tying labels to selected images, feelings, memories, and other labels, after-the-fact.

Squinty eyed guy

Willie's image

Lacking time and resources you and I 'test' our conclusions by mentally selecting and tying suspects to events based on fuzzy memories and personal and cultural biases.

Testing

Willie

Ideally rigorously testing the connections between 'real' objects or events.

Observations: tying labels to 'real' objects, after-the-fact.

and knees under the basket. So Carl knows, consciously and unconsciously, about nasty squinty-eyed characters. Carl has access to all the information and *emotional anchors* he needs to reach a trusted conclusion about who 'caused' Willie to die.

Carl, doing what comes naturally, is behaving exactly how our four experts, discussed in Chapter 2, would predict. He's cutting his problem down to mind-size by relying on a *premise* or bias (à la Simon), supported by a *readily accessible*, emotionally anchored bit of evidence (à la Kahneman), released from its brackets (à la Shoham), and thus avoiding overwhelming his bounded rationality, or encountering a dangerous way of thinking (à la Minsky).

Now we recognize that Carl jumped to his conclusion on the basis of both very fuzzy evidence and precious little critical thinking. Nevertheless, we and Carl do exactly the same thing every day.

Now, if you're thinking 'Wait a minute, I don't always jump to naïve conclusions,' you'd be right. For special people or projects we do focus our attention, shifting it from other people and events, thus reserving our bounded rationality for one person or project, for a short while.

So does Carl. Sometimes, operating in the left corner of his PST, he conscientiously focuses his attention on past events. He checks his observations and critically analyzes what he remembers, thinking hard about which dots to connect. For instance he plays and replays past basketball games. And before an economics exam he even puts basketball aside, clears space in his bounded rationality, and conscientiously studies his lecture notes and his highlighted textbooks (the past).

So, while we 'solve' most of our after-the-fact problems by jumping to conclusions while zipping around our PSTs, at times we reserve and protect a portion of our bounded rationality for special projects. Our solutions may still be fallible but at least they're not flippant or casual. When we specialize we may not always get it right but at least we spend more time at all three corners of the triangle, we don't jump to as many naïve conclusions.

Are we perhaps being overly critical of Carl, the common-sense problem-solver using the-after-the fact method? After all, if we've been using it for thousands of years, and we're still here, it must *work* a lot of the time.

How Come the After-the-Fact Method *Works*?

If it's so flawed, how is it that this method seems to 'work' every minute of every hour of every day? How come this 'doing what comes naturally' *works* even with our slipshod performance at all three corners of the PST?

It works—or seems to work—for a variety of reasons. *Temporal, Subjective*

First, notice that *it works* for Carl. As far as he's concerned he's solved the problem. He's convinced he knows who killed Willie. The detectives don't know yet, the judge and jury don't know yet, the appeal courts don't know yet, but Carl *knows*, and that knowledge is linked to an old memory, anchored to a still hot emotion of hate.

Second, after-the-fact methods work because, for complex problems, the *answers* are typically delayed, fuzzy, or endlessly revised. For many, maybe most, of life's complex puzzles there are no absolute answers. So, when using this method, we can't be absolutely certain who is *right*. Like us, Carl can often *get away* with his gut-based conclusions for days, months, or even years.

Third, even if the jury finds squinty-eye not guilty, Carl will likely maintain that they're wrong, and notice he doesn't suffer any negative consequence for disagreeing. He knows the right answer in his own mind, heart, and gut. Even if an appeal court eventually declares squinty-eye 'not guilty' Carl probably won't buy it: 'Too many bleeding heart liberals sitting on the bench and in the jury box these days.'

If you remember only one thing about solving complex problems let it be this: For many problems there are no currently available, clear-cut solutions. The after-the-fact method *works* because even though it requires little time and effort it enables us to achieve subjective certainty for now, potentially even for life, in an objectively uncertain world. And certainty is a valuable commodity in an uncertain world.

If you can mentally afford to remember one other thing about the after-the-fact method, then remember this: Because we can't mentally or emotionally afford too many doubts, we not only jump to conclusions but we've also developed automatic damage control methods to help us defend those conclusions, and to maintain our self confidence.

What damage control strategies do we use? We stay away from people who ask too many whys and who lead us into dangerous ways of thinking (à la Minsky). We keep exceptions bracketed away in mental closets (à la Shoham). We have quick, ready-made responses for critics or for people who disagree with us. For instance, when the jury came up with the not guilty verdict for squinty-eye, Carl didn't open up his mind—his bounded rationality—to that possibility. Instead he automatically discredited the judge and the jury, thus keeping his limited attention span, memory capacity, and critical thinking available for basketball, for increasing his height, and for an economics exam on Friday.[1]

For special projects we focus our limited attention, but most of the time we jump to conclusions on the basis of simple rules and biases and *it works*.

A bias for all occasions

But what about all those puzzles that crop up every day loaded with questions for which you have no mind-shrinking, emotionally anchored biases or no trusted 'If A then B' rule?

Good point. Although you may have no beliefs about the specific issue, Simon's mantra would suggest, and we agree, that you still use a trusted, all-purpose premise or assumption to reach a conclusion. We propose that you still use time-saving, mind-shrinking rules to handle all such situations.

The rule may be as simple as: 'Believe or remember the last answer you heard.' Experimental psychologists call this the 'recency effect'. This helps explain why, if we have no particular culturally acquired bias, we fall back on a neurological bias and tend to remember the last thing we heard, the one still

---

[1] Notice how quickly our minds automatically erase most of the information we've studied for an exam. It's as though our brain dumps it as soon as we walk out of the exam room. Forgetting helps protect our bounded rationality from overload.

cycling around our neurons. In Kahneman's terms recent memories are more *accessible*, and so more likely to be included in our conclusions.

Or, the general-purpose mind-shrinker may be another simple 'If A then B rule'. The rule may be 'If A says it, then B, it must be true.' 'A' may be your favourite news anchor,[2] politician, professor, rock star, or sports hero. Simon's simple mantra still works.

Rapid rates of change and complexity lead to personal uncertainty and breed an exponential growth of *experts* of all types with premises for sale. Lacking strong premises of our own we increasingly rely on these mobile bags of premises and rituals, providing a kind of Simon 'rent-all service' for the rest of us, providing us with a temporary premise and ritual to help get us over yet another patch of uncertainty.

The after-the-fact tool may not be our best route to 'the truth', nevertheless, when the *truth* isn't readily accessible, this crude, but affordable, method helps us construct and maintain enough certainty to stay in the game, to walk into the future with confidence, based on incomplete information and naïve premises though it may be.

We've seen how the crude after-the-fact method can generate different and trusted *realities* for different problem solvers working on the same complex problem (e.g., determining guilt or innocence, electing a leader, etc.). We've seen how the after-the-fact method works as we sprint around our PST when there's no affordable way of rigorously testing our *solution* down in the lower right corner. Now let's see how this primitive, pre-scientific method *works* when we commit more conscious time and effort at all three corners of the problem solving triangle. We'll present two examples: a case for the courts, and a case for the physician.

A Case for the Courts

In the last section we saw how Carl rapidly reconstructed the past and jumped to a subjectively certain conclusion on the basis of flimsy, but emotionally anchored evidence—flimsy to us, not to him.

Give Carl a gun, instead of a club, and you have the makings of high-tech caveman justice. Bring half a dozen gun-toting Carls together and you have vigilante justice. Add a hanging judge to the mix, and you have the Wild West. Our judicial system is far from perfect. No system forced to rely on the after-the-fact method can be. But it's a big step forward from frontier justice.

---

[2]You may recall that during the last Presidential election there was a fuss created when trusted news anchor Dan Rather reported, and initially defended, an erroneous story about Bush's military service. Some speculated that a loss in his credibility led to his retiring in 2006, just before reaching his 25th anniversary as anchor. Millions of people rely on their favourite news anchors for 'the truth', for selecting and connecting the dots, for drawing reliable maps of the past.

Through centuries of quick and dirty, trial and error justice, through pooling our bounded rationality, we've learned a thing or two. Society has slowly evolved some rules of evidence while providing our courts with the time and resources to conscientiously cycle around the PST—more conscientiously than Carl or you can 'afford' to do it.

Rather than jumping to conclusions, the courts invest time and attention in the left corner of the triangle, to examine the reliability of observations, and at the top of the triangle, to critically examine alternative explanations or suspects. Then, in the bottom right corner, the judge or jury conscientiously—but not rigorously—tests the premise, and produces a guilty or not guilty verdict.

Because of the nature of after-the-fact puzzles, the courts—unlike scientists—don't have the luxury of rigorously testing their conclusions through controlled experiments. Nevertheless, a judge or jury does a much more conscientious job than the cave dwellers, a lynch mob, or even Carl, in reaching a carefully considered conclusion.

To illustrate the difference, let's examine how the courts, using the after-the-fact decision-making tool, deal with Willie's murder.

Shrinking the problem down to court size

Whereas Carl invested very little conscious effort at the lower left corner of the PST, the courts invest a great deal.

However, like anyone attempting to make sense out of past events (after-the-fact events), the courts must face the basic fact that, like Carl, like historians, like physicians, they must try to map the past while relying on incomplete information by relying on fuzzy and missing dots.

Remember, the after-the-fact model is simple. An observation (O) is made. A murdered man is found, or a patient is diagnosed as depressed, or Diana slaps Derek. Next we attempt to decide what previous event, (X), led to (O), or what previous events were necessary in order for (O) to occur. In the language of common sense we are asking what *caused* (O). In the language of science we are asking what key antecedent(s) (Xs) were linked to the selected consequence (O). There are usually several possible (Xs), that is, several antecedents (causes) that could lead to a given consequence. The problem we face at the top of the PST is to select the most probable one(s): X_1? X_2? X_3? . . . X_n?

When Willie's murder occurred the police uncovered a variety of possible suspects—a large number of Xs, including squinty-eye.

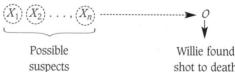

Possible	Willie found
suspects	shot to death

We place the Xs inside dotted circles and use a dotted arrow to indicate that there is uncertainty surrounding each suspect and its connection to the murder.

How does the justice system cut the number of suspects down to mind-size? What aids does the legal system use to sort the most likely suspects from the least likely? One decision aid is *time*. When the time of death is determined to within two hours, all suspects who have *reasonable* alibis for the estimated killing time (1:00 AM to 3:00 AM) are separated from those who do not.

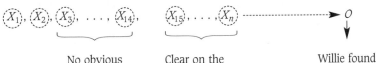

These suspects are excluded on the basis that they were not present when Willie was murdered

Willie found shot to death

Thus, we reduce the load on our bounded rationality—our limited memory—by excluding many of the original suspects, many fewer dots to connect.

The list of suspects, and our rational load, can be reduced still further, this time using the decision aid of *motive*. Twelve additional suspects are eliminated because they have no *obvious* motive. Notice we say no 'obvious' motive because determining motive is an imprecise process—it's best to leave dotted circles of uncertainty around each suspect.

The courts rely heavily on motive as a decision aid (it's a core premise or assumption, à la Simon). That's one of the reasons why a gang or a mob might use a 'hired gun' from out of town; that person will have no prior connections to the victim, therefore, no obvious motive.

No obvious motive

Clear on the basis of time that Willie was murdered

Willie found shot to death

Of the suspects who still remain after the *time* and *motive* screening, the focus shifts to suspect #1 when it is discovered that the murder weapon is his. This, plus the fact that he had a motive and no alibi, links his dot to Willie's death with three lines of evidence. Nevertheless, suspect #1 is quickly replaced by suspect #2 when the latter's fingerprints are found on the murder weapon.

As well as being the suspect most closely tied to the murder weapon, he also has a motive and no alibi.

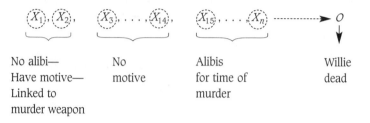

No alibi—	No	Alibis	Willie
Have motive—	motive	for time of	dead
Linked to		murder	
murder weapon			

Though limited to the pre-scientific after-the-fact method, notice how the court imports whatever scientific technology it can to supplement its pre-scientific problem solving. Using DNA to connect previously excluded or unknown suspects to crimes is a modern instance. Though not foolproof—even lab technologists make mistakes or may accept bribes—DNA is still an almost miraculous way of connecting apparently unconnected dots, allowing connections to be made across towns, across years, even across the centuries.

A controlled and adversarial process for reaching closure

Apart from science, our courts, in their efforts to solve after-the-fact problems, set the gold standard for conscientious efforts at all three corners of the PST.

Prosecution and defense

The courts—in particular the invention of the adversarial system in which the defense and prosecution lawyers critically examine and challenge each other's evidence, premises, and arguments—are a cultural invention that significantly raises the level of critical thinking. The adversarial process commences with jury selection, with each side attempting to exclude *biased* jurors (i.e., those holding a premise opposite to the lawyer's). Even if they've never heard of Simon, lawyers are well aware of his mantra: 'No conclusions without premises'. They want to find jurors likely to support their position, or at least not biased against it.

The adversaries continue this critical process by challenging the reliability of the information provided by each side's witnesses. Perhaps lawyers are familiar with the astonishing witness misperceptions evident in the classroom demonstration discussed in Chapter 2.

So, although still using the after-the-fact method, the courts conscientiously attempt to identify the more reliable observations at the left corner of the PST, and also use more critical thinking at the top of the PST than Carl, or Ellie, or you can afford. Of course, the lawyers play on the elasticity of after-the-fact problem solving. They know full well that unconscious emotional anchors play a large role in decision-making and they employ courtroom theatrics to trigger strong emotions likely to sway jurors for or against the suspect. Carl's decision was based largely on just such an anchor, his emotionally charged memory of a 'dirty', squinty-eyed basketball player.

Lawyers appreciate that when engaged in after-the-fact problem solving that the believing-is-seeing rule is the name of the game.

The judge and the jury

While the prosecution and the defense use every trick of their craft (rational, sneaky, and emotional) to sway the jurors, the more or less 'unbiased' judge,[3] supported by evolved rules of evidence, acts as a referee to control the lawyers' more outrageous distortions of the evidence. The judge instructs the jury before they begin to make a decision, indicating which evidence is acceptable and which *must*[4] be ignored. So, in terms of critical thinking at the top of the PST, the opposing lawyers critique each other's thinking and the judge attempts to serve as a reasonable arbiter.

Finally, in the bottom right corner of the PST, relying on a judge or jury, the courts provide conscientious, but not rigorous, testing of the question of guilt or innocence.

Again we run right into the major limitation of the after-the-fact method. By its very nature we can't rerun the event, in this case Willie's murder, to rigorously test our conclusions. Nevertheless, the courts at least make a much more serious effort than Carl did to *test* alternative explanations.

Solving or resolving?

The Necessity for Closure: Not only does the controlled adversarial system of the courts commit significant resources at all three corners of the PST, but it also serves another vital function. The courts may not be able to accurately reconstruct the past, that is, they may not be able to *solve* complex after-the-fact problems, but they provide a socially acceptable way of *resolving* them in order to reach closure.

The courts provide a form of closure for open-ended questions for which there is often no clear-cut, absolute answer. Often, the best they can do is to identify the *smoking gun*. They have no other choice. Complex problems

---

[3]In North America, the Supreme Court judges are screened and appointed to reflect the political values (biases?) of the party in power. Judges—like the rest of us—dance to Simon's tune. Their decisions reflect not only the laws of the land, but also their particular interpretations (premises) concerning those laws. Some legal scholars (e.g., Reynolds, 2005) suggested that some items in the US constitution, far from being clear rules, are as fuzzy as an indecipherable 'inkblot'. Since Supreme Court justices frequently disagree, we have clear examples of 'believing-is-seeing' in action in the highest court of the land.

[4]Clever lawyers sneak in emotionally loaded evidence because they know that once it has escaped from its brackets it can't be ignored, no matter how the judge instructs the jury.

invariably involve missing, incomplete, fuzzy, conflicting, or distorted evidence. There will always be plausible alternative interpretations. Providing socially accepted forms of closure helps protect individuals and groups from the festering effects of endless, debilitating debate.

Peer pressure

Notice how the jury system forces closure. In delegating the final decision to the jury the courts must rely on whatever indeterminate mix of wisdom and bias those particular 12 people bring to bear. But also notice that individual jurors are often not allowed to individually express their opinion on a secret ballot. Rather they are locked away as a group so that focused peer pressure can operate in producing unanimous decisions.

Social scientists have demonstrated the potent power of peer pressure, not only on influencing teenage dress codes, bullying, music preferences, and adult voting behaviour, but also on simple objective tasks such as judging the length of lines. Peer pressure can influence not only what we believe, but also what we *see* or say we *see*.

We typically achieve closure on complex questions not by rational, empirical means but because we run out of resources such as time, energy, and patience. We frequently do a rational cop-out. On occasion we rely on a trivial but affordable decision aid: we flip a coin, go with the flow, or follow the leader.

In brief, when working on complex, after-the-fact problems, institutions such as the courts, parliaments, and Congress, must have built-in closure 'rules', just like individuals. They must have rules, wired-in by both genetics and culture, that signal 'enough already', rules that signal that it's time to 'stop cycling' endlessly around this particular PST, make a decision—right or wrong—and move on. You probably know individuals who waste large portions of their lives procrastinating, unable to make an important decision, or unable to stop endlessly recycling a loss or misfortune . . . unable to achieve closure.

In future chapters, as we progress from the pre-scientific to scientific methods, keep in mind the court's inventions for resolving, if not solving, after-the-fact problems. Keep in mind the resource commitment at all three corners of the PST through the controlled and adversarial closure processes. Also keep in mind three specific decision aids the courts employ to cut complex problems down to manageable size: a time frame, a theory frame, and *experts* or specialists.

Time frames, theory frames, and specialization
Time frames

Remember how the court ruled out suspects, or reduced the number of dots, by relying on the estimate of the *time* of death? We simplify after-the-fact problem resolution whenever we can establish a time marker for past events. George concentrates on identifying *when* Joyce started acting cool towards him, and what he had said or done just prior to *that time*. The courts focus on the *time* of death and where each of the suspects was at that *time*. Doctors focus on the *time* at which your stomach pains first appeared and what you had eaten in the period just preceding that *time*.

We rely heavily on time frames to help us rule in, and rule out, suspected causes. Notice that we are also relying on the premise or the assumption that events are the result of factors immediately preceding them. This assumption works unless the 'cause' has a delayed action such as conception and birth, or early childhood trauma and adult personality disorders.

Whenever a long period of time separates the cause and the effect—whenever there are many dots occurring in that interval—then all problem solving (pre-scientific and scientific) becomes more complicated, more prone to error, and more likely to be *truth free*.

Think how long it must have taken Oog and Oola to identify what led to the birth of a child. There are an infinite string of dots that can serve as possible suspects in that nine-month period. As we explore other pre-scientific and scientific methods, pay attention to how often we rely on time frames to reduce the number of suspects.

Theory frames

Remember how the justice system relied heavily on the premise, on *the theory*, that crimes are driven by motives (e.g., greed, jealousy, lust, or hate)? While time markers help shrink problems to mind-size, theory frames (premises, assumptions, and biases) shrink them still further.

Theories are premises, or sets of assumptions, about how the world works. Since we can't see into the future, we walk into it on bridges of belief, on our pet theories. All of us do it. Even scientists.

We will be encountering this general premise repeatedly throughout the book because theory frames typically play a definitive role in all problem-solving methods: common sense, pre-scientific, and scientific.

Carl relied on the premise that physical characteristics—in this case squinty-eyes—reflect a flawed

| |
| We are restating the 'believing-is-seeing' premise to read 'no conclusions without theories.' |

character. When it is time to select a jury, the judges and lawyers try to eliminate jurors with well-established theory frames (prejudices) about what 'types' of people commit crimes (males, foreigners, blacks, etc.). The courts appreciate that people's theory frames—their basic premises—determine which dots they notice, which dots they connect, and which dots they stuff into simplified, and often reprehensible, categories.

Specialization

In addition to time and theory frames, the courts rely on specialists to help them shrink problems to mind-size. By definition, that's what specialists or experts do.

They focus their bounded rationality and limited attention on certain kinds of dots: DNA dots, blood dots, time of death dots, fingerprint dots, money dots, political dots, and psychological dots.

Down at the bottom left corner of the PST experts wear blinders, they narrow their search so that they can focus on specific dots. Then, moving up to the top of the PST, they analyze how their 'pet' dots are connected. To reach conclusions they must rely on professional rules, rituals, and theories.

If you view experts as mobile bags of premises and associated rituals you can better understand their behaviour. They share some of their guiding premises with other members of their craft (the current conventional wisdom of the trade or profession), while other of their premises and rituals arise from that individual's unique combination of genes and experience.

Viewing experts in this way helps explain why, on occasion, they disagree; their professionally deviant premises lead them to emphasize and connect different dots—real, fuzzy, and imaginary.

Both the prosecution and the defense have no trouble providing their own experts, all with the same impeccable credentials but with diametrically opposed perceptions of the evidence. What kind of experts are these? The jury has to decide which expert is the most believable. We're back to Simon's 'believing is seeing' mantra. This basic challenge faces anyone using the after-the-fact method.

The Supreme Court

The highest court of the land faces formidable challenges. The Supreme Court is called on to provide final closure on selected cases on which the lower courts disagreed. In a way, the Supreme Court is like the last jury, composed of politically appointed members—some liberal, some conservative. Operating up at the top of the nation's PST, they receive written arguments (briefs) from vested interests and hear adversarial lawyers argue. The evidence they hear is not only after-the fact, but also second- and third-hand vested-interest constructions of *reality*.

How do they make their decisions? On the basis of premises (conceptual constraints) including their individual interpretations of the constitution, the laws of the land, their personal beliefs and biases, and peer pressure from other members of the court. Because the constitution and the laws are open to widely different interpretations, the justices' political and personal beliefs play critical roles in constructing a majority interpretation. For a fascinating peek inside the Supreme Court of the United States see Breyer (2005).

> Certainly, the justice system can be improved, but we must remember that it has a challenging task. Limited to using the after-the-fact method—to reconstructing the past out of fragments of information—the courts must attempt to resolve, rather than solve, a problem. The courts must reach a 'conclusion' in a culturally affordable and acceptable way. And that conclusion holds until a later court *sees* a different truth.

Because many vitally important decisions (e.g., concerning segregated schools, abortion, putting evolution onto school curriculums, etc.) result in a 5–4 ruling, the loss of a sitting member, and the appointment of a replacement, creates a great deal of political excitement and debate. The premises, beliefs, and biases of one new member of the court can tilt the critical thinking at the top of the judicial PST—it can shape the course of justice for decades.

Nevertheless, it is important to remember that our courts, at all levels, face an impossible task of attempting to reach rational decisions on the basis of after-the-fact, fuzzy, distorted, and incomplete evidence. They serve us not so much by discovering valid solutions but rather by establishing affordable *resolutions*.

Liberals and Conservatives, Democrats and Republicans, rely on different beliefs and biases concerning the role of government and the courts in our personal lives. The low, but affordable, level of critical thinking, on both extremes, consists of simply labelling their opponents soft-headed or hard-hearted.

Stretching the limits

To be fair, not all reconstructions are so simple-minded. Unlike editorial writers and political hacks, some legislators, columnists, and jurists periodically stretch their critical thinking to the breaking point by attempting to acknowledge opposing positions or premises. Swing vote justices provide an example of this extra effort. As noted earlier, the courts resolve, rather than solve, problems. Unless their often-arbitrary resolutions attract wide public support, they eventually become dysfunctional.

We may frequently disagree with a judicial decision but we should at least respect the awesome stretching of human bounded rationality that both the adversarial system and peer pressure involve. We're more likely to respect similar rational stretching when great novelists, playwrights, and storytellers do it, as they reconstruct the past in rich and fascinating ways.

Few of us remember the names of the Supreme Court Justices whose vote helped integrate the schools and reshaped the future. However, we know the names of some of the scientists whose theoretical maps revised our view of the future. For instance, Freud and Einstein are known to almost everyone. Their theories helped thousands of researchers decide what dots to look for, what dots to connect, and what connections to rigorously test. Many of Freud's dots and connections turned out to be too fuzzy to test rigorously, while some of Einstein's hypothesized connections tested true and changed our world.

Some scholars claim that a good theory is the most practical thing in the world because it cuts complex problems down to mind-size and, sometimes, changes not only the way we think, but also the way we act.

A Case for a Physician

As noted earlier, in pre-scientific applications the courts set the gold standard for systematically committing resources to all three corners of the PST while attempting to resolve after-the-fact problems. But you and I haven't had much direct contact with the courts. We need an example that is closer to home.

We've all had personal experience with doctors as they cycle around their PSTs. Discussing doctors will provide us with first-hand observations about how 'experts' attempt to separate fact from fancy while still burdened with the after-the-fact method. We will take a closer, if somewhat disturbing, look at how physicians attempt to make sense out of the buzzing confusion of dots that we drag into their waiting rooms.

Medical practitioners deserve medals for their individual heroics of managing both their own and their patients' uncertainty in dealing with an overwhelming array of complex—maybe life-threatening—after-the-fact problems.[5] Patients of all ages—in all states of health—continually arrive at the physician's door with unrealistic expectations of immediately obtaining clear diagnoses and miracle treatments.

In this discussion it is important to distinguish between medical practitioners and medical researchers. Medical practitioners are the general practitioners and specialists that we consult. They employ pre-scientific methods[6] such as the after-the-fact method. Medical researchers employ many of the scientific methods—particularly rigorous testing, to their work.

Just as the courts rely on theory frames, time frames, and specialists, so too do doctors. Doctors rely on current medical practice and theory, both of which help them shrink the problem to mind-size and enable them to choose one suspect, or group of suspects, over others.

Consider a familiar situation in which the after-the-fact tool is employed. You suffer from periodic painful stomach aches and you present your case to the physician.

You deliver a flow of words at the bottom left corner of your doctor's PST. Words are our most efficient, though certainly not our most reliable, mind-shrinkers. Notice how we condense a vast number of different dots into one fuzzy word[7] or phrase like: 'It sort of hurts some of the time.'

---

[5]Of course, there are incompetent and unethical people in the medical profession, as there are in all walks of life. But most of them, we know, are trying their best under increasingly difficult circumstances.

[6]While your GP or specialist may rely on specific tests generated from scientific research, their problem solving methods are nevertheless pre-scientific, and involve reconstructing the past based on a mix of observations or dots: reliable, incomplete, and fuzzy, including those regurgitated from patients' flawed memories.

[7]Stop and think about the vast number of different dots we cram into words such as black or white, liberal or conservative, good or bad, healthy or sick, etc.

Your physician has to select a few dots out of the fuzzy flow and connect them into a diagnosis. He or she is faced with the same problem as the courts: the past must be reconstructed.

Doctors combine your memories—clear, fuzzy, and erroneous—with their observations—both reliable and unreliable—and premises—both wise and biased—in order to select one or more suspects from a group of 'possibles'.

Travelling rapidly up and down the left side of his or her PST, your doctor constructs a diagnosis based on your stream of fuzzy dots, and a treatment from his or her bounded storehouse of connections. Out of your flow of words, and perhaps a physical examination, they construct a target symptom or 'observation' (O) and a list of contributing suspects (Xs).

$$X_1, X_2, X_3, X_4, X_5, X_6, \ldots, X_n \longrightarrow O$$

Stomachache

Forget finding absolute solutions to complex after-the-fact problems. Such solutions usually lie beyond the reach of even our best medical practitioners. But hope springs eternal and there is some order in the universe.

Good news

Just as there are reliable patterns in physical nature, so too there are reliable and detectable patterns in biological nature: most colds last about two weeks, most stomach aches disappear, antibiotics kill lots of bugs, etc. So, between nature's curative powers and your doctor's training and experience—supported by the profession's current conventional wisdom—we're all healthier than we've ever been.

Furthermore, some doctors, like some scientists, are intuitively brilliant at identifying subtle patterns in the flow of fuzzy dots. After many exposures to symptom flows from many patients, they experience that wonderful high that expresses itself as 'Ah ha!': 'Ah ha! My patients who developed this symptom had all been on blood pressure pills!' or 'Ah ha! Most of my patients who have trouble maintaining stable interpersonal relationships were all separated from their mothers at an early age.'

We are all blessed with such 'Ah ha!'-highs once in a while. Some even turn out to be 'true' in the sense that they are accepted by our friends or colleagues, or even by society, such as Semmilweis's intuition that doctors should *really* wash their hands, not just wipe them off on their trousers, before coming into direct contact with their patient's open wounds or newborn babies.

But, as the complexity of the problems rise and the patterns of connected dots become subtler and lie just beyond the reach of our bounded rationality, modern technology, and even beyond the reach of our most brilliant intuitive minds, then we encounter the profound limitations of the after-the-fact method.

Time frames are important. Specialists are important.[8] Theory frames are vital.

Theory frames

While you're unloading your fuzzy flow of symptom dots at the bottom of your physician's PST, various alternative explanations are popping into his or her consciousness up at the top. Some are remembered from medical school (the profession's current conventional wisdom), some have been encountered frequently in practice, and others are remembered from reading recent articles.

Your doctor may have just had a visit from a drug company representative promoting a new combination of drugs for stomach problems based on company-sponsored research. The drug company's underlying premise, or theory, is that such symptoms are the result of a specific kind of bacteria and too much stomach acid. The drug company's wonder pill combo is designed specifically to treat both of these conditions—to kill bacteria and to reduce acid.

Yes, but

While appealing in its simplicity the proposal encounters a conflicting premise in your doctor's mind: the bacteria–acid problem combination seems to occur in an older age group, and the patient is still relatively young.

Furthermore, patients who test positive for those specific bacteria frequently don't have stomach pain or ulcers. The rule isn't as simple as the drug company would like us to believe. Instead, it's 'If A then sometimes B'. And we don't know why. Apparently the real rule reads: 'If A and If A_1, A_2, . . . A_n then probably B', and doctors don't know what A_1, A_2, or A_n are. They could be age, diet, or prior illnesses—or something else entirely. It creates a buzzing confusion of 'ifs' and 'maybes'.

As with most after-the-fact puzzles, the more critical thinking your doctor applies at the top of his or her PST in an attempt to 'cover all possibilities', the more complicated the problem becomes, and the greater the risk of drifting into dangerous ways of thinking. As noted in Chapter 2, we can mentally afford to keep a few exceptions to a rule bracketed in a closet in our mind, but if we pack in too many exceptions and qualifications we can't close the closet door and the 'Yes, buts' will keep spilling out to mess up our thinking, threaten our bounded rationality, and make decision making difficult or impossible.

---

[8]Recall the old folk saying: 'Experts [specialists] are people who know more and more about less and less.' As one wit commented: 'My medical specialist only works on the right eye of left-handed red-heads.'

Physicians face this dilemma frequently. They need a trusted theory frame to help them cut down the search space so as to capture a few suspects inside the box while excluding the distracting majority. But many theory frames conflict and as a result doctors often rely on simplifying rules of thumb (mini-theories) such as: 'If the patient is young and healthy use a conservative "wait and see" treatment because the current symptom will probably pass.'

As Kahneman suggests (see Chapter 2), in order to avoid mental overload we must all rely on a collection of simple 'If A then B rules'. For your doctor, the rule may be: 'If A_1 (young) and A_2 (healthy) then B_1 (wait and see); If A_3 (high fever) then B_2 (prescribe antibiotic); If A_4 (chronic illness) then B_3 (reduce discomfort); If $A_5, A_6 \ldots A_n$, then B_4 (refer to a specialist)'.

Doctors maintain a mental closet for each of these simple rules, out of awareness, in which they store a mentally affordable number of exceptions to their simple rules. That closet remains closed, protecting their bounded rationality, until an *exceptional* (attention-grabbing) observation automatically unlocks the closed door, releasing those extended rules into consciousness. For instance, 'If A_1 (young and healthy) then B_1 (wait and see) *unless* A_4 (family history of stomach cancer)'. When that A_4 observation becomes clearly accessible it trumps the A_1 observation, releasing a new cancer-related rule into awareness.

Your medical practitioners must trust their mini-rules. Like us, they can't rationally or emotionally afford to have a little voice inside their heads continuously yapping: 'But what if you missed something? What if you're wrong?'

They must lock that little voice away most of the time and *believe* in most of their simple rules in order to *see*, in order to decide. They must trust their beliefs, premises, and rules in order to make timely treatment decisions with enough confidence to maintain their own sanity (avoid dangerous ways of thinking), while, at the same time, maintaining the patient's confidence and trust in the doctor–patient relationship.

As well as mini-theories, physicians rely on *mega-theories*. For example, some doctors are more willing to see psychological stress as a major suspect in many illnesses while, for others, such a theoretical orientation smacks of *mind-over-matter* processes and echoes of the supernatural. They focus their attention on bugs and lumps—on things they can see or feel—rather than on what they consider to be fuzzies.

Keeping score and keeping up

While your physicians benefit from the findings of medical researchers (new treatments and technology) they face two daunting tasks: keeping score and keeping up.

Keeping score

How can your doctor move down to the right corner of his or her PST and rigorously test the effectiveness of his or her treatments? With great difficulty.

Anyone limited to pre-scientific methods has to settle for less. They must rely on their simple rules while waiting for researchers to continue the seemingly endless process of rigorously testing and extending medical rules.

Doctors, because they must rely on the after-the-fact method, don't have the time or resources to rigorously test their treatments, much less the seemingly impossible challenge of recording, retrieving, and analyzing patient feedback. Doctors can't afford to record and keep detailed records on all their patients; instead, they keep brief notes. And even if they kept detailed records, what would they contain? What would your doctor have to work with? At the bottom left corner of his or her PST he or she must rely mainly on patient self-reports, an indeterminate mix of reliable observations and fuzzy and incomplete memories, and outright lies about medical history, symptoms, and habits, as well as those not wanting to confess that, for whatever reasons, they did not follow their treatment regime (e.g., couldn't afford the drugs, forgot to take their pills, fell off the wagon, etc.).[9] Furthermore, some patients don't come back, so there's no feedback from them—good, bad, or indifferent.

Doctors do have access to the results of laboratory tests, but because of continuing research, these results are always under revision. Not really a solid place to stand!

Keeping up

Doctors face a second challenge. If they do attempt to keep up with even a small, specialized area of current medical research, they soon become overwhelmed with conflicting findings. Noisy messages flood forth from all corners of the medical research PST. It can take years of trial and error investigations, case studies and clinical trials, false starts, and hopes before a new treatment passes all the hurdles involved in its rigorous testing. Only then do these treatments start slowly wending their way into medical practice as they gradually overcome economic, bureaucratic, political, and professional barriers.

Our doctors deserve to be well paid. They fight on the front lines of health care, relying, as they must, on the flawed after-the-fact method and on incomplete or unreliable information at all three corners of their PSTs. They battle on, dependent on their trusted mini and mega rules. But they're smart. Smart enough to periodically recognize their limitations and smart enough to periodically suffer dangerous ways of thinking.

After reading all of that, don't you have more respect for your physicians and the challenges they face every time you limp or wheeze into their examining room expecting a clear diagnosis and a miracle cure? Don't you now feel

---

[9]Have you seen the television show *House*? It involves a brilliant diagnostician whose patients frequently lie to him, making their symptoms all the more mysterious. For example, one female patient didn't want children but her spouse did so she was secretly taking contraceptive medication while at the same time undergoing fertility treatments in order to please her husband. The result was, of course, a very confusing pattern of symptoms.

they should all be awarded medals for heroic service performed while having to carry the after-the-fact albatross on their backs?

All of us—experts and scientists—must trust most of the beliefs and rules we've accumulated thus far, while awaiting the arrival of revisions and extensions. Most of the time we're unaware of the flaws in the after-the-fact method. In this sense 'ignorance is bliss.' However, periodically, one or more of the naïve conclusions we've jumped to comes back to haunt us, and we come face to face with that ignorance. We endure some painful, even dangerous, ways of thinking, but sooner or later we leap back in the game. It's called living.

You may be wondering why we're spending time on common sense and pre-scientific problem-solving. It's because they provide the foundations on which scientific methods are built, and because only then can you appreciate both the strengths and limitations of science. Furthermore, case studies (after-the-fact studies) serve as a major source of 'knowledge' in medicine and business.

Scientists Use the After-the-Fact Method Too

As noted at the beginning of this chapter, scientists must also rely on this most popular of methods, and not only when they hang up their white coats and join the rest of us.

Scientists rely on the after-the-fact, mentally affordable method whenever they select particular observations and ideas from the endless flow of past experience. They use it after a day in the laboratory to make sense of what they observed. They use it on their way home from a scientific conference to make sense of what they've heard. They use it after reviewing the scientific literature to make sense of what they've read.

Most importantly, scientists rely on the elastic after-the-fact method to generate hunches, hypotheses, and theories. In one sense, theories are the most practical thing in the world because without them scientists can neither make sense of gaps in the past nor confidently travel into the unknown future. As Simon says 'No conclusions without premises', and premises are theories.

Using the flawed after-the-fact method, scientists sometimes guess right, sometimes they guess wrong. They're often right if they're making guesses about small space/time frames that have occurred in the immediate past or are about to unfold in the near future. The bigger the space/time frame is, then the bigger the guess will be, and the more likely they are to guess incorrectly and trigger the derisive laughter of the Gods.

SUMMARY

The after-the-method involves reconstructing the past (e.g., deciding who murdered Willie, or what's causing your stomach ache) from accessible bits and pieces. Since we must rely on a messy mix of dots (clear, fuzzy, and missing), and faulty memories, mapping the past is a creative process, often a guessing process.

We rely on beliefs and biases to shrink the problem down to mind-size, to help us select and connect the dots (e.g., Carl selects and connects different dots than the court.) Simon's mantra suggests that different beliefs lead to different reconstructions, and that different premises lead to different conclusions. To put it another way, our reconstructions reflect our beliefs and biases rather than accommodating *all the facts*, which are rarely, if ever, accessible.

Our reconstructions of the past can be weird, wonderful, or disastrous. Weird reconstructions include science fiction and psychotic thinking. Wonderful reconstructions include fascinating tales told by storytellers, and intuitively brilliant theories generated by great thinkers. Disastrous reconstructions can lead to devastating lies, voodoo economics, lethal medical errors, hanging the wrong man, or fighting the wrong war.

As we cycle round our PSTs, we must rely on the after-the-fact method for most of our day-to-day reconstructions and the decisions that arise from them. We have no choice because most of our decisions are based on past experience, bits of evidence, and faulty memories.

Even though it's fallible, the after-the-fact method *works*. It works in the sense that:

1. this method takes little time and effort so it's mentally affordable;
2. there are no clear cut, objective answers to many complex after-the-fact puzzles so we can't easily be proven wrong; and
3. since there are few objective answers to such puzzles we fall back on culturally approved and acceptable answers—we *go with the flow*; we may be objectively wrong, but nevertheless, we can be *culturally and politically correct*.

Even though most of our after-the-fact *solutions* are, of necessity, based on beliefs and biases rather than hard evidence, for special problems we make a special effort. We devote extra time and effort at one or more corners of the PST.

On such occasions, at the bottom of the PST, we make an extra effort to seek and examine more evidence, more dots. At the top, we generate and critically evaluate more connections, more alternative interpretations. And sometimes, down at the right corner, we make sincere, if not rigorous, attempts to test one or more of these alternatives.

Our courts set the gold standard for conscientiously applying the fallible after-the-fact tool to resolve pressing social problems. The controlled, adversarial system, the evolved rules of evidence, the judge and the jury all combine to increase resource commitment at all three corners of the PST. This commitment doesn't necessarily produce solutions but it does usually produce culturally acceptable *resolutions*. The process produces *closure*. It's an affordable way of managing complex social problems.

In applying this pre-scientific method, the courts rely on theory frames, time frames, and specialists to help them cut complex after-the-fact puzzles down to mind-size. Like the courts, experts or specialists (e.g., lawyers, physicians) focus their bounded rationality on particular bits and pieces of evidence at one or more corners of the PST.

You also specialize. We periodically stop racing around our PSTs and temporarily focus on special people (sharing treasured bits, pieces, and reconstructed memories from our respective pasts), or on special projects or hobbies (critically examining sports, cooking or chess events, or investment strategies).

Notice, it's when we periodically step out of life's hectic traffic and focus our attention on a special project, concentrating on one or more corners of the PST that we move from quick and dirty common sense problem solving, to the conscientious pre-scientific variety, practiced by experts and specialists.

And also notice that when we focus our attention and efforts down at the bottom right corner (rigorous testing) we may even be employing scientific methods. We do so when we systematically control and manipulate a selected sample of dots, as do chefs and laboratory scientists.

The after-the-fact method remains our most popular and most elastic problem-solving tool. As we make use of this method, we rely on the *believing-is-seeing* premise. As long as we all believe the same thing, then we *see* similar things, and therefore reach similar conclusions. The alternative is that we each see different realities, discover different truths, vote for different parties, and worship different Gods.

All of us must trust most of the beliefs and rules that we've accumulated along the way, while awaiting the arrival of mentally and culturally affordable revisions and extensions. Most of the time we're unaware of the flaws in the after-the-fact method. In this sense 'ignorance is bliss.' Periodically, though, one or more of the naïve conclusions we've jumped to comes back to haunt us. Then, we come face-to-face with our ignorance. We endure painful, even dangerous, ways of thinking. But, sooner or later, we drift back into the game. We have no choice.

Scientists rely on the after-the-fact method not only when they take off their white coats, but as one method in the process of exploring a problem. Unlike the rest of us, they don't rely on it as a main method of reaching conclusions but rather as a source through which hunches and hypotheses are generated and subsequently critically examined and rigorously tested.

In the next chapter we discuss another pre-scientific process, the *before-and-after method*. It has the advantage of radically reducing the number of potential suspects. We use it as crude method of travelling down to the right corner of our PST and *testing* a hunch or a conclusion. We use it whenever we ask: 'I wonder what will happen if . . . ?' Scientists use it in preliminary or pilot studies.

student's notebook

Professor Creek gave us a 'hot' assignment on the after-the-fact chapter. At least it was hot enough so that I'm no longer talking to Derek and my parents are barely being civil to each other.

After a lot of pogo-sticking around, I came up with an interesting after-the-fact obser-vation, namely: 'How come, after all these years, and the feminist movement, many more men than women still occupy the seats of power in government, corporations, universi-ties, and at home?'

I decided not to spend time documenting the power differences between the sexes, but to take it as a given, as a trusted premise. Those two guys who won Nobel Prizes (Simon and Kahneman) made the point: 'no conclusions without premises', that is, you can't make decisions without first shrinking the problem down to mind-size with the aid of hunches, or beliefs, or theories, or hypotheses, or biases.

So call my mind-shrinker what you will—I call it an obvious fact. I take the power differences between the sexes to be a very reliable observation. Next, I travelled up to the top of my PST to do some critical thinking, and to consider the cause(s) of the second-class status women seem stuck with.

Here's how I started out my assignment. This is the bit of science that got me into so much trouble.

How Come Men Still Rule the Roost?

Every once in a while a scientific finding shakes the world, literally, like the atom bomb, or socially, like the genome project.

Recently two genome researchers at Duke University (a man and a woman)[10] highlighted the fact that the male's genetic blueprint is much simpler than the females. They noted that while men have only one complex X chromosome and a very simple Y chromosome, women have two complex and information rich X chromosomes.

Since chromosomes carry the genetic wisdom of life it would appear that men have much less of it than women.

But before we jump to that conclusion, let's do a little critical thinking.

Geneticists agree that the Y chromosome carries much less information about how to build and operate a human being than X chromosomes. Y's main job is to make sure that males are adequately equipped sexually, and carry a chip

---

[10]I've got to get that reference—I think it was in the journal *Nature*. Oh boy! Dr Frund told me 'Diana, don't lose your references!' Update: Derek found it—Maureen Dowd, *New York Times* 20 March 2005.

on their shoulder—that is, to make sure they have high levels of aggression (testosterone).

The two big, information-rich, X chromosomes of women are more complex, have many more genetic moves, and more subtle shades of grey, in contrast to the male's simple black and white genetic inheritance—their black and white worldview.

Dr Willard, a male and one of the researchers says: ' . . . genetically speaking, if you meet one man, you've met them all. We are, I hate to say it, predictable. You can't say that about women. Men and women are farther apart than we ever knew.'

That's as far as I got with my assignment before I showed it to Derek. That's when everything hit the fan.

I should mention that Derek has red hair. When he read what I'd written you could hardly see where his red hair stopped and his red face started.

He stood up. He sneered. He said: 'Donald Duck has ten times the critical thinking skill you demonstrated in that diatribe!' and then he stormed off. I called after him: 'I wasn't talking about you . . . you're an exception . . . ', but he kept walking. Now Derek's really smart, so maybe he's right. Maybe I should go back to the drawing board. But then I showed my mother what I'd written. She thought it was wonderful, and at dinner she read it to my Dad and brother.

Wise people say you shouldn't talk about religion or politics at the table. Well I'll add another topic to that forbidden list. Don't talk about genetics either. Wow!

My mother told me to keep at it, saying: 'We women need all the ammunition we can get.'

I sent Derek a peace offering by e-mail. No response.

So I kept writing.

Theories of Human Behaviour
By Diana Dodds, for Research Methods 201

All theories are simplifications so that they'll fit into our brains, into our bounded rationality. They're like maps; they leave out a lot of detail in order to help you get from point A to point B without too many distractions along the way.

One main theory of human behaviour is 'B = E + g', which means that behaviour depends mainly on big 'E' (your early upbringing and environment) and little 'g' (genetics). The opposing theory is 'B = G + e', which means that behaviour depends mainly on big 'G' (genetics) and little 'e' (the social environment).

In the past, feminist researchers[11] have dismissed the big 'G' theory and based their hopes for improved opportunities for women on the big 'E' theory. That is, for example, they hoped that by changing the institutional rules of admission and promotion that a fairer representation of women would end up occupying the seats of power.

But it's been a slow process, and many more men than women still control our major institutions.

Last year, in my History of Civilization course we learned that, in the beginning, when hunting and tribal warfare prevailed, male strength and aggressiveness understandably gave them power and social dominance. Even in the middle ages, as long as groups and nations fought, and as long as the weapons involved heavy armour and broadswords, men, with their big Y chromosome, dominated.

But as agriculture and manufacturing grew, the need for brute force and aggression waned. The need for subtle distinctions grew, yet males still continued to dominate. Why?

Because by that time the routes to power had been blindly accepted. The rules for admission and seniority have become ingrained in our major institutions: government, business, religion, education, and family—and those rules (premises) favour men.

What started out as a genetic advantage continued as institutional habits, even when men put away their heavy swords. According to sociological theory, large and established institutions are like great ocean liners, once they start going in one direction they have so much inertia it takes a long time after you turn the tiller before they change direction. Maybe women just have to be patient—we're gradually turning the tiller but it takes decades for the great ship of state to respond.

Equalizers of Physical Power

Not only have females been gaining access to some of the wheels of power, but gunpowder, the lever, and the electric motor have all served to help level the playing field concerning physical strength.

The big, simple Y chromosome has given men a muscular advantage for centuries. But not anymore. Handbag-sized guns and electric and gasoline motors each deliver massive power with only the twitch of a finger—even a weak, smooth, French manicured finger.

So, logically, physical power should no longer be a determining factor in the

---

[11] I need to dig out some references in the theoretical and research literature to support this statement.

equation deciding the balance of power between males and females. But the marked imbalance persists. Yes, a few women have occupied the seats of great influence in government, corporations, and universities. But even with these token females in high-sounding positions, the glass ceiling remains firmly in place. Women typically get the *soft power* advisory positions like human resources and planning, not the *hard power* positions that steer the ship.

The president of Harvard University was forced to resign for raising the possibility that part of the explanation might be genetic. I don't think he went completely for the simple big 'G' theory.

Derek and I are speaking again! What turned the trick was that our birthdays fall on the same day. We have a long (two-year) tradition of celebrating them together. So I sent him an e-mail which read 'Happy birthday Big Guy, love Donald Duck.'

He invited me out to the pub. It was like old times. We agreed not to discuss my paper, at least not until after our celebration. But he said he had some ideas that might help. And did he ever! I put them in my paper and gave him credit. Sort of. Here's what I wrote:

Why Does the Big Y Still Rule the Roost?

Even in the face of increased feminist awareness, all the social efforts made to level the playing field, and the female advantage provided by the two wisdom-rich X chromosomes, the question still remains: how come men still rule most roosts?

Recent discussions with a sociological scholar[12] may provide a clue. In fact, it may even provide an answer.

Most sociologists adhere to the '$B = E + g$' theory of human behaviour. While they acknowledge that the Y chromosome may lack much information, the little it does include is still potent.

Stop and think. How do we ultimately resolve arguments when social negations fail? Often, as a last resort, we resort to physical force or threat of force.

Next, recall Simon and Kahneman's mantra: 'no conclusions without premises'. Wouldn't it be fair to say that a basic premise buried deep in the minds of all males and females alike, in every society, in every institution, is simply this:

---

[12]I'm not sure how to reference advice from a friend in a formal paper? Particularly when a lot of the stuff is his.

'When all else fails (and sometime before) males (waving their big 'Y') are more likely than females to resort to aggression and physical force'?

When all else fails is physical force the premise of last resort?

Notice that I'm not saying males even have to use it. But as long as it's there, as long as men feel it's there, as long as, deep down, females feel it's there, it tilts the game in the men's favour. The wired-in aggressive tendencies and physical strength that 'Y' provides acts like an ever-present big brother standing in the wings, ever-ready to come to his little brother's aid if needed.

Wouldn't this social internalization in both sexes of the simple but potential power of 'Y' help account for the persistence of male dominance, even in the face of the benefits bestowed on females by their two large information-rich X chromosomes?

Summary

I tried to apply critical thinking to the after-the-fact observation of persistent male dominance in most of our powerful social institutions. My initial theoretical orientation was that behaviour is mainly a function of large social influences and smaller genetic ones. While I still prefer that big 'E' position, recent genetic research suggests that because females possess two large and information-rich 'X' chromosomes, women should have some major advantages over men, who are handicapped in this regard because half of their genetic wisdom is carried by the information-impoverished 'Y' chromosome.

Historically, there have been a variety of significant social attempts to redress the power imbalance: the vote, legal and civil rights, equal employment opportunities, feminist awareness, and more equal higher education. Nevertheless, competent and ambitious females keep bumping their heads against the glass ceiling while watching men take the best jobs, tutored by strong mentors, and advance up the ladder with the help of the established male network.

Environmental, social, or cultural explanations seem to require super-human patience and a model of change involving small steps and centuries of waiting. Maybe that required patience is in one of the genes relegated to the X chromosomes?

Genetic explanations, on the other hand, that favour males based on hard wired aggression, physical strength, and maybe male bonding, help account for both their early dominance by direct action, and their subsequent dominance through both institutionalization of early dominance, and the hidden, implicit presence of physical force and 'big brother' effect.

Any explanation arrived at using the after-the-fact method remains open to question. This is particularly true when the potential 'suspects' are many, fuzzy, and are scattered over centuries. Plus, we're dealing with emotionally anchored premises on both sides of the sexual divide.

I prefer an explanation based on 'E' even if it involves a long time delay before significant changes can be seen in large established institutions—the inertia hypothesis. But, I must admit that the hypothesis that over the centuries the 'big brother' effect has been embedded in all our minds and institutions has an unfortunate ring of plausibility. So, like all after-the-fact investigations, this one remains a work in progress.

I'm not sure how to rigorously test this disturbing hypothesis. A first step might be to see if there's a correlation between testosterone level and different measures of power or dominance?

I really should give Derek more credit for this last section. First, because it's hard for a sociologist to give that much credit to a genetic influence, and second, for his ingenuity in maintaining a reason for male dominance. He was almost preening when he explained it to me. Although at the same time, he assured me that whenever he was with me he left his big brother, 'Bruto' at home.

When I discussed the 'big brother' theory with a strong feminist colleague she was not amused. She said: 'Hasn't your cretinous boyfriend heard of gunpowder? That's the equalizer. I carry my "big brother" in my purse, and if a man makes a false move it's POW.'

When I told Derek what she said, he didn't seem upset. He just replied: 'Tell her that she always has to remember to carry her "big brother" with her everywhere she goes—to the store, to bed, even in the shower. Whereas, Bruto is with me wherever I go. I know it. And she knows it.'

I'm unhappy with this so-called explanation, but I haven't come up with a more convincing one to explain the persistence of male dominance in all cultures,[13] throughout the ages. Certainly the two big X chromosomes give me hope, but what have they been doing through the centuries when we needed them? I know that old saying about 'the hand that rocks the cradle rules the world,' but we've got to start rocking differently if we're going to break through the glass ceiling.

Oh, I must remember to tell Dr Frund that I'm still relying on summarizing and recall for most of my studying. When recalling main ideas from my lectures or texts I scribble them out on the front of index cards, and list a few supporting details or examples on the back. So I study from these cards and only go back to my notes or text if I can't figure out what my index cards mean.

---

[13]Yes, I've heard about the odd culture where females dominate, but they're always in the distant past. And we know the kind of trouble historians have with after-the-fact dots buried way back there.

Note

Check out the major fallacy in your thinking on the student website at http://www.oup.com/ca/he/companion/agnewpyke.

REVIEW TRUE OR FALSE QUIZ

T F	
T F	1. The after-the-fact method allows us to believe whatever we want to believe.
T F	2. All the decisions we make are based on fallible or unproven presuppositions, beliefs, or biases.
T F	3. The after-the-fact method is based on the premise that seeing-is-believing.
T F	4. Use of the after-the-fact method involves reliance on first-hand evidence and reliable observations.
T F	5. Use of the after-the-fact method requires confidence in your beliefs.
T F	6. One of the problems with the after-the-fact method is that it doesn't permit the rigorous testing of conclusions.
T F	7. Another problem with the after-the-fact method is that there are too many potential suspects with connections to the problem to be solved.
T F	8. This problem (see #7 above) is handled by a careful listing of all potential suspects and their interconnections.
T F	9. One of the reasons that the after-the-fact method works is that for complex problems there are often no clear-cut solutions.
T F	10. Individual applications of the after-the-fact method that generate wrong answers often lead to negative consequences.
T F	11. Believing or remembering the last answer you heard is an all-purpose premise or assumption and is known as the primacy effect.
T F	12. Courts using the after-the-fact method invest significantly more resources in its application than do individual problem solvers and hence are able to enhance the reliability of the observations.
T F	13. In order to reduce the number of antecedents that lead to a given consequence, various decision aids are used including a time frame and a theory frame.
T F	14. Premises or sets of assumptions or prejudices are essentially theories about how the world works.
T F	15. The courts, using the after-the-fact method, an adversarial process and peer pressure, are highly successful in generating valid solutions to the problems brought before the courts.

T F	16. Extended rules intrude into consciousness (e.g., if A_1 and A_2 and A_3 and A_4, then B) when triggered by exceptional observations.
T F	17. Scientists rely on the after-the-fact method as a source of hypotheses to be subsequently explored with more rigorous methods.
T F	18. The X chromosome carries much less genetic information than the Y chromosome.
T F	19. Diana argues that when all else fails, physical force is the premise of last resort.

4

The Before-and-After Method

Chapter Goal

- To introduce the *before-and-after method* of problem solving. This *pre-scientific* method helps overcome some of the limitations of the *after-the-fact* method discussed in Chapter 3.

However, this more powerful tool remains at the mercy of four rogue suspects, rogues that trick us into having false confidence in our conclusions. Scientists often use this method in pilot studies to estimate whether one of their hunches warrants more rigorous testing by the control-group method to be discussed in the next chapter.

Introduction

'Beware of the four rogues!'

The before-and-after method is also referred to the *test-retest* model. Although it is more rational than the after-the-fact process discussed in Chapter 3, it remains pre-scientific, at the mercy of four rogues that lead us to naïve or false conclusions.

Whenever we travel down to the bottom right corner of our PST and ask ourselves 'I wonder what will happen if . . . ' we rely on this before-and-after, or test-retest, method of problem solving.

For instance, in Chapter 1 Ellie used it when she tested the newest wonder lotion on her skin rash. She observed (O_1) her skin rash 'before' treatment, then she applied the latest lotion (X), and then 'after' that she observed (O_2) her rash again to see if there was any change. In other words she conducted a little before-and-after experiment ($O_1 \ldots X \ldots O_2$).

Carl also conducted a before-and-after experiment, first observing his height (O_1) and then introducing his new stretching and diet treatment (X), after which he tested the result by measuring his height again (O_2).

Using this pre-scientific method Ellie and Carl both observed positive changes and gave credit to their respective 'treatments', to the their pet X. But recall that when we applied a bit of critical thinking to their conclusions we found major loopholes in their logic—beware of loopy logic.

Because this test-retest tool serves as the major stepping-stone between the pre-scientific and the scientific methods, it is important that we appreciate the differences. And particularly, we must critically examine the tricks that <u>the four rogues play</u>, one or more of which can lure even experienced scientists into practicing loopy logic (see Figure 4.1).

Familiarity with these four tricksters will boost your critical thinking capacity at the top of your PST, will significantly increase your ability to spot

Fig 4.1 ■ THE BEFORE-AND-AFTER PROBLEM-SOLVING TRIANGLE (PST)

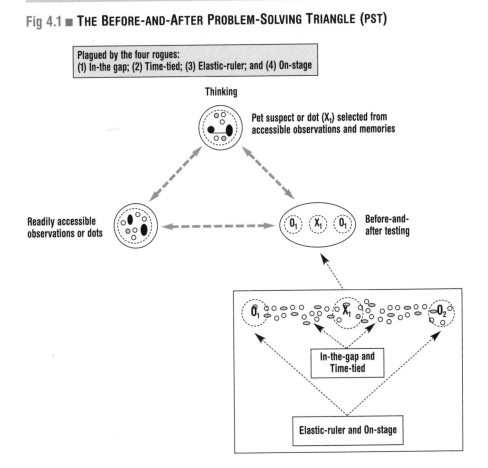

Plagued by the four rogues:
(1) In-the gap; (2) Time-tied; (3) Elastic-ruler; and (4) On-stage

Thinking

Pet suspect or dot (X_1) selected from accessible observations and memories

Readily accessible observations or dots

Before-and-after testing

In-the-gap and Time-tied

Elastic-ruler and On-stage

strengths and weaknesses at all three corners, and will make you a more discriminating consumer of 'the news', including scientific news.

The Four Rogues

A psychiatrist decides to evaluate a new drug for depressed patients. Down at the bottom of his PST he rates the patient's degree of depression on a five-point scale (O_1). Then, over a six-week period, he administers the drug treatment (X_1). Patients take two of the new pills three times a day. They are hospitalized to ensure that they all take their pills, and experience the same controlled environment, diet, nursing care, etc. At the end of the treatment the doctor again rates the patient's degree of depression and concludes that 75 per cent of them have improved.

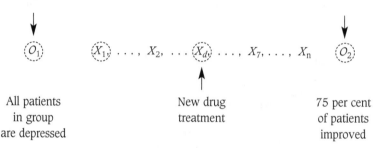

$$O_1 \qquad X_1, \ldots, X_2, \ldots X_d, \ldots, X_7, \ldots, X_n \qquad O_2$$

All patients	New drug	75 per cent
in group	treatment	of patients
are depressed		improved

Pleased with his results the psychiatrist publishes his article in a medical journal. A scientist[1] reads the article and writes a critical letter to the journal editor complaining that the psychiatrist's research is badly flawed. Keeping in mind the loopholes in Ellie's (skin rash) and Carl's (height) before-and-after experiments, can you guess what some of the criticisms were?

What four frequent, but ignored, alternative explanations—the rogues—could account for the patients' apparent improvement between O_1 and O_2?

1. in-the-gap (historical),
2. time-tied (maturational),
3. elastic-ruler (instrument decay),
4. on-stage (testing).

Let's examine each rogue in turn. As we do, notice when you have been tricked in the past—you've probably been conned by one or more of them in the last hour.

---

[1] Recall that we make a distinction between medical practitioners, who spend their time treating patients, and medical scientists, who spend their time doing research.

Table 4.1   Common Suspect Types

Type		Examples
Historical (in-the-gap)	(X)	Exam
		Stock market crash
		Catching cold
		Death of mother
		Hangover
Maturational (time-tied)	(X_1)	Hungry
		Tired
		Older
		Natural healing
		Rested
		Menstruating
		Male midlife crisis
Instrument-decay (elastic ruler)	(O_2)	Boredom, fatigue, or mood of researcher
		Instrument wear or breakdown
		Bias of researcher, practice
Testing (on-stage)	(O_2)	Putting best foot forward
		Lying

In-the-gap suspects

What other changes, in addition to the drug treatment, occurred 'in-the-gap', or in the period between O_1 and O_2, that may have helped the patients? Remember that any other change in the routine of the patients' lives, in the interval between O_1 and O_2, becomes a legitimate suspect and could contribute to improvement.

For instance, the hospitalization of each patient led to a complete change in lifestyle: healthy diet, getting away from family problems, regular bedtime, etc. Any one, or combination, of these factors may have accounted for part or all of the improvement the psychiatrist reported.

Keep in mind many 'wonder drugs' turn out to be duds. The psychiatrist was focusing on this pet pill, so it received the credit while other plausible suspects/factors were ignored. Remember, Kahneman received his Nobel Prize for demonstrating that we rely on the most easily accessible observations and thoughts to guide our problem-solving. In the other words, the history—the gap—between O_1 and O_2 is invariably filled with ignored suspects in addition to the pet treatment (X) the researcher is investigating.

We typically focus attention on our pet suspect—in this case the drug—which, like a noisy

Anything that occurs between O_1 and O_2 is an in-the-gap suspect, or rogue, which may influence O_2.

child, cries 'look at me . . . look at me!' Whereas other possible, and even plausible, suspects remain neglected, *inaccessible*, out of sight, and more importantly, out of mind. This is one of the reasons why the conclusions we jump to using the before-and-after (or test-retest) method are so prone to error and are considered pre-scientific.

Recall Simon's mantra: 'No conclusions without premises'. We can't pay attention to, or think about, everything that's happening in-the-gap between O_1 and O_2. So, we cut that gap down to mind-size by making assumptions, by consciously and unconsciously ignoring many suspects or alternative explanations. We use a theory frame, or premise, to help us decide which dots to attend to and which to ignore.

Our psychiatrist, like the rest of us, relies on a mind-shrinking premise. In particular, he sees depression from a *biological perspective*. As a result, he generally ignores environmental suspects, while focusing on biological factors—or dots—and tries to knock them out with drugs. He tries to change his patient's *brain* through psychopharmacology. Other psychiatrists, with different mind-shrinking theoretical perspectives, might focus on psychological or social suspects, and try to *fix* the patient's *mind* through psychotherapy.

At the top of their respective PSTs, both groups—those with a biological bias and those with a psychological/social bias—can claim success because the after-the-fact, as well as the before-and-after method, are fluid making it possible for them to go on seeing what they want to see, and so go on believing what they want to believe.

Next consider a rogue you met in Chapter 3, one connected to time.

Time-tied suspects

In her letter to the editor criticizing the psychiatrist's research, the scientist asks: 'What percentage of the patients would have improved over the six-week period without drug treatment? Or without any treatment at all?'

Remember Ellie's rash? Remember Carl's growth? Carl's growth is tied to his maturation, that is, to a time-tied suspect. Any change that is systematically linked to time or aging is called *maturational*.[2]

Most things change over time no matter what you do. Not only do a lot of unpredictable suspects get dumped into the gap between O_1 and O_2 (like a new ward supervisor or chef), but some suspects are predictable; some are tied to time, like teenage growth, aging, or spontaneous recovery. The scientist's question is valid: 'How many patients would have improved naturally without the drug: 25 per cent, 50 per cent, 75 per cent, 90 per cent? Maybe the drug actually delayed the natural recovery of some patients.'

---

[2]Notice that time-tied suspects, are also in-the-gap suspects, but they are so ubiquitous, and so often ignored, that we give them their own category.

Using the pre-scientific before-and-after method we have no way of knowing. The before-and-after, or test-retest, process doesn't allow us to answer the critic's questions.

This idea is reflected in the old folk wisdom: 'The doctor keeps the patient busy while nature works the cure.'

Because we tend to focus our attention on our pet treatment—it remains the most obvious and the most accessible explanation—we forget that time alone may account for some, or maybe all, of the changes in O_2.

> If time alone, without any specific treatment, can produce systematic changes in O_2 then we are dealing with a maturational, or time-tied, rogue.

Our scientific critic has pointed out two problems with the psychiatrist's drug study. First, there are too many unpredictable and unknown suspects, or dots, pouring into the gap between O_1 and O_2. Second, some of those suspects may be natural time-tied forces that can push O_2 up or down as illustrated at the bottom right corner of Figure 4.1.

And, as if those aren't enough flaws, she points out a third rogue.

Elastic-ruler suspects

Up until now the scientist focused her criticism on the influence of suspects (in addition to the new drug) operating in the gap between O_1 and O_2 that could change O_2. Now she travels down to the bottom right corner of the PST and raises questions about the elasticity of O_1 and O_2.

> All measuring instruments, human or otherwise, fluctuate for a variety of reasons (temperature, low batteries, fatigue, mood, personal bias, etc.), so scientists must protect against such measurement biases or fluctuations that affect O_1 and O_2.

How did the psychiatrist measure the degree of a patient's depression? He doesn't have a *depressionometer* like a thermometer. *What* yardstick did he use to determine the initial amount of depression (O_1) and the post-treatment degree of depression (O_2)?

The psychiatrist was the 'meter', he was the human yardstick. After interviewing each patient he rated his or her degree of depression on a five-point scale. But is he a reliable ruler for measuring depression? It's his judgment alone that determines which of the five numbers he ticks off against a given patient's name. Would a different psychiatrist tick differently? We know that when dealing with complex, multidimensional phenomena human judgment fluctuates like an elastic-ruler; the same observer will change his or her mind, and different observers will tick off different numbers on the five-point scale for a given patient.

The psychiatrist failed to provide any protection against elastic-ruler effects, such as having an *independent* observer rate each patient's degree of depression before and after the treatment. Preferably the independent observer would not be someone employed by the drug company promoting the new wonder pills or paying for the study—because the one who pays the piper often calls the tune!

On-stage suspects

Finally, the critic pointed out one more deficiency in the psychiatrist's research, namely that he failed to appreciate that the very act of testing someone, or putting them 'on-stage' can change their behaviour; it can make them nervous or trigger 'a performance'.

People, unlike bricks or billiard-balls, can stretch or shrink their behaviour to fit the situation at hand. For instance, many people respond positively to any new treatment. This is called the 'placebo effect'.[3] If you tell patients that you've prescribed a new wonder pill—even if it's filled with nothing but sugar—a significant number will experience improvement. How many of the psychiatrist's patients were placebo responders. We don't know.

Also, on the final interview (O_2), how many patients tried to appear better so they could go home, or so that they could help the nice young doctor with his work? We don't know. And neither does the psychiatrist.

Such on-stage suspects usually remain outside our range of attention, or *outside the box*. They lie beyond our bounded rationality and beyond our theory frame. Since they are *inaccessible* we ignore them, and give credit for any positive change to our pet treatment.

So 'on-stage' effects are the fourth reason the scientist found fault with the way the psychiatrist tested his theory and, in the end, favoured the new wonder drug.

> Many humans, regardless of the effects of any specific 'treatment', change between O_1 and O_2 merely because they are 'on display' or being studied. When this happens we are dealing with 'on-stage' rogues that can distort our measurements at the bottom of the PST.

A noble, if flawed, effort

Let's not be too hard on the psychiatrist. He has less time, less research training, and fewer resources than a scientist. And, unlike most of us, he at least went to the trouble of travelling down to the right corner of his PST—he tried to test his theory through further observation. As we've seen, it wasn't a rigorous test, but at least it was a conscientious one. Like Ellie and Carl, though, he focused on a pet explanation—his wonder drug.

Furthermore, unlike most of us, before he did his 'testing' he spent time down at the left corner of his PST working with and carefully observing depressed patients. And, up at the top of his PST, he invested time reading up on some of the psychiatric literature and research about depression, and did some critical thinking that led him to conclude—to create the premise—that a biological

---

[3]While researchers still argue about the biological or psychological mechanisms underlying placebo effects, they now agree that they *work* and remain a prime suspect in all treatment studies.

manipulation of a patient's biochemistry using a drug treatment was the best way to create a positive change.

But, like others before him who have relied on the before-and-after method, he was unwittingly at the mercy of the four rogues. Consequently, he couldn't draw any conclusions with confidence about the effects of the new pill on depressed patients.

Summarizing, we can think of a variety of suspects, other than the magic pills, that could well account for the claimed improvements:

1. Removing patients from the stresses at home and work and placing them in a protected hospital environment may have done wonders—a change, any change, is as good as a rest (in-the-gap suspects like pretty nurses and nutritious food, good night's sleep, etc.),

2. The psychiatrist doesn't know for sure what percentage of his patients would have improved over that period with no treatment due to the time-tied rogue;

3. He doesn't know how much his desire to 'see' improvement (believing is seeing) unwittingly shaped how he scored their degree of depression on his O_2 rating (elastic-ruler rogue); and,

4. He doesn't know how much his patients stretched themselves during O_2 to appear better so that they could go home (on-stage rogue).

In choosing the pre-scientific before-and-after method the psychiatrist innocently and unwittingly invited the four rogues aboard. If he'd had more research training—more critical thinking at the top of his PST—he'd have chosen the 'control-group method', which we will discuss in the next chapter. This scientific procedure helps *control* the rogues, or helps prevent them from causing so much research mayhem.

But don't reject the before-and-after method out of hand. Under some conditions it can help us reach useful conclusions.

Note how much simpler it is to control the four rogues when experimenting with *brainless material* like billiard balls. You don't have to make an appointment and wonder whether the ball will show up on time, be in a bad mood, be a secret drinker, etc. You don't have to worry whether they have 'a thing' for female experimenters that will make them expand and shrink their behaviour unpredictably. You don't have to fret about whether the billiard ball will understand your instructions and sit still for O_1, X_d, and O_2. You don't have to wonder whether the ball heard about your experiment from another ball and thinks it would be fun to freak out the experimenter by deciding not to travel in a straight line or to roll up instead of down the incline.

Skilled Use of the Before-and-After Method

The before-and-after method can help us reach reasonable conclusions under five conditions, all of which help reduce the distortions generated by the four rogues:

1. The observation under study (O_1) has remained stable for an extended period of time (e.g., your skin rash has persisted for months);
2. A quick acting remedy is employed (e.g., it *cures* the rash in two days);
3. The number of suspects pouring into the short time gap between O_1 and O_2 is controlled by the researcher (as in lab studies);
4. The same remedy *works* on repeated tests; and
5. The research participants are unaware that they are being observed (and so are not altering their behaviour to look good).

Stable observations

The before-and-after tool can work if, at the bottom left corner of your PST, you are working with an observation O_1 that can be reliably observed and that provides a stable pre-treatment baseline for an appreciable period of time. This can be represented as follows:

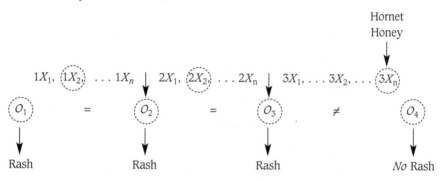

In this instance, over a baseline period of a month, different observers can agree that O_1 equals O_2 equals O_3. Notice that during the period there are various in-the-gap suspects ($1X_1$, $2X_1$, etc.) that have had ample opportunity to affect the rash, but it still persists. Then, after the third observation (O_3), we introduce a new treatment—a miracle salve called Hornet Honey ($3X_n$)—and we find a rapid, clear reduction in the rash; O_3 does not equal O_4. Now we probably have more justification in getting excited about Hornet Honey because the rash has been exposed to a wide variety of other suspects in-the-gap between O_1 and O_3 with no obvious changes.

Similarly, the other rogues (time-tied, elastic-ruler, on-stage) have had considerable opportunity to affect O_1, O_2, and O_3 prior to introducing Hornet Honey with no evidence of change.

Of course the *possibility* still remains that there would have been a shift in O_4 even without Hornet Honey. That is, that the natural life span of the rash could have run its course between O_3 and O_4 (an extended time-tied suspect at work) and that the improvement at O_4 represents a spontaneous recovery coinciding, by chance, with the administration of Hornet Honey.

Not likely, but possible. So to be sure you continue your testing.

Repeat testing

Let's assume that following O_4 we stop using Hornet Honey and that by O_5 the rash returns. Now we reintroduce the Hornet Honey and by O_6 the rash disappears, again. And independent observers agree that the rash is gone. So, it appears that the initial improvement at O_4 was not just a coincidence resulting from the introduction of Hornet Honey at the same time that a time-tied suspect had run its natural course.

At this point our confidence increases that the improvement is *somehow* connected to Hornet Honey. It may be that hype about Hornet Honey has reduced the patient's anxiety, thereby creating a placebo effect. Or the positive result may be directly linked to some chemical in the honey. Regardless, we have increased confidence that some part of our treatment ritual is helpful. Now, travel up to the top of your PST, put on your critical thinking hat, and notice how quick-acting treatments deserve our respect.

Quick-acting treatments

The before-and-after method gains additional power when we introduce a quick-acting and powerful treatment X_d into the gap between O_1 and O_2. For instance, it is much easier to detect the effect of a cure for a rash that takes only one day to work than one that takes three months. Obviously, that's because fewer alternative suspects, in addition to X_t, pour into the 24-hour gap than into a 3-month gap.

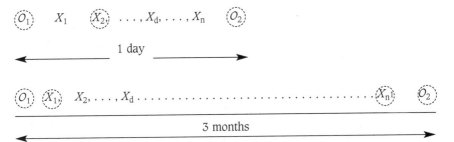

Penicillin is a good example of a quick-acting treatment (X_t). With the administration of such an antibiotic the patient's temperature rapidly returns to normal and the reliable signs of infection disappear.

However, some of the long-term negative side effects (a slow-acting, time-tied rogue) took longer to detect. It took scientists quite some time to link negative effects to antibiotics because of all the other in-the-gap suspects pouring into the time frame between the end of the course of antibiotics and the emergence of the side effects such as penicillin-resistant bugs.

Slow acting suspects (X_s), whether diseases or treatments, challenge our bounded rationality and confound our best critical thinking. When suspecting such delayed action effects we must be prepared for relatively slow progress, sometimes enduring years of frustrating trial and error guesses and 'treatments' with highly touted but fictional 'cures'. On the other hand, scientists may give up on a slow acting but powerful treatment because its effects didn't show up before their patience, or grant money, ran out.

Elimination of stray suspects

Obviously, if we can somehow reduce the number of historical or time-tied rogues pouring into the gap between O_1 and O_2 it would be simpler to test whether our treatment (X_t) can be credited with any change in O_2.

> Whenever we're trying to predict or control the behaviour of dots possessing brains it's like trying to herd cats.

We noted that quick acting 'treatments' that lead to a rapid change from O_1 to O_2 (a small gap) reduce the number of stray suspects. Furthermore, if we can somehow shield the gap between O_1 and O_2 from stray suspects (e.g., keep them in the hospital, lab, or freezer) then we enhance the utility of the test-retest method.

We can protect the gap from stray suspects much more readily in the physical sciences than in the social sciences. In classical physics we can practice 'hot house' research where we conduct our experiments 'under glass'. Laboratories are controlled, shielded environments where various stray suspects that might affect O_1 or O_2 are excluded (e.g., dirt, germs, etc.) or controlled (e.g., temperature, humidity, etc.).

Of course, when doing research with humans you can't completely control their lives between O_1 and O_2 (unless you had a captive group of some sort, such as prisoners, in-patients, or laboratory subjects). You can't control what they eat, drink, read on the Internet, hear from their friends, and certainly not what they think. You can't control whether they adhere to the 'treatment' instructions: whether they take the prescribed pills and/or self-medicate, follow the diet; do the exercises, or whatever the treatment schedule (X_t) calls for.

Some behavioural scientists add precision to their work by focusing on more or less stable research subjects. Some, for instance, use pseudo billiard balls with small brains and long tails, more commonly known as white rats. Also, by working with the tiny-minded rodents in lab settings scientists can protect the gap between O_1 and O_2. Such factors as diet, love life, hangovers, and on-stage shenanigans can either be controlled or assumed to be irrelevant.

Generally, though, the rogue suspects cannot be directly controlled in the social and behavioural sciences. As a result, we must shift from pre-scientific to scientific designs such as the *control-group* method (Chapter 5).

SUMMARY

Whether called the before-and-after, test-retest, or the case study method, this type of research—despite its popularity, despite its improvement on the after-the-fact method—is still seriously flawed. When used to test a hunch or hypothesis at the bottom right corner of the PST, the concept of believing-is-seeing rules the roost. Our beliefs, or premises, blind us, thus enabling us to ignore the rogues and focus our limited attention on our pet treatment. Our X_t shouts 'Look at me . . . look at me!' as it absorbs all of our attention, making it easy to ignore the many other plausible suspects that could be sneaking into the gap between O_1 and O_2.

Four rogue suspects plague most before-and-after studies. Two of the rogues (elastic-ruler and on-stage) typically distort O_2 in favour of the pet treatment. The other two rogues (in-the-gap and time-tied) occur either in addition to or entangled with the treatment. Therefore, using this pre-scientific method we usually have trouble separating the influence of the rogues from those of the treatment (X_t).

In a clinical study, if the patients improve we don't know which suspect, or combination of suspects, to hold responsible. It may be that the new pills are useless, but the rest in hospital performed wonders. Or perhaps the pills improved the patients' mood two points, but being away from their families set them back three points for a net loss of one point.

Like the after-the-fact method, the before-and-after method allows us to jump to erroneous and naïve conclusions, thus providing many belly laughs for Einstein's judgmental Gods.

Although seriously flawed, under certain stable and sheltered conditions, this method becomes a useful research tool. Under these conditions you and the scientists can and do discover some pretty shells (remember Newton), some local truths. Once in a while we make a lucky guess and discover a BIG truth.

An excellent way to learn the principles of sound research, and wrestle with the four rogues first hand, is to conduct a brief before-and-after study of your own behaviour. We provide an example in the Appendix. Not only will you learn more about yourself, but also you'll acquire additional critical thinking skills. You'll be better able to spot the flaws in other people's arguments, in testimonials, and more easily spot the junk research that tries to pass itself off as scientific news.

But, like the after-the-fact tool, the before-and-after method remains pre-scientific. In order to rigorously test a hunch or a theory down at the right corner of the PST we must control the four rogues. The clearest way to do this is to use a classic scientific strategy, such as the control-group method.

student's notebook

I'm having fun with the before-and-after method. I'm doing a secret experiment.

My boyfriend, Derek, talks more than he listens. With a bit of psychological theory and the before-and-after method I'm going to change that—if the theory works.

We're doing a lab project with Professor Creek. We modify rat behaviour by giving and withholding reinforcements or rewards. The theory (behaviourism) is that responses that are rewarded increase in frequency and those that aren't decrease. It's sort of a psychologist's way of saying that you can catch more bees with honey than vinegar.

I'm going to try this theory on Derek. Every time he pays attention to what I'm saying, I'll smile and touch him. When he doesn't, I'll withdraw my attention from him (look away, drum my fingers on the table, ignore what he's saying,[4] etc.).

I wonder if this is ethical? You know, is it a form of 'mind control'? I think I'll see if it works first, and then I'll worry about the ethics.

I've already used the before-and-after method[5] when I did my study skills project: I took a baseline measure (O_1) then introduced my treatment (X_1) (summarizing and recalling my notes), then did daily observations for four weeks (O_2, O_3, etc.,) to see if I was actually carrying out my treatments religiously and to see if I was doing what I resolved to do.

I'd never heard of the four rogues back then, so I didn't worry about them. I didn't get an A from Dr Frund, though, and now I can see why.

So far in this class we've covered two pre-scientific tools: the after-the-fact and the before-and-after, or test-retest, methods of solving problems.

Professor Creek repeated the points from the previous chapters concerning the PST (the importance of reliable observations, testable predictions, and rigorous and repeated testing of those predictions). Then he posed a question. Let's say you start down at the bottom of your PST and identify three reliable dots—you can see them and independent observers can see them. Next, you cycle up to the top and conclude (guess) that dot A is connected to dot B which in turn is connected to dot C. Now you cycle down to the bottom right corner and test your prediction.

The question, then, is how many successful tests (replications) do you need before you have confidence in your conclusion that the dots are indeed connected? How many successful replications before you decide that your conclusion is true?

He got different answers from class members ranging from 'at least two' to the politically correct but weasly 'as many as possible'.

Professor Creek then told us a weird story.

The story goes like this. Every morning at sunrise a farmer comes out his back door and throws corn on the ground for his turkeys. He does it day after day. One smart turkey figures out the rule and scratched it out in the sand: If A (the sun comes up) then B_1 (the farmer comes out), then B_2 (he throws corn on the ground).

All the other turkeys were so impressed that this smart turkey was chosen to receive the Gobble Gobble Award—the turkey equivalent of the Nobel Prize. But he doesn't show up on the day of the award ceremony—it was Thanksgiving! Ha Ha!

Professor Creek says the smart turkey had 364 successful replications of his rule, far more than Nobel Prize winners ever have.

So what's a simple student supposed to do with that story?

That afternoon I told our pub group the turkey story. Derek says it's just a joke and that 'Creek got bored with his own lecture so woke himself up with it, and probably you as well.'

---

[4] Ignoring what he says will be hard—he has some pretty good ideas!

[5] See Prologue.

But a guy from the physics program, and a girl from philosophy, both disagreed with Derek. They claimed that Professor Creek was planting the seed of a thought experiment in the class—apparently Einstein was famous for them. You take a question, like how many successful replications of a prediction is enough—and push it as far as you can.

So these two students did a thought experiment—right then and there—playing off each other.

'OK, so 364 successful replications are not enough, but it's a lifetime; it's forever for a turkey.'

'So a rule, or a law, that lasts forever for a turkey only lasts a year for us, so for us it's a time-limited rule.'

'And a rule that lasts a long time for us (e.g., a lifetime), only lasts a blink for an archeologist . . . for them an 80-year-old law is a flash in the pan—a few ticks of the geological clock.'

'And a rule that lasts forever for an archeologist (e.g., evolution) only lasts a blink for . . .'

Derek interrupted the game, pleading: 'Get to the point!'

The physicist concluded: 'A rule that seems like forever for an archeologist only lasts a blink for time travellers from another galaxy, hovering over our planet in a spaceship. They run out of grant money, so have to lasso their sun and go home.'

So that's the end of the thought experiment.

Since all laws are time-limited, they should carry a 'best before' date stamped on them. Except nobody knows when that is. So the number of replications is not the only yardstick to use in deciding when a theory has been rigorously tested.

I can hear Minsky saying: 'Now that's a dangerous way of thinking!' And I can hear Simon saying: 'No conclusions without thought-bounding premises.' And I can hear Einstein saying: 'Did any of you hear the snicker of the Turkey Gods.'

So, I'll lock that unanswerable puzzle safely away inside brackets within brackets and hopefully never think of it again. Now I have to do an assignment focusing on something in Chapter 4.

A Popular but Flawed Way of 'Testing' Our Pet Conclusions
By Diana Dodds, for Research Methods 201

We've covered two pre-scientific research designs, the after-the-fact and the before-and-after procedures. Using these methods we can cycle around our PSTs and still end up believing what we want to believe.

I look forward to the next chapter, where we'll shift from pre-scientific to scientific methods. I look forward to seeing how researchers can better control the four rogues. I look forward to seeing how scientific tools can help us supplement but still protect our bounded rationality. Maybe even mine?

The first thing that struck me about this chapter is how much we rely on the unreliable before-and-after method to generate supporting evidence for our pet beliefs. And not just me and you, but experts too, including our doctors.

But what really stuck in my mind was how much we depend on unreliable or fuzzy observations down at both corners of the PST. And that's what we have to work with up top—garbage goes in; no wonder garbage comes out.

I'm especially interested in the tricks the on-stage rogue plays on us.

Big On-Stage Effects

Testimonials provide a classic instance of the fallibility of the before-and-after method in general, and unreliable observations in particular.

Let's say you're an advertiser and you *test* your pet *treatment* on 20 people. Your treatment may be any of the following: a new shampoo, mouthwash, diet, tranquilizer, cosmetic, self-help book, investment strategy, new management fad, or anything, really.

Now notice that, in order to obtain a testimonial, all you need are one or two people (paid or not) to *claim* improvement from O_1 to O_2. Your pet treatment in combination with other in-the-gap suspects, plus elastic-ruler and on-stage effects, *worked* for a couple of people out of 20. And so you use those two to advertise your treatment on TV. You merely neglect to mention that it *worked* for only two out of 20. And, of course, those two *successes* were probably due to one or more of the four rogues. Remember Ellie and Carl?

Consider how often testimonials literally capitalize solely on *on-stage* effects. For instance, hundreds of times each day we are inundated by commercials using paid actors who are dressed up as doctors, scientists, or experts proclaiming, *with deepest sincerity*, that they have a cure for everything from sore feet to hemorrhoids to shyness.

Or, we can feast our envious eyes on a gorgeous model with a flawless complexion and luscious, shiny hair just shampooed with 'Formula X', recently discovered by Dr Y, shown in his glowing white coat in his lab with colourful flasks bubbling merrily in the background. The so-called doctor probably doesn't know the difference between a stethoscope and a horoscope.

Talk about an 'on-stage' effect! A staged event using a paid model whose hair is probably always luscious and shiny, even if she washes it with yellow laundry soap, and of course it looks even better after being 'shined' by the make-up artist or Photoshop expert.

The before-and-after method gives advertisers, and con-artists, a perfect opportunity to capitalize on the elastic-ruler and on-stage rogues to manipulate O_1 and O_2 to make X_t look good.

It seems to me that the only time the average citizen can have confidence in the before-and-after method is when you have personal experience with a quick-acting treatment, carried out on a hitherto stable O_1, which then shifts quickly to a significantly different O_2. For example, you have a long-term leaky tap (stable O_1), and a plumber comes and *treats* (X_t) the tap, and immediately the tap stops leaking (O_2). In such simple, billiard ball circumstances *seeing-is-believing*.

Unfortunately, when employing the before-and-after method to solve people puzzles (dots with brains) it's usually impossible to control all the rogues so you can end up seeing what you want to see, and believing what you want to believe—*believing becomes seeing*. You have unstable O_1s (at the mercy of the elastic-ruler and on-stage rogues), and your pet treatment is tangled up with time-tied and other in-the-gap rogues, followed by O_2, also at the mercy of elastic-ruler and on-stage effects. Under such flexible conditions ANYTHING GOES! And unscrupulous advertisers and con artists can have a field day.

I'm now compulsively examining ads and identifying the fuzzies and the slippery language. For example, you see the weasel phrase 'up to' everywhere you look: 'with this new diet you can *lose up to* forty pounds in two months', or 'come in for our great sale with *up to* 80 per cent off'. When you stop and think about it, they're safe but sneaky promises. It could be a one pound weight loss and one per cent price reductions, but they would still meet the legal requirements of the advertisement—sneakily, the ad didn't specify a minimum guarantee. Since the *sellers* can manipulate (wittingly or otherwise) the O_2 that you see, they can guarantee a positive result. If seeing-is-believing, and they 'control' much of what we see, then we'll believe them. At least for a little while.

No wonder we have trouble trying to ferret out the truth from a chain of messages when the messengers are consciously manipulating the news with elastic-ruler distortions and on-stage misrepresentations.

Most of what we know is based on an endless cycle in which a bit of seeing leads to believing, which leads to selective seeing, which then leads to confirmed believing. These self-fulfilling beliefs fit our bounded rationality, which we protect by learning to avoid too many Minskian 'whys'.

It seems to my very bounded rationality that this generalization holds whether we're talking about shampoo commercials, politician's promises, corporate annual reports, professional advice,[6] or even some scientific reports!

---

[6]Notice that, for many ailments, we must rely on our doctor's high tech 'readings' of our entrails to tell us whether we're sick or getting better. We don't have direct access to those O_1s or O_2s. We don't have direct access to most 'news'. We must rely on 'experts' to tell us 'how we're doing'. If we look too carefully we find that our world is a buzzing confusion of dots. We rely on 'experts' to select out a few, connect them, stretch them this way and that, and tell us 'the truth' about our innards, our personalities, our career prospects, or our future. Talk about elastic-rulers!

All these *promisers* can create supporting *evidence*, deviously or sincerely, with the co-operation of the four rogues inherent in the before-and-after method. Dangerous thinking!

I'm having more success changing the behaviour of rats in Professor Creek's lab than changing Derek's listening behaviour.

My O_1 (his talking and poor listening habits) has been stable, for as long as I've known him. My treatment (X_t) has been to reward him (smiles and touching) when he listens and to withdraw attention (look away, yawn, drum my fingers) when he talks too much.

The problem is that he doesn't seem to notice when I withdraw my attention—he just keeps talking anyway $O_1 = O_2 = O_3 = O_4$. Talk about a stable behaviour! I don't get much chance to reward him for listening, because I don't get a chance to talk.

This behaviour modification theory is not as simple as it seems. It's the old problem of how to change the direction of billiard balls with brains.

Dr Frund says most research involves some false starts. Mine sure does. I've got to try something different. So, now when he talks too much, instead of just yawning and looking away, I'm going to get up and leave. I wonder if he'll notice?

Oops, I still need two news stories for my report!

News Stories

I came across two science stories, one on the effects of eating fish and the other about the effects of hypnosis on the brain.

Brain food

This study[7] suggests that those who ate fish reduced the normal aging decline of brain functions, like recalling details of a story.

The authors studied almost 4,000 seniors, testing them three times over a six-year period. Talk about a commitment of time and resources. The authors report that those who ate fish once a week reduced their normal cognitive decline by 10 per cent, whereas those that ate fish twice a week slowed the decline by 13 per cent.

That's not a huge difference, but it looks like it might be a trend—two observational check points (based on a large sample). The kinds of questions that come to mind include:

---

[7]'Fish Fights Aging In The Brain'. Available at http://www.cbsnews.com/stories/2005/10/10/health/webmd/main931654.shtml (accessed 4 August 2006).

1. What other in-the-gap suspects might account for the effect (e.g., are people who eat fish more likely to be health nuts with a good diet, less alcohol, and more exercise?)

2. How reliable are the data on diet reported by seniors? My Grampa can't remember *if* he ate, never mind *what* he ate.

3. How precise are the tests for measuring mental functioning?

When you look at all the work involved in this study, you can see why we can answer many more questions than scientists. We don't have to bother sweating it out down at the right corner of the PST. We don't go near there; we just jump to a convenient conclusion up at the top.

We can also see why it can take so long for scientists to provide good answers to what looks like a simple question. Never mind trying to control some of the elastic-ruler, on-stage, and in-the-gap rogues, just doing an independent replication of the study would take another six years.

Hypnosis: believing is seeing

What happens to the brain when you hypnotize its owner? Do they see, hear, feel, and think differently, and do their *brain images* change?

As far as I can see this is a before-and-after study[8] where O_1 (you observe the pre-treatment brain images), then you introduce X (hypnosis), then you take O2 (second observation of brain images during treatment).[9] I know nothing about the reliability of reading brain images, but let's say it's OK. But I do know that determining whether someone is hypnotized, and how deeply, is still fuzzy—so the X in this case would have a large uncertainty circle around it.

Anyway, the study reports big changes in brain images under hypnosis, and changes in what the research participants report they see, hear, feel, and think. Apparently the messages streaming in from outside get radically modified under hypnosis—believing-is-seeing. These researchers are big believers in the powerful top-down effects of beliefs and expectations on perception.

According to the news report there are *ten times more* nerves carrying messages down from the brain, as there are carrying messages up. So no wonder our premises and biases can overrule the observational messages flowing up. No wonder the amputee could feel pain in his non-existent toes. No conclusions about what's flowing up without selective and controlling premises flowing down? Does that mean that the messages flowing up only get one neurological vote, while those flowing down get ten . . . particularly about fuzzy messages from the bottom of the PST?

---

[8]'Believing is Seeing', *New York Times*, 22 November 2005, F1.

[9]For comparison they used some non-hypnotized subjects, the value of which I'll presumably find out about in the next chapter dealing with the control group.

115

> I think I want to talk about this some more with Professor Creek—this is strong stuff!

Note

Be sure to check out the poem inspired by Dr Seuss on the student website at http://www.oup.com/ca/he/companion/agnewpyke.

REVIEW TRUE OR FALSE QUIZ

T F	
T F	1. The before-and-after method is sometimes known as the test-retest method.
T F	2. Natural healing is an example of an historical or in-the-gap rogue.
T F	3. In the drug study described in this chapter, having two independent raters assess the degree of depression provides some protection against the on-stage effect.
T F	4. The placebo effect refers to a positive response to an assumed treatment.
T F	5. Making sure that the research participants are unaware that they are being observed is a way of controlling the elastic-ruler rogue.
T F	6. A problem with testimonials is that they frequently capitalize on on-stage effects.
T F	7. The before-and-after method capitalizes on the effective use of a limited time frame.
T F	8. The before-and-after method is a less powerful method than the case study approach.
T F	9. The before-and-after method pretends to be scientific but would not be regarded so by most scientists.
T F	10. If time alone can produce changes in O_2 without any specific treatment, then we are dealing with a historical suspect.
T F	11. Some organisms (including humans) may change their behaviour merely because they are 'on display' or being studied.
T F	12. 'Four classes, or types, of suspects plague every before-and-after study.
T F	13. The before-and-after method can be used to advantage when a quick-acting remedy (or treatment) is being tested.
T F	14. One problem with the before-and-after method is that measuring instruments can change or deteriorate between O_1 and O_2.
T F	15. 'If an observation (O_1) has remained the same or stable for an appreciable period, then the before-and-after method should not be used.

T F	16.	Reducing the number of stray suspects pouring into the interval between O_1 and O_2 strengthens the power of the before-and-after method.
T F	17.	Relatively simple research methods such as the before-and-after method are typically quite inadequate for studies in the physical sciences.
T F	18.	Collecting baseline data is a necessary first step to testing the effectiveness of any technique to change individual behaviour.
T F	19.	Eating fish appears to reduce the normal aging decline of brain functions.
T F	20.	The number of nerves carrying messages up to the brain far exceeds the number carrying messages down from the brain.

5

The Control-Group Method

Chapter Goal

- To introduce the classic control-group method.

A giant step from pre-scientific to scientific problem solving, the control-group method is a research tool that does not eliminate but 'controls' the four rogues. It is a tool that, in one step, helps to overcome the major flaws of both the after-the-fact and before-and-after methods.

Introduction

Although the pre-scientific methods 'work' because they help us make timely decisions (e.g., jump to conclusions), and although some of those decisions 'work' in that they don't result in immediate disaster, those methods neverthe-less contain so many loopholes that different people can end up believing almost anything they want to believe regardless of the evidence.

In one simple step, by including a comparison group, the control-group method closes major loopholes. By including a comparison group that doesn't get the pet treatment (X_t), we expose the dirty tricks the four rogues play.

> With treatment a depression only lasts 90 days.
> Whereas without treatment it lasts three months.

Relying on the before-and-after method we can write the first line (about depression lasting only 90 days) and gain false confidence that the treatment (X_t) did the trick.

However, with the help of the control-group method—by studying an untreated comparison group—we expose the truth by adding the second line to the story, showing that patients get better just as quickly without the pet treat-ment. It doesn't matter whether they took the treatment or the placebo,[1] the duration was the same. This suggests that time alone (the time-tied rogue), that natural healing, accounts for the positive results.

As we'll see, a control group helps you to better control the rogues but not eliminate them from the experiment.

As you know, when you try to fix a human (a billiard ball with brains) it's not as easy as trying to fix a leaking tap. Humans won't sit still, physically or mentally. When measuring people, scientists often rely on elastic-rulers, and not only do their research participants often stretch themselves out of shape while putting on an act, but uncontrolled suspects pour into the gap (e.g., between O_1 and O_2), along with the proposed, and often favoured, treatment.

Nevertheless, if O_2 changes for the better, even *experts* jump to the conclu-sion that it must be their action or advice that *fixed* things. However, as we learned in the last chapter, a little critical thinking tells us we can't be sure that the change isn't due to one or more of the four rogues, for instance the mere pas-sage of time—the universal healer.

In the social and behavioural sciences we face the challenge of observing, understanding, and predicting the behaviour of complex dots, of dots with brains.

The Control-Group Method and the PST

A shift from pre-scientific methods to the scientific control-group design requires committing extra resources to all three corners of the PST.

This researcher is better able to rigorously test her treatment than was the psychiatrist in the last chapter. He not only lacked the grant support, but because he was untrained in research methods, he maintained naïve confidence in the flawed before-and-after method.

Operating down at the right corner of Figure 5.1 our researcher has two options. She can compare her treatment group with an untreated control. In this example the untreated control group indicates the amount of change the four rogues can accomplish on their own. While the treatment group indicates the amount of change the treatment, in combination with the rogues, can achieve. Our naïve psychiatrist didn't have the comparison control group, so naturally he attributed all the changes in O_2 to his treatment, all the while naïvely unaware of the powerful influence the rogues can have.

Or, as indicated in the graphic, the researcher can compare her treatment group (X_t) with a placebo control group (X_p). Not very long ago drug researchers were unaware of the powerful effect of belief, or expectation, on human behaviour. Gradually, they learned that any pill in which the patient has confidence can affect symptoms, even if it contains no active ingredient.

---

[1] Some patients improve, as noted previously, as long as they believe that they're getting a potent treat-ment (believing is seeing). This kind of change is called a *placebo effect*.

Imagination and expectation (top down influences) can work wonders. Thereafter, to control both for the rogues and for this expectation effect, researchers increasingly included a placebo control group, where patients received a pill that looked exactly like the treatment pill, but which, unknown to them, contained an innocuous substance like sugar.

Observe how this reflects Simon's mantra: no conclusions without premises. If a patient believes (holds the premise) strongly enough that the treatment will work, they unwittingly produce improved symptoms—a spontaneous on-stage effect: a very clear illustration of the believing-is-seeing phenomenon.

When you read scientific literature you will encounter the terms _dependent variables and independent variables. Dependent variables_ are what we refer to as Os, and _independent variables_ as Xs. They are called variables because they can take different values. We expect that our dependent variable, our observation (an O) will change as we introduce our treatment (X_t), our independent variable. For instance, if we are doing a drug study we would expect that (O_2) would vary as we increased, or varied, the drug dosage (X_t).

Notice how our researcher attempts to sort fact from fancy using the placebo control-group design illustrated at the bottom right corner of Figure 5.1:

- The difference between O_1 and O_2 measures the effect of the drug treatment (X_t) plus the influence of the four rogues.
- The difference between O_{1a} and O_{2a} measures the effect of the four rogues combined with a sugar pill (X_p), a dummy treatment or placebo.
- The difference between O_2 and O_{2a} estimates the effect of the treatment over and above the effects of the four rogues.[2]

> Notice that the control-group method does not eliminate either the individual or combined influence of the four rogues. Rather, this scientific method ideally provides the rogues with equal access to both groups.

Let's explore in more detail how the researcher attempts to _control_ the rogues.

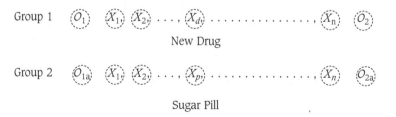

Group 1 O_1 X_1 X_2 ..., X_d ...., X_n O_2

New Drug

Group 2 O_{1a} X_1 X_2 ..., X_p ...., X_n O_{2a}

Sugar Pill

[2] This estimate assumes that the only way in which the two groups differ is that one group gets a treatment (X_t) and the other does not. As we shall see, this is often easier said than done—the rogues are sneaky. This design assumes that O_1 equals O_{1a}, that is, the two groups started out the same. How can we help ensure that happens? Keep an eye open for discussions of 'matching' and 'random assignment'.

Fig 5.1 ■ THE CONTROL GROUP METHOD OF PROBLEM-SOLVING

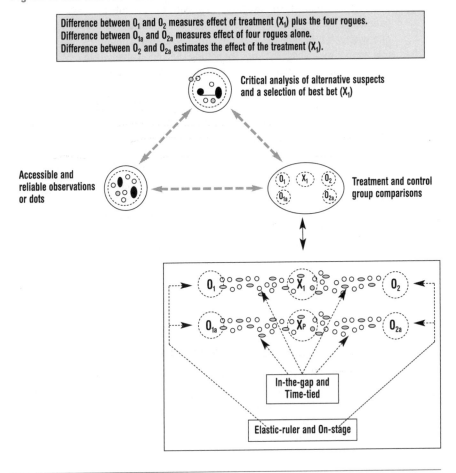

Difference between O_1 and O_2 measures effect of treatment (X_1) plus the four rogues.
Difference between O_{1a} and O_{2a} measures effect of four rogues alone.
Difference between O_2 and O_{2a} estimates the effect of the treatment (X_1).

Critical analysis of alternative suspects and a selection of best bet (X_1)

Accessible and reliable observations or dots

Treatment and control group comparisons

In-the-gap and Time-tied

Elastic-ruler and On-stage

Thus the two groups start out with supposedly identical amounts of depression—that is $O_1 = O_{1a}$—or, in other words, one group does not include more seriously depressed patients than the other does. Following treatment we see whether O_2 is less than O_{2a}—whether the level of depression is now less for Group 1 than for Group 2.

Rogue Suspects

Historical (in-the-gap) suspects

Our research goal is to run the experiment so that the individuals in the two groups are treated exactly the same, except for one suspect—the drug X_d. We are attempting to make sure that the same Xs pour into the gap between O_1 and O_2 as between O_{1a} and O_{2a}. To ensure that the nursing staff does not spend more time with the patients in one group than with the patients in the other, that the patients in the two groups are mixed up or made indistinguishable as far as any-one who can influence the experiment is concerned. The nurses and other doctors are not told which patients are getting the new wonder drug (X_d) and which are getting the sugar pill (X_p). All patients receive pills that look identical.

By not letting the doctors, nurses, or patients know who is receiving the drug and who is receiving the sugar pill, you're keeping both groups 'blind' as to the design of the study—this is called a 'double-blind' study because neither the doctor nor the patients know who is getting the magic pill. Double-blind studies help control elastic-ruler, in-the-gap, and on-stage rogues.

If both groups are to be open to influence by the same historical or time-tied suspects, then both groups must occupy the same space and time frame. For example, they must occupy the same hospital ward at the same time for the same duration. You can't test the treatment group first and the control group second. If you did run one group before the other, your groups would not only differ in terms of the specific treatment but in other ways as well. For example, they might have different nursing staff, cooks, or weather, all of which might lead to different in-the-gap suspects. Furthermore, the people doing the evaluation of patients may not observe things in the same way—if they become bored with the study an elastic-ruler effect will be introduced.

Instrument-decay (elastic-ruler) suspects

If the experiment is run properly, the doctor who measures the depression at the beginning and at the end doesn't know which patients received X_d and which received X_p, so the physician's biases—or elastic-ruler effects—cannot systematically influence the doctor's assessment of one group over the other, either during the study or when deciding which patients have improved and which have not. The double-blind procedure helps protect against elastic-ruler and on-stage effects. Only the researcher knows the code that will identify one group from the other, and the code is not disclosed until O_2 and O_{2a} are completed.

Testing (on-stage) suspects

The on-stage effects of having been observed and interviewed would influence patients in both groups. In both groups there will be patients who want to impress upon the doctor that they are well enough to go home, as well as some who merely want to 'help the nice young doctor'. Because such individuals can be found in both groups, if the groups were randomly selected, then we assume that the resulting influence on O_2 and O_{2a} will be about the same—both groups will probably show similar amounts of on-stage improvement apart from any effect of the treatment.

Maturational (time-tied) suspects

Furthermore, spontaneous recovery should be similar for both groups since the time between O_1 and O_2 is the same as between O_{1a} and O_{2a}. And the end result? Time-tied, or natural recovery, suspects should affect each group the same way.

Now What?

Notice that the control-group method does not eliminate either the individual or combined influences of the four rogues; rather, *the control-group design provides the rogues with* equal *access to both groups*. Thus O_2 reflects the influence of the four rogues combined with the drug, while O_{2a} reflects the influence of the rogues combined with the sugar pill.

We should not be surprised, then, if both groups show some improvement: O_2 shows an improvement over O_1, and O_{2a} shows an improvement over O_{1a}. These changes reflect the effects of such suspects as spontaneous recovery (time-tied), a biased doctor (elastic-ruler), a nice ward supervisor (in-the-gap), and a desire to go home (on-stage). If, in addition, X_d has had an effect greater than X_p, we should have O_2 showing a greater shift than O_{2a}. If the two groups were the same to begin with, the difference between O_2 and O_{2a} provides us with a measure of the effect of X_d over X_p.

This is in contrast to the simple before-and-after model where the X_d effects were all mixed up with the effects of the other suspects, and there was no way to untangle them. It was this kind of tangle that led some wit to wisely observe that a good doctor keeps the patient occupied while nature works the cure. It is easier to wait for a natural change when under the illusion that some potion is bringing it about.

When we divide a group in two to make the two sections as identical as possible and then give them exactly the same treatment except for one X, we are using a control-group method—a much more precise sieve than the after-the-fact or the before-and-after sieves discussed earlier. Representing a remarkable leap forward in helping us produce packages of durable information, in one stroke the control-group method permits researchers to assess the effects of their treatment over and above the effects of the four rogues alone. Of course, this applies only if the groups are equivalent to begin with. And that is a big 'if'.

Selection of the Control Comparison Group

Unless Groups 1 and 2 are 'more or less' equivalent at O_1 and O_{1a}, our efforts to rule out alternative suspects are thwarted. Random assignment to each group is an affordable and commonly employed technique to help insure that all relevant or influential suspects are equally represented or distributed across the two groups. It is the luck of the draw that determines whether an individual patient will be sorted into the treatment or the control (placebo) group. Random assignment, however, does not necessarily produce a balanced outcome, at least in the short run or with small samples, as anyone who plays cards knows. By the luck of the draw one of your opponents can end up with a larger number of face cards than you, just as the placebo group, by the luck of the draw, may end up with a larger number of heavy drinkers than the experimental group. This confounding factor could lead to abnormally high depression scores (O_2) thus not serving as a relevant control group. This is a risk all researchers face, that's why the golden rule of science is to have independent investigators repeat the study, in order to help avoid being lead astray by the tricks of chance.

It is possible to test the assumption of equivalence, on a few relevant variables, of the treatment and control groups by comparing the two groups before the introduction of the treatment or placebo. That is, does $O_1 = O_{1a}$? Are the patients in the two groups roughly the same age? Have they been hospitalized for about the same amount of time? Do they include similar numbers of heavy drinkers, smokers, etc.? Even if the patients in each group are equally depressed, differences in other relevant dimensions may affect observations at O_2 and O_{2a}.

Another strategy for creating a control group is to pair each individual in the treatment group with a 'matched' partner in the control group. Each control-group patient is matched in the sense of being similar on most dimensions to a patient in the treatment group. This is easier said than done because we may not know in advance what all the relevant variables are, and we may not have access to a sufficiently large or appropriate pool of potential research participants.

As you can see, perfect matching is an impossible task. That's why researchers rely so heavily on random assignment of participants to experimental and control groups, and replicating studies. That's why it's so important to use large samples and to repeat studies.

The following example details a research study that was done by Dr Ames (Ames & Carter, 1992). It vividly captures the difficult decisions and trade-offs surrounding the selection of the 'best' control group when operating outside narrow laboratory conditions.

The purpose of Ames and Carter's research was to determine the effects of institutionalization on the subsequent development of Romanian children who had been adopted into a North American family. Before adoption, these children had been institutionalized in Romanian orphanages under conditions of appalling deprivation. Many children were severely undernourished and suffering from various illnesses, and most were developmentally delayed in some way—for example, the average 2-year-old could neither walk nor talk.

What is the appropriate comparison (control) group for these Romanian adoptees? To separate the effects of institutionalization from those of adoption, the researchers would have needed to find a matched group of adopted children who had not previously been institutionalized but who were adopted at the same ages as the Romanian sample. Such a comparison group does not exist because only rarely does a child move directly from the birth home to the adoptive home between one to four years of age. More typically adopted children of this age have either spent some time in an institution or have been through a series of foster homes.

'Alternatively,' commented Dr Ames, 'one could conceive of a sample of children institutionalized but not adopted. This would tell us how much better off our children are than those left behind in Romania (but that is probably pretty obvious anyway), and such a study would not tell us anything about how our children compare with children reared at home.'

What about a comparison group that was both institutionalized and adopted, but whose institutional experience was vastly different from that of the Romanian children? Perhaps children adopted from Peruvian or Mexican orphanages? To locate such a sample would be extremely difficult. Consider that the research would have to find a 37-month-old boy who had been adopted from a non-Romanian orphanage at the age of 2 years and 1 month in order to match one specific Romanian child, and then repeat the process for all of the Romanian children in the study. Even then there might still be a confounding variable of darker skin colour leading to biased responses.

Dr Ames observed: 'Finally, we might wait for the children adopted as new-borns from Romanian hospitals—children who would have gone to orphanages had they not been adopted—to grow to the ages at which our orphanage children were adopted. This would be the best group to help control for background variables.'

The conclusion that may be drawn from this analysis is that different types of control or comparison groups answer different kinds of questions. Some good control groups are simply not available or feasible. In the above research the comparison group ultimately selected was a group of never institutionalized, non-adopted children living with their biological parents. These children were matched with a Romanian child on the basis of sex; age; parents' educations, occupations, and ages; family income; and the number of children in the family. Subsequent statistical testing of the differences between the two samples revealed no significant differences on the matching variables.

In brief, if you recall the problems created by the four rogues you will appreciate that a control group that controls for even one of the rogues is better than no control group at all.

Elaboration of the Control-Group Method

Suppose that in our example of depressed patients all them had been given a stimulant pill each day as part of the regular hospital routine. At the time of the study, Group 1 individuals would receive both the new wonder drug in addition to their regular stimulant. Group 2 patients, however, would receive only the regular stimulant.

Group 1 (X_s) (O_1) (X_1) (X_2) $\ldots,(X_d)$ $\ldots,$ (X_n) (O_2)

      Stimulant   Wonder Drug

Group 2 (X_s) (O_{1a}) (X_1) (X_2) $\ldots,(X_p)$ $\ldots,$ (X_n) (O_{2a})

      Stimulant   Sugar Pill

Can we conclude that if O_2 is different from O_{2a} the difference is due to the wonder drug? One is tempted to answer yes and to argue that, since both groups were given the stimulant, any difference between the groups must be due to the difference between X_d and X_p. It is possible, however, that it was the *combination* or interaction of the stimulant and the wonder drug that led to improvement and that the wonder drug alone may be ineffective. In this situation, repeating the study with two other groups of patients while omitting the stimulant pills would measure improvement resulting from the wonder drug alone. Similarly, the effect of making the first observation (O_1) may get mixed or combined with the treatment, and so we may want to know the effect of: (1) observing or measuring alone, (2) the effects of treatment alone, and (3) the combination or interaction of the two.[3]

Consider another example. Assume we're interested in determining whether providing children with training in physical coordination will improve their intellectual ability. We design a control-group study to test this idea. In order to ensure that our two groups are comparable in intellectual ability to begin with, we administer an intelligence test to all of the children, and then divide them into two groups with similar numbers of bright, average, and dull children in each group. Group 1 is then given two weeks of training and subsequently both groups are retested.

If the difference between O_2 and O_1 is greater than the difference between O_{2a} and O_{1a}, we may conclude that coordination training improves intelligence

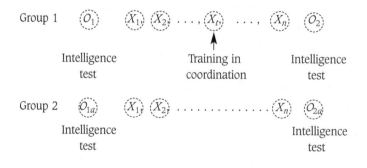

Group 1 (O_1) (X_1) (X_2) $\ldots,(X_t)$ $\ldots$ (X_n) (O_2)

    Intelligence   Training in   Intelligence
      test   coordination   test

Group 2 (O_{1a}) (X_1) (X_2) $\ldots\ldots\ldots\ldots(X_n)$ (O_{2a})

    Intelligence   Intelligence
      test   test

---

[3]The distinction between O and X can become somewhat vague or arbitrary. In essence an O may be considered as a suspect, or X, when the first O has effects on subsequent observations.

test scores. But a sophisticated critic argues: 'You may have controlled for the four rogues, but you still don't know whether the improvement is due to a combination or interaction of the pretest (O_1) and the training (X_1). Maybe the children in the first group were just more familiar with the experimental setting. The relaxation that comes with familiarity, plus the extra attention during training may have produced the difference between O_2 and O_{2a}.'

How can we answer this critic? One way is to randomly select two extra groups of children from the same classroom. Neither group is given the intelligence test but we assume, since they were picked at random from the same class, that they would have the same average IQ scores as other groups. In addition, we give training to one of the groups but not the other. The model then becomes:

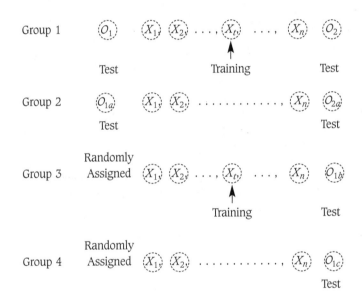

Assume that we obtain the following results:

$O_1 = 60$ $O_2 = 110$ $O_{1b} = 85$

$O_{1a} = 60$ $O_{2a} = 80$ $O_{1c} = 60$

If we compare O_2 and O_{2a}, we have a measure of the effectiveness of training combined with a pretest—30 units of difference. A comparison of O_{1b} with O_{1a} gives an indication of the effect of the treatment alone—25 units difference. The difference between O_{1c} and O_{2a} gives a measure of the pre-test effect—20 units difference.

We now conclude that training plus test practice accounted for the greatest improvement. Testing alone and training alone were not as effective as the two combined. Knowing the size of the test effect alone and the training effect alone would not lead to the correct prediction regarding the size of the two effects 'interacting' together.

When there is a strong possibility of an interaction between a treatment (X) and a measurement or observation (O) it's advisable to test those effects separately and in combination.

By using the control-group design and by assigning subjects randomly to groups, we try to reduce the risk of the four rogues or of chance factors influencing one group more than the other. Nevertheless, even under such circumstances, the hand of chance may play a hidden part by (1) dealing more quick-healing subjects into the experimental group and letting the new wonder drug receive unwarranted credit, (2) unpredictable shifts in the sensitivity or bias of the measuring instrument that happens to favour the treatment group, or (3) mistakes in transcribing or calculating the results.

The best defense against such chance factors leading to faulty conclusions is to consider the conclusions tentative until the study has been repeated and similar results obtained. Chance, being a fickle customer, shouldn't play the same tricks twice in a row. Another defense against chance factors making the independent variable (treatment) look unwarrantedly good is a so-called crossover design. In this design each group serves as a treatment *and* as a control group— that is, each group is tested under the influence of the independent variable and also tested without its influence, with the order of testing being counterbalanced. For example, to test the effects of threat of shock on errors of addition, we would use the following design:

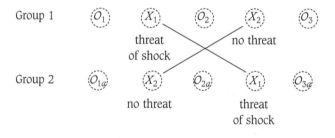

If the performance of *both* is impaired under threat of shock, you have increased confidence that your independent variable is having a predictable influence. It is a form of replication of the study, with each participant serving as his or her own control.

The crossover design is particularly appropriate when studying processes that can readily be reversed. For example, Agnew, Pyke, and Pylyshyn (1966), employed a multiple crossover design to investigate the effects of arousal (induced muscle tension) on absolute judgment of distance, using heart rate as an index of arousal. Figure 5.2 provides reassuring evidence that we were not

Fig 5.2 ■ HEART RATE (BEATS PER MINUTE) UNDER STRONG AND MILD TENSION AND REST CONDITIONS

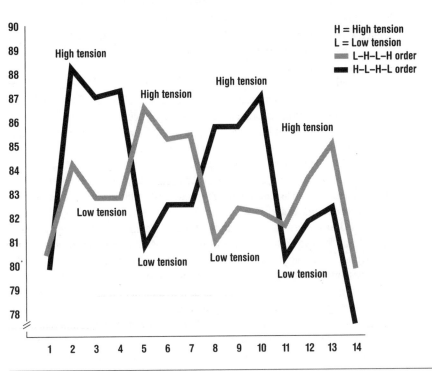

dealing with mere chance fluctuations in heart rate, but rather that our independent variable (X, brief induced muscle tension) was having a systematic and replicable effect on heart rate. This design is, of course, not viable for the research described earlier with Romanian children.

In addition to the four rogues already discussed, three more difficulties plague attempts to untangle the influence of the experimental treatment from that of the rogues, acting singly or in combination: statistical regression, differential mortality, and biased selection.

Statistical regression

Statistical regression (*drift toward the average*) reflects the fact that, even without treatment, people with extreme scores subsequently score closer to the group average. That is, high scorers, on retest, tend to score relatively lower, and low scorers, on retest, tend to score relatively higher.

Many students find this regression effect difficult to understand. Intuitively, however, you encounter this phenomenon when you do exceptionally well on an exam, when *everything* has worked in your favour—you studied all the right material, didn't have a cold, had a good night's sleep, wrote the exam at your 'best time' of the day, etc. In other words, the invisible hand of chance arranged everything in your favour. Thus, the high mark you obtained doesn't necessarily provide a reliable or fair estimate of your ability alone; rather, it provides an inflated estimate. Therefore, under less ideal conditions, your mark would have been relatively lower, would have been a more typical reflection of your ability, and would have been closer to the class average.

Similarly, when you do exceptionally poorly on a test, this usually reflects not only that you weren't prepared academically but also that chance arranged everything against you—by chance you missed a crucial lecture, you had a cold, you didn't sleep well, and the bus broke down and you were late for the exam, which was held during your 'worst time' of the day.

Therefore, statistical regression refers to the fact that extreme scores typically reflect an unusual constellation of forces, unlikely to be repeated on retest. On retest the scores will reflect a more typical constellation of factors, and so produce a less extreme score.

Statistical regression reflects the natural tendency of extreme measures to gravitate back toward the average, of extreme behaviour to return to 'normal' even without treatment. For example, when you're feeling low, or when you've 'bottomed out', there's only one direction to go—up. But when you're low, or when things are bad, is also when you're most likely to take a 'treatment'. Therefore, corrective measures frequently occur when a natural, or spontaneous, return to normal is most likely—and, of course, the treatment gets the credit. This can be seen as a special case of a time-tied suspect (maturation), but also, as a case of statistical regression, in which extreme measurements reflect a floor or a ceiling effect, and then move, or regress, toward the mean, or the average. Whenever dealing with extreme values, whether they concern *low* moods, or *high* temperatures, you need a control group to estimate the contribution of statistical regression effects alone.

Differential mortality

Differential mortality (*biased dropout*) occurs when, during an experiment, you lose subjects from your experimental or control group for whatever reasons. For example, the subjects you lose from your experimental group (subject attrition) may be, unknown to you, the sickest subjects. Therefore your treatment group improves more than your control group, not because the treatment worked but because it happened, by chance, that the sickest patients dropped out. Differential mortality is difficult to control. Some safeguards include:

1. attempting to use matched pairs of subjects in the experimental and control groups, so if one drops out the other member of the pair is also excluded from the analysis;

2. carefully reporting the number, and characteristics, of dropouts when you publish your results; and
3. viewing your results as tentative until the experiment has been repeated.

Biased selections

Just as the experimental and control groups may end up different because of biased dropouts, so too can they start out different. As noted previously, no error-proof method exists for matching the control and experimental groups on all relevant connections—some of which remain unknown. Nevertheless, four safeguards against biased selection include: matching subjects on obvious dimensions; assigning individuals at random to the two groups; using large groups; and having the experiment replicated by an independent investigator.

Finally, while we include *experimenter bias* as a form of elastic-ruler, or instrument decay, others assign it a separate category. So, if you prefer, you can reserve the concept of instrument decay to describe changes in the sensitivity of measurement equipment, which can be controlled by the use of the standard control-group design.

Experimenter bias, on the other hand, is more difficult to control. You can use 'blind' procedures so that the experimenter doesn't know which subjects are in the experimental group and which in the control group. However, when blind controls are not possible, the main protection against experimenter bias is having the experiment repeated by an 'independent' investigator.

Summarizing, then, we can say that:

1. Science has no perfect methods for collecting and packaging knowledge or information;
2. Scientists use a variety of methods, which differ in precision and cost;
3. A sieve or a scientific method is useful to the extent that it assists a scientist to make decisions by reducing the number of suspects involved; and
4. It is not always possible to use a fine sieve on a problem—a coarse sieve often becomes acceptable if it helps control one of the rogues, if it reduces our ignorance even a little bit.

Consumers of science need to be told, or to determine for themselves, which sieve(s) of science were used in naming prime suspects; otherwise it is impossible to decide how much confidence to place in the pronouncements of 'experts'.

Limitations of the Control-Group Method

Replacing after-the-fact and before-and-after methods with a control-group design yields increasing confidence in our results. For example, even when taking into account the influence of the rogues, we find that the new drug did indeed help reduce depression under our particular experimental conditions.

Under our particular experimental conditions? Aye, there's the rub. Although we have high confidence that the drug works with that particular group of patients, on that particular ward, with that particular ward staff, diet, routines, support therapies, and so forth, we still don't know whether the drug will work on a different group of depressed patients, treated by a different doctor, housed on another ward, in another hospital or clinic, in another country.

To Specified

We face a dilemma. In order to be increasingly confident that it was our treatment that did the trick, we try to 'control' the possible influence of other factors such as diet, age, sex, duration of illness, physical health, ward atmosphere, and other treatments. We usually control such factors by narrowing them—for example, by limiting the patients who can get into the study to females under 40 with no previous history of depression, with no major physical disability, all living on the same ward with the same nursing and medical staff. In doing so we limit the number of *external* factors that might affect the results. We test the drug under internal 'hothouse' conditions.

If we get a difference between our experimental and control groups under such protected hothouse conditions, we can be relatively certain that it was due to our drug and not to chance influences like variations in diet between the two groups. But we buy such confidence at a price, for while we are busy eliminating external influences to establish the internal hothouse effectiveness, or validity, of our drug, at the same time we narrow the claims we can make about its efficacy *beyond* the hothouse conditions. Each restriction or control we introduce into our study (e.g., only including female patients under thirty), also restricts the generalizations we can make about the drug's effectiveness (e.g., we don't know whether it will work with male patients, or with females over forty).

So scientists face a dilemma. Should they focus on obtaining small world (hothouse) certainty, or gamble (throw manure (X) to the winds) and hope for a large world harvest, a big truth?

Extending the Control-Group Method

There are at least three experimental paradigms, based on the control-group model, which help overcome some of the limits of traditional restrictions on laboratory and small sample research: (1) the natural experiment, (2) the field experiment, and (3) simulation research. Each of these approaches to scientific investigation maintains the manipulative feature of laboratory work but allows for the intrusion of a great many external factors. You hope that your treatment (X) is strong enough to *work* outside highly controlled experimental settings (strong enough to influence behaviour in predictable ways) in large random samples and in different *real world* situations.

The natural experiment

Campbell (1969) provides us with an elegant example of the use of the natural experimental design. In 1956 Senator Ribicoff of Connecticut instituted a crackdown on speeding as a result of a very high traffic fatality rate the previous year. Was his program effective? Apparently. Forty fewer deaths occurred in 1956 than in 1955, but if 1956 had exceptionally dry weather, we would expect fewer accidents due to lack of rain or snow. Or perhaps the price of snow tires dropped dramatically, and hundreds of drivers availed themselves of the opportunity to purchase safety at a bargain. Or perhaps the state had invested in a mammoth highway improvement program. These in-the-gap variables confound our interpretation of the simple pre-versus-post model.

Public knowledge of the high fatality rate might have produced the reduction in 1956 (on-stage effect), or the accuracy or techniques of recording accidents may have changed concurrently with the crackdown (instrument decay).

Traffic fatalities fluctuate yearly, and perhaps the drop after the crackdown merely reflects this normal up-and-down fluctuation. Plotting the number of traffic fatalities for the five-year period preceding, and subsequent to, the crackdown provides a stable baseline helping to rule out some of the rogue suspects. A control group, consisting of the traffic fatality rates in neighbouring states where there was no crackdown, further reduces the number of competing suspects and helps confirm that the crackdown did indeed have a beneficial effect.

The field experiment

Experiments are often conducted in natural (non-laboratory) settings thus reducing or eliminating the confounding effects of on-stage suspects and so enhance external validity. These advantages are of course counterbalanced by the minimal control that the investigator has over many components of the experimental situation—the four rogues are on the loose—so the treatment effect has to be strong enough to shine through in spite of their tricks. Nevertheless, the method has great utility for the study of certain phenomena that are not suitable for laboratory investigation.

One classic experiment of this type was reported by Milgram, Bickman, and Berkowitz (1969). These researchers arranged for small groups of research confederates to stop in the middle of the sidewalk of a busy thoroughfare and gaze upward at a building across the street. The size of the group of confederates, ranging from 1–15 people, was the treatment (X), that is, the independent variable, or the experimental manipulation.[4] To what extent would passers-by also stop and glance up, and would a larger group of confederates be more influential in inducing more of them to stop and stare? Many more passers-by looked

---

[4]This experiment is analogous to comparing the new wonder drug, not with a placebo (or non-treated control) group, but rather with the current popular treatment.

up than stopped, and even one research confederate gazing upward was enough to produce imitative behaviour in 40 per cent of the passers-by. But a similar percentage of passers-by were induced to stop when all 15 confederates looked up. So all it took was one confederate to demonstrate the full effect of that particular treatment.

Simulation research

Zimbardo and his colleagues have produced a most dramatic example of simulation research (Haney, Banks, & Zimbardo, 1973). In a very realistic mock-up of a prison, university students role-played either prisoners or guards. In a matter of days the guards developed and utilized oppressive and domineering tactics on the prisoners, while the latter degenerated into passive, dependent, pathetic creatures. The experiment was terminated prematurely because of the pathological reactions of both groups.

Again this type of experimental paradigm may be employed to investigate—under systematic, controlled conditions—events that are otherwise outside the realm of scientific study, events such as international negotiations. Subject awareness, however, has unknown effects on the results obtained, and thus conclusions derived from simulation research of this type are only suggestive.

Unobtrusive Measures

Extensions of the control-group model expand our scientific reach into natural settings. So does the use of unobtrusive measures. Such measures may be employed in many types of research paradigms—most commonly in field studies, and they may also be used in laboratory experiments.

When we eavesdrop on the conversation of the diners at the next table, watch the air flight attendant handle the drunken passenger, or admire someone on the subway, we're making unobtrusive observations. A minimum of deception, feigned indifference, or a studied air of passionate absorption in a newspaper provides us with abundant opportunities to observe how people behave when they don't know they're being watched.

For example, one student, curious about what police officers talked about while cruising, adopted an unobtrusive measure by hiding in the back seat of a cruiser. In so doing he obtained a radically different picture of the content and style of police officer conversations than he had obtained through questionnaires, interviews, and archival research. However, when the officers stopped for coffee and our researcher tried to leave the cruiser as unobtrusively as he had entered, he learned to his dismay that, in the back seat of police cruisers, there are no handles on the inside of the doors. He was apprehended, and only after careful examination of his person and his credentials and after repeated assurances that it was only a college prank was our trembling novice researcher sent on his humble way. Unobtrusive probes, if discovered, can teach you more than you bargained for.

The Watergate scandal remains a classic example of a politically motivated unobtrusive probe that not only failed, but also shook a nation in the process. The ethical implications of applying unobtrusive measures are serious and complex, and any student would be well advised to consult faculty advisors before launching into this important—but sometimes risky—extension of research methodology. Also notice that archival sources provide a rich, ethical, and safe source of unobtrusive data.

In brief, for most of the day-to-day problems we face, using the classic control-group design is impossible, impractical, or inappropriate. It's impossible because we can't move the real world into the laboratory; it refuses to relocate for our benefit. It's impractical because the problems are too big to fit, and even if they did it's too expensive. It's inappropriate because we want to understand and predict many kinds of behaviour in their natural setting, minus on-stage effects that can occur beyond the laboratory footlights and proscenium arch.

True, when studying billiard balls with brains, sometimes we want to study their billiard ball qualities (e.g., weigh them in a study of low-fat diets), and can do so under highly controlled lab conditions without encountering on-stage distortions. But as soon as we start studying their brain/mind qualities we increasingly rely on extensions to the control-group design. We rely on control-groups wherever possible and appropriate—we follow the spirit of the control-group law, but not necessarily the letter of that law.

Mendelson, Sholar, Goletiani, Siegel, and Mello (2005) provide an impressive example of a multi-measure research design on the effects of smoking. They use a control group design to examine the effects of both cigarettes and placebos on hormones, cardiovascular measures, subjective responses (e.g., mood), and the relationships between the measures. For instance, they report that within four puffs of a cigarette (but not of a nicotine free placebo) that both the level of nicotine in the blood and heart rate increased, followed by subjective reports of a 'high' or a 'rush'.

This study is important for several reasons: it addresses a serious health problem, it uses a scientific method (control-group design), it includes a variety of measuring tools ranging from quantitative (heart rate) to qualitative (mood judgments), and by demonstrating the chemical and physiological mechanisms that trigger elevated mood it helps us understand addiction and why it is so difficult to quit the habit.

Smoking appears to provide an example of a strong bottom-up message system (i.e., smoking-is-feeling) a physical stimulus triggering a predictable neuro/chemical response. A response against which top-down messages (i.e., New Year's Resolutions) usually have little effect. Some rabid anti-smokers might even propose that smokers' behaviour is so predictable that they're like billiard balls without brains, without top down controls.

Control groups of various kinds have enabled social scientists to increasingly evolve from pre-scientific to scientific problem solving. You won't hear as many belly laughs from Einstein's derisive Gods when you use a control-group design. Nor will there be as many loopholes in your logic. Furthermore, the walls of your playpen move in closer and your mind bumps into solid empirical constraints when it tries to jump directly to naïve conclusions.

Research Design Checklist

The following checklist may help you decide how much confidence to place in a given research finding:

1. Does the investigator demonstrate that he or she has made a careful attempt to control the four rogue suspects? For example, would you have more confidence if a control-group design had been used than if a before-and-after design had been used?
2. If two or more groups were used, was there a reasonable attempt made to ensure that they were equal to begin with (randomization)?
3. Did the investigator use enough people in each group to make you feel that the samples adequately represented the target population the investigator wanted to end up talking about (children of different ages and from different socioeconomic backgrounds)?
4. Does the particular dependent variable represent a reliable and valid means of measuring the target behaviour under study?
5. What prior evidence is presented to justify the selection of the particular treatment, to assume it is strong enough to influence the target behaviour significantly?
6. How representative is the research context or treatment settings?
7. Did the investigator publish or make available raw data so you could check the investigator's calculations or data packaging procedures?
8. Did the investigator repeat the study and get similar results?
9. Is the investigator established and has his or her work usually proved to be durable in the past?
10. Has another investigator repeated this study and published similar findings?
11. If so, was the second investigator independent of the first investigator (not his or her graduate student or employee)?
12. Do the findings make sense in terms of other durable findings in the same field?

SUMMARY

The classic control-group problem solving method adds great power to our research repertoire, permitting scientists to assess the impact of treatment, or independent variables, over and above the impacts of the four rogues. In skilled hands this method enables us to untangle an increasing number of scientific knots and to have increasing confidence in our conclusions.

However, just as the behaviour of bodies in a vacuum is different from their behaviour under *uncontrolled* conditions of pressure, temperature, and wind, so too will some aspects of human behaviour, when studied in more natural situations, differ from that displayed in a protected laboratory or control-group setting.

The good news is that the use of control groups warrants increased confidence in our conclusions. The bad news is two-fold: (1) our generalizations are limited to the controlled (restricted) conditions of our study, and (2) because control-group studies typically require extra time and resources we must often wait for the answers to pressing questions. For example, when deciding whether or not to have a major operation, you and your doctor may have to make a decision on the basis of flawed after-the-fact or before-and-after studies because the control-group studies of that particular operation remain to be done on a large representative sample including people like you (e.g., age, sex, etc.), or such a study has not yet reached the head of the very long research priority line.

Unfortunately, we in particular, and society in general, have far more pressing problems to be solved than society has scientific resources to generate both affordable and trusted answers.

In the following chapters we explore how citizens and scientists alike must rely on a combination of affordable methods to reach affordable conclusions. In the next chapter we discuss the reach of science as it tries to extend some of its ideas and laboratory or small sample findings beyond the protected experimental hothouse into the noisy, windy world.

Situations make a difference. One of the characteristics of human behaviour is that much of it depends on the situation in which it occurs, on on-stage effects (e.g., we act differently in a lab setting than when relaxing with friends, we don't smoke in church, or laugh out loud during a funeral service).

The concept of *external validity* refers to the degree to which results garnered in one controlled condition can be generalized or exported to the relatively uncontrolled world in which we live. Scientists must always ask themselves how fragile are their laboratory findings, how similar are they to hothouse flowers that can't survive outside such a controlled environment? Will the successful drug treatment, generated in the protected, resource rich, University Hospital still work in the small general hospital in Podunk, and in the tiny clinic in Bangladesh?

To answer this question we rely on extensions of the control-group method. We rely on research strategies such as natural and field experiments, simulations, qualitative and unobtrusive measures, which help us further test and extend the external validity of our conclusions.

Since Lady Luck always sits in on the science game (dealing the four rogue wild cards into any study), our best defense against being tricked is to repeat the experiment. Every time a study is successfully replicated we gain confidence that we're mapping the shape of nature rather than tracing the shape of our own expectations, while being hoodwinked by chance or the rogues, or being conned by phony data generated by a naïve, sloppy, or dishonest researcher.

In the next chapter we take a closer look at how we measure the *internal* (small playpen) and *external* (big playpen) validity of our research results.

student's notebook

Project Derek, Progress Report: Well, I think my attempt to change Derek's behaviour is having an effect. I started with a simple before-and-after design: O_1 (him not listening to me) was a long-standing, predictable behaviour, a stable baseline ($O_1 = O_2 = O_3$, etc.). Any real change would be noticeable and astonishing.

My treatments included rewarding him any time he really listened to what I was saying (X_1) and withdrawing my attention (X_2) when he ignored what I said. Sort of a 'double whammy' treatment.

The problem is that I rarely get a chance to apply X_1 (rewards) because he never really listens, except when he wants something. And when he talks on and on, even when I withdraw my attention (X_2) by looking at the ceiling or reading a book, he doesn't seem to notice—he just continues to natter.

So, I strengthened my X_2. Instead of looking away, yawning, drumming my fingers on the table, and reading when he ignored what I said, I got up and left. He noticed that! He came after me. We had a little chat. I told him why I was mad. But of course I didn't tell him I was running an experiment with him as the rat. I guess my little temper tantrum is another in-the-gap treatment (X_3).

After I blew off steam I had all kinds of opportunity to talk. Now he just sits there like a stump saying absolutely nothing. It's hard to apply X_1 to a stump. It's hard to reward it, to smile warmly at it, to touch or admire it.

But I'm trying. I'll give it another week.

What if it seems to work? How can I rigorously test it? It's still only a before-and-after study so it's at the mercy of the four rogues. But because it is such a stable baseline it seems unlikely that the rogues are too involved. The rogues have had two years to work and the baseline never varies.

I've been trying to figure out how to use a control group. I thought I might try a counterbalanced design. You apply the treatment and then the non-treatment (control) conditions to the same research participants. That is, if the miraculous occurred and Derek did really start listening, if we really did start having conversations as a result of my combined X_1 and X_2 treatments, then I could try shifting to a no-treatment condition, (no rewards, no walk away) and see how long it took before he flipped back to his old habits.

But hey, I'm not sure I want to risk it. I'll only do so much for the sake of science. Instead, I might try this behaviour-shaping trick on someone else, like my bratty brother, as a kind of replication. After all, he has no shortage of obnoxious behaviours to reshape.

Right now I've got bigger fish to fry. Professor Creek gave us a tough term assignment based on this chapter. He divided the class into two-person teams and said he wanted each pair to actually conduct a control-group study. He said he didn't expect a perfect experiment, but he wanted us to gain first hand scientific experience. We had to:

1. *doing some critical thinking;*
2. *then choose a researchable question (one that we could afford to do with our time limits and resources);*
3. *design a study that tried to control for the four rogues; then,*
4. *cycle down to the bottom right corner of our PST and testing our hypotheses as rigorously as time permitted; and finally*
5. *critically analyze the results.*

Well, it took us a month. You wouldn't believe the trouble we had agreeing on a research question. But there's nothing like a hard deadline (or a bias) to cut a problem down to mind-size. My research partner is trying to give up smoking and he'd reviewed some of the literature, so that's where we got our hypothesis. I liked it because the theory fit in with the behaviour-shaping attempt I'm trying on Derek.

Here's what we handed in.

Why Do People Keep Smoking?
By Diana Dodds, Class Project for Research Methods 201

We chose to research why people keep smoking. Many smokers want to kick the habit but can't, even though they know that smoking can, and likely will, lead to major health problems including lung cancer. When rational people persist in irrational behaviour one common explanation is that they are somehow addicted. Another explanation is that they have the lung cancer information safely bracketed away out of awareness (à la Shoham's theory discussed in Chapter 2).

In reviewing the scientific literature we selected two findings to guide our own research. Mendelson et al. (2005), mentioned in Chapter 5 of *The Science Game*, report that smoking produces an increased heart rate followed by a mood elevating 'high'. Therefore, one of the reasons why so many people can't kick the habit is because every time they inhale they feel energized by the increased heart rate, blood flow, and psychological 'high'. With every puff they're reinforcing themselves. Not only can smoking pick you up when you feel tired, but it has the additional effect of calming you if you are tense or stressed.

The purpose of our research is to use a control-group study to see if smoking does raise heart rates and thus serving as a physiological stimulant. As well as providing us with first-hand research experience this study will serve to test the reliability (through replication) of earlier studies.

Procedure

Through naturalistic observation we selected 10 heavy smokers from a large introductory psychology class to participate in our study. Two said they were too busy, so we selected two more. We told them that we were studying memory, so it was a single-blind study, the participants didn't know that we were really studying the effects of smoking.

We divided them at random into two groups by drawing their names out of a hat. All subjects were tested individually. The general procedure is outlined below.

After they arrived at our laboratory, which was a spare office in the psychology building, they were asked to sit down and were told this was a study to test the effects of relaxation on memory. They read a short passage, were tested for recall, and were allowed relax and have a cigarette. Then they read another passage and were tested for recall again. Group 2 subjects followed the same procedure, but they were not allowed to smoke.

To see how well they were relaxing, a pulsemeter (San-Ei Pulsemeter, Medical Systems Corp., Great Neck, NY) was used. The pulsemeter dial reads heartbeats per minute. The pulsemeter is about the size of a pocket calculator. A metal finger sleeve serves as a single slip-on electrode. We used the middle finger of the non-writing hand, first cleaning it vigorously with alcohol.

After the participants were hooked up to the pulsemeter, they read from the procedure section of a mirror-drawing experiment for three minutes. Meanwhile, one of the experimenters recorded pulse rates every 30 seconds (O_1). Following the three-minute reading, subjects were asked to answer a number of standard questions about the passage they had just read. Then members of the experimental group were told that they were welcome to take a break, have a cigarette, and relax for 10 minutes (X_t). The members of the control group were told to relax for 10 minutes but were not allowed to smoke (X_c). During the 10 minute relaxation period, the subjects' pulse rates were recorded every 60 seconds (O_2).

We were supposed to observe to see if the smokers were deep inhalers but forgot to do it for two of them; from memory we concluded that they were, so all members of the experimental group were inhalers.

At the end of 10 minutes, each subject read for three minutes from another standard passage and was questioned, during which time pulse rate was recorded every 30 seconds (O_3). The subjects were not told the real purpose of the experiment at this time for fear their knowledge would affect the results. Instead, they were informed of the real purpose of our study when we reported our results back to their class.

Results

We calculated the average pulse rate for each group at each recording point, but we did not do statistical tests because we had so few participants. This kind of small sample investigation is apparently called as a pilot study, where you test out your procedure and equipment and see if you get trends suggesting that a proper large sample study is warranted.

From the graph in Figure 5.3, you can see that the groups started out with approximately the same pulse rate at the beginning of the investigation and at the commencement of the 10-minute rest. While during the rest period both groups showed a decline in pulse rate, the smokers experience less of a decrease, suggesting some support for the hypothesis that smoking maintains a higher heart rate even during relaxation. Also, the smokers' pulse rate continued to be somewhat higher during the second reading passage, indicating that the nicotine was still working.

Figure 5.3 • Heart Rate Changes as a Function of Smoking

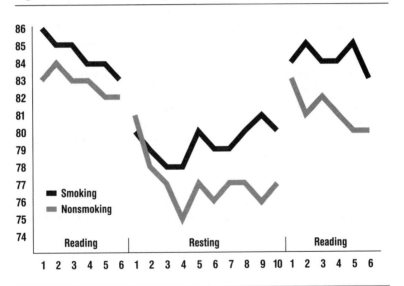

Discussion

Our results support the hypothesis that smoking produces increased heart rate. However, we should not get too confident about these results for several reasons.

We had only five students in each group, so our samples were small. Also, we made an error and tested all the experimental participants before the control group. Therefore our design looked like this:

Group 1 (O_1) (O_2X_1) (O_3)

           Reading   Resting   Reading
                         and
                     Smoking

Group 2 (O_{1a}) (O_{2a}) (O_{3a})

                                 Reading   Resting   Reading

This means that in-the-gap and elastic-ruler rogues could be different for the two groups. For example, a possible in-the-gap suspect operating differently on the two groups could have been experimenter relaxation. By the time we tested the control group, we knew what we were doing and so we were more relaxed ourselves. This may have had a relaxing effect on the test Group 2 participants.

There are also obvious elastic-ruler and instrument-decay suspects. The pulsemeter is battery-operated and it could have been losing some of its charge toward the end of the study. This would have resulted in lower pulse rate readings for the control group. The graph shows that while they were not much lower to start with, they were a little lower. Whether this was due merely to chance or to the pulsemeter's gradual loss of power, we don't know.

It was poor planning not to test each experimental and control-group participants alternately. By not doing this we failed to take advantage of the strength of the control-group method. Correcting this mistake and working with a larger group of participants would have greatly improved this study. Also we should have used a standardized test for memory to see whether smoking really did affect memory as well as heart rate.

References

Mendelson, J.H., et al. 2005. 'Effects of Low- and High-Nicotine Cigarette Smoking on Mood States and the HP A Axis in Men', *Neuropsychopharmacology*: 1–13.

Well, as you can see we really goofed. Not only at the top of the PST (lack of critical thinking), but also at the bottom by ignoring the elastic-ruler rogue by not regularly testing the battery in the pulsemeter. There was also the really big mistake of running the experimental and control groups at different times, thus permitting different in-the-gap suspects to affect the results. We defeated the whole purpose of the control-group design. We ended up with two before-and-after studies.

Well, at least we used a single-blind design—the research participants didn't know the real purpose of the experiment so that controlled some of the on-stage rogues. Also, we should earn some brownie points from Professor Creek for doing a laboratory type of study. Unlike Frund, he prefers hothouse research and he has a thing for internal validity.

What's done is done. Now back to Derek. His behaviour is currently all over the board: at times he sits there like a sullen stump, at times he actually listens, and at times he flips back to being his old self and rattles on while paying absolutely no attention to me or my futile treatments (X_1, X_2, or X_3).

I wonder if that's what happens when you disrupt or reshape a habit? Maybe you don't get a smooth transition to a new pattern of behaviour but instead you end up with a bunch of trial and error floundering? Anyway, I'm hanging in there with good old X_1 (rewards), X_{2light} (withdraw attention), and X_{2heavy} (get up and leave in a huff.) I may have to resort to good old-fashioned yelling and screaming. Only time will tell!

Note

Check out the sins committed against the control-group method at http://www.oup.com/ca/he/companion/agnewpyke.

REVIEW TRUE OR FALSE QUIZ

T	F	1. The placebo effect is an example of 'seeing-is-believing'.
T	F	2. With the control-group method, the difference between O_1 and O_2 reflects the effects of the treatment plus that of the four rogues.
T	F	3. The concept of external validity refers to the extent to which research results can be generalized to the real world.
T	F	4. Use of qualitative and unobtrusive measures extends the internal validity of our conclusions.
T	F	5. An independent variable refers to the response of the research participant.
T	F	6. The difference between O_1 and O_2 is referred to as the dependent variable.
T	F	7. Use of a control group ensures that the researcher will come up with the correct suspect.
T	F	8. A placebo is intended to enhance the co-operativeness of the research participants.

T F	9. To help ensure that bias isn't operating in the placement of research participants in specific experimental conditions, the researcher assigns individuals randomly to groups (i.e., treatment group and control group).
T F	10. Use of a double-blind procedure means that neither the research participants nor the researcher is aware of the experimental condition to which each participant has been assigned.
T F	11. Spontaneous recovery is an example of the operation of an elastic-ruler suspect.
T F	12. A control-group design eliminates the individual and combined influences of the four types of rogue suspects.
T F	13. The control-group method permits researchers to assess the effects of their treatment over and above the effects of the four rogues alone.
T F	14. Choice of an appropriate comparison group depends on the kind of question the researcher is asking.
T F	15. To address the possibility that it is the combination of a pretest with the treatment that is responsible for the effect, researchers may expand their design to include two additional groups that are not given a pretest.
T F	16. In a crossover design, each individual participates in both the experimental group and the control group.
T F	17. People who score high on a measure tend, on retest, to score relatively lower and low scorers tend to score relatively higher on retest.
T F	18. The effects of differential mortality (the biased dropout of subjects) can be minimized through the use of matched pairs of subjects in the experimental and control groups.
T F	19. Field experiments and simulation research overcome to some extent the limits of the traditional laboratory model.
T F	20. In trying to shape Derek's behaviour, Diana used four treatments: rewards, withdrawing attention, getting up and leaving, and yelling and screaming.
T F	21. In Diana's smoking study, testing all the experimental participants before testing the control participants meant that in-the-gap and elastic-ruler suspects could be different for the two groups.

From Local to General Truths

Most research is *local*. It involves observing a small sample of people in one laboratory, classroom, factory, or street corner at a given time, on a given day.

There's nothing wrong with that. We learn something about that sample, in that setting, at that time. And that's important. In fact, local knowledge is what you and I gather every day—it's what's going on around us.

But that's not the job of science.

We pay social scientists not to tell us merely what this small sample of people think and feel, but rather what large numbers of people think and feel; men, women, Conservatives, Liberals, members of Parliament, police officers, and prostitutes. We expect them to be able to gather and analyze their data so that they can go beyond their small, local samples and generalize to larger populations of people.

We expect scientists to generate truths that can travel beyond local settings, beyond local space and time, to larger spaces and longer times. We're not particularly interested in how the small group of depressed patients on this particular ward responded to the new drug. We want to know how depressed patients on other wards, in other hospitals, will respond. We expect scientists to come up with big truths.

In Chapter 6 we discuss how scientists attempt to travel beyond local observations and local conclusions to observations and conclusions that cover more people and more places. We're not only interested in whether the new drug helped patients in different hospitals to get better, but we also want to know if they stayed better. We want to know how well a local truth travels in both space and time.

In Chapter 7 we discuss the ways scientists study what happens to how people think, feel, and behave over time—from birth to death.

6

Validity:
The Reach of
Science

Chapter Goal

- To explore the reach of science, to explore its *validity*.

We discuss two types of validity: top of the PST validity (beliefs) and bottom of the PST validity (observations). Each of these two types of validity comes in two sizes: small playpen truths (internal validity) and large playpen truths (external validity).

Introduction

You're already familiar with the word *validity* as it is used in the context of a 'valid' drivers' license or a 'valid' passport. Used in this way, the term validity is a like a travel permit. Because the permit is valid, it grants a person permission to cross geographical boundaries. Similarly, different scientific passports determine how easily different ideas and observations can pass across scientific boundaries, or can pass from small playpens to larger ones. Validity judgments determine how easily ideas and observations are allowed to travel from scientist to scientist across disciplinary boundaries and gain a secure place as trusted beliefs or premises at the top of PSTs, or as trusted observations at the bottom.

When scientists mistakenly issue a valid passport to flawed ideas or unreliable observations, sooner or later, they're embarrassed by the laughter of the gods. The gods also giggle when scientists reject deviant ideas or observations out of hand. But with their bounded rationality what are poor researchers to do? Get used to periodic godly giggles, that's what!

For instance . . .

Until very recently the *BIG truth* about ulcers stated that they were caused by *stomach acid and stress*. That truth had a universal passport allowing it to travel freely across cultural and scientific boundaries. That particular truth had acquired loads of *big playpen validity*—everyone, everywhere *believed* it at the top of their PSTs and saw it down at the bottom.

But in the early 1980s, unknown to medical science, in a small playpen, two Australian researchers were committing scientific heresy.[1] On the basis of their observations, their critical thinking up-top (they remembered good old germ theory), and their rigorous testing down below (actually, and heroically, growing an experimental ulcer in the stomach of one of the researchers) they concluded that most ulcers were caused, not by acid or stress, but by a particular bacteria. These researchers challenged the conventional wisdom that acid and stress caused most ulcers, and proposed that this universal travel permit be revoked, or at least restricted.

When the upstart Aussies published their heresy, what do you think doctors and medical researchers around the world did?

NOTHING!

Most of them never *heard* or *saw* the news. Remember, Kahneman[2] received his Nobel Prize for pointing out that, because of our bounded rationality we make decisions on the basis of information that is readily *accessible*, not on the basis of *all* available information. Ideas or premises need to be accessible at the top of our PSTs, and observations need to be accessible at the bottom before we honour them with our rationed attention.

The Aussie heresy wasn't issued a travel permit in the US; it wasn't readily accessible at the top or bottom of American PSTs. Busy doctors don't have the time or inclination to look outside their current medical box because:

1. they were busy seeing a new patient every 8.7 minutes;
2. they already *knew* (emotionally anchored premise) what causes ulcers and how to treat them (drugs, diet, relaxation);
3. they were not paid to keep detailed records and do careful follow-ups of all their patients to see what works (limited time for critical thinking or rigorous testing);
4. everyone has stomach acid and stress, so like bad air, these accessible, familiar, in-the-gap suspects can always be blamed as repeat offenders (believing-is-seeing);

---

[1] Mayne Florey Medal 1998 Award, for the discovery of the *Helicobacter Pylori*, the causative agent in Gastritis and Gastric Ulceration. Available at http://www.tallpoppies.net.au/floreymedal/winner1998.htm.

[2] See Chapter 2.

5. most physicians are medical practitioners, not trained medical scientists, and therefore are not familiar with all the tricks the four rogues can play; and finally,

6. medical researchers, who are trained in research design, can only afford to critically evaluate (top of their PST) and rigorously test (bottom of their PST) a tiny fraction of the fledgling premises or theories and observations flooding the literature from small medical playpens all over the world.

So for years the *truth* from down under failed to travel beyond the Outback. For years it failed to penetrate the protective boundaries (busy-ness and biases) operating both at the top and bottom of North American PSTs. It was a case of believing-is-seeing and the entrenched beliefs of our physicians and medical researchers prevented them from even *thinking seriously* about this fledgling truth, let alone *seeing* it.

The few who did glance at it protected their bounded rationality by promptly forgetting it, or by bracketing[3] it safely away, out of awareness.

As Simon says: 'No conclusions without premises', and the Aussie premise—lacking a scientific travel permit—couldn't gain entry into North America. Organized medicine already had a mentally affordable and trusted 'If A then B then C rule': If A (ulcer), then B (too much acid), then C (prescribe acid reducing pills).

It took decades for the North American medical and scientific establishments to loosen up their conceptual borders enough to allow the Australian theory and observations to leak through and be carefully considered and rigorously tested.

The Aussie truth is granted a universal passport

Finally, in 2005, the two previously ignored Australian medical pioneers were awarded the Nobel Prize. This award is as close as we come to issuing a universal travel permit to a scientific truth, the closest we come to officially placing a 'big playpen' *validity* stamp upon the theory and its supporting observations.

As we noted in Chapter 2, both Simon and Kahneman's theories and observations concerning bounded rationality were awarded the very same Nobel travel permit. So far there's no expiry date on their *truths*.

Great scientific truths rise and fall. They start out small and local (small playpens) and then gather enough strength to travel, and eventually to be widely considered, and to find a foothold in the establishment's dense network of emotionally anchored beliefs, biases, and habits of thinking and seeing. Only then is the fledgling truth widely and rigorously tested. Only then does it rapidly

---

[3]See the discussion about Shoham in Chapter 2 and his premise that we protect our bounded rationality and pet decision rules by bracketing exceptions safely out of awareness until peer pressure, or the repeated and obvious failure of the emotionally anchored rule, forces the brackets open, and lets suppressed memories and new ideas flow into awareness.

blossom into a BIG truth with a universal passport, before gradually retreating back to occupy a territory larger than its local beginnings but much smaller than the whole world. That rise and partial shrinkage happens to all theory, even to Einstein's great theory of relativity, as well as to Freud's psychoanalysis, and Skinner's learning theory.

Actually, no scientific theory deserves to receive a passport authorizing universal travel. Acquiring *external validity* is always a work in progress. No scientific theory or observation can be rigorously tested in *all* places, under *all* conditions, for *all* time. No scientific theory can have 'forever' stamped on its travel permit in the space provided for *expiry date*. The best we can do is to stamp 'unknown' on that line.

Scholars Study Scientists

Scholars not only study the physical, biological, and social world, but they study SCIENCE itself, and they study individual scientists, too. These scholars study the history of science (remember Ignaz Semmilweis and hand washing), the philosophy of science (what scientists believe and how they establish their truths), the psychology of science (how individual scientists think and behave), and the sociology of science (how science as an institution establishes cliques and hierarchies, and how it punishes or ignores deviants).

But how do scientists make decisions when observations are incomplete or unavailable? Neither they nor we can see the future. When scholars hold their mirrors up to science, big questions are reflected back: how do scientists determine *the truth*? How do they determine how much confidence to place in their always-imperfect conclusions and incomplete observations? In brief, how do they determine the *validity* of their observations and theories? How do they try to avoid being shipwrecked by the laughter of the gods?

Models of truth or validity

Wouldn't it be nice if there were one resounding and crystal clear answer about *the truth*, an answer about which all scholars agreed? But of course there's not. However there are two conventional answers.

The first, the *correspondence* model of truth, or validity, is based on how well the answer or speculation *fits the facts*, that is, how well it fits trusted observational checkpoints at the bottom of the PST.

The second, the *consistency* theory of truth, or validity, is based on how well the answer or speculation fits in with what we already *believe* to be true up at the top of the PST. We need this up-top, belief-based, *consistency theory of truth* because we rarely have all the facts about the present and precious few, if any, about the future. So we have no choice but to make life-shaping decisions on the basis of beliefs, not facts. Scientists invest years, even a lifetime, investigating a particular theory. To make that kind of commitment they've got to *believe* that it's valid. String theory (the theory of *everything*) is a modern case in point.

We're most familiar with the correspondence model of truth, which examines how closely reliable observational stepping-stones follow along the path sketched on the up-top speculative maps. Of course we don't always have access to trusted observational checkpoints, nevertheless, we must still make decisions, and commitments of great consequence about career choices, getting married, trying new drugs, global warming, going to war, etc. How do we, or scientists, decide what's true and trustworthy, or *valid*, when we, or they, have to make these life shaping decisions without reliable observational stepping-stones.

We do so, as Simon says, by relying on emotionally anchored premises, beliefs, or theories. Or if you prefer, we make major decisions based on bias. We assign a truth-value, or validity, to our speculative maps according to how consistently they fit our expectations distilled from past experience. In doing so we assume that the future will be just like the past. Auto accidents, cheating partners, strokes, and 9/11 terrorist attacks challenge that assumption.

Or, if we lack relevant experience, we rely on what trusted authorities say or write (hearsay evidence), and on how well they pass trusted mental and emotional litmus tests (e.g., logical, mathematical, folklore, religious, etc.).

So, lacking trusted *observational* stepping-stones at the bottom of our PSTs, we have no choice but to make vitally important decisions on the basis of trusted *mental or conceptual* stepping-stones at the top. We accept as true those ideas that follow a familiar and trusted way of thinking. In brief, we tend to accept as valid new ideas that are consistent with our current habits of thinking, or our popular biases and theories.

For those of you planning to do graduate work in the social or behavioural sciences, the *mental* stepping-stones are called conceptual variables or *constructs* (e.g. 'intelligence'). The *observational* stepping-stones are called operational variables, defined in terms of the operations involved to identify them (e.g., intelligence is what an intelligence test measures). Millions of conceptual variables (speculations) float around at the top of the PST without observational anchors down at the bottom.[4]

In addition to the two types of validity discussed earlier—consistency and correspondence—we now discuss the two sizes of validity, those generated in small local playpens and those supposedly valid in global playpens.

Top-of-the-PST Validity: Internal and External

In scientific literature the terms *internal* and *external* validity typically refer to reliable observations and rigorous testing carried out at the bottom right corner

---

[4]In some cases the concepts are beyond the reach of operational definitions (e.g., those dealing with the supernatural or fantasy worlds). In other cases they're too vague (e.g., many of Freud's constructs). In other instances no one has developed operational definitions or tested their reliability and validity.

of the PST. They typically refer to the observational, seeing-is-believing, part of science.

However, as noted above, the authors take the position that the terms apply equally well to the top of the PST. In other words, we accept two kinds of validity: ideational/*conceptual*/logical validity at the top and observational/*perceptual*/empirical validity at the bottom.

Fig 6.1 ■ INTERNAL AND EXTERNAL VALIDITY

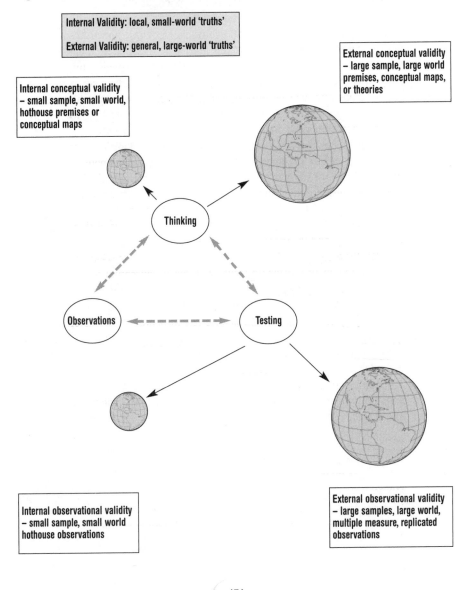

Internal Validity: local, small-world 'truths'

External Validity: general, large-world 'truths'

External conceptual validity – large sample, large world premises, conceptual maps, or theories

Internal conceptual validity – small sample, small world, hothouse premises or conceptual maps

Thinking

Observations   Testing

Internal observational validity – small sample, small world hothouse observations

External observational validity – large samples, large world, multiple measure, replicated observations

In keeping with the consistency model of truth discussed earlier, we propose that validity judgments apply to the *believing-is-seeing* part of science, as well as to the *seeing-is-believing* part.

Operating conceptually up at the top of their PSTs, researchers must have sufficient belief in the *theoretical validity* of their premises—their hypotheses—to warrant travelling down to the bottom right corner and investing the research time, energy, and mental effort required to rigorously test, through observation after observation, the *empirical validity* of the fledgling theory's predictions.

Therefore, as indicated in Figure 6.1, we apply the terms internal and external validity at the top and the bottom of the scientific PST.

Keeping Semmilweis's 'dirty hands' theory and the Aussie ulcer theory in mind, we propose that new scientific truths evolve. These new truths might start with a surprising observation at the bottom left corner of the PST (maybe Semmilweis noticed a doctor, coming from the morgue on his way to deliver a baby, wiping autopsy remains onto his trousers). Or, maybe a surprising idea or premise pops into mind at the top of the PST (Semmilweis may have dreamed about a swinging door between the morgue and the gynecology ward, only to wake up, remember the door, and then make the *connection*).

Scientists may focus their limited attention on making more observations, or on more critical thinking, or on both by cycling and recycling around their PSTs. At first, operating in a small playpen, they attempt to establish a local truth. They need to establish enough local, internal validity (theoretical or observational) to assure them that they're on to something *real*.

If they're theoretical scientists, like Einstein, they slave away at the top of their PSTs, endlessly scribbling possible expansions of their small truth and making out-of-the-box predictions. With luck they establish enough conceptual validity (internal and external) to attract the attention of other theoretical scientists and empirical researchers. Lacking relevant and reliable observations, theoretical scientists like Einstein rely on elaborate logical or mathematical arguments to bolster and extend the conceptual validity of their speculations, while waiting for researchers to buy into their idea and rigorously test their theory.[5]

Mathematical maps are mathematical speculations of where observational checkpoints will be found *if the theory is right*.

If—at the top of the PST—a theory can be stated mathematically, many scientists automatically think of it as valid, even though its predictions have not been rigorously tested down at the bottom.[6]

---

[5]Unlike Einstein, some scientists like Skinner travel endlessly back and forth from the top to the bottom of the their PSTs, making and testing their own predictions.

[6]This is very similar to the way that you and I believe many of our ideas are *valid* even if they lack any observational evidence supporting them. Maybe, if you and I learned to state our beliefs in mathematical lingo, others who doubt our genius would pay more attention and let us get away with our brilliant believing-is-seeing decisions (e.g., '3 + 4 of Harold's statements = 0 truth'). Or, if we stated them in sophisticated philosophical lingo (e.g., 'Harold's statements are truth free.').

Some modest scientists, operating at the top (see Figure 6.1), admit that their theory covers a small local conceptual domain (internal validity). In contrast, other scientists *think big* and *believe* their theoretical map covers the whole world (big external validity), even though it still lacks rigorous testing down below (i.e., lacks empirical validity). It took years before Einstein's *theory of relativity* faced its first rigorous observational test. Prior to that it was only mathematically valid—'E = mc²' was merely a mathematically elegant promissory note floating at the top of the PST without supporting, reliable, observational stepping-stones at the bottom of the PST to support the theory's predictions.

Moving from small to large playpens

If other theoretical scientists pick up and extend a fledgling speculation generated and tested in a small playpen, then the theory starts travelling. It starts covering more and more theoretical space, expanding its external validity at the top of the scientific PST. Modern string theory in physics—sometimes touted as a theory of *everything*—is an example. In spite of its mathematical elegance and the theoretical excitement it generates at the top of the PST, it has yet to acquire local, internal, empirical validity at the bottom. This is because in some cases scientists can't make—and may never be able to make—the necessary observations to rigorously test it. But don't knock it. Einstein's theory started out the same way, as did Semmilweis's; there were no microscopes at the time to prove the existence of the germs. In fact, 150 years later experts are still trying to get the rest of us, including doctors, to wash our hands. Some big truths travel *very* slowly . . . they remain outside our limited attention, our perceptual radar.

If a new top-of-the-PST theory is to acquire *observational* or *empirical* validity at the bottom of the PST it has to attract a growing number of hard-nosed researchers willing to put the new theory's predictions to the test through rigorous testing and replications. It has to fight for a space in the minds, grants, journals, and laboratories of busy researchers.

Great scientific theories typically demonstrate an evolution from local, internal validity, at the top of the PST, to expanding external validity. Such theoretical maps gradually expand to cover more and more imaginative territory. While the theory gains status at the top of the PST, researchers start testing and replicating an increasing number of its predictions at the bottom of the PST, thus sprinkling that expanding conceptual map with an increasing number of trusted observational checkpoints.

> In *large playpens* externally valid theories are generally right and specifically wrong. Whereas, in *small playpens* internally valid theories are usually specifically right and generally wrong.

That is, in large playpens the best that externally valid theories can provide is a general lay of land—the big picture—but lacking detail. In small playpens the best that internally valid theories can do is provide specific information about a local territory, but not much beyond it.

Now that you have an overview of internal and external validity it is important to consider some of the threats to each.

Threats to Internal and External Validity

You already know many of the threats to rational thinking at the top of PST (e.g., our bounded rationality) and to reliable observing at the bottom (e.g., the four rogues). We will quickly review known threats and introduce a few new ones.

Threats to internal validity

For this discussion, please refer to Figure 6.2 and keep in mind the idea that different *ideas and observations* deserve different travel permits, some local and some international.

Fig 6.2 ■ MAPPING *THE TRUTH* AT THE TOP AND BOTTOM OF THE PST

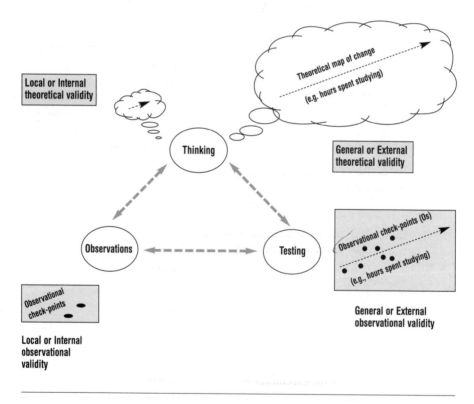

Top-of-the-PST internal validity

Operating at the top of the PST, an idea or premise gains conceptual internal validity to the degree that it is believed locally—that is, to the extent it passes a local believing-is-seeing test. As Simon says: 'no conclusions without premises.' Freud, Einstein, and Skinner started small with personally trusted premises—emotionally anchored beliefs. On that basis, all three challenged the BIG truths of the time. Einstein challenged Newton's universally accepted view of the universe; Freud rattled the status quo by proposing that what we thought and did were under the control of naughty unconscious urges; while Skinner confidently insisted that we throw out our most precious possession—our minds and focus on behaviour.

When operating at the top of a PST, the main threats to internal validity are our personal, emotionally anchored premises and biases, which provide no mental space for alternative ideas or for critical thinking to get a foothold. The main threats consist of our bounded rationality, limited attention span, and habitual rules of thinking (e.g., 'If A, then B'—if female, then emotional; if male, then horny; if squinty-eyed, then dangerous; if ulcer, then too much stomach acid; if bad behaviour, then bad genes.)

A given premise starts gaining up-top, local, internal validity to the degree that it is *believed* by given individuals (citizens or scientists) and their immediate peers operating in a small playpen or laboratory. It gains local validity to the extent that it meets their particular local tests of *good* thinking. For them it must pass the test of time, must continue to ring their emotional chimes, or must pass pet logical or mathematical tests. It must *add up* mentally and emotionally, even though as yet it remains unknown or unsupported by other scientists outside their group, or by any reliable observations at the bottom of the PST.

> When an up-top premise or idea survives all the critically thinking that an individual or small group can afford to put it through, then it acquires internal theoretical validity.

Bottom-of-the-PST internal validity

You already know the major threats to observational validity that occur at the bottom of the PST, namely the four rogues as discussed in Chapters 4 and 5. The first time an observation is demonstrated to be reliable it acquires some local observational validity. Local researchers, such as those in that lab, begin trusting the novel observation (e.g., the Aussie researchers).

To the extent they controlled the four rogues (e.g., by using a control group) it gains internal validity. But will it be able to travel? Will other researchers in different places, different playpens, and different times, be able to repeat the observations or the experiment and get similar results? Will it earn an extended travel permit? Will it acquire external observational validity through rigorous testing?

The following list summarizes the threats to internal validity involving observations at the bottom of the PST:[7]

1. In-the-gap suspects, in addition to your pet suspect.
2. Time-tied suspects—a major threat (e.g., natural healing).
3. On-stage suspects—all the world's a stage.
4. Elastic ruler suspects—believing-is-seeing.
5. Statistical regression—extreme scores drift toward the average.
6. Sampling bias—pretreatment differences between treatment and control groups (e.g., not assigning large numbers of research participants randomly to treatment and control groups).
7. Data loss or mortality—a biasing attrition of research participants, from either the treatment or control group.
8. Interactions—any of the above may combine with the treatment (prime it, magnify it, depress it).
9. Fraud (some scientists lie and diddle their data).
10. Mathematical errors in analyzing and reporting the results.
11. Failure to replicate.

By skillfully managing these eleven items we address questions of internal, or local, validity of our observations. We help assure ourselves and skeptical others that our *specific treatment*, conducted by *specific* researchers, does indeed lead to significant differences between our *specific* samples of subjects or patients, on our *specific* measures, in our *specific* research context or laboratory, at the *specific* time, using that *specific* statistical test.

The eleven threats to internal validity listed above complicate, or confound, our ability to make decisions. Therefore, they are called *confounding variables*. They make it difficult, at times impossible, to decide what leads to what and to determine if any of the changes that occurred in-the-gap between O_1 to O_2 are the result of the researcher's pet treatment (X_t) or due to one or more of these eleven confounding suspects.

Therefore, given the many threats, establishing internal validity in small playpens—top and bottom—is no small accomplishment. Nevertheless, it's not the main goal of scientific research. Instead, the scientific goal is to conduct research in such a way that local thinking and observations are robust enough to travel from our small world out far and wide into the big world, to earn a universal travel permit.

The purpose of using a specific sample is to represent a larger population of subjects or patients. The purpose of using a specific treatment is to represent a class of similar treatments, the purpose of using a specific research context is to

---

[7]In later chapters we'll discuss additional threats to both internal and external validity through the use of inappropriate statistical methods when analyzing research results. These threats arise from researchers unwittingly bending or breaking the rules for tying numbers to objects and events.

represent other research contexts, and so on. Because the goal of science is to establish external validity, and because individual researchers tend to concentrate on internal validity, it's necessary to appreciate the major threats to external validity.

Threats to external validity

Now we shift from considering threats to internal validity to those plaguing external validity both at the top and at the bottom of the PST.

Up-top threats to external validity

When operating at the top of our PST, external validity is compromised when, through lack of time or brain space, we have difficulty critically examining our current big beliefs or big generalizations about human behaviour and when we have difficulty seriously entertaining alternative beliefs, premises, or explanations.

While making it difficult to establish internal validity in small playpens, our bounded rationality makes it doubly difficult to generate external validity in large ones. The same threats operate. Threats to external validity include our lack of brain space, our bounded rationality, our limited attention span, and our individual and institutional emotionally anchored premises, beliefs, and biases. Semmilweis, Freud, Einstein, Skinner, and the Australian researchers all encountered this problem. They all ran smack into the stone wall of human bounded rationality, protecting itself with mind-size solutions, with the biased beliefs and conventional wisdoms (*truths*) of their time.

For both citizens and scientists, changing habits of thinking—changing emotionally anchored world views or paradigms[8] has all the implications of doing a brain transplant. Fortunately, the degree of bias about given issues varies from scientist to scientist. To the degree that a specific idea or premise at the top of the PST can find welcome mats in an increasing number of small playpens around the world is the degree to which our local *premise* gains external theoretical validity.

Down-below threats to external validity

Meanwhile, at the bottom of the PST, researchers are staking out local claims on the currently popular theoretical maps by testing specific, local predictions in their small playpens. Most of their experiments or studies will involve small claims, local predictions aimed at establishing internal validity at one small spot on a large map.

---

[8]More recent research (Kraus, 1995) analyzed 88 attitude-behaviour studies demonstrating that while there is a relationship between what people say or do, it's not a strong relationship. More often than not, what people say on attitude questionnaires will not enable you to reliably predict their behaviour.

In the following diagrams the large dotted circles represent the big picture, the larger population or territory that scientists eventually want to understand (e.g., human attitudes and behaviour in general, not just the attitudes of the small sample included in a particular study). The small solid circles represent the tiny sample of people (local attitudes and behaviour) that you can *afford* to observe and that represent your small, local, staked claim on the large theoretical map.

Four major threats to external validity

Sample restrictions occur when the people studied, or observed, are not a representative sample of the target population, that is, of the people you really want to study.

The degree to which a theory gains external validity at the bottom of the PST and increases its theoretical validity at the top of the PST is dependent on the extent to which lots of different researchers, in different playpens, stake local claims at different points of the theoretical map, and to the extent that their observational stepping-stones fall on the path the theory predicts.

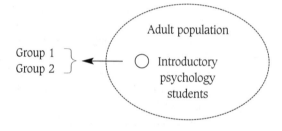

Do you think introductory psychology students fairly 'represent' our adult population in terms of factors such as age, education, values, and work experience? What about our psychiatrist's small sample of depressed patients? How representative were they of depressed patients in general? How representative were the Romanian adopted children of all the institutionalized children in Romanian orphanages?

Measurement restrictions occur when the specific observations you make are not a representative sample of the target behaviour that you really want to study and understand (e.g., predict or change.) Do you think questionnaire or interview responses provide reliable predictions of how people actually behave?

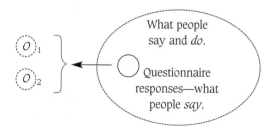

Do you think the interview responses depressed patients gave the psychiatrist provide reliable records or maps of their experience?

Treatment restrictions occur when the specific treatment you apply is not a representative sample of the target treatment that you really want to study and evaluate.

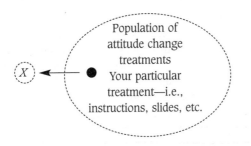

Do you think coloured slides of starving Ethiopians have as much impact on attitudes as television pictures? Or as you actually being there and witnessing the starvation? Do you think the psychiatrist's 'magic pill' was a good representative of drug treatments for depression?

Research context restrictions occur when your specific research context is not a representative sample of target contexts. In other words, the 'hothouse' conditions place restrictions on how far you can generalize to field conditions.

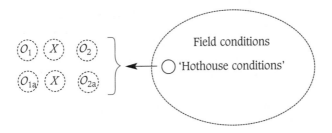

Do you think how you behave in a laboratory experiment on cheating is a fair indicator of how honest you are outside the laboratory? Do you think that the psychiatrist's ward and staff in a university teaching hospital are a fair representative of the kinds of ward and staff in small town general hospitals?

Sampling restrictions

In considering threats to external validity, remember that researchers may not be able, or even willing, to select a representative sample of subjects from their target populations. Instead, for convenience, they end up studying attitude change in undergraduate psychology students a readily accessible captive audience. That isn't a problem; as long as you recognize the resulting sampling restriction and recognize the limitations this restricted sampling places on the generalizations you subsequently make. Ask yourself how similar are the dots inside your research box to the ones you want to talk about outside that small sample box.

Such small, non-random, sampling results obviously cannot be generalized to adult North Americans—you can generalize only to introductory psychology students. Can you even generalize your results from this sample to introductory psychology students? No, only to those who have a chance of getting into your sample—only those on a particular campus. If you had put all the names of all the first-year psychology students on that particular campus into a hat and then drawn your sample at random, you would be able to generalize to the first-year psychology students on a particular campus. But that sort of sampling is rarely done. More often, researchers use students from Professor X's introductory class because it's readily accessible; perhaps he's interested in the same research topic or he's only to happy to give up an hour's lecture time. You can now generalize to all introductory psychology students in Professor X's class. Or can you? You can, if you put all the names in a hat and draw your sample at random, or if you included the whole class in your study. But you may have had to settle for volunteers. So you put the names of the volunteers in a hat and select your experimental and control group samples—now you can generalize to volunteer introductory psychology students in Professor X's first semester psychology class.

Such restrictions result in a drastic shrinkage from the adult American target population. It is even a drastic shrinkage from the general population of introductory psychology students. As a practitioner or a consumer of science, you can see how important it is that you identify the actual population the experimental sample represents—it includes only the people who had an equal chance of getting their names into the hat. If they were a random sample of volunteers from Professor X's psychology class, then you can generalize the results you obtained from the sample of volunteers to the hatful of volunteers from which you drew that sample.

But surely that's being unduly cautious. Why not generalize to Professor X's whole class? In fact, why not generalize to psychology students on that campus or to all introductory psychology students?

Such generalizations are unwarranted for a variety of reasons. Let's say you're conducting a study on attitudes toward different ethnic groups testing volunteer subjects from Professor X's Psychology class. You could obtain atypical responses because: volunteers frequently respond differently from non-volunteers, or because Professor X lectures long and loud on the evils of prejudice and so has probably primed his students, or because this particular university has very high entrance standards and so the students are not intellectually or academically representative of psychology students on many other campuses.

In brief, sampling restrictions usually place strong limitations on the external validity, or generalizability, of social science research. Researchers frequently generate sample-biased research by studying only males, but presenting their findings as a study of the general population. For example, the respected Swiss child psychologist Jean Piaget, who developed a widely accepted theory of cognitive development, did almost all of his research with boys. As you can see, doing ideal science is impossible, so scientists in practice do the best they can with the time and resources available.

Measurement restrictions

Just as the samples you select might under-represent the people you wish to study, so too might the measure or dependent variable you select be a limited measure of the behaviour you wish to study. Just as the limited sample of people you select restrict the generalizations you can make about people, so too the specific measuring scales you select and apply further restricts your generalizations to the behaviour accessible through that measuring scale or that method of observation.

Therefore if we select a particular questionnaire to study attitude change and use only volunteers from Professor X's class, our generalizations are doubly restricted. First, we can only generalize to the hatful of volunteers from which we drew our research sample; second, we can only generalize to changes in *questionnaire* behaviour. We may legitimately claim that, following treatment, our subjects can indeed 'talk' a better game, but we can't claim that they can play a better game—not unless we also employ unobtrusive follow-up observations in our sample of dependent measures.

How far you can generalize from what people say they will do to what they *actually* do is an issue of great concern to a growing number of social scientists. While the details of the debate lie beyond this discussion, consumers of science should be aware that the strong relationship assumed to exist between attitudes and behaviour appears to be much more flimsy than we once supposed (Ajzen & Fishbein, 1980). Wise consumers of science will be cautious about generalizing too far from observations of behaviour obtained by questionnaires, ratings, and interviews because people appear to talk a better game than they play—whether the target behaviour is fishing, bridge, tennis, or tolerance for minorities.

Before considering the validity of tests and questionnaires, recall that measuring scales should be reliable as well as valid. A clock is reliable if it keeps *consistent* time. The clock is valid if it keeps the *correct* time. If your clock is consistently two hours behind the official time, it is nevertheless a reliable clock—it measures time consistently, but it is not a valid measure of the time in your zone. Therefore you can have a measure that is reliable but invalid; however, to be valid, a measure must also be reasonably reliable.

Since so much social science and educational research employs tests and questionnaires, the validity of such instruments deserves special attention and discussion.

Types of test validity

When you complete a test or questionnaire you usually want to know what your score is and what that score means. There are at least four related kinds of larger meanings, or validity, associated with a test: content validity, predictive validity, concurrent validity, and construct validity.

If we critically examine the items on a test—say a mathematical aptitude test—and determine that they include a representative sample of simple, average, and difficult questions drawn from each of the domains of arithmetic, algebra, trigonometry, and calculus, we conclude that the test has reasonable *content validity*—that is, it fairly represents the population of mathematical questions.

Next, the degree to which your score on one test helps estimate your current score on a different test presumably relevant to mathematical aptitude, illustrates that the first test shows *concurrent validity* with the second. For example, if by knowing you scored two standard deviations above the mean in a mathematical ability test, we can then accurately estimate your *current* score on a mechanical aptitude test to be one to two standard derivations above the mean, then we would have evidence of concurrent validity.

Furthermore, if, on the basis of your high score in mathematical ability, we can make a better-than-chance prediction that in two years you will graduate in the top half of your class in electrical engineering, we have evidence of *predictive validity*—predictive validity involves a significant interval of time between the two measurements or observations.

Now we come to *construct validity*, which, while important, is also difficult to explain. A construct is a complex, speculative dimension (for instance, anxiety, intelligence, sociability) that represents a network of relationships. No single test or study defines a construct. In fact, a given test may be related to several constructs—for example, observed performance on a mathematical test may help infer mathematical ability, intelligence level, anxiety level, and vocational interest.

Estimating the validity of a construct—intelligence, for example—is an ongoing research activity that involves exploring the emerging network of concurrent and predictive relationships through which 'intelligence' appears to run.

The value of a construct lies not only in helping you organize and simplify a network of current knowledge but also in enabling you to make valid and surprising predictions.

Since no single measuring instrument can adequately represent a complex construct like intelligence or love, conscientious researchers rely on more than one type of measure. Thus, they are better able to represent the complex of ideas and observations that such constructs imply, and so increase the validity of estimation. Such multi-measure methods are called *triangulation* to indicate that the construct is being viewed from different angles.

The value of a construct lies not only in helping us organize and simplify our current knowledge about a complex topic, but also enable us to test its reach—its range of application. For example, while tests of intelligence enable us to make valid predictions concerning performance on a variety of high school subjects, IQ tests are not so helpful in making predictions about future success out in the rough and tumble of the *real world*.

While the four types of validity listed above apply to tests and question-naires, the underlying principles apply to all forms of measurement (all Os). A measure lacks reliability and scientific reach to the degree that it lacks content, concurrent, predictive, and construct validity.

Treatment restrictions

Just as the specific sample of people and the specific measures you select may both under-represent your target populations, so too may your specific treatment under-represent the general treatments (or treatment construct) you wish to study.

For example, your hypothesis may be that attitudes change toward minority group members following an emotionally involving experience in which the experimental group members witness a majority group member helping a minority group member out of a crisis. It's your belief that the experience of witness-ing the rescue scene should be as realistic as possible. Since such scenes are difficult to engineer, you settle for a movie scene—you restrict your population of treatments to film simulations. In order to get your experimental subjects emo-tionally involved (to identify with the 'hero' and the 'victim'), you want them to watch the whole movie. However, you can only have 50 minutes of Professor X's class time for everything: pretest (O_1), film (treatment X_t), and post-test (O_2). Therefore you have to settle for a film clip—further restricting the size of your treatment population (hatful of possible treatments) to accessible film clips.

As if that weren't bad enough, the sound on the film clip is poor at times, and you're not sure whether it 'broke the mood' of those who were emotionally involved.

So now your specific *treatment* has deteriorated to a poor representative of what you had in mind. Nevertheless, you did get a shift in questionnaire responses in the predicted direction. What kind of generalizations can you make? Well, you can make them only to Professor X's volunteers, tested on that questionnaire, before and after that particular and lousy film clip. The best laid plans. . . .

Next time, you decide you'll prescreen a series of appropriate film clips and draw one at random—then you can generalize to all the treatments (all the film clips) you examined, as well as to all the students who volunteered. If you draw your questionnaire at random from a hatful of appropriate questionnaires, you can generalize to those as well—keeping in mind the tricks that chance plays with small samples (e.g., by chance you might select the worst questionnaire in the hat).

But don't forget, textbooks often present worst-case scenarios to make a point. Whereas, once you get involved in a scientific treasure hunt you take lit-tle bumps along the way in stride—you'll probably become addicted.

Research context restrictions

Just as the specific sample of people, *and* the particular measures, *and* the specific treatment all under-represent your target populations of people, measures, and treatments, so too does the specific experimental context in which you do your study under-represent the population of contexts you would like to study and to which you would like to generalize.

A host of features of the research context come to mind: the room was hot, the study was conducted in the late afternoon, Professor X made a long introduction which not only made you rush your testing, but also hinted at the real purpose of the study increasing the chance of on-stage effects.

Research context restrictions include rogues that can idiosyncratically shape your results so as to reduce the generalizations you can make and, in turn, reduce your external validity. Major rogues to watch for include:

1. in-the-gap suspects combining with your treatment (hot room, poor lighting, noisy);
2. time-tied suspects combining with a treatment (late in day, tired, cranky);
3. pretest or post-test priming (Professor X's hints at the purpose of the study);
4. temporary effects (easy to change your prejudice for half an hour or so); and
5. experimenter effects (experimenter characteristics—e.g., gender or colour affect participant responses).

Oh yes, we forgot to mention the experimenter in the study was black—maybe the subjects changed their 'attitudes' (questionnaire responses) because they sympathized with him, not with the 'victim' in the lousy film clip. What if a white experimenter were to replicate this study? Would it change the results? Some experimental results may be difficult to interpret because the results may be attributable—in whole or in part—to characteristics of the research context, like the ethnicity of the experimenter, and not to the specific manipulation of the independent variable or 'treatment'. Such results are called *demand characteristics* because such cues seem to elicit or 'demand' certain types of biased responses from the research participants.

Surely we're not now going to suggest that to increase generalizability a researcher should describe various and relevant research contexts, including researcher characteristics, place them all in a hat, draw one at random, and then use that one to guide a particular piece of research. Theoretically, it's not a bad idea and this approach is not so practically far-fetched as it seems.

In a curious way the large community of scientists practices what we've been preaching—in a haphazard, semi-random way, different researchers dip into these various hats and draw out this sample of subjects, that dependent variable (O), this independent variable (X), that research context, that set of experimenter characteristics. Taken one study at a time the external validity of any given study remains highly circumscribed and drastically restricted. But taken together the many researchers add up to . . . to what? To just one hat dipper after another? No, they create a host of loosely co-ordinated explorers driven by curiosity and probing accessible nooks and crannies of a multi-layered reality.

Loosely co-ordinated explorers? What forces co-ordinate them? The scientific culture, the language and logic of science, the currently popular dependent and independent variables all help co-ordinate them. For example, psychologists in various countries draw samples of introductory psychology students from a subject pool hat and subject them to an array of measures—Os—drawn from dependent variable hats, before and after subjecting them to an array of treatments—Xs—drawn from independent variable hats, conducting their studies in an array of classrooms and laboratories drawn from the research context hat.

But couldn't all this be done in a more coordinated manner? Yes, but to the extent that you co-ordinate, you also control the size and content of the hats—you place restrictions on the explorations of multi-layered nature. You would not only control the kinds of questions that get asked but to a certain extent the kinds of answers that get given. You run the risk of enforcing politically correct research (as drug companies and governments are accused of attempting to do) just because they provide the money.

The truly creative scientist is one who draws from a larger or different hat, who draws out a powerful new construct, or who builds a new dependent or independent variable. Creative scientists frequently work on the fringes of their discipline—too much co-ordination shrinks their workspace, crowds them out of the game. Too much co-ordination may eliminate some sources of error but also discourages precious creativity.

Nevertheless, in a flexible system one creative person or promising idea can provide an opportunity for semi-co-ordinated explorations by many others. Co-ordinated or programmatic research leads to a systematic investigation of a given population (for instance, autistic children) using a sample of measures representing a given dependent variable (social interaction) or a sample of treatments representing a given independent variable (reinforcement) within a sample of research contexts (schools, hospitals, and private homes.)

Such studies represent one small segment of a much larger series of studies focusing on *reinforcement* as an important independent variable—as *the* most important independent variable, according to B.F. Skinner. Thus an independent variable can become the focus for coordinating the research of thousands of researchers. These researchers draw samples from many population hats, draw sample measures from many dependent variable hats, draw a variety of treatments from many reinforcement hats, and conduct their studies in a variety of research contexts. Surely then we now have a reasonable example of external validity as applied to reinforcement. Yes, this is so, except the follow-up time of many conditioning studies on humans has been nonexistent or brief. Therefore, we are restricted in the generalizations we can make concerning the durability of many of the changes brought about through selective reinforcement—many of the changes lasting no longer than a New Year's resolution? Time will tell!

Notice that external validity issues are never settled; external validity refers to the expanding reach of research in the exploration of multi-layered shifting nature. External validity, like the future, always lies around the corner.

Up at the top of the PST, ways of thinking (theories, beliefs, biases) are seen as locally or globally valid not necessarily based on how well they're observationally anchored at the bottom of the PST, but rather on how well they fit in with the network of emotionally anchored premises and biases ruling the theoretical roost and on how much we rely upon them in making important decisions about the unknown, and unknowable.

Science survives and thrives because of its adversarial system. Science, somehow, accommodates enough contrary, deviant thinkers willing to challenge entrenched premises. Even in the face of repeated rejection, these thinkers confidently (arrogantly?) promote theoretical heresies and, in doing so, help ensure that science remains our most trusted news service.

Kuhn (1970) and Fuller (2003) saw researchers as busily sprinkling observational checkpoints on a currently popular theoretical map or *paradigm*.[9] Periodically, and gradually, a paradigm shift would occur, such as those stimulated by creative deviants (e.g., Freud, Einstein, and Skinner) drawing new theoretical maps. Then, as the result of a growing number of theoretical inconsistencies and/or observational deviations, some creative, young researchers will shift their focus to the theoretical margins, stake out new small claims, and start sprinkling a revised or alternative theoretical map with local (hopefully internally valid) observations.

As illustrated in Figure 6.3, *internal validity* refers to small playpens, to local truths and observations involving small samples in local contexts over a short time (e.g., the early days of the Aussie research on ulcers). Whereas, establishing *external validity*—always a work in progress—involves conceptually mapping and observing increasingly large space–time frames, using larger representative or random samples, drawn from different places, repeatedly tested in different research contexts (e.g., the gradual spread of the Aussie theory and supporting observations around the world).

Notice we use a large dotted rectangle at the outer edges of Figure 6.3 to indicate that there is no boundary for external validity—that large space–time frame is infinite both conceptually at top of the PST and observationally at the bottom. This is so not only because questions of external validity include currently available but yet to be seriously considered hypothesis or theories, and currently available but yet to be tested samples, but also include questions

---

[9]A paradigm is a general map or widely accepted theory covering a large playpen. It strongly influences the thinking and research of many scientists staking out different claims both at the top and bottom of the PST (e.g., behaviourism).

Fig 6.3 ■ VALIDITY

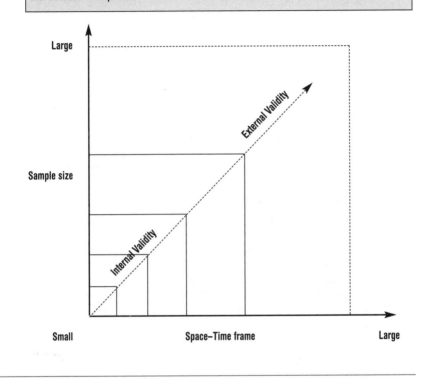

Internal Validity (small playpens): Small sample of premises (top of PST) or observations (bottom), with limited travel permits.

External Validity (large playpens): Large sample of premises (top of PST), or observations (bottom), with extended travel permits.

concerning the validity of current truths in the unknown future, questions concerning the expiry dates of their scientific travel permit.

Gradually researchers produce more and more observational stepping-stones, some falling on the predicted path generated by the currently popular theoretical map. While others lie off the path, a little or a lot. Believers in the theory publicize the positive evidence while wrestling with the negative. Adversaries publicize the negative evidence while wrestling with the positive. And the cycle continues, revising, cutting, fitting, and sometimes even dumping one previously trusted theory while gradually constructing and testing its replacement. Observing all molecules or all people, in all places, at all times, is obviously impossible. True external validity forever remains over the moving horizon.

The best we can do is sprinkle increasingly large space–time frames with increasing numbers of internally valid, conceptual and observational, checkpoints. Researchers establish such markers by focusing on restricted samples of hypotheses and people in circumscribed space–time contexts. Empirically we hope that those small observational stepping-stones fall along the paths in the space–time frame predicted by the currently trusted theory.

In brief, trying to establish the external validity of a general theory (universal validity) is like chasing shadows. True believers see it here, they see it there but can't quite follow it everywhere

SUMMARY

We discussed two types of validity, top-of-the-PST *beliefs*, and bottom-of-the-PST *observations*. We also discussed *internal validity*, covering small speculative and small observational playpens, and *external validity*, aiming to cover larger and larger speculative and observational spaces.

Our bounded rationality, narrow attention span, and limited access to relevant and timely information restrict our ability to establish internal and particularly external validity.

In addition to our bounded rationality and related emotionally anchored premises that limit what we can think and see, we listed various threats to internal validity, once again highlighting the tricks of the four rogues. The smaller the playpen—the given conceptual or observational space—the simpler it is to explore and control. But the resulting certainty comes at a high price. Our certain knowledge is confined to a small speculative space, at the top of our PST, or a small observational space at the bottom. In brief, in attempting to establish internal validity (small playpen truths) individual scientists sacrifice external validity (big playpen truths).

But we don't provide scientists with extra training, time, and resources to find tiny truths. We want big trusted truths about the past, present, and future. Where did we come from? What's with cancer? When can scientists provide me with a trusted map of my future in which I end up healthy, wealthy, and wise? And while they're at it, can they also provide guaranteed defenses against hemorrhoids, pandemics, global warming, terrorism, and slow dreadful deaths?

Yes, we want our scientists to generate external validity—grand truths that provide trusted maps into the ever-expanding future. Threats to the Nirvana of *external validity* restrict the generalizations scientists can make—restrictions imposed by small biased samples of premises and people, measuring tools (Os), treatments (Xs), and research contexts.

But things aren't as bad as they might seem. While individual researchers typically focus on establishing internal validity, the loosely co-ordinated and adversarial community of scientists—spread haphazardly across the world—explore pet hypotheses at the top of their PSTs and stake out small empirical claims at the bottom. While the external validity of a particular research study by a particular scientist will be restricted, the large community of researchers investigating a given topic helps extend its validity:

1. by sampling from a variety of populations, thereby extending sampling validity;
2. by employing different variations of popular dependent variables (Os) thereby extending measurement validity;
3. by experimenting with different versions and amounts of popular independent variables (Xs), thereby extending treatment validity;
4. by conducting their studies in a variety of research settings, thereby extending the context validity; and finally,
5. by spending time at the top of their PSTs, and taking a wide angle view of these haphazard theoretical and observational local playpens, brilliant theorists, like Einstein and Simon, detect big picture patterns, and discover/construct external validity with an extended travel permit. This provides large treasure maps that keep future generations of researchers exploring, digging, and debating.

Summarizing, external validity is enhanced through the haphazard, semi-random behaviour of a set of loosely co-ordinated independent researchers exploring various aspects of a research question using different subjects, measures, and research contexts

The expanding production of individual research studies, and the progressive reduction in the validity of some theories, and the extension of others, consumes the scientific enterprise in its dedicated and compulsive exploration of our expanding multi-layered experience. In the next three chapters we will discuss methods of extending your observations and speculations beyond the space–time constraints many small playpen research contexts impose.

student's notebook

I'm in TROUBLE! I made the mistake of asking Dr Frund for advice about 'Project Derek', you know, about trying to shape his listening behaviour by using Skinner's conditioning techniques. Well, Dr Frund blew her top! You would have thought I was the devil trying to con innocent children into robbing little old ladies. Anyway, why was she so mad when the project wasn't even working? I wasn't controlling his behaviour at all . . . it's all over the board.

I think the main reason Dr Frund got her knickers in a knot was that she felt partially responsible. She was the one who introduced me to behaviorism, to Skinner's conditioning stuff, and to shaping my own studying behaviour. I guess she felt guilty for failing to warn me not to play around with other people's brains or behaviour. Besides, Derek manipulates me all the time—he just doesn't use science.

Dr Frund read me the ethics riot act. Apparently it's one thing to use psychological science to change your own mind or behaviour, but unless you get permission from the *person you're trying to change using psycho-technology you aren't supposed to try to change them. And you can't get away with just his or her naïve permission—you have to get informed consent. The same kind of permission a surgeon is supposed to obtain before cutting anything off. They're supposed to level with you: 'If I cut this bit off your heart, it might not like it and might stop doing its job.'*

This seems a bit over the top to me. You would think Skinner's stuff was powerful enough to let you rule the world, judging from Dr Frund's reaction. All it did was get Derek going around in circles.

I guess Dr Frund saw that I wasn't taking her too seriously. Then she came down real hard. She reeled off examples of how therapists had lost their licenses to practice, and even gone to jail, for sneakily leading patients astray with psychological tricks. She even threatened me and said that if I ever did anything like this again she'd drop me 'like a hot tamale'. She would even consider bringing an ethics complaint against me and possibly have me kicked out of the program. Wow!

So, I finally understood that this was serious. I promised to stop 'Project Derek' immediately. Dr Frund said that wasn't enough, though. I had to tell Derek the complete truth about what I'd been doing.

I met him at the pub, and I even bought the drinks. After a couple of false starts I finally told him everything, including Dr Frund's flaying me alive. He didn't say anything. He looked down and kind of covered his forehead with his hand and started to tremble. He was starting to cry! I'd never ever seen him cry. I leaned forward, put my hand on his shoulder.

Wait a minute! He wasn't crying. He was giggling! Now it was his turn to confess. He admitted that, at first, he was confused but then he figured out what I was up to—he had studied Skinner's stuff, too. So he had purposely shifted into different behaviours to confuse me, to see what I would do when I didn't know whether I was going to be rewarded, ignored, or punished.

He even took a cartoon out of his wallet showing two rats in a maze. One rat says to the other: 'Look how I've trained white coat to give me a food pellet merely by turning right or left when I run the maze.' Derek boasted: 'Just as the rat was conditioning the researcher in the cartoon, I conditioned you!'

Then, of course, I got mad. He teased me for not liking a dose of my own medicine, and told me to 'grow up'. I got up to leave. Then I started to giggle! Finally, after we apologized, we talked about each other's current class projects, both of which are due next Friday. I told him about internal and external validity, and the threats to each. He listened. He took notes. He never does that. Why would he start now?

Psychological territory versus sociological territory

It turns out he's doing a paper on the sociology of science and his courses don't cover the same kind of stuff we do. For example, they don't cover much of what goes on at the bottom right corner of the PST—stuff like the four rogues and control groups. They focus most of their attention at the top. But they think more about large groups and their theoretical biases instead of focusing on emotionally anchored premises, and the peer pressure on scientists to conform to the popular research theories and methods of the day. He wanted my references about the Australian ulcer researchers who couldn't break through the 'groupthink' operating at the top of the North American medical and research establishment but later won the Nobel Prize.

One of his professors said that psychologists and sociologists had an unwritten agreement to stay out of each other's territories. Psychologists focus on individuals and tiny groups whereas sociologists focus on large groups and institutions. We tend to ignore each other's truths.

For example, sociologists believe that most knowledge is culturally determined, that is, determined by institutional and cultural beliefs and biases at the top of the big PST. So, for him, what happens at the bottom wasn't considered to be important. Now he understands that there are bottom-up influences as well.

Groupthink breaks down

Then, in return for my help, Derek gave me some good stuff about how beliefs and biases operating at the top of the PST can be a bit elastic. Just like with teens, pressure from peers to toe the party line (e.g., dress and language codes) is not 100 per cent effective. There are those at the centre of any group who follow the current trends slavishly, there are some who make slight modifications, and there are also a few mavericks who make radical changes, or do their own thing; they might even start a whole new fad.

According to Derek, the same things happen in science. And sociologists still haven't figured out when a 'groupthink' trend will break down or which currently out-of-the-box marginal premise will move inside and take over. We can't predict which of the deviants— mild or far out—will provide the seed from which the next trend, theory, or cult will spring.

That's why sociologists and anthropologists are observing scientists. They study them as if lab scientists were primitive tribes. The sociologists report on their rituals, customs, superstitions, and power structures (e.g., when there's doubt about an in-the-gap suspect, conflicting observations, or research results, who in the scientific pecking order decides which scientist gets believed and which data gets published?).

These sociological snoops hang out in scientific laboratories. They study how scientists debate and reach decisions, how they make sense of the world when dealing with fuzzy and conflicting observations. There they go again—deviant billiard balls with brains.

Derek says that when groupthink wins—when the hit parade theoretical map wins—the deviant dots are explained away, poured down the sink, swept under the scientific carpet. Of course, that view fits in with Simon's bounded rationality stuff—keeps it mentally affordable, keeps it in line.

But not always. Just as in teen groups, there are scientific mavericks that deviate, some a little and some a lot—dangerous thinking or scientific breakthrough?

As I've learned in this course so far, there seems to be no sure-fire way of finding the whole truth or of even determining that internal validity isn't error free. And it seems as though external validity is never completely established. It always involves chasing shadows. Therefore, scientists have to negotiate and create the truth to some degree—like the authors said in this chapter, whether we like it or not every truth has a travel permit with an expiry date, we just don't know ahead of time when that is.

Derek and I are going to exchange notes and references. His stuff on scientific peer pressure, power structures, and changes in scientific groupthink should help me ace this assignment, particularly by providing examples of what goes on at the top of the PST in trying to establish external validity.

News stories

Two news stories, both about the conflict between evolution and intelligent design, caught my attention while we were studying this chapter of *The Science Game*.

Teaching evolution and intelligent design in our schools

The media is bursting out all over with arguments about whether the biblical account of the origins of life, and a pre-scientific interpretation of same (intelligent design), should be taught in the schools, even in science classes.

Derek and I belong to a mixed bag of students who meet regularly at the pub—it's called The Brew and Bull Club. It started with five members of Derek's touch football team all majoring in different subjects: sociology, biology, math, etc., and then it grew. With all these experts, the B&B club solves all the world's problems. Here's my take on their take on the debate about evolution versus intelligent design.

Some religious citizens and school boards propose that intelligent design should be presented as an alterative to Darwin's theory of evolution—that modern life evolved over millions of years of random (trial and error) selections of the fittest, with us 'fitter' than the apes.

In one of his lectures, Professor Creek said it should be called the 'survival of the fittingest' to describe species that happen to fit a given environment at that time. If there were a nuclear war, the only survivors that would be most fitting in that environment would probably be cockroaches. They would be 'fitter' than us—they would be the 'fittingest' for that particular environment.

Intelligent design supporters argue that life is so complex that it's highly unlikely that it could have evolved through random combinations of molecules. It needed a helping hand, the hand of an intelligent designer (e.g., God).

A Gallup poll in 2004 reported[10] that 45 per cent of Americans believe that God created human beings, essentially as we are now, within the last 10,000

---

[10] J. Wilgren, 'Seeing Creation and Evolution in the Grand Canyon', *New York Times*, 6 October 2005. Available at http://select.nytimes.com/search/restricted/article?res=F30713FC35540C758CDDA90994DD404482.

years. In contrast, evolutionary theory claims that two legged human-like creatures appeared about 4 million years ago, and ancestors with our brain size maybe 200,000 years ago, plus or minus a few thousand years.

A second Gallup poll found that only about 5 per cent of scientists, in general, and only 1 per cent of earth and life scientists bought the young earth premise as described in the Bible.

It looks like the theory of evolution has a valid passport to travel pretty well everywhere in the sciences, but is stopped at the border of beliefs by almost half of the US population—there's no universal welcome mat in the United States for Darwin or his theory.

Most scientists find this public rejection incomprehensible. Perhaps they should pay more attention to one of their own, a Nobel Prize winner: Herbert Simon and his mantra, 'No conclusions without premises.' The majority of the American public does not share the Darwinian premise, for whatever reasons (ignorance, religious beliefs, etc.). And of course, according to Simon, for complex puzzles, the top down rule of believing-is-seeing wins, simple as that. Most scientists accept the external validity of evolutionary theory and evidence. Most of the public apparently does not.

Up-top truth strong, down-bottom truth so-so

According to the B&B club members, both truths—evolution and intelligent design—are emotionally anchored at the top of the PST and are weak at the bottom. The intelligent design promoters can't produce photos of God, and the evolutionists face big gaps in the fossil record. One anthropologist[11] estimates that you could dump all the human fossil bones found so far into the back of a pickup truck.

Neither of the opposing truths has established absolute external observational validity. However, the evolutionists have accumulated more local, internal observational validity in the form of a chain of ancient fossils sprinkled along a very long historical timeline. That truck full of hominid bones rates higher scientifically than the shroud of Turin, or the slivers of wood alleged to be from the cross.

So according to the B&B experts, lacking a high density of observational stepping-stones down below, the real debate must occur at the top of the PST—a debate about anchored premises (à la Simon), while each side cherry-picks selective evidence to support their own arguments.

---

[11]See B. Bryson's *A Short History of Nearly Everything* (2004), referring to Ian Tattersall, curator of anthropology at the American Museum of Natural History in New York.

How do the anchored premises differ? The first big difference is that one side accepts supernatural explanations and the other demands *natural* explanations. Sound familiar? It's been going on for thousands of years. Secondly, both groups stand on an emotionally anchored premise as the original source of the truth—both sides have a book—the Bible versus Darwin's *Origin of Species*. So even though neither side can make an unassailable case for observational validity (internal or external) at the bottom of the PST, both sides claim victory at the top—even though neither truth has a travel permit accepted by the opposition.

How much can chance accomplish?

The intelligent designers don't buy that human life evolved by chance from a random shaking of molecules—humans are too complex for that. It's too improbable. Four aces in a poker hand once in a while, that's believable. But, an Elvis Presley, a Billy Graham, an Einstein, and a Wayne Gretzky all popping up by shaking molecules—no way.

To be fair, there are religious laypeople and religious scientists who, by stretching their bounded rationality at the top of their PSTs, conclude that evolution and intelligent design can work together. For instance, some intelligent designers accept evolutionary theory as helping explain earthly things, but rely on religion to help explain questions beyond the reach of science. Similarly some scientists see religion and science as managing different territories or human experiences, and as 'responsible for mapping different space–time frames'.

Our resident B&B mathematician thinks that incomplete bits and pieces of the past and present flow through our brain and then our brain automatically 'calculates' the future—usually in straight lines. That's what brains do. To mathematicians, our brains are calculators. To chemists, they're bone bowls full of chemical soup.

The B&B philosopher, not to be outdone, pronounced that regardless of its fancy computations, science has nothing to say for sure about the future—it only offers guesses and probabilities. In contrast, religion is not committed to concrete observations and instead promises certainty—'believe and thou wilt see.'

As I see it, this all boils down to an after-the-fact argument where the number of possible suspects covers a period of 6,000 years in one case (the Bible and intelligent designers) and billions of years (evolutionists).

If you believe in evolution, in your calmer moments you have to admit that the number of reliable observations (bottom of the PST) scattered over your staked-out space–time territory (billions of years) is pretty sparse and incomplete (the fossil record).

And if you're an intelligent designer, in your calmer moments you have to admit that the reliable, independent observations of God are noticeable by their absence. Even organized religions are nervous about single sightings.

So it looks to my bounded rationality that both sides are relying very heavily on emotionally anchored premises, and interestingly enough, increasingly on mathematical arguments, specifically probability theory.

Both Derek and I were brought up on evolutionary theory so that premise seems valid to us. My parents don't seem to be concerned with either theory. On the other hand, Derek's parents have changed positions over the last few years when they became born-again Christians. They now feel strongly that children should be exposed to both evolution and intelligent design at school, but don't believe in teaching the strict Bible view.

The members of the B&B group are split down the middle. Half of them believe that science and religion cover different territories while half felt there was only one acceptable option—science, in general, and evolution, in particular—particularly now with DNA evidence available to track our ancestries.

Note

How similar are the dots and connections inside the box you study to those outside that you want to talk about? Visit the student website at http://www.oup.com/ca/he/companion/agnewpyke.

REVIEW TRUE OR FALSE QUIZ

T F	1. The conclusion of the Australian researchers that ulcers were caused by particular bacteria received instant recognition and endorsement from the medical community.
T F	2. We protect our bounded rationality and pet decision rules by bracketing exceptions out of awareness.
T F	3. Acquiring external validity is always a work in progress.
T F	4. The correspondence model of truth refers to how well the 'truth' fits with what we believe to be true.
T F	5. Validity judgments apply only to the seeing-is-believing, or observational, part of science.
T F	6. A theory that can be stated mathematically is automatically empirically valid.
T F	7. Scientific theories typically demonstrate an evolution from local, internal validity to expanding external validity.
T F	8. The main threats to internal and external conceptual validity are our personal, emotionally anchored, premises and biases.

T F	9.	Threats to internal observational validity include the operation of the four rogues, fraud, and mathematical errors in analyzing the results.
T F	10.	Statistical regression refers to a biased attrition of research participants.
T F	11.	Local research results acquire external validity to the extent that local samples, treatments, measures, and contexts are representative.
T F	12.	Results of studies employing introductory psychology students from Yale as research participants may not be generalized to adult Americans but may be generalized to all introductory psychology students.
T F	13.	What people say they will do in a given situation is a very good indicator of how they will actually behave in that situation; hence, it is quite legitimate to generalize from questionnaire and interview responses to real behaviour.
T F	14.	A clock is valid if it keeps the correct time and it is reliable if it keeps consistent time.
T F	15.	It is possible for a measure to be unreliable but valid.
T F	16.	The content validity of a test refers to the extent to which it represents the population of questions relevant to the factor the test is designed to measure.
T F	17.	Predictive validity means that two different scorers marking the same test at different times produce the same result.
T F	18.	Multi-measure methods are called triangulation to indicate that the construct is being viewed from different angles.
T F	19.	The demand characteristics of an experiment channel or limit the potential range of responses.
T F	20.	External validity is enhanced through the haphazard, semi-random behaviour of a set of loosely co-ordinated independent researchers exploring various aspects of a research question using different subjects, measures, and research contexts.
T F	21.	The eleven threats to internal validity are called operational variables.
T F	22.	Dr Frund was concerned about Diana's project on Derek on ethical grounds.
T F	23.	In contrast to psychologists, sociologists focus on individuals and small groups.
T F	24.	The debate between intelligent design and Darwinian theory primarily involves activity at the top of the PST.

7

Developmental and Longitudinal Studies

Chapter Goal

- To explore how we study change in behaviour over time.

The after-the-fact, before-and-after, and control-group designs typically base their conclusions on one or two snapshots of behaviour (Os). In this chapter we consider longitudinal methods that base their conclusions on several observations (Os) covering an extended period. You can think of them as time-lapse maps that help capture the internally and externally valid rhythms of behaviour. Such methods extend the temporal reach of science.

Introduction

One way to extend the reach of science—its external validity—is to look for patterns of behaviour over extended periods of time. Such patterns enable us to generalize our findings—to extend the expiry dates on the travel permits of our *truths*. Notice, as we identify such patterns we not only increase our current understanding but also our ability to predict the future.

For instance, we need longitudinal studies to be able to predict, with confidence, the temporal validity of our treatments (will they last?). We need them to predict the path into the future that our observational stepping-stones will follow, to determine whether our new treatment will not only reduce the length and severity of a particular depressive episode but also reduce the likelihood of further attacks.

In this chapter we explore *time-lapse* research methods that enable us to draw temporal maps, to take repeated snapshots over time to capture the rhythms of behaviour. Things change, babies grow up and then grow old; some memories fade while some keep coming back, people fall in and out of love; governments and corporations rise and fall.

From both happy and bitter experiences, everyone knows that change happens—fast and slow—and often in unpredictable directions. In this chapter we examine the various methods researchers use to map the direction and rate of change.

Maps of Change

You can draw short and long maps of change. The ones you draw in your imagination at the top of your PST are usually smooth and can be as long as you like: 'I *plan* to lose three pounds a month for the next year.' Or consider the marriage map: 'I intend to love and cherish my husband as long as we both shall live.' Now there's an off-the-top of your PST map into the future. One that gets rigorously tested down the at bottom . . . and fails over 50 per cent of the time!

But unlike the long, smooth maps of change that you so easily whip off at the top (plans, hopes, theories), the ones you observe at the bottom are relatively short and zigzagging. Making and mapping a series of reliable observations at the bottom of the triangle takes longer—you have to wait for the dots to make their appearance as the future unfolds. Furthermore, they're not as well behaved as mental maps. That's why rigorously explored observational maps rarely travel in a nice straight line like mind maps (premises, hopes, hunches, hypotheses, theories, and mathematical formula).

Up-top maps are highly compelling, not only because they're easy to imagine or draw but because they're often so optimistic and they go on forever. Your mind is a time machine, gliding over the past and soaring over the present into the future.

In contrast, observational maps anchor us in the present, provide only scattered fragments of the past (e.g., the fossil record, photo albums, love letters) and neither you nor I can actually see beyond our local horizons. The future always remains out of sight. At best, maps of the future are promissory notes.

Note that if, at the top of her or his PST, someone is unable to draw trusted mental maps of the future (emotionally anchored maps they believe to be externally valid) then that person—citizen or scientist—is *future deprived*. Their *truths* have no travel permits; their little truths stay anchored depressingly close to home.

> Mental maps are all about *believing-is-seeing*, and beliefs have universal passports. Observational maps are about *seeing-is-believing*, and so only possess local travel permits.

Theories play the same role in science as hopes and dreams play in everyday life. That's why science depends so much on theories—without them there's no future. And everyone needs a future. In that sense, trusted theories are the most practical thing in the world.

Fortunately, most of us harbour trusted mental maps and blithely travel with confidence into the observationally uncertain future. Such maps are usually both optimistic and naïve. In our mind's eye we see the things that we want (e.g., health, friendship, safety, etc.) stretching ahead of us in a nice straight line, upward and onward. In our imagination, we see the things we don't like (e.g., indigestion, hives, debt, a cranky boss, etc.) conveniently travelling rapidly down a sloping line and, like most other dangerous ways of thinking, conveniently disappearing with the trash.

Upward and onward

Now, let's cycle up to the top of the PST and, as shown in the first box of Figure 7.1, draw one of those simple and optimistic mental maps of change that head for the stars.

Fig 7.1 ■ MAPS OF CHANGE

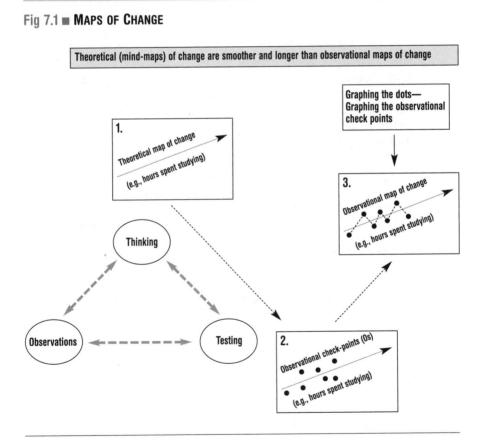

For instance, the first map (#1) displays the steadily increasing time you *plan* to spend studying, or perhaps the rate you *plan* to enrich your savings account—sort of a New Year's Resolution map . . . upward and onward.

To start *testing* the theoretical map we cycle down to the bottom right corner of the PST, as seen in the second map (#2). As your behaviour unfolds over the first week we see seven dots, seven observational checkpoints (Os).[1] Notice, how they zigzag—dots with brains rarely follow a straight line. It's often hard to determine where the dots are heading. With only those seven spaced-out dots to work with, we're uncertain whether they're following our hopes, our theoretical map, or not.

To help decide, we take the seven observations back up top and do some critical thinking. We start by connecting them into a graph (#3). However, the observations are so variable, and cover such a short section of the time-line, that it's hard to be sure where they're heading—it's not a safe bet. Furthermore, it would really shake our confidence if the next dot fell far below the line. Scientists doing longitudinal research, studying behaviour as it unfolds over extended periods (e.g., growth, language skills, habit change, etc.) need patience and tenacity. How do they manage to stay the course?

They persist when they have confidence in their premise, in their theoretical map, in its top-of-the-PST external validity. As the observational dots slowly emerge, any dot within shouting distance of their theoretical map is cheered. Early into the project, longitudinal researchers must play a believing-is-seeing game. They must rely on an emotionally anchored premise or theory to carry them confidently into the future—the initial zigzagging dots rarely do. To do much critical thinking in the early stages of a longitudinal study is a dangerous way of thinking.

Skeptics can't afford to conduct longitudinal studies.

When the slowly emerging observational stepping-stones keep following the theoretical map—when the dots behave—it's only then that longitudinal researchers enjoy a scientific high!

Rates and level of change

When you draw maps of change, be sure to note that they tend to differ in at least two respects: the rate of change and the level of change.

Individuals or organizations frequently differ in how slowly or rapidly they change, and how rapidly they reach a certain state or level of performance (see Figure 7.2).

---

[1] When we refer to observations (Os), we're referring to activity at either the left or right corner at the bottom of the PST. Observations are transformed into memories or concepts, (into abstract, dotted circles) at the top of the PST. They are empirically free, they can travel in imaginary space, and they have no necessary ties or obligations to the bottom of the PST, *to reality*. Concepts are only constrained by the limits of your imagination, by acquired cultural rules and rituals (e.g., biases, images, dreams, logics, and mathematics), and by Minsky-ian conceptual and emotional danger signs that you're heading into dangerous conceptual space.

Fig 7.2 ■ RATES OF CHANGE

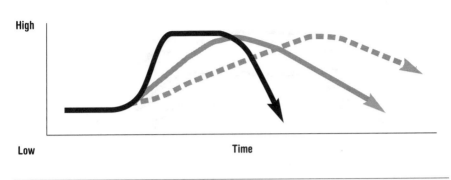

All children learn a variety of skills—toilet training, walking, talking—but at different rates of acquisition. Similarly, adults lose their capacities at different rates of decline—some losing their memory, eyesight, or co-ordination much faster than others. Moreover, there can also be regular cycles of change in hormonal secretions, in alertness, in mood, in market activity, and so on. Organizations also differ in the rate that they achieve certain organizational states: the rate at which they reach a certain size, degree of specialization, rate of return on investment, or market penetration.

Important developmental and longitudinal research questions focus on such rates of growth and decline and on possible factors that may hasten or retard them—genetic, nutritional, maturational, technological, political, or market factors.

Upper limits of change

Not only do individuals and organizations differ in their rates of change on selected measures but they differ also in the levels they reach (see Figure7.3).

For example, children differ not only in the rate of growth, but also in the maximum height they reach. Why is that? What combination of genetic, nutritional, and maturational factors help establish such *ceiling* effects? We observe such apparent ceilings, or limits, in individual measures of intelligence and in organizational measures such as span of control—the number of people or operations that an executive can manage.

Thus we see change taking many routes: the common up-and-down route can vary in terms of rate of growth or decline, the ceiling—or limits—it reaches, and the duration of such limits or plateaus.

Now that we have seen how change may take various routes at variable rates to different levels, we need to examine how we can stake out and at least partially map the zigzag courses of change. We rely mainly on three research

Fig 7.3 ■ LEVELS OF CHANGE

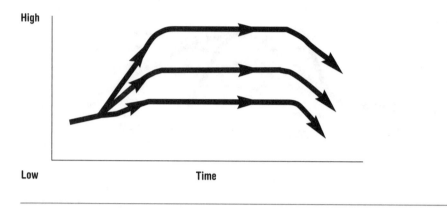

Methods of Mapping Change

Cross-sectional studies

strategies to provide observational checkpoints: cross-sectional studies, retrospective (after-the-fact) studies, and longitudinal studies.

This affordable method provides most of the observational checkpoints in developmental psychology—with this method we map, from birth to death, the growth rates, ceiling effects, and declines in physical and psychological characteristics.

It's called *cross-sectional* because researchers take samples of people of different ages at a given time (e.g., April 2006) and measure given characteristics (Os), such as height, weight, IQ, or income. Then they compute the averages of each age group and draw a map of change based on those different samples of people (see Figure 7.4).

The cross-sectional method allows you to map such curves without taking 70 or 80 years to follow *one* large sample from birth to death. It is a relatively quick method to get average trends—that is its advantage. For curves that are strongly determined by age alone, the method is adequate.

Where age is only one of several strong factors influencing the rate of change, the cross-sectional method can be misleading. If some samples used to represent the height of a certain age group have either benefited from or been hampered by other strong factors, then that sample is not typical and so should not be compared with other points on the curve.

For example, it is assumed that height, which reaches its ceiling, or limit, in early adulthood, starts to decline when people reach their fifties or sixties, but there is some evidence that this 'decline' may be an artifact of cross-sectional

Fig 7.4 ■ CROSS-SECTIONAL RESEARCH

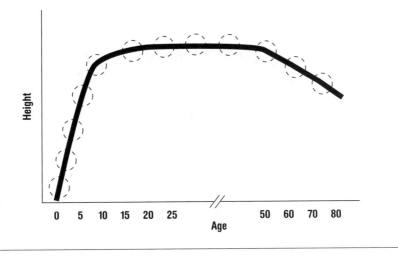

data because our current 20-year-olds are taller than their fathers and grand-fathers. Therefore, it may not be that fathers are shrinking; rather their sons, who are large, produce sons who are even larger, thus providing an inappropri-ately taller baseline against which the fathers are compared.

Briefly, the cross-sectional method provides an average curve for age-related characteristics, but given points on the curve may be pushed up or down by other strong factors not related to age, for example, nutrition. Such atypical points on the curve, supposedly comparable to all other points, are not actually comparable and so distort the age curve. Therefore, when using the cross-sec-tional method, you must be cautious and must repeatedly ask yourself the ques-tion: 'In what other important ways, besides age, do my samples differ?' It is a safe bet the samples do differ in various ways, and so, rather than using a fine line curve you would do well to at least visualize a curve surrounded by a region of uncertainty (see Figure 7.5)

Visualizing it in this way is clear acknowledgement that cross-sectional curves represent crude estimates that may deviate significantly from a curve that is based on following and measuring the *same* individual through time (longitu-dinal method). Maps of change based on cross-sectional studies should be updated frequently and compared with earlier cross-sectional curves for evidence of atypical bulges or dips so that particular points of uncertainty are highlighted and used with caution.

The obvious way to increase the comparability of points on the curve is to avoid cross-sectional studies, to go to longitudinal investigations where you study the same people over time rather than a cross-section of people at the

Fig 7.5 ■ UNCERTAINTY BAND

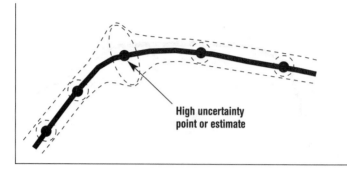

High uncertainty
point or estimate

same time. Alternatively, we can obtain cheap and crude estimates using retro-spective studies.

Retrospective studies

Rather than trying to determine whether 60- or 70-year-olds are shrinking by comparing them with 20-year-olds (cross-sectional studies), we can compare their current height with a *recalled* height at age 20 or in early adulthood. This solves one problem—you are now comparing a person against himself or herself rather than against a 20-year-old stand-in. However, you run smack into another problem—namely, the unreliability of recalled data—the problem of the fallibility of human memory (elastic ruler).

When recalled data are compared with data recorded at the time of the event, we find ample evidence of distortions in memory, not just random distor-tions, but also on-stage, rose-coloured distortions.

For example, mothers are unreliable sources of recalled information con-cerning the length of labour, their health during pregnancy, or their baby's weight and health. Mothers may also provide 'favourable' distortions concern-ing the age at which their child's toilet training and weaning occurred.

There may be instances when only a retrospective approach is viable. Consider an investigation of the developmental aspects of supervisory relation-ships for graduate students. How does the supervisory relationship change as one moves from honours BA to MA to PhD years, and within the PhD years how does it change? It would be preferable to collect these data as students advance through the system, while the information is still fresh in their minds and less distorted by forgetting. However, many students will be understandably reluctant to criticize their supervisors until they are safely out from under the supervisors' influence, or until they have the diploma securely in hand. In such situations a retrospective approach, although not ideal, may be the only feasible method. In brief, beware of recalled data as a means of charting maps of change for any characteristics, unless you are using it only in a supplementary manner:

1. to help check cross-sectional data
2. with some archival data[2] to back it up, or
3. to fill in gaps in a longitudinal study.

In any case, enclose such recalled estimates within a large uncertainty circle.

Longitudinal studies

In order to avoid the unreliability of recall that affects many retrospective studies and to avoid the confounding due to the fact that the different samples used in cross-sectional studies differ in more ways than age, we should, whenever possible, use a proper longitudinal study to map the curves of change.

The longitudinal study differs from the cross-sectional study in that the same subjects are observed repeatedly during the period under investigation; it differs from the retrospective study in that current observations—rather than recalled or archival data—are involved. Furthermore, longitudinal studies provide a way of mapping not only general group trends in the growth and decline of various physical and psychological characteristics (that is, boys versus girls or identical twins versus fraternal twins), but also information about individual differences in rates of change, levels achieved, duration of plateaus, and onset and rates of decline.

Although the longitudinal method represents a major improvement over the cross-sectional and retrospective designs, it, too, poses problems, including the following:

1. sample shrinkage—subjects disappear because of change in residence, illness, boredom, or death;
2. testing effects—repeatedly measuring the same people with the same yardsticks can lead to instrument decay (elastic-ruler effect), boredom, and loss of motivation—that is, to systematic on-stage effects;
3. external validity limits—the societal conditions under which this sample grew up (nutritional, social, educational) may shift so that this sample's developmental curve no longer provides a valid picture, or map, of the curve that would emerge with a new sample of people under current environmental conditions.

---

[2]When you have adequate archival data (see Chapter 8), retrospective research deserves increased confidence.

Hence, longitudinal studies require large samples to counteract the effects of sample shrinkage. Such studies also require non-reactive, or alternate form, measures to help counteract the effects of boredom and practice. Finally, these studies must be periodically updated by contemporary longitudinal studies using new samples to reflect the influence of shifting environmental conditions on developmental curves.

Nevertheless, in spite of these reservations, the longitudinal study represents an important research tool, not only in psychology, education, and organizational behaviour, but also in anthropology and sociology (historical method) and in economics (time series). Because of its many applications we now examine some of its variations.

In considering the following research designs, remember that, like any designs, they can't tell the whole story of 'what leads to what'—the best that any research method can do is to help reduce the number of suspects. Furthermore, because longitudinal studies are usually conducted outside the laboratory, large numbers of uncontrolled influences can affect the results and raise serious questions about their internal validity (Coolican, 1999).

Interrupted time series

This design involves a series of observations or measurements before and after the particular 'treatment' or event occurs (see Figure 7.6). The term *interrupted time series* comes from the fact that the 'treatment' interrupts the time series of observations.

Which of the seven time-series mapped in Figure 7.6 would you pick as likely demonstrating a reliable treatment effect over and above the four rogues? The first four have stable baselines followed by a shift upward closely associated with the treatment. If replicated—good news. In contrast, series 5, 6, and 7 warrant no bets at all. Series 7 is incomplete (no follow-up), while series 6 reflects the variable map of change typical of many of life's processes: health, mood, and energy level. Because of the zigzag pre-treatment and post-treatment course of this series, we usually have little confidence in any study of such a time series unless we have major shifts in behaviour, or unless a control group is employed.

It is important to note that the time series is a variation of the before-and-after design discussed in Chapter 4, and is therefore subject to the same limitations. It gains in power to the degree that the pre-treatment observations are stable and precise so that the post-treatment changes stand out. It also gains in power to the degree that the treatment is potent and quick acting; otherwise, historical and maturational suspects can produce changes in the treatment group that are wrongly attributed to the treatment.

This design is also at the mercy of elastic-ruler effects, as is any repeat measurement design. It is particularly vulnerable to experimenter bias, to the

Fig 7.6 ■ INTERRUPTED TIME SERIES

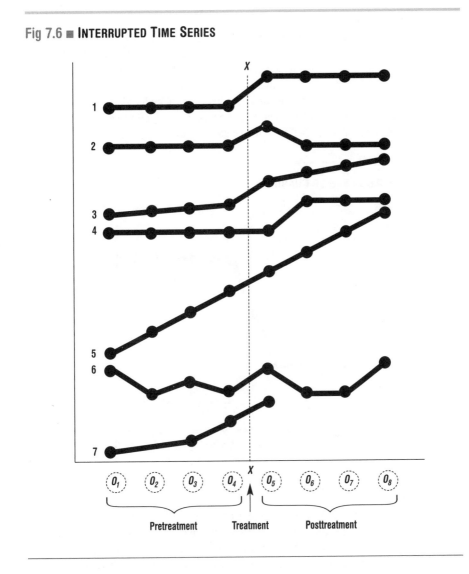

degree that the observations are unreliable or subjective—that is, to the extent that large areas of uncertainty surround the observations.

A repeated interrupted time series, where feasible, provides increased confidence in the treatment—that is, when the introduction of the treatment leads to a significant shift from a pre-treatment baseline, and then a withdrawal of the treatment results in a return to the pre-treatment baseline.

Evaluation research—an example

As an example of a question that lends itself to longitudinal research of the time series variety, consider the introduction of a management training program into an organization—how are such programs typically evaluated?

The desired map of change will probably look like that in Figure 7.7. This curve, presenting management skills, portrays a multitude of characteristics: delegation of responsibility, clarity of communication, effective use of time, and morale building—in brief, a multifaceted measure.

Fig 7.7 ■ DESIRED CURVE OF CHANGE

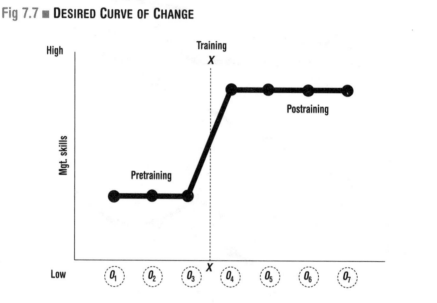

Typically, in most management training a pre-treatment baseline is rarely measured, or, it is estimated by retrospective methods—that is, by supervisors or trainees *recalling* how they performed before treatment. We recognize this as a notoriously unreliable method of establishing observational checkpoints, so we should enclose the pre-treatment curve within a large band of uncertainty.

Now we come to the treatment (training), which is usually a stew of treatments (audiovisual displays, lectures, handouts, discussion groups, workshops, individual assignments, parties). Probably neither the people paying for the training program nor the people providing it have any precise idea at the top of their PSTs about rates or levels of change beyond the crude picture in Figure 7.7.

However, from an outsider's viewpoint it would be reasonable to assume that if the training program has any effect at all there will be individual differences in

Fig 7.8 ■ INDIVIDUAL RATES OF CHANGE

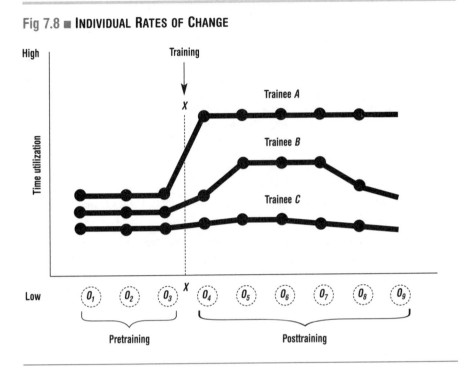

rate, level, and dimension of change. On any given dimension (for instance, more efficient use of work time), we might at least visualize the following curves reflecting individual differences in rate and level of change (see Figure 7.8). In Figure 7.8, trainee A shows a rapid rate and a high level of stable or durable change, whereas Trainee B demonstrates a lower rate, a lower level, and less stable change, and Trainee C exhibits little change at all. On the basis of a post-training questionnaire (O_4), we find most trainees reporting a Type A curve —that is, they're using a *recalled* pre-treatment baseline and *reporting*, after training, a rapid rate and significant levels of improvement.

So, using a self-report measure, we obtain a rosy picture of both the rate of change and the level of change. The personnel department that sponsored the training program is happy, the president is happy, and the consultants who put on the program are happy with their extended contract to train more managers. But what kind of questions might you raise about the results? Appropriate questions might be based on the following:

1. a recalled pre-treatment baseline is probably highly unreliable;
2. on-stage and elastic-ruler effects strongly influence how individuals respond to ratings and questionnaires (for instance, the training seminars

sure beat working; can you really admit you learned little or nothing; you had a good time and would like to go next year); and,

3. you've only got a soft measure to estimate rate, level, and duration of change, and that's a self-report measure, notoriously open to bias.

Now a new president takes over the firm and is concerned about the costs (time away from work, consultant fees) of all this training. Furthermore, the president is not convinced that it does all that much good, in spite of the post-training questionnaire results. The president hires you to help evaluate the 'real' effects of training. What might you do?

Improved research design

The following are examples of how you might improve the evaluation procedures:

1. At the bottom of your PST, increase the reliability and duration of the pre-training and post-training observations—that is, have trainees keep pre-training and post-training diaries of how they utilize their time. Furthermore, supplement these estimates with unobtrusive pre-training and post-training observations in order to provide a check on diary accu-

Fig 7.9 ■ EFFICIENCY TIME UTILIZATION

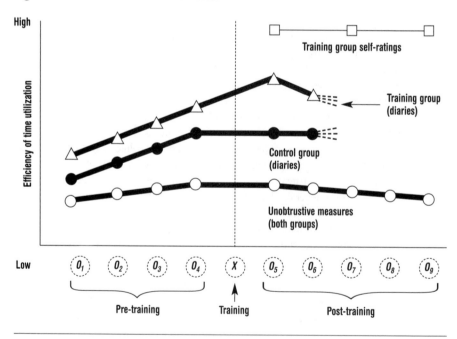

racy.

2. Delay training for half the participants (selected at random) to measure the effects of keeping a diary alone during the period the other group is training. The first part of the study consists of a simple control-group design comparing training and diary keeping, with diary keeping alone. The second part involves a crossover where the control group receives training, and the experimental group merely continues to keep diaries.

Fig 7.10 ■ INTERRUPTED TIME SERIES CONTROL GROUP DESIGN

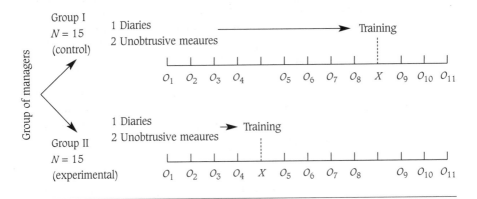

Now you return to the president with the following results (see Figure 7.9)

On the basis of these results, you report that:

1. Diary reports of efficient time utilization show marked increases *before* training for both experimental and control groups; here we have evidence of a testing or on-stage effect—that is, merely keeping track of how you spend your time leads to 'reporting' more efficient time utilization.

2. Unobtrusive time-sampling surveillance of a random sample of both experimental and control-group members before training reflects only very small increases in efficiency of time utilization.

3. Following training the experimental group diary reports continue to claim increased time utilization efficiency; however marked individual differences soon start to appear, and quality and number of diary reports diminishes markedly—sample shrinkage and data mortality.

4. The no-training, control-group diary reports do not show the post-training 'booster' effect shown by the experimental group, but they do soon show similar sample shrinkage and data loss.

5. The unobtrusive measure has settled back to the pre-treatment, pre-testing baseline for both experimental and control groups, except for one

member *in each group* who continues to maintain pre-treatment gains—that is, a subject by treatment interaction. (For instance, while most participants fail to show significant or stable unobtrusive measure gains resulting from diary keeping or training, one manager from each group, *for unknown reasons*, did show such gains. Further study of these two may provide productive hypotheses for further research.)

6. Questionnaire ratings of the overall value of training by trainees remain high for 3, 6, and 12 months following the training (on-stage effects?).

Summarizing, if we base our conclusions on unobtrusive measure data, we conclude that diary-keeping alone or in combination with training has little enduring effect on efficient time utilization. If we rely on diary reports, we conclude that diary keeping and training increase *reported*, but not necessarily actual, efficiency of time utilization before training and for a short time after training. If we rely on general self-report ratings by trainees following training, we conclude the training leads to rapid and significant improvements on a variety of dimensions.

While acknowledging that you are measuring only one dimension of managerial skill (time utilization), the new president places most confidence in the unobtrusive measure and decides such workshops may build morale but probably are an ineffective means of training—at least concerning the dimension of more efficient time utilization.

Notice, though, that even if an equivalent control group, as was used in this study, is impossible, a *non-equivalent* control group can be useful in obtaining estimates of the role of testing or time in shaping the curve of change. For example, you could have probably obtained a fair estimate of the effect of keeping diaries even if the control group had been run at a different time from the experimental group or in a different plant. Certainly it's not as powerful a control, but it's better than no control. For example, notice that in this study the greatest increase in *reported* time efficiency and unobtrusive estimates of time efficiency occurred *before* the training.

Also observe that if you want to map precisely the rate of increase or decline of a characteristic, you require multiple measures over the relevant time period. The diaries recorded time utilization for every 15-minute period during the working day for four weeks before the training and supposedly for three months following the training. Thus, the diary method is designed to provide a fine-grained measure of change—15-minute units over a 16-week time span. The fact that these 15-minute units were filled with rose-coloured data indicates that you can also end up with fine-grained *distortions* of the rate of change. How might the time taken to complete the diaries affect the dependent variable (time utilization)? Is this an instance where your measurement methods influence or confound the thing being measured?

The unobtrusive measure likewise sampled 15-minute units, but only one per morning and one per afternoon for each participant, taken more or less at random, and then compared with the same time period in diary reports. As noted, the unobtrusive measure data not only differ markedly from diary data but also reflect a much-deflated rate and level of change for comparable time periods. Unobtrusive measures also picked up interesting, 'casual' comments: 'I'm three days behind in my diary and I've got to get caught up by Friday' (thus the diaries in some cases reflected *recalled* data), 'What kind of things are they looking for in these damned diaries anyway?' (this person seems to be asking what kind of on-stage performance one should give), and 'We better get together on our diaries; we don't want to turn in conflicting information.'

Not only do these comments raise important questions regarding the reliability of the diary reports, but they also place grave ethical responsibilities on the researchers—people's jobs and careers could be placed in jeopardy as a result of identifying their source.

We've indicated the importance of having relatively fine-grained and objective estimates to map rates of change. The same requirements apply in order to map the duration of change. Failure to conduct fine-grained, objective, post-treatment follow-ups probably constitutes the most glaring weakness in studies of change; consider, for example, the famous Hawthorne effect.

The Hawthorne effect

At the top of our PST the basic up-and-down curve of change is a powerful model for describing many time-related phenomena including charting the course of problem-solving intelligence from birth to old age, mapping the 'melt rate' of New Year's resolutions from 27 December to 27 January, or plotting the course of management skills from before training to a few weeks after (see Figure 7.11).

Fig 7.11 ■ NEW YEAR'S RESOLUTION MELTDOWN—A CLASSIC HAWTHORNE EFFECT

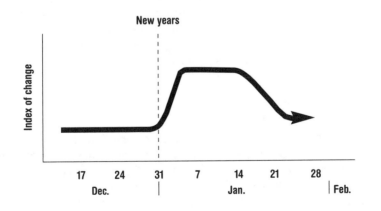

Among the most famous investigations of organizational change are the Hawthorne studies (Roethlisberger & Dickson, 1948). From this research has emerged a phenomenon known as the *Hawthorne effect*, which describes temporary changes that are due mainly to on-stage or testing effects or to the effects of novelty. For example, in the Hawthorne studies it was found that when lighting levels were raised, production in the factory increased temporarily. But it was also found that when illumination levels were lowered, production also increased briefly. The important point to note is that *novelty*, like New Year's resolutions, can produce change, but not necessarily enduring change.

In evaluating longitudinal studies, consumers of science must ask one critical question: 'How do I decide how many of the ups and downs of human or organizational behaviour to assign to chance (that is, to the rogues) and how much to specific "treatments"?'

In brief, you decide by obtaining some estimate of the range of variation in the behaviour without the influence of some selected treatment or intervention. Then you add your 'treatment' and determine whether the behaviour obviously shifts to a new higher or lower range, maintains the new range (longer than a New Year's resolution), and is maintained when using observations that are not readily open to on-stage and elastic-ruler effects. Science is in the business of mapping heavyweight changes in behaviour over significant periods.

You can analyze shifts in behaviour by plotting the maps of change and making eyeball assessments of whether there has been an 'impressive' shift. If a neutral observer agrees with you, then your conclusions warrant increased confidence. If a hostile observer agrees with you—one who doesn't believe in your treatment—your discovery is astonishing.

With the advent of computers and complicated statistical models, science relies less on eyeball analysis; rather, we compare statistical estimates of day-to-day variability and statistical estimates of whether the shift is larger following an experimental intervention that can 'reasonably' be expected by chance, larger than the four rogues usually produce on their own. The four rogues, singly and in combination, can engineer some remarkable shifts in the ranges of human behaviour. Therefore it is wise to use a control group, equivalent or otherwise, whenever possible, or lacking a control group, to use extended baseline and follow-up observations involving non-reactive measures and treatment reversal designs.

Regression toward the mean

In discussing the value of the control-group method in Chapter 5, we briefly referred to statistical regression. This effect pervades many longitudinal studies and warrants further discussion at this time. When you do unusually well on an exam, or unusually poorly, what will likely happen on the next exam? Before you answer, think of all the reasons you can about why you did better or worse than usual. Then answer the question: 'How will you likely do on the next one?'

The answer is that you probably won't do as well, or as poorly, on the next test. That's because we usually perform better or worse than usual because of an *unusual combination of circumstances*—a combination of positive or negative events that is unlikely to occur again. A person who performs worse than usual can take heart that their grade will likely rise, and the person who performs better than usual can prepare for a lower grade next time. In other words, unusually high or low scores tend to gravitate toward the average or mean score, hence, referred to as 'regression toward the mean'.

Unusual combinations of circumstances influence your behaviour, moving it up above, or below, the usual level. Therefore, anytime you see a score describing human performance—like a test score—you should see it as the end result of a combination of two influences: the person's ability or skill and chance factors associated with that particular testing session. Because a different combination of chance factors will likely be at work on the next testing occasion, they will have a different influence on the score. Therefore, even if ability and skill remain relatively constant, performance scores will change up or down as a result of different chance factors operating on different testing occasions.

SUMMARY

Longitudinal research involves drawing timelines into the past[3] and future and then looking for reliable observational stepping-stones that fall on the path that the up-top scientists predicted. Longitudinal research extends, or shrinks, the temporal validity or travel permit of a theoretical prediction.

Archeologists and paleontologists draw mind-maps of the distant past and, every time they discover an ancient bit of bone they plot in another an observational checkpoint. Life-span researchers draw shorter mind-maps of the future and, as it flows by into the past, gradually test their theory against observational checkpoints. Developmental psychologists focus on theoretical maps, which typically cover the first six years of life and predict rapid rates of change in mobility, language acquisition, height, puzzle solving, social skills, etc.

When drawing observational maps researchers find zigzag variability. Children march to their own drummer and some march slower than others; some deviate above *the line*, some below it, and so they will attract attention.

As a teacher, and particularly as a parent, you may question where scientists draw *the line*, particularly if your pupil or child falls below it. As you become a more sophisticated consumer of science you will ask questions about the samples, their size, from what population were they drawn, and why did the researchers rely upon these samples to determine whether their pet theoretical map was observationally valid? What kind of travel permit does their pet *line*

---

[3]Darwin's theory of evolution consists of a very large playpen extending into the distant past, sprinkled with observational checkpoints with researchers constantly digging for more Os to help fill in the gaps.

deserve? What about elastic-ruler effects? How far below the line does my son have to be, and for how long, before he is noticed for further observation? Furthermore, what suspect, or combination of suspects, *causes* such deviations (e.g., what combinations of genes and environment)? Finally, what treatment do they recommend? Does it work?[4] Did they use control groups and if they used longitudinal methods, you have to keep the following points in mind:

1. Cross-sectional studies and retrospective studies provide very crude maps of the curves of change.
2. Interrupted time series gain in power:
   a. when control groups—equivalent or nonequivalent—are used or when treatment reversals are feasible;
   b. when at least some of the observations or measures are robust—are relatively resistant to on-stage and elastic-ruler effects; and
   c. when such robust measures are continued long enough to determine whether you have a change over and above a New Year's resolution meltdown or a Hawthorne effect.

Longitudinal investigations help us extend the reach of science by exploring an extended time frame. In the next two chapters, we discuss additional methods that help us look for patterns in space/time frames beyond the confines of the laboratory or the control-group method.

student's notebook

It's really weird, but despite Dr Frund's warning about the ethical dangers of manipulating other people's behaviour, on occasion I still slip back into giving Derek the old Skinner treatment—rewarding him for listening and sort of punishing him when he isn't. What's more, I think he's doing it me too—when he does listen he does it in such a way that sort of says: 'OK, look I'm listening, but not really.' It's sort of like he's training me not to talk.

This ethics stuff isn't simple. Does it boil down to this: If you know you're manipulating people, then it's unethical, but if you don't realize you're doing it, then it's alright?

Maybe I'll ask Professor Creek—I'm a little gun-shy of Dr Frund at the moment.

I found this chapter interesting because I've done a bit of longitudinal research trying to improve my study skills.[5] My scientific playpen lasted six weeks, and I was taking multiple observations every day. So my study had six weeks worth of external observational validity. But since it involved observing only one person—me—it had almost no external validity in terms of sample size. So, at the bottom of my PST, I can't generalize the observations I made in my tiny longitudinal study to anyone else.

---

[4] Are you feeling a bit of information overload? The old bounded rationality starting to complain a bit? At the same time are you realizing why, and how much, we must depend on 'experts' to shrink all this stuff to fit inside our brains?

[5] See Prologue.

But, up-top, I really believe it will work for anyone who follows the instructions. I believe it has up-top external validity. Anyway, it's still working for me.

I appreciate that longitudinal takes patience and tenacity—imagine if you were following a group of children from birth to six years of age, or to their teenage years, or to retirement. My God! Think of the observations, dots, and records! And think of the critical thinking!

To do that kind of longitudinal research you'd really have to have almost blind faith in your theoretical map. That map would have to be really emotionally anchored at the top of your PST. In this sense, a theory that drives that kind of longitudinal research is very practical.

I had a relatively short time period (six weeks) but it still took a lot of work. My theoretical map was an upward slanting line, like the one in Figure 7.1. Since I started with a baseline of zero for my target behaviours (summarizing and recall), any change at the bottom of my PST was obvious. Eyeballing my data was sufficient to show the steady upward trend—except on weekends.

What were the emotional anchors for my theoretical map of change? I can think of three: a fear of failing, a desire to impress Dr Frund, and a sense of pride in doing well at university, which I think is a little different from a general fear of failure.

But a little critical thinking makes me question my first and third reasons. I've always crammed until this year. How come fear and pride didn't work in the past? I suspect that the main emotional anchor was that I wanted to impress Dr Frund. Plus, she was encouraging and continued to give advice and supervision as I went along.

I suppose that means I can't take much of the credit for its success. It's not particularly reassuring that changing my own irresponsible behaviour was dependent on the emotional anchors provided by other people. That suggests that I rely on authority figures (and maybe impressing peers like Derek) in order to smarten up.

I told you so
Derek would say: 'I told you so.' As a sociologist he goes on and on about how individual behaviour is at the mercy of cultural institutional forces. Social psychologists would go on and on about how individual behaviour is at the mercy of peer pressure. Probably clinical psychologists would claim I was trying to impress a mother figure (Dr Frund). Every discipline has its own map, its own favourite observational checkpoints. But I think there are some common and trusted up-top beliefs—sort of master maps.

Free will
For example, I believe, as do most people I know, that an individual has free will—each person is the master of his or her fate, captain of his or her soul.

How would you do longitudinal research on that question? How would you design a study to help separate the effects of individual planning and will power, on the one hand, as opposed to group influences, on the other, in leading to significant behaviour change over the long haul.

There are tons of before-and-after studies to suggest that individual planning and will power aren't worth much when it comes to changing bad habits (e.g., repeatedly failed New Year's Resolutions). A lot of people have to join a group (Weight Watchers, AA, etc.,) to make a change. But I don't know whether, in these cases, the testimonials are based on flawed before-and-after studies, or whether there's control-group evidence. Plus, are there long term follow-ups to see if change for the better persists? Those help groups aren't likely to publish negative evidence about their program—they don't publicize what percentage of people dropped out.

Creek's assignment

For this assignment Professor Creek instructed us to travel to the top of our PSTs, select the most personally valid theoretical maps of change we could find stored in there, and give examples of behaviour that fit each map. I think I'll try to jot down my ideas right now, and then type it up later in the week.

First, as I suggested earlier, the horizontal, no change, theoretical map fits all kinds of observable habits (e.g., food and drink preferences; addictions like smoking, drinking, and drugs; which side of the bed you sleep on; language and patterns of speech, etc.). Steady, straight-line stuff.

Second, the theoretical map sloping down to the right covers all kinds of observable biologically based behaviour (e.g., people's mental and physiological functions start to decline perceptibly in middle age) or even earlier (e.g., reaction time, vision, memory, sexual energy, etc.).

Third, a theoretical map starting out level, rising for a short time, and then returning back to a baseline accurately describes observational maps resulting from resolutions or good intentions (e.g., to lose weight), or adult training programs (e.g., take a yoga class), and temporary changes in situations (e.g., going on holidays, spending time with new friends). The Hawthorne effect is a classic example of this map, where novelty brings about a temporary change. As the novelty wears off, behaviour slides back to baseline.

The fourth one is the reverse of the third, often reflecting the effects of stressful situations (e.g., can't sleep, indigestion, etc.). The line starts out level, then decreases, then gradually returns to the normal or original level, that is, to the baseline.

The fifth, and often neglected, theoretical map of change, refers to cyclical, rhythmic, or periodic changes in behaviour linked to changing psychological or physical states (e.g., mood swings, energy levels, wakefulness, attention, etc.). I'd like to know what kinds of research methods you could use to map this? My mood and energy levels seem to shift wildly up and down over time for no obvious reason—often I can't identify the guilty in-the-gap suspect.

Mapping shifts in moods and feelings must be tricky because they're kind of fuzzy (elastic-ruler) and may be linked to several in-the-gap suspects such as time of day, day of the week, the situation, and who is there (on-stage rogues). Come to think of it, Dr Frund and Derek frequently appear 'in-the-gap' prior to shifts in my mood, both good and bad.

So, I now see why drawing developmental and longitudinal maps tends to be much easier at the top of my PST instead of at the bottom, particularly with fuzzy Os. You need hard-edged ones like height or number of words written. And any archeologist will tell you that it's easier to find people's skulls than their minds in the distant past.

News stories

No shortage of stories in the media that map, or at least claim to map, the truth over long time periods.

Roll them bones

Speaking of archeologists and skulls, you can get a lot of information about where humans came from just by surfing the Internet. For example, Google 'intelligent design'. Wow! Literally millions of results come up! Derek finds this interesting, so we spent a whole afternoon pogo-sticking around the online world, starting with the Wikipedia site.[6]

Those who believe in intelligent design focus on the gaps in the fossil record, and on the problems with random variation and probability theory. Related to that, we found a really great quote at www.origins.org: 'Anyone who considers arithmetical methods of producing random digits is, of course, in a state of sin.' This quote is attributed to John von Neumann, who is credited with inventing the modern computer. So, this genius is saying that statistical foundations of evolutionary theory are maybe a bit wobbly?

And yet scientists rely on probability theory to help them sort chance relationships from 'causal' ones. And, of course, on the Internet you can find the latest news on the fossil record very easily.

We quickly realized that anyone trying to get up to speed on this debate becomes overwhelmed in minutes—you quickly run off the edge of your bounded rationality. You really appreciate why scientists need to cut the problem down to mind-size by generating a premise, point of view, or theoretical map at the top of their PST, to tell them where to look, what to look for, and most importantly, what to ignore. Otherwise it's a buzzing confusion that leads to dangerous ways of thinking.

Derek's bias

It would be easier to be selective if I had as strong a bias as Derek does. I kind of lean toward Darwin, but I'm not married to the guy. You'd think Derek was his son. He's really pro-evolution and anti-intelligent design. He 'cherry-picks' good

---

[6]'Intelligent design' in *Wikipedia, The Free Encyclopedia.* Available at http://en.wikipedia.org/w/index.php?title=Intelligent_design&oldid=60037643 (accessed 23 June 2006).

news about evolution and bad news about intelligent design and then shoves it in your face. He says I do the same to him when we're talking about feminism. Anyway, he thinks that most of the intelligent design 'scholars' probably got their PhD's via mail order from universities for $20. Sounds a bit biased, doesn't he?

During our Internet afternoon, when I pointed out the problems with evolution that popped up in what we were reading, he became decidedly cranky. He didn't like me pointing out that one website said that you could load all the hominid fossil bones (all the observational checkpoints sprinkled over a four million mile map) into the bed of half-ton truck. And he was not amused when we read about the recent discovery of a million-year-old skull and some tools. This find was different because the skull was so small it fell way off the evolutionary map—that dot was way outta line! How could someone with such a small brain have tools? According to the evolutionists, you would need bigger brains—like our cave-dwelling ancestors; people with the same size brains as ours, in order to make and use tools.

Derek has a point

What do scientists do when they find a deviant, but rock solid, dot like that? Derek recovers and says: 'They fight about it, which is what science is all about. At least they collect and fight over facts, unlike the intelligent design nerds who play word games at the top of their PSTs and never expose their emotionally anchored biases to hard data.' Well, it's hard to collect hard data in heaven . . . you can't get it through customs.

I think he's probably right that evolutionary theory makes more sense up top and down below, particularly now with dna evidence to help map our ancestral record. But I just don't feel comfortable believing that I'm merely the chance result of shaking a bag of dust for four million years.[7]

Politics and birth rate

Now that I've discussed sprinkling a few observational checkpoints on a theoretical map that stretches back millions of years, I think I'll move on to talk about a theoretical map that only started in the year 2000 and will stretch into the future.

As I understand it, the theory is[8] that in the United States, liberals (represented by the blue states) marry later and have fewer children than conservatives

---

[7]From *New Scientist* 1 July 2004.

[8]Tamar Lewin, *New York Times* 13 October 2005.

(the red states). So, if the theory continues to be observationally valid, Republicans may rule the political roost until liberals start conceiving and raising more Democratic babies.

This theory apparently started as a result of examining census data on marriage, fertility, and socio-economic class by state and using a pretty big sample—three million people. What they found was that, between 2000–3, people in the North East (politically liberal states) are more likely to marry later and are less likely to become teen-age mothers than those in the south. Also, men in the North East marry later than men in the Midwest, West, and South.

This is kind of a neat theoretical map. At least it's triggered by some pretty reliable observational checkpoints, and is open to testing by big sample, reliable dots. It will be interesting to see if the current connections between the dots hold up, whether liberals get the message and starting birthing more liberal babies.

So, here we have two examples of longitudinal research. The first, evolution, concerns a scientifically popular theoretical map extending back millions of years, sparsely sprinkled with observational checkpoints, but with researchers constantly looking for more. Their work is critically analyzed within an adversarial institution—Science—as well as criticized from those outside science, such as the intelligent designer supporters, in an up-top speculative map that is empirically un-testable. There are no observational stepping-stones to Heaven.

The second example of longitudinal research, of a more recent origin, concerns the production of conservative and liberal babies stretching into the future, and open to rigorous observational testing by anyone taking the trouble to access easily accessible (à la Kahneman) census data on the Internet.

I also stumbled across, electronically speaking, a 30-year—and counting—longitudinal study of more than 1,000 children in New Zealand which, among other things, predicts which kids will fall into risky sexual behaviours.

Professor Creek's assignment on longitudinal research makes me appreciate how emotionally anchored a theoretical map must be in order for a researcher to devote his or her life to rigorously testing it, by slowly creating an observational map stretching back into the past, or out into the future. I can understand why a lot of researchers go for internal validity, or for local, time-limited truths. Acquiring a long-term travel permit for your truth is hard work.

Earning an external validity passport, down at the bottom of the pst takes a lot of research sweat. I think I'll settle for being a famous theorist spending my time merrily scribbling astonishing speculative maps all over the blackboard.

Note

Check out the 'world leader' of longitudinal studies at http://www.oup.com/ca/he/companion/agnewpyke.

REVIEW TRUE OR FALSE QUIZ

T F	1.	Observational maps are about seeing-is-believing and have universal passports.
T F	2.	Theoretical maps of change are smoother and longer than observational maps of change.
T F	3.	Changes differ in their rates of growth or decline, the ceiling or limits to a change, and the duration of such limits or plateaus.
T F	4.	The research methods employed to assess change are the correlational method, the cross-sectional method, and the interrupted time series design.
T F	5.	When researchers sample people of different ages and test them all at about the same time, they are using the cross-sectional method.
T F	6.	The cross-sectional method provides an average curve for age-related characteristics, but given points on the curve may be affected by factors not related to age.
T F	7.	Retrospective studies provide considerable protection from elastic-ruler effects.
T F	8.	Retrospective studies gain strength when there is supporting archival data.
T F	9.	When researchers sample the same subjects repeatedly over time, they are using the retrospective method.
T F	10.	Problems with the longitudinal method include sample shrinkage and systematic on-stage effects.
T F	11.	With an interrupted time series design, the treatment interrupts the time series of observations.
T F	12.	The interrupted time series design gains in power when the pre-treatment observations are stable and when the treatment is slow acting.
T F	13.	One strategy to improve the power of evaluation research is to use an interrupted time series control-group design.
T F	14.	Use of non-equivalent control groups should be avoided because they are no better than having no control at all.
T F	15.	The most glaring weakness in studies of change is the failure to conduct fine-grained, objective, post-treatment follow-ups.

T F	16. The Hawthorne effect derives from studies of organization change and refers to permanent and enduring changes that are due mainly to on-stage or testing effects, or to the effects of novelty.
T F	17. Unusually high or low scores on an initial test tend to gravitate toward the average or mean score on the next test.
T F	18. Longitudinal research extends the temporal validity of a theoretical prediction.
T F	19. Diana's longitudinal research on improving her study skills had observational validity.
T F	20. A theoretical map of change which is initially level, rises briefly and then returns to baseline levels, describes observational maps of biologically based behaviour.
T F	21. Diana reports a news story indicating that Liberals marry earlier and have more offspring than Conservatives.

Beyond the Laboratory

A great deal of human behaviour occurs in places beyond the reach of traditional scientific instruments, like inside our heads and bedrooms.

Lacking appropriate physical yardsticks and quantitative methods, we rely on humans to peek inside their own heads, bedrooms, patrol cars, pubs, backroom meetings, etc., and tell us what's going on. We call these reports *qualitative methods*.

In Chapter 8 we will examine the pros and cons of three such methods: questionnaires, attitudes and personality scales, and interviews. In Chapter 9 we will consider naturalistic observation and archival research.

8

Qualitative Methods: Questionnaires, Attitude Scales, and Interviews

Chapter Goal

- To examine the methods scientists use to access subjective information, namely, what people think, feel, and plan to do.

Lacking valid physical probes and quantifiers, researchers rely on various *qualitative methods* to collect, analyze, and display these subjective messages. These self-reports provide a view of what the top and bottom of your PST look like from the inside—from your perspective.

Introduction

If a scientist wants to measure your temperature he or she sticks a thermometer inside your mouth and reads off the number. However, if he or she wants to measure your thoughts or feelings, he or she has no physical instrument to stick inside your head and read off the number.

Instead researchers must rely on the only instrument available, a human measuring instrument—that human instrument is you. So, you go inside, peek into your brain, and provide scientists with *qualitative messages* about what's happening. Instead of using numbers, you usually use words. You wouldn't normally say 'I'm feeling nine out of ten', though. Instead you would say 'I'm feeling pretty darn good.'

Of course, if you're filling out a mood scale you may translate your fuzzy feelings into a number message, such as 'I'm feeling about 8 out 10.'

Unlike your temperature, the number you report on a questionnaire includes the influence of elastic-ruler and on-stage rogues. You both wittingly and unwittingly manipulate your subjectively generated numbers to fit your emotionally anchored premises, and in order to look 'good'. For want of a better term we call those elastic numbers 'sort-of-quantitative'.

Recognizing this problem, researchers use a variety of qualitative methods to by-pass or correct these distortions in order to access the most important information in the world—the *subjective information* you, we, and our leaders use to make life-shaping and world changing decisions.

We choose careers, mates, and send troops to war in Iraq not so much on the basis of quantitative facts but rather on the basis of qualitative, emotionally anchored beliefs or premises.

To access the subjective information that resides at the top of our PSTs, qualitative researchers ask us to go inside our heads and attend to our memories, thoughts, and feelings. From our feedback they then try to identify the emotionally anchored working premises, entrenched biases, and habits that guide our thinking and shape our behaviour.

Of course, you can't always control where your insider observations or consciousness will focus. Often it's impossible to get it to focus on the ideas or feelings you want it to. At other times you can't get the pig-headed beast to stop regurgitating memories, ideas, or emotions that you really want to avoid.

Qualitative Research is Like a News Service

Earlier we proposed that science is like a news service. So is qualitative research.

In Figure 8.1 scientific research is presented as a chain of messengers and messages. Let's assume that you're the person being studied. If you are involved in a quantitative experiment the message chain typically involves attaching you to a physical yardstick (e.g., a thermometer, lie detector polygraph, an MRI machine, etc.) that will transform, more or less accurately, one of your physiological functions into numbers or graphs on the screen.

Human messengers

However, lacking accessible or trusted quantitative hardware to *measure* what's going on inside your mind, researchers must rely on human detectors to access, package, and verbally report current subjective memories, thoughts, feelings, and resolutions.

In Figure 8.1 notice that every messenger in the chain—hardware or human—typically transforms, edits or distorts, to some degree, whatever information it, he, or she receives. In brief, research consists of a chain of messages more or less distorted by elastic-ruler and/or on-stage effects. Even the most precise physical measuring instrument has some elasticity and includes some measurement error in its numbers. The longer the message chain, the greater the accumulation of edits or error.

Furthermore, note what happens when researchers include a physical instrument in the chain. The on-stage effects are eliminated and the elastic-ruler

Fig 8.1 ■ SCIENCE IS LIKE A NEWS SERVICE

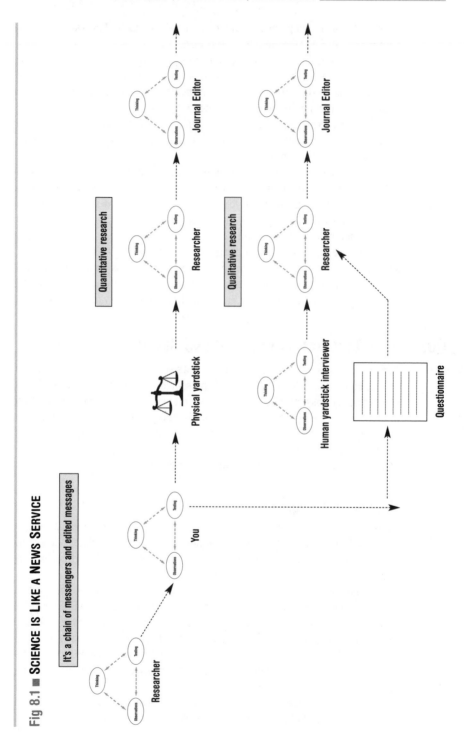

effects are reduced, but only at that particular link in the chain. Both prior to and following that link human messengers run the show, and with them the rogues are sure to go.

Before and after the physical measurement, the limitations of the observer's bounded rationality prevail. As human messengers cycle around their PSTs they cut the flow of messages—whatever their source—down to mind-size. They select and connect *accessible* dots to accommodate their up-top expectations and premises. They pass these highly edited messages along the chain for further editing by other messengers in the chain.

Comparing the research process to a chain of messages generated and transmitted by bounded rationality messengers has profound implications. Is it any wonder that scientists conscientiously investigating the same theory may disagree, or when rigorously testing the same predictions obtain different results? Is it any wonder that journal editors reject novel theories and surprising research results (e.g., the Aussie research on ulcers referred to in earlier chapters)? Is it any wonder that the press and public unwittingly distort scientific messages? Is it any wonder that, with all the elasticity in the chain, some ambitious researchers take advantage and adjust their data in order to get their fifteen minutes of fame?

> Junk science involves pseudo-scientists playing 'Rumour' in white coats. Serious science requires conscientiously checking the reliability and validity of each message in the chain, regardless of the quantitative or qualitative methods used.

Instead, it's surprising that science gets it right as often as it does. It's a credit to the conscientious dedication of most researchers, and to their feisty scientific adversarial system.

When thinking of any chain of messages, think of 'Rumour', the party game, where the flow of messages gets unwittingly edited—sometimes a little, sometimes a lot—by each person transmitting the message.

Now let's consider the challenges serious scientists face using qualitative methods.

Cycling Around the PST Qualitatively

We now cycle around the scientific PST to see how social scientists generate their answers and how they attempt to identify valid messages in the endless and elastic chain.

First, notice that Figure 8.2 uses dotted circles to indicate that a *region of uncertainty* surrounds all observations or measurements (which are indicated by solid circles), including those based upon physical yardsticks. To some degree all yardsticks are elastic-rulers.

Typically, qualitative measures based on human judgments contain a larger area of uncertainty, as indicated at the bottom of the PST in Figure 8.2. For example, when you measure someone's head size with a tape measure you expect a

Fig 8.2 ■ QUALITATIVE METHODS

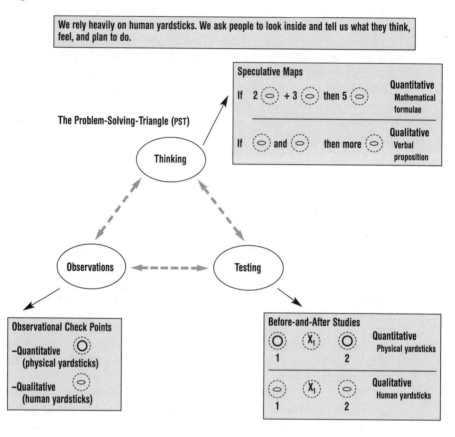

We rely heavily on human yardsticks. We ask people to look inside and tell us what they think, feel, and plan to do.

smaller region of uncertainty or error than when you measure his or her *thoughts* (e.g., his or her *stated resolution* to lose weight).

Nevertheless, lacking valid physical yardsticks able to access vital insider information,[1] researchers work long and hard to develop and test the reliability and validity of their qualitative measures (questionnaires, surveys, interviews, etc.) to establish trusted observational stepping stones at the bottom of the PST.

---

[1]Two hundred and fifty years ago scholars *discovered* a physical yardstick for measuring minds, namely bumps on the skull (phrenology). But the travel permit of this particular *truth* was revoked. Recently, scientific excitement has been generated by 'artificial intelligence' (computer models of the brain), the genome project, and MRI imaging, all issuing promissory notes that we have, or would soon have, physical yardsticks for measuring human thinking and feeling. It will take time to estimate their reliability and validity. Only time will tell what kind of travel permits they deserve.

Meantime, notice that up-top all their theories—their speculative maps—are *promissory notes*. For the most part they're based on predictions describing imaginary observations that have yet to be made. Those up-top speculative *images* all either have a large area of uncertainty surrounding them or are empirically empty.

Even if it's a theoretical map filled with mathematical symbols, those are still only promissory numbers, while the main players in the formula—the promised observations—remain uncertain, unknown, imaginary. And they remain imaginary until the scientists move back down to the bottom of the PST and make reliable observations to rigorously test the promise or prediction, that is, to check and see if the observed numbers are the same as the predicted ones. In brief, whether the promissory note is worth the paper, or the backboard, it was written on.

It's important to remember that the term 'quantitative' refers to different things when used at the top as opposed to the bottom of the PST. When used at the top it usually refers to speculative mathematical maps or formulae. Quantitative symbols are used to portray detailed but abstract descriptions and predictions. But such formulae are still only promissory notes using mathematical lingo, composed of observationally empty symbols. For example, Einstein's famous formula $E = mc^2$ remained a top-of-the-PST speculation, lacking observational facts, until it was possible to travel to the bottom right corner and rigorously and empirically test it, years later.

It was only then that the second, and more familiar, meaning of the term 'quantitative' came into play. It was only then that numbers were reliably tied to actual and reliable observations; instead of remaining up at the top as free floating abstract symbols. Sometimes scientists fall in love with their premises, with the elegance of their mathematics, with playing and navigating in symbol space, delegating the empirical research, down below in the trenches, to others.

As scientists accumulate qualitative observations through rigorous testing, they travel back up to the top to see how their observations fit the theoretical predictions. For instance, did the prediction that treatment X_t would increase reported self-confidence in a sample of college undergrads turn out to be accurate?

Because qualitative measures of 'self-confidence' are vulnerable to large elastic-ruler and on-stage effects, most serious researchers use several qualitative methods: interviews, questionnaires, and unobtrusive measures. To the degree that the students in the research sample showed increased self-confidence on all three measures, the researcher gains confidence in the local validity of his predictions. If so, he tests additional samples of students to increase the external validity. If the results don't hold, then it's back to the drawing board: perhaps fine-tuning his questionnaire, or testing others before reluctantly climbing laboriously back up to the top of his PST to painfully stretch or shrink his beloved theory.

As we describe various qualitative methods, try to identify those most vulnerable to the elastic-ruler and on-stage rogues. The quality of critical thinking that a qualitative researcher demonstrates is reflected in how well he or she has controlled the four rogues at the bottom and how well he or she avoids jumping to conclusions at the top.

Qualitative Methods

Social and behavioural scientists rely on a variety of qualitative methods to access your thoughts, feelings, and plans, including:

- Questionnaires (open ended and structured)
- Attitude scales (positive and negative ratings)
- Interviews (open-ended and structured)
- Clinical interviews (case studies)
- Naturalistic observation (unobtrusive and participant)
- Archival research (diaries, letters, historical records, etc.)

In this chapter we discuss questionnaires, attitude scales, and interview methods. Chapter 9 will address naturalistic observation and archival research.

Scientists develop and employ a variety of research tools—too many to be covered in an introductory text. Rather than trying to be all-inclusive, we'll provide you with the basic principles enabling you to become a more sophisticated consumer of scientific messages—less open to sloppy news and junk science, less vulnerable to the tricks of the four rogues and spin-doctors.

Questionnaires are one inexpensive method scientists use to obtain reliable messages about what's going on inside your head. *Attitude scales* are another paper and pencil method that involve asking whether you agree or disagree with ready-made statements. A third, more time consuming and analysis intensive, method—*interviews*—provides you with more freedom to answer questions more freely and to express subtle shades of agreement or disagreement with statements.

All three methods involve a chain of messages passing between those being studied and the social scientist doing the studying, as he or she attempts to elicit carefully considered and honest answers. But remember, whenever a message is generated and transmitted it's open to editing and distortion—witting and unwitting—both by the research participant and the researcher.

Just as the nervous system of an amputee can generate and transmit a pain message from missing toes, so too can your brain generate and transmit messages about almost anything—real, distorted, or imaginary. That challenge keeps qualitative researchers *on their toes*.

Questionnaires

If you're a student, your academic survival is at the mercy of questionnaires: multiple-choice and open-ended exams. We've all responded to too many surveys and suffered brow-wrinkling experiences trying to answer attitude and personality scales.

Those among you who love details and want to *share* your unique and subtle story become frustrated with the mental straight jacket imposed by multiple choice and short answer questionnaires. Justifiably question their external validity. After all, those methods aren't getting a valid picture of *all* you know; they're just getting tiny samples and isolated bits and pieces.

Trading off validity for reliability

While you may disagree with multiple-choice questions, from the point of view of the university multiple choice and true or false questionnaires have two vitally important advantages. First, they're cheap to mark. Most can be fed directly into a computer and the grades are displayed on the course website—unseen by professorial eyes, untouched by faculty fingers (except the ones that fall off the bottom *of the curve*). Even if the computer does not score them, relatively inexpensive grad students using templates can grade them *reliably*.

Second, they're reliable. Multiple-choice questionnaires may not always yield a completely valid picture of everything you know on a given topic, but at least different markers usually assign the same score—valid or not. In contrast, with essay type questions different markers frequently disagree about what grade to assign to these long chains of fuzzy dots and strings of vague messages.

In brief, if we use a multiple-choice questionnaire we trade off some *validity* (a complete and *true* picture of your knowledge), for *reliability* (an agreed upon picture of the answers you got *right* and *wrong* on this particular test).

The bureaucratic beauty of multiple-choice questionnaires is that anyone with normal vision can score them—seeing-is-believing. The more open ended and longer the answer, the more the grade also reflects what the marker believes—believing is seeing. The more open-ended the answer, the more Simon and his premises sit in on the game, and the more the truth lies not on the page but in the mind of the marker.

In the face of massive enrolments and course sizes, we settle for reliability, until graduate school where lower enrolments make a search for increased validity affordable.

Now that you appreciate the practical necessity of multiple-choice-type questionnaires (this category can include true or false questions, and fill in the blank questions, too), let's look at a non-academic example that deals with a sensitive issue.

Questionnaire: Erotic Contact with Blood Relatives

Please answer the following questions as honestly and truthfully as you can. Note that this questionnaire is to be completely anonymous. Do not put your name on the form. For the purposes of this questionnaire, please understand erotic contact to mean any behaviour intended to arouse or satisfy sexual desire.

Age: _____   Marital Status: _____   Sex: _____

Do you have any children related to you by blood?
Yes_____   No _____

Erotic contact between parents and their biological children is harmful.

_____	_____	_____	_____	_____
Strongly	Agree	No	Disagree	Strongly
agree	somewhat	opinion	somewhat	disagree

Have you ever engaged in erotic contact with one of your biological parents (excluding sexual intercourse)?

| _____ | _____ | _____ | _____ | _____ |
| Never | Rarely | Occasionally | Frequently | Very frequently |

If yes, which parent?
Mother _____   Father _____   Both _____

Who initiated this erotic contact?
You _____   Parent _____   Not sure _____

Have you ever had sexual intercourse with one of your biological parents?

| _____ | _____ | _____ | _____ | _____ |
| Never | Rarely | Occasionally | Frequently | Very frequently |

If yes, which parent?
Mother _____   Father _____   Both _____

Have you ever engaged in erotic contact with any other relative (excluding parents) related by blood?

| _____ | _____ | _____ | _____ | _____ |
| Never | Rarely | Occasionally | Frequently | Very frequently |

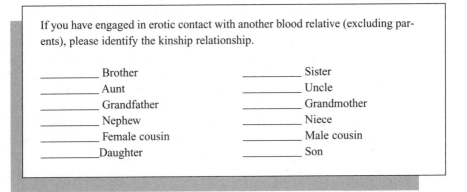

If you have engaged in erotic contact with another blood relative (excluding parents), please identify the kinship relationship.

_____ Brother	_____ Sister
_____ Aunt	_____ Uncle
_____ Grandfather	_____ Grandmother
_____ Nephew	_____ Niece
_____ Female cousin	_____ Male cousin
_____ Daughter	_____ Son

Even though we indicate to respondents that their replies are anonymous (to encourage truth telling and to maintain confidentiality), because of the sensitive issues explored we may nevertheless be justifiably suspicious about the honesty of the answers. Would you answer the above questionnaire honestly if it had been distributed in your college class? If not, under what conditions would you be willing to share that sensitive information? With a same-sex scientist? In a one-on-one interview? Or anonymously over the phone?

Researchers face challenges in writing clear questions and instructions, but the greatest challenge is designing questionnaires that encourage honest responding. While most of you may never design a questionnaire, you will to be pestered to fill them out. And you won't be aware when you're unconsciously responding in a biased manner (e.g., controlled by emotionally anchored premises). But, with the next questionnaire you complete, try to detect when an on-stage rogue pushes your pencil.

Biased responding

A common form of response bias that occurs in questionnaires, personality tests, attitude measures, and interviews is the *social desirability* bias. Most people want to present themselves in the best possible light, and often this means pretending to conform to cultural ideals—that is, respondents can often determine which option of the alternatives presented is the socially desirable one—the response blessed by society's prescriptions. This option may be selected even though it does not reflect your deeply held personal views or behaviours (e.g., your answer includes large on-stage effects).

Incestuous relationships are not socially sanctioned, so it's probable that some respondents who selected the first alternative on Item 2 were responding in the socially endorsed direction instead of providing us with their 'true' opinion. Indeed, almost every question on our instrument is prey to the operation of this socially sanctioned distortion performed by the on-stage rogue.

Researchers sensitive to this potential source of error sometimes include a scale (a few questions) in their questionnaire packet that is especially designed to measure the extent to which a subject consistently opts for the socially desirable response. Data deriving from high scorers on these particular politically correct questions are then discarded on the grounds that the subjects' propensity to endorse socially desirable alternatives is probably disguising their 'real' views.

'Faking bad', the opposite of being politically correct, occurs if there is some advantage for the respondent to appear markedly deviant. Brain-injured victims of car accidents engaged in litigation for damages may be motivated to fake bad—to exaggerate the seriousness of their disabilities. Likewise, a respondent, irritated with the invasion of their privacy, might be motivated to scuttle the research by faking bad, or simply refuse to provide the information. For instance, in the TV show *M*A*S*H*, Corporal Klinger (Jamie Farr), who faked being a transvestite soldier in order to be discharged on psychiatric grounds provides a dramatic and humorous example of this bias. Again, some personality tests include a special set of items designed to assess the strength of the faking bad bias.

Another form of bias—'nay-saying'—occurs when the respondent tends to respond consistently to items in a negative direction regardless of their content. 'Yea-saying' is the exact opposite form of response bias—agreeing with items regardless of the nature of the items.

Some individuals display a *response extremity* bias when they consistently select the most extreme positive or negative alternative. On Items 6 and 8 of our questionnaire, consistent choices of 'Never' or 'Very frequently' suggest such a bias, although we would require more items with this response format (and items which are less likely to be responded to with extreme choices) in order to be certain. Items employing dichotomous response alternatives ('Yes' or 'No') avoid this problem. Conversely, the tendency to consistently check the middle or neutral category on items providing a range of choices similar to Items 2, 6, and 8 might be termed the 'cop-out' bias.

Inconsistent responding constitutes a form of response bias as well. If respondents are not motivated to complete the questionnaire in a conscientious fashion, their careless—even capricious—responding may be revealed by contradictory responses. For example, if one of our research participants indicates that he or she has engaged in erotic practices with a son or daughter (Item 9) and also reports that he or she does not have any children (Item 1), we might legitimately be skeptical about the validity of his or her responses.

Other issues

In addition to these more or less standard forms of response bias (sometimes called *response sets*), surveyors must guard against the creation of idiosyncratic biases. The manner in which questions are worded can play a big role in shaping the respondent's replies. Suppose, for example, the third question on our questionnaire had been worded as follows: 'Have you ever been sexually assaulted by one of your biological parents?' This form of the question has a heavy emotional charge, and some respondents might be loath to label their experience in this way. Thus they may select the 'Never' alternative when in fact the more accurate response might be 'Rarely'. Questions of the 'When did you stop beating your wife?' variety are similarly avoided. Questionnaire designers attempt to employ terminology that is objective and clear, that permits only one interpretation, and that is as emotionally neutral (non-evaluative) as possible—an ideal continuously sought and rarely, if ever, achieved.

Miller's (1991) guide to questionnaire construction includes advice such as

- keep the questions short,
- start with easy and interesting questions (not the biographical items as in the example questionnaire),
- keep open-ended questions to a minimum and place them at the end of the questionnaire (assuming this does not destroy the logical progression of the questions), and
- pre-test the instrument with individuals representative of your ultimate sample to ensure that the questions are appropriate, understandable, and answerable.

Attitude and personality inventories

Not only have you completed multiple choice and fill-in-the-blanks questionnaires, but probably you have also responded to attitude and personality inventories. Instead of asking you questions, many of these qualitative methods contain a series of statements to which you are asked to agree or disagree on a given scale ranging from high to low. Different researchers use different types of scales (e.g., Likert, social distance, etc.) to help you, or them, assign numbers to your subjective responses. For example, a social distance scale measuring attitudes toward an ethnic minority might ask you to endorse statements ranging from willingness to have contact at work to intermarriage.

Designing and standardizing[2] a personality inventory is a highly specialized undertaking. At the top of the PST the researcher must generate a theoretical model of how many dimensions are required to validly represent human personality—five, fourteen, sixteen? Which particular dimensions must be included (depression, masculinity/femininity, introversion/extraversion, tough-mindedness, conservatism, etc.)?

---

[2]Standardization involves administering the test to various samples of your target population (e.g., undergraduate college students). Using different tests of reliability (e.g., test–retest) and of validity (e.g., predicts scores on other measures of the attitude being measured) test items are dropped or modified to accurately reflect the population. Once such a norm, or standard, is established you can compare your score to that standard and determine whether you score at the high or low end of that population (e.g., more or less prejudiced, or anxious, or extraverted, etc.).

Next, they must design it in such a way that encourages us to go inside our heads and *conscientiously* access our personal supply of each of those dimensions while trying to keep our elastic-ruler and on-stage rogues under control. As you can imagine, the wording of inventory statements demands great skill. You know how frustratingly easy it is for other people to misinterpret your own crystal clear statements. Researchers learn the hard way that no matter how much time, effort, and rewriting they commit to constructing transparently clear and concise statements, some creative, or rushed, or lazy, human respondents will misinterpret them.

During the analytical stage the researcher, or a computer, through sophisticated statistical analysis assigns numbers to your subjective responses in order to display the intensity of each dimension of your personality profile.

Of course, other researchers get into the adversarial act, critically evaluating the validity of the inventory. They decide how well that particular inventory fits in with their map or model of personality (e.g., not enough dimensions, too many dimensions) and question how well it helps us understand and predict human behaviour.

In the above accounts you can recognize the chain of edited messages flowing first from the researcher to you, then from you to the paper and pencil attitude scale, then back to the researcher for scoring, then pooled with others for statistical and critical analysis. Does it fit the researcher's pet theory (e.g., female undergrads are less prejudiced than males)? Eventually the findings will be written into a paper, suitable for publication in a scholarly journal. And the chain will continue to flow on through journal editors, to readers, to their friends and colleagues—each person in the flow adding their professional or personal spin.

How do you decide when a researcher *gets it right*?

No universally accepted yardstick exists against which to judge the validity of personality inventories. You and your significant others judge its *internal validity*—how well it *appears* to describe and predict your behaviour. The adversarial battles (both at the top and bottom of the PST) among personality researchers, journal editors, and the purchasers of such inventories, all help determine the scale's reliability and validity—its travel permit and its expiry dates.

In Chapter 6 we discussed issues of reliability and validity. Researchers who design questionnaires and attitude and personality scales, work hard to ensure that their products are, first of all, reliable (i.e., they measure the behaviour *consistently*), and gradually demonstrate increasing validity (e.g., they consistently measure what they *claim* to measure). A biased person is consistent, but their observations are not necessarily accurate (valid).

Researchers work to reduce the amount of elasticity in these qualitative rulers and to reduce the influence of the on-stage rogue. However, establishing validity is always a challenge; the on-stage rogue is always trying to nudge your mind, and your pencil, in the direction that helps you look good, nudging you to give answers that are socially and politically correct, even though those answers may not necessarily reflect your usual or true feelings. The next time you complete one of those scales, pay attention to see if you can sense the nudging. Try to catch the rogues in action!

In addition to questionnaires and attitude scales that can be distributed by hand in a classroom, a shopping centre, or in the workplace, researchers conduct surveys by mail, phone, and the Internet in order to obtain a larger and more representative sample. For example the 'erotic contact' questionnaire discussed earlier could be mailed out to potential respondents or conducted over the phone. The larger and more representative the sample, the greater the external validity your findings possess. The greater the number of people contributing their opinion, the broader the generalizations you can make, and the larger the population your conclusions can cover.

Qualitative researchers joke that most of what we know about human behaviour is based on what first year psychology students *say* that they think and feel. They're sitting ducks—a captive audience for academic researchers testing one of their latest attitude or personality scales. They are a *readily accessible* source of information. But to assume that first year psychology students think and feel just like the rest of us is not only naïve, it's scary. Fortunately, that kind of biased sampling is no longer as common as it once was, thus the external validity of scales has been extended.

To standardize a test on readily accessible undergraduates (a cognitively and emotionally volatile segment of the population) unfortunately establishes a convenient and affordable standard for what's considered normal thinking and feeling about a given topic. Therefore, if your *score* differs significantly from that particular *norm* then by definition you're *abnormal*. You can see that to assume that first year university students validly represent normal thinking, feeling, and behaviour against which the normality of rest of us are judged is, to say the least, bizarre.

Therefore, when evaluating the validity of a questionnaire, attitude scale, or personality scale you should not only judge how easy it is to fake good results, but determine how representative of the target population is the sample of people used to develop or standardize it.

Questionnaires and inventories enable us to determine what a large number of people say that they think and feel on a particular occasion. In order to obtain more in-depth information researchers conduct phone or personal interviews. In doing so they are searching for more internal validity—specific to that person—than a questionnaire or scale typically provides. A skilled interviewer can help you go to places inside your head that questionnaires never reach.

Interviews: digging deeper

One of the disadvantages of a mailed questionnaire or attitude scale is the relatively low return rate, which is, on average, about 48 per cent. As an alternative, telephone interviews have gained in popularity. Much higher return rates are achieved through telephone interviews and the costs are still significantly less than face-face interviews.

Personal interviews

Perhaps the best way to illustrate the differences between a questionnaire approach and an in-depth personal interview is to describe an actual interview study.[3] Elizabeth Church (2004) wanted an answer to the question of why it is so hard to be a stepmother. To find out about the experiences of others in this role, she interviewed 104 stepmothers who volunteered to participate in her study in response to solicitations to family physicians, media interviews, notices, and talks to community organizations. The sample was a fairly homogenous group of white middle and professional-class Canadian women living with a man who had children from a previous relationship. The interviews were framed by a series of questions (e.g., what are the positive and negative aspects of step-mothering) but respondents had an opportunity to raise any additional issues that they thought were relevant. Taped interviews ranged from one and a half to three hours in duration and were subsequently transcribed and subjected to conent analysis.

Based on repeated readings of the transcripts, frequently occurring themes were tabulated. 'Once a list of common themes was generated, all the inerviews were coded using these categories and the conext for the themes was identified. Jealousy, for instance, was a theme that frequently appeared among the step-mothers' (297). One major categorization involved the identification of seven main sources of stress for stepmothers: the image of the wicked stepmother; unrealistic initial expectations; the notion of the perfect mother; dealing with the 'real mother'; relationships with the stepchildren; unsupportive partners; part-ner's unwillingness to have more children.

A second main classification derived from the interviews had to do with dif-ferent approaches to motherhood. Five models were identified based on how the women defined their place in the stepfamily, relationships within and outside the stepfamily unit, conflicts experienced and emotional reactions (the nuclear model, the biological model, the retreat model, the couple model, and the extended model). A working definition was developed for each model. Using these definitions, an independent coder read two-thirds of the interview tran-scripts and assigned each interviewee to one of the models. An 80 per cent agreement was found between Church's assignment and that of the coder. In the nuclear model, for example, the focus is on family defined as mother, father, and all biologically related children. The stepmom tries to reduce the influence of in-laws and sees the biological mother as the 'fly in the ointment.' Underappreci-ation may be the down side for women in this model who believe they should perform all the mother activities.

---

[3]See Belenky, Clinchy, Galdberer and Tarule (1986) for another example.

As a clinical psychologist, Church was also interested in the assistance these stepmothers sought and received from professionals, self-help strategies, support networks, and the like and this was also explored in the interviews. Synthesizing the information obtained through the interviews, Church concludes her study by describing seven principles that appeared to guide the behaviour of the happiest stepmothers.

An interview strategy permits investigation of a huge problem space, brings the researcher much closer to the reality to be explored, allows analysis of an issue in a context, and generates a massively complex and fantastically rich data pool. But, as sophisticated science consumers, we have some questions. Are the interviewee reports accurate and complete representations of the experiences sampled by the interviewers? Would other interviewers using the same interview schedule with the same set of interviewees have elicited similar responses? Would other analysts generate a similar coding scheme from the interview transcripts? If so, would individual responses be similarly classified? And would the research participants themselves agree with Church's assignment of them to one or the other of the five family models? To what extent did Church's personal experiences as a stepmother influence her data? Are these findings generalizable to all women? Some women? Which women?

You can recognize a familiar challenge in these questions. To what extent do researchers provide us with answers based primarily with valid data collected at the bottom of the PSTS (seeing-is-believing), and to what extent unwittingly based on their personal or professional distortions at the top (believing-is-seeing)?

Focus groups

Interviews can be conducted with groups as well as individuals. To supplement information obtained by individual interviews, or surveys, some researchers conduct a kind of group interview or 'focus group'. Particularly popular with market researchers, customers are asked to comment on, and discuss their feelings about a product, or planned product, or what they like and don't like about a particular company. Once they get warmed up, focus groups generate spontaneous interactions and novel ideas that are less likely to emerge in more controlled individual and survey-type contexts. But because they are less controlled they are also open to very large elastic-ruler effects; that is, we are not sure whether the final analysis and report mainly reflects the ideas of the group, or of the researcher. Nevertheless, this method provides an excellent way to generate creative hypotheses that can then be investigated more systematically by other methods.

Making sense of qualitative data

Qualitative measures typically cover more psychological ground than quantitative methods. That's both their strength, and their limitation. When you try to explore large territories you run the risk of learning less about more. To reduce that risk researchers use a variety of methods to help them separate fact from fancy. They do so both in the way they design their questionnaires and structure their interviews, and also in the way they critically analyze the results. Without such controls we run the risk of learning more about what the researcher thinks and feels than what the people he interviewed, or who responded to his questionnaires, think and feel. This is a complex research area so, in the space available, we will only provide a few examples of the various controls social scientists employ.

Q Methodology

Imposing a structure on qualitative data, on the pages and pages of free-flowing prose transcribed from interview protocols or open-ended questionnaires, is a daunting task—all the more so because of the infinite opportunities for researcher characteristics (e.g., bias) to shape perceived patterns. To achieve a measure of objectivity, researchers precisely define coding categories, provide examples, develop procedures for their recognition or identification, train others in the application of these coding strategies, and determine the extent to which various coders agree in the assignment of categories. However, such codes or categories belong to the researcher, not the subjects, and reliable coders may be those who successfully grasp or intuit the researcher's biases. A recently resurrected qualitative approach that helps to address these difficulties (but does not totally eliminate them) is the Q methodology.[4]

The essence of the Q-technique or Q-sort (Stephenson, 1935), as it is sometimes called, involves the presentation of a set of statements (or objects or pictures) to research participants, who then sort the items into piles according to some system of categorization (i.e., 'most like me' to 'least like me'). It is then possible (using objective factor analytic techniques rather than researcher-generated categories) to identify clusters of individuals with similar rankings. Celia Kitzinger (1986, 1987; Kitzinger and Rogers, 1985) for example, used the Q methodology in her explorations of the nature of lesbian identities. How do homosexual women understand or interpret the development/origin of their sexual preference? Do lesbians view themselves as sick or deviant, or do they see themselves as challenging these socially constructed conceptions?

Selection of the items to be sorted is, of course, a key issue. If the researcher creates/invents the item pool, then this technique approaches a Likert-type questionnaire situation, with its attendant constraints on tapping the subjective realities of the respondents. However, the Q researcher attempts to span the domain so that the item pool covers or does justice to both the breadth and diversity of

---

[4]Brown (1980) describes numerous examples of the use of this technique from a political science perspective.

the phenomena to be studied. Kitzinger derived her items directly from interviews with a sample of lesbians to help ensure their validity and to make them user friendly by using verbatim comments. Her interview sample was non-random because the objective was to achieve representativeness (i.e., to obtain the broadest possible spectrum of views); in any case, because the parameters of the lesbian population are unknown, a random selection is not possible. Use of the Q methodology, unlike more traditional approaches, does not require the testing of large numbers of randomly selected respondents. In the interviews, Kitzinger attempted to capture personal meanings of lesbian identity—the idiosyncratic subjective conceptualizations of individual lesbians.

Interviewee comments about their views of their own lesbianism were transferred to cards (e.g., 'My relationship with my father helps to explain why I am a lesbian,' 'I believe I was born lesbian,' and 'I feel good about being different.'). At this step in the research process, we perceive an opportunity for researcher edits (which of the myriad interviewee statements will find their way to the Q-cards and which will be discarded?). These cards are then subsequently sorted by the interviewees themselves (which provides a useful check on the researcher's selection), or by others—or by both—into a quasi-normal distribution using 11 categories ranging from +5 ('most agree that the statement applies to me') to –5 ('most disagree that the statement applies to me'). If the deck of items consisted of 80 cards, the distribution might be as follows:

Scale:	–5	–4	–3	–2	–1	0	+1	+2	+3	+4	+5
Items:	5	6	7	8	9	10	9	8	7	6	5

Completed Q sorts are then subjected to a statistical procedure (factor analysis) that essentially assesses the extent to which different individual sortings are intercorrelated. In effect, the analysis distinguishes subgroups of individuals who rank-ordered the items similarly. Kitzinger's data analysis yielded seven different patterns of lesbian identity. Unlike content analysis techniques or the interpretation of unstructured interviews, which oblige the researcher to create coding or scoring categories and thus allow ample room for the biases of the researcher to influence the results, analysis of the Q-sort is objective in the sense that the commonalities are determined statistically.

However, an element of researcher bias may still seep in with the interpretation of these patterns, so they are presented to the research participants as a validity check. Articulating the distinctiveness and advantages of this research strategy, Kitzinger and Rogers comment, 'Unlike normative methodologies, the use of Q sorts does not impose a structure in advance; and unlike the 'qualitative' methodologies (such as participant observation, in-depth interviewing, etc.), the use of Q sorts does not require the investigator to impose a structure *after* the data have been gathered (through content analysis, for example): respondents in the process of sorting the items create their own structure' (1985: 170).

Grounded theory

Not everyone believes our top-of-the-PST assumption that premises, beliefs, and biases play the key role in selecting and editing messages flowing up from the bottom. For example, grounded theorists adopt a bottom-up premise, proposing that bottom observations can generate up-top premises. And they're not talking about billiard balls. They're talking about inputs from thinking, feeling, and planning clinical clients.

The researcher attempts to take a blank slate approach to the input (e.g., a live or taped interview with a client). In a sense the researcher is trying to become the perfect listener—listening for psychological nuance: he or she is gradually determining the content of the thematic message in the chain based on what the client actually says and does, rather than simply reflecting the therapist's or researcher's expectations or premises. The psychological categories and connections ideally emerge from the client's discourse, as opposed to having been shaped to fit the researchers pre-existing categories. Grounded theorists don't support Simon's mantra of 'no conclusions without premises' as wholeheartedly as the authors of this text, do. They're prepared to believe that the clinician can adopt a relatively clean mental slate for the patient to write on.

In simplified form, the final message the researcher receives and delivers is ideally based on the client's dots and connections as delivered by the client. It is not necessarily a message that accommodates the researcher's pet theory. The researcher's goal is to become the perfect measuring instrument—one that doesn't distort the psychological meaning of the messages being transmitted.

We accept their bottom-up premise concerning the impact of firmly packaged and salient observations (e.g., needles, skunk musk, and hot stoves). We also acknowledge, through two-way arrows, that information affects flow in all directions around the PST, bottom up, top down.

Furthermore, we respect the remarkably conscientious efforts of grounded theorists[5] who spend hours and hours, even weeks, seeking the client's patterns of thoughts and feelings in a brief one-hour segment of a clinical interview.

They do sincerely try to put aside their personal and theoretical premises and biases in an effort to let the natural structure embedded in the clients flow display itself on the blank slate of their minds. In brief, when dealing with clinical clients, grounded theorists attempt to adopt a seeing-is-believing perspective by putting their own beliefs on the back burner.

You may have noticed that we, the authors, are painfully stretching our bounded rationality trying to explain this opposing view. These differences between our perspective and that of the grounded theorists do not mean that the grounded theorists are wrong. It just means that we can't afford, at the top of our own PSTs, to accept their way of thinking. To do so would mean dismantling

---

[5]See Rennie (In Press), for further discussion by a sophisticated researcher who understands both the philosophical, theoretical, and methodological challenges involved in grounded theory research.

our network of emotionally anchored beliefs. In short, we would have to rewrite this book.

We can accept Pidgeon and Henwood's (1977) 'flip-flop' model involving continuous shifts between theory and data, between the top and bottom of the PST. But, for all but billiard ball experience, we continue to presume that up-top premises hold the trump cards. Time will decide what kind of travel permit grounded theory acquires in the future.

Sample selection

All scientists, whether they work in the lab or in the field, struggle with decisions about sample selection. If researchers could have their druthers, all their subject samples would be representative of the total population of *Homo sapiens*. Ah, what a dream of glory—to be able to generalize our findings to every single human being on (and off) the planet! But if wishes were horses, beggars would ride. The study based on such a sample has yet to be done, although computers may soon provide the technology to transform this daydream into a nightmarish reality.

Meanwhile researchers must compromise by limiting or curtailing the parent population from which they draw their samples. For obvious reasons one of the most popular populations from which samples are selected and studied is the undergraduate university population. However, survey researchers frequently pose questions that necessitate selection from larger and more diverse populations. How will the country vote in the next election? Polling the voting preferences of a sample of university students will not help us predict, with any degree of confidence, which party will capture the majority of congressional seats. Therefore, pollsters and other investigators interested in predicting or identifying national trends adopt more sophisticated (and more expensive) sampling techniques. First, the total population—all members of the population over voting age—is categorized in terms of certain characteristics believed to be relevant to voting preference (e.g., minority group affiliation, religion, age, geographic area, and socioeconomic status). Subjects are then selected so that they reflect the proportion of these characteristics in the total population. For example, if the population is 49 per cent male and 51 per cent female, then this sex ratio will be maintained in the sample. Similarly, if 10 per cent of the total population as defined is unemployed, then 10 per cent of the sample will consist of unemployed respondents. This procedure, known as *quota sampling*, is popular with pollsters.

Many other strategies for sample selection have been devised. None are perfect in that none of them can guarantee that the sample is an exact miniature replica of the target population. Studies will differ, however, in the extent to which they approximate the population. Before we buy the most recent statistic on the percentage of the population favouring capital punishment, or the number of dentists recommending a specific brand of toothpaste, or the degree of opposition to gun control legislation, we would be well advised to assess the quality of the sampling procedure. Perhaps the statistic was based on responses to a telephone poll conducted on a one-hour TV talk show last Saturday. Such haphazard sampling is totally inadequate, and we reject those types of findings out of hand.

Maybe the *area-sampling* approach was employed with dwellings within each precinct in Des Moines being randomly sampled. We may accept the accuracy of the statistic for those Des Moines residents who were at home when the researcher called. We may be willing to go even further and generalize the findings to those from the same socio-economic group who didn't happen to be home. Some of us might even include people living in comparably sized Midwest cities, but most of us would be justifiably reluctant to apply the statistic to natives of say New York City.

The *panel technique*, defined as interviewing the same group of people on two or more occasions, has become an important sampling strategy. This approach is most appropriate for studying behaviour, attitude, or opinion consistency and fluctuations. Mortality (sample attrition) and the effects of repeat interviewing are potential problems (see Chapter 7).

Next time someone tries to hustle you with a survey statistic, finger it, stretch it, prod it, and sniff it. How was the sample selected, and does this selection procedure offer reasonable assurance that the sample is representative of the target population? Ask three simple questions:

1. Who was left out?
2. What percentage of the population does this omission represent?
3. How do non-respondents compare with respondents?

Administration

The most carefully constructed questionnaire or interview schedule, combined with the most sophisticated sampling strategy, may still fail to produce accurate results if the administrative procedures are faulty. Obviously surveys based on interviews are more influenced by interviewer techniques, but the return rate of mailed-out questionnaires can also be affected by the content, and tone, of instructions.

Response rates to mailed questionnaires vary enormously, but on average 48 per cent of those who receive a single mailing return the form. Follow-up mailings yield, on average, an additional 20, 12, and 10 per cent return rate in response respectively to second, third, and fourth mailings. So, although at first glance the mailed questionnaire seems to be a relatively inexpensive means of gathering huge amounts of data, the need to implement follow-up procedures enhances research costs considerably. Personal interviews produce the best response rates.

Research examining the effects of interviewer characteristics on subject responses has established that the interviewer's sex, social class, age, and race may affect interviewee answers. Further, just as the hypotheses of the experimenter may shape the data he or she collects in the lab, so too may the expectations and attitudes of the interviewer channel the replies obtained from interviewees. Interviewers may unknowingly reinforce the expression of opinions that fit well with their own views—with a nod, a smile, an uh-huh, or, in the extreme, with a spontaneous comment like, 'You're absolutely right. I couldn't agree more!' Interview responses obtained by naïve interviewers often tell us more about the investigator than they do about the respondent.

Various techniques may be employed to reduce the impact of interviewer characteristics on the data. An infrequently used tactic is to match interviewers with their interviewees on certain demographic characteristics such as age, sex, social class, and race. An alternative strategy (equally rare) requires heterogeneity of interviewers on these variables—that is, equal numbers of male and female interviewers, black and white interviewers, and so on are sent out to the field. Then, even though the harvest reaped by each interviewer is biased, we have avoided a systematic bias; we hope to average out our biases.

Careful training of interviewers may help to overcome the problem of the intrusion of the interviewer's personality, expectations, and attitudes into the interview protocol. Training is aimed at standardization. Ideally we would like to rule out the interviewer as a rogue suspect, and so we attempt to train each interviewer to follow a specific uniform procedure. Each interview is to begin with the same introductory comments; the questions are to be asked in a designated order; the wording of each question must be followed exactly; probing techniques are to be specified and instructions provided as to when to probe. Additionally, interviewers may be taught how to establish and maintain a pleasant relationship with the interviewee—how to develop good rapport. The assumption is that if the respondents feel comfortable and relatively relaxed in the interview they will be more responsive, more open, and more co-operative.

The next time you watch an interview on television, try to identify the interviewer's techniques. Try to assess whether this interviewer is likely to elicit accurate responses. Does the interviewer victimize the respondent by employing a brusque, aggressive, non-accepting stance? Whose views do you learn more about—the interviewer's or the guest's?

Strengths and weaknesses

Survey methods have the advantage of getting the responses of large samples of people, even of large random samples, at relatively low cost. But notice that the responses are 'lightweight' ones. Your research subjects are 'telling you' what they would do—and you know that more often than not there is a world of difference between what people say they would do (or did) in a given situation and what they actually do (or did). In 1949 some 920 Denver residents were asked whether they had made contributions to a charity organization. Of those who replied in the affirmative, 34 per cent had not actually done so (Parry and

Crossley, cited in Oskamp, 1977).[6] Most of us recognize this inconsistency in ourselves—for example, the parent admonishes little Jane, 'Do what I say, not what I do.' Nevertheless, our critics, little or big, rarely miss an opportunity to point out this deficit—'I can't hear what you're saying because I'm watching what you're doing.' Notice that on a questionnaire we have only to move the pencil a few inches to shift our scores from being a bigot to being a humanitarian. We don't have to move our heavyweight (actual) behaviour at all. Hanson (1980) has reviewed the research investigating the association between attitudes and behaviour. Almost half of the studies he examined (20 of 46) failed to demonstrate a positive relationship between attitudes and behaviour.

Lack of correspondence between questionnaire responses and behaviour may reflect a lack of *internal validity—our* survey procedures were inadequate, and so we did not obtain an accurate picture of the respondent's attitudes. Or, the discrepancy between the verbal and behavioural domains may suggest an *external validity* problem in that, like the control-group model discussed in Chapter 5, survey research data may not generalize to life outside the survey. Still another interpretation is that humans are well able to tolerate such incongruency. One of our colleagues, who was accused of behaving inconsistently, replied quite unabashed, 'What's so great about consistency? Consistency is the refuge of closed minds.' A fourth possibility is that, in fact, attitudes and behaviour agree but are almost continually in a state of flux. At 10:00 AM on Election Day Mr Jones responds to the interviewer firmly, sincerely, and without a moment's hesitation, 'Oh, I intend to vote for President Bush.' If the election had taken place before 6 November, Mr Jones would indeed have voted as he indicated; but perhaps his verbal, lightweight response changed after that, and his X on the ballot followed suit.

The use of simple physical evidence can markedly extend the validity of laboratory and questionnaire data. For example, following a campaign to encourage drivers to wear seat belts, a questionnaire study indicated a large increase in the number of drivers reporting that they had begun to wear seat belts. Two students supplemented this data by interviewing gas station attendants and by doing spot-checks at stoplights and service stations. Gas station attendants reported little or no shift in the percentage of customers wearing seat belts before or after the campaign, and observational spot-checkers revealed a much lower percentage of drivers wearing seat belts than the questionnaire data estimated.

Questionnaire and interview techniques permit us to extend scientific horizons—to go back in time, to go forward into the future, to explore new terrain, to expand our data pool. In so doing they take us out of the lab and classrooms into street corners, back alleys, living rooms, bars, churches, funeral homes, clinics, etc. As is the case with all the other sieves of science, naïve use of the

---

[6]Note that this study provides evidence of the operation of the social desirability response bias.

survey approach will allow much that is valid to escape through the mesh and much that is nonsense to remain trapped—looking for all the world, to our believing-is-seeing perspective like fact, not fancy.

SUMMARY

Social scientists need to access subjective information. They need to know what people think, feel, and plan to do. Lacking physical probes and quantifiers researchers rely on qualitative methods to collect, analyze, and display these subjective messages. These self-reports provide a view of what the bottom and top of your PST look like from the inside—from your unique perspective.

Questionnaires, attitude scales, and interviews extend the observational validity of our explorations of people's thoughts, feelings, and plans. They enable us to travel outside the sheltered laboratory, to see if of our small truths can survive in the rough and tumble of less protected, less controlled environments. As usual, there is a kicker—the elastic-rulers comes back to haunt us. Paper and pencil and interview responses are notoriously ephemeral, distorted by self-serving on-stage effects, blown away by memory loss, twisted by deceit, capriciously fluttering here and there at the mercy of personal whim and situational breezes.

Some qualitative methods allow researchers considerable latitude for imposing top down, believing-is-seeing distortions on the research participant's chain of messages, on their *realities*. Nevertheless, some of that elasticity may be removed through careful and sophisticated instrument design, sample selection, and testing and scoring procedures.

Stop and think about what percentage of the endless chain of messages you process every minute, of every hour, of every day consists of your own subjective self-reports, and those of others? Plus or minus 90 per cent?

Stop and think of how much fun the rogues are having editing (correcting? distorting?) accessible messages to accommodate your bounded rationality, your emotionally anchored premises? And yet it seems to *work* most of the time. How can that be? Does it mean that many of those blind premises must be based on genetic and cultural wisdom distilled over centuries of trial and error gambits to fit our particular physical and cultural environments?

student's notebook

I don't think Professor Creek likes this chapter. Being a quantitative experimental kind of guy, I get the feeling he's a bit twitchy about the lack of control that qualitative researchers face when operating down at the noisy bottom of their PSTs.

In fact, I've heard Professor Creek and Dr Frund arguing over that very issue. He says that qualitative research is like throwing seeds to the wind and then trying to find the flowers hidden in a field of weeds. She says that it is better than growing tiny flowers

under a microscope and wondering why they died when you took them out of the sheltered greenhouse (laboratory).

Professor Creek followed up by saying that at least he could state his conclusions (up
at the top of his PST) with mathematical precision, which was better than the fuzzy, wordy
logic qualitative researchers used. And Dr Frund countered by saying that if he wanted to
spend his life computing the 'square root of sweet fanny all to four decimal points', then
he should just go ahead, but anyone with common sense knew it was better to be reasonably certain about a wide angle observation than to be completely certain about how
many hairs there were on a bee's knee.

It's sort of exciting to overhear Professors fight!

But, in the end, maybe there's something to be said for both sides. From Professor
Creek's perspective you can learn certain things by studying a few animals under the controlled conditions of a zoo. From Dr Frund's viewpoint you can learn other things from
observing a lot of animals in the wild. From Professor Creek's perspective you can learn
some things in a lab by recording MRI images of people's brains. From Dr Frund's viewpoint you can learn what they're thinking by skillfully interviewing them and unobtrusively
observing them as they go about the business of living.

From where I sit—alone and lonely in the library on a Friday afternoon—
researchers would learn still more by combining quantitative and qualitative observations. It's nice to know that blood is probably rushing to the primitive part of Derek's brain
whenever he sees me. But knowing that doesn't make me as happy as seeing his eyes light
up and seeing him smile when we meet. Those are qualitative, out-of-lab observations,
though. Maybe he's not really smiling. Maybe he's grimacing because the chilidog he ate
for lunch is giving him indigestion.

Have you noticed that most arguments seem to be driven by either/or assumptions?
It's either nature or nurture. It's either true or false. Of course it gets much more complicated when you replace 'or' with 'and': it's both nature and nurture; it's both true and
false. I guess it's too complicated, too many dots, too many possible connections for our
bounded rationality to handle. Is that because, as we zip around our PSTs, we can't afford
to get our heads around more than one main answer per big question? But surely
Professor Creek and Dr Frund are different. As professors they must have both the time
and critical thinking capacity to consider, weigh, and integrate the good ideas flowing out
of nature and nurture, both quantitative and qualitative methods? At least they must have
the time when they are teaching, as opposed to when they're using up all their time fighting. Lots of behaviour, including theirs seems to be specific to certain situations—internally valid for one situation but not for another. Restricted travel permits, I guess.

I suppose Derek's right. He says that when scientists take off their white coats they're
just like us. Their brains are the same size as ours, but they can usually camouflage their
biases with a fancier vocabulary.

Even when wearing their white coats, I guess it takes all the bounded rationality
they've got to investigate a single complex question, without overloading their brain with
too many competing premises and too many different research methods. Trying to learn

the details about both quantitative and qualitative research methods overloads the old brain. Trying to get their big academic heads around too many alternatives leads to information overload, which, of course, leads to dangerous ways of thinking, academic fights, and giggling Gods.

Without a strong premise, no strong conclusions, no coherent lectures, no publications, no grant applications, no career! And no interesting fights!

I discussed this with Dr Frund. Well, actually, I asked her whether she thought I should take Professor Creek's advanced course involving a lot of lab research with animals.

She surprised me. She said that the kind of research you end up doing—quantitative or qualitative—depends a lot on your personality. In her opinion, lab-based quantitative research requires not only brains but also a great deal of patience, attention to detail, and in some cases, a good background in math. It takes great patience because, as she heard an award-winning neuropsychologist, Dr Brenda Milner,[7] say, it can be a long time between positive results.

I guess with quantitative research you usually find out more quickly that you're wrong than with qualitative research—the quantitative ruler isn't quite so elastic. Dr Frund's advice was to take Professor Creek's course and see how I liked it. I might become addicted to lab research.

As I was leaving she mentioned that one of the founders of modern psychology—a guy named William James[8]—apparently said: 'We do what we must and call it by the best name we know.' Then she said, 'I like qualitative research and call it by the best names I know—it suits my temperament, my core premises, my biases.'

Interesting. Do I have enough patience to be a lab researcher—a hard-nosed quantitative psychologist? Maybe I'd become famous studying the topic of patience, quantitatively and qualitatively. How would I do that?

Brainstorming

I posed these questions to our pub group: How would you study patience scientifically? Here's some of the answers I got.

Quantitatively you could look for a persistence gene in animals. That is, are there genetic differences between those animals that persist until they drop when trying to solve an impossible task, those animals that give it a good shot and then sit down and scratch themselves, and those animals that give up early and take a nap?

With people you could record how long they pay attention or persist at an unsolvable task. You could do a longitudinal study starting with babies and keep retesting them every year. Are there DNA differences between those showing low persistence versus those

[7]Brenda Milner. 2006. Available at http://en.wikipedia.org/w/index.php?title=Brenda_Milner&oldid=54392577 (accessed on 24 June 2006).

[8]William James. 2006. Available at http://en.wikipedia.org/w/index.php?title=William_James&oldid=60062139 (accessed on 24 June 2006).

showing high persistence on quantitative measures? If you follow them long enough how many of each group would become lab researchers themselves?

And qualitatively, you could check to see if differences in persistent behaviour (measured by surveys, unobtrusive measures, etc.) show up in identical twins raised apart. If identical twins differ significantly, then it would seem that persistence might not be influenced as much by genes as it is by early environmental influences like training and role models.

Some of the B&B members were still debating this question—still persisting at their attempts to solve the problem—when Derek and I left to go to a movie. Come to think of it, the guys who continued arguing were lab jockeys (according to my naturalistic observation, right?).

In order to get this chapter to fit my bounded rationality I decided that the major difference between quantitative and qualitative methods is simply this: with quantitative methods you focus on reliability and internal validity. And with qualitative methods you trade off some (but hopefully not too much) reliability and internal validity in order to get a wide-angle picture—to get more external validity.

Anyway, in spite of Creek's preference for lab research, he made us do a major qualitative assignment—an interview study based on what we learned in this chapter. Three of us pooled our resources. Here are our results.

Police and Prostitutes—A Research Paper
By Diana Dodds, for Research Methods 201

Introduction

The purpose of this study is to determine whether police officials accurately perceive the behaviour and attitudes of prostitutes and to investigate the nature of the interactions between prostitutes and police.

Method

Participants

Thirteen subjects were interviewed: eight prostitutes and five police officers. At the time of the interview, the prostitutes—who ranged in age from 18–50—were all incarcerated for offenses connected with prostitution. The police officers were all connected with morality work and included two constables, two sergeants, and an inspector. All police subjects were male and their ages ranged from 30–50. Permission to interview a random sample of police officers in the city was sought but not obtained.

Materials

An interview form containing nine questions was designed to provide specific information concerning the behaviour and opinions of prostitutes and the nature of their interactions with the police. Similar questions, but appropriately reworded, were administered to the police to determine their perceptions of prostitutes. A copy of the interview form follows.

Interview

We are students working on a project dealing with the relationship between prostitutes and the police. We would like to ask you some questions, if you don't mind. If there are any questions you would prefer not to answer, that's fine. We would appreciate any information you would like to give. Please be assured that you will remain anonymous and your answers will be kept strictly confidential.

1. Do you tend to work a regular area?
   a. Yes
   b. No
2. How do you get your tricks?
   a. Street contacts
   b. Bars
   c. Pimps
   d. Bar or hotel employees
   e. Regular customers
   f. Police
   g. Taxi drivers
   h. Telephone
3. Do you get the same amount of money for each trick or does it vary?
   a. Same
   b. Varies
4. Are you friends with other prostitutes?
   a. Yes
   b. No
5. What is your relationship with the police?
   a. Occasionally have a drink with police?
   b. Call certain officers by their first name?
   c. Discuss personal matters with them?
   d. Ask for advice from them?
   e. Are sarcastic and/or unfriendly to them?
   f. Avoid speaking to them?
6. Do you ever make deals or bargains with the police?
   a. Inform the police about criminal acts (pushers, thieves) in return for easy or lenient treatment?
   b. Co-operate with the police to get rid of your competition?
   c. Turn a trick with a police officer to avoid getting busted?

7. Do you always keep your part of the deal or bargain?
   a. Yes
   b. No
8. Do you think the police treat you fairly?
   a. Yes
   b. No
9. Do you think the laws on prostitution should be changed?
   a. Made clearer
   b. Male prostitution should be illegal
   c. Prostitution should be legalized
   d. Rehabilitation should be offered instead of fines and jail sentences

Procedure

The three researchers conducted the interviews together, with one researcher directing the questions and the other two recording the responses. The interviews were approximately one hour in duration. Two of the police interviews were conducted in the home of one of the researchers, and the others were held in the office of the interviewees. All the prostitutes were interviewed in a small room in the jail provided for visiting purposes. At the conclusion of the interview, all participants were thanked for their time and co-operation.

In an effort to establish rapport before commencing the interview proper, the researchers described the course under which auspices we were conducting the research. We also explored with interviewees some personal history and shared cigarettes.

Results

The percentage of prostitutes and police providing each response alternative is presented in Table 8.1. The greater the disparity between the two percentages, the greater the misperception on the part of the police.

Table 8.1 Accuracy of Police Perceptions of Prostitutes

Question	Prostitutes	Police	Question	Prostitutes	Police
1. a	88	80	5. aa	25	0
b	13	20	b	13	0
2. aa	25	20	c	0	0
b	75	80	d	0	0
c	13	20	e	38	100
d	13	40	f	50	0
e	0	0	6. a	0	20
f	0	0	b	0	20

Question	Prostitutes	Police	Question	Prostitutes	Police
g	13	20	c	0	0
h	0	20	7. a	–	20
3. a	88	80	b	–	20
b	13	20	8. a	13	40
4. a	100	100	b	88	60
b	0	0	9. a[a]	0	20
			b	3	20
			c	100	20
			d	50	40

[a]Percentages total more than 100 because several response alternatives were provided by the interviewees on these questions.

Discussion

To illustrate the experiences and lifestyle of the prostitutes, a typical case is described. At the time of the interview, this prostitute had so many convictions on her record that she could not remember the exact number. She had been 'busted' (arrested) seven times within the last 11 months by the same detective. She had been released from jail the previous week but was apprehended again three days later. She reported that she had had the assurance of a job, which was to start in three weeks. Given this information the police advised her to plead guilty in the hope of a remand for two weeks. However, she received a sentence of two months. Unable to qualify for legal aid and not able to afford a lawyer, she had little chance of escaping conviction. When she is released, she will have no job and no money and will be forced to return to prostitution in order to support herself. Thus she must risk yet another conviction. In a sense the predictable and repeated chain of events is analogous to being caught in a revolving door.

The results obtained from the interviews suggest that the perception of the police with respect to the behaviour of prostitutes is reasonably accurate on many points. The most obvious discrepancies occurred in responses about the nature of the interactions between the prostitutes and the police. Prostitutes report more friendly or intimate contacts than the police do.

The major weakness of this research is the small size of the samples. As indicated earlier, it was not possible to obtain permission to randomly sample police officials. In the case of the prostitutes, permission had been obtained to solicit interviewees in one jail. At the time the interviews were conducted, a total of 14 prostitutes were inmates in the jail, but four refused to participate, one was released before she could be interviewed, and one woman, who stated that she was a prostitute but had never been arrested for this offense, was excluded.

When all was said and done, Professor Creek made the following comments.

Instructor's comments

You are to be congratulated for attempting to tackle a significant issue—one that requires the collection of data from groups that are under-researched due to the difficulties in obtaining sufficiently large samples. You made a valiant (albeit unsuccessful) effort to follow 'good' research practices with respect to sample selection. Your interview form has several strengths—particularly evident is your attempt to use the vernacular of your interviewees and the effective use of probes. Your sensitivity to the need for good rapport is also noteworthy. How successful do you feel you were in establishing rapport? One concern, which you did not express, relates to the accuracy (truthfulness) of the responses obtained. Apparently you probed for some demographic information (such as number of convictions); perhaps you might have been able to check this information against official records to provide a crude indication of response 'slippage'. It would have been of interest to have recorded and reported the demographic data.

The use of three interviewers is puzzling. Perhaps you felt intimidated by your interviewees and wanted the moral support of a colleague. Having one person conduct the interview while another records the responses is also a good strategy. However, an interviewee might feel overwhelmed and be more circumspect (on-stage) in the presence of three interviewers. Since two people were recording, you had an opportunity to assess the reliability of the recording process, yet you do not appear to have compared recorders' responses.

Given the small sample it is inappropriate to generalize beyond your specific samples. While the five police officers may have been reasonably accurate in their perceptions of the eight prostitutes, we cannot assume that this degree of congruence would hold with more representative samples.

News reports

I didn't forget my news reports this week, and I think I found two really good pieces of news to discuss. I've included a copy of this assignment below.

Physical yardsticks of the mind

Speaking, as this chapter does, of developing physical yardsticks for measuring what you're thinking and feeling, MRI imaging is on a roll.[9] An MRI measures

---

[9]'Magnetic resonance imaging'. 2006. Available at http://en.wikipedia.org/w/index.php?title= Magnetic_resonance_imaging&oldid=60177418 (accessed on 24 June 2006). Also, see *Time magazine*, 24 October 2005: 64–5.

blood flow to different parts of your brain while you're looking at different pictures, or answering different questions, or experiencing different emotions. So, what researchers are trying to do is connect those different internal, subjective experiences to different patterns of blood flow in different parts of your brain. For example what kinds of stimuli lead to increased blood flow to the thinking part of the brain and which to the feeling part?

Researchers see all kinds of possibilities, like being able to get access to your mind without having to trust your self-reports.

Of course advertisers are mad about the possibilities. They see big bucks rolling in by generating ads that bypass our thinking brains and make direct contact with our emotional brains. Using MRI data, they found out that more blood flows to the emotional brain when you're shown a bottle of Coke than when shown a bottle of Pepsi—even for people who claim to be loyal Pepsi drinkers.

The advertisers are probably hoping MRIs will tell them which of their staged truths will sneak by our bounded rational brain and light up pleasure centres buried deep in our primitive psyche, and, of course, make you reach automatically for your wallet.

As I see it, these scientists are currently trying to determine the reliability and internal validity of the method—do they get consistent results from the same individual? But how will they ever measure the external validity? To be measured in an MRI machine, you have to lie perfectly still inside a great hollow tube. How do they do MRIs when you're out in the real world—studying, watching TV, chatting with the B&B group at the pub, or alone in your bedroom?

And, now that I'm thinking about it, why do Pepsi drinkers still drink Pepsi, even though the sight of a bottle of Coke delivers more blood to their emotional brain? It looks like a problem of external validity to me. I think that MRI data, at present, only deserves a limited travel permit.

Mona Lisa was 83 per cent happy

I came across a hilarious news report[10] out of the University of Amsterdam. Researchers tested a new 'emotion recognition' software package on the famous Mona Lisa painting in Paris to get a quantitative reading on her strange smile.

The new computer program decided that Mona was 83 per cent happy, 9 per cent disgusted, 6 per cent fearful, 2 per cent angry, and less than 1 per cent neutral.

It's not actually clear from the news report whether the researchers were serious or just kidding. But the software program is real; it was developed by a group of researchers in Holland who collaborated with a group at the University of Illinois.

---

[10]LiveScience.com. 'Mona Lisa was 83 Per cent Happy'. Available at http://www.livescience.com/history/ap_051215_mona_lisa.html.

I look forward to future reports where the software is tested on live people in combination with qualitative methods, but the math wizard in our B&B club says the program is based on 'fuzzy sets theory' where, instead of using either/or categories, they discuss your degree of membership in a category. For example, rather than talking about whether you're male or female, they might determine that Derek was 92 per cent male, 5 per cent female, and 3 per cent neutral. Can you imagine the fuss if these researchers applied this sort of study to Hollywood stars, reporting that the macho-est of men were actually 60 per cent female, 10 per cent male, and 30 per cent undecided? The tabloids would feel like they had hit the jackpot of exploitative gossip!

Well, I'm 100 per cent sleepy.

Note

Check out the classic study showing that what people say and do are two different things at http://www.oup.com/ca/he/companion/agnewpyke.

REVIEW TRUE OR FALSE QUIZ

T F	1.	Research, whether involving physical or human yardsticks, consists of a chain of messages, more or less distorted by elastic-ruler and/or on-stage effects.
T F	2.	Typically, observations based on qualitative measures contain a smaller area of uncertainty than those derived from quantitative yardsticks.
T F	3.	The images at the top of the PST, if involving numbers and mathematical symbols, have a small area of uncertainty surrounding the promised observations.
T F	4.	Qualitative methods include questionnaires, attitude scales, interviews, case studies, and naturalistic observation but not archival records.
T F	5.	Multiple-choice exams may not necessarily provide a valid picture of what you know and are typically unreliable.
T F	6.	With more open-ended questionnaire answers, the more the grading process becomes a believing-is-seeing process.
T F	7.	Common forms of response bias that can occur in questionnaire and attitude measures are the social desirability bias, yea-saying, nay-saying, and inconsistent responding.

T F	8.	Corporal Klinger (actor Jamie Farr), who appeared as a transvestite soldier in the television show *M*A*S*H*, provided a humorous example of the response extremity bias.
T F	9.	Open-ended questions in questionnaires should be kept to a minimum and should be placed at the end of the questionnaire.
T F	10.	A social distance scale asks about willingness to have contact with a specific group under various conditions such as dating and marriage.
T F	11.	Standardization of a test involves administration of the test twice to the same group of subjects.
T F	12.	The return rate of a mailed questionnaire or attitude scale is about 25 per cent.
T F	13.	Researchers who use interviews as their data-collecting tool, rather than questionnaires, are searching for more internal validity.
T F	14.	A major flaw in the Church study of stepmothers is that no independent coder analyzed the interview transcripts to determine the degree of agreement with Church's assignment of interviewees to one of the five different approaches to stepmothering.
T F	15.	Focus groups, popular with market researchers, are open to very large elastic-ruler effects.
T F	16.	Q methodology provides an objective technique for identifying clusters of individuals with similar rankings of items.
T F	17.	Q methodology, in keeping with more traditional approaches, requires the testing of large numbers of randomly selected respondents.
T F	18.	Grounded theorists attempt to adopt a seeing-is-believing (bottom up) perspective by putting their own beliefs aside.
T F	19.	Quota sampling is defined as interviewing the same group of people on two or more occasions and is used for studying opinion consistency and fluctuations.
T F	20.	Employing a heterogeneous group of interviewers or matching interviewers with interviewees on certain demographic variables may reduce a systematic bias of the impact of interviewer characteristics on the data.
T F	21.	Lack of correspondence between interview or questionnaire responses and behaviour may reflect a lack of internal validity and/or a lack of external validity and/or a tolerance for incongruency.
T F	22.	A major weakness of the study of the perceptions of police and prostitutes reported by Diana is the small sample size.
T F	23.	As Diana describes Dr Frund and Professor Creek, the former seems to favour qualitative research methods while the latter prefers quantitative methods.

T F	24. If identical twins reared apart show very similar persistence patterns this suggest that persistence is affected by environmental influences.
T F	25. Diana concludes that with quantitative methods, the focus is on external validity whereas with qualitative methods the focus is on reliability and internal validity.

9

Qualitative Methods: Naturalistic Observation and Archival Research

Chapter Goal

- To introduce you to two wide-angle qualitative methods: naturalistic observation and archival research.

These methods enable researchers to collect and analyze large samples of behaviour from people living, working, and writing in their natural environments, rather than from people confined to laboratories or classrooms. Studying people in their natural environments helps control the on-stage rogue.

Introduction

The goal of social science is to identify patterns of thinking, feeling, and acting. To achieve this goal researchers harvest quantitative observations from highly controlled situations like laboratories. The patterns researchers detect in these constrained contexts often demonstrate high reliability and internal validity. Nevertheless, such studies may not help us understand and predict behaviour outside those sheltered situations—they may not demonstrate external validity.

In contrast, questionnaires, attitude scales, and interviews harvest subjective messages—memories, thoughts, and feelings. These qualitative methods enable us to gather data from large samples of people in different settings. However, the messages collected by these research tools are highly vulnerable. They're vulnerable to both on-stage and elastic-ruler effects, and to the influence of researcher premises and biases, which unwittingly stretch coding categories to make the data fit the predictions of a pet theory.

Wide-Angle Qualitative Methods

Naturalistic observation and archival research, the qualitative methods discussed in this chapter, provide several advantages over paper-and-pencil tests and interviews:

1. They reduce the influence of the on-stage rogues.
2. They provide access to an abundance of wide-ranging thoughts, feelings, and behaviours (messages) occurring in natural—*real life*—settings, where control group studies would be impossible.
3. They can check the reliability and validity of the findings of scientific colleagues because unobtrusive video records and archival documents are accessible to independent investigators.

But the selection of research methods doesn't have to be an either/or decision. Why couldn't a researcher use a combination of measures?

Multi-method research

Given adequate resources, scientists can bring multi-method research strategies to bear on a given puzzle. For instance, suppose we want to study the thinking, feeling, and behaviour of laboratory scientists (i.e., scientists studying scientists).[1] We could have anthropologists conducting naturalistic observations of *tribal* rituals inside the laboratory; social psychologists studying cliques among scientists that cause inter-group conflicts; psychometricians measuring IQs, attitudes, and personalities; sociologists studying the power structure within the lab; and archival researchers examining the recorded chain of messages. All of these various research approaches are looking for the same thing—they are looking for the influence on scientific thinking that results from outside forces such as peer groups, grant committees, journal editors, and constraining government policies that pressure scientists to conduct politically correct research and to publish culturally correct findings.

Such multi-method research projects, though expensive, provide the ability to sample messages from the multi-layered reality of human thinking, feeling, and acting. Note, however, that even playing with the idea of such a rational approach threatens our bounded rationality. We're on the verge of dangerous ways of thinking. Stop and contemplate the logistics of designing and conducting such a study, of the time and expense. Contemplate the multiple streams of messages arriving from the various researchers. They combine into a mammoth tsunami, flood into the scientific PST, and swamp its information processing capacity.

So, although this grandiose idea is momentarily exciting, we must now retreat to the affordable, mind-sized, yet important, role that naturalistic

---

[1]For examples see: Knorr-Cetina (1987), Latour (1987), and Campbell (1993).

Fig 9.1 ■ Science is Like a News Service

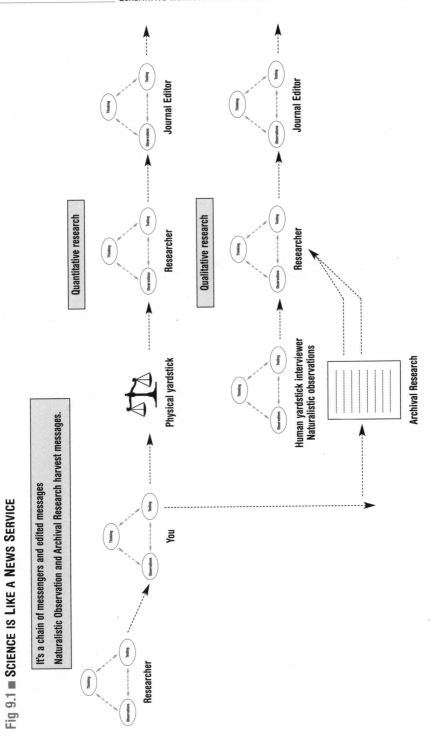

It's a chain of messengers and edited messages
Naturalistic Observation and Archival Research harvest messages.

observation and archival research can play in extending the reach of science and in expanding its external validity.

These two wide-angle qualitative methods harvest messages from natural settings and from documents (e.g., letters, reports, books, photos, websites, etc.).

As indicated in Figure 9.1, these methods add a rich new source of wide ranging messages to the data chain; beyond those available in the laboratory and the classroom, messages that extend both the theoretical and empirical reach of science. Both methods provide exciting opportunities to test the external validity of a hunch or theory. Furthermore, they provide career opportunities

Fig 9.2 ■ WIDE-ANGLE QUALITATIVE METHODS

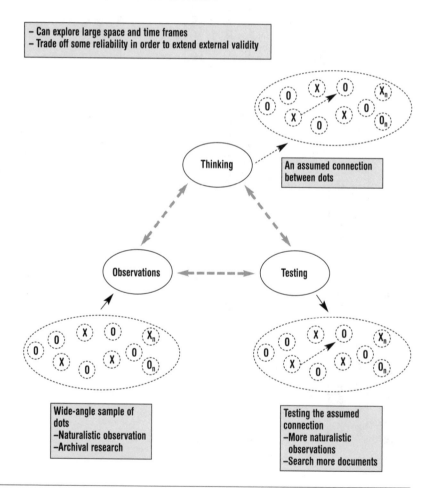

for both outdoor and bookish scientists—the ones conducting naturalistic observations, the others poring over dusty documents.

However, like most qualitative methods, they involve trade-offs. They trade off some reliability and lack of control for increased external validity and for an extended observational and theoretical reach. They also trade the convenience of working with the neatly packaged messages typical of most laboratory research and of research based on computer-scored questionnaires and personality inventories.

Naturalistic observations and archival research rapidly generate mountains of messages that often require months to condense into elastic, mind-sized (theory friendly?) categories. As a result, it's important to appreciate that the arrows flowing from naturalistic observation and archival research back into the message chain carry a lot of freight and place a heavy organizational and analytical burden on the PST of the researcher(s).

Yes, such research involves a lot of work, but we mustn't overlook the accompanying excitement, the scientific 'Ah Ha!s', the driving childlike curiosity that makes it all worthwhile. It's just another kind of treasure hunt but in a much bigger playpen.

Naturalistic Observation: Ethnographic Research

Naturalistic observation is the principal technique of ethnographic research or the field-study method. This method moves science out of the laboratory. Borrowed from ethnologists studying animal behaviour in their natural environments, this method greatly extends the reach of social science in both space and time, and it significantly increases the number of messages it can access from different levels of experience.

Classic early studies include the work done by Leon Festinger,[2] who embedded himself in a small religious group convinced that the world was coming to an end on a specific day and time. The group members were so convinced of their 'truth' that they had disposed of their worldly goods. Festinger unobtrusively observed their thinking and behaviour up to the fateful moment—and beyond—in order to study first hand what happens when an emotionally anchored prophecy fails. The leader's explanation: God had merely been testing their faith and new dates were set.

What's your guess? What's your prediction about how different members of the cult might respond to a failed prediction in which they had invested so heavily emotionally and financially. Some dropped out of the group, others become more committed.

Social scientists have engaged in some unusual behaviour in the name of unobtrusive observation. Some have joined street gangs. Others have had

---

[2]Leon Festinger. 2006. Available at http://en.wikipedia.org/w/index.php?title=Leon_Festinger&oldid=59985073 (accessed 24 June 2006).

themselves secretly admitted as patients into mental hospitals (one anthropologist had himself committed to a schizophrenic ward to see whether, over time, these patients created a culture of their own or if they remained socially isolated).

If you want to know the rituals practiced by pygmies in their worship of the forest god Ituri, or what people do when they win a lottery, or whether bees exhibit social behaviour, or how apes communicate, or whether teachers encourage creative thinking in their students, the most obvious recourse is to 'go and see'. In some scientific circles the technique of crude observation of events without technical apparatus is known as the *eyeball technique*, and this is the core of ethnographic research, of the field-study method.

The essence of this science sieve is the observation, description, and interpretation of events as they occur in nature or naturally (a stew of observational and speculative maps). This method requires no manipulation and no controlled experimentation, but rather the careful observation of episodes as they take place in their usual surroundings. It is perhaps the earliest (and, in some ways, crudest) of science's methods. The 'primitive' strategies of careful, methodical observation and classification predate the use of complex experimental designs and elaborate apparatus. However, even with the more advanced methods, observational skills are essential, and increasing awareness of the limitations of laboratory technologies has prompted a revival of interest in the field-study and its principal technique—naturalistic observation.

Darwin's (1936) picture of evolution provides an excellent example of this method. By his own admission Darwin devoted five years to the careful, detailed 'field' observation of thousands of plants and animals, both domestic and wild. These observations were meticulously (even compulsively) recorded in prose and picture form and subsequently grouped into categories, which in turn led to a grand speculation—*the theory of evolution*. If we were to represent this process

$$(O_1), \ (O_2), \ (O_3), \ (O_4), \ (O_5), \ (O_6), \ (O_7), \ (O_8), \ (O_9) \ \dots \ (O_n)$$

$$(O_1) \ = \ (O_2) \quad \text{in some respects}$$

$$(O_1) \ \neq \ (O_2) \quad \text{in other respects}$$

$$(O_3) \ < \ (O_4) \quad \text{in some respects}$$

$$(O_3) \ > \ (O_4) \quad \text{in other respects}$$

$$(O_5) \ \text{linked to} \ (O_6)$$

$$(O_7) \ \text{never found with} \ (O_8)$$

schematically, we would start with a series of Os (observations) and then impose some grouping scheme on our Os so that they were combined according to certain rules.

There are four key components to the field-study strategy:

1. the setting,
2. the observational task,
3. the role of the observer, and
4. the classification of observations.

In the discussion to follow, we examine each of these in turn. In actual practice, however, these facets of the method do not necessarily operate sequentially or independently.

The setting

Field studies obviously belong in field settings—that is, in non-laboratory environments—but research in the field implies a lack of control, which in turn implies unpredictability. Although investigators have hunches about how their observations are causally linked, cause–effect relationships cannot be established via this method of research; it is descriptive rather than inferential. If other science sieves promise more precision, why use a field approach? As we gain precision and control, we lose external validity. Would people in a laboratory, who passively obey an experimenter's instruction to shock an innocent victim, display this same blind obedience in a real-life setting? Perhaps not. There is good reason to assume that people behave differently in natural settings than they do in the lab where they may be on their 'best', most compliant behaviour. Also, some areas of interest (for example, the reaction to natural catastrophes) cannot be duplicated *realistically* in a laboratory environment. For these very important reasons the field-study is an essential arrow in the scientific quiver.

Once investigators decide what they want to know, the next decision involves selecting the setting(s). Choosing the setting depends on various factors, including the question to be answered and the feasibility and cost of the appropriate setting, a factor that is dependent on how broadly or narrowly the researchers wish to apply their findings. Suppose our budding scientists are interested in the characteristics of people who burglarize and vandalize abandoned vehicles. They live in New York so they observe an abandoned car in the Bronx. Within the first ten minutes they see a family of three remove the car battery and the contents of both the trunk and the glove compartment. By the end of the day, adult vandals have extracted every removable part from the automobile. Acts of random destruction (breaking windows, denting the hood) occur over the next several days, primarily perpetrated by well-dressed adults. As a result, our researchers conclude that vandalism is primarily an adult activity that will occur in any urban center. But is it legitimate to draw this conclusion?

Zimbardo (1970), who actually conducted this classic study, reports not only that a car similarly abandoned in Palo Alto, California, was not vandalized, but also that a passerby thoughtfully lowered the hood of the car when it was raining so the engine wouldn't get wet. Zimbardo's speculation is that high population density creates conditions of anonymity and loss of identity. Such conditions, he argues, foster a reduction in one's sense of responsibility and social consciousness. Hence the individual performs acts that appear reprehensible. Certainly Zimbardo's analysis is supported by much of the available data, but it is worth noting that the two settings employed (New York and Palo Alto) differ in many respects, not just population density (Milgram, 1970), and some of these other factors may be just as relevant.

Researchers must address a number of questions when choosing an appropriate setting: (1) Is this a setting in which the event(s) of interest are likely to occur? (2) Is this a representative setting in terms of most settings in which the event(s) of interest are likely to occur, or is it unique in the entire world? If the latter, then as consumers of science, we have less confidence that this particular research project provides us with 'the big picture'.

The observational task

Contemporary ethnographic research often combines a potpourri of methods including archival analysis and personal interviews as additional data collection tools or in lieu of naturalistic observation. This multi-method approach enhances the validity of the findings. Issues related to naturalistic observation are presented below, followed by a discussion of archival techniques

Harry's old Chevy died—much to his disgust—five blocks from the 'greasy spoon' where he works as a short-order cook. He decides to walk to work and call the tow truck from the cafe. As he trudges crankily past the school playground, he glances idly at the children playing. Two future NHL stars are high-sticking each other on the ice, another boy is inscribing a particularly nasty piece of graffiti on the school wall, a big girl is washing a small boy's face with snow, and one little imp, noticing Harry's interest, hurls a snowball with deadly accuracy, hitting him on the temple. Harry angrily shakes his fist and speculates, 'Bloody juvenile delinquents could sure use a kick in the ass.'

Harry has observed a number of events in their natural surroundings, integrated or grouped them together, and generated some speculations. However, Harry's observational procedure is casual. We should question the validity of both his observations and his conclusion. For example, Harry didn't notice that the feisty hockey players were really just trying to disentangle their sticks, which were caught in skate blades. Ineptitude, rather than aggression, accounted for their behaviour. Harry also failed to observe the dancing pair of figure skaters at the other end of the rink. Harry was already gone when the big girl picked up the little boy, hugged him, dusted off the snow on him, and carefully re-tied the laces of his boot. And how could Harry know that the snowball thrower had actually been aiming for the fence post?

Defining what to look for in any observational task becomes the most crucial aspect of the field-study method. As consumers of science we must focus on the quality of the data, or the observational checkpoints, that researchers use in generating their speculations.

Distortion

Personal experience in observing an event is obviously not a guarantee of truth. Since human senses are fallible, what we think we see isn't always what has occurred. Our observations are not pure—that is, we do not perceive only forms, contours, and certain wavelengths of light or sound; rather we perform symbolic transformations of these stimuli. One might say with some justification that we do not see light waves of 75 microns; we see red. Similarly, we do not hear a sound of 80 decibels; we hear a pneumatic drill. Therefore, any event that is observed is not experienced 'in the raw', so to speak, but is altered by our past learning or, as in Harry's case, our mood. Sometimes our interpretations (organization) of what we see can be quite misleading. For example, psychologists have constructed rooms built on a slant in which an individual standing at one side of the room looks like a midget. Viewers, instead of perceiving the room as distorted, distort the size of the individual in the room. If we press this argument further, it will be seen that our opinions, beliefs, and attitudes can also alter our observations. If we were observing the movement of planets, the pelvic bone structure of the apes, the strength of a magnetic field, or the electrical conducting properties of copper, you might argue that political affiliation, religious denomination, skin colour, or nationality would not affect our observations. Is this really the case? Religious beliefs supporting the theory that the earth was flat prevented many people from making the simple observation that the mast of a ship appeared on the horizon before the rest of the ship. If the area under study involves human behaviour, how much more will we distort our observations to fit our beliefs, hopes, or fears?

Scientists using the field-study method and the techniques of naturalistic observation strive to be as objective as possible; they consciously try to observe without evaluating. They try not to make value judgments like good or bad, wrong or right, beautiful or ugly. In other words, they attempt to prevent their own biases, opinions, values, and beliefs from colouring their observations— they try to keep observations as pure as possible. Although scientists have set an impossible task for themselves, at least knowing how beliefs can distort observations makes them more careful and more cautious about accepting observations—either their own or others'—at face value. Also, scientific training and the use of certain instruments, like hidden cameras, can help in obtaining a more objective picture to increase the size of the empirical chunk relative to its surrounding speculative space.

Selection

We know that biases play a role in the selection of information. In other words, we see or notice those things we want to see and screen out information that doesn't fit in with our particular point of view. For example, the biased observer, convinced that civilization corrupts and believing that people living in so-called primitive societies are happier, may fail to notice many negative aspects of the 'simpler' life. The poverty, the suffering due to lack of medical attention, the grueling hard work with improvised tools—these things escape attention. Scientists, being aware of this pitfall, attempt to make *detailed, value-free observations* at the bottom of their PSTs.

Selection operates not only on our observations but also on our recording and report writing. We don't see everything that happens nor do we record everything we see. We can't record all our observations (even if we wanted to) because we forget things, and we forget selectively. We tend to forget those things that don't fit well with our established biases and expectations and to remember those things that do. We have no trouble remembering an appointment to go out for dinner but the dentist appointment may be forgotten. In addition, time can distort the top the PST memories of observations. Since our memories are both leaky and creative, it is essential to make accurate notes when making observations, a practice most good researchers have developed. Alternatively, in order to avoid relying on our imperfect and creative memories, we may use tape recordings, films, sketches, graphs, or counters. There is still the danger that valuable data may be lost, but such recorded observations are not as subject to distortion, decay, or growth as are the ones we deposit in memory. A further advantage accrues because the data may be perused in all its rich detail at some later date and may be examined again and again, by us or by others. New technologies permitting the devious distortion of photos, videos, and tapes not only confound the media and the courts, but present new challenges to scientists evaluating the work of others, particularly archival material.

Even if our memories did not erase some observations from our minds, we still can't record everything that we observe. Secretaries know that exact reproduction of even a short conversation leads to a copious report. Minutes of meetings represent highly condensed and abbreviated versions of what actually occurred to avoid overload; much of the discussion must be omitted. Similarly, researchers must select (cherry-pick) from what they remember of the events observed. They must decide what to record and what to omit, ignoring material that is not relevant to the thesis being developed. Notice that while not consciously trying to discard observations that contradict their views, they still must discard those observations that add nothing to the point of the research. Such observations are tangential to the topic under study. If one wishes to describe the puberty rites of the Hopi Indians, it is perhaps irrelevant to record that homes of the Indians are constructed of thatched straw and adobe.

Researchers' biases or points of view help them select what is worth recording. Such biases may prevent them from considering alternatives but are vital in terms of providing guidelines for selections from the flood of data surrounding them.

An example

If Harry were to become really serious about studying the aggressive behaviour of little girls and boys on the playground, he would first have to make decisions on the following questions:

1. What constitutes aggression?
2. Which particular sample of children he will watch? (He can't observe all of them.)
3. At what time of the day will he observe them?
4. For how long will he observe them?
5. Who will do the observing and recording?
6. How many observers he will need?
7. How will the observations will be recorded and checked for accuracy?

To illustrate the complexity of the observational task, consider the following excerpt from a laboratory experiment (Bem, 1975). Bem investigated the extent to which a person's playfulness with a kitten was related to the individual's sex and sex-role orientation. Although not a field study, the observational strategies employed were similar to those that might be adopted in a field setting. Specifically, notice how the experimenter established reliable observational checkpoints.

> During the period of forced and spontaneous play, the subject's interaction with the kitten was time-sampled every 10 seconds by one of four female coders, all of whom were blind with respect to the subject's sex role attitudes and all of whom observed an approximately equal number of masculine, androgynous, and feminine subjects of each sex. For each subject, the coder made 30 2-second observations during forced play and 60 2-second observations during spontaneous play. Ten behaviors were coded as present or absent: Was the subject looking at the kitten? Speaking to the kitten? Petting the kitten? Nuzzling the kitten? Was the subject playing with the kitten? If so, was he holding it in his hand, on his lap, on his chest, or face-to-face?

> In order to establish the reliability of these various measures, two of the four coders simultaneously observed 12 subjects. These double coding sessions were scheduled so that all possible pairs of coders were together twice and so that two subjects from every sex role received double coding. The reliability of a given behavior was determined by combining forced and spontaneous play for a total of 90 observations per subject and then by calculating the percentage of observations on which the two coders agreed perfectly. The results indicated very high reliability (over 95% perfect agreement) for all 10 behaviors. (Bem, 1975: 640)

Do you have any questions about the independence of observers? Do we know from this description whether they peeked at each other's notes during the session? How might independence have been assured? Would it have been better to use male and female coders? Why?

The role of the observer

Knowledge that one is the object of study, a participant in a research investigation, or simply being watched, can have an enormous impact on behaviour (the on-stage rogue). In naturally occurring settings, this knowledge, of course, derives from the degree of the participant's awareness of the researcher's presence. To the extent that the researcher can minimize this awareness or its salience, the participant's behaviour will more closely approximate its typical form—that is, what the behaviour is when the researcher isn't there or isn't watching. Field-study researchers have adopted various strategies to minimize this on-stage effect. However, even when such efforts are successful, researchers still do not rule themselves out of the picture. They know that their own symbolic transformations of what they see continue to shape and edit the picture. Nonetheless, some of the strategies designed to reduce the impact of the on-stage rogue do double duty in helping to attenuate the magnitude of 'researcher variance'.

Invisible observers

In an effort to eliminate themselves as one of the suspects (Xs) influencing the phenomenon under investigation, researchers employ twenty-first century equivalents to Harry Potter's handy invisibility cloak—they hide in blinds or replace themselves with cameras, microphones, electronic tracking signals, and the like. These are the strategies of naturalists studying birds, bats, and beasts. Laboratory researchers may approximate this strategy through use of the one-way mirror, as did Bem (1975).

Covert observers

Field experimenters (Chapter 5) are covert observers. Participants in these staged research projects don't know they are involved in an experiment; hence, subject reactivity or related on-stage suspects are eliminated. Similarly, researchers employing the field-study method may disguise their data collection aims, blending in with the surroundings like well-trained, unobtrusive spies. Field studies conducted to examine such issues as courtroom behaviours, what draws people to accidents and fires, scalper strategies at ball games, the return of shopping carts to supermarkets, and the popularity of tourist attractions (e.g., noting the out-of-state license plates) may be amenable to a covert observer strategy.

Unobtrusive observers must be alert to the possibility that their cover has been 'blown'. Data gathered when there is reason to believe anonymity has been penetrated should be discarded. Another problem with covert observation is that it may run us afoul of ethical considerations. In fact, strict adherence to ethical principles (Chapter 13) requires that subjects be aware of the nature of their participation (principle of informed consent).

Non-participant observers

Anthropologists, such as Margaret Mead, who study so-called primitive or pre-literate societies, rely heavily on the field-study method. Invisibility or covert operations are not options for these researchers—their purpose is to describe and understand the complexities of entire cultures, or some significant aspect of them. Although the presence of the observer cannot be disguised, the researcher adopts or is assigned an outsider's role; he or she is visibly present, but not an active participant or legitimate group member.

Although the observer influences the group to an unknown degree, he or she nevertheless endeavors to minimize this impact by staying on the sidelines, by maintaining passivity, by eschewing active participation, except when required to maintain acceptance or enhance understanding. One procedure commonly used by field researchers to counteract this on-stage effect involves observing the group (being present in the group) for some time before beginning the formal data collection process. This gives the group members a chance to acclimatize themselves to the outsider. Eventually the researcher more or less fades into the woodwork.

Trice (1970) argues persuasively in favour of the outsider's role, noting that disinterested (uninvolved) outsiders may be the recipients of privileged information—private information that would not be shared with other members of the clan, club, or company. On the other hand, attempts to ingratiate oneself—to be integrated or accepted as just 'one of the gang'—may be viewed with suspicion and distrust, as Trice discovered in his study of hospitalized alcoholics and members of Alcoholics Anonymous. In such cases, the researcher may fall into the outsider's role by default.

Participant observers

Another creative strategy for overcoming the reactivity problem is to employ undercover confederates who infiltrate and become active participant members of the society, organization, or group. Alternatively the researcher, or his or her confederate, may already have membership in the group or organization under study. Since qualitative researchers strive to uncover and understand the meanings of behaviours to the actors, rather than simply describing the acts themselves, they argue that some degree of researcher involvement is a *sine qua non* of such research.

Sullivan, Queen, and Patrick (1970) detail many of the complexities of this form of field-study research when describing their experiences using participant observation in the investigation of an Air Force training program. Other fascinating studies of this ilk include Festinger et al.'s (1956) analysis of the reaction of members of an occult group to a failed prophecy, Whyte's (1943) classic study of street corner gangs, and Goffman's (1962) investigation of a mental institution.

Participant observers walk a tightrope between detachment and involvement. They run the risk of being absorbed by the culture of the group or organization under study. Alternatively, care must be taken to ensure that a confederate does not shape or mold the group to perform in a manner dictated by the investigator's expectations or pet theory. Participant observation also raises some thorny ethical issues.

Barker and Schoggen (1973) adopted an alternative approach in their comparison study of life in two small towns—one in the US Midwest and the other in England. The researchers and their families established residences in the towns and fully explained the purpose of the study to the local inhabitants. They attempted to participate normally in community affairs, following their own interests but avoided initiating new activities.

Multiple observers—multiple observations

Making several observations and having several observers make repeated observations of the same event (the strategies employed by Bem in 1975) increases the probability of producing durable packages of information. Those practicing the technique of naturalistic observation utilize this principle. In an attempt to partially overcome or reduce observer bias, scientific investigations often make use of two or more independent observers who later come together and discard any observations on which they do not agree. Or, more commonly, a third observer is called in to resolve the disagreement. Also, the same observer may try to observe the same event many times in order to ensure that all the relevant details are observed and recorded and to rule out the possibility that the initial observation was a once-in-a-lifetime event. As a result, anthropologists may visit the same primitive tribe many times and observe the tribe's activities over long periods. For the same reason another investigator may repeat a colleague's experiment, and the extent of similarity in their findings adds to the durability of their observations. As you can see, sometimes it gets a bit crowded at the bottom of the scientific PST.

Classification or interpretation

The final component of the field-study method involves top of the PST classification of dots collected at the bottom—their linkages, orders, or patterns. This discovery, construction or invention, of pattern is the basis of science.

The development of the periodic table in chemistry represents a most fruitful use of one aspect of the field-study method—classification. In the nineteenth century, elements were being discovered rapidly, but as each element had different properties, no obvious sense of order or relationship could be perceived among elements. However, science doesn't just create facts; it puts facts into a speculative, conceptual framework. Several investigators, including chemists and a geologist, made attempts to classify, group, or arrange the elements into some kind of order. Mendeleev's periodic table was the most successful attempt at classification. Mendeleev believed that the properties of elements were more important than their atomic number; when arrangement by number would not work neatly, Mendeleev left holes in the table for elements still to be discovered. He even predicted the properties of some of the missing elements on the basis of his table. With the knowledge of the hypothesized properties of these missing elements, their eventual discovery was stimulated. It's easier to find something if you know what specifically what you're looking for.

The development of the system for the classification of plants and animals by the Swedish botanist Carolus Linnaeus (1707–78) is another famous example of the fruitfulness of taxonomy to science. Classification of organisms—both past and present—into kingdoms, phyla, classes, orders, families, genera, and species is an obvious example of an attempt to replace disorder and confusion with order. To develop such a taxonomic system, close observation of the properties of organisms had to be undertaken. Again, the technique of naturalistic observation proved invaluable.

Barker and Schoggen (1973), whose field study was briefly described earlier, attempted to produce a complete inventory and classification of the behaviour settings (public places or occasions) in each community. The Midwest town was found to have considerably more public behaviour settings, which in turn was reflected in the different activities of the inhabitants, ranging from public attention toward children to religious pursuits.

The construction of classification systems is very much a function of top of the PST beliefs, biases, or points of view. In fact, classification can be seen as a primitive form of theorizing that allows for the expression of opinion, inference, or speculation. With any set of data there are usually a variety of ways in which these data may be ordered or grouped, and the researchers' hunches or biases determine which particular grouping they will develop. Will the researchers group people on the basis of intelligence, skin colour, sex, political persuasion, aggression, genetics, or some other category? The possibilities often seem endless.

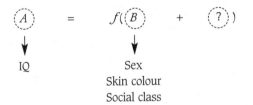

$$A = f(B + ?)$$

IQ   Sex
Skin colour
Social class

An important item in every researcher's tool kit

Just because naturalistic observation is employed to study behaviour units and requires little in the way of elaborate equipment, don't conclude that it is no longer in vogue, has outlived its usefulness, or is a simple method that requires little training. All these assumptions are wrong. There are many areas of study in both small and large playpens in which it is impossible—for ethical, moral, political, or practical reasons—for the researcher to manipulate events or to experiment. In addition, certain kinds of information can only be obtained in field or naturalistic studies. For example, if we wanted to investigate the phenomenon of hibernation, famine, or juvenile gangs, we would need to use naturalistic observation for at least a portion of our study. The work of Piaget, the famous child psychologist, was based on the technique of naturalistic observation and is the foundation for much of the current research in some areas of psychology today. Although it is a crude sieve, in the hands of a skilled researcher, the field study remains a valuable source of important and durable data.

One obvious advantage of this method is its superiority to casual observation and hit-or-miss recording, or tabulating, of events. A second advantage accrues because it does not require manipulating or controlling events; therefore many subjects that would normally be taboo to experimental science become open to this form of study. Furthermore, the four principles of the field study (the setting, the observational task, the role of the observer, and the grouping or classification) apply, to some degree, to all the other sieves of science. Often the data gathered by the field-study method provide guidelines for later inquiry with more sophisticated sieves, as has been the case with Piaget's work. Finally, young student scientists with limited resources can practice this method. By being analytical, unobtrusive, and accurate, the novice researcher can establish important observational checkpoints and can offer fascinating speculations.

In brief, naturalistic observation provides researchers entry into multi-layered aspects of human behaviour inaccessible by other means. A nagging and persistent question drags along behind all such studies: how much did the act of observing, and the presence of the observer, influence the results. In a word, in spite of various attempts to remove it from the research equation, how much did it allow, or encourage, the on-stage rogue to get into the act, how much was the observer one of the main in-the-gap suspects? How much were the act of observing and the presence of the observer a distorting influence on the chain of messages flowing around the PST?

Because unobtrusive observation is often difficult or impossible, the issue surrounds the impact of obvious observers in natural settings. The question remains open. Some studies continue to raise doubts, while others offer reassurance that the observer can be confined to a minor, if not an insignificant, role. For example, Jacob et al. (1994) reported that neither high nor low level obtrusive observations distorted mealtime behaviour of families. Whereas Zegoib et al. (1975) found that under observation, mothers changed their patterns of interaction with their children for the better, and Brody et al. (1984) reported that siblings did less teasing and quarrelling.

The main point to remember is that naturalistic observation is a powerful tool for increasing external validity, but appreciate that the on-stage rogue rides on the observer's shoulder. Our premise is that familiarity breeds acceptance and that in most instances people forget that they're being observed and revert back to *normal* behaviour.

Archival Research

In many instances you don't have to observe behaviour directly to know what has occurred; you only have to observe the marks, tracks, spoor, or deposits it leaves. One of the by-products of the revolution in communications technology is the development of information pools of oceanic proportions—data pools that are rich and ready for the nets of eager scientific fisher-folk. Newspapers, magazines, books, films, plays, songs, census statistics, radio broadcasts, suicide notes, letters, diaries, gravestones, and paintings all provide valuable information for researchers.

Gribbin (1984), in the book *In Search of Schrodinger's Cat*, tells us that most mammals determine and mark their territories by leaving excretions that define the size and shape of the claimed turf. Domesticated primates (humans) however, mark their territories by excretions of ink on paper. The analysis of these excretions, of these people-tracks or traces, is known as *archival research*. Employing this method allows the scientist to capitalize on and exploit already collected or deposited data chunks. Moving away from direct observation, the investigator relies on the accumulated behavioural spoor and he or she creatively analyzes, groups, combines, and juxtaposes these indirect data.

A study by Sir Francis Galton (cited in Webb, Campbell, Schwartz, & Sechrest, 1966) provides an example of the creative use of archival research. Since the long life of a monarch was prayed for more frequently than was the case for less august persons, it was theorized that greater longevity should be observed for royal personages, if praying is effective. The data revealed that, in fact, royalty had shorter life spans than did the gentry. As sophisticated consumers of science you are quick to note that people of royal birth differ from gentry on a host of other variables, and Galton's study doesn't seem to have taken these other differences into account—some of them, like inbreeding, are perhaps much more relevant in affecting life span than prayer. So, in the end, Galton's research on this question has only anecdotal value.

Content analysis

Just as the principal technique of the field-study is naturalistic observation, one of the frequently employed tools of the archival researcher is *content analysis—* what Simon (1969) refers to as a method of measuring the unmeasurable.

Naturalistic observation, it will be recalled, involves detailed, objective, and systematic observation of events in their typical surroundings. Similarly, content analysis requires detailed, objective, and systematic observation of verbal or symbolic communications.

Consider the following research question derived from a study by Pyke (1976): 'To what extent do children's books depict traditional sex roles?' Assume that two researchers collect a representative sample of books. They then undertake an analysis of the prose and picture (verbal and symbolic) content of these books. Two coding categories are established: (1) a female figure is performing a traditional female sex-role function (mother squirrel is dusting the nest with her tail); (2) a male figure is performing a traditional male sex-role activity (a fireman is holding the net for the lady in the burning building). For comparison purposes the researchers include two more categories that are the converse of those examples: male or female figures engaged in cross-sex activities (a male cooking; a female operating a backhoe). Each researcher takes half the books and proceeds with the analysis—identifying for each figure depicted in both illustrations and text whether the figure portrayed is performing traditional sex-role functions or functions of the opposite sex role. One hundred books are analyzed; the researchers meet and share their findings.

'Why did you categorize Mary as performing a cross-sex function when she was climbing a tree? Girls climb trees,' argues Researcher A. Researcher B similarly questions A's judgments, 'You've got the Daddy coded here as a traditional sex-role item, but surely shopping is a traditional female activity so he should be coded as cross-sex.' 'Yes, but it's a hardware store,' rebuts A. 'OK, but what do we do if we don't know what kind of store it is?' responds Researcher B. Echoes of elastic-ruler effects?

Although these researchers have coded their observations in a detailed and systematic fashion, they have failed to satisfy the basic criterion of objectivity—independent and consistent labelling. Their understanding of what constituted a traditional sex-role activity was subjective or pragmatic. They were including a great deal of speculation but had assumed they were operating on the observational or objective level, involving a large amount of solid information.

The problem was resolved by simply coding the activity or occupation (reading, sewing, driving, fighting) and by determining whether this activity or occupation was being performed by a male or female figure. With this more objective coding scheme, the two researchers achieved a high level of agreement in their individual assignment of codes. Their observational checkpoints had reduced areas of argument or speculation.

Many researchers lack the luxury of readily identifiable (objective) coding categories for their content analysis of archival material. Jacobs (1979), for example, reports a phenomenological study of 112 suicide notes, one of which is reproduced below.

It is hard to say why you don't want to live. I have only one real reason. The three people I have in the world which I love don't want me.

Tom, I love you so dearly but you have told me you don't want me and don't love me. I never thought you would let me go this far, but I am now at the end, which is the best thing for you. You have so many problems and I am sorry I added to them.

Daddy, I hurt you so much and I guess I really hurt myself. You only wanted the very best for me and you must believe this is it.

Mommy, you tried so hard to make me happy and to make things right for all of us. I love you too so very much. You did not fail, I did.

I had no place to go so I am back where I always seem to find peace. I have failed in everything I have done and I hope I do not fail in this.

I love you all dearly and am sorry this is the way I have to say goodbye.

Please forgive me and be happy.

Your wife and your daughter.[3]

How would you tackle the analysis of this material, distilling key variables? Jacobs, relying heavily on a theoretical model developed by Durkheim, indicated that 35 of the 112 notes (including the one above) fit the pattern described by Durkheim in reflecting the following themes: (1) others created the problem; (2) long history of problems; (3) recent escalation of problems; (4) death seen as necessary; (5) begging indulgence; and (6) awareness of the act. Try to identify which elements of the note exemplify these themes. Are there components not covered? Would a different classification system serve as well? Although the note allows access to the phenomenological world of the suicide, the analysis provides the researcher with ample opportunity to stretch or shrink or otherwise misinterpret this world.

Content analysis brings with it a host of concerns. The quality of the information derived from this technique depends on the adequacy of source sampling (was the sample of children's books or suicide notes a representative sample?), the appropriateness and relevance of the coding units, and the reliability of the coding—that is, its independence and consistency.

Spoor analysis

Although the term *archival* suggests some form of document (from a music score to sales records), archival research encompasses a broader band of materials, including physical evidence, such as garbage, ancient pottery shards, dust, and other remnants. For example, an architect consulted a psychologist, asking where sidewalks should be built on a new campus to accommodate traffic flows. The

---

[3]Reprinted by permission of the Society for the Study of Social Problems.

architect said, 'You're an expert on human behaviour, tell me where people will walk.' The psychologist, having an empirical bent, visited several established campuses and carried out naturalistic observations of traffic flows. He noted that, in addition to the sidewalks, a variety of paths had been worn across the lawns. He consulted the head groundskeeper, who maintained that once a path was established, it was nearly impossible to discourage its continued use. The psychologist advised the architect to design his sidewalks so they covered the shortest distance between any two entrances. He also advised the architect to save part of his budget to be spent a year later to put in additional sidewalks where newly trodden paths would indicate natural, but unpredictable, traffic flows.

People leave traces indicating behavioural flows everywhere: worn linoleum, dog-eared library books, picnic sites, etc. Analyzing garbage, not only of famous people but also of different socioeconomic classes, provides measures of certain aspects of their behaviour. Furthermore, a longitudinal study of people's ashtrays can provide crude indices of patterns of stress; such a study could also provide a relatively objective index of the efficacy of New Year's resolutions to give up smoking or the impact of antismoking campaigns.

Let's consider another example of the use of physical evidence as a source of research data. Suppose, as the owner of a car rental agency, you wonder about the value of the radio advertising you've commissioned. Do many people actually hear your creative jingle on station OHM? An archival approach might involve maintaining a record of the radio dial position on all cars returned after rental. This provides a measure of the popularity of the various stations, and so you can use the most popular station (ERG) to carry your advertising (adapted from Webb et al., 1966). A moment's reflection, though, raises a question. Don't you want to reach the *potential* car renters rather than, or in addition to, those who actually use your agency? Perhaps the former group listens predominantly to station WATT rather than ERG.

Webb and colleagues (1966) provide many examples of the analysis of physical traces, including measuring the food consumption of institutionalized patients by weighing the trucks bringing in food supplies and the trucks carting garbage out; estimating the differential activity level of children by comparing the degree of wear on their shoes; determining the height of individuals in the Middle Ages by measuring the height of suits of armour; and judging the popularity of library texts by measuring the degree of wear and tear on the pages.

Strengths and weaknesses

Archival research is perhaps one of the least exploited research methods, even though its unobtrusive quality offers some protection against a prime villain—reactivity (the on-stage effect). It is hard to imagine that a student might deliberately deface a text so that the next archival researcher who comes along will judge it to have been well or frequently read. It's equally difficult to accept the idea of a tombstone carver gleefully altering birth dates so as to mislead future generations of scientists. The man whose height is being estimated from his suit of armour can't throw our measurement off by standing on his tiptoes. Nor will the rental car clients fake their radio-listening behaviour—they don't know it is being researched. Thus archival research involves the use of unobtrusive, or non-reactive, measures. Researchers using this method usually need not be concerned that their observations are distorted by subjects' awareness that they are objects of study.

The value of conclusions derived from spoor analysis depends, of course, on how much of the original deposit remains available for analysis. The Nixon tapes offer a classic example of a mammoth attempt to provide a relatively complete verbal record of his office behaviour, not all of which record was retained, including the infamous 18-minute erasure. Such records can be incomplete by design or by accident; they can be edited by the crude hand of sloth and decay or by the fine hand of deceit. In either case, running or episodic records provide ingenious social scientists with further fixes on human behaviour—with views that go beyond the sheltered laboratory.

While deceit and incompetence can affect the amount of information available in written and taped documents, so too can systematic changes in record-keeping procedures. For example, records of crime show that rates shift in some cases as a result of improved record keeping, in other cases because of increased detection. In order to differentiate between these two influences, social scientists relying on archival records must be no less sophisticated than when working in the laboratory. They must be record-wise. For example, rates of alcoholism in a given region are frequently based on liver cirrhosis death rates. However, such estimates are frequently low because of the stigma surrounding that cause of death appearing on the certificate. Unless investigators become familiar with the practices surrounding the production of archival records, they can be badly misled.

Given the revolution in data storage and retrieval systems arising from the development and spread of computer facilities, the prognosis for archival research is excellent. How much money did consumers invest in children's toys last December? What's the unemployment rate for university graduates? How many non-nationals are currently employed in the country? Is there a sex difference in the incidence of mental disorders? How much income tax did people in the $80,000-a-year bracket pay last year? Questions such as these may soon be answered with a press of a button—data literally at our fingertips. If you think this is an idle fancy or a futuristic view, listen to a major league baseball broadcast. Every imaginable statistic is available for the pressing.

Although archival data may be more readily accessible, assessment of the quality of these data is still of concern. We referred earlier to the use by computer programmers of an acronym GIGO (garbage in, garbage out), which captures the notion that the computer record, or memory, is only as accurate and detailed as the information that is fed into it. Problems of lost and distorted data still apply. The many film plots depicting the mad, irresponsible, or criminal computer genius who erases information, plants misinformation, or otherwise deliberately distorts the computer record for his or her own ends suggest we must adopt a critical stance. Add to deliberate deception the inaccuracies deriving from carelessness and human error, and the problem is compounded. Yet the seductive computer carries with it an aura of precision and accuracy. At first glance it seems the answer to a researcher's prayer, but let the user beware.

For the imaginative and record-wise researcher, archival records—whether they are laundry lists or Supreme Court rulings, classified advertisements or death certificates—provide rich opportunities to increase the external validity of our observations. In many instances, they also provide auxiliary information about the adequacy of such data in terms of biases affecting what was recorded and what was retained.

Perhaps the optimum use of archival research arises when it is employed in combination with other methods. Indeed, to the extent that an observational checkpoint is revealed by more than one of science's methods, our confidence in the validity of the observation is enhanced; it has picked up more 'empirical robustness'. In this sense all research methods are supplementary. The multi-method bracketing of hypotheses by imaginative and tenacious researchers warrants massive encouragement. A case in point is one student's attempt to study the effects of frustration on eating behaviour, in which he extended his laboratory observations from studying rats to checking the records of the hometown fans' consumption of hot dogs when attending losing, as opposed to winning, football games.

Internet access to archival data

With the advent of computer scanning, the electronic storage of documents, and easy access to such data through the Internet, archival exploration and research is blossoming.

Researchers can now readily access vast quantities of statistical data from the national archives of many countries, facilitating inter-region comparison, as well as studying behaviour change over time.

Levitt and Dubner (2005) explore a cornucopia of fascinating questions by accessing such publicly available data. In one example, they propose that parents should be much more concerned about their children dying in swimming pools than from guns. In the United States, 550 children under ten years of age died from drowning, compared to 175 from guns. Let's assume that this data proves to be reliable—confirmed by independent investigators over a significant time period. What recommendations would you make? What kinds of public policy messages, delivered in what manner, might impact on the emotionally anchored premises and behaviour of parents? And would your policy initiatives have a more immediate impact on the parents' behaviour than the Australian[4] researchers' messages had on the premises and practices of American doctors?

[4] Mayne Florey Medal 1998. Awarded for the discovery of the *Helicobacter Pylori*, the causative agent in Gastritis and Gastric Ulceration. Available at http://www.tallpoppies.net.au/floreymedal/winner1998.htm.

Levitt and Dubmer reported another provocative correlation and proposed that the significant drop in the US crime rate over the last ten years may be linked to the increasing number of abortions. Now, how many of us have ever connected—or would ever have thought to connect—those two dots?

Such a surprising, outside-the-box finding cries out for multi-method exploration and testing. But it is one very hot potato, both politically and religiously. Those powerful forces will impact at all levels of the scientific PST. Is the finding reliable? What other alternative suspects are there? You can be sure many, many alternatives will be proposed by various opposing camps. With your bounded rationality how do you reconcile two opposing, emotionally anchored premises? For example, let's say that on the one hand you really want to reduce the crime rate, but at the same time you're really against abortion? How, by cycling around your PST, can you resolve those two diametrically opposed messages? How do you eliminate the emerging connection between those two dots?

We can look forward to archival research becoming one of the major sources of scientific hypotheses, and also a qualitative method of testing hypotheses.[5] Every time you read a newspaper or do a Google search, you're engaged in archival research.

SUMMARY

The two qualitative methods described in this chapter—the field study and archival research—have distinct advantages over the casual observation and reading we rely on every day to infer what people are thinking, feeling, and planning. Although lacking the precision of the control-group model, they enable us to explore spaces that control groups can't reach.

Naturalistic observation techniques employ sophisticated observational strategies down at the bottom of the PST (e.g., unobtrusive filming). And, up top, they apply critical thinking designed to identify stable patterns in the chain of messages, and to map them against current theoretical speculations. All scientific methods, including the field study and archival research, rely on these basic critical thinking tools in mapping multi-layered physical and human nature.

Archival research examines behavioural remnants—tracks of past behaviour. The major strength of this method is that those tracks aren't usually putting on a show[6]—they aren't dancing to the music of the on-stage rogue. But those tracks still reflect the hidden-hand editing of the person who originated them, as well as time-tied message decay effects, and, of course, whatever transformations occur as they pass through the researcher's hands, eyes, and brain.

---

[5] Both of these examples report a possible linkage (correlation) between two variables (deaths and swimming pools, and crime rates and abortion). In Chapters 11 and 12 we discuss the dangers of jumping to conclusions on the basis of such correlational data.

[6] Yes, some archival messages are contrived 'plants' deliberately designed to mislead. Experienced archival researchers don't blindly accept all messages at face value.

Nevertheless, in skilled and conscientious hands, naturalistic observations and archival research extend the reach of social science into multi-layered *reality* and into wondrous and private places that more controlled research methods cannot go.

student's notebook

Creek gave us our mid-term grades today. I did OK, so to celebrate I skipped my political science lecture and met Derek at the pub. Interesting. He's changed a bit—for the better—since my Skinner-esque experimenting. I know it was a simple, naturalistic, before-and-after study, but since he didn't know he was a guinea pig it didn't have any on-stage effects. Well, at least not in the beginning.

I suppose the positive changes I think I've seen are the result of my own wishful thinking (elastic-ruler)? Or, maybe the change was a temporary blip in the message chain, like the kind we saw in longitudinal time series studies in Chapter 7. Anyway, the 'experiment' didn't have clear enough results, not results that have lasted for a long enough period of time, for me to get excited enough to start shouting my proven hypothesis from the rooftops. At least he got the message—that I wanted, and needed, some talking time. Whether or not I get it, well, only time will tell.

When we got to the pub the B&B club was already out in force—Friday afternoons tend to be like that around campus.

I mentioned the stuff from class about more kids drowning in pools than being killed by guns. The talk bubbled right along, with the two 'shooters' in the group giving self-righteous lectures to the rest of us, who are pretty much all on the 'pro-gun-control' side of things. Of course, neither side was noticeably swayed. You know how it goes: 'No strong conclusions without biased premises.'

While the conversation had bubbled along when we were discussing gun control, it boiled over when I mentioned the stuff about the effects of abortion on crime rate. Everything started out calmly, and people discussed whether or not the data were any good. How reliable are the abortion statistics? How many years did the archival records cover? Did it include data from all states, for all types of crime? These were all rational, mind size questions.

Then Derek, I suppose thinking he was helping to move the discussion along, said: 'Let's do a thought experiment. Let's suppose that the statistics are sound and let's assume that the data clearly show that as the number of abortions goes up, the crime rate goes down. What does that mean?'

Everyone took a moment to travel to the top of the their PSTs, dragged their critical thinking skills out of the closet, and started sniping at each other.

Now, I'm against abortions for personal, rather than for religious, reasons. I just don't want anyone messing around 'knife-wise' with my body. I'm not overly concerned about what other women decide, so I was cool with the right-to-choose movement.

At first the debate centred on what you could and couldn't decide from statistics. Our resident math wizard pronounced: 'You can prove anything with statistics. You can prove that buying bathing suits causes you to buy ice cream, or visa versa, since one usually follows the other.'

Everyone agreed that was stupid, everyone knew that buying bathing suits and ice cream were caused by warm weather. Weather was the big in-the-gap cause and ice cream and bathing suits simply went along for the ride.

So, the thing to consider was what might be the big in-the-gap cause—besides increased abortions—for the falling crime rate? It sounded like a reasonable question, but as soon as someone proposed an alternative cause—namely decreased poverty, or better education—the gloves came off.

When premises collide

The 'poverty' proposal triggered someone to play the 'race' card proposal, and away we went! A chain of messages started to spew forth from the race premise.

One person argued: 'Everyone knows the crime rate is higher among blacks than whites, and so are teen pregnancies. So . . . more babies are born to poor, black, single mothers; the babies grow up in poverty; can't get decent jobs, and as a result, commit more crimes. But then, in the mid-1990s, abortions become more accessible; so fewer black babies were born to single teen mothers, to grow up in poverty, and to commit crimes. The crime rates fall. Therefore, it only makes sense that racial poverty is the in-the-gap suspect.' All of a sudden everyone's premises started colliding, people starting banging on the table and yelling at each other!

'What about white collar crimes that never get recorded?'

'What about all the poor blacks that don't commit crimes?'

'What about the police biases—they pick up more blacks on suspicion, so more blacks get tried, and more black people are convicted?'

'What about the white people who have access to better lawyers, or who are part of the 'old boys' network?'

And so it went. And so Derek and I went—off to celebrate both my grade in Creek's class and the fact it's Friday.

In reviewing the pub 'discussion' the next day, we wondered why the 'religion card' wasn't played. If it had been brought into the mix, how would the chain of messages differ? There would have to be an alternative in-the-gap explanation to replace the abortion premise, because it would be unacceptable to the right-to-life movement. What would the alternative be—poverty, work ethic, faith, family values? I'm sure Derek will stir things up and start another 'discussion' at the pub next week.

Treasure maps

At the moment Derek is more excited about the idea of using the Internet for archival research than he is about causing another uproar at the pub. There are all kinds of treasure maps, all kinds of ways to ask sociological questions on what in-the-gap suspects (in addition to, or other than, abortions) are related to reduced crime rates: income level, *religious affiliation, types of crime, age at which abortions are performed, etc. All you have to do is use the right combination of search terms to find more information than you could possibly use.*

In his lectures Creek pointed out that archival research was both an after-the-fact and a before-and-after method. While it is great for generating hypotheses, he said, we have to remember that it is also subject to the same limitations of those methods. You can also use archival methods for testing how stable the observations are over time, and testing the trend into the future. If the pattern proved to be reliable, then you can start considering and researching alternative suspects (e.g., other than or in addition to abortion) in the growing chain of messages.

Then, after all that preliminary work, you can rigorously test your hypothesis using more powerful methods, such as the control-group method (testing for the effects of: religious affiliation, peer groups, socio-economic status, etc.).

News reports

I'm hooked. I'm a junkie. I need a regular 'fix' of scientific news whether I have to or not. Several times a day I go online to check the flow of scientific messages on the World Wide Web. I use it to access current breakthroughs, promised breakthroughs, and scholarly fights, and as an archive that lets me 'pogo-stick' back and forth across the history of science.

For this week's assignment I've selected one current and one ancient piece of scientific news. The current news article describes a field-study of the speculated relationship between cancer and stress. The ancient message comes from Iganz Semmilweis, the guy who told doctors over 150 years ago to wash their hands before delivering babies or performing surgery.

Stress causes cancer, or does it?

A popular truth, or speculation, residing comfortably at the top of our PSTs is that the cancer dot is connected to the stress dot.

Well, you can hardly do a control-group study on this question. You really can't load one big group into a bag and draw them out at random, half going to the experimental group that will then be placed under stress, while the other group sits around in the lab watching re-runs of *Friends*, and then test each group to see which one ends up with the most cancer cells. Far more unethical than my behaviour experiment with Derek!

So what do you do?

A number of scientists[7] around the world have travelled down to the bottom of their PSTs, and done longitudinal follow-ups of people who have undergone

---

[7]G. Kolata. 2005. 'Is there a Link between Stress and Cancer?', *New York Times*, 29 Novermber 2005. Available at http://www.nytimes.com/2005/11/29/health/29canc.html?ex=1151294400&en=c642376f5bfb53a6&ei=5070.

stress in their natural environment—a naturalistic observation type of experiment. I guess they wanted to find out whether this speculated connection was a superficial one, like the ice cream–bathing suit linkage.

For example, researchers checked for cancer: (1) in the parents of children who had cancer; (2) in parents who had lost a child; and (3) in parents who had a child with schizophrenia. Then they compared their cancer rates with those of parents who hadn't experienced the same stress. They found there was no significant difference between the two groups. Score one for archival research!

Of course, those aren't the only parts of the population you could study. They could have studied cancer rates in war-torn countries, or in the parents of US soldiers who died overseas, or in the husbands and wives of 9/11 victims. There's really no end to the list.

So you don't have to give up scientifically on a big problem just because you can't do a control-group study. Natural experiments like these deliver some pretty potent messages, even if they rely on pre-scientific methods like after-the-fact, or before-and-after methods.

A voice from the past

You no longer have to sneeze your way through dusty documents to do archival research—just hop online and away you go! I Googled 'Semmilweis' and struck gold! Not only was there a ton of biographical information, but there were also quotes from the man himself.[8]

Writing about the 'Understanding and Prevention of Childbed Fever', Ignaz says:

> In the excited condition in which I was, it rushed into my mind with irresistible clearness the disease from which Kolletschka [a surgeon] had died was identical with that from which I had seen so many hundreds of lying in women die . . . the cause of the disease of the lying in women and that of Kolletschka must be the same . . . cadaveric material. In examinations of pregnant . . . women, the hand made unclean by cadaveric material [from autopsies] was brought into contact with the genitals.

Semmilweis went on to explain that doctors did rinse obvious 'cadaveric material' off their hands but that was for their own comfort, not to protect patients from contamination. And even after washing, their hands still smelled of the cadaver—invisible 'somethings', but not 'unsmellable somthings'. So Ignaz

---

[8]See pp. 48–51 of Sinclair's 1909 publication, *Semmelweis, His Life and His Doctrine.*

> was relying on some bottom-of-the-PST inputs to put his theory together. Both the visual and nasal messages in the flow were available to lots of other people too, but only Semmilweis travelled up to the top and made the crucial connection.
>
> It was kind of eerie . . . I could almost hear him speaking to me across the years. Archival research is pretty interesting stuff!

Note

Discover archival treasures related to this chapter at http://www.oup.com/ca/he/companion/agnewpyke.

REVIEW TRUE OR FALSE QUIZ

T F	1. Compared to tests, questionnaires, and interviews, archival research reduces the influence of the on-stage rogue.
T F	2. In general, the use of quantitative methods enhances external validity.
T F	3. In general, the use of qualitative methods involves a trade-off of external validity for increased internal validity.
T F	4. Ethnographic research refers to laboratory-based experimental research.
T F	5. The eyeball technique is the core of the field-study method.
T F	6. Cause–effect relationships cannot be established via the field-study method because it is descriptive rather than inferential.
T F	7. As the researcher gains precision and control, he or she loses external validity.
T F	8. Components of the field-study method include, the setting, the observational task, the role of the observer and classification or analysis.
T F	9. Remembered observations are subject to biased selection, distortion, decay (loss), or growth.
T F	10. Bem's procedure for coding her subjects' interactions with a kitten involved the independent coding by two raters of all research participants.
T F	11. In a field study involving naturalistic observation, observers may be invisible, covert, or visible non-participants but should not be participants in the phenomena under study.
T F	12. The development of the periodic table in chemistry represents a fruitful use of the classification aspect of the field-study method.

T F	13.	Naturalistic observation is a simple method requiring little training and is no longer in vogue.
T F	14.	The analysis of people-tracks, or traces, is known as archival research.
T F	15.	One of the frequently employed tools of the archival researcher is context analysis.
T F	16.	Archival research encompasses only a narrow band of materials—that is, some form of document.
T F	17.	The unobtrusive character of archival research offers some protection against reactivity (on-stage) effects.
T F	18.	Systematic changes in record-keeping procedures constitute one source of error for archival researchers.
T F	19.	The advent of the computer solved the problem with the accuracy of the data derived from archival records.
T F	20.	A declining crime rate has been linked to a reduction in the number of abortions.
T F	21.	'Googling' the Internet is a form of archival research.
T F	22.	In her discussion of the connection noted in #20, Diana discussed a possible on-stage factor that could account for the linkage between crime and abortion.
T F	23.	The investigation of the relationship between cancer rates and stress reported by Diana is an example of a natural experiment.

Walking on Numerical Stepping-stones

In the next three chapters we will discuss how we tie numbers to ideas, feelings, objects, and events. This is the number game, and, like any game it has rules that we sometimes break, unwittingly and disastrously.

Sometimes we make mistakes. We inadvertently tie a phone number to the wrong person, or assign someone the wrong age number. Sometimes we lie. We purposefully tie the wrong age, weight, or income number to ourselves. We unwittingly, or wittingly, alter *the score* of the game. CEOs of giant corporations do the same thing when they fix their books—they break the rules for tying numbers to company assets.

Since scientists are human, they also inadvertently make mistakes and tie the wrong numbers to some of their observations, or make mistakes in their calculations. Since they often use elastic-rulers, it's hard to be accurate all the time. And it's easy to innocently stretch the ruler to get the numbers you want. And, unavoidably, since scientists are human, some of them will diddle their data in an attempt to win the game.

You already know most of the rules of the number game, you just haven't written them down—we'll do just that in the next three chapters. Once you recognize the rules, you'll be in a better position to detect phony numbers, devious advertising and 'junk science'.

You'll also be in a better position to appreciate why scientists rely so heavily on numbers. Numbers are necessary to cut complex problems down to mind-size, to construct mathematical stepping-stones to fill in the gaps between observations, and to travel into the unobservable future.

In Chapter 10, we review the basic rules for tying numbers to objects and events (e.g., age and weight numbers). In Chapter 11, we discuss how we use numbers to summarize and describe large amounts of information (e.g., averages and descriptive statistics). In Chapter 12, we explain how to use mathematical bridges to travel from the known to the unknown (e.g., predicting your grade point average in college on the basis of your high school grades).

10

The Number Game

Chapter Goals

- To demonstrate how numbers and science go together and how we benefit from that marriage.
- To present the rules of the game for tying numbers to packages of experience as they flow up from the bottom of the PST.
- To show how we—either unwittingly or deviously—break the rules of the number game and, in so doing, deceive both others and ourselves.

Introduction

Language involves tying symbols to packages of experience as they flow up from the bottom of the PST. Mostly we tie words, rather than numbers, to those packages (e.g., dog, Willie, car, good, bad). When we use words to identify a package of experience we usually call it a *qualitative* label or category.

We also tie numbers to certain packages (e.g., 123 pounds, 10 dollars, 115 intelligence points). When we use numbers to identify a package of experience we call it a *quantitative* label or category.

Sometimes, for personal reasons, we break the rules of the number game. For example, some people have been known to change their age number by quite a bit within the same day, let alone the same year. Sometimes we tie numbers to fuzzies: 'I have 5 real friends. Maybe 4. . . . Well, 3 for sure.' Counting friends is harder than counting billiard balls.

The rules of counting assume that you're counting things that have hard, stable boundaries, not vague, elastic boundaries like friendship, how much money you think you have in your bank account, how much weight you plan to lose, or the untrustworthy CEO's annual report of company assets.

273

Measurement and the PST

Measurement is a language. Its symbols are numerals. Numbers help us both combine and divide packages of experience into mind-sized chunks. Our manipulation of numbers up at the top of the PST may or may not reflect *reality* at the bottom of the PST. It's usually easier to change number labels than to change the packages of reality they represent. It's easier to take a pencil and change the numbers in your bankbook, than to change the actual number of dollars in your bank account. In short, it's easier to talk a good number game than to play one.

Fig 10.1 ■ THE NUMBER GAME

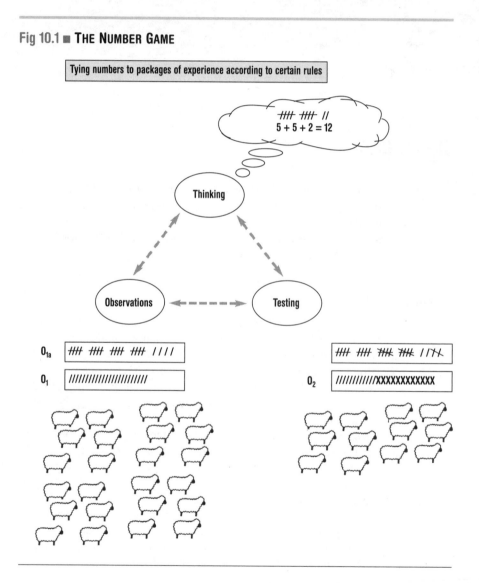

In Figure 10.1 we hop in our time machine and travel back to ancient times. At the bottom left corner of the PST you see a *bunch* of sheep. A 'bunch' is a fuzzy, qualitative category. Over thousands of years human nervous systems learned to chunk light and sound waves flowing in at the bottom of the PST into qualitative packages (e.g., sheep, people, rocks, sabre-toothed tigers, etc.). We acquired such qualitative packages—mental images and categories—before we had numbers.[1]

So, before our ancestors invented numbers, a shepherd had no way to mentally represent a bunch of sheep in *quantitative detail*. All he could retain, up-top, with his bounded rationality—his limited short-term memory—was a vague image of a *bunch*, or rely on the crude qualitative categories *few* or *many*.

Then, *somehow*, the number game got its start.[2] Perhaps some lonely shepherd, sitting on a rock and whittling away on a stick made that first step toward inventing numbers. He might have carved a mark on his stick for each sheep, like this: / / / / / / (see O_1 in the figure). This was a shorthand way of keeping detailed *quantitative* track of a *bunch* of observations.

This quantitative invention had many advantages. It took a load off the shepherd's memory, off his bounded rationality. And the marks helped him *keep score* when he ran out of fingers. With this shorthand invention a shepherd could show other shepherds the size of his flock by showing them the marks on his stick. He no longer had to herd his sheep here and there to show prospective buyers. Quantity received a travel permit.

If the size of his flock changed—a before-and-after situation—the shepherd could modify the marks on his stick. For example, if he sold half his flock he could carve a line through their marks (see O_2 in Figure 10.1). If two shepherds wanted to combine flocks they could keep quantitative track by putting their sticks together—a physical form of addition.

Finally, if someone wanted to buy the whole flock, the purchaser could *rigorously* test the reliability and validity of the measuring stick. Operating at the bottom of the PST, as each sheep was herded through the gate, the purchaser would be able to check the sheep's presence against the marks on the seller's stick(s).

With the markings on the stick, our shepherd was still operating at the bottom of his PST. He had progressed from seeing actual sheep, to *seeing* their simple representatives—their marks on sticks—but he's still playing a clumsy *seeing-is-believing* game as far as quantity is concerned. Then a very clever person simplified the system further by grouping the marks (see O_{1a} in the figure) into packages of five. (Can you guess why *five* was the magic number?) It's a miracle! Why?

---

[1] Ken Wilber, *Integral Psychology* (2000), sees preconscious qualitative packages as integrating experience, and conscious, quantitative packages as analytic, perhaps even divisive.

[2] Since we don't have reliable archival records of the period no one knows for sure how counting got started. Probably using fingers, but then running into trouble with quantities over ten.

Mind-size quantities

At the bottom of his PST, a shepherd was able to carry around twenty-four individual marks on a stick, but at the top of the PST it was impossible to hold that many separate marks in his short-term visual memory, or his bounded rationality. His memory could accommodate the categories *few* or *many*, but not twenty-four individual units.

A psychologist, George Miller, wrote a classic paper (1956) proposing that our short-term memory can only retain seven, plus or minus two, separate units at a time.[3] That is to say that we only have the short-term memory capacity to manage about seven distinct chunks of information at a time before we begin to forget and/or distort some of them. Notice the trouble we have remembering a new ten-digit phone number.

By packaging the 24 marks into groups of five the shepherd could now afford to carry them around up-top—*four* units of five and *four* units of one, which is eight units total, one less than Miller's upper limit, the *dangerous nine*.[4]

A major invention

Finally, the Arabs went beyond marks on a stick and invented numbers, thus miraculously reducing the memory load still further. Instead of having to remember a chunk made of four diagonal strokes with a line through them, we only had to remember the simple symbol '5'. Thus, mind-size numbers replaced groups of marks on a stick. The invention of simple arithmetic enabled humans to map and modify more of their big world, even with their bounded rationality.

With the additional inventions of *division* and *multiplication* we were able to think of, and explore, both astonishingly tiny and massive space and time worlds, in our heads, on blackboards, and on computers.

It is important to note that while many of our quantitative speculative maps are *mathematically valid*, with unlimited up-top travel permits, their validity down below remains, at best, only partially tested. Science is a work in progress. Some of our scientific theories are *true*, some are *kind of true*, and some are *truth free*. We just don't always know which one falls into which category.

> Our mathematical imagination can map much more space and time on its blackboard than any reearcher can explore observationally down at the bottom of his or her PST.

As a consequence, we become increasingly and dangerously, dependent upon speculative maps of the present (e.g., a bank account) constructed of numbers. Numbers that are

---

[3]You can test his premise by trying to remember a new phone 9-digit number while walking across the room to make a call at a noisy party.

[4]Notice how packages of 10, 100, 1000, etc., each allow us to carry more and more chunked or numerically corseted quantitative information in our limited short-term memory.

based on missing, flimsy, or fraudulent observational checkpoints, and particularly on maps of the future (a planned bank account), which are completely lacking any observational anchors at all.

Yes, maps can be mathematically valid up-top (add up accurately) and, at the same time, observationally empty down below (bankrupt).

Remember that modern mathematics—on the blackboard, computer screen, or piece of paper—is nothing more than a promissory note using numbers, the equivalent to the marks on an ancient stick, but generated by modern *shepherds*, sincerely, or deviously, trying to sell you imaginary sheep. Some of them are careful carvers but lousy or dishonest observers, some of them are reliable observers but clumsy or fraudulent carvers, and some are skilled carvers and observers. But you can't tell ahead of time whether they're honest but number numb, geniuses, or mathematical con artists. That's why science has evolved into an adversarial system in which scientists attempt to replicate each other's work, and why they demand to see more than your blackboard scribbles and computer printouts. That's why hard-nosed researchers demand: 'Show me the sheep!' Admittedly there are some *scientists* (particularly in Theoretical Physics and Economics) who fall in love with the number game, and buy mathematical promissory notes because they're so elegant—this is akin to naïvely believing the ancient shepherd simply because the notches on his stick were so elegantly carved—even though he had no sheep to back up his stylish carving.

That being said, much of modern science travels via mathematical maps. By learning to chunk quantity into smaller and smaller memory-sized packages (numbers) humans moved beyond crude qualitative maps of local observational experience to refined quantitative maps. Even a tiny, but valid, mathematical scribble can move the world—$E=mc^2$. When such maps are valid representatives, or labels, of down-below observations, they enable us to both detect and imagine finer distinctions and more subtle changes in the flow of experience.

The goal of quantitative science is to locate reliable observations (down-below) and tie them to stable mathematical symbols (up-top) and hope that the observations behave the way the mathematical model predicts they should. If so, then by merely manipulating the lightweight symbols we can economically describe a current *reality* and, hopefully, predict the unknown future.

However, such quantitative packaging and manipulation works better on some parts of our experience (e.g., sheep and body weight) than on other parts (e.g., love and hate). Some of our most personally important kinds of experience (love, fear, pain) defy neat and tidy numerical packaging, so we still rely heavily on qualitative categories. Nevertheless, for those parts that can be neatly packaged we can achieve astonishing powers of prediction and control, both at the top and bottom of selected parts of the PST, resulting from quantitative categories and their mathematical manipulation.

Numbers can be dangerous

Unfortunately, such knowledge is a two edged sword, which can be used for good or ill. In ancient times the rule was one mark for one sheep. *As soon as the stick and the flock are separated* we face the possibility of honest errors or cunning skullduggery—of accidentally or deviously breaking the one mark for one sheep rule.

Some modern CEOs have practiced such skullduggery on a massive scale. They've played a dirty number game involving the carving of many more marks on their stick—or financial statements—than they have sheep. The average purchaser (shareholder) has no affordable way of counting the corporate sheep, particularly when greedy auditors join the fraudulent number game.

In our modern world we spend less and less time with *the sheep*—less time in the relatively simple natural environment—and more and more time navigating complex and changing artificial environments. We spend more time up-top counting imaginary sheep than down below actually observing real ones. We spend more time manipulating invented qualitative and quantitative categories at the top of our PSTs, than we do making reliable observations down at the bottom. Sun-time and biological rhythms have been replaced by digital time and the electronic blips in the heart of your bank's computer have become our *reality*. We can no longer see most of the things we believe. So, if at the top of our PST, the qualitative categories feel right and if the numbers add up mathematically, then they must be valid; they must be *real*.

> Believing-is-seeing increaingly becomes the name of the game when you can't *see* the sheep.

Notice that your identification number is so real that if someone steals it then the *physical you* no longer exists as far as governments, banks, insurance companies, and credit card companies are concerned. In the modern world your number is more important than you are. In can take months to get your number reattached to you, for you to become really real again. We live in a world where the notched sticks are becoming more important than the sheep.

We rely on experts to package and number the *reality* we can't see. In most cases we have to take their numbers on faith. That's why the adversarial system of science remains our most trusted news service. Researchers make an effort to test the reliability and validity of the marks on each other's sticks. While most scientists subscribe to the motto 'Show me the sheep!' it's easier said than done.[5]

---

[5] However, as our world becomes more complex, of necessity our scientists are starting to spend increasing amounts of time at the top of their PSTs, and in front of computers. They spend more and more time generating and running elegant mathematical models of an imagined down-below reality that's too complicated, or invisible, or too large, or too expensive to observe or test (e.g., string theory in physics, and multi-variable statistical models in social science). This is why we see a renewed interest in less precise but more mentally and observationally affordable qualitative methods, this is also why we see more fraudulent junk science. It's easier and easier to change the numbers and harder and harder to check their reliability and validity.

278

Working away at the bottom of the PST, hard-nosed empirical researchers aren't interested in promises or advertisements about sheep, they are not interested in listening to overpaid actors tell lies about sheep, and they're not interested in corporate executives giving fancy PowerPoint presentations with coloured slides telling tall tales about sheep. Instead, they insist on seeing the sheep. Bottom dwelling empirical researchers are hooked on the *seeing-and-measuring-is-believing* way to the truth. While ultimately aiming for external validity, they attempt to patiently build one internally valid stepping-stone at a time.

In this chapter we describe the four kinds of yardsticks scientists use to tie numbers to packages of experience, and the rules for using them. And, for the 'number-numb': don't worry. These rules are 'user friendly'.

On being number-numb

When children break rules while tying number words to objects and events, we laugh. When researchers do it, it's not so funny. It's also not as obvious and it can be disastrous.

Have you noticed how otherwise very competent people are number-numb? A fellow faculty member is a case in point. He speaks of numbers as 'those ugly little squiggles that are the constituents of a black art'. When the abolition of child labour in mines and factories freed children from punishing physical work, he claims the evil powers rushed in with arithmetic, algebra, trigonometry, and statistics as new forms of child torture.

Measurement Scales and Rules

Those of you who major in psychology or become social scientists will encounter many different types of measurement scales that range from crude to precise. An appropriate measurement scale will help you locate an important phenomenon or discover a subtle change in behaviour; a crude or inappropriate scale will miss the very differences and changes for which you are looking. Since the scientific method rests on systematic observation, and since measurement is the fundamental tool of observation, you need to know how to select and evaluate, and perhaps even construct, these vital observational tools.

The four major types of scale encountered in social science are: (1) nominal, (2) ordinal, (3) interval, and (4) ratio scales. To understand the construction and application of these scales, and to appreciate their relative power to detect differences in human behaviour, it helps to know the different rules upon which each one rests. Knowing them helps you avoid being conned by sleazy advertisers, salesman, and crooked CEOs.

At this point we could list and describe some of the logical rules for combining number symbols, such as the nominal rule, the ordinal rule, and the interval rule. Instead, let's discover the logical operations by examining a concrete example of their application.

Measurement can be defined as rules for tying numbers to packages of experience—to objects and events. A familiar example of tying numbers to an object is an ordinary one-foot ruler.

one-foot ruler

In the case of the ruler, someone has printed numbers, rather than carved notches, on this flat piece of wood. What rules were followed? Examine the ruler for a moment; notice the symbols; observe how they are placed. If you examine another school ruler, even one made by a different manufacturer, you will find many similarities. While the colour of the wood or the paint or the plastic may differ, the two rulers will have several characteristics in common—the placement of the numerals in all cases has followed the same rules.

Nominal rule

Notice first that different symbols are used to label different points on the ruler. If this were not the case we could be faced with a silly ruler of the following type:

The nominal rule—the naming or labelling rule—demands that you apply different, agreed-on labels (names, numbers, symbols) to different objects or events.

Some scientists do not consider this rule as a form of measurement. They point out that it is merely a labelling operation, useful for identification purposes, but in no way does it tell us anything about 'more than' or 'less than' relationships. Nevertheless, since counting is a form of measurement and since it is based on the assumption that we have met the requirements of the nominal rule, it is important to include it as one of the rules of measurement. In other words, since the nominal rule is fundamental to all other measuring rules, it should be included.

For example, your phone number is reliably tied to you. It is your number. If it changed every few days it would not only confuse you and your friends, but it would also break the nominal rule. Similarly, think how confusing it would be if the numbers on your currency changed at random, if the number 10 on ten dollar bill suddenly became a five, and the number one on a 100 dollar bill suddenly became the number 20. But it might change again before you got to the store. You would never be able to *reliably* count how much money you had.

When students cheat by using another student's ID, or when psychiatrists can't agree which patients should be labelled as depressed, they are breaking the nominal rule. The naming rule requires that observers must be able to agree what qualitative or quantitative label is tied to an object or an event. If you're planning to do graduate work, keep an eye on nominal scaling and category theory, which offer rich

> The nominal rule would be repeatedly broken if the names or number labels attached to objects and events changed unpredictably.

opportunities for conceptual and empirical breakthroughs. Clinical psychologists become famous by discovering/inventing new illnesses and naming them. Drug companies seem to discover/invent new illnesses and, of course, the pills to cure them every month. To name something, to make a special mark for it at the top of the PST, usually leads us to believe that it must be really there down at the bottom (oil wells, gold mines, love, diseases, cures, etc.).

Ordinal rule

Not only are different numbers assigned to different objects and events, but the numbers have a reserved place in the number series—this is the ordinal rule. If it were otherwise, we would encounter rulers such as the following, where different rulers have their numbers in different orders.

1	2	3	4	5	6	7	8	9	10	11	12

9	5	11	1	3	12	4	10	8	7	2	6

An object measured by the first ruler might be assigned the number 2, but when measured by the second ruler, it would be assigned the number 5. If numbers on a ruler, or in the number series generally, were permitted to play musical chairs we couldn't use the numbers to talk about order or to indicate where in the series a given object or event occurs. Think of the problems involved in a simple example:

> *You:* How did Sally make out in the 100-metre freestyle?
> *Paul:* She came in second.
> *George:* She came in fifth.

In an effort to resolve the conflicting answers, you ask Ringo. He replies, 'Sally came in *B*.' Ringo doesn't like numbers and will use them only when no alternative method is available. The three foregoing systems for describing order are outlined as follows:

Paul: 1, 2, 3, 4, 5, 6, 7, etc.
George: 9, 5, 11, 1, 3, 12, 4, etc.
Ringo: A, B, C, D, E, F, G, etc.

It is important to remember that the symbols we use and the position they're assigned in the series are mere customs. As long as Paul, George, and Ringo use the same rules consistently, they are playing the game. Paul's number series has the advantage of being in common use (large-group rules)—it is blessed by custom. Notice, however, that when George's number series (individual rules) is put next to Paul's, there is no contradiction in their replies to our question. In both instances Sally was assigned the position right after the beginning position—that is, Position *B* in Ringo's terms. If George wants to persist in having his own individual ordinal scale and he uses it consistently, we can learn to translate it into our own terms. He plays by the shareable rules of language, and anyone who wants to learn his system can do so. If, however, the positions of the numbers change—if George haphazardly changes them from day to day—then this would be an unstable system, and George would be breaking the 'reserved-place' ordinal rule.

It should be noted that in these examples the nominal rule is also violated. You will recall that we stated that, in the case of the nominal rule, different agreed upon labels are assigned to different objects or events. In our examples, although different labels are applied to different objects or events (marks on the ruler), they are not agreed upon—that is, there does not appear to be a consensus as to the label for second place. In one case it's 2, in another 5, and in Ringo's system it is *B*. Each of the rules builds on preceding ones, so that in order to develop an ordinal scale, you must first satisfy the assumptions of the nominal rule.

So far we have considered two rules of the number system: Rule 1—by custom, different objects and events are assigned different and agreed upon symbols or numerals; Rule 2—by custom, the symbols or numerals are assigned a reserved position in the series of numerals. The alphabet, as well as the whole number system, fulfills these two rules. Thus, if you want to label events or simply talk about their order, the alphabet will do as well as the number system, providing you don't have to talk about more than 26 objects or events. While the alphabet is a useful system for labelling events and describing their order, and although it can be used to describe relations such as 'earlier than' and 'bigger than', it's not as useful if we want to talk about 'how much bigger' one object is than another?

The interval rule

Returning to our standard 12-inch ruler, notice that the symbols are placed equal distances apart. A ruler is divided into a series of equal-sized units. But how far apart are the letters of the alphabet? One alph? You see that the order rule makes no assumptions about how far apart the symbols are. All of the following scales meet the ordinal rule:

Scale 1

| 1 | 2 | 3 | 4 |

Scale 2

| 1 | 2 3 4 | 5 |

Scale 3

| 1 2 3 | 4 5 |

> *You:* How did our team make out in the 100-metre freestyle?
> *Reply:* We placed first, second, and third.

Does that mean by Scale 1, Scale 2, or Scale 3? Usually when we ask such a question, we are not concerned about how big an interval separates the swimmers but only about the order they came in, regardless of interval. If we want to know the swimmers' times, or the distances separating the best jumps of three pole-vaulters, we can't answer that question with only an ordinal scale? Suppose Elvis vaulted 13'9", Blane vaulted 14'0", and Turk vaulted 14'6". How do we communicate this information with only an ordinal scale? We could say Blane beat Elvis by a bit and Turk beat Blane by more than that. So we have communicated more than just 'order' information.

We have communicated some distance or interval information as well. How did we do it? By selecting a standard that we call 'a bit' (the distance separating Elvis and Blane) and comparing it to the distance separating Turk and Blane, we decided that the latter distance was bigger than 'a bit'.

The important point, of course, is that to talk about 'more than' and 'less than', we need to know what a 'than' is; if we want to talk about 'more than a bit' and 'less than a bit', we need to know what a 'bit' is.

Selecting a standard, or basic, unit is an arbitrary decision. When faced with this problem, you look around for a readily available standard and make that your 'bit'. People's feet were usually readily available, and so 'one foot' became an early unit for measuring distance. Using people's real feet for measuring distances must have led to certain inequalities and inconveniences. When Dad's farm was divided, the son with the biggest 'foot' did better. Eventually someone, probably someone with smaller feet, recommended that there should be one special foot to avoid arguments; everyone agreed, and of course they decided to use the king's foot.

Now a king doesn't go traipsing all over the countryside pacing out distances to help people divide up farms. So they cut off one of his feet to be sent around for the purpose. That left the king with only one foot, hence the origin of the term *the one-foot ruler*. We're sure that a little archival research on your part will confirm this explanation!

The point is that if we want to talk about how much more than or less than one object is in relation to another, we need a unit—a standard interval that is easy to apply. It often takes years to develop such a unit and then to sell others on using that particular interval, whether it is a second, a bushel, a micromercury, a megaton, an ounce, a degree of temperature, a unit of anxiety, intelligence, depression, or a foot.

In summary, if all we want to do is to label or identify objects or packages of data by using numbers, we follow the nominal rule (different objects get different numbers). We can do this as long as we can tell the objects or the qualities of objects apart. If we also want to describe order relationships among objects by using numbers, we must include the ordinal rule. We can do this as long as we can reliably order the objects (from earliest to latest, or smallest to biggest). Then, we assign the first number, 1, in the number series to the first object in the ordered series and the second number, 2 to the second object in the ordered series, and so on. If, in addition to labelling and ordering, we want to describe with numbers the interval separating objects, then we must use the interval rule and select or develop a measuring instrument that is divided into equal units.

There is one more characteristic about our one-foot ruler that deserves comment. Notice that it has a zero point. This is so obvious that its importance is often overlooked.

The ratio (zero point) rule

Unless a measuring instrument has a zero point, it is impossible to say anything about how many times bigger or smaller one object or quantity is than another. Without assuming that there is such a thing as zero age, we would not be able to say that Harry is twice as old as Mary. Consider an example. In a test of knowledge of French nouns, we have the following results:

Vladimir knew none of the words.
Hamish knew 5.
George knew 10.
Gloria knew 15.

We can portray the results in the following way:

| Vladimir | Hamish | George | Gloria |
| 0 | 5 | 10 | 15 | 20 |
| French noun test |

Thus our test of French nouns is a measuring instrument that appears to have all the characteristics of an ordinary ruler—that is, it appears to meet the nominal, ordinal, interval, and absolute-zero rules. If this is so, then we can say that George knows twice as many French nouns as Hamish knows, and that Gloria knows three times as many as Hamish knows. We can do so only if we are able to agree on where zero belongs on the scale. As you can guess, certain very simple French nouns weren't included on the test the teacher gave—words like *l'amour* and *la bouche*. Therefore it is quite likely that there are at least five French nouns that even Vladimir knows, and that if they had been included on the test, everyone would get some of the answers correct. This would involve moving the zero point on our scale five points to the left. Now look at the old scale alongside the new, and see how this affects what we can say about how many more nouns Gloria knows than Hamish or Vladimir. In the case of the first scale, we had concluded that George knew twice as many French nouns as Hamish knew, but with the new zero point, this is no longer the case. Similarly, on the original scale Gloria knew three times as many French nouns as Hamish knew, whereas on the new scale, she knows only twice as many.

| Vladimir | Hamish | George | Gloria |
| 0 | 5 | 10 | 15 | 20 |

| Vladimir | Hamish | George | Gloria |
| 0 | 5 | 10 | 15 | 20 | 25 |

It is apparent, then, that if we want to talk about how many times greater or smaller one object is in relation to another, we must have a way of deciding where absolute zero is on the scale. In many cases, such as most test scores (arithmetic, French, intelligence, anxiety, beauty, and musical talent), we use an arbitrary zero. In those cases where we are not sure where zero lies, we should not (1) attempt to say how many times bigger or smaller one score is than another or (2) attempt to use any statistical procedures that involve multiplying or dividing the scores. Many social science researchers ignore these rules.

Arbitrary zero

You may say that one way around the problem is simply to report that, in the case of our original French test, George knew twice as many of the words as Hamish did on *that particular test* (internal validity). This way you are making no claim about whether George knows twice as many of all French nouns (external validity). And, of course, you would be perfectly right in doing so. However, most tests are designed to estimate an amount of knowledge in a given field, with the test questions representing only a small sample of all possible questions in that area. Thus while it is relatively easy to say whether someone gets a score of zero on the particular sample of the questions selected, it is extremely difficult to decide whether that person would get zero if all possible questions dealing with the topic had been asked—that's too large a playpen to cover with observational stepping-stones.

Most students who receive poor test grades know what we are talking about. When they say the test was unfair, they are saying that it was a bad sample of questions, and by poor luck, the teacher just happened to select the only questions the student didn't know. In your friend's eyes, your score of 80 and his score of 10 certainly does not indicate that you know eight times more about the field than he does. In fact, by the time he finishes complaining, he might have implied that he could answer hundreds of questions about the topic, whereas you were able to answer only the eight particular questions the teacher selected. So he goes away mumbling, concluding that he knows more about the field than you do but that the professor is almost diabolical in his or her ability to select those few questions for which he has no answers.

This is a critical problem facing educators, particularly with the present knowledge explosion. We can no longer expect physics professors to know everything about physics or psychology professors to know everything about psychology. The professors solve this dilemma by becoming more and more specialized, by carving out smaller and smaller areas—playpens—within their very large playpen of their own discipline, in which they attempt to become very knowledgeable. They then dump all that knowledge in the student's lap.

But how is the student to face the dilemma of information overload at exam time? The naïve student attempts to learn all the material that the professor presents, as well as to cover the outside readings. Wise students know how to study strategically. They've learned to spend more time on some of the course material than on others. They've learned to *read the professor*, to identify his or her preferences based on how much time they spend on different topics, noting which topics appear to excite them, seeing what sorts of questions their professor traditionally asks, looking over exam papers from the previous year, and by grilling former students.

This strategic approach to learning may appear to be unscholarly. Certainly some students carry it to the extreme, devoting almost all their time attempting to predict the few questions that will be asked, and then applying their very limited remaining time and energy to studying these few. This is, of course, a self-defeating approach to learning. Nevertheless, serious students facing the impossible task of preparing for all possible questions rely not only on their own particular interests but also on the biases of the professor in guiding them towards what aspects of the topic require more concentrated work than others, what parts of the playpen to concentrate upon, which parts to pass over lightly, and which to stop and do some digging.

This discussion is not just a bit of friendly advice on successfully surviving university. The rational way to estimate a student's knowledge of a given area (external validity) would be to have all competent professors in that area write out a list of all conceivable questions. These questions would then be put into huge drums grouped into classes from most important to least important. On a given examination a sample of 10, 15, or 50 questions would be drawn out of each drum and would constitute the exam—the number of questions drawn depends on the amount of time available for the examination. Such a list of questions would constitute a random sample of hard, average, and easy questions.

In contrast, under the present circumstances, a more affordable method—institutionally and professorially—is employed in which your professor decides which questions to ask and you're presented with a cherry-picked sample of questions, reflecting your professor's personal playpen of interests in that field. If a student repeatedly does well on the series of exams based on the large random sampling procedure noted earlier, we would conclude that the student knows the topic well. When a student does well on tests designed by a given professor, we are not sure whether he or she knows the topic well or *knows the professor well*.

Similarly, when you read the results of a poll concerning who will be the next president of the United States or concerning premarital sexual relations, are you getting the answers from a cross-section of the population in the country, or are you getting the answers from the friends and colleagues of the person who carried out the poll? In other words, are you learning about the topic, or are you learning more about the biases of the person who conducted the poll? *Absolute-zero scales* refer to external validity covering large space and time frames and total populations. *Arbitrary-zero scales* refer to restricted samples of questions and people.

In the example of our test of French nouns, we were not talking about how many of all (population) French nouns the student knew, but only about how many of those selected for that particular test (a small sample). Thus we were using an arbitrary zero, so it is impossible to talk about whether Gloria knows 2 times or 20 times as many French nouns as Hamish does. If we wanted to be able to make such statements with confidence, we would have to test the students on *all* French nouns. If we wanted to make an approximation, we could test them on several samples of French nouns picked at random from a data pool of all French nouns. Arbitrary zero scales are typically interval scales masquerading as ratio scales.

Before discussing how science and measurement go together, we shall summarize measurement rules. Nominal scales are used when we compare objects or data clusters and can decide which ones are the same and which ones are different. After this we *can count* how many objects fall into each category. Ordinal scales enable us to talk about relations such as 'more than' or 'less than', or 'earlier than' or 'later than'. As long as independent observers *can rank-order objects* or events on some less-to-more dimension, they have an ordinal scale.

In some cases we want to know more than who came first and second. We also want to know by *how much* one swimmer beat the other. In instances where we want to describe by how much objects or events differ, we use an interval scale. Finally, absolute-zero scales are used when we want to compare one event, not merely with another person or sample, but with *an absolute-zero or population value* (knowledge of *all* French nouns).

Each of the four scales, then, has a different purpose, but each succeeding scale assumes that the rules of the preceding scales have been met. If an ordinal scale is to be used, it is assumed that the nominal rule has been met. If an interval scale is to be used, it is assumed that, in addition to the interval rule, the nominal and ordinal rules have also been met.

In relatively new disciplines like the social and medical sciences, remember that nominal and ordinal scales can be of invaluable assistance in describing or packaging data. For example, even before we had thermometers how might you 'measure' someone's temperature using a crude ordinal scale? The way every parent does: by putting your hand on the person's forehead and seeing if it feels hot. Hotter than what? Hotter than your hand. This works well, providing the parent's temperature is 'normal', and the child has a high fever. Just as a crude thermometer is better than no thermometer, so crude measures of anxiety, or management ability, or patient improvement are better than no measure, better than casual observation. Furthermore, what may start out to be crude measures are, with experience, gradually refined and transformed into more sensitive measures that can detect smaller and smaller differences and changes. So we move from nominal scale (normal temperature, abnormal temperature), to an ordinal scale (normal temperature, moderately high temperature, high temperature), to an internal scale with the aid of a thermometer (98 degrees, 100 degrees, 102 degrees, 104 degrees). What would be an absolute zero scale for measuring body temperature?

In the section to follow, we will have an opportunity to examine some of the challenges involved in constructing simple nominal and ordinal data-packaging methods.

Science and Measurement Go Together

Everyone knows that science and measurement go together, but not everyone appreciates the importance of the relationship. You now have some familiarity with many different scientific and pre-scientific methods, including natural experiments, after-the-fact, field experiments, archival research, simulation methods, survey research, unobtrusive measures, before-and-after, developmental and longitudinal methods, control-group method, interrupted time series, and treatment reversal (cross-over) designs. And you are also familiar with the four measurement scales: nominal, ordinal, interval, and ratio (absolute zero) that are used to clearly describe suspects (Xs) and observations (Os). So the various scientific methods and measurements go together—the methods include measurement scales, involve (Os).

Dependent and independent variables

In order to understand science you have to learn a bit of its special lingo. For instance, scientists technically refer to suspects (Xs) as *independent* variables and to observations (Os) as *dependent* variables. They are variables in the sense that they can take different values, and the changes in the dependent variable are assumed to *depend* on changes in the independent variable. Just as moving from the after-the-fact sieve to the control-group sieve increases confidence in your findings, so too moving up from nominal scales to ordinal, interval, and ratio scales increases the precision of your measurement and reduces regions of uncertainty.

Recall the control-group study (treating depressed patients with a new drug) in Chapter 5. This study can be conducted at different levels of precision, depending on the precision used to manipulate the independent variable (the drug) and the degree of precision used to measure the dependent variable (the degree of depression). At the crudest level we could manipulate the independent variable on a nominal scale (Drug A versus Drug B) and measure the dependent variable also at a crude nominal scale level (depressed versus non-depressed).[6] The following figure displays the research design as well as the results of the study:

	O_1	X	O_2
Group 1 ($N = 10$)	10 depressed 0 not depressed	Drug A	8 depressed 2 not depressed
Group 2 ($N = 10$)	10 depressed 0 not depressed	Drug B	9 depressed 1 not depressed

Not very encouraging results. But is it because the drugs have similar effects or that the scale is too crude to detect the differences? Note that the dependent variable can only take two values—depressed versus non-depressed. There is no provision for shifts in the degree of depression; it may well be that Drug A helps

---

[6] You can think of this as a two-point ordinal scale rather than the two-category nominal scale, if you prefer.

relieve the depression of significantly more patients than does Drug B, but this result cannot show up in this study since, for example, there is no category for mild depression.

Now look what happens to our results when we increase the degree of precision by using a four-category ordinal scale instead of a two-unit nominal scale for assessing depression:

	O_1	X	O_2
Group 1 (N = 20)	10 severe 10 marked 0 moderate 0 mild	Drug A	2 severe 6 marked 7 moderate 5 mild
Group 2 (N = 20)	10 severe 10 marked 0 moderate 0 mild	Drug B	7 severe 12 marked 1 moderate 0 mild

Following treatment with Drug A, 12 out of 20 patients are well enough to go home, having shifted down to mild or moderate depression, whereas only one patient was well enough to go home following Drug B treatment.

If Drug A *had* been a miracle drug, a drug capable of shifting most patients from a seriously depressed state to a state of no depression, then we could detect its effect with a crude two-category nominal scale. However, although not a miracle drug, it is significantly better than Drug B, being capable of shifting severely depressed patients to a state of only moderate or mild depression. With a four-point ordinal scale, we detect this important new information; with only a crude two-point nominal scale, we missed it.

We still don't know anything about the effects of different amounts of our independent variable (Drug A), since we previously used only one dosage level. In certain amounts it may indeed prove to be a miracle drug. To find out about the effects of different amounts, we can conduct a study in which we manipulate the independent variable on a milligram scale (a ratio scale with an absolute zero and equal units). The results of this study follow:

> Remember that the cruder the measuring scale used to detect shifts in our dependent variable, the stronger must be the effects of your independent varible.

	O_1	X		O_2
Group 1 (N = 20)	10 severe 10 marked 0 moderate 0 mild	Drug A	150 milligrams	2 severe 3 marked 8 moderate 8 mild
Group 2 (N = 20)	10 severe 10 marked 0 moderate 0 mild	Drug A	100 milligrams	2 severe 6 marked 7 moderate 5 mild
Group 3 (N = 20)	10 severe 10 marked 0 moderate 0 mild	Drug A	50 milligrams	4 severe 8 marked 5 moderate 3 mild

As the dosage becomes larger, a larger number of patients improved. Also note that we don't know what a dosage larger than what we have tried would do; it might be even more effective, or it might start causing negative side effects—obvious ones like hives and drowsiness that can be detected by casual observation involving crude nominal and ordinal scales, or subtle ones like subsequent difficulties in carrying a baby to full term, or long term ones like reduced life span, which may take years to link to the drug. There is no practical way to pre-test the long-term effects of a new drug—its external validity—how it affects different patients over the long haul. That's why we see surprising recalls of well-known drugs after decades of use by millions of people. The best that researchers can do is a series of small playpen tests over time and hope for the best, and hope that the adversarial system of science will lead to early warning signals.

By combining the control-group method with increased precision in the measuring scales used both to measure our dependent variables and to manipulate our independent variables, we are able to get a clearer picture of nature's rhythms. For example, Agnew and Ernest (1971), using human subjects, compared the effects over time of three dosage levels of a sedative drug and three levels of a stimulant drug with a placebo on a variety of measurement scales. The results obtained from one of the self-rating mood scales used are given in Figure 10.2.

In this large study the effects of all three independent variables (type of drug, dosage, and time since drug taken) all show up clearly on a variety of qualitative rating scales but not on certain quantitative perceptual and cognitive tests. Therefore, not only is it appropriate to have sufficient degrees of precision in your measuring scales, but it is also important to select scales that measure relevant aspects of the behaviour under study. This selection is influenced both by past experience and by theoretical hunch. In this particular study, the qualitative self-reports were more accurate in detecting drug type and dosages than were the quantitative 'objective' tests.

It is clear that science and measurement go hand in hand. If you believe your independent variable has a strong effect on your dependent variable, you can probably detect such an effect with a crude nominal or interval scale. If, however, you suspect only a mild or moderate effect, you should use a more precise measuring scale—one with small units able to detect small differences. If you are not sure what aspect of behaviour will be affected, you had better use several different scales.

Fig 10.2 ■ THE INFLUENCE OF A SEDATIVE AND OF A STIMULANT ON MOOD

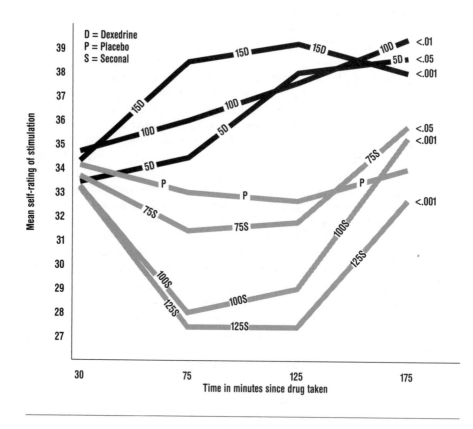

Most wise researchers carry out naturalistic observations or conduct pilot studies to get a 'feel' for the strength and rhythm of the relationship between the dependent and independent variable before launching into elaborate research projects. You would probably be wise to do the same.

What to Look for in Pilot Studies

A pilot study familiarizes you with some of the characteristics of your independent and dependent variables. What appeared under casual observation to be clear suspects and observations, on closer examination turned out to be fuzzy categories—the drug changes colour from day to day and the patients' responses are highly variable.

Indeed, as well as giving some crude estimates of the potency of your independent variable, a pilot study helps you decide how you should scale your independent and dependent variables. Whether you need a few or many categories for each and whether those categories lend themselves to nominal, ordinal, interval, or ratio scaling becomes more obvious. Whether or not observations lend themselves to one scale or another can be determined by asking certain key questions—for example, we need to know how many categories we would need in order to describe the independent variable and its range of impact upon the dependent variable. If we use too few categories, we lose valuable information—as was the case when we used only two nominal categories to detect the effect of our drug on depression in the previously discussed drug study. On the other hand, if we use too many categories, we raise the cost of our study and probably overtax the ability of our observers to make fine discriminations.

Many factors affect our decisions, including theoretical assumptions, past experience (our own and those described in the literature), and the availability of resources and measuring instruments.

For example, once you have satisfied yourself, on the basis of a pilot study, that you are working with an ordinal scale the next key question is how many scale points or categories should you use. Too few categories in an ordinal scale can cause trouble, but so can too many. Consider the case of a therapist who is interested in evaluating the effectiveness of a new treatment for neurosis. She sets up a five-point ordinal scale as follows:

Markedly worse	Modertely worse	No change	Moderately improved	Markedly improved
1	2	3	4	5

Improvement scale

Category 3 is to be assigned to patients who demonstrate no change; Category 4 is to be assigned to those showing moderate improvement; Category 5 to those showing marked improvement; Category 2 to those who seem to be moderately worse following treatment; and Category 1 to those who seem to become markedly worse.

Our researcher has a therapist examine the patients before and after treatment and assign each individual to one of the five categories. She has another therapist independently follow the same procedure. You will recall from our discussion of nominal scales that one of the ways of determining whether you have clear categories (i.e., that the categories can be consistently applied, and your measure is reliable) is to see if different observers can *independently* label the objects or events the same way. We are essentially following the same procedure here with ordinal scales.

The worst that can happen with the ratings of our two observers is almost no agreement between them in assigning patients to categories—that is, had the patients been assigned their categories by drawing the numbers out of two hats rather than having them assigned by therapists, the results would have been similar. Or perhaps there may be large disagreements between the two—that is, therapist B has assigned some patients to Category 5, and therapist A has assigned some of the same patients to Category 1, and vice versa. Under either of the preceding conditions, it is apparent that (1) the scale is inadequate and (2) at least one of the therapists has a very personal or pragmatic view of improvement. However, if the differences occur around scale points 2, 3, and 4, the researcher will recognize that Categories 2 and 4 are fuzzy, that they contain large areas of uncertainty, and so she collapses them into one category by combining them with Category 3.

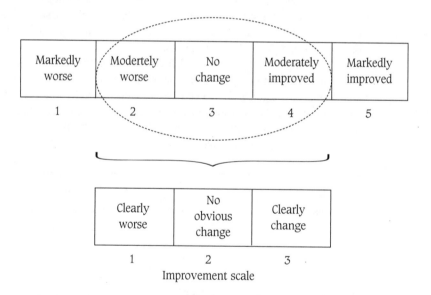

Markedly worse	Modertely worse	No change	Moderately improved	Markedly improved
1	2	3	4	5

Clearly worse	No obvious change	Clearly change
1	2	3

Improvement scale

If this is the case, she has a crude three category ordinal scale that can only detect the results of treatments that have a large effect. Even a crude scale like this is preferable to no scale at all or, in other words, to individual bias.

But she may decide she wants to develop a scale that will be sensitive not only to strong treatments but also to moderate treatments. If so, she devotes time attempting to clarify the distinction between Category 3 (no appreciable change) and Category 4 (moderate improvement) of her original five-point scale. She can attempt to make these categories more distinctive by giving examples of what she considers to be moderate improvement: 'patient may still have severe nightmares but not as frequently'; 'patient still experiences strong anxiety in presenting class paper but is attending class more regularly.' After attempting to clarify distinctions between the middle categories, she tests this scale again to see if she is now getting more agreement among independent judges in the use of the middle categories. If so, she has reduced the region of uncertainty in her original Category 4, and she has increased the sensitivity of her scale in detecting moderate, as well as marked, changes.

Everyone needs maps of the future

Travelling blindly into the future isn't simple, is it? As we indicated in Chapter 6 when discussing validity, we can't see the real sheep over the horizon, only the imaginary ones at the top of the PST. When dealing with speculative maps covering large spaces and long times—particularly those mapping the future—we can't see, and so we can't count real things. No one can! Instead, we make-up or invent the future, quantitatively (with mathematics) and qualitatively (with words).

Nevertheless, you and I desperately need a map of the future. Everyone does. So we buy a speculative *map*, and then promptly forget that it's speculative—if we didn't forget we would move quickly towards dangerous ways of thinking. We bet our lives on those maps and on the promissory notes they contain: concerning mates, careers, children, health, and retirement. Concerning the future, in the global economy, in the expanding universe, we have no choice but to increasingly shift to a believing-is-seeing trajectory to the *truth*.

Like us, empirical researchers have to buy one of these speculative maps. They have to trust it enough to commit their time and talent to rigorously testing it, to searching for the promised sheep. Quantitative (number game) researchers like to work with speculative *mathematical maps*—most popular are the ones describing sheep that will be all standing in a straight line with numbers tied to them, so that researchers don't have to bother searching as far and wide as the qualitative field researchers and naturalistic observers do.

Qualitative researchers, also operating at the bottom of the PST, don't have as much faith in either numbers or straight lines in their imagined futures. They buy speculative qualitative maps that tell interesting word stories, cover more space and time, and include some zigs and zags, some wayward sheep. It's a bigger space so they may discover sheep the quantitative researchers miss. But qualitative researchers can also get lost in those big playpens.

SUMMARY

Using a common one-foot ruler as an example, we described four types of measurement scales: nominal, ordinal, interval, and ratio (absolute zero). Naturalistic observations and pilot studies can help you get a feel for how you might measure your dependent variable. You also get some idea of the 'power' of your independent variable. If it generates a big effect then you can get by with a crude nominal or ordinal scale, whereas if its effect is weak you require a more precise interval or ratio scale. Or perhaps you should look for a more powerful independent variable, one that more obviously pushes your dependent variable—your Os—up or down.

The results you report depend not only on the type and precision of your measurement scales but also on the kind of analysis you perform. Statistics play a large role in shaping the results of science. Among other valuable functions, statistics serve to summarize the results of applying your measurement scales. The next chapter describes some of the vital descriptive functions that statistics perform in the service of science.

The invention of numbers has had a profound impact on our ability to map and manipulate subjective experience at the top of our PSTs, and to package and scale experience down at the bottom. But it is a world where all of us—sometimes innocently, sometimes deviously, and sometimes creatively—break the rules of the number game. It is also a world where science remains our most trusted new service, where theorists map the future, and where conscientious researchers say: 'Don't just show me the map, show me the sheep.'

As researchers accumulate observations at the bottom of the PST, they must critically analyze their pile of data in order to connect the dots. Qualitative and quantitative researchers rely on various statistical methods both to help them package their observations—*descriptive statistics*—and to help them make predictions—*inferential statistics*.

student's notebook

I'm 'number numb'. I'm one of those mathematically challenged losers *referred to in the text. At the sight of a string of digits my brain dives for cover. My already bounded rationality curls up in a fetal position and whimpers. If someone wanted to finish me off, all they'd have to do would be to ask: 'What's the square root of 64?' So before I could work on this chapter I had to lure my bounded brain out of hiding. It turns out that Derek is very good at thinking with numbers, and was actually helpful.*

I like the way the authors started with the observable sheep at the bottom of the PST. I like the word 'bunch' when they moved it up to the top. I get the mental images of the sticks with the hash marks. I even followed along when they started to group the hash marks into sets of five. But my bounded brain started to whine when they moved from hatch marks to NUMBERS. By the time they started discussing the different scales, I'd seized up. That's when Derek rode in and rescued me.

'You're being silly. You think abstractly all the time with words. You can do it with numbers.' He took out his pencil and drew a ruler with evenly distributed marks—but no numbers. Then he drew a balloon tied to each mark on the ruler—that flat stick. Next he told me to write a couple of words inside each balloon. I did. In the first balloon I wrote 'a bit', in the next: 'a bit more', in the next: 'a bit more still'. Well you get the idea.

Derek took back his pencil and erased the string tying each balloon to each mark, leaving the marks below and the unattached balloons floating above them.

A light went on. My brain uncurled. It stood up, straight and tall. Untying the balloons did it. They still had the words inside, but tied to nothing below.

Now, of course, I've tied word-filled balloons to packages of experience all my life. And up-top I cut them free and string my word-balloons together into sentences, in any way I please: 'How do I love thee, let me count the ways.' Delightful, free floating, abstract nonsense, symbols, fuzzy words—all tied to nothing below but to each other at the top. Conceptual stepping-stones without any solid connection to clear observational stepping stones down below, like what happens when you're imagining things, planning your future, daydreaming, or lying.

Now I can do the same with number balloons—play with them. Cut 'em free and string 'em together into math sentences (formulas), in anyway I choose. I can play by the rules mathematicians made up, or make up my own, just like when I make up word rules when talking to babies or pets or lovers.

You've probably known that for years. I didn't. My troubles started about half way through the first grade. I'd was fine when we added ducks. One duck plus two ducks equals three ducks. But things went rapidly down hill when we starting killing off the ducks—four ducks minus three ducks equals one duck. I started to cry. What happened to the three ducks? Then the teacher introduced division and fractions, and started cutting up the ducks. They had to call my mother to come and take me home.

They never told me you could untie the ducks from the numbers. So ever since numbers have always had real ducks tied to them. I'd go to the bank and be on the verge of asking: 'How many ducks do I have in my account?' I was like the ancient shepherd before he invented the notched stick. He spent years adding, subtracting, and dividing real live sheep.

Now I'm a liberated woman! Now I can blithely untie the number balloons and play with them. I now boss the numbers around, rather than letting them bully me. And I can't stop talking about it. I wonder if Derek wishes he hadn't explained things so clearly?

I even wrote a science fiction story in which I changed Einstein's famous formula from $E = mc^2$ into $E = mc^4$. It was a very short story because when they set off their first atom bomb it was so powerful it blew up the whole planet.

Now, when I read about fancy math formula in physics—like string theory, the theory of everything, or one in Economics, like a math model of the world economy—I realize that number crunchers are sitting up at the top of their PSTs playing games with numbers—playing with free-floating number balloons, with hardly any of them tied to anything down below. They're creating speculative mathematical maps.

I can relax now because I don't have to worry about what awful things they're doing to all those ducks.

I appreciate that there are some rules in the number game. Just like there are grammatical rules saying how you should string word balloons together, there are also math rules saying how you should string number balloons together. But now I realize that people made those rules. Humans made them up; they weren't issued from on high. You have no idea what a relief that is!

You can play with strings of word balloons without worrying about what they're tied to: Like in the Songs of Solomon, in the Bible, it says: 'I liken you, my darling to a mare, harnessed to one of the chariots of Pharaoh.' Now that string of word balloons may be grammatical, but it isn't tied to any reality, or any row of ducks, that I know.

I now realize that I can also be creative with number balloons. I can horse around at the top of my PST and decide $1 + 1 + 1 = 1$. I even included this new mathematical truth in my short story: the government of Fuddleland decreed a law to reduce the consumption of alcoholic beverages. In one simple step they cut the number of drinks by 300 per cent in one year. When the opposition challenged these statistics, the Secretary of Mathematics stood up in the house declaring: 'Our calculation is based on the new law of liquid combinatorials. That law states that if you take three glasses of booze and pour them all into another glass, you end up with one glass of booze. So, by unassailable logic: $1 + 1 + 1 = 1$.' You can see why I'm driving Derek crazy.

Now, that mathematics is duck-free, the chapter makes sense. I'm cool about nominal, ordinal, interval, and absolute zero scales. I can now play the number game—almost anything goes!

Besides number liberation—a real biggie—the other important thing I learned concerns nominal scales. While counting seems quantitative, if what you're counting is hard to see—like thoughts and feelings—then it's like counting ghosts. Now, when I notice that a nominal scale is used, I'll keep an eye on reliability. Folk wisdom addresses that problem clearly—'don't count your chickens before they're hatched'—but I never appreciated it before. That warning applies to all the scales, when you get right down to it. From now on, anyone playing with numbers better not mess with me. I know the game!

News stories

I was glancing through the *New Scientist*[7] and a bunch of number game stories caught my attention.

---

[7]'Climate meeting may turn out to be pyrrhic vistory', *New Scientist*, 17 December 2005, p. 3.

The first story said that 'every square meter of the planet's surface is absorbing about one watt more heat than it can release into space.' (7). In the old days, BNL (Before Number Liberation) I would have blindly accepted that statement. This time I stopped and asked myself: 'How many people with wattmeters did it take to measure every square metre of the planet? They must have used Wal-Mart staff on their days off. I hope they fed the ducks.'

Now that I know better, I know that these researchers were at the top of their PSTs playing the number game. They were generating an up-top chain of numerical messages, a speculative map that covers the whole planet. And what's that map tied to? It's tied to the readings on battery-operated wattmeters, and performed on a teensy weensy percentage—a miniscule sample—of the planet's square metres. Talk about a few observational stepping-stones anchoring a massive speculative map.

Furthermore, it just makes sense that there were probably some older batteries in use on some of the wattmeters, so the elastic-ruler strikes again. These researchers, using battery-operated instruments of measurements and a tiny sample of the earth's surface, then travelled to the top of their PST and multiplied, or projected, their small sample findings over the whole globe—inventing external validity.

What those researchers have given us is a massive map of the planet sprinkled with relatively few observation checkpoints. And we don't know how many of the researchers harboured pro- or anti-global warming premises or biases, and so may have unwittingly 'edited' the flow of messages, regardless of what kind of scale a wattmeter uses: ordinal, interval, or absolute zero. Or maybe they used satellite imaging?

The second news story that caught my eye in the New Scientist[8] was on the very next page. It's not good news for everyone who religiously eats their fibre: over the course of 13 studies covering 725,628 people (nominal counting scale), for 20 years (absolute zero scale), about 8,000 developed bowel cancer (archival nominal count). This was in spite of how much fibre the participants ate (qualitative, elastic-ruler, questionnaire reporting subjective estimates of quantities of fibre—including inputs from on-stage and elastic-ruler rogues).

The conclusion? Eating more fibre did not reduce the rates of bowel cancer.

What a study! A flood of messages, dedicated researchers, and a massive sample size tested over an extended time period! Who cares if there's a bit of elasticity in their results? The message is clear. As the headline reads: 'Rough on fiber'.

But that's not the end of the story. A different study, based on a mere 500,000 Europeans in ten countries (pretty good external validity), analyzed their own

---

[8]'Dietary fiber may not prevent bowel cancer after all', New Scientist, 17 December 2005, p. 4.

questionnaire data and concluded that eating fibre reduces the risk of bowel cancer by 40 per cent.

Before my number liberation, I would have been completely flummoxed by these conflicting results. Particularly because the huge samples suggest that there should be a lot of external validity in both studies, except they contradict each other. But now, viewing research as a flood of messages passing through a bunch of messengers, I expect surprises in the results. Well, maybe not whoppers like this!

Even though they conflict, these two studies are great examples of both research tenacity and the adversarial system of science?

As with a lot of scientific research, you'll probably only remember whichever research findings fit your own premises, and you'll forget or file away the findings that don't match safely out of sight behind brackets. I'm not a big fan of fibre—like my Gran says, trying to eat shredded wheat is like chewing on a small bale of hay—so I'll probably remember the first study.

Even though I've now filled my required quota of stories for this week's assignment, there was an interesting article[9] about linking people to a piece of electronic hardware and concluding from the resulting message flow that the hardware resulted in a reduction in chronic pain. Eight volunteer chronic pain patients (nominal, qualitative pain scale, but working at one extreme end) received feedback (colourful but qualitative computer images of brain blood flow) from an MRI machine. Following three 13-minute sessions of feedback, five out of eight patients reported more than 50 per cent pain reduction on a questionnaire (qualitative, elastic-ruler, on-stage, ordinal scale measure).

This is a great example of a chain of messages containing a mix of quantitative and qualitative information, including messengers, who may or may not have taken advantage of the elasticity of some of these measures (pain intensity). And we don't know about the on-stage effects arising from being treated with the fancy new machine. Nevertheless, I recognize this as one of an increasing number of studies in which hardware is used in combination with subjective reports to read thoughts and feelings. It involves searching for treasure inside small playpens. Using a few research subjects—on-stage—trying to link elastic blood flow messages to elastic self-report messages. It's a fascinating 'early in-the-game' message chain which may or may not be granted a universal passport.

Speaking of possible messenger bias distorting the chain of messages, the prestigious *New England Journal of Medicine*[10] pointed an accusing finger at a

[9]'Power of the mind can lessen chronic pain', *New Scientist*, 17 December 2005, p. 19.

[10]'Editorial', *New York Times*, 11 December 2005.

large drug company for omitting data from a research paper in order to hide the risks of heart attack from taking one of it's drugs. Apparently an internal company memo was leaked to the media. The memo revealed that company researchers 'knowingly' deleted critical data. Subsequently, one messenger in the chain 'blew the whistle'.

So, even in the hallowed halls of science, an old truth pops up: 'He who pays the piper calls the tune.' Not only do blind, emotionally anchored premises edit or distort messages in the chain, but so too do conscious, profit-driven premises.

You may think that my interpretations of this scientific news are a bit extreme. I may be flexing my newly discovered math muscles, and maybe I'm being a bit too suspicious of the number balloons and of those who pull, or even cut, their strings.

I'll end this week on a high note, though. It's an odd story. Surgeons in the Czech Republic were able to reattach a boy's nose. The odd part? The nose had been in a dog's stomach for two hours.[11] The plastic surgeon claimed: 'We have looked, in vain . . . for an earlier case where a nose was sewed back that had stayed for two hours in a dog's stomach. We are the first to do this.' This seems to be a proud claim for local, internal validity. Let's hope no one has to test its external validity on more noses extracted from more stomachs.

Note

Explore more treasure maps for this chapter at http://www.oup.com/ca/he/companion/agnewpyke.

REVIEW TRUE OR FALSE QUIZ

T F	1.	Our short-term memory capacity is sufficient to manage between five and 12 separate chunks of information at a time.
T F	2.	Maps can be mathematically valid but conceptually empty.
T F	3.	Empirical researchers are hooked on the believing-is-seeing way to the truth.
T F	4.	The four major types of scale encountered in social science are: ratio, interval, ordinal, and nominal.

[11]*New Scientist*, 17 December 2005.

T F	5.	The ordinal rule demands that you apply different agreed-on labels to different objects or events.
T F	6.	The alphabet satisfies both the nominal rule and the ordinal rule.
T F	7.	A measuring instrument that is divided into equal units is an example of an interval scale.
T F	8.	Only an interval scale will allow us to decide how many times greater or smaller one object is in relation to another.
T F	9.	Absolute zero scales refer to topics and total populations while arbitrary zero scales refer to samples and biased groups of one kind or another.
T F	10.	Arbitrary zero scales are typically interval scales masquerading as ratio scales.
T F	11.	Changes in the independent variable are assumed to depend on changes in the dependent variable.
T F	12.	The cruder the measuring scale used to detect shifts in the dependent variable, the stronger must be the effects of the independent variable.
T F	13.	A pilot study gives the researcher a crude estimate of the potency of the independent variable and the degree of precision necessary to measure the dependent variable effectively.
T F	14.	Measurement consists of rules for tying numbers to packages of experience.
T F	15.	A typical test of a grade 9 student's knowledge of French nouns is illustrative of an absolute zero scale.
T F	16.	The determination and application of a psychiatric diagnosis to a patient is a good example of the use of the nominal rule.
T F	17.	The experience of quantity was initially qualitative.
T F	18.	Diana's new law of liquid combinatorials states that $1 + 1 + 1 = 1$.
T F	19.	The news story that 'every square meter of the planet's surface is absorbing about one watt more heat than it can release into space' is a good example of external validity.
T F	20.	The conflicting results of the studies on the connection between fibre and bowel cancer provide a good example of the adversarial system of science.
T F	21.	Results of the chronic pain study revealed that after three 13-minute (relative zero scale) feedback sessions, 5 of 8 patients reported more than 50 per cent pain reduction on a questionnaire (qualitative, elastic-ruler, on-stage, ratio scale measure).

11

Statistical Foundations: Packaging Information

Chapter Goal

- To introduce you to descriptive statistics.

We use it to package observations into mind-sized chunks. Your grade point average is an example. It rounds up all your different grades and condenses them into one number. It's a gross oversimplification of your university life but it's sure easy to remember.

Introduction

One death is a tragedy; a thousand deaths is a statistic.

This chilling statement illustrates that statistics not only condense information but, in doing so, strip it of some meaning. You're already familiar with using statistics to summarize information. You're familiar with the flow of creative statistics: the average worker earns $668.54 per week, comes from a family of 2.3 members, has completed 12.3 years of education, and before dying at the age of 76.6 years has consumed 18,250.5 hamburgers and 23,802.4 Tums.

In this chapter we discuss *descriptive statistics*, which help us describe a pile of observations in a manner that fits our bounded rationality by shrinking a bunch of dots into one or two numbers. As researchers conscientiously explore their playpens they accumulate heaps of observations and tie descriptive number signs to them.

In the next chapter we focus on *inferential statistics*, which help us make educated predictions about a lot of people on the basis of observing or measuring a small sample of people.

Like any summary, descriptive statistics tell you something about everyone in general and nothing about anyone in particular. Nevertheless, such numerical summaries simplify communication when large quantities of information must be transferred.

For example, listen in on the following dialogue between two professors:

Professor Blender:	You have a large introductory psychology class this year—over 400 students, I believe.
Professor Makan:	It's a pain teaching such a mob. What can they learn?
Professor Blender:	How did they do on their exam?
Professor Makan:	Sit down and I'll tell you. Aaron got 97.1, Abbott got 73.5, Agnew got 34.2, . . .
Professor Blender:	I don't want to know what each individual student got. Don't you know the class average?
Professor Makan:	Of course; it was 78. But what does that tell you?
Professor Blender:	It tells me that your class average is higher than anyone else's. You must have smart students.
Professor Makan:	From the average you can tell that? How do you know I'm not just an easy marker? One student got 97, but I've got some real dummies, too. Another student only got 18.

From this brief dialogue you appreciate that an average doesn't really tell you a lot by itself. Even when you also know that the scores ranged from 18 to 97, you still don't know whether most students scored below the class average of 78, with a few very smart ones scoring high enough to pull the average up, or whether approximately half scored above and half scored below. It is the purpose of descriptive statistics not only to summarize data but also to do so with a minimum loss of important information.

There are two major types of descriptive statistics. One deals with descriptions of central values like *averages*, and the second deals with descriptions of variability like *ranges*.

Descriptive Statistics and the PST

Down in the bottom left corner of our PST we collect, package, and label observations. As experience flows by we cherry-pick bits and pieces, selecting only a tiny fraction from the flood of dots. To protect our bounded rationality we ignore most of them, forget a lot of them, and shrink the selected dots into mind-size chunks using automatic 'data shrinkers'—like averages or numerical stereotypes.

Limited by our bounded rationality, that's the only way we can afford to make sense of experience as it streams by. Typically, to save brain space, we bracket the extremes away out of awareness until reality temporarily dissolves

Fig 11.1 ■ Descriptive Statistics Help Shrink Data Floods Into Mind-Size Packages Like Averages and Extremes

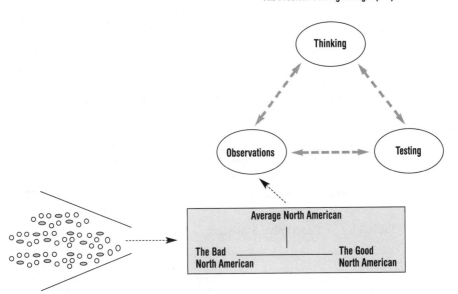

The Problem-Solving Triangle (PST)

the mythical average. On such occasions, when stereotypes are threatened, we keep an exception—an extreme—available in storage (e.g., the generous Scot; the financially responsible Democrat; the romantic, post-coital male). By trotting the exception out once in a while we demonstrate that we're not completely simple-minded. And producing the rare exception 'proves the rule'—it justifies the mind-shrinking stereotype.

Now that we've shrunk descriptive statistics to extremely simple size, let's open it up a bit. We will discuss two major types of descriptive statistics. The first deals with descriptions of central values and the second deals with descriptions of variability.

Central values

There are three main ways of describing the centre of gravity of a data pile or distribution:

The mean is the average score obtained by adding all the scores and dividing by the number of scores. For the scores in Column A of Table 11.1,

$$\overline{X} = \text{Mean} = \frac{\Sigma S}{N} = \frac{300}{15} = 20$$

This mean represents the arithmetic centre of gravity in interval and ratio-scale distributions.

The median is the middle score, on either side of which lie the low half of the scores and the high half of the scores. For the scores in Column A of Table 11.1, the median = 19. There are seven scores higher than 19 and seven scores lower than 19. This is the *middle* score, rather than the average score, and is a particularly useful description of the central position when dealing with ordinal scale data.

The mode is the most common or most frequently occurring score or category. For the scores in Column A of Table 11.1, the mode = 17. Three students obtained a score of 17. The mode doesn't tell you how well they did relative to other students; it merely identifies the score that the largest number of students achieved. The mode is generally useful for describing concentrations of people or events in nominal categories.

Each of these measures alone tells us something about the centre of gravity of a set of scores. The mean describes the arithmetic balance point; the median describes the middle balance point; and the mode describes the frequency concentration point or heaviest category. Taken individually none of

Table 11.1   Descriptive Statistics

Patient		Anxiety Score X	Deviation from Mean $\bar{X}-X$	Squared Deviation x^2
Hamish		27	+7	49
Irv		25	+5	25
Vera		25	+5	25
Bob		24	+4	16
Jane		23	+3	9
Norm		20	0	0
	Mean			
Joan		20	0	0
Laura	Median	19	−1	1
Dave		18	−2	4
Igor		18	−2	4
Anne		17	−3	9
Lucy	Mode	17	−3	9
Mary		17	−3	9
Charlie		16	−4	16
Neil		14	−6	36
		300	0	212
		Col. A	Col. B	Col. C

these measures tells us anything about the shape of the distribution of scores, but taken together they give us some hints. For example, we have a balanced or symmetrical distribution if all three of these indices lie on the same score.

Although knowing all three measures of central tendency for a given distribution tells you more than knowing only one, you still know relatively little about the *differences* between the scores in the set. To describe such score differences—that is, to tell you how spread out the scores are around the mean—three further descriptive statistics are used: the range, the variance, and the standard deviation.

Measures of variability

The range

This statistic describes the difference between the highest and the lowest scores. In Column A of Table 11.1, the range equals 13. The range tells you what range of possible scores your particular distribution covers. For example, in Professor Makan's psychology quiz we discussed earlier, the mean was 78 and the grades range from 18 to 97, indicating large differences between individual students. While the range indicates the extremes of the distribution of scores, it is based on only two scores and may therefore give a false impression of variability. For example, the student scoring 18 may have been the only failure in the class, and without him the range may have been 58 to 97. Therefore although the range adds to your information about individual differences in performance, because it is based on only two scores, it is not very representative. The next statistic is much more representative because it is based on *every* score.

The variance (σ^2)

This important statistic, applicable to measures on interval and ratio scales, is the *average of the squared deviations from the mean*. For example, in Column B of Table 11.1, we listed how much each individual score deviates from the mean—a plus sign indicates how much a given score is above the mean and a minus sign indicates how much a given score is below the mean. To get rid of these signs, we squared these deviations (as in Column C) and added them to get a so-called sum of squares.

$$\Sigma x^2 = 212$$

To determine the variance, we divide the sum of squares by N—that is, by the number of scores:

$$\text{Variance} = \sigma^2 = \frac{\Sigma x^2}{N} = \frac{212}{15}$$

$$= 14.13$$

But squaring the deviation scores to get rid of the signs leaves us with an average of *squared* deviations, which gives a misleadingly large number. We need an average of deviations regardless of signs. The next statistic does just that.

The standard deviation (σ)

This most widely used measure of variability is merely the square root of the variance:

$$\text{Standard Deviation} = \sigma = \sqrt{\frac{\Sigma x^2}{N}} = \sqrt{\frac{212}{15}} = 3.8$$

Now we have a measure of variability that

1. is based on the deviation of *all* scores from the mean,
2. treats negative and positive deviations the same, and
3. is expressed in the same units of measurement as those from which it was derived, rather than on their squares.

Measures of variability help describe individual differences in a group. The standard deviation is of particular value in that it provides a standard unit for such comparisons—one that can be used on any interval or ratio scale. Suppose your class takes two tests—one in psychology and one in physics—and that you score 78 in psychology and 68 in physics. In which test did you do better? In psychology?

Maybe, but that assumes it is as easy to get one grade point in psychology as it is in physics. Maybe each grade point in psychology is easier to get than a grade point in physics. We can then ask, 'How well did you do relative to the rest of your group?' The group's average in physics was 53, and in psychology it was 63. This suggests that it may be easier to get a point in psychology than in physics, even though you are 15 marks above the group average in each. Does *that* mean you did equally well in both? Well, that depends on how much the marks vary around the mean—and that's why we use the standard deviation. We note that the psychology scores are much more variable than the physics scores. Although you are 15 points from the mean in both distributions, you were much closer to the top of the distribution in physics with a score of 68 than in psychology with a score of 78. In fact, when we calculate the standard deviations (σ) for each distribution, we find that you are 2.6 standard deviation units above the mean in physics and only 1.2 standard deviations above the mean in psychology. Thus relative to your classmates, you did better in physics than you did in psychology.

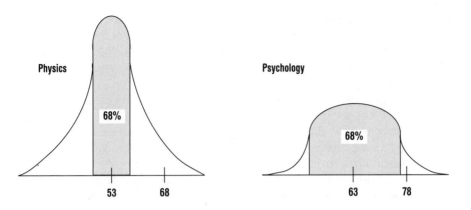

In addition to helping describe and compare individual differences in performance, the standard deviation helps us describe and analyze different data piles or distributions. Although it isn't particularly useful for describing misshapen or skewed distributions like the following skewed curve, the standard deviation is very useful in describing symmetrical distributions called normal, or bell, curves.

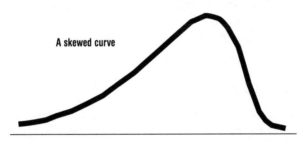

The elegantly simple bell curve serves as a mind-sized map for much of the statistical analysis that social scientists perform. In practice, the curve almost collapses under this unfair burden. The social sciences borrowed it from simpler worlds—worlds in which things behave themselves, *brainless* things like height, rolling dice and billiard balls without brains.

We use the curve, appropriately and inappropriately, as a rough approximation of some human characteristics. It's a pretty good approximation of the distribution of some physical characteristics—for example, the height of first-year, male university students—particularly if it's based on a large random sample. If not, the resulting curve may have very limited validity.

Lumps and corsets

A particular normal curve may only apply to a special segment of the first-year students that happen to be included in your non-random sample—by simple chance the first-year psychology class you tested might have included a lot of male bas-ketball players. Your so-called *normal curve* of the height of first-year male stu-dents doesn't fairly represent the population of first-year students. Its *internal validity* is mainly limited to a small biased sample loaded with tall males who play basketball.

Random sampling is important, and so is the elasticity of the human char-acteristic being measured. Height is relatively stable (reliable), whereas there are many measures that are more elastic, like mood and attitudes, so it's difficult to get reliable data on which to base the curve. Unlike height, you would get dif-ferent curves on different days.

Furthermore, people have been known to alter the data to make them *'fit the curve'*. College presidents, for example, don't like to see grade curves with a big hump at the low end—it makes their institution look bad and it's not good for recruiting students. To fix this, professors are sometimes *encouraged* to 'nor-malize them', to make them academically correct. Sometimes normal curves look normal because they're wearing corrective corsets.

You should view the bell curve as a speculative map, not a God-given graphic, for describing all human behaviour. In the following discussion, and particularly in the next chapter, it's important to keep this point in mind. Most of the statistical tests we will describe are based on the premise that the character-istics being analyzed fit the normal curve. And we now know ad nauseam the mantra: 'no conclusions without premises', or similarly, lots of wrong conclu-sions flow from faulty premises.

The normal curve

The normal curve has approximately 50 per cent of the scores lying above, and 50 per cent lying below the mean. Thirty-four per cent of its area lies between the mean and +1 standard deviation, 14 per cent of its area between +1 and +2 standard deviations, and 2 per cent lying between +2 and +3 standard deviation units. Since the normal curve is symmetrical, the mean, median, and mode all lie at the same point.

A useful statistic is one that summarizes data with a minimum loss of infor-mation. The standard deviation, in combination with the normal curve, is such a statistic. Notice how little information is acquired from merely knowing that your score on a given test is 72. Did you do relatively well or very poorly? If a normal distribution shows that your score was 2 standard deviation units below the mean, it becomes clear that only 2 per cent of the class obtained lower scores than yours. If your actual score is 72 and the standard deviation is equal to 4, then the mean can be estimated to be 80 (your score of 72 plus 2 standard devi-ations) and the highest score can be estimated to be 92 (your score plus 5 stan-dard deviations).

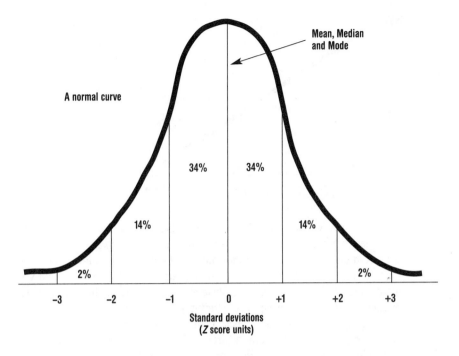

You can see that the standard deviation (or *Z score*, as it is frequently called) combined with the normal curve becomes a powerful descriptive statistic. Knowing where your score lies in *Z* score units tells you where your score lies in relation to all other scores in that distribution. Furthermore, because the *Z* score describes your relative position in a set of scores, it can be used to *compare* your relative position in two or more score sets. For example, if you scored 21 in Anxiety and 104 in ESP, that tells you very little about your results. But if you knew that your *Z* score in Anxiety was +2 and your *Z* score in ESP was zero, then you would know that you scored relatively high in Anxiety and only average (at the mean) in ESP. If you also knew that your *Z* score for time spent in the pub is +3 and your *Z* score in math is –3, then it would become clear that you lead your group in pub time and trail the group in math. Some people might even wonder if the two *Z* scores are connected.

Correlation

To say that two variables are *related* indicates they are somehow tied together—like pub time and math grades. For example, two variables may be negatively related; as one score goes up, the other score goes down.

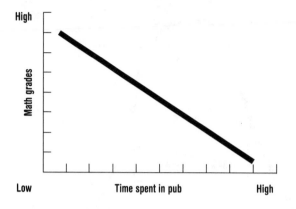

Or the two variables may be positively related; as one score goes up, so too does the other one. If hours of study and math grades were *perfectly* correlated, we would expect that each pair of scores would occupy the same relative position on their respective distributions—that your hours-of-study score and your math score would each lie the same distance, in *Z* score units, from their respective means. If, for your group, your study-time score was +2 *Z* scores above the group mean, then we would expect your math grade to also lie +2 *Z* scores above the group mean in math, as seen in Figure 11.2. In the case of a perfect correlation, when you plot score pairs for each individual in the group, the plots lie along a straight line.

Fig 11.2 ■ Perfect Positive Correlation

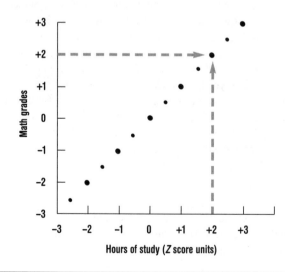

However, rarely, if ever, are two variables perfectly correlated. There are always a few people who study very little and still get good math grades, and others who study a great deal and persist in getting low grades. Thus, when we

Fig 11.3 ■ Strong Positive Correlation

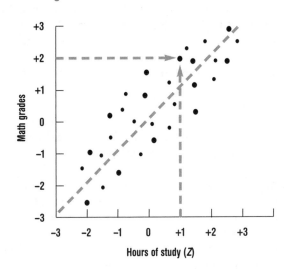

Fig 11.4 ■ No Correlation

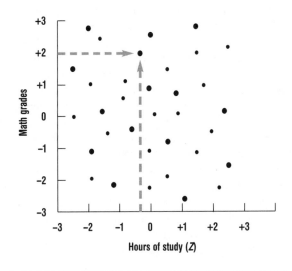

plot score pairs for two human characteristics, we don't expect to see them lie neatly on the straight line of a perfect correlation; we expect to see them marching fairly closely around such an imaginary line, as in Figure 11.3, or, in the case of unrelated variables, to be scattered all over the place, as in Figure 11.4.

By an 'eyeball' analysis of these figures, you can *see* different degrees of correlation: perfect correlation in Figure 11.2, strong positive correlation in Figure 11.3, and no obvious correlation in Figure 11.4. One way for you to determine the degree of correlation is to plot the score pairs—in raw, or in Z score units— and see to what degree the plots cluster around a positive or negative diagonal. This *scattergram* provides an excellent way to get a feel for your data, for its variability, and we strongly recommend you make such plots, or let your computer do it for you.

If you require a more precise and shorthand measure of the degree of relationship, you can calculate a *correlation coefficient*. This is nothing more than a statistical means of describing the differences between pairs of Z scores. In brief, if a pair of scores has similar positions (in Z score units) in their respective distributions, their correlation approaches 1.0, or a perfect positive relationship. However, if any given pair of scores occupy very different, or unpredictable, relative positions—if they have very different Z scores—then their correlation approaches zero. If you calculate a correlation coefficient greater than 1.0 you have made an error—numerically, 1.0 is as high as correlations go. If you discover a correlation higher than 0.90 when studying human behaviour, check your calculations and increase your sample size—such a correlation is suspiciously high. Humans rarely march in linear unison along such a straight line.

Using a small sample of the data from Figure 11.3, we show in Table 11.2 how to calculate a Pearson product-moment correlation, which is represented by the symbol γ, which you can think of as meaning 'degree of relationship'.

In the case of the relationship between hours of study and math grades, how much confidence do you have in the very high correlation (0.94) that we reported? First, notice that we used a very small sample of subjects, or observational checkpoints—only six. There is no magic sample size, but it is generally recommended that you use at least 100 subjects to estimate degree of correlation.

Nevertheless, apart from sample size, on the basis of your own experience how much confidence would you place on such a high correlation? What other variable, or characteristic, probably influences math grades besides hours of study? Mathematical aptitude and background are obvious additional suspects. Therefore you might anticipate a curved relationship between hours of study and math grades—the highest grade coming from people with mathematical aptitude who study a medium amount, low grades from people who don't study, and medium and low grades from people without math aptitude who study a lot, but to little avail. Perhaps the relationship might resemble that mapped in Figure 11.5.

The Pearson product-moment correlation is designed to measure straight-line relations (linear), not curvilinear ones, as shown in Figure 11.5. You can do thought experiments by proposing variables, which, on the basis of casual

Table 11.2   Pearson Correlation Coefficient

| | Raw Data | | | | | | |
| | Hours of Study | Math Grades | Deviations from Means | | | | |
Ss	X	Y	x	y	xy	x^2	y^2
A.B.	27	88	11	28	308	121	784
B.J.	23	78	7	18	126	49	324
C.W.	22	69	6	9	54	36	81
D.N.	10	50	−6	−10	60	36	100
E.R.	8	30	−8	−30	240	64	900
F.G.	6	45	10	−15	150	100	225

Sum: $\Sigma X = 96$ $\Sigma Y = 360$ $\Sigma xy = 938$ $\Sigma x^2 = 406$ $\Sigma y^2 = 2414$

Mean: $X = 16$ $Y = 60$

Standard Deviations (σ):

$$\sigma X = \frac{\Sigma x^2}{N} = \frac{406}{6} = 8.22$$

$$\sigma X = \frac{\Sigma y^2}{N} = \frac{2414}{6} = 20.06$$

Correlation (γ):

$$r = \frac{\Sigma xy}{N \sigma x \sigma y} = \frac{938}{6(8.23)(20.06)} = \frac{938}{6(165.09)} = \frac{938}{990.54}$$

$r = 0.947$

Note: If you have a large number of subjects, you can calculate correlations using raw score data on a small computer or desk calculator—consult the machine handbook for the simple procedure:
i.e.,

$$r = \frac{\Sigma XY - \dfrac{(\Sigma X)(\Sigma Y)}{N}}{\left[\Sigma X^2 - \dfrac{\Sigma x^2}{N}\right]\left[\Sigma Y^2 - \dfrac{\Sigma y^2}{N}\right]}$$

Fig 11.5 ■ Curvilinear Correlation

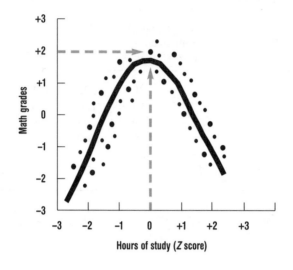

observation, should be highly correlated (for example, having the same subjects repeat an intelligence test one week later) or by proposing other variables that are probably not correlated at all (people's heights and their score on math exams). Great arguments ensue, and some even lead to worthy research speculations.

What does a correlation tell you?

Although it is simple to calculate a correlation coefficient, it is not so simple to decide what to conclude from a high coefficient. While a high correlation tells you that score pairs occupy similar relative positions on the two distributions, it does not tell you if they are tied together intimately like Siamese twins—when one moves, the other must move—or only related casually like two strangers travelling on the same subway train—when the train moves, they both move. But they don't necessarily move together because, unlike Siamese twins, one can move to another car without the other, and furthermore one can leave the train or the 'relationship' without the other. Movement is made in relation to the subway; it's to that third variable that they're connected, not to each other.

Don't leap to the conclusion that, because one variable appears to be moving with another, the first one 'causes' the other. Many supposed relationships turn out to be pseudo-relationships, like the young lady travelling by train from New York to San Francisco who reported to the conductor that a strange man was following her. Indeed he was; his seat was located just two spots behind hers! But he was related to the train, not the young lady—except in her imagination. There are many instances where two variables appear to be related, but are really only incidentally related to each other through a third variable (the train, in this instance). For example, there is a strong positive correlation between the purchase of bathing suits and the sale of ice cream, but you don't conclude that buying bathing suits makes you eat ice cream; rather you say a third variable, temperature, is the independent variable to which ice cream consumption and bathing suit purchases are related.

Whenever you are tempted to conclude that a variable is dependent upon, or moves with, another variable, stop and think, 'Does it make sense on the basis of logic and experience?' Moreover, always look for a third variable to which the two may be tied—as in the preceding cases of temperature and trains.

Beware of correlations

You probably wouldn't be surprised to learn of a negative correlation between being a Boy Scout and getting into trouble with the law—that is, relatively few Boy Scouts end up formally charged and convicted of crimes. Also, it would not surprise you to learn about a positive correlation between university education and above-average income.

It is, however, quite possible that both of these relationships 'ride' on a third *hidden* variable—namely, socioeconomic status. Most Boy Scouts *happen* to be middle- and upper-class kids, and middle-class kids rarely get booked or convicted, even if they are caught doing something wrong—whether they are Boy Scouts or not. Similarly, if you took a sample of middle- and upper-class people who hadn't graduated from a university, you would probably find their subsequent incomes to be comparable to those of university graduates—the implication being that it is not so much the university education that is related to subsequent income as it is middle- and upper-class contacts and opportunities.

You may disagree with these speculations. Good! Such disagreements stimulate further research. How would you go about testing either of these hypotheses linking criminal conviction negatively and income positively to the socioeconomic status of parents?

Correlation, regression, and prediction

Before moving to the chapter on prediction, we must point out that some of the statistics discussed in this chapter can also be used for prediction. For example, if you want to guess, or predict, the IQ of a given individual and you know the average (mean) IQ score of his or her group, you can use the group mean as a rough guess. If you also know the variance of IQs around the mean for that group you gain some notion of how much confidence you can have in making that guess. That is, if the variability around the mean is very large, then you know your guess could be way off, whereas if the variability is small you have high confidence that your guess will be pretty accurate. Correlation provides a more interesting example.

Suppose you have collected data on study time and math grades from 50 students and plotted the results, as in Figure 11.3. You can use this plot to predict the math scores of additional students just on the basis of their study score alone. If, for example, you know George's study score is +1 Z score units, you can follow the line up from +1 on the 'Hours of Study' scale to the diagonal line representing the correlation: you can then use that as your best-bet prediction of his math grade (e.g., a Z score of approximately +1.3) by drawing a horizontal line from the intercept over to the 'Math Grade' scale. However, you will not be surprised if you find that his actual math grade is a bit higher or lower than the one you predicted because you already know from the scattergram you plotted that people with the same 'Hours of Study' Z score can get math scores a bit above and below the predicted point on the correlation or linear regression line. This straight line is calculated to best represent, or 'best fit', all the points on your plot. It is a kind of average of the points scattered on either side of it. Standard statistics texts include detailed discussions and formulae covering regression and errors of estimate in making predictions. Here, we merely want to relate predictions to correlations.

How far above and below the correlation line the scores scatter can be seen by visual inspection, and depends on the degree of relationship between the two variables. A more precise method of estimating the kind of error of prediction you might make is called the *standard error of estimate*. How might that be determined? As you can guess, it is based on the differences between, in our example, the math scores you predict on the basis of hours of study, and the actual math scores obtained. Such an estimate will be expressed as an 'average' of those differences. For strong correlations (low scatter around the line), the error of estimate will be small, whereas for low or weak correlations (large scatter around the line), the error of estimate will, of course, be large.

Internal validity

In a control group study, internal validity means demonstrating that it was your independent or treatment variable (X_t) that caused the observed change in your dependent measure, the change from (O_1) to (O_2), for that particular sample of participants. You do that by attempting to rule out all the threats to internal validity, as listed in Chapter 6, including the four rogues.

In a correlation study, internal validity typically involves showing that changes in the value of one test score (O_{t1}) are strongly linked to changes in another test score (O_{t2}). Note, however, that any time a correlation is less than 1.0 (perfect) it means additional forces (e.g., rogues) are pushing the scores around. So these confounding forces threaten the validity of the correlation.

When variables combine in such a way that they cannot be separated—as they usually do in after-the-fact, before-and-after, and correlation studies—we call them *confounding variables*.

Since very few correlations in the social sciences approach 1.0, it means confounding variables plague the internal validity of most correlations. You can see the increasing effects of confounding variables by observing the markedly increased scattering of scores when comparing Figure 11.3 with Figure 11.4.

While confounding variables, such as the rogues, occur in all investigations, researchers tend to ignore them in correlational studies. Too often they rely instead on statistical *tests of significance*, which are poor substitutes for practical or social significance. In brief, too often statistical significance is an unreliable basis for making real life predictions.

We'll discuss these statistical tests in the next chapter, but for now it's important to think of validity in terms of the degree of scatter in a scattergram, and to keep in mind that if you have a large enough sample a correlation can be shown to have statistical significance, even though there is so much scattering of the scores you can have little confidence in even roughly predicting one score from the other.

Before relying on statistical tests, the validity of a correlation should be judged by:

- the scattergram,
- random sampling of participants,
- the reliability and validity of the psychological tests scores used (control of elastic ruler and on-stage rogues), and
- confounding factors in the testing situation (e.g., too hot, too cold, too noisy, time of day, vague instructions, etc.)

But how are you going to evaluate all that? Advice to consumers of science: 'Don't bet any money on a correlation until it's been replicated by an independent investigator on a large representative sample.'

Correlations and factor analysis

In examining college grades for a variety of students, you notice that some students seem to do well in almost all their subjects, ranging from psychology to computer science (their Z scores, regardless of course of study, are high), whereas another group of students seems to get average grades in most of their courses (their Z scores, regardless of course of study, are in the middle), whereas yet another group gets low grades in almost all their courses. In addition, there are, of course, a fair number of students whose grades range from high to low—that is, their scores are all over the board.

Given a large amount of data—comprising perhaps several hundred students and say 10 or 20 test scores for each—how do you make sense of such a data pile; how do you reduce it to mind-size? One way to do this is to reduce the search space by focusing on those students who are more or less consistent in their performance: the highs, the average, and the lows. Can you reduce all that data to a simpler form, to one or two antecedents? With a little thought you conclude that you can *make sense of* the data on the basis of two variables: intelligence and work habits. You're not sure how they combine, or which is most important in given subjects or individuals. Nevertheless, with these two premises, or guesses, you've radically reduced the data to mind-size, even though as yet you have no measure of intelligence or work habits to use as an observational checkpoint. For example, do your students with consistently high grades score high on both intelligence and work habits, and your students with consistently low grades score lower on intelligence and work habits? If you wanted to address the same question and be more precise in your conclusions and more objective in your analysis, you might use one or another form of factor analysis.

Factor analysis is a formal way of reducing a large set of variables or measures to a much smaller number called a factor. More importantly, it describes how those factors are related to each other and to the original set of measures. So, what we did intuitively—reducing a large set of measures to a small one—factor analysis can help you do formally, and in a way that is more replicable and less subjective. More importantly, it specifies which of the reduced number of variables (factors) are most important in explaining and predicting certain relationships in the original data set. If we apply factor analysis to the data we used in our preceding example, it is hoped we will address our theoretical speculation or hunch by moving down to the bottom of you PST and including reliable measures of intelligence and work habits in your analysis, to determine empirically whether or not most of the other test scores are correlated with intelligence scores and/or work habits.

Of course, the quality of the factors you extract, and the explanatory and predictive power of their structure, depends on the quality of the data you input—garbage in, garbage out, no matter how powerful the computer or sophisticated the software. Cross-validation (replication) of factor analytic studies has not been common because of the time and effort required to accumulate a large data set (multiple tests on multiple people). Therefore, the external validity of the factors and their structure, extracted in a given study, is often unknown because replicating them is costly. Furthermore, not only do such studies involve complicated statistics, but extracting and identifying factors is not cut and dried—it involves some believing-is-seeing top-of-the-PST adjustments.

Standard statistical texts explain and provide examples of various forms of factor analysis, and with the advent of computer software, factor analysis becomes much more feasible than it once was.

SUMMARY

Descriptive statistics help package information in mind-sized bites in which one number is used to describe a set of observations. Some of these statistics describe the centres of gravity of a distribution (mean, median, and mode), whereas others describe the variability or dispersion of scores (range, variance, and standard deviation). The normal curve is a mathematical invention that helps summarize a great deal of information about bell-shaped distributions. (This invention can even help predict the score you receive on an exam. How so?)

High correlations tell you that score pairs (e.g., IQ and math grades) occupy similar relative positions on the two distributions of scores—people who scored high on one tended to score high on the other, and people who scored low on one tended to score low on the other. But, beware of correlations; the relationships they describe could result from a variety of reasons, from a hidden third influence that you overlooked.

In the next chapter we move from focusing on packaging information down at the bottom left corner of the PST to testing theoretical predictions. We do so by relying on statistical bridges (inferential statistics) to help us move from a small sample of observations (small playpens) to conclusions about large populations (large playpens). This involves drawing conclusions about lots of people we haven't even observed, and never will!

student's notebook

When I first cracked this chapter and saw the word 'statistics' I panicked. But then I firmly reminded myself that I was no longer 'number numb'. I'm now the boss of numbers! Well, most numbers—some remain beyond my control like my declining bank account, and the specific date of my death. But I 'own' the stuff in this chapter.

Professor Creek told us we didn't need to do a commentary on this chapter, or the next, because we'd be spending time in the stats lab running statistical thought experiments. But doing the commentary is a painless study aid, and I'm in the habit now—the old Premack Principle rides again. The commentary sort of just happens automatically.

In the stats lab there are software packages available to perform almost any kind of statistical analysis you can dream up, or have nightmares about. You don't even need to bring your own data. The programs include data sets on every conceivable human characteristic, from quantitative data like height, weight, and reaction time, to quasi-quantitative stuff like IQ and personality profiles, to qualitative measures like ordinal scale self-ratings of mood, or nominal (either/or) judgments of good–bad, sick–healthy, and Democrat–Republican.

Or you can feed in your own data, like ordinal rankings of how boring your different classes are, or of the sex appeal of the guys in the B&B club. You've got to be sneaky about plotting graphs on this personal stuff or the lab attendants decide that you are goofing around and boot you out so serious students can use your computer space. It's best not to attract the attendant's attention anyway, because most of them are not too friendly. If you ask them a question they ask you questions right back. Like: 'Do you know what "homoscedacticity" means?'

I thought it might be some kind of sexual preference. Not so. Apparently it means the data in your sample follows the normal curve.

News reports

Ever since Kinsey, researchers have been tying numbers to the duration of fore-play and intercourse in humans.[1] For instance the average duration of foreplay reported by men and women was 12 minutes, and three-quarters of the men reported an intercourse duration of less than two minutes. Using a multiple choice questionnaire to indicate the 'ideal' duration of foreplay, the respondents selected foreplay times ranging from less than five minutes to more than 30 min-utes. However, since only one member of the pair reported, we don't know whether the partner agreed.

Something to consider: how accurate is a person's estimate of time when engaged in an attention-grabbing activity?

Animal researchers don't have to rely on qualitative self-reports—they peek and use stopwatches. Apparently the average length of foreplay and intercourse combined for chimpanzees is seven seconds. Against that, the human male's two minutes is at least an improvement.

The second interesting news story this week was about computer anxiety, as measured by using the qualitative Computer Anxiety Index (CAIN). Being a sweaty palm computer user myself, I found the topic interesting. In a before-and-after study, the researchers used two students who started out performing one standard deviation above the mean anxiety score of their group (i.e., 83 per cent scored lower than them). The in-the-gap treatment included increased supervised practice time on computers. One of the students showed a marked drop in anxi-ety (two standard deviations) while the other student scored even higher on the post-test than on the already high pre-test anxiety score.

I like this study for several reasons: it focuses on an important practical problem; it uses a pilot study so the researcher gets a feel for the power of the treatment and the precision of the qualitative scale to pick up changes in per-formance; and it uses standard deviations as a yardstick of variability and com-parison.

What I don't like about the study is that it doesn't help a particular individ-ual (e.g., me) predict the probability of whether I'll become more or less anxious with computer practice. But that's unfortunately what group research let's you do, predict how most members of a group will respond to a given treatment. So, if the average anxiety score of the group dropped, then that would help me make

---

[1] Miller and Byers (2004).

a positive decision. But the only way to be sure it will work is for me to try myself.

Apparently journals are more likely to publish group studies, so that's what researchers concentrate on—predicting and testing what will happen to a group average following treatment. How much variability there is on either side of the average or mean score gives you some idea of how different individuals differ in their response to the treatment. It gives you an idea of the validity or power of the treatment.

I guess I'll just have to wait for further research.

I wonder if Professor Creek would accept computer anxiety as an excuse for not completing my computer assignments? 'Dear Professor Creek, please excuse me from attending the stat labs. I suffer from a pathological case of CA (computer anxiety) and, according to a thorough review of the research literature, I find that there is no valid treatment—only conflicting experimental results.' He might actually buy it. Yeah, right!

Note

Breeding horses to make them better is different from breeding people. Learn more on the student website at http://www.oup.com/ca/he/companion/agnewpyke.

REVIEW TRUE OR FALSE QUIZ

T F	1.	Inferential statistics help us make educated predictions on the basis of a small sample of observations.
T F	2.	An average class mark of 57 tells you that approximately half the class scored above 57 and about half received a mark below 57.
T F	3.	Descriptions of variability deal with central values like averages.
T F	4.	The mean represents the arithmetic centre of gravity in interval and ratio-scale distributions.
T F	5.	The most frequently occurring score is the median.
T F	6.	The mode is generally useful for describing concentrations of people or events in nominal categories.
T F	7.	The difference between the highest and lowest scores of a distribution is the variance.

T F	8. The standard deviation is the square root of the variance.
T F	9. The standard deviation is especially useful in describing skewed distributions.
T F	10. The normal curve has approximately 68 per cent of its area lying between +1 and −1 standard deviations.
T F	11. Since the normal curve is symmetrical, the mean, median, and mode all lie at the same point.
T F	12. In the case of a perfect correlation, when you plot score pairs for each individual in a group, the plots lie along a straight line.
T F	13. A perfect positive correlation is +0.50.
T F	14. To estimate the degree of correlation one should have a sample of at least 500 subjects.
T F	15. When two variables are correlated, one is the cause of the other.
T F	16. Factor analysis is a formal way of reducing a large set of variables or measures to a much smaller number called a factor.
T F	17. Factor analysis specifies which of the reduced number of variables are most important in explaining and predicting certain relationships in the original data set.
T F	18. The internal validity of the normal curve of a particular measurement, such as height, may be limited unless based on a large random sample.
T F	19. Confounding variables affect the internal validity of most correlations.
T F	20. Homoscedacticity means that the data in your sample follows the normal curve.
T F	21. In the study on duration of foreplay in humans, a high positive correlation was observed between the paired respondents.
T F	22. Diana likes the study on computer anxiety because the researcher conducted a pilot study and used standard deviation as a yardstick of variability and comparison.

12

Statistical Foundations: Prediction

Chapter Goal

- To show how researchers make predictions on the basis of small samples of experience.

You do it every hour of every day, often successfully, even if you don't know the statistical assumptions or premises that guide you. The main presumption is that the truths you discover or invent in your small playpen are valid in other places and future times.

Introduction

As you cycle around your PST you travel from observations to speculations to predictions, back to observations to more speculations, and so on.

As we cycle, we shrink the flood of experience down to mind-size. We automatically select and connect dots to fit our neurological and cultural expectations.

For instance, based on personal samples we construct mentally affordable simplifications: the *stereotypical* American, the stereotypical Republican, or lawyer, or man, or woman, etc.

Furthermore, these stereotypes *work*—believing-is-seeing. And because mental economy trumps accuracy, stereotypes are widely accepted by others in our culture as valid packages of information.

Of course, we also construct a few exceptions: the honest lawyer, the romantic male, the softhearted Conservative, the hardheaded Liberal. But we bracket them away for special occasions and trot them out only to justify our stereotype: 'exceptions prove the rule.' In other words, the perception of the soft-hearted Conservative is so rare that one will stand out from the majority! All of

Fig 12.1 ■ STATISTICAL FOUNDATIONS: THEORETICAL PREDICTIONS AND RIGOROUS TESTING

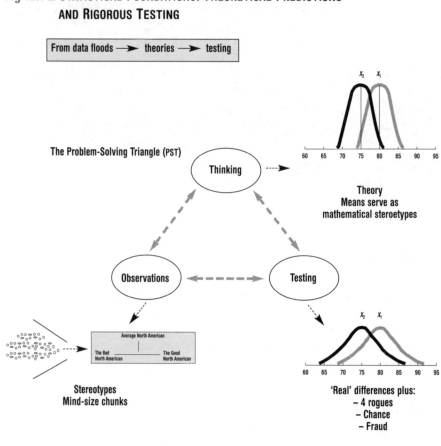

us, citizens and scientists, rely heavily on stereotypes, or fuzzy generalizations, to accommodate our bounded rationality. In statistical jargon we call our mathematical stereotypes 'averages' or 'means'. Like all stereotypes, averages condense data into oversimplified, mind-size chunks.

Theoretical predications

For instance, in the upper right corner of Figure 12.1 we present a speculative map. After sampling the research literature and doing some critical thinking, a theorist condenses the flow of messages into a conclusion. He generates a prediction that the average score for Democrats (X_1) will be higher on attitudes toward government spending than the average score for Republicans (X_2).

This is a neat and tidy speculation, a prediction that involves little overlap in scores between the two groups. It's easier to get people to do what you want them to do in theory than it is in fact. That's why theories and daydreams are so popular. As long as we stay at the top of our PSTs, as long as we don't travel down and rigorously test our generalizations, we can believe that the world is dancing to our tune. We can believe our emotionally anchored stereotype. Believing-is-seeing, it's both mentally affordable and reassuring, helps you maintain the illusion that you understand and can predict behaviour.

Rigorous testing: 'Show me the sheep!'

However, nothing is perfect. Although you or I might be happy with our pet theory, sooner or later a skeptical empirical researcher will borrow the generalization—the speculative map—travel down to the bottom right corner, and rigorously *test* our prediction.

She draws two random samples, one of Democrats and one of Republicans, and tests them on a standardized scale designed to measure political attitudes. She then graphs her results and compares them to those predicted by the armchair theorist. In her observational map the two groups overlap more than in the speculative theoretical map. This is, of course, no surprise. Up-top premises, theories, or biases divide the world into clear, simple packages of dots. However, when we travel down to the bottom of the PST we find that many 'dots with brains' don't stay put inside our stereotypical categories. We inevitably find more variability within groups, and more overlap in performance between groups, certainly more than we predicted, and more than fits comfortably within our bounded rationality. For instance Democrats not only fight with Republicans, but with each other as well. Upon closer examination, like most categories, stereotypes are elastic, stereotypes leak.

If you remember one thing from this chapter remember this: When you and I—and theorists—make predictions we tend to underestimate the variability of the behaviour of any given individual and the differences between individuals who we might have assigned to the same category.

Nevertheless, to accommodate our bounded rationality we usually ignore this truism. We rely on our over-simplifications to avoid information overload and dangerous ways of thinking even though our stereotypes distort reality and lead to naïve predictions and unpleasant surprises. We usually get away with such flawed predictions because we rarely expose our conclusions to either intense critical thinking or rigorous observational testing. Ignorance is bliss, after all.

However, scientists don't enjoy the same luxury for very long. Instead, they operate in the self-corrective and adversarial system of science. A scientist's theory typically undergoes both more critical analysis up top and more rigorous empirical testing down below than the scientist desires, but no more than he or she deserves.

While theorists usually provide for more variability in behaviour than do you or I, they typically underestimate the variability that is eventually discovered through the empirical testing of their speculative predictions.

Forces pushing scores up and down the measurement scale

Re-examine the observational map at the bottom of Figure 12.1. Why is there more overlap between these two groups than between the two well-behaved groups displayed in the theoretical map at the top? Because there are more forces pushing observations around down below than there are pushing around the theorists' pet theories at the top. Those bottom forces include any *real* differences in attitude that move a score up or down the scale. In addition, they also include unknown combinations of forces arising from the four rogues, plus fickle chance and sneaky fraud.

The statistical procedures discussed in this chapter help us understand and estimate the influence of *chance* forces on the movement of scores up or down the scale. For instance, let's do a thought experiment up at the top of the PST. With aid of stereotypical thinking we *assume* that if we measured *all* Democrats and all Republicans on our attitude scale (which we can't afford to do) we would obtain a clear difference in their *mean score* with relatively little overlap between the two groups. But we have not had—and will not have—the luxury of access to all that data. Therefore, we have to settle for much less, will have to base our conclusions on relatively small samples.

When we work with small samples, we allow chance to sit in on the game. In the study shown at the bottom of Figure 12.1 we may, *by chance*, have drawn two deviant samples that don't validly represent their total group. That is, we may have—by chance—drawn a sample of liberal Republicans and conservative Democrats, a situation which would explain the large overlap.

If, on the basis of this small playpen data, we jumped to the conclusion that there's no difference between Republicans and Democrats, the empirical state of affairs at the bottom of the PST would be misrepresented.

Our goal in this chapter is to explore how—with the aid of statistical assumptions—we can avoid those kinds of misrepresentation of *reality* and to explore how we can *reasonably* move from small samples of experience to larger generalizations (e.g., from *small truths* about local samples of Republicans and Democrats, to larger *truths* about Republicans and Democrats in general).

> In generalizing from small samples to large populations, don't just look at the average score of the sample. Also look at the variability—at the individual differences—between members of the same group.

Lady Luck sits in on every game

If he tosses 10 heads in a row . . . get a new coin!

Just as the hand of Lady Luck helps determine whether the coin comes up heads or tails, so too does she help to determine whether your depressed patient 'comes up' improved or not improved. In the case of the coin we have a 50–50 rule that helps us decide what to expect from chance, or random, influences alone over a long series of tosses. If the results deviate 'too far' from the rule (50 per cent heads and 50 per cent tails) then we conclude that non-random influences are operating on the coin.

In the case of human behaviour, various statistical rules help us decide whether our results are due merely to good luck, or to good treatment—to *real* non-random influences in the treatment. For example, our control group on the 'sugar pill' provides a way of estimating the effects of random, or rogue, influences on our depressed patients. For instance, in Chapter 5 we described a study comparing the effects of a new drug treatment for depressions, against the effects of a control group on a sugar-pill placebo. The control group provides an estimate of how many patients we can expect to improve without treatment—say 75 per cent improve just from the effects of random in-the-gap and time-tied suspects. Therefore, to be accepted the new drug has to significantly beat the 75–25 rule we derived from our control group. It is important to note that if we ran several control groups, we would get somewhat different rules (e.g., 78–22, 72–28, 74–26, etc.). Remember that the rule provided by any single control group is only an estimate of the influence of chance factors. Statistical tests help us decide by how much our treatment must beat the particular control group generated-rule before we decide the results are worth taking seriously.

What if, after our 'magic pill' treatment, we find 80 per cent of the patients improved and 20 per cent did not? How much must our treatment results surpass the control-group results before we decide that, in addition to lady luck and the rogues, our treatment is having a systematic effect? Statistical tests help us make those decisions in a disciplined, standardized, way. But always remember, the best means of determining whether your positive results were due to lady luck or your treatment is to repeat the study. Or, better still, have an independent researcher repeat the study.

Inferential Statistics

Most social science experiments compare differences between two or more means or averages. For example, suppose we study the effects of two methods of teaching mathematics—one employing a text using programmed instruction à la B.F. Skinner and another based on the same material but written in a traditional manner. We divide our class at random into two groups:

| Group 1 | X_1 | O_1 |
| Group 2 | X_2 | O_2 |

One group studies from the programmed text (X_1) and the other studies from the traditional text (X_2). Then both groups write the same exam, and we calculate the means:

$$O_1 = 80$$
$$O_2 = 75$$

We obtained a difference. So what? Even if we had used the same text with both groups, we probably would have obtained 'a difference'. Groups rarely yield precisely the same means even when treated identically, because we never control the operation of all chance factors. The question is not, 'Did we get a difference?' but rather, 'Did we get a difference worth talking about?' In statistical language we want to know whether we got a *significant difference*.

At least four common factors produce a significant difference:

1. The operation of chance. By luck we ended up with more bright students in Group 1 than in Group 2, even though we drew the names out of a hat.
2. The operation of the chosen independent variable. The programmed text was a more effective teaching aid, and so Group 1 students did better on the exam.
3. The operation of error. A mistake was made in scoring the tests or in adding the scores that favoured Group 1.
4. The operation of fraud. The researcher fraudulently manipulated the data in favour of Group 1 to accommodate the professor's bias.[1]

Therefore, while statistical tests help you decide whether you obtained a reliable or significant difference between your two group means, such tests do not tell you whether such differences arise from the operation of your independent variable, from errors in calculation, or from fraud. Such tests don't even completely rule out the possibility of chance, but such tests do *help you identify inferences that do not occur frequently by chance alone*.

When you conduct a statistical test on your data and obtain a significant result, you have some confidence that such a large difference is not likely due to chance—although such large differences may occur, say, five times in a hundred due to chance alone. However, you choose to decide that, rather than an unusual chance event, the difference was 'caused' by something else. Having done your statistical test to control for the operation of obvious chance factors and having found a significant difference, you then puzzle over the alternatives of whether the significant difference results from the impact of your independent variable, or error, or even fraud.

---

[1] Of course, it could be the result of two or more of these factors in combination.

Parenthetically, while fraud appears as a viable alternative in fringe research areas like ESP, it is rarely so listed in traditional research areas or in research design courses—perhaps because researchers are less fraudulently inclined than are other segments of the population, or perhaps because fraud represents an alternative too threatening to the research enterprise to be contemplated openly. (A discussion of instances of possible fraud perpetrated by a famous psychologist appears at the end of Chapter 13.)

Maps of chance

To determine whether our differences arise from chance factors, we compare our results with what we would expect by chance; we compare our results with maps or models of chance. You already know about such maps. If I flip a coin producing 10 heads in a row, you might say, 'Hey, wait a minute!' Why? Because my results deviate significantly from your map of chance—my results were surprising. Your map of chance for tossing coins is 50–50. The further my results deviate from a 50–50 distribution of heads and tails, the more willingly you entertain the possibility of the operation of 'something' in addition to chance. Like what? Like an independent variable: like a biased coin or a biased tosser—*something* more than chance.

If you keep this example in mind, you need have no fear of inferential statistics; such statistics are merely maps of chance against which you can compare your findings and decide whether your results—your experimental tosses—have gone beyond the limits of what you willingly accept as mere chance happenings. Inferential statistics provide a model against which to compare your results. If nothing else but chance is influencing our results, inferential statistics provide you with the distribution of differences you should expect. When you get a difference that occurs rarely by chance, you have two choices open: you can either decide you obtained one of those rare, large, but unreliable differences delivered by chance, or you can decide to credit the difference to the operation of your independent, or treatment, variable. By using inferential statistics, you never rule out the operation of chance but you do make it a less likely explanation.

Sampling theory

Inferential statistics rest on sampling theory, and you already have a solid background in this theory, even though you may not know it. Sampling theory deals with the relationship between 'samples' of experience and 'total' experience.

For example, that sample of 10 heads in a row went against your total experience of coin tossing; that sample didn't belong to your population of coin-tossing experience. It was a sample that seemed to belong to another population of experience—to experiences characteristic of fraud and trickery. Similarly, a host of samples make up your total experience (population of experience) concerning friendship. When a friend acts unfriendly once or twice, you take it in stride as part of the chance 'ups and downs' of friendship. But if the unfriendliness continues, the time will arrive when you say, 'No, this is too far out from friendship.' These samples of behaviour come from another population of experiences—an unfriendly population. That person is no longer classed as 'cranky friend' but is now classed as 'non-friend' or even 'new enemy'.

Sampling theory is a statistical means of deciding to which population a given sample belongs when such a sample may be found in both populations; unfriendly samples or bits of behaviour emerge from cranky friends as well as from enemies. Similarly, friendly samples of behaviour emerge from both friends and con-artists. To which population does the person producing this particular sample belong? Five heads in a row can result from both tossing a legal coin and tossing a biased coin; from which population does this particular coin come? Ordinarily you decide such questions by getting more samples—by continuing to toss the coin or by continuing to closely observe your 'friend'. If in the *long run* heads or unfriendliness continue, you conclude these are not normal chance variations but rather reflect a coin that is biased toward heads and a person who is biased toward unfriendliness.

Often we must make such judgments without the benefit of long-run experience. We must make judgments on the basis of short-run experience, on the basis of small *samples*. Inferential statistics and sampling theory provide help in comparing short-term sample results with the results to be expected by chance in the long run.

Sampling error theory

Some research design principles are really worth learning because they apply to all research studies, because they'll help make you a much more discriminating consumer of scientific news; they help you sort junk science and preliminary studies from serious reliable research results. Sampling error theory is one of those important principles.

We have indicated how the information contained in short-run samples of experience can differ from the information contained in long-run populations of experience. Research in the social sciences involves sampling; it involves conducting observations on a few individuals—on a sample—to provide estimates about the total group or population that the sample represents. When we observe the impact of a new drug on a sample of depressed patients, or the impact of a new teaching technique on a sample of students, we don't merely want to know how it affected that small sample of people (descriptive statistics); we want to estimate from the sample results what the impact of our independent variable will be on depressed patients in general or on students in general.

But because the members of a population differ from one another—some are very depressed, some are less depressed—and because chance factors invariably play a part in determining which individuals end up in a given sample—the patients in our treatment group may be less depressed than most—the mean or standard deviation obtained from a sample is sure to differ from the mean or standard deviation obtained from observing *all* members of the population, that is to say, all the depressed patients. *Therefore, sample 'facts' remain crude estimates of population 'facts'.*

How reliable are such estimates? This is the question that sampling theory addresses. To appreciate the simple logic involved, consider the following example. Suppose you wish to know the mean height of North American females. Measuring the height of millions of females is prohibitively expensive, both in terms of time and money, so instead you take a sample. Your sample consists of the first 10 females who enter the lobby of a large hotel. You determine their average height to be 5 feet 2 inches. How good an estimate is this of the average height of all North American females? You decide two estimates are better than one. Just as you are about to take your second sample, much to your surprise, you see some Japanese women entering the hotel. What luck! Now you can compare the height of North American women and Japanese women. You measure and average the heights of the cooperative volunteers and find the average to be 5 feet 8 inches. What's going on? Japanese people are generally considered to be shorter than North Americans, not taller.

After a little inquiry you discover that the hotel is housing the athletes attending an international athletic event. *By chance* you happened to measured 10 members of the Canadian women's gymnastic team and then, by chance, 10 members of the Japanese women's basketball team—hardly typical or representative samples of either respective population.

From this example we learn three points about the reliability of estimates of population values based on sample values. These three points can be framed into questions you should ask about any sample:

1. How representative is the sample of the population that I want to talk about? Was it a *random* sample—that is, did every member of the population have an equal chance of getting into the sample? To the extent that this is so, you have increased the likelihood that your sample fact will provide a reliable estimate of your population fact.

2. Does this sample 'feel' representative? Before you get too far into your study, try to decide on the basis of your previous experience whether you have drawn a typical sample. For example, in our sample of American females, you may have noticed that they all smoke, or that most of them are young, or that they all carry basketballs. Your past experience can frequently guide you in assessing the representativeness, and so the reliability, of your sample data.

3. Do you have a large enough sample to obtain a reliable estimate? Intuitively you are familiar with this question. Intuitively you know that large samples of experience give more reliable estimates than small samples, whether we are estimating friendship or height. In estimating the height of North American women, the means of several small samples

will vary more (will prove less reliable) than the means of several large samples. The *sampling error*, or variability, of the means of small samples is larger than the sampling error of the means of large samples. As a brilliant friend observed: 'The *n* justifies the means.'

This third point is addressed by inferential statistics—the issue of how much confidence we can afford to have in comparing the average or mean of the experimental group with that of the control group when we know that the small sample means are unreliable. The haunting question remains: 'Is the difference we find between the two means due to our treatment or merely due to the fact that small sample means bounce around even without treatment?' We remain caught on the horns of a dilemma. On the one hand we can't afford to measure very large numbers of subjects in order to determine the *population* mean accurately; yet on the other hand we know the means of small samples provide unreliable estimates of the populations they are supposed to represent.

We need some rational and mind-sized way of helping us decide when sample means are reasonably accurate estimates of their respective population means—methods of deciding when sample 'facts' are reliable estimates of population 'facts'. The rational solution we rely upon is called *sampling theory*. A detailed examination of this topic lies beyond the scope of our discussion; nevertheless if you keep the following principles in mind, you are less likely to be hoodwinked by chance playing tricks with sample means:

1. Sample means become an increasingly accurate estimate of their population means as you increase the size of your samples. We recommend that you use sample sizes of 30 or more per group when you want to compare an experimental sample with a control sample.
2. When deciding whether you have obtained a significant difference between your experimental and control groups, you must take into account:
   a. The size of the difference between their means, and
   b. The variability (i.e., standard deviation) of the two samples—the size of the variability in each sample and the similarity of the variability in each sample, and
   c. How much the two samples overlap each other.

Particularly when you're getting started on social science research, it is wise to obtain this information by plotting your results.[2] Notice in the following three figures how the two means remain the same, but the variability and the degree of overlap differ; particularly notice how such differences suggest very different conclusions.

The three figures (12.2, 12.3, and 12.4) present different versions of an experiment to test whether students using a program instruction text (Group 1)

---

[2]Computer programs available in statistics labs and on the Internet make this a simple task.

perform better on a math exam than students using a standard instruction manual (Group 2). As noted in all three examples, the experimental group scores five points higher than does the control group on the math exam. But notice in Figure 12.2 how the samples show wide variability and large overlap—such differences between samples occur frequently by chance. Therefore we conclude since such differences occur relatively frequently in random sampling we can have little or no confidence that the program text is responsible—that is, we can frequently expect such differences even in two samples receiving identical treatments, e.g., both groups using the same text.

Fig 12.2 ■ Large Overlap in Group 1 and Group 2 Scores

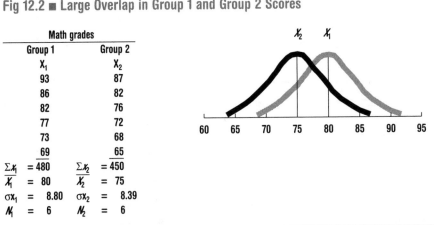

Math grades	
Group 1	**Group 2**
X_1	X_2
93	87
86	82
82	76
77	72
73	68
69	65
$\Sigma X_1 = 480$	$\Sigma X_2 = 450$
$\bar{X}_1 = 80$	$\bar{X}_2 = 75$
$\sigma X_1 = 8.80$	$\sigma X_2 = 8.39$
$N_1 = 6$	$N_2 = 6$

In Figure 12.3 the difference between the means remains the same (5), but the sample variability is less and so is the degree of overlap. Although such differences between samples occur by chance more frequently than 5 times in 100 sample pairs, the result is promising and warrants increasing the sample sizes to see if the differences hold.

In the third case we can be relatively certain we have a difference 'worth talking about'—the sample variance and overlap is relatively small, while the difference between the means remains at 5.

While eyeball examinations increase our confidence in the results presented in Figure 12.4 over those in Figures 12.2 and 12.3, we can gain additional confidence by performing a statistical test (a *t* test). This test is designed to measure the 'significance' of a difference between independent samples by comparing the difference you obtained with the difference chance alone can deal an experimenter. The procedure outlined in Table 12.1 uses data reflecting the differences we observed in Figure 12.4

Fig 12.3 ■ Some Overlap in Scores

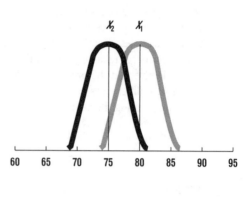

Math grades			
Group 1		Group 2	
X_1		X_2	
86		81	
82		78	
81		76	
80		73	
77		72	
74		70	
ΣX_1 = 480		ΣX_2 = 450	
$\bar{X}_1$ = 80		$\bar{X}_2$ = 75	
σX_1 = 4.14		σX_2 = 4.09	
N_1 = 6		N_2 = 6	

Fig 12.4 ■ Almost No Overlap in Scores

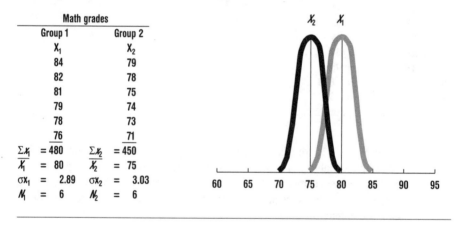

Math grades			
Group 1		Group 2	
X_1		X_2	
84		79	
82		78	
81		75	
79		74	
78		73	
76		71	
ΣX_1 = 480		ΣX_2 = 450	
$\bar{X}_1$ = 80		$\bar{X}_2$ = 75	
σX_1 = 2.89		σX_2 = 3.03	
N_1 = 6		N_2 = 6	

If we go to an appropriate map of chance (t table), we discover that for samples of this size, this particular t value would occur rarely by chance alone—that is, if 100 such comparisons were made between *control* groups of this size, we would expect such a large t value to occur less than 5 times in 100 trials. We can decide either that we have stumbled on one of these rare tricks of chance, or that it was not the work of chance but the influence of our treatment (the programmed text) that 'pushed' the samples apart.

Samples of raw data for the other two cases are listed in the figures, so for those who wish to examine the likelihood of obtaining these sample differences by chance alone, one can compare the resulting t values with those provided in

Table 12.1   Test for Small Independent Samples

Math Grades

| Group 1[a] | Group 2[b] | Deviations | | | |
X_1	X_2	x_1	x_2	x_1^2	x_2^2
84	79	4	4	16	16
82	78	2	3	4	9
81	75	1	0	1	0
79	74	−1	−1	1	1
78	73	−2	−2	4	4
76	71	−4	−4	16	16

$$\Sigma X_1 = 480 \quad \Sigma X_2 = 450 \qquad \Sigma X_1^2 = 42 \quad \Sigma X_2^2 = 46$$
$$\overline{X}_1 = 80 \quad \overline{X}_2 = 75 \qquad \Sigma X_1^2 = 42 \quad \Sigma X_2^2 = 46$$
$$N_1 = 6 \quad N_2 = 6 \qquad \Sigma X_1^2 = 42 \quad \Sigma X_2^2 = 46$$

$$t = \frac{\overline{X}_1 - \overline{X}_2}{\sqrt{\frac{\Sigma X_1^2 + \Sigma X_2^2}{N_1 + N_2 - 2}\left(\frac{N_1 + N_2}{N_1 \bullet N_2}\right)}}$$

$$t = \frac{80 - 75}{\sqrt{\frac{42 + 46}{6 + 6 - 2}\left(\frac{6 + 6}{6 \bullet 6}\right)}} = \frac{5}{\sqrt{\frac{88}{10}\left(\frac{12}{36}\right)}}$$

$$t = \frac{5}{\sqrt{2.93}} = 2.92$$

For $df = 10, p < 0.05$[c]

---

[a]Group 1 studied from programmed text (Experimental).

[b]Group 2 studied from standard text (Control).

[c]For degrees of freedom = 10 ($N_1 + N_2 - 2$) probability (p) of obtaining $t = 2.92$ by chnce is less than 5 in 100.

---

the t tables of any standard statistical text (for degrees of freedom = 10, or $N^1 + N^2 - 2$).

Analysis of Variance (ANOVA)

Just as a t test can help you decide whether your experimental and control groups differ by more than the hand of chance, an F test, ANOVA, helps you decide whether your experimental group and several comparison groups are separated by differences greater than you would expect by chance alone.

One-way analysis of variance (one independent variable)

Let's say that you are studying the effects of alcohol (independent variable) on coordination (dependent variable) using a control group, group 1 (12 ounces of Coke); and three experimental groups: group 2 (12 ounces of Coke plus 1 ounce of alcohol); group 3 (12 ounces of Coke plus 2 ounces of alcohol); group 4 (12 ounces of Coke plus 3 ounces of alcohol). You speculate that as alcohol consumption increases, so too will errors in coordination, but when you plot your results (Figure 12.5), it doesn't look that way—group 3 has the lowest, not the second highest, error rate.

Fig 12.5 ■ Effects of Alcohol on Errors of Coordination

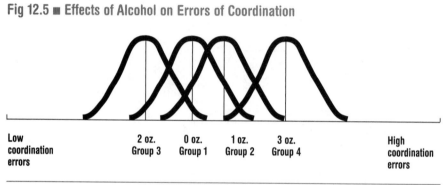

| Low coordination errors | | 2 oz. Group 3 | 0 oz. Group 1 | 1 oz. Group 2 | 3 oz. Group 4 | | High coordination errors |

The question is whether these are more than chance differences. An analysis of variance (F test) helps you decide whether two or more of these groups differ by more than chance expectancy. An F test is based on the differences between the means, in relation to the variability and the size of the groups. A significant F test, in this alcohol experiment, tells us that two or more of the groups differ by more than expected usual tricks of chance.

Having obtained a significant F we can now use eyeball analysis and t tests to decide which particular pairs of groups differ. We find that group 4 differs significantly from all of the groups; that groups 1 (no alcohol) and 2 (1 oz.) did not differ, nor did groups 1 (0 oz.) and 3 (2oz.), but that groups 2 (1 oz.) and 3 (2 oz.) did differ. On the basis of *this* study and this sample we conclude that 3 ounces of alcohol disrupts coordination, and tentatively decide that 2 ounces may facilitate coordination.[3]

---

[3]Did you notice any differences between the groups besides the quantity of alcohol consumed? What about the ounces of liquid?

You are probably wondering why one would bother doing an analysis of variance at all, since the *t* tests have to be done anyway. There are two important reasons. First, if you fail to get a significant *F* test, this tells you the differences you observe are likely due to chance, and so you stop the analysis right there, saving yourself from doing a series of *t* tests (six in our example). Second, when comparing several groups, an initial *F* test provides more protection against flukes of chance than you get by starting with a series of *t* tests.

But ANOVA has another great advantage: it enables researchers to measure the combined effects of two or more treatment variables; it enables us to measure what are called *interaction* effects.

Two-way analysis of variance (two independent variables)

In the foregoing example we studied the effect on coordination of one treatment variable (alcohol—a one-way analysis of variance). But suppose we wanted to add another treatment variable, such as drinking history. We now have two independent or treatment variables. This involves a *two-way* analysis of variance, the columns representing the one treatment variable (four levels of alcohol) and the rows representing the other treatment variable (two levels of drinking history).

	Alcohol			
	0 oz.	1 oz.	2 oz.	3oz.
Novice drinkers	Group 1	Group 2	Group 3	Group 4
Practiced drinkers	Group 5	Group 6	Group 7	Group 8

The *F* tests in 2-by-4 analysis of variance can measure quantitatively what we observe in Figure 12.6.

From these observed results (Figure 12.6) we can't say that more alcohol leads to significantly more errors in coordination—you *can't* make any across-the-board generalization about the effects of alcohol in this study. In addition, you can't, for example, say that being a novice drinker leads to significantly fewer errors—you *can't* make any across-the-board generalizations about drinking history. However, you can say 'It all depends'; it depends on special combinations of amounts of alcohol and drinking history—that's an interaction effect.

We usually hope for straightforward simple effects like those in Figure 12.6a. In this tidy speculation, errors of coordination increase with the amount of alcohol consumed. They increase for both novice and for practiced drinkers, but more so for novice drinkers. Now these are results that make sense, results that are simple enough to remember.

Instead of such simple results, however, we frequently obtain results like those plotted in Figure 12.6b; we obtain effects where factors combine in 'funny' ways (novice drinkers show the fewest errors on 2 ounces of alcohol, while

Fig 12.6 ■ Effects of Alcohol and Drinking History on Errors of Coordination

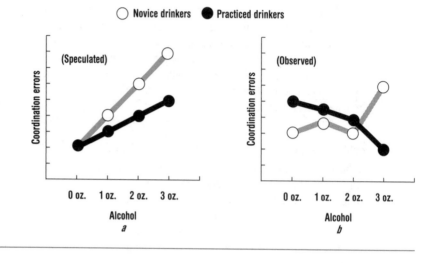

practiced drinkers show the fewest number of errors on 3 ounces of alcohol). Analyses of variance enable researchers to measure the statistical significance of complex effects of various treatment combinations using two-way, three-way, or four-way ANOVA designs.

When examining social science research, look for interaction effects, and expect some treatments and some people to combine in surprising ways. Look for interaction effects in the graphs, in the statistical analyses, and in the discussion. How does alcohol affect coordination? It all depends on the amount of alcohol, *and* on drinking history, *and* etc.

A closer look

If you plan to become a practitioner of science, as well as an inevitable daily consumer, you'd best take a closer look at sampling theory and at studies employing more than one treatment or independent variable at a time. First, let's take a closer look at sampling theory.

Unloaded and loaded dice

A control group study can be viewed as comparing two groups: a control group playing with unloaded dice and an experimental group that *might* be playing with loaded dice. Using unloaded dice, the control group's scores should reflect the *normal* distribution of scores you'd expect with rolling unbiased dice.

However, if you've introduced a valid (loaded) independent variable in the experimental group's dice, that treatment should push their scores out of the normal shape, that is, the shape that would be produced if only random forces were at play.

The central limits theorem

The concept of the normal distribution of random variables at play is called *the central limits theorem*. This theorem helps us predict the outcome of combining the results of a bunch of random events, such as rolling dice.

If you repeatedly roll a number of dice and record your results in the form of a histogram, its shape will approach that of a normal (bell-shaped) curve. At either end you will have relatively rare or improbable events. For example, if you rolled five dice, then at the low end you would record the number of times you rolled 5 ones, and at the high end you would record the number of times you rolled 5 sixes. In between you would record the number of times you rolled various combinations of ones, twos, threes, fours, fives, and sixes.

The practical value of this theorem and the normal curve is that it provides a model or map of how random events combine. If observed results—in the real world—take similar forms, then we assume that random forces are at play. The distribution of people's height in a population, for example, takes the form of a normal curve. This suggests that random forces are at play, and in this particular example it involves a random combination of genes.

Alternatively, to the degree the observations in an experiment deviate from the characteristics of a normal curve, we suspect that non-random (loaded) independent variables are involved—the kind of deviations you would get using loaded dice. In the case of an experiment, we hope our independent variable is loaded to the extent that it pushes the scores into a non-random form, with more of the patients who got the new drug being moved to the high end of the curve, while the scores of patients in the control group behave *normally*—as if only random forces are at play—as if there is no loaded therapeutic factor at work.

Factorial Designs

First, it's important to learn the language. A *factor* is the same as an independent variable or treatment (X_t). You can have different *levels* of a given factor. In the above study of the effects of alcohol consumption on coordination we used a factorial design: factor #1 was alcohol (using 4 levels of consumption) and factor #2 was drinking history (using 2 levels, novice and practiced). Since we assigned people to the groups at random it's called a *4 by 2 random assignment factorial design*. It involves 8 groups (4 x 2).

Main and interaction effects

Examine the left hand panel of Figure 12.6. Sitting comfortably at the top of our PST we confidently predicted that alcohol consumption would lead to more errors of coordination among novice than among practiced drinkers. That is, we speculated that if you added up all the errors made by all the novice drinkers in the study, they would be reliably (significantly) higher than those made by all practiced drinkers. Such a consistent result associated with one of the independent variables, or factors, is called a *main effect*.

However, obtaining such consistent results is more a hope than a reality in social science research. Billiard balls with brains don't necessary follow predictions and instead they tend to wander all over scientific graphs. That's of course what we discovered when we moved down to the bottom right corner of our PST and empirically tested our neat and tidy prediction. That prediction turned out to be naively optimistic. As indicated, on the right side of the figure we found that the effects of factor # 1 (alcohol consumption) were not consistent across either the novice or the experienced drinkers.

Instead, the graphs zigzagged, even crossing over each other. Mixed results such as these are known as *interaction effects*. They can take many forms but if the graph lines of the different factors are not parallel when you do a visual inspection, then you should suspect an interaction effect. As we noted previously, this is why it's generally naïve to make simple generalizations like 'Novice drinkers will make a greater number of coordination errors.' When the results come in you end up having to stretch your own and your reader's bounded rationality with the qualification of 'It all depends': 'It all depends *on both* the amount of alcohol consumed, *and* the person's past experience with booze, *and* chance, *and* the rogues.'

You can have *both* main and interaction effects in the same study. We predicted a systematic (main) difference between the two independent variables, but we also predicted an increasing, rather than a parallel, difference on coordination errors.

Chance sits in on the game

Up until now we've been assuming the results in Figure 12.6 are reliable. But some, or all, of these results may be due to chance as a result of sampling error. By chance more clumsy people may have been sorted in to one group than another. They're naturally clumsy, with or without the alcohol.

To estimate the reliability of the diagramed differences arising in factorial designs we rely on the previously noted statistical method called *analysis of variance*.[4] As you know, that analysis is based on the degree of variability (variance) spreading out on either side of the means in each group (remember the normal curve?). In this case we're looking at the degree to which individual participants within each group differ in their response to the particular dosage of

---

[4]The assumptions underlying this method (e.g., normal distributions and linearity), and how to do the calculations, in case you don't have access to a statistics lab, are available in standard statistical texts. One of our statistics Professors used to say that if you know enough statistics you could torture the data until it confesses the truth. . .or at least tells you what you want to hear.

alcohol. The greater the spread of these scores around their group means, and the greater the overlap of scores from one group with another, the less confidence you can have in your results, and the less their practical significance.

In brief, the larger the within-group variance is, the less likely we our to obtain statistically, or practically, significant results. The greater the individual differences within each group, then the more certain we are that chance and the rogues are in control and pushing the scores around.

And the rogues will play

When trying to change behaviour, the results you obtain depend upon the strength of the independent variables or treatments (X_ts), the reliability and validity of your dependent variables (Os), the role of chance in sorting people into groups, and of course to the tricks of the rogues and their gang[5]—all of them pushing and shoving scores this way and that way. That's why we shrink the problem down to mind-size by relying so heavily on graphing group averages (means), to blind us to the variability.

And the more complicated factorial designs become then the greater the opportunity for both chance and the rogues to control the game. The more factors and levels and dependent variables you employ the larger the playpen. If researchers are lucky they obtain increased external validity. If not, then the rogues have a field day messing up scientific graphs, or producing an exciting but unreliable interaction effect. You can explore different factorial designs by Googling 'factorial designs' on the Internet.[6]

As we discuss factorial designs you are probably feeling an increasing load on your bounded rationality. This is bound to happen as we move from a typical control-group study (one factor, one level) to factorial designs where you can have multiple factors, multiple levels, and multiple dependent measures. For instance, it's relatively easy to remember the well-behaved graph in the left panel of Figure 12.6, but probably impossible to remember the location of the eight wandering data points graphed on the right panel.

Multi-measure factorial designs

We limited the above study to one dependent variable (O)—namely coordination errors—for the sake of simplicity. But that's putting all our dependent variable eggs in one basket. One or more of our independent variables may be having a positive effect but our dependent measure (O) is too crude to detect it. Some measures are more sensitive than others. For example we could have used a multi-measure

---

[5]Recall the eleven threats to internal validity discussed in Chapter 6.

[6]David et al. (1986) used a 4 x 2 x 16 factorial design—that's 128 cells. That works out to be a lot more than the short-term memory limit (7 plus or minus 2), and is a threat to our bounded rationality.

factorial design by adding such measures as reaction time, error rates in a simu-lated (virtual reality) driving test, measures of short-term memory, etc.

But notice that every time we add another independent variable or depend-ent measure to a factorial design, we add another cell to be filled with data. Such data must be collected and analyzed, which means more samples of research participants. And the observed data can move up and down on whatever scales you're using, influenced by the treatments (singly or in combination), and/or by chance, and/or by the gang of eleven.

No wonder we provide scientists with extra time, training, and fancy equip-ment. No wonder we provide them with extensions to their senses, to their mem-ories, and to their computational skills. When they discover a reliable and valid pattern buried in nature's buzzing confusion, they deserve our gratitude and a BIG prize. And, when they get it wrong, they deserve our understanding, sym-pathy, and continued support. Unless they're caught cheating—then they deserve a good swift kick in their scientific pants.

Summarizing, we now have the scattergram to help us decide *visually* how closely two measures (taken on the same individuals) are related, and the cor-relation coefficient to help us decide *quantitatively* how closely the measures move together, and we have the *t* test to help us decide *quantitatively* the sta-tistical significance of the differences between two groups, and analysis of vari-ance (ANOVA) to help us decide quantitatively the statistical significance of the difference between more than two groups.

Meta-analysis

The first, or at least an early, phase of any project involves an assessment of the current knowledge about the particular topic of interest. Typically, students, researchers, and theorists will review the scientific literature applying an after-the-fact method. They go back in time and select or cherry-pick from the hun-dreds—perhaps thousands—of relevant studies, a few that pique their interest, that are easy to access from the close-at-hand journals and texts, and that have been identified as classic, highly-trusted studies of the topic, rightly or wrongly. Suppose you are required to do a review of the research on psychotherapeutic outcome: Does psychotherapy really help people? After reading your selective (non-random) sample of studies you write up your review, indicating which studies reported positive results and which reported negative results, along with your conclusions. Since this is an after-the-fact study, your conclusions will reflect your 'theory frame' applied to the articles in your limited 'time frame' sample of studies.

We would predict that if you believe in the efficacy of psychotherapy, you would conclude that it works if applied properly. If you don't believe in psy-chotherapy—if it doesn't 'fit into your theory frame', you'll probably conclude it doesn't work. Even in those few studies where it seemed to work, you can con-clude that there were certain weaknesses in the research methods (e.g., the four rogues were not controlled, therapist bias entered into the evaluation of the results, the investigator didn't use double-blind procedures, etc.).

A critical literature review of this traditional type has been referred to as the narrative approach (Matlin, 1992) and it forms the introductory chapter of most graduate student theses. Maccoby and Jacklin (1974) employed a 'box score' approach tabulating the number of statistically significant gender differences on a host of independent variables such as mathematical ability and aggressiveness. They used a pool of 1,600 studies from which to draw their data. From their review we know how many of those studies investigating male and female differences in mathematical ability, for example, revealed statistically significant findings and how many showed no sex differences. Although this information is of great interest, it would be even more useful to know which of these statistically significant differences are of conceptual or practical significance. In other words are they statistical differences that made a social difference?

What alternative methods are available for obtaining more systematic and 'objective' evaluations of a large body of literature? Enter meta-analysis.

Meta-analysis provides a quantitative method for drawing conclusions about the overall results of different studies that use a variety of dependent variables, but all of which presumably study the same type of independent variable (e.g., psychotherapy). In fact, Smith and Glass (1977) did such a study of nearly 400 control-group studies of psychotherapy. Even though Smith and Glass would have to rely on their theory frame, as well as a time frame, to determine which studies were selected and which excluded, nevertheless 400 studies is a much larger and more representative 'sample' than the typical review article would normally cover.

Although there are a number of ways to compare studies, these authors subtracted the mean of the control-group outcome from that of the treatment group and divided the difference by the standard deviation of the control group—and they did this for each study. In effect, they were transforming the differences into Z scores, which, as you will recall from discussions in the last chapter, allow you to make comparisons of relative position on different measures (e.g., psychology and physics grades). In any case, Smith and Glass concluded that, in terms of relative position, the average treated patient was superior to 75 per cent of the control-group patients. Although, like any method, this is not a foolproof procedure, and although researchers with a different theory frame will find much to criticize, meta-analysis techniques provide a more powerful and more objective method of drawing large playpen conclusions, or testing speculations, than traditional after-the-fact methods.

More recent examples of meta-analysis involve the use of the d statistic. A d value provides an index of the overall size of the effect of the treatment variable on the dependent variable of interest. This approach has the advantage over other literature review strategies because it allows for an interpretation of the practical significance of a statistical difference. To illustrate, anything less than a d value of .20 is not worth getting excited about, that is, the variable in question (e.g., a new drug) has only a minimal impact on the dependent variable (e.g., depression). A moderate difference, worthy of a raised eyebrow or two, would be represented by d values of .50, and a d greater than .80 is the theorist's or researcher's dream—an effect worth shouting about.

A major limitation of psychotherapy research, identified by meta-analysis, is the lack of long-term follow-up (Bradley, Green, Russ, Dutra & Westen, 2005).

Chi Square

Another popular and useful statistical tool—the chi square test—helps us decide whether the distribution, particularly of nominal scale data, deviates significantly from chance. For example, one student proposed the provocative hypothesis that women are both more soft-hearted and soft-headed than men. He also speculated that, since Republicans are more hard-hearted and practical than Democrats, women would tend to support the Democratic Party.

To test his hypothesis he drew two samples at random of 60 women and 60 men from a large introductory psychology class. He then had each individual indicate his or her political preference for one of the two main parties. He got usable data from 50 males and 50 females (that is, the number remaining within the sample, after refusals and after elimination of those choosing other parties.

He reported the following results:

	Female	Male
Republican	10	30
Democrat	40	20

Based on visual inspection he concluded his hypothesis was supported—females tended to be more Democratic or liberal. On being challenged to provide evidence that such a difference was not merely due to chance (to sampling error), he performed a chi square test—very simply, as outlined in Table 12.2.

Notice that in Table 12.2 the expected cell frequencies appear in the small boxes within each cell. If you have a complex table, consult a standard statistics text for help in computing these expected frequencies. In our table we simply went to the row totals and assumed an *expected frequency* of 50–50, half women and half men.

For 2 x 2 tables, a raw score formula allows you to avoid calculating expected frequencies by merely using the observed frequencies in each cell (A, B, C, D).[7]

---

[7]X^2 for raw score formula will closely approximate that found by calculating differences between observed and expected frequencies.

	A	B
	C	D

		Female		Male	
Republican	A	10	B	30	40
Democrat	C	40	D	20	60
		50		50	100 (N)

$$X^2 = \frac{N(AD - BC)^2}{(A + B)\,(C + D)\,(A + C)\,(B + D)}$$

$$X^2 = \frac{100(10 \times 20 - 30 \times 40)^2}{(10 + 30)\,(40 + 20)\,(10 + 40)\,(30 + 20)}$$
$$= 16.6$$

$$d.f. = 1 \qquad p < 0.001$$

Having demonstrated that such a combination of cell frequencies is likely to occur less than one time in 1,000 by chance, the student expresses greater confidence in his hypothesis. An unconvinced student repeats the study and she obtains less dramatic but still significant results.

	Female	Male
Republican	18	28
Democrat	32	22

$$X^2 = 4.03 \qquad p < 0.05$$

The student decides that there is some evidence that women do indeed tend to support the Democrats, not because they are soft-hearted and soft-headed, but rather because 'intelligent' people tend to support the Democratic party, whereas simple-minded people support the Republicans. She then did a study showing that Democrats have higher grade-point averages than Republicans do:

Academic Performance

	Above Median	Below Median	
Republican	$\boxed{23}$ 19	$\boxed{23}$ 27	46
Democrat	$\boxed{27}$ 31	$\boxed{27}$ 23	54
	50	50	100

$\chi^2 = 2.58$ $d.f. = 1$ $p < 0.20$

In this study the researcher drew a random sample of 100 students from another introductory psychology class and obtained the results tabulated in the preceding contingency table. It turned out, by chance, that there were 46 Republicans in her sample, and so if there was no relationship between political affiliation and academic performance, you would expect, by chance, a 50–50 split—expected frequencies (*fe*) of 23 above the whole group median and 23 below. Similarly, for the Democrats a 50–50 split would lead to expected frequencies of 27 above and 27 below the median academic performance.

On the basis of eyeball analysis the researcher is pleased with the results—more Democrats than Republicans scored above the academic median, quite a few more. Of course there were more Democrats in the sample, so that is why it is important to figure out the expected frequencies for each cell; that is why it is important to do an appropriate statistical test like a chi square. The researcher finds, to her disappointment, that a chi square of 2.58 (*d.f.* = 1) can occur by chance close to 20 times in 100 random trials. Therefore she hasn't obtained a *statistically* significant result—which by custom is set at less than 5 times in 100 random trials. Nevertheless, it is an *emotionally* significant result, and she argues that her findings represent a strong trend supporting her hypothesis—she will increase her sample size and prove her hypothesis next semester. Others who disagree with her hypothesis (quite a few Republicans, for example) accuse her of trying to read her own bias into the results, rather than accepting the quantitative judgment of her own statistical test.

As you can imagine, the argument continues and will continue. The chi square provides a simple and useful tool to help wage this kind of war *quantitatively* and provides a simple map of chance against which to compare your research results.

But notice that when you establish chi square categories or cells (a contingency table), you provide opportunities to test how fuzzy the categories are—to test how large a region of uncertainty they contain. For example, arguments about whether someone belongs to the male or female category rarely arise,

Table 12.2   Chi Square Test

1. General Chi Square (X^2) Forumla:

$$X^2 = \sum_{r=1}^{r} \sum_{c=1}^{c} \frac{(fo - fe)^2}{fe}$$

where: fo = Observed frequency in a given cell
fe = Expected frequency in that cell

The Chi Square is obtained by adding the differences between fo and fe (according to the formula) over all cells—the cells in the rows (r), and columns (c) of the table.

2. Example of Chi Square for 2 by 2 contingency table:

	Women	Men	
	$fe =$ 20	20	
Republican	$fo =$ 10	30	40
	30	30	
Democrat	40	20	60
50	20	50	100

$$X^2 = \frac{(10 - 20)^2}{20} + \frac{(30 - 20)^2}{20} + \frac{(40 - 30)^2}{30} + \frac{(20 - 30)^2}{30}$$

$$= 5 + 5 + 3.3 + 3.3$$

$$= 16.6. \quad df = 1, \quad p < 0.001^a$$

[a]For degrees of freedom = 1 (number of row − 1) (number of columns −1), probability of X^2 = 16.6 less than one chance in 1000.

Experts disagree over the need for a Yates' correction for small cell frequencies and for all tables with degrees of freedom less than 2. Our practice is to use the correction if a cell frequency is less than 10, or if the chi square level of significance is borderline around the 0.05 level. We follow Guilfford (1956, p. 237): "The correlation is particularly important when chi square turns out to be near a point of division between critical regions." With the correction, the chi formula becomes:

$$X^2 = \sum_{r=1}^{r} \sum_{c=1}^{c} \frac{[(fo - fe] - 0.5)^2}{fe}$$

apart from at the Olympics. However, whether to categorize someone as a Republican or a Democrat can become tricky. Do you accept as reliable evidence the fact that they put a pencil mark after Republican or after Democrat on one question on a questionnaire? Or do you ask for evidence of party membership? Or do you ask for evidence of active party support for at least three years? Until such issues are resolved, the various categories or cells of our first chi square table should perhaps be drawn as follows:

	Female	*Male*	*?*
Republican	10	30	40
Democrat	40	20	60
	50	50	100

Therefore keep an eye open for the fuzziness of the categories of all scales, but particularly with nominal scale data of the type used in the cells of chi square contingency tables. When you find such fuzziness—independent observers can't agree on who goes into which cell—take the results with a grain of salt.

Which Statistical Test?

Consumers as well as practitioners of science must learn to 'read' graphic and quantitative descriptions of the degree of relationship between observational samples (scattergrams and correlations) and the differences between observational samples (distribution plots, contingency tables, t tests, analyses of variance, chi squares).

You will encounter a host of statistical tools. Some, called *parametric statistics*, are based on the assumption that your samples have been drawn from populations that are normally distributed and have the *same variability*. Other statistical tests, called *nonparametric*, do not assume normalcy, or variance equivalence (homogeneity) in populations, and so can be applied to a wide range of observations.

Arguments among experts continue over when to use a given statistical test —some preferring to use nonparametric statistics when sample data suggest the parent populations are non-normal (skewed) and/or the experimental and control populations have markedly different variances. Other experts believe that, since parametric tests are more powerful—that is, they can detect finer differences—and are not all that sensitive to violations of the normalcy and variance assumptions, the parametric test should ordinarily be used. Our bias is to examine the data from several angles: plot it and examine it visually; do parametric tests where possible; do nonparametric tests when in doubt or when parametric tests aren't available.

The following brief list of nonparametric and parametric statistical tests are more or less matched in terms of the kind of relationships, or differences, they are designed to measure:

Nonparametric	Parametric
Spearman rank-order correlation.............. Pearson product-moment correlation	
Sign test ⎤ .... —t test for related samples (e.g., two	
Wilcoxon test ⎦ two measures on the same subjects)	
Mann-Whitney U test ⎤ .... —t test for independent samples	
Median test ⎦	
Kruskal Wallis one-way link test ⎤ .... One-way analysis of variance	
Median test ⎦	
Freedman two-way ranks test.................One-way analysis of variance with repeat measures	
Chi square test.. No comparable parametric test	

The detailed procedures for doing these tests can be found not only in statistical texts but also increasingly in the instruction manuals for desk calculators, computers, and on the Internet.

However, if in doubt, plot your data or a random sample of it. If you are a consumer, keep an eye open for information that lets you do rough plots in your mind's eye of sample sizes, variances, and overlap, and also watch for fuzzy categories or scales as well.

The preceding lists represent different statistical ways of helping you to quantitatively describe your observations—nominal scale observations, ordinal scale observations, or interval and ratio scale observations. Each method lends itself to certain scales, and each method also provides a suitable map of chance so you can determine how often the differences, or changes, you observed would likely occur by chance alone or between a series of two groups receiving no treatment or between a series of groups receiving the same treatment.

Statistical tests help to identify which of the many observations you make are worth talking about—worth talking about in the sense that they are statistically improbable. By custom social scientists consider differences that occur less than 5 times in 100 by chance alone as *statistically improbable*. So when you read, 'A finding is significant at the 0.05 level of confidence,' or 'p is less than 0.05,' it simply means that the researcher is reporting that such a difference between the experimental and control groups would probably occur less than 5 times in 100 if they had been drawn from the same population—that is, if both groups were given the same treatment.

But if the 0.05 level (5 times in 100 trials) is merely set by custom as the arbitrary boundary line of statistically improbable events, wouldn't it be safer to set an even more stringent boundary line? For example, why not define a statistically improbable event as one that occurs only once in 100 trials or once in 1,000 trials? Then if you turned up such a rare event in your experiment, you could be almost certain it wasn't due to chance playing a trick on you. Well, the reason is that by reducing the risk of being hoodwinked by chance you increase the risk of throwing the baby out with the bathwater. By reducing the risk of one kind of error, you increase the risk of another.

Type I and Type II errors

As noted, maps of chance provide no ironclad protection against error—particularly against two types of error. For example, in deciding whether a coin is biased, if you're 'trigger happy' you can accuse the tosser of using a biased coin too soon, after perhaps five heads in a row. By rejecting the possible role of chance, you commit a *Type I error*.

On the other hand, you can be too cautious and decide not to accuse the tosser of using a biased coin until 12 or 15 heads in a row have been tossed. By rejecting the possible influence of bias you commit a *Type II error*.

Technically we are talking about accepting or rejecting the *null hypothesis*. The null hypothesis states that there is no real difference between the pre-test and post-test, or between the experimental group and the control group. It presumes that whatever differences do exist are due to random chance fluctuations.

A Type I error occurs when you erroneously reject the null hypothesis—when you mistake a chance difference for a treatment difference, when you mistake a chance grimace for a hostile look, when you mistake a useless drug for a curative one, when you mistake a true coin for a biased one.

But just as you can be too trigger happy—seeing real differences where only chance differences exist—you can also be overly cautious—refusing to recognize 'real' differences. When you go on betting tails after the tosser has thrown 15 heads in a row, well, you're making a mistake and that kind of mistake is called a Type II error.

Someone who cries, 'Wolf', when a spring breeze rustles the leaves commits a Type I error, whereas someone who says, 'Nice puppy', as the wolf snaps at his hand commits a Type II error.

The likelihood of committing one or the other of these types of errors may be related to personality characteristics such as the tendency to take or avoid risks. However, another way of thinking about the likelihood of making a Type I error is in terms of the maps of chance you use to decide whether you've got a difference worth talking about. If you wish to reduce the risk of Type I errors, you only accept differences, or results, that occur very rarely by chance—that is, once in 100 trials or once in 1,000 trials. On the other hand, if you wish to reduce the risk of making Type II errors, you move in the other direction by accepting experimental results that could occur by chance 5 times, 10 times, or even 20 times out of 100 random trials.

As you can see, reducing the risk of one kind of error increases the risk of making the other. Therefore, it is not merely a question of trying to avoid making an error; it becomes a question of avoiding a high-cost error. If you're betting pennies on whether a given coin is biased or not, the cost of making a Type I or a Type II error is probably no more than 25 cents, so who cares? But if you're betting your life on a new surgical treatment for your brain tumour, you care; your family and friends care; the surgeon cares.

In such a situation you look at the results to date: of 10 patients with your kind of tumour who have had the new surgery, 3 are dead and 7 are living and somewhat improved. Is it really a 7 out of 10—70 per cent chance of success? Or is it really 50–50 or 30–70? Only more trials will decide! Should you wait for the results of more 'experiments' or accept surgery now? You can decide that the surgery works (has more than a 50–50 success rate), elect to undergo surgery, risk a Type I error, and maybe die under the knife. Or you can decide to wait for more data, risk a Type II error, and die from an enlarged, inoperable tumour.

Therefore Type I and Type II errors represent more than esoteric statistical phrases; rather, they represent a rational approach by bounded rationality researchers to analyzing the risks involved in making decisions under uncertain and sometimes critical conditions.

Fortunately most decisions don't present us with such pressing, high-risk situations. Under more mundane circumstances how should you, a consumer of science, respond to a statistically improbably research result—one that in your opinion balances the risks of Type I and Type II errors? What questions might an informed consumer of science ask? You might consider the following:

1. 'Yes, I understand your finding is statistically improbable, but it could still be due to chance. Therefore before I assign it a high level of personal confidence, I would like to see some independent researcher repeat the study and obtain similar results.'

2. 'Granted, you obtained a statistically improbable result, but it could be due, not to your treatment, but to some other shaping influence:
   a. to an unusual trick of chance,
   b. to error in data recording or calculating, or
   c. to (I hesitate to say it) fraud.

Therefore before I assign it a high level of personal confidence, I'd like to see some independent researcher repeat the study and obtain similar results with larger samples of people than you used.'

Independent and consistent labelling is the hallmark of objective language. Independent and consistent replication of observations is the hallmark of objective science. Statistically significant results from one-shot experiments are no substitute for independent and consistent replication of experiments. While statistical tools are helpful, they remain just that—tools. In skilled hands, they help us explore a multi-layered reality. In unskilled or irresponsible hands, they help foul the media and the scientific literature with false claims and numerical noise.

N-of-1 Research (Studying One Case)

Just as Rodney Dangerfield 'don't get no respect', so, too, is single-case research ill-respected. There are at least two reasons for this: first, *n-of*-1 research is frequently associated with the error-prone after-the-fact or case method approach; second, widely accepted statistical tests that would give us added confidence in whatever changes we see between baseline and treatment observations are lacking.

However, the ultimate criteria we apply in judging the reliability of any finding is replication, not statistical significance. Therefore, if we can replicate a reliable difference between the baseline and treatment conditions, we have met the standards of good research. Appropriately, then, *n*-of-1 studies typically take the form of a series of baseline-treatment trials on the same subject, and are typically described as *ABA*, or *ABAB* treatment reversal designs, where *A* stands for baseline observations and *B* for treatment observations. For example, Figure 12.7 maps the percentage of time a young student spent out of his seat under two conditions of teaching—*A*, a lecture method (baseline), and *B*, a game method of teaching (treatment). The second *AB* series serves as a replication and produces, in this case, a reliable result. We can analyze such results in this kind of study, as in other interrupted time series designs, in a variety of disciplined ways without relying on statistics. For example, we can compare the means; the slopes as you move from one block of observations to the next; abrupt shifts in performance from block to block; a similar pattern of changes as the treatment is introduced and withdrawn, etc. (Kazdin, 1989).

Fig 12.7 ■ *ABAB* Reversal Design

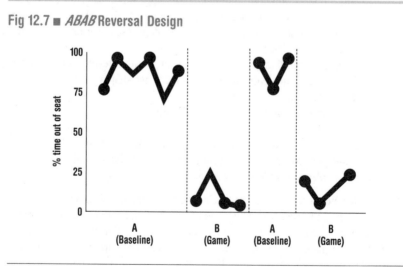

A student used a series of n-of-1 cases to map studying behaviour in average and above-average university students. Different students kept diaries for 16 weeks in which they coded their daily behaviour into various categories (e.g., studying, recreation, transportations, etc.). The researcher extracted a time series for each student that mapped the rise and fall of studying behaviour. We see these as n-of-1 studies, rather than a small group study, because different students encountered different in-the-gap, on-stage, maturational, and elastic-ruler rogues, and because our primary focus was the individual. If similarities between them appeared the researcher could use them as hypotheses for larger generalizations via group studies.

Following a baseline period each student participated in a 6-week time-management program, after which they continued their diaries over a follow-up period. Although time spent studying rose for some students during the time-management program, performance later gravitated back toward baseline. However, for all students, regardless of the operation of different rogues, one powerful factor was associated with increased study time, and that, of course, was exam and essay deadlines. All subjects showed the procrastination and cramming pattern associated with deadlines, although above-average students maintained a modestly higher baseline rate of studying.

Interviews with the students suggested that they were programmed to work to weekly deadlines in high school, and without that regular structure they fell behind in those university courses with long periods between deadlines. Setting personal deadlines and drawing up study schedules did not lead to significantly increased study time for most students. Deadlines, to be effective motivators, apparently have to be strict, set and monitored by authority figures. Otherwise, if only you make 'em, usually you break 'em!

Finally, not only do n-of-1 studies provide researchers with a more in-depth look at human behaviour and the subsequent generation of interesting hypotheses, but such investigations also provide individuals with an opportunity to study their own behaviour. Is there a more fascinating topic than that?

There is a solid tradition within science (e.g., biology) and outside science for relying on n-of-1 data for drawing important conclusions about your behaviour. As you can guess, it becomes particularly powerful when you are familiar with the individual or animal being observed. In other words, you have a good intuitive sense of the baseline and the degree of variability over long time frames. In time you learn to identify the rhythms in a friend's behaviour. And just as you know how a familiar song will unfold from the first few bars, so you can predict the unfolding behaviour of a friend on the basis of the first few bits of their familiar behaviour patterns. Thus, the n-of-1 method becomes a powerful method of predicting behaviour in certain hands; for example, most mothers, and old-time general practitioners, represent skilled pattern detectors and predictors using the $n = 1$ design.

Statistical methods are increasingly available which can be used to supplement disciplined visual inspection rather than to replace it. The statistical principles are the same for group or individual analysis, the main difference being the kind of generalizations you want to make. In the *n*-of-1 study, the population of behaviour you want to generalize to is that of an individual rather than a group. However, when making comparisons between two samples of an individual's behaviour, as in Figure 12.7, you keep the same points in mind as when making comparisons between two groups—namely, (1) the size of the differences between the means of each block of observations; (2) the size of the variability within each block; and (3) the degree of overlap of the observations between blocks. In the case of Figure 12.7, it is clear that the means of the baseline and game blocks differ markedly; the within block variability is low; and there is no overlap between the observations—that is, none of the observations in the treatment blocks are as high as any of the observations in the baseline blocks.

Once you have established a reliable difference between baseline and treatment conditions for the single subject, you can then work toward generalizing your results. You can test a larger time and/or a different dependent variable for that subject. In the case of our example, does the game method of teaching keep working, or does the child start reverting back to his old habits? In addition to spending more time in his seat, are there other changes as well (e.g., improvement in grades, or in relations with other students and parents, etc.)? Also, you can check to see if the method works with other, similarly restless students. Now you are starting to see if your results might generalize to a larger population, to the behaviour not just of one child, but of a particular, defined group of children. You are extending its external validity, or its travel permit.

Finally, if your results are not as clear-cut as those in Figure 12.7—if the means are closer together, or if the within-block variability is higher so that there is some overlap in the observations from block to block—then, as noted earlier, there are statistical tests available to help you draw conclusions from such fuzzy data (see Barlow & Hersen, 1984). Nevertheless, we strongly recommend that you plot your data first, so that you get a good feel for the variability, and thus for the degree of overlap, between observations in the treatment blocks and those in the baseline blocks. If you're interested in *n*-of-1 studies, start by using yourself as a subject.

SUMMARY

In the toolbox of social science, statistical devices abound. Descriptive statistics help package observations into mind-sized bites. Inferential statistics help us defend ourselves from being perpetually hoodwinked by capricious chance.

But remember that *statistically significant* findings represent a beginning, not a research climax. A statistically significant finding encourages further investigation but does not bestow a label of truth on your results. After having obtained an 'improbable' research finding, you write up your research project and submit it to a journal. Several reviewers familiar with your research area then critically examine your manuscript, and they decide whether your experimental procedure, your maps of chance, and your calculations seem appropriate and also whether your conclusions appear reasonable. Only if you pass all these tests is your manuscript then published. Then, other investigators can check your findings on new samples of people, perhaps controlling more carefully against the rogues, taking longer baseline measurements, or using larger samples.

In brief, although statistical tests (like t tests and chi squares) help you decide whether you have obtained a statistically significant result, it still requires experience, critical judgment, and continued research to determine whether you have obtained a result of scientific import or social consequence. Research requires not only tenacity but also courage. The researchers' code might well be taken from W.E. Henley's famous poem 'Invictus': 'Under the bludgeonings of chance my head is bloody, but unbowed.'

student's notebook

Dr Creek has us glued to computers doing assignments for this chapter. We're merrily feeding data sets into canned programs. All we have to do is punch the buttons and the programs figure out stuff like means, medians, modes, correlations, standard deviations, chi squares, analyses of variance, tests of significance, tables, and graphs.

Creek told us he never met an average or a mean he liked unless it was holding hands with some measure of variability, like a range or standard deviation. Without such measures you fall into the trap of accepting the mean as a valid representation for all the scores, and it's not! It's like accepting the average person of a group as a spokesperson for all the other members.

I like the idea of the mean as a 'mathematical stereotype', and measures of variability as representatives of statistical democracy.

Also, before we used any canned programs on correlations, he made us do several scattergrams by hand. That way you get a clear visual message of data variability—the unruly behaviour of dots with brains. You also appreciate that the straight line, which supposedly represents all those dots, is a gross oversimplification. And furthermore, that the number supposedly representing the degree of relationship between two scales (e.g., r = 0.60) only represents a minority of the dots.[8]

Creek also emphasized the difference between a statistically and a socially significant finding. For example, a given correlation between two measures may be statistically significant, but personally useless, like the one discussed above. Similarly t tests and F tests may be statistically significant in describing differences between groups but be of little or no practical value. You can be number numb and appreciate this point, merely by

---

[8] Apparently you square the correlation to estimate how much of the variance it represents. So a correlation of 0.60 only accounts for 36 per cent of the variance in the data. So, as I understand it, in this example, if you were going to predict a score on one measure (e.g., grade point average) from a score on the other (say, IQ), you would be wrong more often than right *even though you had a statistically significant correlation*.

observing the degree of overlap between two groups, as presented in the bottom right hand corner of Figure 12.1. So what if the means are different? The two groups overlap so much that they share pretty much the same behavioural space and the same attitudes.

Finally, in relation to analysis of variance, he advised us not to forget an earlier discussion in the text concerning interaction effects. The authors used the example of combining alcoholic drinks to demonstrate the big difference between simple additive effects as opposed to multiplicative effects (interactions), where small additions make a big difference, like adding the extra ounce to a novice drinker's glass, or like adding one bee to a picnic.

News stories

And now for my discussion of this week's news items.

Fraud in science

Did you notice, down at the bottom right corner of Figure 12.1, that the authors include fraud as one of the suspects influencing the outcome of rigorous testing? How big a problem is it? Is it just a few bad apples in the big barrel of science?

According to a recent news report,[9] the self-critical, adversarial safeguards of science are stretched to the breaking point. Some researchers claim that the problem of fraud is only getting worse, as research projects, and journals that publish fraudulent findings, soar in number.

In brief, research results are flooding out of the labs—and off the presses—faster than they can be critically reviewed or replicated. Therefore it's becoming less risky for irresponsible scientists to diddle their data, more tempting for them to desperately grasp for a grant renewal, a publication in a prestigious journal, a promotion, a scientific prize.

A survey of 3,427 scientists reported that a third of the respondents had ignored or stretched ethical guidelines by omitting or falsifying data. I guess that the influence of the on-stage rogue makes that a conservative estimate. There are, of course, attempts to reverse this disturbing trend. The US Federal Government established the Office of Research Integrity to encourage greater surveillance of scientific research and coordinate efforts. Journal editors from around the world established the Committee on Publication Ethics (COPE) to address the problem on an international level. But it's not that simple.

Consider this: there are more than 54,000 scientific journals published around the world. Just checking for blemishes on a small sample of that many publications boggles the imagination. Imagine the time and money involved in critically checking that many journals for fraudulent articles.

---

[9]Altman and Broad, 'Global Trend: More Science, More Fraud', *New York Times* 20 December 2005.

Headlines screaming 'Scientific Fraud' inundated the international media recently. A South Korean stem cell researcher faced disgrace over his research. In his defense, he claimed his method really works, despite some honest mistakes. But others close to the scene claim it was a case of intentional fabrication.

How do you police science? It's easy enough to innocently distort a short message, like in a simple game of rumour. Can you imagine monitoring the reliability and validity of the flow of messages flooding out of 54,000 journals?

Recent incidents of scientific fraud, which seem to be increasing, are discouraging. However, encouraging signs include the efforts by professional and governmental agencies worldwide to reverse the trend, to protect the premise that science will continue to be our most trusted news service.

Spoons with brains

I can't find my reference for this news story (it's a good thing we don't have to hand anything in this week), but I read that researchers in Australia secretly numbered 70 teaspoons in a cafeteria and tracked them over five months. Eighty per cent of them vanished. The scientists generated three theories to account for their results:

1. The spoons were secretly migrating to a spoon-friendly planet.
2. Teaspoons have a natural aversion to humans.
3. The customers might be taking them.

Derek and I are polling individual members of the B&B club to determine which alternative explanations they choose. We plan to build a personality inventory on the basis of our results. The inventory will measure a person's capacity to think outside the box. So far items 1 and 2 are tied, and only our waiter has chosen #3. I wonder if his mental brackets are opening and releasing a conventional way of thinking—a bias against student customers?

Note

Check out the rocky relationship between truth and statistics at http://www.oup.com/ca/he/companion/agnewpyke.

REVIEW TRUE OR FALSE QUIZ

T F	
T F	1. A mean is a statistical stereotype.
T F	2. In making predictions, we tend to overestimate the variability of the behaviour of any given individual.
T F	3. The best means of determining whether positive results are due to chance or the independent variable is to have an independent researcher repeat the study.
T F	4. A significant difference may be due to chance, to fraud, to the effect of the independent variable, or to error.
T F	5. With inferential statistics, the operation of chance in influencing the results obtained is ruled out.
T F	6. Sampling theory is a statistical means of deciding to which population a given sample belongs.
T F	7. Inferential statistics and sampling theory help in comparing short-term sample results with the results to be expected by chance in the long run.
T F	8. A random sample is a biased sample in that every member of the population did not have an equal chance of getting into the sample.
T F	9. The sampling error or variability of the means of small samples is larger than the sampling error of the means of large samples.
T F	10. The means of small samples provide reliable estimates of the populations they represent.
T F	11. Determining whether a significant difference has been obtained between two groups requires taking into account the size of the difference between the means, the variability of the two samples, and the degree of overlap of the two samples.
T F	12. A t test is a statistical test that measures the significance of a difference between independent samples to see if it is larger than what would occur by chance alone.
T F	13. An F test or ANOVA is used to determine whether several comparison groups are separated by differences greater than expected by chance alone.
T F	14. In order to test for interaction effects, it is necessary to do a meta-analysis.
T F	15. A quantitative method for drawing conclusions about the overall results of different studies that focused on the same topic is known as the narrative approach.
T F	16. In meta-analysis, a d value of .20 suggests that the variable in question has only a small or minimal impact on the dependent variable.
T F	17. Chi square is a useful statistical technique to employ with ratio scale data.

T F	18.	A Yates' correction for small cell frequencies is important to use with the correlation statistic.
T F	19.	Parametric statistics assume that samples have been drawn from normally distributed populations and have the same variability (homogeneity).
T F	20.	By rejecting the possible influence of bias, you have committed a Type 1 error, refusing to recognize real differences.
T F	21.	The central limits theorem helps us predict the outcome of combining the results of a bunch of random events.
T F	22.	If the distribution of a variable takes the form of a normal curve, this suggests that non-random forces are at play.
T F	23.	The study of the effects of alcohol consumption and drinking history on coordination is an example of a 4 x 2 factorial design.
T F	24.	It is not possible to obtain both main and interaction effects in the same study.
T F	25.	Diana notes that the square of a correlation provides an estimate of how much variance it represents.
T F	26.	A statistically significant difference is a guarantee that the finding has important socially significant implications.

Being Good
and Being Clear

The first chapter in this section explores an explosion of ethical challenges as science pushes its way into every nook and cranny of our lives, from preventing our conception to hastening our exit, from mapping our private thoughts to plumbing our deepest feelings.

A code of ethics must mark a fine line between ensuring proper conduct, on the one hand, and not smothering the goose that lays the golden scientific eggs, on the other.

The second chapter focuses on how scientists communicate their scientific news. The gold standard of science is being able to repeat another researcher's investigation and obtain the same results. In order to do so, the procedure followed must be clear, must be described in step-by-step detail. This research procedure is like a recipe, with no room for 'fuzzies', such as 'a pinch of this' or 'a bit of that'.

13

Ethics

Chapter Goal

- To expose you to the complexities of ethical issues vis-à-vis research, in particular, the relativity of ethical codes, their restrictive and shaping influences and the extent to which bias, stereotypes, politics, and self-interest determine the specific content and adherence to or rejection of ethical standards.

Introduction

Ethical principles and codes help individuals reach conclusions about *proper* behaviour.

Remember, there can be no conclusions without premises. A code of ethics is a set of premises concerning acceptable and unacceptable conduct, within various contexts. What's considered acceptable behaviour in the bedrooms of the nation is not necessarily considered acceptable in the boardrooms of the nation.

Each of us harbours a personal set of ethical premises or rules at the top of our PST. However, we keep many of these ethical rules safely bracketed out of awareness, only letting them out on special occasions. Others are kept off to one side; we might preach them, but not necessarily practice them.

Sigmund Freud called the personal enforcer of these cultural 'shoulds' and 'should-nots' the Super-ego. Most professions have a formal code of ethics designed to assist our conscience to do battle with the forces of darkness, to warn us when we falter, and punish us when we fail. In this chapter we examine how scientific organizations develop quantitative and qualitative ethical guidelines, and try to both encourage and enforce professional conduct.

This is not a simple thing. The odds favouring deviant behaviour are formidable. They include:

1. our bounded rationality trying to do battle with opportunistic greed and lust while vainly attempting to navigate the increasingly complex maze of ethical restrictions;
2. our inability to see what's going on behind closed doors—most unethical behaviour is observationally inaccessible;
3. the self-interest of professional organizations in protecting their members; and,
4. the reluctance or inability of victims to get a fair hearing before our feeble moral courts.

Ethics regulation—the development, revision, and enforcement of codes of ethics—is currently a growth industry. At a recent convention of the American Psychological Association (APA), over 30 sessions had an ethics component and a new prize has been developed to recognize dissertations focusing on psychology and ethics. There are specific journals devoted to this theme—*Ethics and Behavior; Journal of Empirical Research on Human Research Ethics* (Behnke, 2005)—and ethics committees abound within disciplines, universities, government agencies supporting research, and within organizations in which research is conducted (i.e., hospitals, schools).

It is easy to see the need for some set of rules of conduct for those professionals providing services of various sorts. Drug addicted physicians should not be allowed to practice medicine; obstetricians should not be permitted to sell unwanted babies to wealthy couples eager to adopt; teachers should not abuse their pupils; priests, of all people, should not sexually molest children, therapists should not have sex with their clients; politicians should not show their gratitude to companies who made huge campaign donations by awarding them juicy government contracts; postal carriers should not destroy the mail they are charged with delivering; service station owners should not gouge their customers by capriciously and unnecessarily increasing the price of a gallon of gasoline; reporters should not deliberately distort or omit relevant information in writing up a story; lawyers should not breach client/lawyer confidentiality privilege; tax payers should report all their income. No doubt you can generate many more 'should not' examples.

But what about scientists? Surely their behaviour is above reproach. By virtue of their extensive education and training, their presumed intelligence and wisdom, and their lofty pursuit of the TRUTH for the betterment of humankind, scientists were simply assumed to naturally behave ethically. Think about how you would describe a scientist. What traits or characteristics come to mind when you think about scientists in general? Although each of us might generate a unique list, at least some of us would no doubt agree on certain adjectives, including, perhaps, intelligent, creative, well-educated, absent-minded, analytical, objective, rational, honest, impartial, fair, and trustworthy. The last four descriptors speak to the ethicality or morality of the researcher. Certainly, science is based on the presumption that the ethical integrity of its disciples is of the highest order. Were we not to make this assumption, the game of science would be an endeavour suitable only for fools, dilettantes, and con artists. This blindly accepted premise of the inherently high level of moral judgment and ethicality of scientists has served to impede the development of formal ethics codes. For example, it was not until the late 1940s and early 1950s that APA recognized the need for the formal establishment of a code of ethics. This recognition culminated in the 1953 publication of *Ethical Standards of Psychologists*. However, as you will soon see, we have been making up for lost time ever since.

No Absolute Standards

Rules of ethics reflect the value substrata of a culture. Just as values and other cultural components vary from society to society, so too will ethical standards. For example, while the Navaho, like many cultures, have prohibitions against lying, stealing, cheating, murder, and rape, the most serious crimes are those of incest and witchcraft (Kluckhohn and Leighton, 1949). Among the Saulteaux of the Berens River, violence of any form (including verbal aggression) is strenuously avoided (Hallowell, 1940); yet, among the Hopi—who also eschew physical aggression—verbal warfare is an ever-present feature of communal life (Eggan, 1943). Both cultures regard competition as being in extremely bad taste and both revere cooperation. This is in contrast to our own society in which merit is selectively attached to both traits. Similarly, ethical concerns related to the expression of sexuality show great cross-cultural variability. For the Keraki males in New Guinea, a period of passive, then active, homosexuality is regarded as a necessary prerequisite to normal heterosexual development (Benedict, 1938).

In addition to cross-cultural variation, ethical standards change over time. As one moves from one historical period to another, we see astonishing modifications in laws and ethical concerns. Throughout much of recorded history, women were regarded as chattels or inferior beings, a view reflected in the 'rule of thumb' of nineteenth-century English common law, which legalized a husband's right to chastise his wife with a rod not thicker than his thumb. Such practices, at the time, created no ethical conflict or burden for the perpetrators of this code of ethics.

Even within a single culture and given time period, considerable variance in the ethical principles accepted and practiced by various sub-groups may be observed. Attitudes among members of the Pentagon toward the ethicality and legality of a particular military policy are likely to be incongruent with the attitudes of their wives (Ellsberg, 1973). And most certainly the ethical stance of some Nazi researchers who used Jewish prisoners as experimental subjects was divergent from that of the German 'man-in-the-street'.

Stereotypes may also exert a powerful influence on ethical decision-making processes. Consider, for example, the stereotype that women are more emotional, immature, and more in need of protection than are men. That stereotype seems to influence a woman's 'right to die' (or more formally, the 'right to refuse life-sustaining treatment'). Miles and August (1990) examined the legal courts' decisions in 'right to die' cases. One of the questions they asked involved the wishes of patients who were on life-sustaining treatment and unable to communicate with anyone. Did the physician try to determine the patient's own preferences for either continuing or terminating life support, based on previous conversations? Or did the courts leave the decision to someone else, such as a family member or hospital policy? In 75 per cent of the cases in which the patient was male—but in only 14 per cent of the cases in which the patient was female—did the physician try to figure out what the individual wanted. So the message is this: If a man is in an irreversible coma, a conversation from 3 years ago can be used as evidence of his wishes either to die or to be sustained; if a woman is in a similar condition, her husband will probably be asked to make the decision about her fate (Matlin, 1993: 402)

The relationship between science and ethics has been fraught with minor spats, hurt silences, martyred expressions, and vicious, acrimonious disputes. At times scientific investigations were severely hindered by ethical concerns stemming from theological teachings. Consider, for example, how progress in medicine was retarded by the religious strictures against mutilation of the dead body. On the other hand, many of us conflate religion, morality, and ethics because—in their simplest form—most ethical standards boil down to the golden rule: Do unto others as you would have them do unto you. It sounds simple, but it's a precept many of us have difficulty following. White (1955) has provided us with an inventory of illustrations that highlight the uneasy association of science and religion.

During a brief halcyon period in the history of science, the primary injunction to scientists was to search for the truth 'no matter what'. Admonitions to seek knowledge for its own sake were the norm, and if unscrupulous minds used such knowledge in an unethical fashion, this was in no way the responsibility of the scientist. This attitude is reflected in Tom Lehr's lyrics about Germany's V2 rockets used in the Second World War.

> Once the rockets are up who cares where they come down;
> That's not my department says Weiner Von Braun.

If research on methods to reduce prejudice, for example, uncovers effective techniques for producing attitude change that are then subsequently employed to manipulate prisoners of war as part of a brainwashing program, it's not the scientist's fault. The more contemporary view, however, recognizes that 'the double-edged potentiality of scientific knowledge poses ethical problems for all scientists' (APA, 1982: 6). What they are saying is that scientists have some responsibility for the monsters they spawn. This modern stance, combined with a general evolution in standards of humanitarianism and respect for the human condition, has forced the scientist into the more philosophical, religious, and politically risky arenas to debate ethical issues.

The moral of the story (to make a bad pun) is that principles of ethics and moral precepts are neither self-evident nor absolute. Being culture-bound and time-tied, ethics are understood only in the context of the culture that espouses them. Our amazement at the atrocities of Genghis Khan, at the horrors of the Crusades, at the child abuse during the Industrial Revolution, at the tortures of the Spanish inquisitors, and at the heartless behaviour of some GIS in Vietnam reflects small playpen perceptions, our own provincial natures and our inability to divest ourselves of our own cultural trappings. In the same way, future generations may well register disgust over many of our current 'ethical' practices.

Ethical Codes for Researchers

As social scientists whose subject matter is animate, reactive, and often human, we are perhaps more sensitized to ethical concerns than is the physicist who measures the aurora borealis from photographs, the geologist who maps rock types on the basis of drill core, or the chemist who analyzes the molecular structure of a complex protein.[1] While the tip of an onion root doesn't object to study or change its behaviour as a result of observation, think how we would react to detailed scrutiny of our behaviour in the intimacy of our own homes—bugged phones and hidden cameras in our nurseries, bedrooms, and bathrooms—all for the sake of exposing the truth about human behaviour? Under what conditions is it ethical to record telephone conversations and intercept e-mail? For science? For national security? Who makes the decision? And who polices the ethics of the people policing and governing us?

Investigations related to altruism, child-rearing patterns, suicide bombings, leadership, authority, incest, fiscal policy, population growth, cancer, cloning, the treatment of schizophrenia, and penal reform all cry out for attention to ethical principles.

Ostensibly the purpose of constructing a code of ethics is to guide our behaviour so as to protect (not contravene) the rights, privileges, and general expectations of others. Other purposes are less lofty. A key reason for designing and encouraging the adoption of a code of ethics is to inflict or impose our current sense of values on our colleagues—'don't go there . . . don't look there . . . don't dig there.' Secondly, the more-or-less uniform acceptance of rules of conduct helps to establish the 'old boy's club'—to guarantee some sense of familiarity and comfort in interacting with other members of one's discipline. To police science, to identify and weed out the incompetent, insincere, or unworthy, and maintain the purity of the profession, is another function of a common code of ethics. Such a code helps protect the public from charlatans—those lacking the training specified for membership in the discipline—and from deviants—those

---

[1] Stem cell research is certainly receiving political and religious scrutiny.

adequately trained but practicing in unethical ways. To protect the individual researcher from pangs of conscience, gnawing doubts, and perhaps even financial ruin brought about by legal suits is another, less publicized, value of an ethics code. How can scientists be faulted if their research project seems to lead to a negative outcome for their participants, especially when they scrupulously followed the rites and rituals (including ethical prohibitions) accepted by their discipline? In some sense, a code of ethics serves the same function in science as *quality control* procedures serve in a factory.

Contemporary ethics standards typically require the researcher to obtain informed consent from the research participants; to eschew the use of deception except under special circumstances; to debrief—i.e., to provide accurate and full information about the study to the subjects as soon as possible following their participation; to ensure the humane treatment of animals used in research; to avoid the fabrication of data and plagiarism; to share research data; and to take authorship credit only for work to which the researcher has substantially contributed (CPA, 2000; Sinclair and Pettifor, 2001; APA, 2002; Smith, 2003). Each one of these general principles subsumes a number of more specific canons. In the discussion to follow two standards from the APA code (2002) are explored in more detail: '8.02 Informed Consent to Research' and '8.09 Humane Care and Use of Animals in Research'.

Informed consent

The purpose of informed consent is to ensure that the person participating in the study is doing so voluntarily and has full knowledge of the relevant risks and benefits of the participation. Typically research participants are asked to read a document that briefly describes the research purpose and procedures, notes the right of the person to decline to participate or to withdraw at any point in the process without penalty, outlines potential benefits and any negative consequences, discusses measures to ensure the confidentiality of the information provided by the participant, identifies any incentives for participation, and identifies who is conducting/supervising the research and how they can be contacted. Participants are asked to sign the document to signal their understanding of the procedures and their willingness to continue. Additional injunctions apply if the study involves an investigation of a treatment using a control-group model or if the participants are below the age of majority. In this latter case, informed consent must be obtained from a parent or guardian. An illustration of an actual consent form, used in an interview study investigating the impact on the lesbian partners of those who decide to embark on female-to-male (FTM) transition (Brown, 2005), appears below.

I agree to participate in an interview with researcher Nicola Brown from York University as part of the work she is doing for her dissertation on queer women partners of FTMs. I understand that the purpose of the interview is to explore my experience as a queer-identified woman who has been or is currently partnered with an FTM (female-to-male). I will be asked about my identity, relationship, and community, as well as turning points and the joys and struggles at different periods during my partner's transition. There are no foreseeable risks in my participation. Because of the personal nature of the questions asked, it is possible that I may experience discomfort in sharing what may be painful periods of time in my life. If this discomfort persists, please contact the researcher for information about accessible and appropriate resources.

There are no explicit gains for my participation. I will be contributing to knowledge about and visibility of this experience, which may be of benefit to others. At best, the interview and subsequent publication of the research findings may be an empowering and validating experience. The researcher cannot guarantee however that I personally will receive any benefits for participating in this study.

Public transport return fare will be provided—not to exceed $5.00. I will be sent a copy of my interview manuscript unless I do not want a copy. Upon completion of the researcher's final paper, I will receive feedback about the study in the form of a summary sheet, unless I do not want one.

The interview will last approximately 2 hours. The session will be audio recorded by the researcher to ensure that my views are accurately recorded. Only the researcher, Nicola Brown, will listen to the interview tapes. My name will not be written anywhere on the tapes. The tapes will be kept privately and locked until the final paper has been submitted, read, and accepted. At that time, the tapes will be destroyed.

My participation is voluntary and I have the right to refrain from answering any questions and/or to stop or leave the interview at any time without prejudice or consequence. I also have the right to answer questions, but ask that the answers not be recorded.

At the end of the interview, I can ask that any of my comments not be used, and up to one week after the interview, I can ask that information I have provided be taken out and not included in the researcher's final product.

The pseudonym I choose for the researcher to refer to me is _____. The pseudonym I choose for my partner is _____. All other identifiable information such as names of organizations or other people will be removed from the transcript for confidentiality, however queer and trans communities are small and this cannot in every eventuality guarantee not being identified by known others.

During the analysis stage, I agree to allow the researcher to share portions of the transcripts with colleagues for consultation purposes.

I agree to allow the data collected (in its written form only) to be used by the researcher in the future for presentations and publications under these same conditions and guarantees of anonymity. I give permission to the researcher to publish verbatim excerpts from the interview under the condition that identifying information is removed.

I may contact the Graduate Program in Psychology at 416-736-5115 for answers to questions about research and about the rights of participation.

I am fully aware of the nature and extent of my participation in this project. My signature is my consent to participate. I acknowledge that I have received a copy of this consent statement.

Signature of participant _____   Date _____
Printed name of participant _____

Signature of the researcher _____   Date _____
Printed name of the researcher <u>Nicola Brown</u>

The animal controversy

Non-human animals comprise important subject populations for many types of research. It has been estimated that about 50 million animals are used in research annually around the world (Gauthier and Griffin, 2005). In 2004, Canadian universities, government, and commercial laboratories used 2,307,232 animals from at least 19 different species for the purposes of research, testing, and teaching (Canadian Council on Animal Care.) Most (89 per cent) were mice, fish, rats, and fowl expressly bred for research purposes.

Concern for the care and use of animals in research is not a recent or unique phenomenon in the scientific community. As noted by Dewsbury (1990), the arguments of the anti-vivisectionists in the Victorian period were not fundamentally different from those of contemporary animal rights activists. The American Society for the Prevention of Cruelty to Animals (ASPCA) was founded in 1866; coincident with the passage of laws in various US states banning or limiting vivisection. More recently, the Animal Welfare Act, first enacted in 1966 and amended by Congress in 1976, regulates the transportation, housing, and care of laboratory animals. Granting agencies, such as the National Institute of Health, have adopted guidelines governing the use of research animals to which grant recipients must adhere. Many scientific organizations have similarly tackled the issue of ensuring appropriate use of animals in research. The APA, for example, first established a committee to address the ethics of animal experimentation in

1925. Current guidelines, approved in 2002, specify that the researcher comply with all government laws and regulations as well as with professional standards, that a scientist trained and experienced in the use of laboratory animals should ensure proper training and supervision of those working with the animals, and that researchers must minimize pain and discomfort to animals in research protocols, in surgical interventions, and with respect to termination procedures. The CPA and The Canadian Council on Animal Care espouse similar guidelines. This latter agency, established in 1968, is the national organization responsible for setting and maintaining standards for the care and use of animals in teaching, testing and research throughout the country.

Such efforts, aimed at the humane treatment of research animals, have not silenced the voices of those concerned about animal rights. Most vociferous among the critics is the Mobilization for Animals Coalition, an international network of hundreds of animal-protectionist organizations (King, 1984). This group has accused experimental psychologists of subjecting animals to such things as repeated, inescapable, painful electric shocks; starvation and dehydration; mutilation; crushing forces which smash bones and rupture organs; and pain and stress intended to make healthy animals psychotic (Coile and Miller, 1984; King, 1984). Even within the scientific community there are those concerned that all animal research meets appropriate ethical standards (Bowd, cited in Carroll, Schneider, and Wesley, 1985; Vonk, 1997). Sometimes research with animals is conducted for its own sake but often the objective is to shed some light on issues relevant to humans. However, Shapiro (1997), questioning this rationale, reports that a majority of clinical psychologists in his sample, who specialized in the treatment of eating disorders, had no knowledge of the animal models of eating disorders.

Additionally, some researchers have expressed dismay at the more specific government-proposed regulations related to the promotion of the psychological well being of non-human primates and dogs (Landers, 1989). The requirements designed to enrich the environments of captive animals include the provision of regular exercise in special pens or housing the animals in substantially larger cages, as well as modifications in feeding regimens to simulate foraging conditions. Among the other concerns of animal researchers are the limits on the number of operations that may be performed on a single animal, the degree of authority granted to veterinarians, and the increased administrative load involved in meeting the requirements. Implementation of these new proposals could have a significant impact on the costs of operating a laboratory and could lead to the curtailment of some research programs even though 80 per cent of APA members residing in the United States support the use of animals in psychological research (Plous, 1996).

Several surveys suggest that a similar curtailment is occurring at the university level. Gallup and Eddy (1990) note that one out of seven graduate departments that previously maintained animals no longer do so. The second most common reason given for closure was 'the prohibitive costs of compliance with existing codes and regulations' (400). Similarly, Benedict and Stoloff (1991) discovered in their survey of 137 of 'America's Best Colleges' that 21 per cent of the 93 schools that previously maintained animal facilities had closed them. Finally, Thomas and Blackman (1992), reporting on events in the United Kingdom, point to a dramatic decline (25 per cent) in the number of psychology departments with animal facilities, a decline in the number of animals used (70 per cent), a decline in animal research (35 per cent), and a decline in the number of graduate students conducting animal studies. This substantial decrease in animal work is attributed to an increasing reluctance of students to participate in projects involving animals out of concern for animal welfare.

That being said, the three Rs (reduction, replacement, and refinement) have become a uniting focus globally for both the scientific and animal welfare communities (Gauthier and Griffin, 2005). Replacement refers to substituting the use of animals with non-animal methods such as computer models or simulations or replacing the whole animal with research at the cellular or molecular level. With respect to reduction, evidence cited above suggests a decrease in the numbers of animals used for scientific purposes. However, there is some reason to believe that the numbers may increase over the next few years as a function of genome research and investigations of the impact of chemicals and environmental changes on human health. The third principle, refinement focuses on mitigating and preventing pain and distress. The use of new and safer anesthetic agents for example and better training of investigators in their use has had beneficial effects.

Recent Considerations

Special ethical considerations have been described in the case of research with particular populations. Fisher, Hoagwood, Boyce, Duster, Frank, Grisso, Levine, Macklin, Spencer, Takanishi, Trimble, and Zayas (2002), for example, have noted the need for knowledge of and sensitivity to cultural values when conducting research with ethnic minority children and youths. Their strictures add a whole new layer of complexity onto an already burdensome process. A sample of some of the advice they provide should be sufficient to make the point:

- Researchers should avoid the use of pan-ethnic labels, such as Black or Hispanic, which neglect the unique differences among racial, ethnic, and cultural groups.
- Researchers should engage in community consultation.
- Researchers should attend to within-group variability.
- Researchers should be on guard with respect to interpreter issues—the use of a family member as an interpreter can result in distortion and breaches of confidentiality.
- Researchers should enhance informed consent through the wide dissemination of information throughout the community and the use of recruitment handbooks.

- Researchers should ensure that all members of the research team are adequately trained with respect to the cultural competencies necessary to conduct the research with the population in question.
- Researchers should consider whether consent to participate is an individual privilege or more properly the prerogative of the family or tribal leader.

There is no question that the quality of research would be enhanced by adherence to the suggested considerations. On the other hand, imposition of these additional hurdles may preclude all but the most athletic researcher from reaching the finish line.

O'Neill (2005) has raised another interesting ethical wrinkle. O'Neill argues that the way in which questions are framed determines or influences the focus of the research—at the level of the system or social environment versus at the individual level. If research strategies focus on the individual as the locus of a social problem then the social structures that maintain inequities tend to be ignored. The shift in the focus of the American government from a war on poverty to a war on drugs reflects this move from a consideration of systemic factors fostering poverty to a focus on addicts and drug lords. Similar changes can be seen in Canadian politics—a war on children's poverty has been replaced by a war on the sexual exploitation of children. The issue of homelessness can similarly be approached as a social or societal issue (e.g., the lack of affordable housing) or as a problem for specific individuals, who lack stable relationships, are alcoholic, or have psychiatric disorders. O'Neill links these shifts to the political orientation of the party in power. A focus on the individual miscreant or deviant is more consistent with a conservative agenda while a more liberal or progressive party may be more sensitive to social conditions. The ethical issues become evident when we reframe the political as personal and, in so doing, 'become complicit in agendas that maintain oppressive and neglectful social conditions' (19). In effect, the way in which we approach researching social problems can have ethical implications.

A third issue relevant to ethics considerations has to do with the extent to which ethical codes pertain to a person only in the context of their professional role or whether these standards should also apply in the personal/private realm (Pipes, Holstein, & Aguirre, 2005). The APA ethics code seemingly permits an individual to behave unethically as long as their professional role is not operative. However, the boundary between the professional and the personal is not always crystal clear. For example, should the code require individuals to specify whether they are speaking in a professional or personal capacity when they make public statements? Is there a problem if the individual writes racist letters to a newspaper editor? Should graduate schools screen applicants for fitness for duty in terms of characteristics such as caring, integrity, and truthfulness? Once again, we see the constraining quality of ethics codes on behaviour; it places limitations on what is designated as acceptable.

Kathryn Becker-Blease and Jennifer Freyd (2006) have recently raised another interesting issue with ethical ramifications. The potential risks associated with asking research participants about their history of abuse has led many researchers to avoid including questions on this matter in their surveys and interviews. Becker-Blease and Freyd outline 10 concerns that preclude such inquiries including: the reluctance of ethics review boards to approve studies directly addressing this issue; the possibility of participant attrition; the potential for causing harm; the ethics of asking participants to disclose stigmatizing information; the view that there are no benefits to participants from disclosure; and the worry that disclosure may trigger traumatic memories. Evidence and argument pertaining to each of the concerns is presented. The consequences of not asking about abuse are also explored. Some research suggests that not disclosing abuse may, in fact, be harmful in the sense of predicting mental health symptoms. Not asking may lead interviewees to think that abuse is unimportant. Eschewing this topic reduces or eliminates the possibility of helping survivors. Connections between abuse and other forms of interpersonal violence and maltreatment may be undiscovered. The authors conclude, 'To the extent that silence is part of the problem—silence impedes scientific discovery, helps abusers, and hurts victims—then this is not trivial matter' (225).

The Review Process for Research with Human Subjects

In the United States, the National Research Act of 1974 authorized the creation of institutional review boards (IRBs) in all organizations receiving federal funds for biomedical or behavioural research. In Canada, the comparable body is the research ethics board (REB) mandated by the Tri-Council Policy Statement on research ethics—a creature of the three major government agencies funding research in the country. The purpose of IRBs and REBs is to both ensure the safety and protect the rights of human research participants. In order to obtain grant funds from any of the three national research councils in Canada, researchers must adhere to these policies. This is always a work in progress as various bodies (e.g., Panel on Research Ethics) examine and comment on the documents and their implications. All university-based research, be it funded or unfunded, and including research conducted by students as part of class assignments, must be approved by the university's REB (in Canada) or the IRB (in the United States). For researchers conducting studies on school children, convicted felons, patients with HIV/AIDS, or voluntary service organizations, ethics clearance must also be obtained from the committees established for this purpose in these various settings.

Critics of the process have identified a number of difficulties and, perhaps unanticipated, consequences of the implementation of these policies:

1. A 'one-size-fits-all' approach has resulted in the application of a biomedical model to the social sciences. Apart from research identified as minimal risk, the standards apply to all types of research from potentially

lethal biomedical interventions to the administration of seemingly innocuous questionnaires.

2. The definition of what exactly constitutes minimal risk research is unclear and variable.

3. Unfortunately, the judgments pertaining to the same project, emanating from the IRBs/REBs of different institutions, are not always consistent (poor reliability).

4. IRBs/REBs appear to have stepped outside their mandate by reviewing not just the ethical implications of a study but also the design of the study itself. One IRB, while lacking familiarity with the subject matter of a project, rejected the proposal and indicated that the poor design would make the participant's involvement a waste of time. Another IRB requested that an item on a standardized test be deleted, apparently without awareness of the implications for the validity of the test.

5. Even minimal-risk research is, in fact, at risk. In one case, in which the potential harm to participants was nothing more severe than boredom, an IRB ruled that 'boring' research is unethical.

6. The composition of IRBs has been questioned. In some instances, the boards consist of members of the public and non-researchers (e.g., professors of English, philosophy, or music) rather than members of the research community.

7. The time required to obtain ethics clearance can be a major stumbling block to the implementation of a research project. As a consequence, a requirement that Honours students conduct empirical theses was dropped from one program; the review process was so time consuming that students would not have completed their projects in time to graduate.

8. The policies and procedures themselves have not been subjected to empirical study. Do they actually lead to more ethical research, or to the minimization of harm to research participants? Do they impede or enhance the research enterprise? The validity of the process needs to be considered.

9. Ethics regulation, as it is currently designed, is an expensive operation. This makes a determination of its effectiveness all the more important.

10. Increasingly, concerns about possible litigation seem to be influencing the decision-making processes of IRBs/REBs. Some claim that this has become more important than protecting research participants from harm.

An obvious consequence of the imposition of an ethics review process is that it inhibits research; not just high-risk research but essentially any type of research from classroom-based student research to investigator-initiated projects. For some researchers, the impediments to carrying out empirical research with human participants have become so substantial that it simply isn't worth the effort. Another ironic consequence of this process takes us to the dark side of ethics regulation—deliberate misconduct. For example, some researchers simply forge ahead and begin data collection in advance of the stamp of approval from their review board (Giles, 2005). Other researchers omit information that might raise a red flag with the adjudicators. A survey of 3,000 researchers has revealed that a third of the respondents had been involved in one of 10 types of misconduct within the past three years. It appears likely that at least some of this misconduct was stimulated by perceived unfair, maybe even unethical, treatment the researchers received from the IRBs/REBs.

From Principles to Practice
Ethical dilemmas

Codes, principles, and standards mandating ethical behaviour are, of necessity, general and abstract. Their application in any given particular situation may be quite uncertain and a decision as to whether there has been a breach of ethics is often a judgment call. The following vignettes, which describe actual ethical dilemmas, have been adapted from Sinclair and Pettifor (2001) and are intended to provide readers with an opportunity to struggle with the difficulties and ambiguities surrounding ethical decision-making in real life.

1. A researcher receives a call at home on the weekend informing her that the animal facility housing her rats will be without heat for at least 48 hours. Realizing that the rats will perish without heat she decides to bring the rats home for the weekend. However, her car won't start and a return taxi trip will cost $60. Considering the fact that the research involving the animals is finished and that the rats are to be destroyed on Tuesday, she wonders if it is worth it.

2. Two professors have collaborated on the production of an article for publication. One author contributed heavily to the conceptual work involved in the study design while the other took major responsibility for writing the article. Both expected to be first authors on the article.

3. A psychologist in the military discovers that his superior officer, also a psychologist, is using the influence of rank to pressure subordinates into participating in psychological research. What should he do?

4. A researcher is given the opportunity to contribute to a new area of cognitive science at a university where similar work has been conducted. The previous work helped develop guidance control and target recognition mechanisms for weapons that were used in a recent war. Although the theoretical work is important and has other uses, the researcher is unsure about her responsibility for its use in future weapons development.

5. A psychologist employed in a hospital is peripherally involved in a longitudinal study of babies with a serious allergy. Babies in both the control and experimental groups are subjected several times a year to a series of tests some of which are uncomfortable, invasive, or painful. Difficulty in obtaining an adequate number of healthy infants for the control group

has lead the investigators to solicit babies from lower socioeconomic neighbourhoods by offering parents several hundred dollars for their co-operation.

6. A university-based REB has received a complaint from a group of high school students about the ethics of research conducted by a psychology professor. The researcher sat in a booth in a restaurant frequented by the students and recorded their conversations with respect to comments praising or criticizing their teachers. When confronted with the complaint, the psychologist argued that the research was a field study that involved public behaviour, that no names or identifying information were recorded, and that there was no attempt to influence the behaviour of the students. The students, however, regarded the research as a gross violation of their privacy.

7. A researcher in a psychiatric hospital has been asked to participate in a study comparing the effects of two different medications for depression against a placebo in combination with and in the absence of cognitive therapy. The research design will leave some participants without any kind of treatment for four weeks, which is about the length of time a client would be on a waiting list. The researcher is informed that any participant in the control condition (placebo, no therapy) who becomes suicidal will receive treatment immediately. The psychologist is concerned about the design and worries about potential harm to clients in the control group.

8. An organizational psychologist is asked by a large security company to evaluate and make recommendations for improvements to a training program for security officers. The company asks that the sample be restricted to male employees because a majority of the employees are male and they would like to keep the costs of the study down.

9. A researcher receives a grant from a foundation to study differences in the assimilation of immigrants from two different countries. A much higher incidence of child abuse, spousal abuse, and other criminal behaviour is found in one of the groups—higher than in the general population and higher than in the other immigrant group. In his report, the researcher notes the long history of violent conflict in the home country of this group and in three other countries populated by the same race. He concludes that the possibility of high aggression and criminality being inbred in this group's genetic pool must be considered. The foundation supporting this study has advocated for more restrictive immigration policies for people from this particular racial group but this reputation is not generally known.

10. A First Nations community offers a psychologist a contract to evaluate the effectiveness of their delivery of child welfare services. She designs a $75,000 study that includes sophisticated client outcome measures with good reliability and validity. Once the study begins, tensions arise.

Representatives of the community tell her that she is being too intrusive, that she is using culturally inappropriate measures, and that they simply want to ask their people if they are satisfied with their services.

Adherence to ethical codes

To what extent do the mechanisms created by scientific organizations ensure that research practices are ethical? Somewhat reassuring is the report by Coile and Miller (1984) that none of the Mobilization for Animals' allegations were found to be true in a survey of 608 published articles involving research with animals. Less reassuring is Bowd's observation that a significant proportion of the published research involving painful animal experimentation was unnecessary and did not contribute new knowledge (cited in Carroll, Schneider, & Wesley, 1985). Still less reassuring is the report by Plous (1997) that training in animal research was not associated with superior knowledge of federal legislation governing animal research. However, the APA committee charged with responsibility for adjudicating complaints of ethical malpractice reported only one case of a failure to ensure the welfare of animal research subjects in a three-year period from 1981 to 1983 (Hall and Hare-Mustin, 1983; Mills, 1984) and in 2004, no cases of complaints regarding animal welfare were received (APA, 2004).

As noted earlier, the screening process to ensure adherence to ethical principles can itself lead to a contravention of the very principles it is intended to enforce. Some investigators have examined the extent to which ethical codes have influenced the conduct of published social psychological research. The survey of 284 empirical studies by Adair, Dushenko, and Lindsay (1985) revealed that researchers rarely state that informed consent was obtained from their subjects or that subjects were aware of their right or freedom to withdraw from the experiment. Although the research, as actually conducted, may have attended to these ethical issues, the failure to report them leaves the question open.

The principle of informed consent implies that research participants must not be misled about the experiment. Nevertheless, deception is permitted under certain special conditions. Given the concern about deception, the finding of Adair and colleagues that experiments involving deception are increasing is surprising although there is more reporting of the use of debriefing procedures. Baumrind (1985) similarly reports that the ethical standards implemented by the APA in 1973 have not decreased the incidence or magnitude of the use of deception in social psychological research and she suggests employment of alternative research strategies.

Adair and associates also highlight a number of methodological problems created by stringent application of current ethical standards. For example, it appears that when conditions of informed consent are instituted, fewer subjects agree to participate. Those who do agree constitute a biased sample. The debriefing procedure required in cases of deception may contaminate subsequent results obtained with later subjects because research participants sworn to secrecy have been found to disclose the nature of the experiment to others.

Maintaining an appropriate balance between the benefits of research and the costs to participants, while at the same time ensuring methodological purity, will tax the creativity and ingenuity of the researcher for some time to come.

Cost–benefit ratio

By and large the legal profession accepts the principle that it is better to let 100 guilty people go free than to convict one innocent person. The costs (damages or harm) attendant on erroneous convictions are deemed to be greater than the benefits of utilizing more stringent procedures that would ensure a higher conviction rate of the guilty but would also entrap some innocent persons. Similarly, many issues in science reflect various mixes of costs and benefits. Some unpleasant, and even dangerous, subjects would not be pursued except that the possible gain to society is great.[2] What about the cost–benefit ratio of brain study? Although some benefits of understanding the operation of the brain are obvious, what about the dangers of a little knowledge, as sensationalized by Michael Crichton in the book *The Terminal Man*? Implanting devices to help someone see or hear is surely beneficial, but what if the appliance ultimately fosters even more serious deterioration in the nervous system? Investigations of the physical and psychological effects of starvation are meritorious, important, and useful, but how much should one try to persuade a volunteer to stay with such a study after nine months when the subject shows an inclination to drop out (Keyes, Brozek, Henschel, Mickelsen, & Taylor, 1950)? How does one balance the costs to monkeys against the benefits derived from the oral Sabin vaccine for polio?

Increasingly, the needs of society influence the nature of the questions attacked by science. Each society has a need to defend itself, so we have research on the development of more deadly (more efficient) weaponry and ever more virulent strains of bacteria. Each society has a need to feed itself, so we have research on undersea farms and new frost-resistant varieties of wheat going hand-in-hand with the development of safer and more effective population control techniques, including abortion. Society has a need for more energy, so researchers strive to locate and discover new sources of energy and to use existing sources more efficiently, even though this may result in oil spills and other forms of pollution that conservationists deplore.

Are the disadvantages (costs) of such research outweighed by the advantages—the greater good for the greater number? Calculation of the total cost–benefit ratio for any of the preceding is a complex, subjective, and incomplete process—never definitive, only suggestive—and the resultant ratio figures

---

[2] The authors are indebted to Dr J. Jenkins for his contributions to the analysis of this issue.

may well differ from one calculator to another. Consensus of judgments as to the ethicality of a particular piece of research is understandably hard to achieve.

Science, Government, and Law

As participants in one of society's most powerful, prestigious institutions, as creators of truth and practitioners of objectivity, scientific disciples understandably appropriated the development, application, and enforcement of ethical standards in research to themselves. Preferring to regulate their disciplines internally, scientists assumed responsibility for the maintenance of high standards and handled contraventions of ethical codes in-house. Current trends suggest that the government and the courts may usurp these functions.

Confronted with essentially unresolvable disputes, social scientists appear to be stepping smartly along in the footprints of the physicians as they search for clarification—not of the moral or ethical bases of their research, but of its legal ramifications and possible liability threats (Nash, 1975; Silverman, 1975). Increasing consumer sophistication regarding the limits of scientific methods and the relativity of the truth product, combined with a clearer articulation and emphasis on human rights, has generated a less gullible, less deferent, less tolerant public. So, there is greater readiness to bring the scientist to task (through litigation) for infringement of civil liberties, for damages resulting from negligence, and the like.

The escalating costs of scientific research, much of it funded from taxpayer coffers, legitimize government's demand for more public accountability while the tentacles of legal and governmental systems scoop up more and more of the ethical issues heretofore residing in the private domain (invasion of privacy; breach of confidentiality; information access; animal care). The erosion of public confidence in scientific ideals, as well as public attitudes of skepticism or cynicism as a consequence of exposure to science's seamy side—its dirty laundry—accelerates these trends.

Erroneous scientific findings stemming from chance factors are to be expected; those resulting from the practice of poor science (based on ignorance of proper methodology) may be forgiven. More heinous, however, are the sins of misconduct (cutting corners and misrepresentation) and fraud (fabricating results with the intent to deceive). Trust in the honesty of research colleagues remains a cornerstone of science. To be tricked by capricious chance is frustrating enough; to be tricked by a sneaky colleague is intolerable.

Evidence surfaced in the late 1970s and early 1980s suggesting that a famous British psychologist, Sir Cyril Burt, fabricated data linking IQ to heredity (Eysenck, 1979; Kamin, 1981). Burt estimated that intelligence level was determined 80 per cent by heredity and only 20 per cent by environment.

The evidence of fraud is indicated on two counts. First, Burt reported data from sources that now appear to be imaginary or non-existent—non-existent theses and research reports. Second, Burt reported identical correlations for supposedly different pieces of research. Since identical results rarely arise from different samples, it would appear that Burt didn't bother calculating new correlation coefficients on the basis of new data but merely used correlations computed on earlier data.

Currently, the debate rages as to whether the evidence proves fraud or is merely an indication of sloppiness and aging on Burt's part. Regardless of the debate's eventual outcome, it raises at least two important issues for us. First, the intensity of the debate provides a current example of how sensitive scientists are to charges of fraud against one of their own number, of how such charges threaten the integrity of science. Second, this debate also provides an example of how scientists, in protecting themselves against chance, also defend themselves against fraud. You will recall that the best way to increase confidence that your findings are reliable is to use large samples and to publish your procedures and findings so that others can check your results.

Fortunately, the hypothesis that intelligence has a large genetic component does not rest on Burt's work alone. A variety of studies by other investigators also support the hypothesis that IQ and inheritance are significantly related (Rimland & Munsinger, 1977). Had such independently arrived-at data not been available, the current debate would be even more acrimonious.

Although we would like to believe that fraud is rare, Dr Jerome Jacobstein suspects that as much as 25 per cent of published work may be based on fudged data (cited in Stewart, 1989). Walter Stewart, the self-proclaimed vigilante of the science world, reports receipt of about 100 allegations of misconduct a year (Stewart, 1989). An Australian researcher 'estimates that for every formal accusation of fraud, there are up to 1,000 cases that go undiscovered or are ignored' (Birenbaum, 1992: 8).

Although Nobel Laureate John Polanyi (1989) places his confidence in the peer review process as science's quality control mechanism, Stewart remains unconvinced of the effectiveness of peer adjudication in protecting science from the offenses of misconduct and fraud. As a case in point, he cites John Darsee's work published in the prestigious *New England Journal of Medicine*. A genealogy was presented in the paper in which a 17-year-old was listed as having four children, one an 8-year-old daughter! Stewart's painstaking investigation of the work of Darsee and colleagues revealed that 35 of Darsee's 47 co-authors had engaged in unacceptable scientific practices. Or, consider the case of American historian Jayme Aaron Skolow, who plagiarized assorted books, articles, and theses on European and American history (Birenbaum, 1992). Similar examples can be found in the *Casebook on Ethical Principles of Psychologists* (APA, 1987). Two of the many cases that, upon investigation, revealed evidence of unethical behaviour, are presented below. In each instance, the Ethics Committee ruled in favour of the complainant, and the maximum sanction of expulsion from the Association was imposed.

> Several faculty members at a foreign university reviewed a colleague's publications in connection with his promotion review, and found that a number of the papers he had

published in their native language appeared to be nearly verbatim plagiarisms of articles and book chapters published elsewhere in English (7).

The chair of a university-sponsored research committee became suspicious of a lengthy vita presented by a psychologist in connection with her application for a sabbatical travel grant. Upon investigation, the chair found that more than half of the nearly 80 articles listed in the vita had never been published and filed a complaint against the psychologist with the Ethics Committee (8).

Material presented in this chapter not only underscores the need for ethical standards, but also reveals great variability in the adherence to and effectiveness of enforcement. Although dismissal from one's collegial network (as represented by learned society affiliation) is unpleasant and may have deleterious effects of some magnitude on career prospects, the justice system brandishes significantly more potent sanctions. In what is perhaps the first case of criminal charges springing from the falsification of research results, psychologist Stephen Breuning (who falsified medical research involving the effects of behavioural-control drugs on the severely mentally disabled) pleaded guilty to two counts of fraud. This plea carries a maximum penalty of 10 years in prison and $20,000 in fines (Bales, 1988). Government agencies are also biting off a chunk of the action with the recent creation of two offices to prevent and investigate scientific fraud and misconduct (Adler, 1989). So, increasingly, the policing of scientific research leaks out of the hands of the scientists to be sucked up by government and the legal system.

An illustrative example: the Freeman affair

An article, published in 1990 in the *Canadian Journal of Physics (CJP)*, authored by Dr Gordon Freeman entitled 'Kinetics of Non-homogeneous Processes in Human Society: Unethical Behaviour and Societal Chaos', aroused considerable consternation in the science community (e.g., Crease, 1992; Lees, cited in Freeman, 1991; Stark-Adamac, 1993; Zimmerman, 1993) and elsewhere (Strauss, 1991; Wolfe, 1991, 1992). In his provocative treatise, Dr Freeman—a university chemistry professor—argues that mothers who participate in the paid labour force are responsible for most social ills—from murder, mayhem, and corrupt politics to drug-taking and student-cheating. The methodology employed in this purportedly sociological study is essentially unsystematic casual observation. Guinan (1992), noting that Freeman has failed to provide precise data in support of this thesis, comments:

The author explains that the study involves 'about 1,300 students' and 'people outside the university' and 2,500 'student controls'. The methods for determining sample size, enrolling subjects, or collecting and analyzing data are not described. No data are given on either the number of subjects with mothers who did or did not work or the number of subjects who cheated on exams. It is impossible to determine whether data was [sic] collected systematically or whether the analysis is sound, since no data or analysis are presented. Significantly, no criteria are given for determining cheaters and non-cheaters (113).

Ironically, given that Freeman is concerned about the ubiquitous nature of unethical behaviour among university students, there appears to be a serious breach of ethics in his own work. Objecting to the artificiality of experiments and surveys, Freeman reports that he collected information unobtrusively. This raises the question of whether Dr Freeman informed his subjects that they were, in fact, participating in a research study.

Despite the lack of supporting data or citation of corroborating research in the social science literature, Dr Freeman proposes dramatic social actions based on the presumed confirmation of his thesis. For example, he advocates substantial tax credits for families in which one parent does not work outside the home, a reduction in tax credits for day care expenses in the case of dual-career families, and discouragement of the creation of on-site day care centres by businesses.

How did this article which is not physics, indeed, not science, come to appear in *CJP*? Dr Freeman was the guest editor for this particular issue of the journal that was to contain the proceedings of the first International Conference on Kinetics of Non-homogeneous Processes. Was the Freeman paper presented at the conference? No, it was not. Did this work pass the scrutiny of any ethics review committee? Apparently not. Had the *CJP* editorial advisory board been consulted concerning publication of this controversial article? No, again, although the regular editor of the journal, Dr Ralph Nicholls, claims that the paper was subjected to peer review and a favourable evaluation received. However, he refuses to provide a copy of the assessment (even with identifying information deleted) to the journal's editorial advisory board. Does this article meet the criteria for scientific publication? Again, we must, in agreement with Zimmerman (1993), conclude no. It does not constitute a significant contribution to the discipline; it is not based on sound methodological or conceptual foundations; it does not use careful and appropriate data analysis procedures to support conclusions.

Following publication, letters expressing reactions to the Freeman article descended on the author, the journal editor, members of the editorial advisory board, and the editor-in-chief of the National Research Council (NRC) Journals. As a consequence of detailed critical analysis and widespread disapprobation, the editor-in-chief, Bruce Dancik, published the following retraction: 'This article does not comprise science and has no place in a scientific journal. The National Research Council Research Journals and the Editor of the *Canadian Journal of Physics* regret that this article was published.' Still unexplained are the procedural irregularities surrounding the publication. Nor was there assurance that steps would be implemented to reduce further harm (e.g., citation of the article as if it were a scholarly piece of research) or to ensure that such an embarrassment would not be repeated. Hence, further actions have been taken such as the following resolution passed by the Royal Society of Canada:

> The Royal Society of Canada, which is strongly committed to the advancement of women in scholarship, hereby expresses its censure of the *Canadian Journal of Physics*. In publishing the article by Gordon R. Freeman, 'Kinetics of non-homogeneous processes in human society: Unethical behaviour and societal chaos,' (*Canadian Journal of Physics.* 68 (1990): 794–8), it displayed a lapse of editorial and scientific responsibility. The article is devoid of scientific content and the title is inappropriate and misleading. The *Canadian Journal of Physics.* failed to publish a timely and adequate retraction. The Royal Society of Canada deplores both the insult to working mothers and the denigration of their children implicit in the published article.

Subsequent responses of NRC constituted more fulsome efforts to redress the damage—i.e., publication of a supplement issue to *CJP* containing commentary solicited from the social science community; organization of a symposium on ethical issues associated with publication practices; greater efforts to ensure representation of women in editorial posts; initiation of a number of formal publication policies; and review of current procedures involved in the publication process for the NRC Research Journals.

The issue here is not whether Professor Freeman's views are accurate, nor is there any quarrel with his right to share his perceptions. It is his abuse of his editorial and professional privileges and obligations that constitutes ethical contravention. Personal bias and prejudice must not be paraded under the guise of legitimate social science research.

SUMMARY

What is considered to be ethical behaviour varies from culture to culture and from time to time, as does compliance with whatever codes are in vogue. Although a given group may be able to agree on a set of ethical principles, it is much more difficult to agree on whether a given principle has been breached in a particular case. Increasingly, government regulations and formal legal criteria and processes are augmenting the self-imposed standards of conduct and enforcement procedures adopted by scientists. The effect of imposing ever more stringent review processes may well act as an inhibiting factor on the conduct of research.

student's notebook

We don't have to do a commentary on this chapter because we attended a full morning of papers and panel discussions on scientific and medical ethics. Wow! They covered some of the same stuff that's in this chapter, but I came away with several points whirling around and colliding with each other at the top of my PST.

First, I appreciate why Dr Frund got her knickers in a knot over my efforts to program Derek to be a listener. It's like big brother pulling our strings, manipulating our behaviour without our consent. But . . . we're all attempting, unannounced, to subtly change and manipulate each other's behaviour every day. You and I do it. Advertisers do it. Politicians do it. Governments do it. Maybe you can control the more blatant attempts, but there's no way you can police most of what's going on. It's like trying to forbid people from passing gas. How are going to identify the guilty party: 'It wasn't me! It must have been the dog.'

How are going to enforce behaviour that you can't monitor?

Talk about bounded rationality. How can we cut the myriad of ethical principles down to mind-size?

On the same point, how are you going to monitor 54,000 'scientific' journals for ethical goofs, including outright fraud? There's a big fuss in the media about a South Korean stem cell researcher who reportedly fabricated his data. Apparently his breakthrough results got medical researchers all over the globe excited about being able to cure all kinds of diseases by treating people with cells identical to their own. So, if your brain wears out, you could just shoot in some new healthy cells that your immune system won't reject, and be as good as new.

There's no way researchers can repeat all the studies flooding out of thousands of journals. Furthermore, it can take years to rigorously test a big theory. Cheating—at all levels, in studies of all sizes—is a growth industry. It's relatively safe and it's rewarding: miracle drugs, billions in profit, personal fame, and fortune.

The second idea arising from that conference is even more upsetting. Two scientists got into a debate about the pros and cons of the explosive growth of codes of ethics. One fellow listed—chapter and verse—all the ways that fraud was eroding away trust in science. The other guy claimed we had moved into overkill. Yes, fraud in science is a problem, but we're building in so many restrictions that creative scientists are giving up, going underground, and accepting jobs in other countries with fewer restrictions.

The B&B group chewed and guzzled over this problem. They even reached a consensus: BIG IS BAD.

Whenever anything—a group, a corporation, a city, or an institution—becomes so big that you can't easily keep an eye on it, devious data fixing is bound to happen. Our brains are just big enough to keep track of relatively few people in one cave. When the cave expands and becomes New York, or London, or the global economy, then we lose track of what's going on. Something bad happens, so we pass more laws, hire more police and more inspectors but it's never enough. And then the cycle starts all over again. For once, none of the smart cats at the B&B had an answer. Big may be beautiful, but it's also unmanageable!

The other big fuss in the realm of ethics right now, of course, is that the US Government is tracking phone calls and e-mails—not just from overseas, but from domestic locations too, all in the name of national security. Of course, they claim that they aren't actually listening to or reading any of the communications. Half of the B&B members disagree and point out that if you can access private messages—regardless of oaths, regulations, and random over-the-shoulder policing—then you will snoop. The US congress is currently debating whether such a level of monitoring is legal. But, regardless of whether or not it's legal, is it ethical?

Note

Did Harvard University create the Unabomber? Visit the student website at http://www.oup.com/ca/he/companion/agnewpyke.

REVIEW TRUE OR FALSE QUIZ

T F	1.	Interest in ethical issues vis-à-vis science has waned in recent times.
T F	2.	There is a remarkable homogeneity or uniformity cross-culturally in ethical standards.
T F	3.	A key reason for designing and encouraging adoption of a code of ethics is to inflict or impose our current sense of values on our colleagues.
T F	4.	Factors favouring ethically deviant behaviour include our bounded rationality and professional self-interest.
T F	5.	Informed consent is generally obtained from subjects participating in field experiments.
T F	6.	Except in extreme cases, we lack uniformity of judgment as to whether an individual study contains a breach of ethics.
T F	7.	Most animals used in research are expressly bred for this purpose.
T F	8.	Concern about animal rights and their abrogation in research is a relatively new phenomenon.
T F	9.	Only about 10 per cent of APA members resident in the United States support of the use of animals in research.
T F	10.	One survey has revealed that one out of seven graduate psychology departments that used to maintain animal facilities have abandoned animal work.
T F	11.	A decline in the number of faculty and students engaged in animal work has been observed in the United Kingdom.
T F	12.	According to O'Neill, a focus on homelessness in terms of the lack of affordable housing reflects a conservative political orientation.

T F	13.	One of the strengths of the scrutiny of research ethics by institutional review boards is the 'one-size-fits-all' approach.
T F	14.	Experiments involving deception appear to be decreasing.
T F	15.	When conditions of informed consent are instituted, fewer individuals agree to participate in the research.
T F	16.	Sir Cyril Burt apparently cited data from sources that do not exist.
T F	17.	One researcher, Dr Jerome Jacobstein, estimates that as much as 75 per cent of published work may be based on fudged data.
T F	18.	Although the Freeman study meets the criteria for scientific publication, given its sociological orientation, it was inappropriate to be published in the *Canadian Journal of Physics*.
T F	19.	Diana identifies the stem cell research by a South Korean as a possible example of fraudulent data.
T F	20.	Comprehensive monitoring of adherence to ethical codes of research publications in scientific journals is nearly impossible.

14

Research Report Writing

Chapter Goal

- To illustrate how researchers describe and organize the complex chain of messages and messengers involved in a scientific study—how they typically tell their story.

Report writing isn't just about jotting the results down on a scrap of paper. The report must contain enough detail so that other scientists can evaluate this work, and repeat it if they so choose.

Introduction

Fiction is fine in its place. But in a research report we want to know not only what was predicted to happen, but also what actually did happen. We want to know what specific operations were carried out from start to finish: what was observed, how the data were analyzed, and what was concluded.

Earlier we proposed that science is like a news service. Empirical scientists[1] report their news in the form of research reports, describing in detail the chain of messengers and messages involved from the beginning to the end of the study.

Figure 14.1 provides a reminder of the research process, of a chain of messengers and messages to be described in the research report. Ideally, the report should be sufficiently detailed so that another researcher could precisely duplicate every aspect of the procedure and rigorously test the reported results.

---

[1] In research reports we're particularly interested in the observational or empirical validity of the work. In theoretical papers we're interested in the up-top validity—in the scientist's premises, speculations, and predictions about which dots are connected to which, and how his or her speculations fit, or don't fit, the prevailing theories of the discipline.

For example, starting with the *researcher* in Figure 14.1 we not only want to know what he or she did, but we want to know their top-of-the-PST premises. We want to know what kind of top-down influences or biases might affect what he or she sees and does. The closest we get to that information is the literature review—appearing at the beginning of most research papers—in which a researcher selects and discusses the theories and methods they consider relevant. The literature review tells us what particular speculative space the researcher plans to explore and what predictions he or she is making. You can often get a sense of how strongly attached the researcher is to his or her theory, that is, how much—at least in the beginning—they are operating in a 'believing-is-seeing' mode.

Next, we move from the researcher to the *research participant*. We want to know about the 'you' in Figure 14.1. We want to know who you are (a first-year psychology student? a depressed patient?), how many of you there are, and how you got involved (volunteered? co-opted? paid?). Knowing these things helps us decide the kind of people the researcher can talk about in the end, a small number of volunteers—local validity—or a large random sample of university students—external validity.

Moving along the message chain, we also need to know how the researcher collected 'the participant's messages, what quantitative or qualitative yardsticks were used, and the reliability and validity of these measures (fresh batteries in the pulsemeter? standardized questionnaire? properly trained interviewer?). We want to know, as quickly and as clearly as possible, how elastic the rulers are and how they may have transformed or distorted the data.

The reappearance of the researcher in the chain is a very important link. He or she receives, analyzes, edits, and packages the second-hand messages—second hand in the sense that they've passed through the quantitative and/or qualitative measuring instruments. The researcher is the most influential link in the chain of messages. He or she, wittingly and unwittingly, selects accessible messages from the flow of observations, at the bottom, and memories at the top of the PSTs—within the limits of his or her neurological capacity and emotionally anchored premises.

After the message collection phase, the researcher travels to the top of his or her PST and decides not only which of your messages will be fed into the statistical program, but also which statistical program to use. There's an old joke among researchers: *'Somewhere there's a statistical method that will let you get whatever results you want . . . or need.'*

Not only is the message-editing influenced by personal, theoretical, and statistical preferences, but to get the results published, the researcher must accommodate, to some degree, the expectations of the discipline as reflected by a particular journal and its editor. Remember the difficulty Aussie researchers had trying to deliver their message about the cause of ulcers to the North American research establishment. It's hard to sell your wares if people won't open their doors.

Fig 14.1 ■ SCIENCE IS LIKE A NEWS SERVICE

It delivers its news in the form of research reports describing a chain of messengers and edited messages

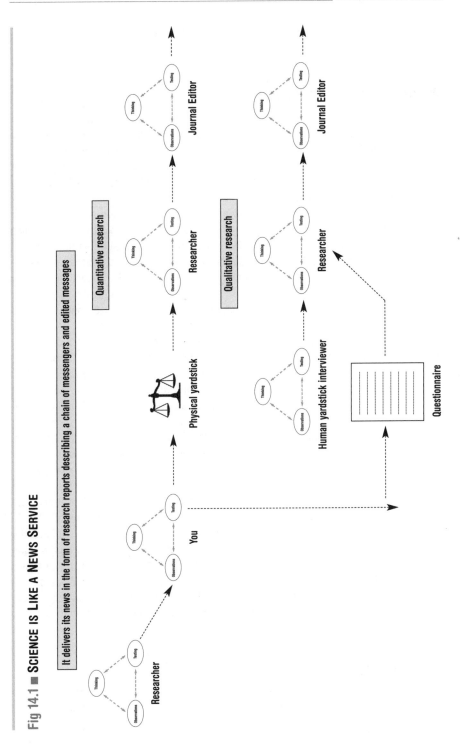

If you keep Figure 14.1 in mind you'll better appreciate, and more easily remember, both the 'what' and the 'why' behind research report writing.

Writing a Research Report

One should always gear one's writing to fit the audience. An article published in *Psychology Today* is going to be very different from a paper published in the *Journal of Experimental Psychology*, because the former is intended for a lay audience while the latter is designed to inform and impress fellow researchers. The rules for popular writing about the social sciences are probably not unlike the rules for accurate journalism, and indeed, most of the interpretations of scientific data for the public are relegated by default to the non-scientist. Taken in the aggregate, scientists are appallingly bad writers—technically unimpeachable but about as interesting as watching paint dry. A typical scientist has an unerring ability to take the most fascinating discovery and milk the intrigue and wonder right out of it, leaving an empty husk behind. Notable exceptions exist, of course, such as Isaac Asimov, B.F. Skinner, J.B. Watson, Margaret Mead, and a few others. Caution, pedantry, and the demands for objectivity, once ingrained, are difficult for most scientists to shed.

The following advice about reports is based in part on the specifications laid out in 2001 by the APA for papers being submitted to its journals. Although originally designed by and for psychologists, the APA model has been adopted by a number of social science disciplines (e.g., anthropology, sociology, nursing, and criminology) and is increasingly becoming an accepted standard format for articles, papers, reports, and texts. This comprehensive document covers virtually all aspects of manuscript preparation from the size of margins to appropriate abbreviations. Additional materials available from the Association intended to assist in mastering the APA style include an *Instructor's Resource Guide* (Gelfand & Walker, 1990a) and a training guide and workbook for students (1990b). These detailed format specifications may appear compulsive and arbitrary—and they are. Their nuisance value, however, is undoubtedly outweighed by the advantages accruing from uniformity. It is much easier to extract information from a report whose organization follows a set pattern. Such an organization, moreover, expedites evaluation of the reports by an editor or professor. Furthermore, in a literature search one can determine the relevance of a piece of research to a particular interest much more rapidly, and can locate the desired information more quickly, in papers that are organized the same way and written in a similar style.

Language and style

A crude autopsy performed on the corpus—research report—reveals that the cause of death is style, not structure; so let us deal with that agent first. The main characteristics of scientific writing style are precision, terseness, and impersonality—all of which combine to produce unambiguous prose. A statement is precise if its implications are eminently clear, that is, if it says one thing and nothing else. To report that the subjects in the study were relatives of the experimenter is not only bad methodology but is also vague. Are they siblings, parents, cousins, or great-aunts? Many statements that pass by unnoticed in the course of normal conversation would be unacceptable in a scientific paper because they are open to a variety of interpretations. Consider your responses and those of a sample of your friends to the following statements and related questions:

- 'Uncle Fred is a moderate smoker.' ▸ How many cigarettes does he smoke in a day?
- 'Senator Fogbound won his seat in the recent election by an overwhelming majority.' ▸ What percentage of the vote did he get?
- 'Ms Simon is a middle-aged woman.' ▸ How old is she?
- 'Aryn read several books last summer.' ▸ How many books did Aryn read?
- 'Kyra bought an inexpensive outfit.' ▸ How much did it cost?

It is apparent that the words *moderate, overwhelming, middle-aged, several*, and *inexpensive* mean different things to different people. Researchers try to avoid ambiguity in their report writing; otherwise their research is not public and shareable, and the scientists find themselves operating at the pragmatic level of language.

A statement is terse if it is economical, if it does not waste words. The aim is to be pithy, to maximize the amount of information per word, and to avoid the kind of redundancy exemplified in this sentence. Since scientists do not have to entertain, but only educate or inform, the need for flowery descriptions is reduced; it is compensated for, to some extent, by the demands of caution. Rarely can researchers make a definitive statement in unequivocal terms about the implications of their findings. The world is filled with reasonable alternative explanations for the same set of data, and even with the admonition to be brief some of those alternatives must be presented for the reader's consideration.

Researchers are increasingly being exhorted to avoid the use of sexist and ethnically biased language. Employment of unbiased, non-sexist language leads to greater precision and avoids inadvertent implicit evaluation. To illustrate the latter, consider the phrase 'culturally deprived'. Use of this term to describe one group of research participants (without supporting data) suggests that there is a universally accepted cultural standard against which others are judged. Similarly, reference to a society as 'primitive' is not only imprecise but also carries a negative connotation.

The most common form of sexist language is found in the inappropriate use of generic nouns and pronouns (e.g., use of 'man' to mean humans or persons or males and females, 'mailman' instead of letter carrier, 'he' to mean he and she, etc.). Generic forms are frequently inaccurate and create ambiguity with regard to the referent. APA recommends the use of plural forms or 'he or she'. Other variants of the sexist use of language occur with non-parallel constructions (e.g., man and wife, instead of husband and wife) and stereotypic depictions (e.g., an aggressive business man and a pushy business woman). Several additional examples of sexist language are presented in Chapter 15.

Accuracy is the mainstay of scientific writing. Slavish adherence to the rules of format (i.e., organization of the research report) and meticulous avoidance of slang, fuzzy terms, sexist language and the like, are no compensation for imprecision or the misuse of terms or conceptual confusion. The following examples have been taken from student reports and illustrate the often humorous but totally inappropriate use of the language. See if you can identify the nature of the problem(s) in these examples.[2]

1. Low levels of androgens in the mother lead to feminism in the male fetus.
2. The main cause of memory loss is brain failure.
3. Spinster muscles help to move food through the digestive tract.
4. When birds are deciding to migrate, they must weigh the costs and benefits.

Structure

In addition to stylistic qualities, most scientific writing shares a number of structural features. In psychology the typical research paper consists of the following sections appearing in the order listed: title, author's name and institutional affiliation, *abstract, introduction, method, results, discussion, references*, and when appropriate, an *appendix*. Each of the main content sections is described in more detail below. Other disciplines may employ a slightly different format, which can be revealed by a quick look through a few recent periodicals.

Abstract

The abstract is written mainly for the benefit of the researcher who is scanning the literature in search of information germane to his or her work. It is most helpful, therefore, if the abstract is brief and summarizes the study accurately. Resemblance of the abstract to the main text is essential, not coincidental; the abstract is a faithful summary of the report—it should not include any new material.

The abstract should describe the hypothesis, together with a brief description of the variables under investigation. The apparatus or measurement devices should be alluded to, and the procedure should be described in general terms. The results and their evaluation should be summarized briefly, while the conclusions based upon them should be listed in more detail.

---

[2]We thank Professor Tony Nield of York University, Toronto, for these examples.

Introduction

The introduction should outline the purpose of the research and describe, in general terms, the nature of the problem under study. A few closely related previous experiments should be cited, and any findings directly pertinent to the study should be described. Any expectations, biases, or predictions you have about how the study will turn out, whether derived from past research, a theory, or a personal hunch, should be specified and a rationale should be provided.

Method

The method portion of a research paper is typically subdivided into three units: (1) participants or subjects, (2) apparatus and materials, and (3) procedure. This section is analogous to recipe instructions. The method section clearly describes what was done and how it was done. It is the empirical cornerstone of your work.

Subjects

This label does not refer to the issues covered by your study, but rather to the people, animals, or organizations that participated—who provided you with the information to answer your initial question. To bake this research cake, the following ingredients in varying amounts are required:

1. How many subjects or participants are in your sample?
2. What are the characteristics of your sample on relevant variables (sex, age, socioeconomic class, diagnosis, education, organizational sizes)?
3. How did you obtain your sample (by asking for volunteers, conscripting friends, etc.)?
4. If you divided your subjects into groups, on what basis was this done (at random, by age, etc.)?
5. How many subjects are in each group?
6. How many potential subjects were contacted in total?
7. How many refused to participate?

It is also important to note adherence to ethical principles in the treatment of the subjects (see Chapter 13).

Apparatus and/or materials

A brief description of each piece of apparatus employed should be presented, but if the apparatus has been described in the literature then a reference to this description will suffice. If you have specially constructed apparatus, use a labelled diagram or photograph. Include a brief description of each kind of material employed (questionnaires, tests, inventories, tasks, drawings, photographs, etc.). The identification of those tests or tasks constitutes the operational definition of the dependent measure. If you are measuring student perceptions of academic climates, you may operationalize the chilly climate concept by employing a scale specifically designed for this purpose (Janz & Pyke, 2000). For certain kinds of reports (theses, but not manuscripts), a copy or example of each type of material should be presented in an appendix. To continue the cookbook analogy, this section of your report refers to the designated oven heat, kind of cake pan, and so on.

Procedure

In this section of the report, instructions are provided for the treatment of the ingredients (fold in the egg whites; boil the syrup mixture until it forms a hard ball; mix at medium speed for two minutes). Describe what you did with your subjects in sufficient detail so that someone unfamiliar to the discipline could duplicate it exactly. One approach is to describe what happened chronologically as the typical subjects performed in the study.

Everything that was done that might *reasonably* have had a bearing on the outcome of a study should be mentioned. While it is probably unnecessary to inform the reader of the experimenter's clothing, other unprogrammed events may be very relevant. Consider, for example, the following project. A study was being conducted to determine the effects of arousal (administration of shock) on speed of recognition of unfamiliar words. In order to ensure that the subjects were actually aroused, heart rate was continuously monitored. To obtain heart rate recordings, electrodes were strapped to each leg. As the male subjects entered the laboratory, they were instructed by a glamorous female experimenter to 'Please roll up your pants and pull down your socks,' in order to prepare for the electrode placement. After about 150 repetitions of these instructions, the experimenter thoughtlessly misspoke, 'Roll up your socks and pull down your pants, please.' Experimenter and subjects alike were of little research value for the next few minutes. This event could well have influenced the performance of this particular group of participants. Subject instructions should be paraphrased in the procedure and quoted verbatim in an appendix, if an appendix is permitted.

Results

Describe how you scored and analyzed your data. Present the results of your significant analyses in clearly labelled tables or figures. Describe each result verbally, but do not repeat information that is already provided in tables or graphs. Analyses that do not yield statistically significant results should be mentioned, but tables illustrating such non-significant findings are typically omitted or placed in an appendix.

Discussion

The results are interpreted in relation to the problem under investigation in the discussion section of the report. Some reference should be made to their reliability, and their limitations should be explained. Aspects of the procedure that might profitably be changed if the study were repeated should be mentioned. Uncontrolled and/or confounded variables should be identified if possible, and ways of avoiding them on subsequent occasions should be suggested. Also, something should be said about the extent to which the results correspond with the predictions and about their agreement or disagreement with the results of previous similar experiments, as well as about their integration with relevant theory. Finally, indicate what conclusions you can draw on the basis of your study and what the practical implications of your results are.

References

In order to report your references correctly, you need to be a trifle compulsive while doing your research. The rules and rituals associated with this component of scientific writing tend to be 'nit-picky'. References are listed alphabetically according to the author's surname. The year of publication (in brackets), and the title of the article, chapter, or book then follows the author's or authors' names; then the source of the item (periodical name and volume number) is provided. For more detailed information about the appropriate format required for listing various types of references (e.g., edited books, journal articles, paper presentations, etc.), refer to the *Publication Manual* (5th edition, 2001) of the APA. References cited in the body of the report require only author identification and year of publication at the point in the text where the reference is made. To illustrate, 'Anderson (2007) found that . . . ', or 'It was found that . . . (Anderson, 2007).'

Appendix

As a crude rule of thumb, the appendix should include any materials which, while important, are not crucial to a general understanding of the study and which, if included in the main body of the report, would be distracting to the reader. Students conducting a research project to fulfill a thesis requirements are typically encouraged to err on the side of over-inclusion and provide copies of all tests, questionnaires, and exercises, as well as tables of mean scores for every measure. In extreme cases a supervisor may even request the incorporation of raw data. Manuscripts prepared for publication in a journal, on the other hand, rarely include an appendix.

Publication Pollution

Like the spread of dandelions, the social science literature proliferates at an alarming rate. The pressure to publish, as a means of attaining job security, status, or even a form of immortality, plagues us all. To cope with the burgeoning mass of articles, new journals are spawned, and into their hungry maws pour tons of tasty manuscripts. PsycINFO is the database for abstracts of published articles with psychological content; the print version of the database appears in *Psychological Abstracts*. Currently, a total of 2,120 journals are reviewed. If each volume of a journal contains about 35 articles that have psychological relevance then almost 75,000 psychology articles are published annually. And we haven't even mentioned the book or thesis markets (see http://www.apa.org/psycinfo/about.colist.html).

Quality control becomes a critical problem under these conditions. Journal editors, who are far from infallible, are ill equipped to deal with the multitude of papers that arrive daily. Most sophisticated researchers are aware that a negative judgment about publication from one journal doesn't automatically mean rejection from others. A rejected manuscript is typically shipped off, often without revision, to the next most prestigious periodical, until publication is attained.

From the point of view of the reader, this cancerous body of literature is overwhelming. What a puerile hope it is to keep abreast of new developments in the field! What an idyllic fancy to assume that key studies, the classic papers, will be easy to identify! Naturally, mechanisms to assist the harassed researcher have emerged. Special journals provide summaries of articles (*Psychological Abstracts, Dissertation Abstracts*), reviews of current research (*Annual Review of Psychology*), reviews of recent texts (*Contemporary Psychology*), theme issues that review the literature on a given topic (*Psychological Review, Psychological Bulletin*). Additionally, computer programs now permit extremely rapid searches of selected literature for specific content areas and spew out abstracts of all articles caught in the scan. As a function of the information overload, scientists must rely increasingly on summaries of research and on secondary sources.

How can we manage this information overload? Perhaps we should propose a kind of eugenics program urging non-publication of 50 per cent of the social science labour force—selected at random, of course. Or maybe there is a technological device that would be more effective—every second article self-destructs after five years. Or only a random sample of submitted, acceptable manuscripts would be published. More realistically, but smacking of censorship, a central clearinghouse co-ordinating all publication vehicles might prevent the shopping around for acceptance by the repeatedly rejected manuscripts described earlier. But under such a radical scheme, we might have missed the contributions of Einstein and Skinner. In the absence of any of these radical procedures, you might pause and consider before adding your personal building blocks to the tower of Babel. Then, add only your 'best' blocks.

SUMMARY

Like a recipe, a research report rests on clarity of procedure and reliability of results. The cornerstone of the research report is the *method* section where the researcher describes—in unambiguous terms—the subjects, apparatus or materials, and procedure. The acid test becomes: 'Are my instructions so clear that another investigator can duplicate my procedure?' Did you ask a 'significant' question? Did you obtain 'important' results? Only time will tell.

student's notebook

Guess what our assignment is for this chapter? We're conducting a research project and writing it up according to professional standards.

Three of us decided to work together and, after much discussion, we decided do investigate extra-sensory perception (ESP). When we told Professor Creek his eyebrows disappeared! Maybe they're still hiding up at the top of his PST!

The main message we all learned from this chapter was to write our report in such a way that if other researchers wanted to exactly repeat our study they could. Of course, they could only do that if the description of our procedure was very precise. Apparently that's easier said than done, because you never know what innocuous bit of behaviour may turn out to influence the research results. Creek told us that when he was a graduate student they used to wander around with their favourite rats in their pockets, fondling them. Then some researcher showed that fondled rats behave differently from non-fondled rats in maze learning studies. So you're never sure when something incidental that you're doing or maybe wearing may turn out to influence your rats, or the billiard balls with brains, and therefore may be a significant in-the-gap variable.

We started with our up-top premises. In the beginning the group had one strong non-believer, one strong believer (me!), and one undecided member.

At the end of our study, I still believed, the non-believer still didn't believe, and the undecided person had come around to my way of thinking. For a little while, anyway. After another discussion she reverted back to being undecided—some temporary elasticity in her up top premise.

Here's our research report.

ESP Ability among Believers and Non-believers
By Diana Dodds, for Research Methods 201

Abstract

Using Zener cards extrasensory ability was compared between five couples who believed they possessed extrasensory powers and five couples who did not. While there was no clear difference between believers and non-believers, there was a trend that favoured believers, some of which was due to cheating.

Introduction

This pilot study was designed to explore the hypothesis that people who believe they possess extrasensory perception (ESP) obtain a higher number of 'hits' in a standard ESP test situation than do non-believers.

Rhine and Pratt (1957) report some evidence that believers perform better than nonbelievers. However, there are major problems with much of the evidence supporting the reality of ESP.

First, much of the evidence is anecdotal and based on 'after-the-fact' information and so it is open to the usual criticism aimed at this primitive research method. For example, a person will hear that a relative died and then recall that they had dreamed about that person the night before. Such evidence is open to serious question because believers are probably more likely to report such incidents than non-believers and perhaps may even be more inclined, unwittingly, to create or modify memories designed to support the cause for ESP. Also, such after-the-fact data fail to include the 'false-positives'—that is, the number of occasions when you dreamed a relative was ill and in fact was not.

Finally, much of the evidence or data is vague enough to be interpreted several ways. For example, if you dream there is 'something wrong' with a relative and then check to see if he or she is having trouble, you can usually find that he or she is, because everybody always has some trouble.

In view of the many difficulties involved in interpreting after-the-fact data about ESP, this study uses the more powerful control-group model to compare ESP performance among believers and non-believers.

Method

Subjects

The participants in this study were volunteers from an introductory psychology class: 10 claimed to be believers in ESP because of personal experience with it and 10 claimed to be non-believers with no personal ESP experience. One member of each pair was designated, at random, as the sender and the other as the receiver of the purported ESP message.

Materials

The test materials were standard Zener cards used at Duke University specifically for ESP research. Each card has one of five geometric figures printed on it; the deck consists of 25 cards, with each figure appearing five times in random order.

Procedure

Each pair of believers and each pair of non-believers completed 50 ESP trials. Believer and non-believer pairs were tested alternately so that the 'four rogue suspects' (Agnew & Pyke, 2007) would not favour one group over another. The procedure for each pair of participants was as follows:

1. The sender was seated in one room and the receiver, out of sight, in an adjoining room with an experimenter present in each room.
2. The experimenter in the sender room shuffled the deck of Zener cards and, without looking at it, handed the top card to the sender, who concentrated on the geometric figure appearing on it for 15 seconds. A bell signaled the end of this period.
3. At the sound of the bell, the receiver indicated on the report sheet which of the five symbols he or she believed was being sent. The card was returned to the experimenter who recorded which one it was on the record sheet, then reinserted it into the deck and reshuffled the deck. This procedure was repeated until 50 such trials had been completed, after which the number of hits was calculated. The participants were informed of the results and all were thanked for their co-operation. During the trials there was no visual contact between the sender and the receiver; experimenters were on the lookout for any sound signals the sender might be using. The sender was instructed not to speak during the trials.

Results

Table 14.1 represents the number of hits out of the 50 trials obtained by each pair of believers and by each pair of non-believers. Since each receiver has a one-fifth chance of being right on any given guess by chance alone, we would expect the average receiver, without ESP ability, to make approximately 10 hits. According to Guilford (1965), 16 or more hits would rarely occur by lucky guessing—it would occur only 5 times in 100 tests like ours. As can be seen, only Pair 3 among the believers reached this significant level of performance; they achieved 19 hits. Pair 5 among the non-believers approached this significant level with 14 hits.

Table 14.1   Number of Hits Out of 50 Trials for Believing and Non-believing Pairs in an ESP Study

Subject Pairs	Believers	Non-believers
Pair 1	11	8
Pair 2	9	10
Pair 3	19	7
Pair 4	12	11
Pair 5	11	14
Total	**62**	**50**

Overall, the believers achieved more hits than the non-believers did.

Discussion

While this pilot study provided no conclusive evidence in support of the hypothesis that believers possess more ESP ability than non-believers, it *appeared* to provide a bit of encouraging evidence. One pair of believers did perform significantly better than we would have expected by chance alone, and the overall trend favoured the believers.

In ESP studies questions concerning unwitting sensory signaling arise, as do questions of cheating. During the experiment no evidence of either was detected.

However, after the experiment was completed, it was disclosed that the high-scoring pair of subjects had, in fact, cheated. The cheating pair used a disarmingly simple plan based on the sender arriving at the experiment coughing and blowing his nose. Therefore the experimenters were not suspicious when he coughed and blew his nose periodically during the experiment. By prior agreement when a particular geometric figure appeared, he would merely cough, thus signalling to the receiver that the figure was before him. Consequently, the receiver got all appearances of that card correct, plus another 9 hits by lucky guessing, giving him an unusually large and significant score. While this deception led to some bitterness, it served to underline the care that must be taken in interpreting experimental results, particularly when the experimenters themselves are believers.

References

Agnew, N.McK., & Pyke, S.W. (2007). *The science game: An introduction to research in the behavioral sciences* (7th ed.) Don Mills, ON: Oxford Press.

Guilford, J.P. (1965). *Fundamental statistics in psychology and education*. New York: McGraw-Hill.

Pitman, J.A., & Owens, N.E. (2004). The effect of manipulating expectations both before and during a test of ESP. *Journal of Parapsychology, 3*, 22.

Rhine, J.G., & Pratt, J.G. (1957). *Para-psychology*. Springfield, IL: Chas. C Thomas.

Professor Creek included the following comments when he returned our graded report:

Instructor's Comments: This is an interesting pilot study in which you introduced yourselves to the topic of ESP and gained a feel for some of the problems and possibilities involved in testing for ESP effects.

Some of the terms used in the introduction require more detailed elaboration. For example, what is the definition of a 'hit'? Also, there seems to be an assumption in the introduction that there is no question about the existence of ESP. You should have indicated that this is still an open question and you should have cited additional references.

Your experimental procedures suggest that ESP can be turned on and off, like a tap, in 15-second spurts. Is that how you conceive it? Was it significant that the experimenter did not know which symbol was being sent? Why?

Learn not to waste data-gathering opportunities. You could have had the sender and the receiver reverse roles for another 50 trials without appreciably increasing your experimental workload but resulting in doubling your data base and also allowing individual differences among senders and receivers to express themselves.

Your bitterness over 'cheating' by two of your subjects is understandable. Deception of subjects by experimenters is commonplace, and we can probably expect increasing incidents of counter-deception by participants. Either way, and as you have discovered first-hand, deception raises important methodological and ethical issues. The cheating subjects should have been replaced, their data omitted from your table, and they should have been only mentioned in a footnote.

Well, Creek was relatively gentle. Or maybe he had one of his graduate students grade our papers.

The thing that most jerked my chain was having two of the research participants cheat. After the all stuff we've covered on fraud you would have thought that we would have been on the lookout. But all the ethics stuff focused on 'hanky panky' by scientists, not by research participants!

Note

Check out 'natural born liars' on the student website at http://www.oup.com/ca/he/companion/agnewpyke.

REVIEW TRUE OR FALSE QUIZ

T F	1. Scientific journal articles tend to follow a more or less consistent organizational pattern.
T F	2. The APA has developed a comprehensive, standardized set of rules for the preparation of manuscripts.

T F	3.	Scientific writing style is characterized by a significant degree of ambiguous prose.
T F	4.	Approximations of quantity (e.g., several, moderate, overwhelming) are helpful descriptors of empirical data in scientific reports.
T F	5.	Use of plural forms is recommended to replace the use of generic pronouns.
T F	6.	An abstract summarizes a report but may also include new material.
T F	7.	Predictions or hypotheses are typically presented in the 'Method' section of a report.
T F	8.	A literature review typically appears in the 'Results' section of a research report.
T F	9.	Researchers typically provide information about the time of day testing occurred, temperature in the laboratory, and details concerning the appearance of the experimenter in the 'Procedure' section of their reports.
T F	10.	All analyses, both statistically significant and non-significant, must be presented in the 'Results' section of the report.
T F	11.	In the 'Discussion' section of a report, the results of the study are interpreted in relation to the problem under investigation.
T F	12.	Scientists increasingly rely on secondary sources.
T F	13.	One reason for writing a research report in great detail is to allow other scientists to evaluate the work and to repeat the study if they choose.
T F	14.	With reference to Diana's study on ESP, Diana was a non-believer.
T F	15.	Diana and her collaborators used Zener cards to test ESP ability.
T F	16.	It was discovered that none of the believers performed significantly better than expected by chance alone.

Wide Angle Views of Sex and Science

The first chapter of Section 7, 'Sex and Science', explores how the social sciences have handled sex. As you'll soon see, it's been at a distance. Everyone has heard the saying 'Children should be seen and not heard.' Social scientists, until relatively recently, behaved as if women should neither be seen nor heard. Not only were they left out of most studies but to add insult to injury, it was also presumed that women were inferior to men on many dimensions.

In the second chapter, 'The Truth Spinners', we take a wide-angle view of social science theory and research as we stand on our tiptoes and attempt to peek into the future.

15

Sex and Science

Chapter Goal

- To illustrate the top down influence of a particular set of emotionally anchored beliefs on the whole of the scientific enterprise—on all three corners of the PST.

Introduction

Given our bounded rationality and the need to traverse a vast landscape with only a few observational stepping-stones we must rely on our emotionally anchored beliefs at the top of our PSTs to guide us as we stride into the unknown. Such beliefs (necessarily oversimplified) provide us with a measure of confidence, however ill founded that confidence may be. A particularly ubiquitous set of trusted beliefs—assumptions, theories, preconceptions, biases, prejudices, stereotypes—relate to the nature of males and females and to why men and women think, feel, and act as they do. The theoretical conceptions associated with these views are so widespread and exportable that, unfortunately, they appear to possess a global passport.

In this chapter we describe how this belief system has permeated every nook and cranny of the science game. But before tackling this task, we need to be a little more specific about the details of this believing-is-seeing model. What thoughts about sex and science emerge as you scoot to the top of your PST: the Masters and Johnson Report?, the identification of genes on the XX and XY chromosomes?, the hunter/gatherer societal system?, the assumption that men have a stronger sex drive than women? Try to dig a bit deeper to reveal the bedrock.

If we start with the premise that we live in a patriarchal society, and if we rely on Simon's mantra, a number of conclusions follow.

Technically, the phrase 'patriarchal society' refers to a form of social organization marked by the supremacy of the father in the clan or family, the legal dependence of wives and children, and the reckoning of decent and inheritance in the male line. More generally, patriarchy refers to the superior position, power, or status accorded to the male members of the society. The majority of organized religions, for example, clearly reflect a patriarchal orientation. Corollaries of this proposition include:

1. that males and females differ on most variables,
2. that these differences have a biological origin (i.e., they are natural and immutable),
3. that the differences are hierarchically ordered and the position of males on these dimensions is regarded as superior to that of females,
4. that males represent the norm or standard against which females are compared,
5. that in those allegedly rare instances where females outperform males, the ability or trait in question is of less importance, of lower value; or, the superior performance of females is probably due to chance, and furthermore, because it is so rare, is a glaring exception that proves the rule.

Evidence is rapidly accumulating that the first assumption lacks empirical support. Maccoby and Jacklin (1974) reviewed about 1,600 studies published between 1966 and 1973 that involved male/female comparisons and concluded that good evidence for gender differences existed in only four areas in the psychological domain: aggression, spatial ability, mathematical ability, and verbal ability. They found that superior verbal ability occurs more frequently in girls, whereas aggression and superior visual/spatial and mathematical abilities occur more frequently in boys.

Janet Hyde (1981), utilizing a more sophisticated statistical technique for summating studies (meta-analysis), reviewed the research on which the Maccoby and Jacklin conclusions were based (excluding studies on aggression). Parenthetically it should be noted that meta-analysis is a statistical method for aggregating research findings across many studies examining the same research question. Hyde found that sex differences in verbal ability, visual/spatial ability, and mathematical ability account for no more than 1–5 per cent of the population variance. So, although these differences are statistically reliable and replicable, they are so small that they lack conceptual or practical significance. In other words, the scores of the two groups overlap almost completely.

Did this evidence, and a host of similar articles, put the gender differences hypothesis to rest? Not at all! Research on this topic has continued unabated. More than 26,000 sex and gender comparison studies were published between 1974 and 1995 (Favreau, 1997). And, the popularity of John Gray's 1992 book, *Men Are from Mars, Women Are from Venus*, which, as of 2003, sold more than 11 million copies in the US and has been published in 38 languages, attests to the fact that the differences hypothesis is flourishing in the public arena (Crawford, 2001; http://www.wayneandtamara.com/johngray.htm).

Very recently, Hyde (2005) published a major review of 46 meta-analyses involving over 100 comparisons of male and female performance derived from more than 6,600 reports. The many indices investigated included mathematics anxiety, spatial ability, talkativeness, smiling, aggression, leadership effectiveness, self-esteem, activity level, cheating, and computer use. Seventy-eight per cent of the gender differences on the myriad variables examined are small or close to zero and hence are of no practical importance. Virtually no support was found for many of the alleged male/female differences underlying the prevalent stereotypes. A few examples of large gender differences were found on measures of motor performance such as throwing distance and throwing velocity, and on some measures of sexuality (attitudes about sex in casual relationships; incidences of masturbation). Clearly, according to Hyde's review, males and females are far more alike than they are different. Indeed, the bottom line with respect to the study of sex differences might well be that never has so much been said by so many about so little.

What is most intriguing is the resilience of the androcentric model. In spite of a multitude of studies spanning three decades supporting the gender similarities hypothesis, the gender differences model is still alive and well. But what is problematic is not that differences exist. After all, there are always differences within individuals and between individuals. The stumbling blocks arise from the remaining propositions of the patriarchal model. Differences which are chiseled in stone (cannot be altered) are hierarchically structured, and in a patriarchal system, males define the 'right', 'appropriate', 'natural', 'correct', 'preferred', or, 'prototypic' position on any difference dimension. Thus, the patriarchal model serves the valuable social function of maintaining privilege for males while engendering serious costs for females. Overthrowing an established, emotionally anchored and institutionally ingrained theory is no easy task.

Meredith Kimball (1995; 2001) makes a strong case that we should continue to explore the similarities and differences both between and among women and men. She argues that gender differences exist on many levels—symbolic, discursive, institutional, interpersonal and individual—and these differences interact with power, authority, and influence, which are linked to male and masculine. A focus on either similarities or differences inevitably leads to an oversimplified partial vision of reality. She recognizes, however, the difficulty of deconstructing hierarchically dichotomies.

But how does all this relate to the science game?

Perspectives on Science

We have tried to make the case that, with a few rare exceptions, we arrive at quick and dirty solutions for the bulk of our problem-solving efforts. Our observational dots are typically spotty, vague, and sparse, and so we fill in the gaps and interconnect the dots relying on the mostly unquestioned but fallible beliefs residing at the top of our PSTs. However, the practice of science is typically portrayed as one of those rare exceptions providing a rational route to the truth. The scientific method and its various refinements are intended to help us avoid leaping to premature conclusions and to protect us from irrationality, emotionality, and subjectivity. And who is best equipped to play the science game? Why males, of course. Patriarchal values assert that male minds are uniquely capable of the logical, rational, objective thought required for scientific pursuits. Above all, emotional detachment—freedom from emotional anchors—is touted as the quintessential element in scientific pursuits and an implicit rule in the science game. Therefore, the stereotype of women as being emotional fosters their exclusion from the centre stage of science. The distinction between the passive object studied (nature) and the active agent or investigator (the scientist) also presents the heroic image of science as a conquering, masculine endeavour.

Most importantly, the objectivity principle implies an immunity or protection from the social, political, and economic influences of society. The scientist—by virtue of natural inclinations or talents (rational mind), training (in habits of thought, critical analysis, and so forth), and appropriate use of scientific methods, techniques, and strategies—presumably produces research that is free from the distorting influence of cultural values, mores, stereotypes, and similar factors. Ideally such research should yield 'pure', or absolute, truth; truth that is uncontaminated by the cultural biases of the scientist or the scientist's society. This conception of science—the seeing is believing model—is known as logical positivism; the truth or reality is independent of the investigator and properly conducted (i.e., objective) research will reveal it. Wilkinson (2001) calls this approach positivist empiricism and defines the criteria for good positivist empirical research as including 'the objectivity of the researcher, the standardization of measures, and the replicability and generalizability of findings' (18).

Critics of this position such as Fee (1976; 1981) argue that society generates the type of scientific knowledge that best fulfills its social, economic, and political needs, valid or not. Kuhn (1970) similarly suggests that our values and biases shape our knowledge of nature more than our objective observations or our rationality.[1] Shields (1975), in a scathing indictment, contends that scientific empiricism does little more than provide a justification for prevailing social values and, in a similar vein, Pyke (1982) implies that prevailing ideologies produce supporting empiricism. Bleier (1984) summarizes this position:

> Science is *not* the neutral, dispassionate, value-free pursuit of Truth
> . . . scientists are not objective, disinterested, or culturally disengaged from the questions they ask of nature or the methods they use to frame their answers. It is, furthermore, impossible for science or scientists to be otherwise, since science is a social

---

[1]For a sophisticated critique of Kuhn's model see Kuhn vs Popper (Fuller, 2003).

activity and a cultural product created by persons who live in the world of science as well as in the societies that bred them (1984: 193).

These authors all argue that the believing-is-seeing orientation is much more reflective of the way the science game is played in the social sciences than is logical positivism. This conception of science—known as social constructionism—posits that investigators 'do not discover independently existing facts through objective observation; rather, they construct knowledge that is influenced by the social context of their inquiry' (Lips, 2006: 47). 'Social constructionists argue that we cannot "know" the external world through observation and measurement (as positivist empiricists contend) or the internal world through reflective introspection or careful listening (as experiential researchers contend) because all knowledge is mediated by—indeed constructed through—the specificities of language' (Wilkinson, 2001: 24).

A third perspective on science is the essentialist position (Crawford, 2001). Proponents of this position accept the first proposition of the patriarchal model that females and males differ but they invert the hierarchical structure and instead argue that it is women, not men, who are superior. According to this orientation, certain characteristics or qualities (e.g., interpersonal sensitivity; unassertive speech style) lie within the person and are an essential part of that person's unique identity. This orientation, sometimes termed the experiential approach (Wilkinson, 2001), stems from philosopher Sandra Harding's standpoint theory: 'Women see the world from a particular perspective, or standpoint, because of the experience of being a woman in a patriarchal world. . . . Knowledge is seen as contingent upon the standpoint of the knower, and as dependent upon the specificities of her experience' (Wilkinson, 2001: 21). This approach has resonated with some feminists to affirm the validity of women's voices and their lived experience, to challenge the male monopoly on truth, and to give positive valence to women's undervalued qualities. Critics argue, however, that an essentialist orientation ignores the diversity among women, and further, that a focus on gender differences may be politically dangerous because any difference may be interpreted as women's inadequacy or deficiency.

Sexism in Science

Evidence of the influence and maintenance of the patriarchal model can be found in the underlying symbolism reflected in science, in the role of women in science, in the history of science, in the topics studied, in preferred research participant samples, in conclusions and inferences derived from research, in language usage, in selection of experimental tasks, in statistics and publication practices, and in theory. Examples of such impacts are briefly presented below.

Science and symbolism

At first blush, science seems to be one of the few human enterprises relatively devoid of sexual connotations. After all, science is touted as the objective search for truth (with a capital T). Scientists, as neutral and dispassionate observers, have no time for the ardor, passion, romanticism, and political polemics permeating other less lofty pursuits. Yet from another perspective, scientists do not so much discover truth as they construct it. Constructed truths (believing is seeing) are manufactured from the values and ideologies of the host society that reside at the top of our PSTs. And given that a patriarchal ideology has guided our society for the past 6,000 years, perhaps we should not be too surprised to learn that the influence of sex on science has been more ubiquitous and invidious than anyone would have supposed.

Science studies nature—physical and human nature—and there has always been a sexual dimension in human thought about nature (Merchant, 1980). In conventional mythology, nature is typically identified as female. Beyond the simple sex label, science eroticizes nature by conceptualizing her as being hidden, enclosed, and having secrets. The role of science, then, is to denude nature, to rip away her veils, to disclose her secrets. In this sense, science appears both voyeuristic and exploitative.

Linnaeus's (1707–78) classification scheme for plants reflects the eroticization of nature in science (Shteir, 1996). Of the myriad characteristics of plants that might be employed to develop a taxonomy, Linnaeus chose the stamens and pistils, the sexual parts of plants. Lascivious descriptions of Linnaeus's system appeared in the scientific literature of the day—a pansy depicted as a loose woman with petals gaping wantonly, pollen presented as titillating dust. Some scientists even attributed deviant sexual desires to women who were interested in botany.

In addition to science's erotic symbolism of nature, science also seeks to control her as she is unpredictable, wild, tumultuous, and potentially destructive. The parallel with the patriarchal view of the need to control females is obvious.

Women's role in science

If you are prepared to accept (or even entertain) the assertions that the common form of social structure of humans in modern history is patriarchy, that ideologies vis-à-vis women and men in patriarchal social systems postulate a subordinate position for women, and that the processes and products of science are heavily influenced by this ideology, then the fringe participation of women in science is easily understood.

Until recently, females were not welcome in mainstream science, into what was seen as an appropriately male activity. Historically, however, women have been very involved on the scientific sidelines. For example, women frequently served as helpmates to scientist husbands, fathers, or brothers. Carl Linnaeus's wife, Prudence, played an essential role in furthering his career by editing his work and handling his voluminous correspondence. Women also served on the fringes of science as 'popularizers' (that is, writing science books for children) and as illustrators. Many women were active amateur scientists, particularly in the fields of botany, geology, and astronomy. Some women practiced medicine both as midwives and as local experts with specialized knowledge of the medicinal properties of plants (Shteir, 1996).

For the most part, though, women were excluded from institutionalized science. As science professionalized itself through the use of Latin and the demand for particular formal education credentials, it became increasingly difficult for women to gain a foothold in this prestigious and exclusive occupation. Indeed, it was not until after the Second World War that the Royal Society was prepared to admit female members (Yount, 1999). And even after this recognition, important scientific contributions by women continued to go unrecognized. Consider the discovery of the double helical structure of DNA. James Watson, along with Crick and Wilkins, won the Nobel Prize for this work in 1962. Rosalind Franklin's unpublished crystallographic images of DNA, reportedly pirated from her locked desk without her knowledge and used by Watson and his colleagues, had direct relevance to untangling the mysteries of DNA, yet her key contribution was never acknowledged (Sayre, 1975).

Kite, Russo, Brehm, Fouad, Hall, Hyde, and Keita (2001) offer a more contemporary perspective. Reviewing the status of women psychologists in academe, they report continuing inequities in the representation of women in full-time faculty positions, in rank and tenure, in compensation, and in top leadership positions. Barriers to success include the accumulated effect of micro-inequities, negative evaluations of female leaders, and gender biases in the classroom.

And, as recently as 2005, Harvard President Larry Summers questioned women's aptitude for high-level science. As evidence, Summers noted the significant disparities that exist between women and men in science despite the increasing presence of women in science. Such disparities—including the higher rate of attrition for women scientists—would seem related more to the particular characteristics of the academic environment, which leads to lowered job satisfaction, productivity, and influence, than to any gender-based differential in aptitude. In a survey of over 200 women scientists with faculty positions, Settles, Cortina, Malley, and Stewart (2006) found that both the personal experience of sexual harassment and gender discrimination, and general perception of a chilly academic climate, have a negative impact on job outcomes (see also Janz & Pyke, 2000; Pyke, 2005). On the other hand, perceptions of a generally positive, non-sexist climate, as well as effective leadership, were related to positive job outcomes.

Historical examples

Sir Francis Galton (1822–1911), considered the father of the modern study of sex differences, was firmly wedded to the patriarchal view that females were inferior to males, not only in terms of physical traits such as strength, but also in terms of their powers of discrimination. Because he believed that sensory discriminatory ability was a valid indicator of intelligence, females were judged to be mentally deficient (Buss, 1976). Galton did not confine himself to passing judgment on alleged sex differences in the physical, sensory, and ability realms; he also made some pungent remarks about personality differences. He regarded women as coy, capricious, and less straightforward than men, subject to petty deceits and allied weaknesses. It will be no surprise to learn that Galton was a member of the British Anti-Suffrage Society.

Stephanie Shields (1975) provided another example of how the accepted doctrine of female inferiority influenced the scientific establishment. Sex differences in the localization of functions in the brain seemed a promising avenue of research. Initially, the frontal lobes were believed to be the seat of the higher functions (for example, abstract reasoning), and it was 'discovered' that males had larger frontal areas whereas females had larger parietal areas. Later, when the parietal region was thought to play a significant role in the higher functions, science reversed itself. It was then 'discovered' that males had larger parietal areas whereas females had larger frontal areas. Here we have a clear instance of empirical findings tracking dominant social values.

More contemporary examples exist illustrating the evolution of evidence. Although females had long been thought to have superior verbal skills, Hyde and Linn (cited in Matlin, 1993) conducted a meta-analysis on gender differences in verbal ability and found virtually no overall difference between the sexes (an average d value of 0.11). However, they discovered that studies conducted before 1974 yielded larger gender differences than the more recent research. Have males improved their verbal competencies or have females lost some of their edge? Or both? Or, is this yet another instance of cultural mores influencing empiricism?

Content

Bias may also be reflected in the questions asked, the research topics studied, or the resources available for research. For example, most funding for cardiovascular research is targeted at understanding predisposing factors for men yet once women reach menopause the incidence of heart disease is the same. Certain topics are under-researched because they pertain especially to women (e.g., maternity, menstruation, menopause, pregnancy, nurturance, dysmenorrhea, incontinency in older women, feminist therapy), and therefore are not regarded as important as issues that are more relevant to men (Denmark, 1994). Although she notes considerable progress as compared with a 1983 review, Denmark reports that the issue of gender bias on research was an obvious gap in the topics covered in a 1993 study of 20 textbooks. Similarly, Rabinowitz and Martin (2001) comment that the fourth edition of the *Handbook of Social Psychology* is remarkably devoid of references to sex and gender issues.

Subject selection

Although preference for male subjects in social science research in the past has been well documented (Carlson and Carlson, 1960; Carlson, 1971), more recent reviews have revealed some improvement. Gannon, Luchetta, Rhodes, Pardie, and Segrist (1992), however, argue that it is too early to be complacent. In two of the eight journals they reviewed (a total sample of almost 5,000 articles), the mean percentages of 'male only' samples continued to be high, as was the number of instances where the sex of participants was unspecified. Failing to include female research participants means that we are relatively ignorant about how females would perform under these various research conditions. However, the problem is even more insidious because studies employing all male samples are more likely to generalize to the opposite sex than those utilizing all female subjects. As a result, the scientific literature may actually perpetuate erroneous information based on the overgeneralizations from research involving males.

Language bias

'Linguistic sexism refers to inequitable treatment of gender issues that is built into the language' (Crawford, 2001: 238) and it can take many forms. Examples include

- the use of non-parallel forms ('man and wife'),
- the generic 'he, his, and man' to refer to people in general,
- the definition of woman in relation to man ('Miss' or 'Mrs'),
- the identification of males as normative, so exceptions to the rule are marked ('woman doctor'),
- the trivialization of females ('authoress'),
- the application of positive terms to males ('master') but negative terms to females ('mistress'),
- the fact that historically many phenomena relevant to women were unnamed (sexual harassment; date rape),
- the linkage of sex with occupation ('cleaning lady'; 'postman')

Consider the form of the following pairs of statements.

A1. Colour blindness occurs more frequently in males than in females.
B1. Girls are more passive than boys.

A2. Learning disabilities are more frequent among males than among females.
B2. Girls are more dependent than boys.

Obviously the paired statements are not linguistically parallel forms. If we were to rephrase the A1 statement to a form analogous to its partner, we would say: 'Males have poorer colour vision than females.' Similarly, the A2 statement would be reworded as, 'Males do not learn as well as females.' There is an inherent inaccuracy in the B statements because they seem to suggest that *all* females are more 'whatever' than *all* males. This implication is not evident in the A constructions. Of particular interest is that the inaccurate B-type assertions are typically applied only to one sex—females.

To keep the patriarchal model intact we assume that whatever males are better at is just generally more valued socially and institutionally than whatever females are better at. This differential evaluation is reflected in our choice of concept labels. For example, the psychological concept of field independence/dependence refers to an individual's propensity to perceive the figures embedded in a surrounding field versus perception of the overall pattern. Guess which sex tends to respond to the field rather than the figure? Females. Equally accurate and appropriate descriptors, but with reverse evaluative connotations, are communicated by the concept labels of 'context awareness' versus 'context insensitivity' or 'context blindness' (Eichler, 1988).

Another form of labelling bias occurs when a generic form is used in contexts where it would be more accurate to be sex-specific. For example, since about 95 per cent of spousal abuse cases involve wife-battering as opposed to husband-battering, the term 'spousal abuse' disguises the sex-specific nature of the phenomenon (Eichler, 1988).

Still other forms of labelling reflect the influence of negative stereotypes. In a control group study of pre-menopausal and menopausal women, the former were referred to as 'normals' while the latter were called 'patients' although none of these women were in hospital or taking medication (Gannon, et al., 1992).

Allegedly generically neutral terms, such as 'he', 'his', and 'man', are presumed, if the context is appropriate, to apply to both sexes. However, many investigators have demonstrated that even in a neutral context such terms are typically interpreted as gender-specific—that is, as referring to males only (Moulton, Robinson, & Elias, 1978; Silveira, 1980).

Crawford (2001) concludes, 'the English language encoded androcentrism and sexism in its structure, content and usage. It portrayed women as different, less important, and unequal to men' (239). This bias was, of course, reflected in the language of science. Feminist language reform has led to the development of guidelines for the non-sexist use of language (Pauwels, 1998). Such policies have been widely adopted by journal editors and text publishers and have proved to be extremely effective in ameliorating linguistic sexism (Gannon, et al., 1992).

Selection, inference and interpretation of evidence

Opportunities for the expression of bias occur when researchers interpret and attempt to export their limited findings from the research situation to the real world. Everyone knows that males are more aggressive than females, right? Yet, Michael Johnson's examination of the evidence regarding relationship violence reveals that, on the one hand, males are the primary perpetrators of domestic violence, and that, on the other, there are essentially no differences between men and women in the incidence of couple violence (cited in Kimball, 2001). How can both of these seemingly contradictory findings be true? Johnson has identified a pattern, which he labels 'patriarchal terrorism', in which the male engages in an escalating, frequent, and severe series of violent attacks when seeking to control his partner. In contrast common couple violence is infrequent, doesn't escalate, isn't motivated by a desire for control, and may be initiated by either partner. One explanation for these disparate findings is that they derive from the investigation of very different samples. Studies of patriarchal terrorism are based on data from divorce courts, battered women's shelters, hospital emergency rooms, and surveys of criminal behaviour. Research on couple violence comes from large, random national surveys. As pointed out by Kimball, in neither case can the samples be regarded as representative. Notice the opportunities that these research results offer for cherry-picking evidence to support opposing hypotheses.

Many people have read, heard, or believe that the following statements are scientifically validated facts:

1. Girls are more social than boys.
2. Girls are more suggestible than boys.
3. Girls have lower self-esteem than boys.
4. Boys are more analytic than girls.
5. Girls lack achievement motivation.

The accumulated available research evidence does not, in fact, support these assertions yet such conclusions continue to appear in the scientific literature and elsewhere. Just as scientists selectively recycle sub-samples of unfounded research findings that support cultural stereotypes, so, too, do they recycle hypotheses based on conventional wisdom—in other words, stereotypes. One example derives from the literature on coping. One of the early taxonomies employed in the study of coping techniques involved the distinction between problem-focused coping (thought to be the preferred strategy of males) and emotionally focused coping (believed to be more common among females). Folkman and Lazarus (1980) tested this sex difference hypothesis and concluded that, contrary to stereotypic beliefs, women and men coped quite similarly. Moreover, they found that both forms of coping occurred in virtually every stress encounter. Although familiar with the work of Folkman and Lazarus, a number of other investigators continue to test, with limited success, the unsupported hypothesis that males and females differ in their coping strategies along the lines dictated by traditional conceptions of the sexes (Billings & Moos, 1981; Marotz-Baden & Colvin, 1986; Stone & Neale, 1984).

Statistical bias

Many scientists use inferential statistical techniques to help decide if their observations are worth getting excited about or even worth sharing with their colleagues (see Chapter 12). Suppose a scientist compares the performance of men and women on a perceptual restructuring task such as identifying a simple figure hidden in a more complex pattern. The scientist's pet theory about the relationship between sex and cognitive/perceptual abilities leads him or her to suspect that the males will be superior on this task. Males obtain an average score of 15, whereas the average for females is 10. To help determine whether this difference is a 'true' difference—one worth shouting about, one that supports the pet theory—the researcher submits the data to a statistical test. Statistical convention requires that the scientist start off with an assumption that the two groups do not differ; this is the null hypothesis. Then, statistical maneuvers are applied that provide information on the probability that a difference of 5 units is a random or chance finding. A probability level of 0.01 ($p < 0.01$) means that there is one chance in 100 that this difference of 5 units is due to sampling error or some other uncontrolled or unknown factor. Our scientist then rejects the null hypothesis and concludes that a real, authentic, true, significant difference does exist between males and females on this task. Note that the scientist could be wrong because there is still that one chance in 100 that the observed difference is artifactual.

What if the investigator had found, after application of a statistical test, a probability value of 0.15? Then our investigator knows that there are 15 chances in 100 that this difference of 5 units is due to chance. Again, by convention, this probability is regarded as too high, or too risky, to permit a conclusion of a real or significant difference in performance between males and females. However, by the rules of statistics, the scientist cannot confirm the null hypothesis and conclude that he or she has discovered that males and females have similar perceptual restructuring abilities. Hence, a failure to obtain a real difference (defined as a probability of 0.05 or less) equals an ambiguous result. Returning to our discussion of sex and science, the implication is that one can never statistically 'prove' that the sexes are similar, that is, that they do not differ. Our main decision aid in science fails to help us make decisions about similarities.

Favreau (1977; 1993; 1997) describes several other problematic features associated with the use of statistical procedures. On a test of mathematical ability, the average score for boys was 40.39; for girls, it was 35.81. This difference proved to be significant at the 0.01 probability level. The conclusion that boys have significantly superior mathematical ability is tempting and implies that all boys perform better than all girls. Yet, as illustrated in Figure 15.1, the lowest scores in the group of boys are as low as those of the lowest girls, and the scores of the best-performing girls are as high as those of the highest boys. In essence, the use of the statistical procedure disguised the extensive overlap between the sexes on this measure of mathematical ability. But while cycling rapidly around

Fig 15.1 ■ MATHEMATICAL ABILITY SCORE

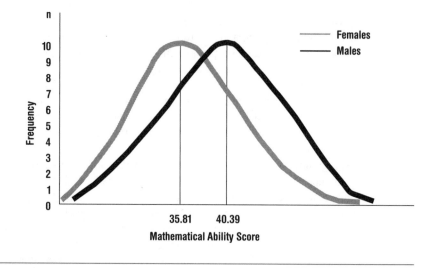

your PST to keep up with the traffic of daily living, it's easier to simply remember that there was a *significant* difference, than to recall that yes there was a statistically significant result, but that the scores of the two groups overlapped almost completely.

Another assumption underlying parametric tests of significance is that the data are normally distributed; an assumption often not tested and frequently not the case. Still another assumption is that the smaller the probability value, the more important the effect. But, we have already seen that a difference that is statistically significant may not be practically significant, may not help you make a personal decision. Finally, significance depends on sample size. The larger the sample, the more likely a given difference will yield a statistically significant, but perhaps socially useless result.

Publication bias

Because of the ambiguity of results that do not permit the investigator to reject the null hypothesis, many scientific journals have an explicit or implicit policy, that only studies reporting statistically significant differences will be published. Consequently, many studies appear in the literature reporting 'real' sex differences when, in actuality, the differences reflect that one chance in 100 for which the difference is artifactual. The other 99 studies that failed to show a sex difference didn't get published. This publication bias then leads us to assume differences between the sexes where, in fact, no such differences exist (a Type I error).

Journal policies may also be biased against publishing reports of sex differences that are contrary to established and accepted findings. Additionally, there seems to be an avoidance of the publication of replications—studies that try to duplicate the procedures of previously published work. Both of these factors tend to augment or exacerbate the problem of accepting those findings that are really attributable to chance as validly authentic. Finally, as Grady (1981) notes, journals may eschew certain research topics or content areas, regarding them as trivial or over-researched. This may be particularly the case for topics related to women's issues.

Design sources of bias

In a fascinating program of research, Rosenthal (1963) and his colleagues demonstrated that a researcher's knowledge of the hypotheses associated with a piece of research might actually shape results in keeping with the hypotheses. In other words, the experimenter's expectation about how the study will turn out works like a self-fulfilling prophecy. Recalling our earlier discussion about premises producing supporting empiricism Pyke (1982) and Weyant (1979) have argued that experimenter expectancy effects serve to enhance the possibility of revealing a sex difference.

The demand characteristics of an experiment (Orne, 1962) are a potential source of bias for any study. A researcher may inadvertently structure an experiment so that the probability of obtaining certain results increases. For example, the particular task assigned to participants may bias the findings. A consistent sex difference cited in the psychological literature has been the greater social conformity of females as compared with males, leading to the conclusion that females were more susceptible than males to group pressure or influence. However, as noted by Weyant (1979), the tasks employed in these conformity studies were typically of the spatial/perceptual variety—a selection that favoured males. When tasks of roughly equal familiarity to both sexes were used, the sex difference in conformity disappeared.

Grady (1981) reviewed studies of aggression and identified a similar source of bias in both the experimental condition used and the type of response option available to the research participants. In studies involving female participants, aggression is typically induced by requiring the participants to read a story presumed to arouse aggression; to measure the amount of aggression so induced, participants complete some sort of questionnaire. When male participants are used, aggression is more actively and directly induced through threat or hostile treatment and the effect is assessed in terms of the administration of shocks to a victim. These demand characteristics could well yield experimental findings supporting a conclusion that males are more aggressive than females.

Researcher bias

We have already learned that characteristics of a researcher may affect the nature of the data obtained. Sex of the investigator appears to be a potential source of bias of some magnitude. Alice Eagly and Linda Carli (1981) conducted a meta-analysis of studies dealing with gender differences in conformity and influenceability. They found that women were more easily influenced than men, but the size of the difference was small and accounted for only one per cent of the variability in influenceability. In the course of this analysis, they uncovered another source of bias—sex of researcher. Male investigators tended to find larger gender differences in influenceability than did female investigators. Intrigued by this discovery, these authors reviewed a body of research dealing with the ability to guess what emotion people are feeling (i.e., sensitivity). Here it was found that female researchers obtained the larger gender differences, revealing that women are more sensitive. As Matlin (1993) notes, 'each gender finds results that are most flattering to their own gender. Male researchers find easily influenced women who are not particularly sensitive to others' feelings. Female researchers find sensitive women, who are not particularly easily influenced' (227).

Theory bias

Observations heaped together on a huge table—like a bargain-basement sale—don't make a science. We rely on theories to help us select observations from the heap, link them into a pattern, and explain them. In one sense, then, a theory functions like a bias. To illustrate the biasing effects of the sorting and interpreting screens of theories, let's examine the provocative theory of sociobiology.

Although sociobiology has many precursors it was E.O. Wilson (1975) who established it as a comprehensive and coherent position that attracted both admiration and admonition from the scientific community. Essentially, 'the basic premise of Sociobiology is that human behaviors and certain aspects of social organization have evolved, like our bodies, through adaptations based on Darwinian natural selection' (Bleier, 1984: 16). According to evolutionary doctrine, organisms are basically in the business of reproduction. Those organisms that survive to leave the maximum number of offspring (or other genetically related kin) are the most fit in the sense that their genetic packages remain in the population gene pool. These gene packages are adaptive because they are associated with maximum fitness (i.e., reproductive success). Natural selection refers to the process whereby certain genes are progressively eliminated from the gene pool because their hosts are less fit; they leave fewer progeny to carry their genetic material forward. Conversely, the representation of other genes in subsequent generations is gradually increased as a function of the reproductive success of their carriers.

From this evolutionary hub, Wilson and his colleagues extrude streamers of theoretical propositions offering genetically based explanations for male sexual promiscuity, altruism, incest taboos, warfare and aggression, homosexuality, ethics and morality, co-operative behaviour, hypergamy (female tendency to marry males of higher status), female infanticide, smiling, phobias, the human sense of free will, the disappearance of slavery, the sexual division of labour, female subordination, selected religious practices, private property, patriarchy, the family as a social structure, the disappearance of the estrous cycle in females, and so on.

For consumers of science, sociobiology has a seductive quality. Its comprehensiveness; its relative simplicity in terms of the reduction of complex, mystifying forms of social behaviour into a fistful of basic propositions; and the personal immediacy or relevance of the phenomena under consideration combine to produce a scientific best-seller. Yet for every one person who reads Wilson's two volumes (1975, 1978) or Dawkins's *The Selfish Gene* (1976), how many people have read the scathing but somewhat pedantic and tedious critiques offered in Montagu (1980)? How many enthusiastic consumers have been exposed to alternate interpretations of the same evidence? Is Wilson's main appeal simplicity, buttressed with catchy anecdotal sketches of the behaviour of subhuman species, or does he provide a valid and powerful insight into complex human behaviour?

To dramatize the potent influence of a theoretical orientation on the selection and interpretation of observations, consider the following two excerpts from Wilson (1978) and Mackie (1983) respectively. They are both discussing the work of Money and Ehrhardt (1972). These latter authors studied 25 genetic females (XX) who were exposed prenatally to heavy doses of androgen (masculinizing hormones), which resulted in a hermaphroditic (adrenogenital syndrome) condition. Corrective genital surgery was performed and the infants were raised as females. Money and Ehrhardt compared this clinical group with a matched control group. Wilson describes this research:

> Did the girls show behavioral changes connected with their hormonal anatomical masculinization? As John Money and Anke Ehrhardt discovered, the changes were both quite marked and correlated with the physical changes. Compared with unaffected girls of otherwise similar social backgrounds, the hormonally altered girls were more commonly regarded as tomboys while they were growing up. They had a greater interest in athletic skills, were readier to play with boys, preferred slacks to dresses and toy guns to dolls. The group with the adrenogenital syndrome was more likely to show dissatisfaction with being assigned to a female role. . . .

> So at birth the twig is already bent a little bit—what are we to make of that? It suggests that the universal existence of sexual division of labor is not entirely an accident of cultural evolution (Wilson, 1978: 132).

Mackie (1983), in summarizing the same research, reports:

> The researchers found that the fetally androgenized females were more interested in masculine clothing, games and toys. Although they regarded themselves as female, they were considered by their mothers and themselves to be tomboys. In comparison with the control group, these subjects were less interested in baby-sitting and future marriage as opposed to careers. Interestingly, no greater incidence of physical aggression was reported. Money and Ehrhardt concluded that the male sex hormone had had a masculinizing effect. However critics point out their behavior is within the normal range for females in our society and further, that female gender identity is not seriously disrupted by the presence of prenatal androgens (Mackie, 1983: 78–9).

In the first account of this research the meager empirical observations with their fuzzy surrounding region of doubt or area of uncertainty are linked into an interpretive pattern supporting a genetic biological determinist position. Mackie weaves the same empirical bits into a cultural determinist tapestry. Who's right? Certainly much can be said for both sides. The point is that most subsets of empirical observations, given their scarcity and ambiguity, can be successfully employed to support even diametrically opposed theoretical models. Thus reliance on secondary sources is a risky business because the empirical data are painted (or tainted) with hues from the theoretical spectrum.

Studies reporting sex differences trigger a bias toward interpreting such differences as biological in origin (the sociobiological position) rather than as environmentally determined. Sex, after all, is a biological variable and therefore (so the reasoning goes) any observed difference between the sexes must have a biological base. Again, this bias appears in non-human primate studies where the tendency to ignore habitat influences on social structure and social behaviour is even more pronounced (Lancaster, 1976).

Another characteristic of the androcentric bias in theory involves utilization of the male condition as the prototype. The position of males is the norm, or the natural estate, or the right condition, with women fitted into the theory later as a footnote (Leonard and Collins, 1979). As Weyant (1979) notes, behavioural scientists have often seemed incapable of viewing women except in relation to a male model.

Bias is a two-way street

It would be wrong to assume that those pointing the 'bias' finger are immune to surreptitious edits of belief systems. Although this chapter is slanted in terms of focusing on examples revealing forms of biases resulting from adoption of a patriarchal ideology, a feminist ideology similarly shapes conclusions. Simon's mantra applies equally to males and females, to feminists and non-feminists.

Cherry-picking from elastic evidence in the service of a theoretical bias may not be limited to male scientists. To illustrate, Jeanne Block (1976) identified several sources of bias evident in the review of the sex difference literature conducted by Maccoby and Jacklin. And taking this one step further, McCormack (1989) notes, 'If we are all white, middle-class feminists, if we replicate ourselves, feminist research will be biased even though our individual studies are beyond reproach' (25).

Celia Kitzinger and Sue Wilkinson (1997) assert that a central tenet of feminism has been the validating of women's experience. What happens when the experience participants report is not consistent with the views of the researcher? When, for example, respondents report that sexual harassment is a non-problem, no big deal or, say they feel responsible for having been raped. Researchers employ a variety of strategies to avoid validating such non-feminist perspectives, ranging from actual data omission to interpretations of brain-washing or male identification, to a search for competing discourses or contradictions to overt disagreement with the interviewee's comments. They conclude, 'there is a conflict for feminist researchers between, on the one hand, simply reflecting and validating whatever women tell us about their experience, and, on the other, providing a feminist critique and challenge to the way in which women's experience is constructed under (hetero)patriarchy' (573).

Restructuring Science

Documenting the pervasive and invidious (if unintentional) impact of the androcentric model on science has had the salubrious effect of promoting greater caution and vigilance in avoiding overgeneralizations, in the more precise use of language, in greater inclusiveness of subject samples, and so on. And, on a variety of fronts, scientists are being exhorted by granting agencies, journal editors, and their professional associations to 'clean up their act'. Stark-Adamec and Kimball (1984), for example, couple their comprehensive description of the many avenues by which sex bias may enter research with a set of guidelines (adopted and endorsed by the Canadian Psychological Association) to aid researchers in their efforts to generate nonsexist research. Comparable guidelines have been developed within American Psychological Assocation (Denmark, Russo, Frieze & Sechzer, 1988; McHugh, Koeske, & Frieze, 1986).

Beyond this, feminist researchers have defined the principles characterizing feminist research. These principles address the inequities extant in traditional or mainstream science and would serve to level the playing field for the game of science. The value of experiential knowledge (Rose, 1986), of a phenomenological approach (Wallston, 1981), of a transcendence of dichotomies (Pyke, 1988), of methodological pluralism (Rabinowitz & Martin, 2001), and of the need to consider the researcher as a relevant variable in the research process are among the characteristics of a feminist perspective on science. On this latter point, Rabinowitz and Martin (2001) have underlined the importance of reflexivity (the relation of the researcher to the researched).

More precise prescriptions for feminist research are articulated by Judith Worell (1990) in defining the mandate for the *Psychology of Women Quarterly*:

> We look for research that meets one or more of the following criteria: (a) challenges traditional or devaluing views of women; (b) uses methods of inquiry that provide alternative views of women's lives; (c) looks at women within the meaningful context of their lives; (d) engages in collaborative efforts with research participants. . . .; (e) solicits samples other than college sophomores, including diversity in age, ethnic and economic status, relational preferences, and so on; (f) considers sex and gender comparisons in context rather than simply looking for 'sex differences'; (g) interprets women's response repertoires (traits, behaviors, cognitions) in ways that do not blame the victims of violence or injustices; (h) explores alternatives that empower women and minorities; (i) examines the structural and interpersonal hierarchies that render women and other minority groups less powerful; and (j) contains implications for social change toward establishing equality and social justice for all oppressed groups (4–5).

More recently, White, Russo and Travis (2001) identified four feminist principles for research: inclusiveness and diversity, context, power and privilege, and activism. With respect to the first principle, researchers are exhorted to be mindful of the fact that gender effects are influenced by variability in immigrant status, race, ethnicity, sexual orientation, physical ability, size, and any of a host of other variables that involve differential access to power and privilege.

The importance of context considerations in understanding and interpreting behaviour has been emphasized in the feminist literature (Yoder, 2002; Yoder & Kahn, 2003). To understand eating disorders, for example, it is necessary to recognize the role of cultural forces for thinness, as well as the roles played by poverty, abuse, racism, classism, and heterosexism.

Feminist researchers are also urged to attend to the dynamics of power and privilege because these factors play a key role in enforcing women's subordination and oppression.

For some scientists, the activism theme in feminist research seems to fly in the face of science's search for truth for its own sake. Feminists unabashedly argue that an explicit goal of their research is to dispel the androcentric model and move toward equality and improvement in the quality of life for both women and men. The goal is to promote a benevolent society in which individual self-actualization is possible (Lott, 1985).

Several volumes have been published in which a feminist orientation to research methodology in the social sciences is described (Nielsen, 1990; Fonow & Cook, 1991; Reinharz, 1992; Zalk & Gordon-Kelter, 1992; Crawford & Kimmel, 1999). Taken in the aggregate these works provide a comprehensive compendium of feminist research methods. Some feminist scholars, pessimistic about the prospects of a revisionist approach and/or distrustful of the inherent masculine orientation in science, are calling for a major restructuring of the social science enterprise (Bleier, 1984; Eichler, 1988; Pyke, 1988; Crawford & Marecek, 1989; McCormack, 1989). Ultimately, however, a restructuring of science (i.e., the creation of a truly non-sexist science) may require a restructuring of society—a move from the male-oriented model of social reality now extant to a model that conceptualizes the social universe as constructed around both women and men. Peplau and Conrad (1989) inject a cautionary note into this discussion. It is their position that any research method (feminist or otherwise) can be applied in sexist ways and they urge appropriate utilization of all research designs.

From Principle to Practice

Rochelle Dalla's 2002 study—which involved an investigation of street-level sex work—illustrates the operation of feminist research principles. Her study revealed that street-walkers by and large do not develop friendships with their colleagues, and although the majority reported substance abuse this behaviour seemed to be the result, rather than the cause, of prostitution; prostitution was a response to financial need, victimization and abuse were a common component of this life style, and emotional relationships were developed with clients, former clients, and/or pimps.

Our review of Dalla's study follows the criteria outlined by Worell (1990) and provides an interesting comparison with the study conducted by the students on the same topic (Chapter 8).

Although sex work generally, and street-level sex work in particular, are regarded as unsavory lifestyles, Dalla's presentation and description of her participants is respectful without any hint of devaluing them or their life choices. Feminist researchers are also sensitive to the exploitation of research participants who typically receive little reward for their cooperation. Dalla's participants were paid for their time.

Dalla employed a qualitative semi-structured interview approach in order to obtain a first-hand account of the lived experiences of these prostitutes. She states, 'Qualitative data provide a vehicle for understanding underlying processes, which are difficult to gauge through quantitative means' (63).

Her approach allowed an exploration of the social context of street prostitution. She notes that her study 'was designed to examine the subculture of street-level sex work, with emphases on the social context of street-walking, patterns of drug use and abuse and the economic implications of such and exposure to violence and victimization' (65). For example, she asked about the nature of relationships with pimps, with clients, and with fellow street-walkers (e.g., Do women on the streets look out for one another? Are they friends?).

Most of Dalla's research participants were involved in an intervention program designed to help women leave the streets. She collaborated with her research participants in the sense that with their permission, she attended the weekly group meetings for 17 months. This procedure helped her to gain credibility and no doubt increased the likelihood that group members would agree to participate in the individual interviews. Further, following data analysis, Dalla consulted several participants and requested their opinions regarding derived conclusions. Two participants reviewed a draft of the study report and their comments and suggestions were incorporated into the final manuscript.

The 43 women interviewed constituted a diverse sample in terms of age (19–56), race (20 Caucasian, 18 Black, 5 Native American), marital status (22 single, 10 married, 9 divorced, 2 separated) and years of education (7 went to college). Not surprisingly, the economic circumstances of these women were relatively homogenous; most lived in shelters or were incarcerated.

Since this study did not involve sex and gender comparisons, this criterion, as laid out by Worell, is not addressed.

Most of the participants in Dalla's study had been exposed to incidents of severe abuse. Rape was a frequently reported experience but apparently not a deterrent in terms of returning to the streets. One respondent matter-of-factly viewed it as simply not getting paid. Dalla speculated: 'Her response likely indicates a coping mechanism that apparently allowed her to return to the dangerous street environment without paralyzing fear and perhaps also with some level of personal dignity intact' (70). Some respondents described the attraction of living on the edge and thriving on the excitement of the streets. Dalla's interpretation of this paradoxical reaction is that 'these women had become so emotionally numb, that life-threatening situations were necessary in order to feel any sensation at all' (70). These interpretations obviously eschew victim blaming.

Based on her findings, Dalla outlines some of the important features that should be included in intervention programs aimed at empowering prostitutes. Such programs should address the self-acceptance of the prostitute label, the prevention and treatment of drug addiction, the facilitation of mutual support among prostitutes, and the provision of job-training or educational opportunities. 'Meeting immediate housing, drug dependence and childcare needs is critically important for women attempting to leave the streets' (71).

While not specifically addressing the structural and interpersonal hierarchies that render women and other minority groups less powerful, Dalla does discuss the role of crack cocaine in generating a pecking order among street prostitutes. Crack addicts will perform sex services more cheaply and thereby lower the price of street-level sex work. In addition, the potential for victimization and violence is exacerbated by the presence of crack cocaine.

As noted above, Dalla discusses some of the implications for social change in the context of defining key ingredients of intervention programs for street-level sex workers.

In sum, Dalla has done a highly credible job of meeting the criteria and principles defined for feminist research. Of course, any study can be improved and Dalla's is no exception. Dalla herself identifies several factors that limit the exportability or generalizability of her findings. Her sample may not be representative of the population of street sex workers in the sense that 40 of her 43 participants were no longer engaged in sex work, relatively few worked for a pimp and more than half were in treatment. The veracity of the interview responses is an unknown and may have been affected by drug use and other factors. A triangulation approach involving archival and survey research methods would have enriched and strengthened the study. In a highly laudable but infrequent research strategy, Dalla (2006) subsequently contacted 18 women from her original sample and interviewed them focusing particularly on their efforts to 'leave the life'. Only 5 women were successful in their exit attempts. Factors relevant to this success included: hitting bottom, formal support services, emotional attachments, ability to earn a living wage, and religion.

Historical Example

The following is an historical example of the impact of ideology on empiricism (Fee, 1976).

A small brain = a small mind

Victorian-era physical anthropologists eagerly embraced Darwin's theory of evolution, published in 1859. Within the patriarchal structure of Victorian society, women were regarded as inferior and subordinate to men. Applying evolutionary theory, many scientists of that period concluded that females represented an earlier stage of evolutionary development. This then explained the lower status of females—socially, economically, and politically. Because they had not climbed as high up the evolutionary ladder as men, women therefore could not be expected to function as creatively, intelligently, and productively as their male counterparts.

A related part of the argument, which helped to explain why in some 'primitive' cultures women held considerable power and status, was the premise that, as one proceeded up the evolutionary scale, the sexes became more and more divergent or differentiated. Hence, the great distinctions between males and females in Victorian England were justified because the Victorian upper class obviously represented the epitome of civilization—the acme of evolutionary progress.

Interest in developing a measure of intelligence led some scientists to resort to the use of brain size as a possible indicator, and so the science of craniology was born. The following predictions regarding brain size might be generated from the propositions outlined above:

1. Females would have smaller brains than males.
2. The difference between male and female brains in primitive cultures would be less than that observed in more advanced cultures.
3. Within more advanced cultures, the difference between male and female brains would be less in lower socioeconomic classes than in higher classes.

As expected, the predictions were confirmed. Women were simply not equipped, as a result of their evolutionary history, to function on a par with men. It seemed they were destined to be always subordinate to men. As George J.

Romanes (1887) put it, 'It must take many centuries for heredity to produce the missing five ounces of the female brain' (cited in Fee, 1976).

As science moved into the twentieth century, patriarchal ideology remained, but changing economic conditions required some adjustment to the evolution paradigm of the Victorian era. Science itself changed its complexion with the trend toward increasing precision and experimentation. At the turn of the present century, Karl Pearson, a statistician of some renown, expressed his disgust with the quality of Victorian evolutionary theorizing and set about to demonstrate the absence of any correlation linking brain size, cranial measurement, and intelligence. Pearson's assault proved fatal to the 'science' of craniology, which disappeared from the scientific scene.

Somewhat reminiscent of the craniology debate is the recent controversy on brain laterality—the extent to which functions or abilities are localized in the right or left hemisphere of the brain. Many researchers assume that being lateralized is preferable to lack of lateralization, primarily because children with various learning problems exhibit ambiguous cerebral dominance. Because the incidence of learning problems in young males is higher than the frequency of these difficulties in young females, and because females are more lateralized for verbal functions than males, it has been hypothesized that males are less lateralized than females. On the other hand, females appear to be less lateralized than males because they show less impairment following damage to either brain hemisphere than do males with a comparable degree of cerebral assault. In some sense, then, females have the best of both worlds. These incongruent findings have led some researchers to conclude that the female brain specializes, that is, lateralizes too early and is thus not able to 'advance' further (Unger, 1979; Pyke, 1982). So, after a hundred years, the Victorian view of female evolution is reborn, albeit in a more sophisticated and elegant guise.

Summary

This chapter highlights the sensitivity of science to belief systems, values, and ideologies—the 'taken for granted' premises and implicit worldview of the scientist. More specifically, we detail the effect of a strong, resilient, emotionally anchored belief system about the nature of females and males (androcentric theory) on various aspects of the science enterprise. Examples of the influence range all the way from women's participation in scientific activities to the operation of sex bias on the topics studied, on the preferred research participants, on the differential evaluation of tasks, on the derivation of inferences, on language, on the selection of evidence, on theory construction, and so on. Principles and criteria defining feminist research, representing a very different ideological perspective, are presented along with an analysis of a specific study in light of these criteria. Recognition of the imperfections and vulnerabilities of the scientific enterprise remains vital for the production of better quality science and is important for all of us if we are to be sophisticated consumers of science's products.

student's notebook

I have a hunch that Professor Creek isn't very comfortable with this chapter. He didn't even give us an assignment. But I have to comment anyway. Derek took me to see the movie Water—part of a trilogy (earth, fire, water)—filmed in Pakistan. Seeing and reviewing Water was a class assignment for one of his courses. The movie is the story of male dominance in India just before Gandhi came to power.

It's scary!

I know it's easier to see faults in other cultures, groups, and individuals. And things have probably changed for the better now. Nevertheless, the movie portrays a shocking degree of male control over almost every aspect of female behaviour, and the absolute power of the caste system.

The story focuses on the powerless and degrading state of widows, one as young as nine years of age. She is sold as a concubine to a rich, high caste man.

OK, it's a movie. But Derek claims that archival documents support the main messages delivered by the film. He says Indian immigrants bring the patriarchal traditions with them to this country and Indian females still have to really fight for their rights. Though I would argue, what female doesn't have to fight, really?

In previous commentaries I've noted evidence of male dominance in North America: the glass ceiling effect in corporations, the brouhaha over the Harvard CEO's comments concerning male dominance in engineering and science, and research indicating prevailing gender differences in accepting responsibility in the home, in particular. But I do try not to go off the deep end on this issue. Major equalizers have been introduced.

When I walked out into the fresh air after Water I was, at least temporarily, very happy with my lot as a North American female. And that contentment lasted. Well, it lasted until a few minutes later when Derek took over the conversation and showered me with pronouncements delivered from on high, from his grandiose and male-oriented perspective.

News story

Wow, did I ever find a humdinger of a news story. Two researchers—Jackson and Rushton (2006)—just reported that males had higher IQs than women. Based on a huge sample of 46,509 males and 56,007 females and some fancy statistical procedures, they state that teenage males scored 3.63 IQ points higher on average than did females. Their data derive from the performance of students on the 1991 Scholastic Aptitude Test from which they calculated a general intelligence factor—'g'. They note that these differences are found at every socioeconomic level, across several ethnic groups and throughout the whole distribution of scores. While they admit that this is small difference favouring males they nevertheless conclude that it is non-trivial. They believe that this intellectual deficit, explains the glass ceiling phenomenon.

Apparently Rushton is the same fellow who achieved notoriety for his work some years ago on race differences. He's the psychologist who claimed that whites are intellectually superior and more sexually restrained as compared with blacks and that those of Asian heritage are superior to both groups. He even goes so far as to attribute the high rates of AIDS in Africa as due to the insatiable sexual appetites of blacks.

In the article just published, the authors reveal their commitment to the patriarchal ideology with their discussion of sex differences in brain size. This seems like a retrogressive step. Karl Pearson, a statistician of some renown, demonstrated over a hundred years ago that brain size, cranial measurement, and intelligence were uncorrelated. Pearson's work led to the demise of the science of craniology, which disappeared from the scientific scene, only to be resurrected in 2006 by Jackson and Rushton it seems. This reminds me of the adage: one step forward, two steps back.

Note

How come women are often treated as second-class citizens? Check the student website at http://www.oup.com/ca/he/companion/agnewpyke.

REVIEW TRUE OR FALSE QUIZ

T F	1. 'Patriarchy' refers to the superior position, power, or status accorded to the male members of a society.
T F	2. Meta-analysis is a statistical method for aggregating research findings across many studies examining the same research topic.
T F	3. Hyde's (2005) review of the research on gender differences revealed that 25 per cent of the differences on the myriad variables examined are small or close to zero.
T F	4. Some of the symbolism in science reflects the eroticization of nature.
T F	5. The Royal Society began admitting female members in 1920, right after the First World War.
T F	6. Research studies on gender differences conducted before 1974 tend to show smaller gender differences than more recent studies.
T F	7. Researchers employing all female samples are more likely to generalize their findings to the opposite sex than those utilizing only male subjects.

T F	8.	Girls are more dependent than boys.
T F	9.	Even in a neutral context, generically neutral terms are typically interpreted as gender specific.
T F	10.	One can never statistically prove that the sexes do not differ.
T F	11.	Statistical procedures can disguise the extensive overlap between the sexes on mathematical ability.
T F	12.	Journal publication policies may lead us to assume gender differences where no such differences exist.
T F	13.	Female investigators tend to find larger gender differences in the susceptibility to influence than do male investigators.
T F	14.	Natural selection refers to the process whereby certain genes are progressively eliminated from the gene pool because their hosts are less fit.
T F	15.	Some subsets of empirical data can be successfully employed to support even diametrically opposed theoretical models.
T F	16.	Attention to context is not one of the principles of feminist research.
T F	17.	The study of street-walkers revealed that prolonged exposure to street work instigates addiction.
T F	18.	Finally, after three decades of support for the gender similarities hypothesis, the gender differences model is no longer accepted.
T F	19.	Scientists are objective, disinterested, and culturally disengaged from the questions they ask of nature and the methods they use to generate their answers.
T F	20.	In the Dalla study, it was discovered that street-walkers have formed support net works (i.e., friendships) with their colleagues.
T F	21.	Pearson's work on the associations between brain size, cranial measurement, and intelligence supported the science of craniology.
T F	22.	Victorians believed that as one advanced up the evolutionary ladder the sexes became more divergent or differentiated.
T F	23.	*Water*, discussed by Diana in her commentary, portrays a shocking degree of male control over almost every aspect of female behaviour.

16

The Truth Spinners

Chapter Goal

Last chapters provide authors with the opportunity to speculate, to think outside the box.

We stand on tiptoes to get glimpses of the future; we stretch our bounded rationality to explore modern controversies, even heresies, operating around the edges of scientific thinking. These heresies range from predicting the end of science, to challenging the American Dream, challenging the sacred truth that we are masters of our fate, captains of our soul.

These heresies are obviously ridiculous! Or are they? Don't forget, once upon a time you could be burned at the stake for having ridiculous ideas, ideas that the world was round, or that women should be treated as equals. Many of yesterday's ridiculous ideas have a habit of becoming today's truths.

Introduction

There are more things in heaven and earth . . . than are dreamt of in your philosophy.
—Shakespeare

Given our bounded rationality and our limited attention span, on the one hand, and the uncertain future we face on the other, it's no wonder there are more things in heaven and earth than are dreamt of in our philosophy! In this chapter we explore the heresies that percolate around the edges of scientific thinking and bubble outside the box.

Such heresies, as briefly mentioned above, include: the end of science, challenges to the sacred truths of conscious control and free will, claims that chance events rule most of our lives, an increased emphasis on the role of theoretical and methodological biases and blind ritual in scientific thinking, and proclaiming that ideas—like endangered species—have to fight for survival.

The End of Science?

We've already proposed that the reach of science has limits. Some problems are just too big for human brains. But how far can science reach? According to John Horgan (1996), in his book *The End of Science*, maybe not much further.

Of course, experts have been wrong before. After all, Columbus didn't sail right off the end of the world and automobiles travelling faster than 30 miles an hour have not resulted in a rash of people dying because they couldn't breathe.

We, as the authors of *The Science Game*, don't believe that we are approaching the end of science, but we do see some fascinating limitations. And we do suspect that a lot of profoundly important problems may lie beyond our scientific reach.

Science has two main claims to fame. The first, *theoretical science*, makes attention-grabbing but speculative predictions such as 'There's enough energy in a rock no bigger than your fist to blow up New York City,' 'There are sexual impulses buried deep in your unconscious that control your behaviour,' 'We're on the verge of a cure for cancer', or 'We'll discover how you can actually keep your New Year's resolutions.' The second, empirical science, builds reliable observational stepping-stones to help us demonstrate that theoretical scientists—like Einstein—are right, or—like Freud—are too fuzzy to be rigorously tested.

We propose there's no end in sight for theoretical science—it's a growth industry. However, a case can be made that empirical science may have seen its best days.

The reach of science

Why do we suggest that theoretical science will roll merrily along, while empirical science may face an uphill struggle?

Simply put, given our bounded rationality and the limitations of our research methods, we may have solved most of the problems that are within our conceptual and empirical grasp. Now we're encountering puzzles that may be too big for our brains and beyond our technical reach, such as the illusive unified theory of everything in physics, or the design and operation of a unified United Nations, or our reliance on violence as the ultimate solution.

In research lingo: we're running out of *main causes and effects*. In other words, *solvable* problems usually have relatively simple solutions because they have one main cause, like gravity or pregnancy. Our bounded rationality can predict the connection between a few dots, and our accessible and affordable empirical methods can test them.

In contrast, complex problems typically result from many causes[1] interacting in various combinations and permutations, such as a cure for cancer, or the maintenance of a successful marriage. Operating in speculative space, at the top of our PST, we delude ourselves into believing that we can *resolve* complex problems, and we go on to do so everyday in daydreams, on blackboards, and in committee meetings. Operating in a speculative or theoretical space we generate *paper solutions*.

> When we can't see in order to believe, we believe in order to see.

Easy to say, hard to prove

For instance, it only takes a few minutes for you to scribble out the factors that you speculate are required for a successful marriage. Your list might include things such as age, education, cultural background, shared interests, proximity of parents, work demands, health, attitude toward marriage, religion, and children. You can even predict which ones are the most important. So, up top, in your mind you're under the illusion that you've solved the problem. But now comes the hard part.

Stop and think about how you would travel down from the top of your PST—where you quickly generated your theory—to the lower right hand corner, where you will rigorously test it? If you plan to conduct a well-designed experiment, how many control groups, and over how many years, would be required?

As an estimate, you might need 60 control groups to help isolate each of the relevant *causes* we so glibly listed, 100 couples for each group (12,000 people), tested at least once a year for thirty years, resulting 360,000 testing sessions.

We haven't even stopped to consider the time and resources required to develop and validate any of the quantitative and qualitative measuring methods you would need, or to consider how you would keep track of the couples in our highly mobile society. Contemplate the length of the message chain such a research project would generate. Consider what happens in the game of rumour every time you add even one new message or messenger in the chain? And, do we dare even consider the idea of repeating the study to test the reliability or validity of the initial findings.

Any complex problem that results from a combination of many causes presents formidable, if not insurmountable, challenges in the lower right corner of the scientific PST. This is always the case, whether that complex problem concerns cancer, addictive drugs, childhood education, fixing the UN, taming teenage hormones, or vainly attempting to keep a New Year's Resolution. Their

---

[1]We use the term 'cause' to designate pet suspects when deciding what leads to what. Philosophically, the term 'cause' is held in disrespect because it presumes a connection when none has been rigorously established. The preferred word is 'antecedent', which merely asserts than one event precedes another, with no necessary connection implied.

empirical complexity propels us back up top of our PSTs to generate affordable, if illusionary, theoretical resolutions. In other words, to generate affordable premises—a few pet causes—enabling us to reach mind-size conclusions.

Do modern physicists know what they're talking about?

Until very recently physicists touted string theory as the unified theory of everything. At a recent international conference one of its early sponsors, Nobel Laureate Paul Gross admitted: 'We don't know what we're talking about.'[2] String theory is a highly sophisticated mathematical model, or speculation, of how particles might interact in a collection of hypothetical universes. It is an exciting theoretical resolution that appears to have fallen down the black hole of its own complexity and lack of empirical support.

Sitting safely at the top of their PSTs, scientists merrily fine-tune their elegant theories, while waiting for poor, old lumbering empirical science to catch up and test the bits and pieces of their speculations. They hope researchers will get lucky and stumble on a major, controllable cause or cure hidden among the many possibilities—a unique particle, a gene, a magic pill, or a self-help book that actually works.

Now you can see why empirical scientists must simplify the abstract speculations that theoretical scientists generate and you can appreciate why they cut down the number of causes—no matter how intuitively plausible they may seem—in order to make the empirical research both mentally and technically affordable.

So as we encounter more complexity (involving combinations of many suspects, or variables, or causes), you can appreciate why empirical researchers must ignore many obvious suspects for practical reasons—too many dots, too many possible connections.

But the scientific future may not be as bleak as we've been painting it. While most big problems may have many causes, some may have one or two major ones.

Archival research to the rescue?

Levitt and Dubner (2005), using affordable archival research methods, generated some surprising correlations when searching statistical archives. For instance, they identified an intriguing connection between the increase in abortions and the reduction in crime (e.g., poor, single mothers have fewer babies raised under deprived circumstances). They hastened to point out that at this stage of the investigation this is merely a correlation, not an established cause–effect relationship.

---

[2]'Baffled in Brussels', *New Scientist* (10 December·2005): 5, 7.

This type of *affordable* archival research involving large numbers of people (big playpen) offers some empirical bridges—wobbly though they may be—between speculations at the top of the PST and empirical testing at the bottom.

For instance, such correlational tip-offs as the one above drastically shrink the massive empirical search space, suggesting that one major reason for the significant reduction in criminal activity may be the increased number of abortions, resulting in fewer young people growing up in underprivileged, desperate e environments. Furthermore, the basic measures are already in place, and can be fine-tuned to increase their reliability and validity (e.g., improve the accuracy of the abortion and crime rate statistics). And note that, readily accessible follow-up data are available from online institutional records.

Additionally, you can extend the validity of your investigation by leaving your computer for short periods and actually tracking a small, random sample of research subjects to identify other *causes* that may have a positive or negative influence on the correlation between abortions and crime rate. You thus help generate additional hypotheses for further rigorous research (e.g., identifying the exceptions, such as regions in which the abortion rate has risen and the crime rate has not fallen).

Pre-scientific and qualitative research methods offer some affordable empirical anchors, helping to prevent the up-top theoretical speculations from completely floating away into 'la la land'. These archival clues enable researchers—using more powerful scientific methods—to test isolated portions of the larger theory and perhaps to establish local reliability and validity within a specific and limited space/time frame.

As data from local playpens accumulate, we gradually gain clues as to where treasures may or may not be buried in bigger playpens and therefore gradually extend the external validity.

Note that the 'end of science' speculation is just that—a conjecture about what we might find in the future. Some speculations turn out to be right (atomic power), while others are wrong (the war to end all wars). When critically examining a speculation you must check out the premises on which it is based. Remember: no conclusions without premises. Our basic premise is that we're running out of mind-sized problems—too many dots and too many possible connections to precisely map at the top of the PST, or to rigorously test at the bottom.

Vote

We presume that we're facing increasingly complicated, multiple cause problems. Maybe too big for our brains. What's your hunch? Should we admit the 'end of science' premise into the scientific box and see it as deserving serious critical analyses?

Strongly Agree	Mildly Agree	Don't Know	Mildly Disagree	Strongly Disagree

Different answers from different students provide the basis for an interesting classroom discussion. For example, 'Why do these authors claim that a good theory is the most practical thing in the world?'

Free Will Versus Determinism

Next we will consider a series of heresies that challenge the sacred premise that we have conscious control over our lives and that we are responsible for our behaviour, that we are masters of our fate, captains of our soul. But before we start, the issue needs to be placed in context.

The goal of science is to identify the *laws* of the universe, including the laws of human behaviour—a form of determinism that assumes that human behaviour is lawful. And yet, subjectively we *know* that we have free will and that we are a law unto ourselves. So, in a sense, we'll explore the modern versions of the age-old argument between free will and determinism.

Who's the boss?

This question has intrigued scholars since the time they learned how to wrinkle their brows. For centuries they thought that *the* BIG bosses were supernatural forces—spirits, demons, gods, and witches. Then scholars gradually shifted ground and accepted a division of power between one God and humans. God we assigned a fuzzy place at the top of the universe. The human power was assigned less exalted, but still fuzzy place at the top of our PSTs. We call it conscious *control* or *free will*, and most of us accept this as an obvious common sense solution, or more commonly, as a *sacred truth*.

However, consciousness and free will are kind of fuzzy; they are kind of *supernatural*. We can't see them, weigh them, or take pictures of them, even with electron microscopes! The 'I'—as in 'I'm the boss of me'—floats somewhere above the brain. We can admit that the 'I' is somehow tied to the brain—it disappears when the brain does—but it's somehow still *the boss*.

As long as we're alive and conscious we presume that, except for basic bodily plumbing and reflexes, our mind runs the show, with the brain carrying out most of our orders, except New Year's Resolutions. One prominent scholar, Dan Dennett, is presently attempting to make the mind—or the 'I'—less fuzzy and more natural. In the process, he's delegating consciousness to the role of a *back seat driver*. Now that's a heresy!

Dennett's teams of mini-robots

Dan Dennett is trying to put your mind in its place. That place is in your brain, instead of its current personification of a ghost-like figure floating somewhere above the brain, while still controlling it.

Like Ignaz Semmilweis, Dennett (2003) prefers natural—as opposed to supernatural—explanations. He's been chewing on this philosophical debate for years. He's smart. He writes well. He tries to present both side of the argument, and yet his critics keep misinterpreting his message. Dennett says that 'We are each made of mindless robots and nothing else, no non-physical, no non-robotic ingredients at all' (2003).[3] Because of this statement his critics immediately leap to the conclusion that he's trying to stripe us of our power by claiming that we aren't the masters of our own fates.

For the purpose of discussion, we'll concede to Dennett that we, the authors, agree that the brain runs some of our life without our awareness or control, including our biochemistry, most physiological functions, and enforcing our obedience to the classic laws of physics. We can argue around the edges of mind-over-matter, and mind control of some physiological functions (e.g., through pain control by means of hypnosis, monks meditating into hibernation, etc.), but in order not to get too bogged down in this discussion, we'll ignore these elements—the exceptions that prove the rule. So, where do consciousness and free will fit in?

The 'I' as back seat driver

What if Dennett's right? Maybe our sense of conscious control is merely an artifact made up of after-the-fact conscious echoes of some of the brain's activity, similar to the awareness of pain—after-the-fact we feel it, but can't control it. What if we have the same degree of control as a back seat driver—when the car goes in the right direction we take credit and when it doesn't we blame somebody else?

After reviewing the evidence, Dennett says, 'When you think you're deciding, you're actually just passively watching a delayed internal videotape . . . of the real deciding that happened unconsciously in your brain quite a while before' (2003: 229). His argument imagines decision-making to be similar to a child who believes that their toy steering wheel controls the car.[4] Note that in this book, up to this point, you have been presented as *the driver* negotiating your PST. In direct contrast, Dennett presents you as a passenger—at best a back seat driver—while your team of mini-robots cycle around the PST. This contrast—this heresy—requires a second look. And to counter Dennett we need a clear case of conscious control.

---

[3]Also see Boag (2005) for a discussion of the single knower within each of us (the little person or homunculus inside calling the shots, as opposed to the case for multiple knowers, or multiple selves).

[4]Gradually the child learns that if he or she turns the wheel when the driver does, then the car turns. From the child's point of view there is a perfect correlation—he or she is in control.

Knocking Dennett's theory out of the park?

Consider Barry Bonds as he decides to swing and hit a baseball, something he does with astonishing regularity.

Initially, it seems like that decision is purely free will. Unfortunately for our side—the captain of my soul, master of my fate side. But is it? Based on what we know about the speed of baseballs and the speed of nerve transmission, Bonds has about a quarter of second to both make a decision and complete his swing. This means that his act of swinging the bat has to be a reflex action[5] because there just isn't enough neurological time from the time the ball leaves the pitcher's hand for Bonds to make a conscious decision, send that message to his arms, and complete his swing. So when we honor baseball batters maybe we should say something like: 'We induct your inherited and acquired reflexes (mini-robots) into the Baseball Hall of fame.'

Doesn't have the quite the same cachet but is apparently more scientifically accurate.

Let's go so far as to agree that our basic bodily functions, and our inherited and learned reflexes, lay mainly beyond our conscious control. But what about all the activity that we are aware of and that we do control, such as consciously deciding to order a drink. If I go into a bar and decide to have martini then 'I' decide, not a team of mindless robots.

Although, come to think of it, maybe that's not such a good example either. If you consider consciousness as an echo of brain activity, then maybe your mindless robots made the decision, and you're just going along for the liquid ride, claiming you're the boss.

Considering this, am I testing my degree of conscious control if I sit at the bar and not order a drink? You can no doubt see right away that this is also not going to support the free will-side of the debate because all kinds of humans consciously decide *not* to have a drink, or a smoke, or a steak, or a second piece of chocolate pecan pie, or stay up watching TV, and . . . it turns out they're not the boss of those either. It may just be the first day of a New Year's resolution which you soon break.

So far Dennett's ideas are coming out on top in this discussion!

Maybe our brain is the boss of *most* of our neurochemistry, reflexes, and behaviour, and our conscious mind is either helplessly out of the action or is a passive bystander futilely issuing orders that the brain has already put in action. But, surely that's not true about really important decisions like choosing careers, friends, political parties, and deciding between right and wrong? Here's where the argument gets really interesting.

---

[5]For a user-friendly account of how the human brain processes speeding objects see Regan et al., 1979 and Regan (1992).

Sending stop and go signals

What's your choice? You can accept the notion that the brain runs the whole show and the mind is at best an ignored bystander erroneously claiming credit. Or, you can extend the role of consciousness beyond merely monitoring some brain activity and include conscious feedback functions that signal simple 'stop' or 'go' orders to a tiny sub-set of robots. In other words, you can assume that there is, at least, an 'I' who controls a few of the robots some of the time.

Sometimes you don't order the second martini or the second piece of chocolate cake, for example, even though your brain chemistry and habits are starting to move your lips to say 'yes'. But the determined *you* hangs tough, overrules them, and says 'No!' You may not be able to control much but you can successfully issue the occasional 'stop' signal. Or, alternatively, you can conclude (as Dennett probably would) that the 'no' signal was issued, not by your 'I', but rather by a term of mini-robots higher up in the robotic chain of command that are overruling the 'local' teams short-sighted inclinations.

 This sounds like a reformulation of Freudian thinking with unconscious forces determining your behaviour. The primitive, raunchy Id (low-level teams of robots) needs a drink, the wise Super Ego (high-level teams of robots) overrules the Id.

The low-level robotic team's program reads: 'If A then B', or 'If in a bar, then order a martini'. The higher-order robotic team's control program reads: 'If A (and not C), then B', or 'If in a bar, and not on a big job interview, then order a martini'. So, the argument states that, in this instance, you don't need a big 'I' sitting on top of your brain to run the show. A biological computer-like program using 'If A (and not C, D or E) then B' rules can do the job by operating automatically with different levels of control.[6]

Dennett's a clever philosopher and he can tie us up in logical knots. For example, as a result of nature–nurture interactions during your lifetime, your brain acquires a massive repertoire of habitual responses to various situational inputs. These situation–response chains are carried out automatically by your multitude of mini-robot teams (networks of neurochemical connections). Some of the responses are highly probable (the brain gets credit); some are more variable and more unpredictable, so we give the mind (the big 'I') credit. Unpredictability and free will justify each other.

As we read Dennett, he'd merely claim the unpredictable variance is still due to the *as yet to be identified robots, because everything is*. That's his conceptually and emotionally anchored premise. At this stage in his theory, it is probably as emotionally anchored and as empirically untestable as Freud's theories.

So the question then becomes whether or not Dennett is another Freud, with an untestable theory, or if he's another Semmilweis, leaving us hanging

---

[6]There were early, grandiose claims that artificial brains would soon do everything human brains could. Increasingly, computers (teams of electronic mini-robots) are able to beat us at chess, steer cars around challenging country roads, and vacuum your living room.

around waiting for a microscope strong enough to take pictures of his mini-robots in action.

Dennett's proposal is a strong example of a speculation, based on a genetic premise, attempting to map the territory of a massive up-top theoretical playpen. For him, treasure is there. We're just waiting for the right shovels (presumably the eventual products of gene mapping, brain imaging, etc.) in order to unearth it. How do we handle currently untestable speculations?

When science can't make testable predictions

Science is in the business of prediction and control. If science can't make testable predictions, then we would have to admit that the world is full of things that scientists can't predict and control. For the time being at least those phenomena are open to explanation by other means—other non-scientific means (e.g., supernatural or religious beliefs).

Scientists who truly believe in the power of science have two obvious responses to alternative explanations:

1. There is a scientific explanation, we just haven't found it yet, and
2. We may never be able to find one, but we know *for sure* that the phenomena are not due to supernatural influences, *because nothing is*! (Now there's an emotionally anchored premise à la Simon.)

These confident scientists reflect Simon's mantra of no conclusions without emotionally anchored premises, and they presume that there is no alternative premise to their own. When you have two powerful institutions (e.g., science and the Church) with conflicting, emotionally anchored premises, effective communication between them becomes challenging, to say the least.

Notice, these scientists would probably even disagree with Shakespeare's statement that: *'There are more things in heaven and earth ... than are dreamt of in your philosophy.'* The nerve!

The pure scientific premise has no room for supernatural answers. This is understandable because many scientists get very nervous around talk of a 'heaven' lacking specific map coordinates, photos of the heavenly furniture, and video clips of flying angels. However, given the direction theoretical physics is heading—way beyond the reach of the bottom right corner of the PST—maybe scientists should be a little less arrogant. String theory, for instance is pretty airy-fairy stuff that is so high up in speculative mathematical space it must be almost bumping up against the bottom of the heaven that doesn't exist.[7] But

---

[7]Gell-Mann, a theoretical physicist in the United States, says: 'At first glance, this theory and our quark theory may seem contradictory. But they may actually be quite compatible—and both may even be right—especially if the quark should turn out to be, as is likely, a useful mathematical figment rather than a concrete building block of matter' (Feynman, 2005: 465). Now physicists would claim that most of their theories are *conceivably*, if not *practically*, empirically testable, whereas supernatural theories are not. They would make the same distinction between evolutionary theory and intelligent design.

these theorists, like Einstein did, spend their time playing at the top of the PST, not conducting rigorous tests down at the bottom.

It may be that future theorists and researchers will indeed shake up the reductionist premises of Dennett and other 'naturalists'. They may provide unequivocal evidence for *the ethereal mind*, evidence so compelling that it puts individuals back in the driver's seat, at least part of the time. What kind of evidence might that be? Because we, as the authors, were raised as naturalists, we aren't very good at generating any theories about this kind of weird evidence. It's hard for us to even find a window, let alone work towards peeking outside our particular box. Maybe the new high resolution brain imaging technology will show a tiny boss-robot, sitting at the top of a brain, cracking a whip and issuing orders to an obedient team of mini-robots?[8]

We think it's more likely that a ship will arrive from outer space, little green aliens will take one look at what we've done to the planet, turn off the master computer aboard that controls our brains . . . and we all fall down

Ethical behaviour

On a more positive note, Dennett suggests that we should take credit for the fact that we have teams of ethical mini-robots that have *learned*—through a mix of neurological hardware and software and trial and error (i.e., have been genetically programmed and socially conditioned) to tolerate short-term pain, frustrations, and deprivation in ·exchange for long-term gain, even for *altruistic* behaviour. The fact that our so-called 'conscious choices' arise from the evolved and automatic, or probabilistic, action of teams of mini-robots, rather than our subjective 'selves', should, in Dennett's view, in no way detract from the social and evolutionary value of our good behaviour. After all, don't we take credit for being beautiful or handsome, even though those qualities are purely due to the luck of the genetic hand?

It's much easier to accept Dennett if you apply his theory to others rather than to yourself. Citizens and scientists alike may agree that the behaviour of others is pre-determined by mini-robots, but not their own behaviour.[9]

Vote

On the basis of the argument outlined above, what's your hunch? Should we at least seriously contemplate Dennett's teams of mini-robots, thus admitting his heresy into the scientific box?

---

[8] For a sophisticated mind-friendly view that is not supernatural, see Searle (1999).

[9] When plea-bargaining we too are willing to invoke forces beyond our control, even to the extent of claiming that alcohol or 'the devil' was ultimately responsible. It's not a big step from blaming neurological misfiring to blaming mini-robots.

Strongly	Mildly	Don't	Mildly	Strongly
Agree	Agree	Know	Disagree	Disagree

Next we consider another heresy that threatens territory currently domi-nated by the ruling premise of conscious control.

Lady Luck

Dennett's theory confiscates a giant chunk of our perceived self-determination.[10] We end up as mere back seat drivers in our own car as we zigzag through life. Now, we'll examine the heresy that our path through life is determined not by mini-robots, but by chance. This heresy claims that, right from conception, chance determines whether or not you'll be able to afford a car, let alone be its back seat driver.

I was dealt a bad hand from a fixed deck

This heresy proclaims that *chance* determines whether you end up successful or unsuccessful,[11] rich or poor, happy or sad. Before you reject this ridiculous idea out of hand, at least entertain the possibility that lady luck plays a bigger role than we usually give her credit for.[12]

Figure 16.1 gives us an overview of the question. You'll recognize the out-line of the so-called normal curve at the bottom. You'll also notice that chance—represented by the triangular pinball apparatus and playing by a 50–50 rule—distributed most of the balls, or people, in the middle, with fewer and fewer being sorted out to the right or the left. It provides a neat way of describing the distribution of all kinds of human characteristics, such as height, intelligence, strength of the immune system, energy level, etc.

---

[10]In his latest book, *Breaking the Spell: Religion as a Natural Phenomenon* (2006) Dennett discusses our need to find supernatural agents in things: selves in people, God in Heaven, etc. At this stage Dennett's theory is like Freud's—his evidence is hidden deep inside your brain. Sheldrake (2006) refers to Dennett's theories as 'evidence-free and highly speculative'.

[11]Burke Brown, in a wonderful chance encounter, rekindled and greatly expanded our understanding of the neglected (repressed) role chance plays in our lives.

[12]See Krantz (1998), who points out that although we're all aware that chance plays a significant role in our lives, social science typically treats it as nuisance, as a temporary source of error, or ignores it alto-gether. Randomness and uncertainty are treated as major players—as irreducible facts of nature—in the-oretical physics. Gigerenzer and Murray (1987; 2001) have not only been major players in the cognitive revolution, but also in bringing the probabilistic revolution to social scientists. Non-linear, dynamic sys-tem theory is starting to knock more loudly on the door of the social science box. It even has its own journal, *Nonlinear Dynamics, Psychology, and Life Sciences*, published by the Society for Chaos Theory.

Fig 16.1 ■ YOU BET YOUR LIFE

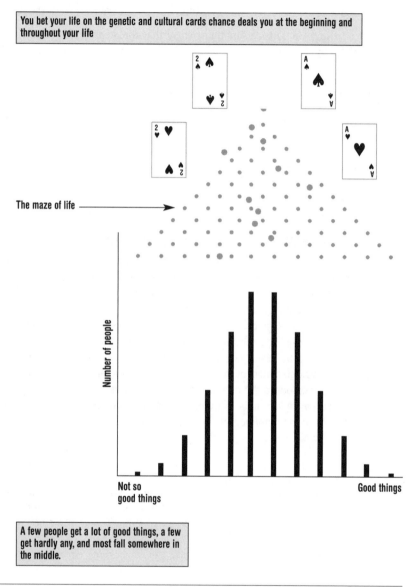

You bet your life on the genetic and cultural cards chance deals you at the beginning and throughout your life

The maze of life ⟶

Number of people

Not so
good things

Good things

A few people get a lot of good things, a few
get hardly any, and most fall somewhere in
the middle.

But what happens if the pinball machine covers the whole world, and instead of chance playing by the 50–50 rule, the coin is a bit biased to favour certain regions (i.e., dealing you a combination of good cards at birth just because you happen to live in one part of the globe rather than another)? For instance, in terms of gaining access to life's goodies, would you rather be born in North America or in Bangladesh?

If you were born in North America then right away chance has dealt you a pretty good hand, for which neither you, nor your 'I', can take personal credit.

In addition, let's say Lady Luck deals you a strong immune system, above average intelligence, and slots you into a nourishing socio-economic niche. Not a bad hand, lots of face cards, and a couple of aces. And still no credit to you.

Fig 16.2 ■

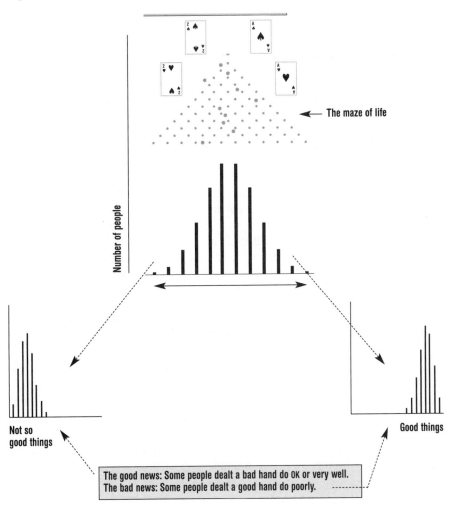

The maze of life

Number of people

Not so good things

Good things

The good news: Some people dealt a bad hand do OK or very well.
The bad news: Some people dealt a good hand do poorly.

The likelihood that you'll end up to the right of the distribution in Figure 16.1 is greatly increased.

Suppose Lady Luck granted you three wishes, you can choose three cards in your very first hand, what would they be? The three we just listed (above average IQ, immune system, and socioeconomic niche), or would you choose others: male or female, ethnic origin, appearance, natural athletic ability, longevity genes, etc?

So, on the day you arrive on earth, chance has already dealt you a hand that you will play for the rest of your life. It is a hand for which you can take no credit and for which you can accept no blame. The chance combination of cards plays an important role in how your path through life unfolds, but the question, ultimately, is how big a role?

How much does Lady Luck control your life?

Does your first hand primarily determine whether you end up on the right side of the tracks, with lots of goodies, (see the right side of Figure 16.2) or the left side, with more than your share of troubles? Or, like most of us, kind of in the middle? The premise underlying the 'American Dream' claims that the hand you're dealt in the beginning need not have an effect in determining your *success*. As proof, we can point to individuals who were dealt a lousy hand and still ended up on top.

Notice that not all those who were dealt a good hand are clustered at the far right. Most of them are above the middle distribution line, but they are spread out. Likewise, those dealt a poor hand aren't all clustered at the far left; they're spread out too. Where does that variability come from: individual self-determination, genetic determinants, cultural determinants, or an irreducible randomness in the molecules, weather, earthquakes, and people?

In short, probability statistics map the distribution of human characteristics. And, sure enough, we find surprises such as individuals who succeed without formal education and individuals who survive fatal diseases. It's *possible* to start with a poor hand and do well, to beat the odds. It's possible, but statistics indicate that it 'ain't ruddy likely!'.

Now, consider what role chance plays throughout the rest of your life. Consider where and when Lady Luck decided to effect major points in your life: your choice of career, accidents, windfalls, choice of mate,[13] (e.g., bad weather delays your flight, you meet someone by chance, you start up a casual conversation with a stranger who eventually becomes your wife).

If you add those subsequent cards, to the ones dealt you in the beginning, how much of your life was determined by chance, and how much by your

---

[13]See Sprott (2004) for an example of applying dynamic, non-linear, chance factors to romantic relationships.

conscious, planned, rational decision making—by your big 'I', by your New Year's resolutions?

Vote

On the basis of the argument outlined above, what's your hunch? Should we admit the premise highlighting the *potency of chance* in shaping our lives, into respectability into the scientific box?

Strongly Agree	Mildly Agree	Don't Know	Mildly Disagree	Strongly Disagree

Next we consider yet another quasi-heresy known as social constructivism. We call it a quasi-heresy because it's more widely accepted than those just considered, but like them, it reduces the regions of choice that are open to individual, conscious, and rational decision-making.

Constructing Reality, Not Discovering It

Gergen (1995, 2005),[14] Mahoney (2004), and Bruner (2005) have convincingly and elegantly developed and documented the theory that our beliefs and habits are both constructed and strongly determined by the particular cultural silos, which by chance, we happen to occupy: 'cultural psychology tends to hold culture as the birthing site for psychological processes. The universal in psychology is replaced with the indigenous' (Gergen, 1995: 32). In other words the culture in which you grew up (nurture) determines your behaviour more than your genes (nature). Bruner (2005) states that '[culture] operates implicitly, as it were, rather like a fish being the last to discover water' (54).

Without consulting the particular individual, we can do a pretty good job of predicting a person's attitudes and behaviour just by knowing the cultural and sub-cultural groups in which they were raised and reside—a form of cultural determinism.[15]

You can relate to this theory by consulting your own experience. You can make better-than-chance predictions about language, food preferences, clothing, and values merely by knowing the person's country of origin. You can make even more accurate predictions by knowing their sub-culture within the country.[16] You also know from personal experience, and from observing others, the

---

[14]See Agnew (2005).

[15]You may be familiar with Dawkins concept of 'meme', a unit of cultural transmission, just as a gene is a unit of biological transmission. It can be thought of as a unit of information or belief passed from one mind to another, or from cultures to individuals.

[16]As young children increasingly experience exposure to multiple cultures at home and abroad, stereotypical predictions should become less naïve.

powerful role peer groups play in shaping the attitudes and behaviours of their members including speech expressions, clothing, and food preferences.

Not only do cultural influences and immediate peer pressures influence such qualitative behaviour, but basic quantitative judgments as well. For example, peer group influences have been reliably demonstrated to affect judgments about lengths of lines. When made alone judgments are typically 100 per cent accurate, but under peer pressure they become uncertain and biased in the direction the peer groups dictate. Jurors may or may not vote by secret ballot. A common practice—unless it is a hung jury—is a verbal go-around or show of hands. Such practices rely on peer pressure to markedly increase the probability of reaching a consensus. Sociologists observing scientists working in their labs conclude that many so-called *facts* are not so much discovered as negotiated under peer group pressure.[17]

Vote

On the basis of the argument outlined above, what's your hunch? Can we afford to admit the *cultural and peer group* premise into full membership in the scientific box? Acknowledging that they provide and sustain the major premises that drive out decisions?

Strongly Agree	Mildly Agree	Don't Know	Mildly Disagree	Strongly Disagree

Therefore, in addition to the influences of Dennett's teams of mini-robots, the hand chance deals us at conception, and subsequently, we now add cultural influences and peer pressure to further reduce the degree of self-control over what we think and do. In brief, we might conclude that chance deals us both our genetic and cultural cards. What the genes don't determine, culture does, leaving the 'I' with precious little, if any, degrees of freedom.

Chance as the Biggest Boss?

Notice how a simple, mind-sized theory emerges when we pool these three heresies together. In one way or another chance turns out to be the big boss.

As indicated earlier, at conception chance deals two very important types of cards that will shape much, if not most, of our future life. The first type includes your genes (male or female, tall or short, strong or weak immune system, etc.). Genes are the major source of Dennett's mini-robots.

The nature–nurture debate talks about the role of chance in determining the nature side of the equation. But consider the other side, the nurture half of the

---

[17]See Knorr-Cetina (1987) and Latour (1987).

debate. It turns out that, at least in the beginning, chance also deals your major *nurture* cards as well. Chance determines your initial physical and cultural environments. Lady Luck decided whether you arrived in Bangladesh or North America, and she decided your socioeconomic sub-culture (ranging from culturally and economically nourished to deprived).

But chance isn't finished with you yet, she still has more cards to deal as you wend your way through the particular physical, social, and inter-personal territory that your genes and your cultural silo provided. Chance can randomly mutate some of your genes (rearrange one or more of your teams of mini-robots) through radiation from medical and dental x-rays, smoking, drugs. Any or all of which can unpredictably and radically alter your destiny. Additional cards can be dealt through chance events occurring within your cultural box; chance events or 'accidents' often determine a career choice or a career change, the choice of spouse, or the location where you buy your house.

But, as noted earlier, not everyone who is dealt a good hand has a good life, and not everyone who is dealt a bad hand has a bad life. The good news is that some people who are dealt a poor genetic and cultural hand do very well. It's this sort of irreducible unpredictability that makes life and science so fascinating.

Well, you, or your genetically and culturally programmed mini-robots, have voted on whether or not to welcome the three heresies into full membership within the scientific box. Regardless of whether you voted yes or no, we don't think you have much cause to worry.

It Takes Persistent Heresies a While to Break into the Box

Our hunch is that your familiar 'I' is safe. It's our bet that all three heresies—the teams of mini-robots, cultural determinism, and the fickle finger of fate—will, at best, be provided low cost housing out in the theoretical suburbs and only invited into the box on special occasions. In other words, they probably won't be offered international passports. Not necessarily because they're wrong, but rather because we can't psychologically or socially afford to give up our core premise of free will and conscious self-control. Our self-image, or 'I', endorses free will, and so do all our major institutions. Or education system, our government, the courts, and our commerce and economy all rest on the presumption of self-control. Dismantling and rebuilding all those institutions to reflect Dennett's idea is prohibitively expensive on conceptual, emotional, and practical levels. Only a few under-financed institutions (e.g., psychiatric hospitals and prisons for the criminally insane) now rest on the premise that teams of mini-robots, or *the devil*, are in charge of inmate behaviour.

Criminal lawyers will no doubt be inviting Dan Dennett as an expert witness supporting *not guilty* pleas by reason that teams of uncontrollable mini-robots 'made my client do it.'

We see the premise of conscious control at least as entrenched as the flat earth truth at the time of Columbus, or the geocentric *truth* at the time of Galileo, but much less open to public disproof than either of those.[18]

Maybe there's a completely dominant gene—part of our immune system—promoting the health-giving illusion of self-control, a genetically programmed Minskian defense against dangerous ways of thinking, against a sense of debilitating helplessness.

We predict that all three heresies will continue to reside in a good safe place, outside the box, and only be invited in on special occasions, like many Christians who only invite Jesus in at Easter.

Ian Stewart (2001) and Bruner (2005) demonstrate how thinking outside the box can be very, very difficult. Along with Minsky, we propose that it can also be very, very dangerous.

Thinking outside the box can be dangerous

As poor Ignaz Semmilweis discovered, thinking outside the box can be dangerous. You could end up in an insane asylum just for telling doctors that their hands are dirty!

Closer to home is the recent suicide of Michael Mahoney a superb psychological theorist and therapist.

He spent his professional career in lonely explorations outside traditional academic boxes, laterally as a critical constructivist, saying: 'No other family of modern theories asks it's adherents to maintain such a degree of self-examining openness, to so painstakingly tolerate and harvest (rather than eliminate) ambiguity, or to so thoroughly question both the answers and the questions by which they inquire. It is not easy to be a constructivist' (1988: 18).

From our bounded rationality viewpoint such a commitment places an impossible burden even on a big brain. From a Minskian perspective it requires a personally dangerous way of thinking. Mahoney lacked the intellectual arrogance required to blind him to the complexity required to cut such a massive undertaking down to a tolerable mind-size.

From personal experience you know that you can be ridiculed merely for putting one foot outside the box—wrong clothes, wrong hair cut, politically incorrect (group incorrect) language.

---

[18]For a delightful yet provocative experience see Stewart (2001) Flatterland, which explores the problem of trying to think outside a box that you don't know you're in—an elaboration of Bruner's metaphor that fish are the last to learn about water. And, if you enjoy conceptual rollercoaster's see Ken Wilber's *Integral Psychology* (2000) in which he sells multiple models of experience rather than assigning supremacy to a reductionistic science. He suggest that if we are made of dirt, it's pretty frisky dirt. Which is like saying to physical reductionists: 'If everything consists of randomly interacting molecules, including scientists, where's the certainty?' Science buys reductionism because it promises certainty, but increasingly many scientific reductionisms are producing uncertainty, complexity, and randomness—including chaos theory. Maybe we should name it 'Frisky, uncertain reductionism?'

The scholarly perpetrators of the three heresies discussed earlier have both feet outside the box into no-no land. When they try to come home and proudly display their souvenirs they're greeted with misinterpretation and/or ridicule

Furthermore, anytime someone leaves the safety of THE BOX and explores outer space, travels into the unknown, they can get lost or abused.

Next we briefly consider mathematics, a common but at times risky way of exploring speculative space.

Dangerous mathematics

When operating at the top of the PST, unexplored mathematical space can be dangerous. Alan Turing (Leavitt, 2005) was a mathematical wizard who not only developed the mathematical model underlying digital computers, but also broke the code of the Nazi Enigma machine, which had been used to send secret messages. Turing, who committed suicide at 42, fits the stereotype of the eccentric genius, of someone who operates outside the conceptual and social box and who got lost along the way.

Levin (2003) provides another sad example:

> Over a century ago the Viennese-born mathematician Ludwig Boltzmann (1844–1906) invented statistical mechanics, a powerful description of atomic behaviour based on probabilities. Opposition to his ideas was harsh and his moods were volatile. Despondent, fearing disintegration of his theories he hanged himself in 1906. It wasn't his first suicide attempt but it was his most successful. Paul Ehrenfest (1880–1933) killed himself nearly thirty years later. I looked at their photos today and searched their eyes for depression and desperation. I didn't see them written there (2003: 1).

Levin, a mathematician, wonders whether isolation and brushes with madness may be occupational hazards of those spending their lives in lonely explorations of outer mathematical space in the speculative space at the top their PSTs. Recall that we suggested earlier that we might be running out of problems with simple solutions and therefore increasingly encountering those beyond the reach of empirical science. Lacking empirical stepping-stones, we must travel into the future on the flimsy bridges of hope and mathematical speculations.

Getting lost in speculative space

If we're correct, then more and more scientists will be spending an increased amount of time playing in the speculative space at the top of their PSTs. Some will fall off the edge—like Semmilweis, Turing, and Boltzmann. Serious explorations in speculative space can be (à la Minsky) dangerous.

To travel without culturally endorsed premises (maps), or conceptual safety lines supported by trusted others, takes courage and tenacity. To travel alone without peer group support, and with the echoes of derision from those you're leaving behind, takes guts.

So, although it's easy to dismiss and deride our modern explorers as they sail dangerously close to the edge of current knowledge and beliefs, and although some of them will disappear *over the edge*, a few will return with compelling maps—promissory notes—of our future, typically lacking any clear warning label of their speculative nature.[19]

As empirical science lags behind, bogged down in complexity, a trusted theory becomes the most practical things in the world because they are the only maps we have of tomorrow's unknowns. Increasingly, believing-is-seeing will probably become acknowledged as the *modus operandi* of science.

As the problems become more complex we will need better theories and better theorists. We know how to turn out good researchers who solve well-defined problems and who can discover/construct local reliability and validity in small playpens. However, we know precious little about turning out great theorists, the Darwins, the Galtons, the Curries, the Einsteins, the Boltzmanns, the Freuds, the Skinners, the Watson and Cricks, the Simons, the Shohams, the Milners, the Minskys, the Kahnemanns, the Dennetts, the Mahoneys, and the Gergens of the future.

Popular conceptions of science have been so focused on the bottom right corner of the PST—on rituals of testing and confirming hypotheses and on producing dogged researchers—that the puzzle of where good theories and creative theorists come from has generally been ignored. Yes, they come from outside the box. But how did they get there, survive there, and then manage to somehow smuggle their heresies back in? Does chance sort those mavericks outside the box but equip them with teams of mini-robots that are also both survival specialists and break-in artists? Semmilweis couldn't break back into the box; Dennett's really hammering at the door, Gergen's got a foot in.[20] Let's consider some others.

Great theorists: confidence, imagination, and analogies?

Biographies and anecdotes give us a place to start when researching the characteristics of brilliant theorists. They suggest a combination of traits: confidence and arrogance, imagination and madness, plus brilliant and weird analogies and metaphors.

---

[19]It is understandable that explorers have to believe in order to rely on strong emotionally anchored premises if they are going to spend years in an outer space, be it a physical, theoretical, mathematical, or spiritual space. Mahoney (2004), a fearless out-of-the-box explorer and strong believer, was an exception because he repeatedly reminds his readers that his maps are his personal constructions and that it's a difficult balancing act to maintain a state of believing and doubting at the same time.

[20]Many of us accept Gergen's cultural constructionism to help explain the behaviour of others, particularly foreigners. But some have trouble accepting the fact that most of our own behaviour is culturally determined. Big 'I' is no more ready to admit that it's under the control of the surrounding culture than it is at the beck and call of a team of mini-robots.

Bryson (2004) presents a compelling portrait of Carolus Linnaeus as a scientist combining arrogance and imagination. Of the famous classifier of plants Bryson writes: 'Rarely has a man been more comfortable with his own greatness. He spent much of his leisure time penning long and flattering portraits of himself, declaring that there had never been a greater botanist or zoologist, and that his system of classification was "the greatest achievement in the realm of science"' (356).

Linnaeus's awesome imagination created the following memorable metaphor:

> Love comes even to the plants. Males and females. . .hold their nuptials. . .showing their sexual organs . . . . the flowers' leaves serve as a bridal bed, which the creator has so gloriously arranged. Adorned with such noble bed curtains and perfumed with so many soft scents that the bridegroom with his bride might here celebrate their nuptials with so much great solemnity. When the bed has thus been made ready, then is the time for the bridegroom to embrace his beloved bride and surrender himself to her (cited in Bryson, 2004: 357).

Without the same aura of voyeurism, Alan Lightman (2005) provides fascinating fly-on-the-wall glimpses of great scientists in less titillating action.[21]

Einstein's gall

Einstein, as a student ranting against his academic supervisor in 1901, threatens: 'But if he has the gall to reject my doctoral thesis, then I'll publish his rejection in cold print together with the thesis and he will have made a fool of himself' (cited in Lightman, 2005: 45). It appears that Linnaeus was not the only scholar to demonstrate a touch of arrogance. Self-confidence may be one of the characteristics of a great scientist.

Only four years later, while working alone as a patent clerk, Einstein published five papers—all in one year—that revolutionized modern physics. Maybe it helps to be not only arrogant but also to be a loner, working outside the theoretical confinements of persistent peer pressure? As documented by Robinson (1990) it also helps to rely heavily on analogies and metaphors, as Einstein did.

Speaking of *analogies*, we used the analogy of the of billiard ball throughout *The Science Game*. We're not the first to have used this imagery to explain a concept. Bryson (2004) notes that Compton, an American physicist, confirmed one of Einstein's theories by shining x-rays at electrons: 'each electron rebounded as if it had been hit by a single tiny *billiard ball*. From the amount and direction of the rebound, Compton could infer that each *billiard ball* of light

---

[21]Physical scientists have been more closely studied than social scientists, and their successes and failures are more obvious. As a result, they provide clearer examples. However, the social sciences are starting to catch up (see Fancher, 1996; Runyan, 2006).

had its own energy and its own definite momentum' (191, emphasis added). Wouldn't it be nice if such simple models worked with people, if billiard balls with brains rebounded by such predictable amounts and in such predictable directions when bombarded with *illumination*?

Heisenberg, famous for his uncertainty principle, says the following about thinking outside the box: 'Usual space–time concepts at cosmological distances [way out] can be justified neither by logic [*up top thinking*] nor by observation [bottom testing]' (cited in Bryson, 2004: 203). So how are such radical concepts justified? By travelling light, by leaving behind established truths about space and time, traditional logic, and trusted observations, by travelling with blind confidence on personal metaphors and imagination, and in many cases, on bridges built of speculative mathematics.

Do great theorists leave old truths behind, or were they merely poor students, like Einstein, who never over-learned them in the first place? And how do they find big new ones?

Where do brilliant ideas come from?

If we must increasingly rely on brilliant theorists to light our way, wouldn't it be nice to know where breakthrough ideas, such as the structure of the atom and DNA, come from? One place, of course, is from other people. Lightman (2005: 370) notes that some historians of science suggest that Watson and Crick got a very good idea from Rosalind Franklin, but didn't give her adequate credit. But we don't know where she got her ideas, so we're still left with the same question: where do brilliant ideas come from?

Using a little circular reasoning, we can come up with the empty answer. Brilliant ideas come from brilliant people. But big ideas can be generated not only by brilliant scientists, but also by liars. When no one knows the right answer, the field becomes a free-for-all. It takes years of research and critical analyses to decide which answer to trust, until next year or next century it becomes an historical curiosity.

Having peeked quickly into the lives of a few great theorists, it becomes obvious that confidence, or arrogance, is a necessary characteristic. Without it, they wouldn't be able to tolerate standing alone outside the box long enough to critically examine it, much less to create a small and revolutionary addition.

Furthermore, as you and I zip around our PSTS we typically jump *with confidence* from one decision to another—about careers, mates, the future, and the driver in the next lane. And do so, in most instances with blind confidence, on the basis of incomplete and conflicting information, and cursory analysis, somehow cut it down to mind-size, to a functional if fallible theory of how our world works.

Managing Uncertainty

In order to have the type of confidence needed to stand outside the box—and indeed to have the confidence to zip blindly around our own PSTs—a way is needed to manage the inevitable uncertainty. Managing uncertainty is a complex question and this textbook provides neither the time nor the space to do it justice. However, based on the discussions throughout *The Science Game* it is evident that a theory to manage uncertainty must include the following:

1. Relying on *premises* that reduce most of the uncertainty (e.g., Simon's 'no conclusions without premises').
2. Lacking premises, we'll rely on *affordable rituals* (heuristics) for selecting (cherry-picking) items from Kahneman's accessible information (e.g., believing the last thing we heard from a friend, a guru, or authority figure).
3. When there's time, we'll rely on both premises and cherry-picking. Maybe we'll adjust our initial premise to more or less reflect some of the more memorable or salient items selected from subsequent flow of accessible information.
4. When managing complex problems (lots of dots, lots of possible connections) everyone is bound to make some mistakes. Items 1, 2, and 3 not only help us avoid dangerous ways of thinking (Minsky) and help us make decisions, but they also help us rationalize our mistakes (e.g., 'It's their fault.').
5. Over time and through trial and error some of our guesses, or premises, will become more accurate and some of our cherry-picking will become more efficient. This will reduce some of our errors, particularly in small space–time playpens.
6. We'll continue to encounter surprises because chance always sits in on the game: tiny games like the random motion and collision of sub-atomic particles; medium size games like fatal accidents, and big games like 9/11, earthquakes, and pandemics.

When considering theories of human behaviour, look for the above six mentally affordable, but fallible, ways of managing daily uncertainties. You'll invariably find the first five. But unlike theoretical physicists, many social and behavioural scientists don't provide a respectable place[22] in their theories for chance or random influences such as those we discussed as heresies earlier in this chapter (e.g., country of birth).

An emerging interest in chaos theory is an exception (e.g., Maasen & Weingart, 2000). This is not the place for a detailed discussion, but you are probably familiar with one premise of chaos theory: the importance of *initial*

---

[22]Yes, they provide for chance and probability theory in their statistical rituals. This is not necessarily because they believe them, but because the scientific institution requires them.

conditions, or of a small early effect having a large subsequent effect (e.g., like a butterfly flapping its wings in Brazil that could eventually lead to a hurricane in Texas, or small spec of lipstick on a collar can lead to a very big divorce).

Overview

In brief, both laypeople and scientists rely on several different premises, or models of reality, to help them to manage uncertainty, to walk with blind confidence into the future:

1. Simple cause–effect models (if A then B) that allow us to make trusted predictions: If you are born (A) then you will die (B).
2. Simple cause–effect models (if A then B + e) that allow us to make accurate predictions about individuals *most of the time*, with some exceptions: If you jump from a ten story building (A) then you will die most of the time (B) unless (e) you have a parachute, land on an awning, etc.
3. Cause–effect relations that allow us to make predictions about *groups* of individuals, but not about specific people: X per cent of 55-year-old males will die of a heart attack before they reach 65.
4. In some cases we can add some accuracy to our model #3 predictions by including more information (If A (and C) then B + e): If you are 55-year-old male (A) who has smoked for more than the last ten years (C) then you have a Y per cent chance (e) of dying of a heart attack before 65 (B).
5. However, in many instances we lack reliable information to help us reduce uncertainty, particularly about the future (e.g., interpersonal relations, job security, health, medical treatments, terrorist attacks, etc.,) and so we must rely on highly speculative top-of-the-PST models, such as on Simon's naïve but trusted premises, mathematical maps—probability theory, string theory, chaos theory, etc.—biases, and hope.

We tend to see scientists as generating the simple models noted as #1 and #2 above. But most of the significant problems facing individuals and society quickly morph into the more complex models detailed as #3, #4, and more importantly, #5, above.

Daily, citizens and scientists confidently walk, drive and fly into the unknown and unknowable future. Usually we travel on simple 'if A then B' speculative stepping-stones. The science game is exciting because we don't know ahead of time how many life-shaping problems will turn out to be based on such simple cause-effect laws enabling precise predictions (as provided for in models #1 and #2), or only permitting probable predictions about groups, not individuals (as provided for in models #3 and #4). We also don't know how many of our individual and social problems will continue to lie, temporarily or forever, beyond the reach of empirical science (as provided for in model #5). Then, we must resolve the ensuing uncertainty at the top of the PST with speculative maps ranging far and wide, from the mathematical to the religious.

SUMMARY

First, we *speculate* that increasing numbers of personal, social, and global problems are becoming empirically intractable—they can't be rigorously tested and solved in the bottom right corner of the PST. Consequently, we must place more reliance on scholars operating up-top and outside the box as they seek and display theoretical *resolutions*, or speculative bridges, into unknown and possibly unknowable futures.

Next, we discussed three such heretical resolutions, all of them challenge one of our entrenched truths: blind belief in omnipotent 'I', in the conscious self enthroned at the top of our PST making decisions, in short, running our particular show. We speculate that the 'I' will successfully resist these threats to its authority, even though these heresies may all be true.

We humans have survived, even thrived, on functional illusions—like the flat earth, horoscopes, perfect rationality, and "til death do us part' dreams. The treasured 'I' may well be another functional but fallible myth holding a universal and timeless passport.

For brief periods all of us stick one toe outside the box playing safely and vicariously through movies, novels, plays, and boozy bull sessions. But many scholars bet their career and even their sanity on lengthy, lonely explorations in high risk, unknown territories. Their newly discovered or constructed truths can be dangerous, can even overwhelm their bounded rationality. And, when the newly constructed truths are displayed back home, they will typically attract derision, rejection, or social and professional punishment. But, if the timing is right, these new truths could open up exciting new futures. These gutsy explorers are our modern-day Ignaz Semmilweis', Newtons, Curries, Freuds, Turings, and Skinners. They forge ahead disregarding complexity and risk. They manage their uncertainty with trusted premises while cherry-picking positive evidence and wrestling with—or ignoring—the negative.

That's why the science game remains the biggest game in town.

Now we close our exploration with the same quotations we used to open it.

I do not know what I may appear to the world, but to myself I seem to have been only a boy playing on the seashore, and diverting myself in now and then finding a smoother pebble or prettier shell than ordinary, whilst the great ocean of truth lay undiscovered before me (Newton, 1972: 929).

Whoever undertakes to set himself up as a judge in the field of truth and knowledge is shipwrecked by the laughter of the Gods (Einstein, 1972: 920).

We hope that these quotations ring your chimes more melodiously now than they may have done when you first encountered them at the beginning of the book.

We hope we have unpackaged the prevailing neat and tidy, stereotypical view of scientists, that you've gained a sense of their infinite variety: ranging all the way from those collecting pretty stones, to those risking their reputations and their sanity outside the box in lonely and dangerous explorations of speculative space, and all of them periodically cowering before the giggles if not the belly laughs of the Gods.

Recall our early proposal that science is a wondrous playpen for grown-ups—a wide open and potentially dangerous place for theorists operating at the top of their PSTs, whereas researchers work in more protected spaces sprinkled with observational stepping-stones. Remember also that we said that when exploring the playpen most scientists would discover small- and medium-sized packages of truth, and periodically run smack into the boundaries of their personal biases, their discipline's biases, cultural ignorance, and the concrete complexity of nature.

A fortunate few will stumble on big truths, and some might even win The Prize!

Although scholars may go on teaching, researching, and publishing for many years, the scientist within them dies when childlike wonder and driving curiosity no longer influence their day-to-day functioning. In such sad instances it's publish and perish.

For most scientists, the addiction is to the mystery and not the prize. And whether you become a professional practitioner of science or continue as an increasingly sophisticated and curious consumer, we hope that you catch the bug, enjoy a second childhood, and glory in the mystery, while managing the uncertainty.

student's notebook

This last chapter gave me a wild ride—it had a lot of information to absorb! I think I'll need to read it through again in a week or so!

I'm able to recall the three heresies. Well to be honest, the interesting thing is I can remember them, and accept them, if I apply them to other people. But not so much when I try to apply them to myself.

OK, I can accept that in the beginning chance played a big part in my life—being a girl born in North America to a functional, middle-class family. So initially, by luck, I was dealt a better hand than most people in the world. Also, since I was born into and raised in an extended family of WASPS, a bunch of my behaviour is culturally determined (language, food preferences, sex roles, views on marriage, religion, etc.)

And I can even see teams of mini-robots (genetically and socially programmed) controlling much (most?) of the behaviour of others—particularly if I don't know or like them very well. But my 'I' is still the boss of me, and of most of my behaviour, most of the time.

With Derek, I vacillate. Sometimes I can predict his behaviour so well that it could well be controlled by mini-robots. Other times, when I can't, I want to hug or strangle his 'I'—probably a miniature red-headed rascal romping around at the top of his PST.

We don't have to hand in a formal assignment, but we do have to submit our relevant news stories for Professor Creek's collection—I think he's writing a book.

You could tell that Professor Creek liked this chapter. He's into neuroscience, so was especially enthusiastic about the idea of mini-robots running the show. I suspect he dreams of doing brain images of rats, before and after they learn a maze, in order to locate the seat of learning in their little brains, to locate the clubhouse where the tiny robots meet, drink rat beer, and decide what to do next.

Dr Frund, on the other hand, seems downright cool towards Dennett's theories, but she's partial to the constructivists like Gergen and Mahoney. I guess she believes the idea that mini-robots run our physiology and habits, but beyond that we still discover and construct chunks of reality on our own. She agrees that, at present, cognitive science (the brain/mind puzzle) tops the social science hit parade.

Dr Frund also acknowledges that chance events have a much larger influence on our lives than we admit, particularly right at the beginning (e.g., where and when you're born, male/female, black/white, strong/weak immune system, socioeconomic status, etc.).

The idea of the 'end of science' was way out of my box. Now my original neat and tidy, seeing-is-believing view fits finding small truths in small playpens. Whereas the end of science heresy applies to big playpens—like the future—where, lacking empirical stepping-stones scientists have to rely on speculative maps, promissory notes, on believing-is-seeing theoretical, or mathematical, stepping-stones.

I guess using the Premack principle to condition myself to do blind recall after a lecture or chapter is like training, or programming, a team of mini-robots. Any conditioned behaviours, or habits, are automatically firing neural networks, which sounds similar to teams of min-robots. Any way the Premack principle—a conditioning method—sure has improved my study skills, my interest, and my grades. Even Dr Frund has to agree with that! So if that behaviour represents the work of a team of mini-robots, then be my guest.

But what about the role of chance beyond the good hand I was dealt at birth? When I stop to think about it, most of my current life seems to depend on one chance encounter after another. I majored in psychology because, by the time I got around to registering, it was the only program that still had enough empty courses for me to declare it a major. I took Dr Frund's course because she added a new section that day. I grabbed the empty course and she became my advisor. I literally ran into Derek coming out of the bookstore one day. He helped me pick up my books, took me for coffee, and now he's my best friend. He was already a member of the B&B group, so now so am I.

To me, it looks like psychology has one group of faculty that backs the brain/genes/neurology/mini-robot theories, and the other group still believes in the power of the mind, dividing it between the 'I' and the environment. Both groups are a long way from rigorous testing and establishing external validity, so for now either side has openings for new disciples.

The idea that our lives are being ruled by mini-robots or chance offends my self-image, though. Derek says Dennett's mini-robots are messenger-boys (he means 'messenger-persons') who are just carrying out instructions from our genes and our environments.

So, all in all, he agrees that we're programmed like robots. But he's still sticking with the simple formula that most important behaviour is programmed by big 'E' cultural influences and small 'e' genetics: $B = E + g$.

We ran all this by the B&B members. Our math geek starting expanding the formula, scribbling strange equations on a series of napkins. Then he sat there giggling to himself, demonstrating the fine line between math and madness. Our resident economist stopped placing 'buy and sell' orders long enough to wave around an article about neuroscience and economics—it was about setting up brain imaging machines at the stock exchange so you could predict people's buy and sell orders before they consciously make the call.

I interrupted to tell them about the six points for managing uncertainty. Big noise followed. It seemed to me the split in beliefs about managing uncertainty depended on whether you were studying billiard balls, or billiard balls with brains, and they acknowledged that the size of the playpen you were exploring had to be a factor.

Small playpen lab researchers took the position that most uncertainty management occurs at the bottom of the PST—relying on reliable observations and rigorous testing—with tidying up occurring at the top. In contrast, non-lab scientists (big playpen types) proclaimed that top-of-the-PST beliefs, biases, axioms, and premises (à la Simon) handled most of the uncertainty, with more or less sophisticated cherry-picking rituals occurring at the bottom.

The philosophy major claimed that quantitative lab researchers were usually specifically right (small playpen internal validity) and generally wrong (lacking external validity). Alternatively, the qualitative researchers were often generally right (rough external validity) but often specifically wrong (lacking specific internal validity).

So, the preferred way of managing uncertainty seemed to depend mainly on the size of the playpen and the size of the brains (rats or people) being studied. The smaller the playpen and the smaller the brains of the research participants, then the more legitimate their claim that they managed uncertainty at the bottom right corner of the pst.

Derek, of course, piped up and said they were all wrong, and that most of their uncertainty was managed by up-top theorists whose predictions told the lab guys specifically where to dig. 'One up-top theorist like Einstein keeps thousands of lab guys shovelling at their local sites for over a century. Otherwise you'd all be standing around scratching' were his exact words, actually. We left right away after that!

I've decided I'm going to try the lab research course with Professor Creek next term, then do some qualitative field research work with Dr Frund following that.

Then I'll decide which kind of famous psychologist I'm going to be.

Note

Check your student website at http://www.oup.com/ca/he/companion/agnewpyke for information about an interview with Dan Dennett.

REVIEW TRUE OR FALSE QUIZ

T F	1.	Examples of the heresies explored in this chapter include the end of science and the claim that chance events rule most of our lives.
T F	2.	A case can be made that theoretical science has seen its best days.
T F	3.	Complex problems potentially involving a combination of many causes present formidable challenges to the lower right corner of the PST.
T F	4.	An increase in abortions is associated with an increase in the crime rate.
T F	5.	To assume that human behaviour follows scientific laws is a form of determinism and a variant of the free will argument.
T F	6.	Dan Dennett (2003) argues that consciousness is a by-product of the operation of the brain.
T F	7.	Dennett's model cannot explain altruistic behaviour.
T F	8.	In theoretical physics, chance factors (i.e., randomness and uncertainty) are regarded as temporary sources of error.
T F	9.	Social constructivism is a concept that describes the operation of chance factors in reducing the regions of choice open to us.
T F	10.	A 'meme' is a unit of cultural transmission, just as a gene is a unit of biological transmission.
T F	11.	Peer pressure can affect qualitative judgments but not quantitative judgments.
T F	12.	It is unlikely that the concept of determinism will win out in the near future because most major institutions rest on the presumption of self-control.
T F	13.	Thinking outside the box can be dangerous.
T F	14.	Mathematicians who thought outside the box and committed suicide include Ludwig Boltzmann, Alan Turing, and Albert Einstein.
T F	15.	Analogies, but not metaphors, provide an adjustable bridge from the known to the unknown.
T F	16.	Confidence and arrogance are key characteristics of great theorists.
T F	17.	Considerable empirical evidence has accumulated in support of string theory.
T F	18.	Archival research may offer some empirical bridges between speculations and rigorous testing.
T F	19.	Managing uncertainty involves guessing, selecting from accessible information, rationalizing errors, and expecting surprises.

T F	20. The philosophy major in Diana's B&B Club claimed that quantitative researchers were usually specifically wrong and generally right.
T F	21. The Google determination of what information is reliable is based, in part, on frequency of appearance or popularity.

Appendix A

N-of-1 Study: Student Self-Change Project

Project instructions

Using as a guide Watson and Tharp's (2002) book, *Self-directed Behaviour: Self-modification for Personal Adjustment*, conduct a study of your own behaviour based on a before-and-after design.

$$O_1 \qquad\qquad X \qquad\qquad O_2$$

pretreatment   treatment   posttreatment
observations or baseline   observation

You will recall that the before-and-after design is weak unless you have a stable pretreatment baseline and also a reasonable posttreatment follow-up, making the improved design look like this:

$$O_{1a} \; O_{1b} \; \ldots\ldots\ldots \; O_{1n} \qquad X \qquad O_{2a} \; O_{2b} \; \ldots\ldots\ldots \; O_{2n}$$

pretreatment baseline of   posttreatment observations
two to three weeks'   and recording of
observation and recording   four to six weeks

Student report

Step 1. Sources of dissatisfaction or desired change

These include wasting a lot of time, skipping classes, smoking heavily, not getting as much out of university—academically, recreationally, or socially—as hoped, not feeling relaxed or acting naturally on most dates (seeming to act a part), and wanting to get more out of both classes and personal relationships.

Step 2. Target behaviours and situations in which they occur

I have chosen the three following target behaviours from the preceding list:

1. *Behaviour:* Chain-smoking or smoking at an increased rate. Smoking, even though I don't enjoy it, is automatic and I regret it the next day.
   Situations: The situations in which this chain-smoking occurs include drinking coffee, keg parties, dates, and tutorials.
2. *Behaviour:* Not paying attention and not asking questions or stating opinions in class.
   Situations: I rarely, if ever, ask questions in any class—large or small. In some tutorials I think of questions and ideas but rarely speak. In large classes I sit at the back where it's easy to daydream or read, though it's harder to avoid participating that way in a tutorial.
3. *Behaviour:* Feeling tense and acting unnatural on dates. I seem to be acting a part, and it's a part I don't know very well, so I suspect neither of us is happy with the performance. I end up talking as if I know everything and also being very critical—not of my date, but of everything else. The behaviour I would like to increase is talking about things I know something about and am interested in, and the behaviour I would like to decrease is acting like a phony, big-time operator.
   Situations: These situations include those where I am on a date and alone with my date. When I'm with a small group, I feel much more relaxed and don't behave like a nerd.

Step 3. Principles of learning as they relate to one of the target behaviours

Not participating in class, for example, can be accounted for by several principles of learning.

1. *Lack of reinforcement.* I can't remember being reinforced or rewarded for past attempts at classroom participation in high school, so I probably never developed skills or habits of this kind. At the university very few professors clearly reinforce students who ask questions, so it is unlikely that such responses will be developed at this stage in my education. Therefore the principle that withholding reinforcers will weaken behaviour helps explain my lack of early development of classroom skills.

2. *Punishment.* My impression is that not only was I not reinforced for participating in class (either asking questions or stating my ideas or opinions); instead I was usually ignored, punished, or ridiculed. (Some of this may have been my own imagination, but whether it was or not, it would probably serve as punishment.) Thus the second learning principle appears to be relevant—namely, behaviour that is punished will occur less often.

3. *Avoidance behaviour.* A third relevant law of behaviour is the principle that behaviour that is punished not only occurs less often but that punishment leads to escape or avoidance behaviour as well. This might account for the fact that I skip classes but also avoid listening when I do attend. Apparently avoidance behaviour, once started, is hard to correct so I may face big trouble trying to ask questions in class. In one sense, I'm rewarding myself by skipping classes and by not asking questions—that way I can sit back, relax and daydream. Then, of course, I feel terrified when exams arrive and I have no lecture notes. Obviously immediate rewards are stronger (reduced tension immediately) than are future punishments (exam time panic). Short-term gain trumps delayed pain.

The professor suggested that we identify the stimuli—things, events, and people—that trigger the behaviours we want to change; in my case, avoiding classes and not asking questions when I go. The mere thought of asking questions makes my palms drip and my heart pound, which in turn triggers silence, which triggers relief and relaxation. Meeting my friends at the pub triggers relaxation, which triggers skipping classes.

Step 4. Selecting target behaviour and the situation in which it occurs

I decided to focus on asking questions in class for several reasons: it's important; it's easy to measure changes; I can test the results down at the bottom right corner of my PST; and I can get enough data to meet the course deadline and complete all the steps.

It is difficult to condense my ideas and feelings. In brief, my behaviour boils down to a general withdrawal of attention, interest, and activity. When I even think of asking a question my heart thumps, and my hands shake. I realize that for the purpose of this project, I must describe a particular target behaviour and also specify the situation or situations in which it is supposed to occur.

The target behaviour I plan to increase is asking questions in class. There are two situations on which I will focus. The first is the small classroom situation, or tutorial. If I am successful there, I will then attempt to ask questions in large lecture classes.

Originally I had decided to increase the time I paid attention in class as the target behaviour. However, it's difficult to keep track of such behaviour because my attention ebbs and flows almost imperceptibly, whereas the number of questions I ask is easily counted. Presumably, if I'm asking questions then I am also paying attention, at least to some degree. In brief, my target behaviour is asking questions, and the specific situation during which the target behaviour is to occur is whenever I am in a classroom.

Step 5. Collecting baseline data

Once the target behaviour and the target situation are clearly defined, and before working out a method to improve the situation, the next step is to determine my current level of performance—that is, to see how frequently I now ask questions so that I have a baseline against which to measure any improvement that might take place following the introduction of a behavioural modification strategy.

In order to keep my record(s) simple, and also to make sure I don't lose them, I simply put a check mark in the upper right-hand corner of my course notebook every time I asked a question in that particular class. I kept a record for one typical week, so all classes were covered—except one that I skipped, which was also typical. Interestingly, I asked a question in my first class of the baseline week, which turned out to be the first and last question of the week. Merely collecting baseline data served to get me to ask one question, but that's all. All of this suggests that I don't ask questions for pretty obvious reasons—not asking questions lets me avoid all that thumping, dripping, and squeaking.

I think the one-week baseline provided a fair picture of how frequently my target behaviour of asking questions in class typically occurs. In fact, it overestimates my base rate by one—I don't remember having asked even one question in my first eight weeks at the university (the ninth week was my baseline week).

Step 6. Reinforcers

According to behaviour theory, the most effective way to increase the frequency of any behaviour is to follow it as soon as possible by a strong reinforcer, reward, or treat.

At first I found it difficult to create a list of personal reinforcers. While I won't cover my whole list here, I included reading mysteries and science fiction, going to rock concerts, horsing around on my guitar, listening to records, sessions at the local pub, watching sports on TV—or better still, going to the games, having a sauna, going swimming, eating chocolate Turtles.

Concerning the Premack principle—that is, things I do habitually to which I can tie in a new behaviour—I shower every morning, I eat three meals a day, and I listen to music and read before going to sleep almost every night. I guess one idea might be to use the Premack principle as follows: I will only listen to my music or read my book if I had asked a question in class that day. However, this seems like punishment, and according to the experts it isn't a good idea to use punishment when attempting to change behaviour. Also, since I already read and listen to music, it can't serve as a reinforcer unless I did more of it every time

I had asked a question. However, as it is, I usually read and listen to records until I fall asleep, so I don't see how I could do more of it.

Step 7. Drawing up a behaviour contract

I had more trouble than I expected drawing up a contract that was clear and that I thought would work. My final contract was as follows:

> On this 17th day of November, 2006, I, _____, make the following commitment to myself—namely, that I will attempt to ask at least one question in each small class I attend and that for each question I ask I will immediately reinforce myself with one Turtle and with a 'token' which is worth 30 minutes at the pub for my regular after-noon session. When I have achieved this goal, I will apply the same contract in large classes.
>
> Signed: _____
> Peter Wheelbarrow

I feel a little silly about the Turtles as a reward; kinda childish—like pasting a gold star in my copy book—but it meets the conditions of an immediate rein-forcer I can afford and it represents an overall gain because I don't normally eat them all that often. However, I worried that I may cheat—that is, if I have Turtles then I'll eat Turtles, whether or not I ask a question.

Also, I almost always attend the regular afternoon pub session, and my contract calls for withholding a strong reinforcer if I fail to carry out the target behaviour of asking questions. Therefore granting myself only one 30-minute period of pub time per question asked turned out to be tough on the days I only asked one question. Once I get there I have a tendency to *stay*.

So, as tokens, I used beer session 'tickets' that I manufactured immediately after I asked a question. I'd scribble on a scrap of paper something different each time, for example: 'Admit this great question-asker to 30 minutes of Golden Happiness—Molson's Golden, of course.' Creating my tickets captured some attention that might have better gone to listening to the lecturer. However, in the beginning of a behaviour modification project, one has to be grateful for even a tiny improvement.

Incidentally, my friends found out about my project and would demand my 'ticket' when I appeared. It would be passed around, and I would be told my 30 minutes were up, and hassled if I did not leave or produce another ticket. I guess I could have cheated and manufactured counterfeit ones, but I didn't. This sup-portive behaviour of my friends helped a lot.

Step 8. Antecedents

Learning theory states that much of my behaviour is under the control of imme-diately preceding events or signals called *antecedent stimuli*. For example, if I

467

happen to run into one of my drinking buddies (antecedent stimulus) between classes, we'll likely go for a beer. One beer becomes the antecedent, or trigger, for another beer, which becomes the trigger for another beer, and so on, until I have wasted the afternoon, and quite often, the evening. Therefore my drinking buddy and I are antecedent signals for each other that start a chain reaction of triggers that control, or strongly influence, our joint behaviour.

Incidentally, running into a drinking buddy is also an antecedent condition for skipping classes that afternoon and also the following morning because I tend to sleep late due to a combination of fatigue, disgust, and (sometimes) a hangover.

The antecedent conditions that affect my not asking questions in class appear also to constitute a chain reaction. If a question pops into my head there is a brief period of interest, which triggers nervousness, which triggers a suppression of any question-asking tendency, which, in turn, triggers withdrawal of attention.

It is difficult to list antecedent conditions that favour asking questions, since I don't ask any. However, asking questions should be increased through any reduction in nervousness, plus the 'awareness' that I will get something I want if I do ask a question. That awareness is an antecedent signal, I guess, if it is conscious. In summary, if my plan to ask questions in class is going to work, I must somehow avoid, or reduce, the potency of certain antecedent triggering conditions by:

1. Steering clear of drinking buddies in the early afternoon, or learning to say no. Come to think of it, sometimes it's me who suggests we go for an early beer, so I am often not under any great pressure from others to go.
2. Reducing the nervousness surrounding the idea of asking a question by practicing relaxation.
3. Increasing my awareness during class of the benefits of asking questions, both in terms of short-term reinforcements and long-term payoffs.

Relaxation. As noted, I get nervous at the thought of asking a question, which serves to suppress question asking. Learning theory suggests that you can replace one response with another through practice. I practiced replacing my 'nervous' response with a 'relaxed' response. I practiced relaxing by:

1. Getting comfortable, loosening any tight clothing, and cutting out as many distractions as possible.
2. Taking three very deep and very slow breaths, exhaling very slowly and completely on each breath. Relaxation experts claim that you can't be tense and breath deeply at the same time. So you can measure how tense you are by how deeply you can breath, or how long you hold your breath.
3. Starting with my feet, tensing and relaxing each set of muscles in my body, coordinating the relaxation with exhaling. This way I learned to recognize when and where I was tense and worked up from the feet to the legs, to the thighs, to the stomach, chest, arms, shoulders, neck, face,

and scalp. My neck and shoulders are frequently very tense. I now notice this and can relax them at will.

I practiced for a couple of weeks just before getting up in the morning. Then when I was lying there relaxed, I would imagine asking simple questions in small classes. Then, I practiced relaxing in class, particularly the neck and shoulders, and deep breathing. The guy sitting next to me thought I was getting ready to vomit or have a fit.

It's easy to forget to practice so I kept a record in my notebook of when I practiced relaxation in class. It's easy to forget to keep a record, so I wrote another contract in which I rewarded myself by ordering a big pizza on Saturday or Sunday when my record-keeping system was complete, or at least more complete, for that week.

Step 9. Behavioural change plan goes into operation

It is difficult to decide exactly when my behaviour modification plan was put into operation. I guess in a way it started the day I started planning it. In another way it started when the period of gathering baseline data ended and I started to record progress. In any case, Table A.1 summarizes my intervention plan.

Table A.1	Intervention Plan
Goal	To increase the frequency with which I ask questions in small and large classes.

Plan	1. Draw up a contract specifying target behaviour and the situation, and also reinforcements to be gained for each behaviour unit performed.
	 2. Select critical antecedent conditions to be modified in order to increase the likelihood of producing the target behaviour. The antecedents to be modified include:
	    a. beer-buddies: not accepting or proposing early afternoon beer sessions
	    b. nervousness: to be reduced through relaxation training
	 3. Record results, including a baseline period.

I believe my behaviour modification commenced the first day I started to work on this assignment, but for the purposes of this section of my report, I'll say it started when I put my contract into operation, after the collection of baseline data.

The key elements of the plan, from my point of view, are avoiding certain antecedents, reducing the potency of others through relaxation, and using strong reinforcers immediately following the performance of the target behaviour. Also, it helped to think of it as a kind of game—a game I was committed to play, but one that included a lot of human interest and humour.

Step 10. Results

I have summarized the results of my project in the figure below. It can be seen that, during the baseline period, I asked only one question, and so this behaviour is very improbable under ordinary circumstances.

For the next three weeks I focused on small classes. I recorded each class day and indicated how many questions I asked. I started off the first week of the intervention plan with two questions on Monday, followed by two on Tuesday, then dropped down to zero toward the end of the week. At the commencement of the second week, I was up to four questions early in the week, dropping to zero at the end of the week. However, by the third week, I seemed to have more or less stabilized, asking questions in small classes at around three or four questions per day. It is interesting to note how the behaviour trailed off at the end of the first two weeks. This is not surprising, since Thursdays and Fridays are typically down days as students prepare for the weekend.

In the fourth week, I continued to ask questions in small classes but also attempted to start asking questions in large classes. From the figure it can be seen that the small-class behaviour change appears to be stabilized, and there is some evidence that I am learning to ask questions in large classes. However, I don't expect the frequency to reach the same level in large classes as in small classes, since question-asking in large classes should not be done frivolously—

Fig A1 ■ Mapping Behaviour Change

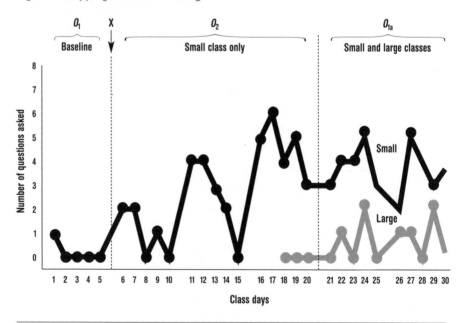

it takes up everyone's time. And some are really stupid like how big can the margins be in our term paper, or will stuff presented by visiting lecturers be on the final exam.

Generally speaking, I am happy with my progress. I am certainly getting more out of my small classes. The questions I ask in large classes are still pretty simple, and I am still not completely relaxed about it—still a few thumps, drips and squeaks.

I plan to continue the same procedure for another two weeks, and if my small-class performance continues, I will let it fly on its own and focus more on the large classes.

I'm still not completely happy about my reinforcements. I've replaced the Turtles with 'girl-watching', with the exception of one tutorial in which I don't seem to need any reinforcements. Also, I use my tokens to buy new CDs rather than to go to the pub, which is a mixed blessing. The relaxation training is working relatively well, except for the odd morning when I oversleep and run out of time; sometimes it works too well and I relax myself right back to sleep. My roommate has agreed to wake me, provided I don't throw things.

I am in the process of drawing up a plan and a contract to tackle another one of the dissatisfactions listed in Step 1 of this project.

In evaluating this before-and-after design, I appreciate the difficulties of deciding just what factors did contribute to my change of behaviour. I am satisfied that it was not an elastic-ruler effect. I did ask more questions; even my professors noted that. But trying to sort out what aspects of my intervention plan—what suspects or combination of suspects—were responsible is very difficult.

For example, I believe the on-stage or testing effects were probably more powerful influences than the reinforcers. If this had not been a class project and if my friends had not been supportive, I don't believe the supposed primary treatment (the contract and the reinforcers) would have had much effect. Time-tied or maturation variables might also contribute—that is, I became more familiar with my classes and the university setting. I don't think so, however, since I have a long history of not asking questions, even in high school.

I can't think of any additional in-the-gap suspects. Towards the end of the study my professor congratulated me, but since I had already started asking questions, that is not a prime suspect, although a reinforcing one.

In summary, I think the prime suspects, or influences, in this study were 'testing' (on-stage effects) and examining my own behaviour—particularly collecting the baseline data. In other words, I think collecting the data motivated me to change more than the so-called reinforcers—the Turtles and the girl-watching. But with this before-and-after design, who knows?

Answers to the Review True or False Quizzes

Chapter 1: From Common Sense to Science

1. False	6. False	11. True	16. False
2. True	7. True	12. True	17. True
3. False	8. False	13. False	18. True
4. False	9. True	14. True	19. True
5. False	10. True	15. True	

Chapter 2: Big Puzzles, Small Brains

1. True	6. False	11. False	16. True
2. False	7. True	12. True	17. True
3. False	8. False	13. True	18. False
4. False	9. True	14. True	19. False
5. True	10. True	15. False	20. False

Chapter 3: The After-the-Fact Method

1. True	6. True	11. False	16. True
2. True	7. True	12. True	17. True
3. False	8. False	13. True	18. False
4. False	9. True	14. True	19. True
5. True	10. False	15. False	

Chapter 4: The Before-and-After Method

1. True	6. True	11. True	16. True
2. False	7. True	12. True	17. False
3. False	8. False	13. True	18. True
4. True	9. True	14. True	19. True
5. False	10. False	15. False	20. False

Chapter 5: The Control-Group Method

1. False	7. False	13. True	19. True
2. True	8. False	14. True	20. False
3. True	9. True	15. True	21. True
4. False	10. True	16. True	
5. False	11. False	17. True	
6. True	12. False	18. True	

Chapter 6: Validity: The Reach of Science

1. False	7. True	13. False	19. True
2. True	8. True	14. True	20. True
3. True	9. True	15. False	21. False
4. False	10. False	16. True	22. True
5. False	11. True	17. False	23. False
6. False	12. False	18. True	24. True

Chapter 7: Developmental and Longitudinal Methods

1. False	7. False	13. True	19. True
2. True	8. True	14. False	20. False
3. True	9. False	15. True	21. False
4. False	10. True	16. False	
5. True	11. True	17. True	
6. True	12. False	18. True	

Chapter 8: Qualitative Methods: Questionnaires, Attitude Scales, and Interviews

1. True	8. False	15. True	22. True
2. False	9. True	16. True	23. True
3. False	10. True	17. False	24. False
4. False	11. False	18. True	25. False
5. False	12. False	19. False	
6. True	13. True	20. True	
7. True	14. False	21. True	

Chapter 9: Qualitative Methods: Naturalistic Observation and Archival Research

1. True	7. True	13. False	19. False
2. False	8. True	14. True	20. False
3. False	9. True	15. False	21. True
4. False	10. False	16. False	22. False
5. True	11. False	17. True	23. True
6. True	12. True	18. True	

Chapter 10: The Number Game

1. False	7. True	13. True	19. False
2. True	8. False	14. True	20. True
3. False	9. True	15. False	21. False
4. True	10. True	16. False	
5. True	11. False	17. True	
6. True	12. True	18. True	

Chapter 11: Statistical Foundations: Packaging Information

1. True	7. False	13. False	19. True
2. False	8. True	14. False	20. True
3. False	9. False	15. False	21. False
4. True	10. True	16. True	22. True
5. False	11. True	17. True	
6. True	12. True	18. True	

Chapter 12: Statistical Foundations: Prediction

1. True	8. False	15. False	22 False
2. False	9. True	16. True	23. True
3. True	10. False	17. False	24. False
4. True	11. True	18. False	25. True
5. False	12. True	19. True	26. False
6. True	13. True	20. False	
7. True	14. False	21. True	

Chapter 13: Ethics

1. False	6. True	11. True	16. True
2. False	7. True	12. False	17. False
3. True	8. False	13. False	18. False
4. True	9. False	14. False	19. True
5. False	10. True	15. True	20. True

Chapter 14: Research Report Writing

1. True	5. True	9. False	13. True
2. True	6. False	10. False	14. False
3. False	7. False	11. True	15. True
4. False	8. False	12. True	16. False

Chapter 15: Sex and Science

1. True	7. False	13. False	19. False
2. True	8. False	14. True	20. False
3. False	9. True	15. True	21. False
4. True	10. True	16. False	22. True
5. False	11. True	17. True	23. True
6. False	12. True	18. False	

Chapter 16: The Truth Spinners

1. True	7. False	13. True	19. True
2. False	8. False	14. False	20. False
3. True	9. True	15. False	21. True
4. False	10. True	16. True	
5. False	11. False	17. False	
6. True	12. True	18. True	

References

Adair, G., Dushenko, T.W., & Lindsay, R.C.I. (1985). Ethical regulations and their impact on research practice. *American Psychologist, 40*, 59–72.

Adler, T. (1989, June). HHS, Congress seeks ways to thwart fraud. *APA Monitor*, 4–5.

Agnew, N. (2005). The meltdown of constructionism? *Constructivism in the Human Sciences, 10*, 11–30.

Agnew, N. McK., Pyke, S.W., & Pylyshyn, Z. (1966). Absolute judgement of distance as a function of induced muscle tension, exposure time and feedback. *Journal of Experimental Psychology, 71*, 649–64.

Agnew, N. McK., & Brown, J.L. (1986). Bounded rationality: Fallible decisions in unbounded problem space. *Behavioral Science, 31*, 148–61.

Agnew, N.M., & Ernest, C.H. (1971). Dose-response and biased set study of an amphetamine and a barbiturate. *Psychopharmacologia, 19*, 282–96.

Agnew, N.M., Ford, K.M., & Hayes, P.J. (1997). Expertise in context: Personally constructed, socially selected and reality-relevant? In P.J. Feltovich, K.M. Ford, et al. (Eds). *Expertise in context: Human and machine*. Menlo Park, CA: AAAI Press, 219–44.

Agnew, N.M., & Pyke, S.W. (1994). *The Science Game*, 6th ed. Englewood Cliffs, NJ: Prentice Hall.

Ajzen, I., & Fishbein, M. (1980). *Understanding attitudes and predicting social behavior*. Englewood Cliffs, NJ: Prentice Hall.

Altman, L.K., & Broad, W.J. (2005, December 20). Global trend: More science, more fraud. *New York Times*.

American Psychological Association. (1982). *Ethical principles in the conduct of research with human participants*. Washington, DC: APA.

———. (1987). *Casebook on ethical principles of psychologists*. Washington, DC: APA.

———. (2001). *Publication manual of the American Psychological Association*, 5th ed. Washington, DC: APA.

———. (2002). Ethical principles of psychologists and code of conduct. *American Psychologist, 57*, 1060–73.

American Psychological Association, Ethics Committee. (2005). Report of the Ethics Committee, 2004. *American Psychologist, 60*, 523–8.

Ames, E.W., & Carter, M.C. (1992, June). A study of Romanian orphanage children in Canada: Background, sample and procedure. In E.W. Ames, Chair. *Development of Romanian orphanage children adopted to Canada.* Symposium presented at the Canadian Psychological Meeting, Quebec.

Andasht, F., & Mchelk, M. (2005). A semiotic reflection on self-interpretation and identity. *Theory and Psychology, 15*(1), 51–75.

Bales, J. (1988, November). Breuning pleads guilty in scientific fraud case. *APA Monitor*, 12.

Barlow, D.J., & Hersen, M. (1984). *Single case experimental designs: Strategies for studying and changing behavior*, 2nd ed. New York: Pergamon Press.

Baumrind, D. (1985). Research using intentional deception: Ethical issues revisited. *American Psychologist, 40*, 165–74.

Becker, H.S. (1986). *Writing for social scientists: How to start and finish your thesis, book or article.* Chicago: University of Chicago Press.

Becker-Blease, K.A., & Freyd, J.J. (2006). Research participants telling the truth about their lives: The ethics of asking and not asking about abuse. *American Psychologist, 61*, 218–26.

Behnke, S. (2005). Ethics at APA's Annual Convention. *Monitor on Psychology, 36*(10), 74–5.

Belenky, M.F., Clinchy, B. McV., Goldberger, N.R., & Tarule, J.M. (1986). *Women's ways of knowing.* New York: Basic Books.

Bem, S.L. (1975). Sex role adaptability: One consequence of psychological androgyny. *Journal of Personality and Social Psychology, 31*, 634–43.

Benedict, J., & Stoloff, M. (1991). Animal laboratory facilities at 'America's Best' undergraduate colleges. *American Psychologist, 46*, 535–6.

Benedict, R. (1938). Continuities and discontinuities in cultural conditioning. *Psychiatry, 1*, 161–7.

Billings, A.G., & Moos, R.H. (1981). The role of coping responses and social resources in attenuating the stress of life events. *Journal of Behavioral Medicine, 4*(2), 139–57.

Birenbaum, R. (1992). Establishing guidelines for research integrity. *University Affairs*, 6–9 May.

Bleier, R. (1984). *Science and gender.* New York: Pergamon Press.

Block, J.H. (1976) Debatable conclusions about sex differences. *Contemporary Psychology, 21*, 517–22.

Boag, S. (2005). Addressing mental plurality. *Theory & Psychology, 15*(6), 747–67.

Bohn, D., & Peat, D. (2000). *Science, order, and creativity.* London: Routledge.

Bradley, R., Green, J., Russ, E., Dutra, L., & Westen, D. (2005). A multidimensional meta-analysis of psychotherapy for PTSD. *American Journal of Psychiatry, 162*, 214–27.

Brewer, N., & Williams, K.D. (Eds.). (2005). *Psychology and law: An empirical perspective.* New York: Guilford Publications.

Breyer, S.G. (2005). *Active liberty: Interpreting our democratic constitution.* Toronto: Random House.

Brody, D.E.B.A.R. (1997). *The science class you wish you had.* New York: Perigree.

Broeder, A., & Schiffer, S. (2003). Bayesian strategy assessment in multi-attribute decision making. *Journal of Behavioral Decision Making, 16*(3), 193–213.

Brooks, M. (2003). The impossible puzzle. *New Scientist,* 5 April, 34–5.

Brown, C., & Seitz, J. (1970). 'You've come a long way baby': Historical perspectives. In R. Morgan (Ed.), *Sisterhood is powerful.* New York: Vintage Books.

Brown, N. (2005). Queer women partners of female-to-male transsexuals: Negotiating self in relationships. Unpublished Dissertation, York University, Toronto.

Bruner, J. (2005). Cultural psychology and its functions. *Constructivism in the Human Sciences, 10,* 53–63.

Bryson, B. (2004). *A short history of nearly everything.* New York: Broadway Books.

Buss, A. (1976). Galton and sex differences. *Journal of the History of the Behavioral Sciences, 12,* 283–5.

Buss, D. (1995). Evolutionary psychology. *Psychological Inquiry, 6,* 1–30.

———. (2001). Cognitive biases and emotional wisdom in evolution of conflict between the sexes. *Current Directions in Psychological Science, 10,* 219–23.

Cacioppo, J.T., Semin, G.R., & Bernston, G.G. (2004). Realism, instrumentalism, and scientific symbiosis: Psychological theory as a search for truth and the discovery of solutions. *American Psychologist, 59,* 214–23.

Camerer, C., Loewenstein, G., & Prelec, D. (2005). Neuroeconomics: How neuroscience can inform economics. *Journal of Economic Literature, XLIII,* 9–64.

Campbell, D. (1993). Plausible co-selection of belief by referent: All the 'objectivity' that is possible. *Perspectives on Science, 1*(1), 88–108.

Campbell, D.T. (1969). Reforms as experiments. *American Psychologist, 24,* 409–29.

Canadian Psychological Association. (2001). *Canadian code of ethics for psychologists, Third Edition.* Ottawa, ON: Canadian Psychological Association.

Canadians for Health Research. (1992). *A true story.* Westmount, QC: Canadians for Health Research.

Carroll, M.A., Schneider, H.G., & Wesley, G.R. (1985). *Ethics in the practice of psychology.* Englewood Cliffs, NJ: Prentice Hall.

Casti, J. (1992). *Searching for certainty.* London: Scribners.

———. (1997). *Would-be worlds: How simulation is changing the frontiers of science.* New York: Wiley.

Cayley, D. (1995). Modes of thought [*Ideas* Program]. Toronto: CBC Radio.

Chronback, L. (1957). The two disciplines of psychology. *American Psychologist, 12,* 671–84.

Chua, H.F., Boland, J.E., & Nisbett, R.E. (2005). Cultural variation in eye movements during scene perception. Proceedings National Academy of Sciences. Published online before print, 22 August 2005. http://www.pnas.org/cgi/content/.

Church, E. (2004). *Understanding stepmothers.* Toronto: Harper Collins.

Clandinin, J., & Connelly, M. (2000). *Narrative inquiry: Experience and story in qualitative research.* San Fransisco, CA: Jossey-Bass.

Coile, D.C., & Miller, N.E. (1984). How radical animal activists try to mislead humane people. *American Psychologist, 39*, 700–1.

Cook, T.D., & Campbell, D.T. (1979). *Quasi-experimentation and analysis issues for field settings*. Boston: Houghton Mifflin.

Coolican, H. (1999). *Research methods and statistics in psychology*, 3rd ed. London: Hodder and Stoughton.

Cowan, N. (2005). Working-memory capacity limits in a theoretical context. In C. Izawa & N. Ohta (Eds.), *Human learning and memory: Advances in theory and application: The fourth international conference on memory*. Mahwah, NJ: Erlbaum, 155–75.

Crawford, M. (2001). Gender and language. In R.K. Unger (Ed.), *Handbook of the psychology of women and gender*. New York: Wiley, 228–44.

Crawford, M., & Kimmel, E.B. (1999). Innovative methods in feminist research. Special issues for *Psychology of Women Quarterly, 23*(1 & 2), 1–436.

Crawford, M. & Marecek, J. (1989). Psychology reconstructs the female 1968–1988. *Psychology of Women Quarterly, 13*, 147–65.

Crease, R.P. (1992). Canadian chemist takes on working women. *Science, 255*, 1065–6.

Cresswell, J.W. (2002). *Qualitative, quantitative, and mixed model research*. Thousand Oaks, CA: Sage.

Crichton, M. (1972). *The terminal man*. London: J. Cape.

Dalla, R.L. (2002). Night moves: A qualitative investigation of street-level sex work. *Psychology of Women Quarterly, 26*, 63–73.

———. (2006). 'You can't hustle all your life': An exploratory investigation of the exit process among street-level prostituted women. *Psychology of Women Quarterly, 30*, 276–90.

Damon, A. (1965). Discrepancies between findings of longitudinal and cross-sectional studies in adult life. *Human Development, 8*, 16–22.

Darwin, C. (1936). *The origin of species*. New York: Random House.

David, S.J., Chapman, A.J., Foot, H.C., & Sheehy, N.P. (1986). Peripheral vision and child pedestrian accidents. *British Journal of Psychology, 77*(4), 12–18.

Dawkins, R. (1976). *The selfish gene*. New York: Oxford University Press.

Delingnieres, D., Fortes, M., & Gregory, N. (2004). The fractal dynamics of self-esteem and physical self. *Chaos Theory in Psychology & Life Sciences, 8*(4), 479–510.

Denmark, F. (1994). Engendering psychology. *American Psychologist, 49*, 329–34.

Denmark, F., Russo, N.R., Frieze, I.H., & Sechzear, J.A. (1988). Guidelines for avoiding sexism in psychological research: A report of the ad hoc committee on nonsexist research. *American Psychologist, 43*, 582–5.

Dennett, D. (2003). *Freedom evolves*. New York: Penguin.

———. (2006). *Breaking the spell: Religion as a natural phenomenon*. New York: Viking.

Dewey, J. (1916). *Democracy and education*. New York: Macmillan.

Dewsbury, D.A. (1990). Early interactions between animal psychologists and animal activists and the founding of the APA Committee on precautions in animal experimentation. *American Psychologist, 45*, 315–27.

DiSessa, A.A. (2003). Changing minds: Computers, learning, and literacy. *Contemporary Psychology, 48*(5), 549–51.

Dixon, L.A., & Colton, J.S. (2000). A process management strategy for re-design: An anchoring and adjustment approach. *Journal of Engineering Design, 11*(2), 159–73.

Doll, W., Fleener, J., Trueit, D., & St Julien, J., (Eds.). (2005). *Chaos, complexity, curriculum, and culture: A conversation.* New York: Peter Lang.

Eagly, A.H., & Carli, L.L. (1981). Sex of researchers and sex-typed communications as determinants of sex differences in influenceability: A meta-analysis of social influence studies. *Psychological Bulletin, 90*, 1–20.

Eggan, D. (1943). The general problem of Hopi adjustment. *American Anthropologist, 45*, 357–73.

Eichler, M. (1988). The relationships between sexist, nonsexist, women-centered, and feminist research. In A.T. McLaren (Ed.), *Gender and society.* Toronto: Copp Clark Pitman, 31–61.

Einstein, A. (1972). Aphorism for Leo. In G. Seldes (Ed.), *The great quotations.* New York: Pocket Books, 920.

———. (1972). Science. In G. Seldes (Ed.), *The great quotations.* New York: Pocket Books, 920.

Elliott, E.A., & Kiel, L.D. (2004). Agent-based modeling in the social and behavioral sciences. *Nonlinear Dynamics,Psychology and Life Sciences, 8*(2), 121–30.

Ellsberg. D. (1973). Women and war. In F. Klagsbrun (Ed.), *The first Ms. Reader.* New York: Warner Paperback Library.

Epley, N., & Gilovich, T. (2001). Putting adjustment back in the anchoring and adjustment heuristic: Differential processing of self-generated and experimenter-provided anchors. *Psychological Science, 12*(5), 391–6.

Epstein, J. M. (1999). Agent-based computational models and generative social science. *Complexity, 4*(5), 41–60.

Eysenck, H.J. (1979). *The structure and measurement of intelligence.* New York: Springer-Verlag.

Faludi. S. (1991), *Backlash.* New York: Crown.

Fancher, R.E. (1996). *Pioneers of psychology.* New York: W.W. Norton.

Favreau. O.E. (1977). Sex bias in psychological research. *Canadian Psychological Review, 18*, 56–65.

———. (1993). Do the Ns justify the means? Null hypothesis testing applied to sex and other differences. *Canadian Psychology, 34*, 65–78.

———. (1997). Sex and gender comparisons: Does null hypothesis testing create a false dichotomy? *Feminism & Psychology, 7*, 63–81.

Fee, E. (1976). Science and the woman problem: Historical perspectives. In M.S. Teitlebaum (Ed.), *Sex differences.* Garden City, NY: Anchor Books.

———. (1981). Is feminism a threat to scientific objectivity? *International Journal of Women's Studies, 4*, 378–92.

Feist, G.F. (2006). The psychology of science. *Special Issue, Review of General Psychology, 10*, 2.

———. (2006). The past and future of the psychology of science. *Special Issue, Review of General Psychology, 10*, 92–7.

Festinger, L. (1946). *When prophecy fails: A social psychological study*. New York: Harper and Row.

Feynman, M. (Ed.). (2005). *Perfectly reasonable deviations from the beaten track*. New York: Basic Books.

Fisher, C.B., Hoagwood, K., Boyce, C., Duster, T., Frank, D.A., Grisso, T., et al. (2002). Research ethics for mental health science involving ethnic minority children and youths. *American Psychologist, 57*, 1024–40.

Fish Fights Aging in the Brain. (2005, October 10). *CBS News*. Retrieved 4 August 2006. http://www.cbsnews.com/stories/2005/10/10/health/wedmd/main931654.shtml.

Fodor, J. (1998). The trouble with psychological Darwinism. *London Review of Books, 2*(2), 1–11.

Folkman, S., & Lazarus, R.S. (1980). An analysis of coping in a middle-aged community sample. *Journal of Health and Social Behavior, 21*, 219–39.

Fonow, M.M., & Cook, J.A. (Eds). (1991). *Beyond methodology: Feminist scholarship as lived research*. Bloomington: Indiana University.

Forbes, G.M., Glaser, M., Cullen, D., Warren, J.R., Marshall, B.J., & Collins, B.J. (1994). Seven year follow-up of duodenal ulcer treated with *H. pylori* eradication therapy. *Lancet, 343*(8892), 258–60.

Foster, K.R., & Huber, P.W. (1999). *Judging science: Scientific knowledge in the federal courts*. Cambridge, MA: MIT Press.

Freeman, G.R. (1990). Kinetics of non-homogeneous processes in human society: unethical behaviour and societal chaos. *Canadian Journal of Physics, 68*, 794–8.

———. (1991, January). Science of complexity. *Physics in Canada, 48*, 5–6.

Fuller, S. (2003). *Kuhn vs Popper*. Cambridge, MA: Icon Books.

Gallup, G.G., Jr., & Eddy, T.J. (1990). Animal facilities survey. *American Psychologist, 45*, 400–1.

Gannon, L., Luchetta, T., Rhodes, K., Pardie, L., & Segrist, D. (1992). Sex bias in psychological research: Progress or complacency? *American Psychologist, 47*, 389–96.

Gauthier, C., & Griffin, G. (2005). Using animals in research, testing and teaching. *Scientific and Technical Review, 24*(2), 735–45.

Gelfand, H., & Walker, C.J. (1990a). *Mastering APA style: Instructor's resource guide*. Washington, DC: APA.

———. (1990b). *Mastering APA style: Student's workbook and training guide*. Washington, DC: APA.

George, M.S., Kozel, F.A., & Padgett, T.M. (2004). A replication study of the neural correlates of deception. *Behavioral Neuroscience, 118*(4), 852–6.

Gergen, K. (1995). Postmodern psychology: Resonance and reflection. *American Psychologist, 50*(5), 394.

———. (2001). Construction in contention: Toward consequential resolutions. *Theory & Psychology, 11*(3), 419–33.

———. (2005). Rationality unbound. *Constructivism in the Human Sciences, 10*, 31–4.

Gigerenzer, G., & Murray, D.J. (1987). *Cognition as intuitive statistics*. London: Erlbaum.

———. (2001). The adaptive toolbox. In R.S.G. Gigerenzer (Ed.), *Bounded rationality: The adaptive toolbox*. Cambridge, MA: MIT Press, 37–50.

Gilbert, K.R. (2001). *The emotional nature of qualitative research*. Boca Raton, FL: CRC Press.

Giles, J. (2005). Researchers break the rules in frustration at review boards. *Nature, 438*, 136–7.

Gladwell, M. (2002). *The tipping point*. New York: Little, Brown and Company.

Goldberg, M. (2006). *Kingdom coming: The rise of Christian nationalism*. New York: W.W. Norton.

Gos, W.W. (1996). Computer anxiety and computer experience: A new look at an old relationship. *The Clearing House, 69*(5), 271–7.

Grady, K.E. (1981). Sex bias in research design. *Psychology of Women Quarterly, 5*, 628–36.

Gravetter, F.J., & Forzano, L.B. (2006). Research methods for the behavioral sciences, 2nd ed. Florence, KY: Thomson Wadsworth.

Gray, J. (1992). *Men are from Mars, women are from Venus*. New York: HarperCollins.

Green, S. B., & Salkind, N.J. (2001). *Using SPSS for Windows and Macintosh*. Upper Saddle River, NJ: Pearson Education.

Gribbin, J.R. (1984). *In search of Schroedinger's cat: Quantum physics and reality*. New York: Bantam Books.

Guilford, J.P. (1956). *Fundamental statistics in psychology and education*. New York: McGraw-Hill.

Guinan, M.E. (1992). A vendetta against working mothers published as science in the *Canadian Journal of Physics:* The editor's role. *Journal of the American Medical Women's Association, 47*, 113–14.

Haack, S. (2003). *Defending science—within reason: Between scientism and cynicism*. Amherst, NY: Prometheus Books.

Haddon, M. (2003). *The curious incident of the dog in the night-time*. Toronto: Anchor Canada.

Hall, J.E., & Hare-Mustin, R.T. (1983). Sanctions and the diversity of ethical complaints against psychologists. *American Psychologist, 38*, 714–29.

Hallowell, A.I. (1940). Aggression in Saulteaux society. *Psychiatry, 3*, 395–407.

Halpern, D.F. (1997). Sex differences in intelligence: Implications for education. *American Psychologist, 52*, 1091–102.

Hanson, D.J. (1980). Relations between methods and findings in attitude–behavior research. *Psychology, 17*, 11–13.

Harris, D.J. (2003). Design theory: From scientific method to humanist practice. *Dissertation Abstracts International Section A: Humanities and Social Sciences, 63*(9-A), 3030.

Heathcote, A., & Elliot, D. (2005). Nonlinear dynamical analysis of noisy time series. *Nonlinear Dynamics, Psychology and the Life Sciences, 9*(4), 399–433.

Horgan, J. (1996). *The end of science: Facing the limits of knowledge in the twilight of the scientific age*. New York: Addison-Wesley.

Howard, I.P. (1974). Proposals for the study of anomalous perceptual schemata. *Perception, 3*, 497–513.

Hunter, J.E., & Schmidt, F.L. (2004). *Methods of meta-analysis.* Thousand Oaks, CA: Sage.

Hyde, J.S. (2005). The gender similarities hypothesis. *American Psychologist, 60,* 581–92.

Jackson, D.N., & Rushton, J.P. (2006). Males have greater g: Sex differences in general mental ability from 100,000 17- to 18-year-olds on the Scholastic Assessment Test. *Intelligence, 34*(5), 479–86.

Jacobs, J. (1979). A phenomenological study of suicide notes. In H. Schwartz & J. Jacobs (Eds.), *Qualitative Sociology.* New York: The Free Press, 156–67.

Janz, T.A., & Pyke, S.W. (2000). A scale to assess student perceptions of academic climates. *Canadian Journal of Higher Education, XXX,* 89–122.

Johnston, W. A. (2005). Third nature: The co-evolution of human behavior, culture, and technology. *Non-linear Dynamics, Psychology, and Life Sciences, 9*(3), 235–80.

Kahneman, D. (2002). *Maps of bounded rationality: A perspective on intuitive judgment and choice.* Paper presented at the Nobel Prize Lecture, Stockholm. http://nobelprize.org/economics/laureates/2002/kahneman-lecture.pdf.

Kahneman, D., Slovic, P., & Tversky, A. (1982). *Judgment under uncertainty: Heuristics and biases.* Cambridge, MA: Cambridge University Press.

Kamin, L.J. (1981). Intelligence. In J.M. Darley, S. Glucksberg, L.J. Kamin, and R.A. Kinchla (Eds.), *Psychology.* Englewood Cliffs, NJ: Prentice Hall.

Kazdin, A.E. (1989). The power to detect differences between alternative treatments in comparative psychotherapy outcome research. *Journal of Consulting and Clinical Psychology, 57,* 138–47.

Kelly, G.A. (1955). *The psychology of personal constructs. Volume 1: A theory of personality. Volume 2: Clinical diagnosis in psychotherapy.* New York: W.W. Norton.

Kern, S. (2004). *A cultural history of causality: Science, murder novels, and systems of thought.* Princeton: Princeton University Press.

Keyes, A., Brozek, J., Henschel, A., Mickelsen, O., & Taylor, H.L. (1950). *The biology of human starvation.* Minneapolis, MN: University of Minnesota Press.

Kiel. L.D., & Elliot, E. (1996). *Chaos theory in the social sciences: Foundations and applications.* Ann Arbor, MI: University of Michigan Press.

Kimball, M. (1995). *Feminist visions of gender similarities and differences.* Binghamton, NY: Haworth Press.

———. (2001). Gender similarities and differences as feminist contradictions. In R.K. Unger (Ed.), *Handbook of the psychology of women and gender.* New York: Wiley, 66–83.

King, F.A. (1984, September). Animals in research: The case for experimentation. *Psychology Today,* 56–8.

Kite, M.E., Russo, N.F., Brehm, S.S., Fouad, N.A., Hall, C.C.I., Hyde, J.S., et al. (2001). Women psychologists in academe: Mixed progress, unwarranted complacency. *American Psychologist, 56,* 1080–98.

Kitzinger, C. (1986). Introducing and developing Q as a feminist methodology: A study of accounts of lesbianism. In S. Wilkinson (Ed.), *Feminist Social Psychology,* Milton Keynes, UK: Open University Press, 151–72.

————. (1987). *The social construction of lesbianism*. London, Sage.

Kitzinger, C., & Rogers, R.S. (1985). A Q-methodological study of lesbian identities. *European Journal of Social Psychology, 15*, 167–87.

Kitzinger, C., & Wilkinson, S. (1997). Validating women's experience? Dilemmas in feminist research. *Feminism & Psychology, 7*, 566–74.

Klages, M. (2003, April 21). *Postmodernism*. Retrieved 8 March 2004. http://www. colorado.edu/English/courses/ENGL2012Klages/pomo.html.

Kleindorfer, P.R., Kunreuther, H.C., & Schoemaker, P.H. (1993). *Decision sciences: An integrated perspective*. New York: Cambridge University Press.

Kluckhohn, C., & Leighton, D. (1949). The Navaho view of life. In L. Wilson & W.L. Kalb (Eds.), *Sociological analysis*. New York: Harcourt, Brace.

Kmenta, J. (1971). *Elements of econometrics*. New York: MacMillan.

Knorr-Cetina, K.D. (1987). Evolutionary epistemology and the sociology of science. In W.C.R. Pinxten (Ed.), *Evolutionary epistemology: A multiparadigm program*. Dordrecht, Holland: D. R. Reidel, 179–201.

Kolato, G. (2005, November 29). Does stress cause cancer? Probably not, research finds. *New York Times*. Retrieved 29 November 2005. http://www.nytimes.com.

Krantz, D. (1998). Taming chance: Social science and everyday narratives. *Psychological Inquiry, 9*(2), 87–94.

Kraus, H.J. (1995). A meta-analysis of the empirical literature. *Personality and Social Psychology Bulletin, 21*, 58–75.

Kuhn, T. (1970). *The structure of scientific revolutions*. Chicago: University of Chicago Press.

Kuther, T.L. (2006). *The psychology major's handbook*. Florence, KY: Thomson Wadsworth.

Lancaster, J.B. (1976). Sex roles in primate societies. In M.S. Teitlebaum (Ed.), *Sex differences*. Garden City, NY: Anchor Books, 22–61.

Landers, S. (1989, June), New animal care rules greeted with grumbles. *APA Monitor, 1*, 4–5.

LaPierre, R.T. (1934). Attitudes vs actions. *Social Forces, 13*, 230–7.

Latour, B. (1987). *Science in action: How to follow scientists and engineers through society*. Cambridge, MA: Harvard University Press.

Lawless, J. (2003). *Statistical models and methods for lifetime data*, 2nd ed. New York: Wiley.

Leavitt, D. (2005). *The man who knew too much: Alan Turing and the invention of the computer*. New York: W.W. Norton.

Leonard, M.M., & Collins, A.M. (1979). Women as footnote. *The Counselling Psychologist, 8*, 6–7.

Levin, J. (2003). *How the universe got its spots*. Toronto: Random House.

Levitt, S.D., & Dubner, S.J. (2005). *Freakonomics: A rogue economist explores the hidden side of everything*. New York: Harper Collins.

Lightman, A. (2005). *The discoveries*. Toronto: Alfred A. Knopf.

Linville, P. (1985). Self-complexity and affective extremity. *Social Cognition, 3*, 94–120.

Lott, B. (1985). The potential enrichment of social/personality psychology through feminist research and vice versa. *American Psychologist, 40*, 155–64.

Maasen, S., & Weingart, P. (2000). *Metaphors and the dynamics of knowledge.* London: Routledge.

Maccoby, E.E., & Jacklin, C.N. (1974). *The psychology of sex differences.* Stanford, CA: Stanford Press.

McCormack, T. (1989). Feminism and the new crisis in methodology. In W. Tomm (Ed.), *The effects of feminist approaches on research and methodologies.* Waterloo, ON: Wilfrid Laurier University Press, 13–30.

McElree, B. (2001). Working memory and focal attention. *Journal of experimental psychology: Learning, Memory & Cognition, 27*(3), 817–35.

McElwain, A.K., Korabik, K., & Rosin, H.M. (2005). An examination of gender differences in work–family conflict. *Canadian Journal of Behavioural Science, 37*(4), 283–98.

McHugh, M.C., Koeske, R.D., & Frieze, I.H. (1986). Issues to consider in conducting nonsexist psychological research: A guide for researchers. *American Psychologist, 41*, 879–90.

Mackie, M. (1983). *Exploring gender relations.* Toronto: Butterworth.

Mahoney, M.J. (1977). Publication prejudice: An experimental study of confirmatory bias in the peer review system. *Cognitive Therapy and Research, 1*(2), 161–75.

Mahoney, M.M. (1988). Constructive meta-theory: I. Basic features and historical foundations. *International Journal of Personal Construct Psychology, 1*, 1–35.

———. (2004). *Scientist as subject: The psychological imperative.* Clinton Corners: Percheron Press.

Malkeil, B.G. (2003). *A random walk down Wall Street.* New York: W.W. Norton.

Marotz-Baden, R., & Colvin, P.L. (1986). Coping strategies: A rural–urban comparison. *Family Relations, 35*, 281–8.

Matlin, M.W. (1993). *The psychology of women*, 2nd ed. Fort Worth, TX: Harcourt Brace Jovanovich.

Mendelson, J.H., Sholar, M.B., Goletiani, N., Siegel, A.J., & Mello, N.K. (2005). Effects of low- and high-nicotine cigarette smoking on mood states and the HPA axis in men. *Neuropsychopharmacology*, 30(9), 1751–63.

Merchant, C. (1980). *The death of nature.* San Francisco, CA: Harper & Row.

Milgram, S. (1970). The experience of living in cities. *Science, 167*, 1461–8.

Miller, D.C. (1991). *Handbook of research design and social measurement*, 5th ed. London: Sage.

Miller, G.A. (1956). The magical number seven plus or minus two: Some limits on our capacity for processing information. *Psychological Review, 63*, 81–97.

Miller, S.A., & Byers, E.S. (2004). Actual desired duration of foreplay and intercourse: Discordance and misperceptions within heterosexual couples. *Journal of Sex Research, 41*, 301–9.

Mills, D.H. (1984). Ethics education and adjudication within psychology. *American Psychologist, 39*, 669–75.

Minsky, M. (1981). Jokes and their relation to the cognitive unconscious. In J. Hintikka (Ed.), *Cognitive constraints on communication.* Boston: Reidel.

———. (1983). Jokes and the logic of the cognitive unconscious. In R. Groner, M. Groner, & W.R. Bischof (Eds.), *Methods of Heuristics.* London: Erlbaum, 171–93.

———. (1994). Negative expertise. *International Journal of Expert Systems, 7*(1), 13–19.

Mintzes, J.J., Wandersee, J.H., & Novak, J.D. (2000). *Assessing science understanding: a human constructivist view*. San Diego, CA: Academic Press.

Money, J., & Ehrhardt, A.A. (1972). *Man and woman, boy and girl: The differentiation and dimorphism of gender identity from conception to maturity*. Baltimore: Johns Hopkins University Press.

Montagu, A. (Ed.). (1980). *Sociobiology examined*. New York: Oxford University Press.

Moulton, J., Robinson, F.M. & Elias, C. (1978). Sex bias in language use. *American Psychologist, 33*, 1032–6.

Nash, M.M. (1975). 'Non-reactive methods and the law.' Additional comments on legal liability in behavior research. *American Psychologist, 30, 777*–80.

Newton, I. (1972). Science. In G. Selds (Ed.), *The Great Quotations*. New York: Pocket Books, 929.

Nielsen, J.M. (Ed). (1990). *Feminist research methods: Exemplary reading in the social sciences*. Boulder, CO: Westview.

Olsen. (2005). Psychopaths could be best financial traders. *Financial Times*, 20 September.

O'Neill, J. (2004). The ethics of problem definition. *Canadian Psychology, 46*, 13–20.

Oppenheimer, D. M. (2003). Not so fast! (and not so frugal!): Rethinking the recognition heuristic. *Cognition, 90*, B1–9.

Orne, M.T. (1962). On the social psychology of the psychological experiment: With particular reference to demand characteristics and their implications. *American Psychologist, 17*, 776–83.

Oscamp, S. (1977). Methods of studying social behavior. In L.S. Wrightsman (Ed.), *Social Psychology*, 2nd ed. Monterey, CA: Brooks/Cole, Chapter 2.

Peirce, C.S. (1955). The scientific attitude and fallibilism. In J.Buchier (Ed.), *Philosophical writings of Peirce*. New York: Dover.

Peplau, L.A., & Conrad, E. (1989). Beyond nonsexist research: The perils of feminist methods in psychology. *Psychology of Women Quarterly, 13*, 379–81.

Pidgeon, N., & Henwood, K. (1997). Using grounded theory in psychological research. In N. Hayes (Ed.), *Doing qualitative analysis in psychology*. Hove: Psychology Press.

Pinker, S. (2003). *The blank slate*. New York: Penguin.

Pipes, R.B., Holstein, J.E., & Aguirre, M.G. (2005). Examining the person–professional distinction: Ethics codes and the difficulty of drawing a boundary. *American Psychologist, 60*, 325–34.

Pitman, J.A., & Owens, N.E. (2004). The effect of manipulating expectations both before and during a test of ESP. *The Journal of Parapsychology, 3*, 22.

Plous, S. (1996). Attitudes toward the use of animals in psychological research and education. *American Psychologist, 51*, 1167–80.

———. (1997). Animal research in psychology. *American Psychologist, 52*, 1250–2.

Polanyi, J. (1989, 1 May). Elation should be tempered until jury has examined experiments. *The Financial Post*, 83(17), 14.

Popper, K. (1959). *The logic of scientific discovery*. New York: Basic Books.

———. (1974). Autobiography of Karl Popper. In P. Schilpp (Ed.), *The philosophy of Karl Popper, Book I*. LaSalle, IL: Open Court.

Procrustes. (2006). *Encyclopedia of Greek Mythology*. Retrieved 4 August 2006. http://www.mythweb.com/encyc/entries/procrustes.html.

Pyke, S.W. (1976). Children's literature: Conceptions of sex roles. In W.C. Mann & L. Wheatcraft (Eds.), *Canada: a sociological profile*, 3rd ed. Toronto: Copp/Clark, 158–71.

———. (1982). Confessions of a reluctant ideologist. *Canadian Psychology, 23*, 125–34.

———. (1988), Dichotomies: An alien perspective. *Atlantis, 14* (1), 56–61.

———. (2005). Access, quality and equity. *Guidance & Counselling, 19*, 201–6.

Rabinowitz, V.C., & Martin, D. (2001). Choice and consequences: Methodolog-ical issues in the study of gender. In R.K. Unger (Ed.), *Handbook of the psychology of women and gender*. New York: Wiley, 29–52.

Regan, M. (1992). Visual judgments and misjudgments in cricket, and the art of flight. *Perception, 21*, 91–115.

Regan, M., Beverley, K., & Cynader, M. (1979). The visual perception of motion in depth. *Scientific American, 241*(1), 139–51.

Rennie, D.L. (In Press). The grounded theory method: Application of a variant of its procedure of constant comparative analysis to psychotherapy research. In C.T. Fisher (Ed.), *Qualitative research: Instructional empirical studies*. New York: Elsevier.

Reinharz, S. (1992). *Feminist methods in social research*. New York: Oxford University Press.

Rhine, J.G., & Pratt, J.G. (1957). *Para-psychology*. Springfield, IL: Chas. C Thomas.

Rimland, B., & Munsinger, H. (1977). Burt's IQ data. *Science, 195*, 248.

Robinson, E.A. (1990). *Einstein's relativity in metaphor and mathematics*. Englewood Cliffs, NJ: Prentice Hall.

Roethlisberger, F.J., & Dickson, W.J. (1948). *Management and the worker*. Cambridge, MA: Harvard University Press.

Roese, N.L. (1997). Counterfactual thinking. *Psychological Bulletin, 121*(1), 133–48.

Rose, H. (1986). Beyond masculinist realities: A feminist epistemology for the sciences. In R. Bleier (Ed.), *Feminist approaches to science*. New York: Pergamon Press, 57–76.

Rose, S. (2005). *The power to mend, modulate and manipulate the mind*. London: Jonathan Cape.

Rosenthal, R. (1963). On the social psychology of the psychological experiment: The experimenter's hypothesis as an unintended determinant of experimental results *American Scientist, 51*, 268–83.

Rozeboom, W.W. (1960). The fallacy of the null-hypothesis significance test. *Psychological Bulletin, 57*, 416–28.

Runyan, W.K. (2006). Psychobiography and the psychology of science: Understanding relations between life and work of individual psychologists. *Review of General Psychology, 10*, 147–62.

Sapsford, R. (1999). *Survey research*. Thousand Oakes, CA: Sage.

Sayre, A. (1975). *Rosalind Franklin and DNA*. New York: Norton.

Schensul, J.J., & Lecompte, M.D. (1999). *Ethnographer's toolkit*. Walnut Creek, CA: AltaMira Press.

Schensul, S.L., Schensul, J.J., & LeCompte., M.D. (1999). *Essential ethnographic methods: Observations, interviews, and questionnaires*. Walnut Creek, CA: AltaMira Press.

Science, Technology, and Law Panel, National Research Council (2001, March). *A convergence of science and law: A summary report of the first meeting of the science, technology, and law panel*. Washington, DC: National Academies Press.

Searle, J. (1992). *The rediscovery of the mind*. Cambridge, MA: MIT Press.

———. (1997). *The mystery of consciousness*. New York: New York Review.

———. (1998). *Mind, language and society: Philosophy in the real world*. New York: Basic Books.

Settles, I.H., Cortina, L.M., Malley, J., & Stewart, A.J. (2006). The climate for women in academic science: The good, the bad, and the changeable. *Psychology of Women Quarterly, 30*, 47–58.

Shadish, W.R., & Fuller, S. (Eds.). (1994). *The social psychology of science*. New York: Guilford Press.

Shapiro, K.J. (1997). The separate world of animal research. *American Psychologist, 52*, 1250.

Sheldrake, R. (2006, 4 February). The unbearable brightness of being right. *The Globe and Mail*, D4.

Shields, S.A. (1975). Functionalism, Darwinism, and the psychology of women: A study in social myth. *American Psychologist, 30*, 739–54.

Shiv, B., Loewenstein, G.B., Bachara, A., Damasio, H., & Damasio, A.R. (2005). Investment behavior and the negative side of emotion. *Psychological Science, 16*(6), 435–9.

Shoham, J. (1989). Time for action: On the relation between time, knowledge and action. Proceedings of the 11th *IJCAI*, 333–42. Detroit.

Shteir, A.B. (1996). *Cultivating women, cultivating science*. Baltimore: Johns Hopkins University Press.

Shumaker, J.F. (2003). The age of insanity: Modernity and mental health. *Contemporary Psychology, 48*(5), 560–2.

Silfe, B.D. (1993). *Time and psychological explanation*. Albany, NY: SUNY Press.

Silveira, J. (1980). Generic masculine words and thinking. *Women's Studies International Quarterly, 3*, 165–78.

Silverman, I. (1975). Non-reactive methods and the law. *American Psychologist, 30*, 764–9.

———. (2003). Confessions of a closet sociobiologist: Personal perspectives on the Darwinian movement in psychology. *Evolutionary Psychology, 1*, 1–9.

Simon, H. (1983). *Reason in human affairs*. Stanford, CA: Stanford University Press.

———. (1995). The information processing theory of mind. *American Psychologist, 50*(7), 507–8.

Sinclair, C., & Pettifor, J. (Eds.). (2001). *Companion manual to the Canadian code of ethics for psychologists*, 3rd ed. Ottawa: Canadian Psychological Association.

Sinclair, W.J. (1909). *Semmelweis, his life and his doctrine*. Manchester, UK: Manchester University Press.

Skinner, B.F. (1938). *The behavior of organisms: An experimental analysis*. New York: Appleton-Century-Crofts.

Sloman, S.A. (1996). The empirical case for two systems of reasoning. *Psychological Bulletin, 119*, 3–22.

Smith, D. (2003). Five principles for research ethics. *Monitor on Psychology, 34*(1), 56–60.

Smith, D., & Johnson, N. (2004). *Evolution management in a complex adaptive system: Engineering the future*. Retrieved 21 September 2004. http://www.citebase. org:org/cgi-bin/citations?id=oai:arXiv.org:cond-mat/0409036.

Smith, M.S., & Glass, A.L. (1977). Meta-analysis of psychotherapy outcome studies. *American Psychologist, 32*, 752–60.

Sprott, J.C. (2004). Dynamical models of love. *Nonlinear Dynamics, Psychology, and Life Sciences, 8*(3), 303–14.

Stam, H.J. (2001). Social constructivism and its critics. *Theory and Psychology, 11*, 291–6.

Stark-Adamec, C. (1993). Social science and scientific responsibility. *Canadian Journal of Physics, 71(3–4)*, 192–6.

Stark-Adamec, C., & Kimball, M. (1984). Science free of sexism: A psychologist's guide to the conduct of nonsexist research. *Canadian Psychology, 25*, 23–34.

Stewart, D. (1989, February), Interview Walter Stewart. *Omni, 11*, 65, 87.

Stewart, I. (2001). *Flatterland: Like flatland only more so*. Cambridge, MA: Perseus Books.

Stewart, I., & Tall, D. (1977). *Foundations of mathematics*. Oxford: Oxford University Press.

Stone, A.A. & Neale, J.M. (1984). New measure of daily coping: Development and preliminary results. *Journal of Personality and Social Psychology, 46*, 892–906.

Strauss, S. (1991, 31 July). Journal apologizes for article. *The Globe and Mail*, A7.

Sullivan, M.A., Queen, S.A. & Patrick, R.C. (1970). Participant observation as employed in the study of a military training program. In W.J. Filstead (Ed.), *Qualitative methodology: Firsthand involvement with the social world*. Chicago: Markham, 91–100.

Taylor, M. (2004, 14 October). *What Derrida really meant*. Retrieved 23 July 2005. http://www.press.uchicago.edu/books/derrida/taylorderrida.html.

Thomas, G.V., & Blackman, D. (1992). The future of animal studies in psychology. *American Psychologist, 47*, 1679.

Trice, H.M. (1970). The 'outsider's' role in field study. In W.J. Filstead (Ed.), *Qualitative methodology: Firsthand involvement with the social world*. Chicago: Markham, 77–82.

Tversky, A. (1977). Features of similarity. *Psychological Review, 84*, 327–52.

Unger, R.K. (1979). Toward a redefinition of sex and gender. *American Psychologist, 34*, 1085–94.

Vonk, R. (1997). Attitudes toward animal research. *American Psychologist, 52*, 1248–9.

Wacome, D.H. (2003). Ways of knowing in psychological science. In S.W. VanderStoep (Ed.), *Science and the soul: Christian faith and psychological research*. Lanham, MD: University Press of America, 25–52.

Walston, B.S. (1981). What are the questions in psychology of women? A feminist approach to research. *Psychology of Women Quarterly, 5*, 597–617.

Watson, D.L., & Tharp, R.G. (2002). *Self-directed behavior*. Belmont, CA: Wadsworth.

Webb, F.J., Campbell, D.T., Schwartz, R.D., & Sechrest, L. (1966). *Unobtrusive measures: Non-reactive research in the social sciences*. Chicago: Rand McNally.

Weizsacker, C.F.V. (1973). Classical and quantum descriptions. In J. Mahra (Ed.), *The physicist's conception of nature*. Boston: Reidel, 635–67.

Wells, B.E., & Twenge, J.M. (2005). Changes in young people's sexual behavior and attitudes, 1943–1999: A cross-temporal meta-analysis. *Review of General Psychology, 9*(3), 249–61.

Weston, D., & Weinberger, J. (2004). When clinical description becomes statistical prediction. *American Psychologist*, 595–613.

Weyant, R.G. (1979). The relationship between psychology and women. *International Journal of Women's Studies, 2*, 358–85.

White, A.D. (1955). *A history of the warfare of science with theology in Christendom*. New York: George Braziller.

White, J.W., Russo, N.F., & Travis, C.B. (2001). Feminism and the decade of behavior. *Psychology of Women Quarterly, 25*, 267–79.

Wiesenthal, D.L. (1974). Reweaving deception's tangled web. *Canadian Psychologist, 15*, 326–36.

Wilber, K. (2000). *Integral psychology*. Boston: Shambhala.

Wilkinson, S. (2001). Theoretical perspectives on women and gender. In R.K. Unger (Ed.), *Handbook of the psychology of women and gender*. New York: Wiley, 17–28.

Wilson, E.O. (1975). *Sociobiology: The new synthesis*. Cambridge, MA: Harvard University Press.

———. (1978). *On human nature*. Cambridge, MA: Harvard University Press.

Wolfe, M. (1991, 18 July). Why does a scholarly journal publish prejudice passed off as science? *The Globe and Mail*, D1.

———. (1992, April 28). Morris Wolfe ponders the NRC's belated action in the Freeman affair. *The Globe and Mail*, C1.

Wood, J.M., & Nezworski, M.T. (2005). Science as a history of corrected mistakes. *American Psychologist, 60*, 657–8.

Worell, J. (1990). Feminist frameworks: Retrospect and prospect. *Psychology of Women Quarterly, 14*, 1–14.

Wright, S.C., Aron, A., McLaughlin-Volpe, T., & Ropp, S.A. (1997). The extended contact effect: Knowledge of cross-group friendships and prejudices. *Journal of Personality and Social Psychology, 73*, 73–90.

Yoder, J.D. (2002). 2001 Division 35 Presidential address. Context matters: Understanding tokenism processes and their impact on women's work. *Psychology of Women Quarterly, 26*, 1–5.

Yoder, J.D., & Kahn, A.S. (2003). Making gender comparisons more meaningful: A call for more attention to social context. *Psychology of Women Quarterly, 27*, 281–90.

Yount, L. (1999). *An a to z of women in science and math*. New York: Facts on File.

Zalk, S.R. & Gordon-Kelter, J. (Eds.). (1992) *Revolution in knowledge: Feminism in the social sciences*. Boulder, CO: Westview.

Zimbardo, P.G. (1970, April). *Symposium on social and developmental issues in moral research*. Paper presented at the meeting of the Western Psychological Association, Los Angeles.

Zimmerman, S. (1993). The National Research Council. *Canadian Journal of Physics: Publication of the Freeman Article. Canadian Society for Cellular and Molecular Biology Bulletin, 17*, 7–9.

Index

Note: Page numbers in **bold type** indicate figures.